"This is a timely—and exciting—book. The technology of extracting financial sentiment from news feeds and other such sources is one that has been slowly growing, supported by the accelerating infrastructure provided by the world wide web. Over the past ten years or so, papers have been appearing showing that useful information can be extracted in this way. Moreover, one can legitimately expect the rate of progress to gather pace, as other supporting web technologies continue to develop.

This book is the first to provide a comprehensive overview of the state of the art. It will attract a lot of attention. From a technical perspective, the area presents some deep and interesting challenges, which are nicely captured here. One is the central issue of fusing entirely different kinds of information, from quite distinct sources, and with very different degrees of reliability. Another is an issue which mining of large observational data sets has to contend with, whatever its area of application, namely the problem of selection bias: it is all too easy to extract a distorted, non-representative data set, so that any analyses based on it are at risk of mistaken conclusions. Overall, this technology is still in its infancy, but the papers presented in this volume provide a perfect launch pad for the future of news analytics in finance.

Just as social statistics enables us both to define and measure the aggregate phenomena that define society, so the work described in this volume will enable us to discern and quantify the forces which steer financial markets."

Professor David J. Hand, Professor of Statistics, Imperial College, London; Chief Scientific Advisor, Winton Capital Management; and President, Royal Statistical Society

"This cutting edge collection of writings offers important insights into the connection between news analytics and sentiment that are rich, deep, and systematic. Investors and academics alike have much to learn from reading this fascinating book."

Hersh Shefrin, Mario L. Belotti Professsor of Finance, Santa Clara University, Leavey School of Business

"Stop the press! At last, we have a substantive book on financial news. This scholarly treatise reaches way beyond how to read the stock pages to provide modern insights on the relationship between news and price formation."

Peter Carr, Global Head of Market Modeling, Morgan Stanley and Executive Director, Masters in MathFinance, NYU

"Technological progress enhances human efficiency including the efficiency of our markets. Trading on news is an integral part of such progress and The Handbook on News Analytics *is a welcome compendium on where we stand with regard to the risks and rewards of news in markets."*

Dilip B. Madan, Professor of Finance, Robert H. Smith School of Business and Consultant to Morgan Stanley and Caspian Capital

"The world runs on information and few areas as directly so as in finance. Now that technology and quantitative techniques have caught up to the live news feed, this volume will be an indispensible addition to the practitioner's library."

Matthew Lee, Head of Research Global Index Equity, BlackRock

"News sentiment is a largely new and unexplored class of data for use in quantitative automated trading. This is a very thorough exploration of what we expect to be a critical element of quantitative trading in the coming years. This book is filled with information and insights that will be of great value to both professional quants and academic researchers."

Steve Bright, Ph.D., Vice President of Quantitative Research, Hyde Park Global Investments LLC

"Quantitative equity portfolio management's continual evolution relies upon the discovery and exploitation of stock price anomalies based on significant systematic investor misperceptions. A vital, and relatively recent, aspect of this process involves exploring the efficacy of non-quantitative information sources, a task for which this book is a particularly important contribution. This volume serves as a very useful introduction to a timely and fascinating area of investment research."

Peter Swank, Ph.D., Tudor Investment Corporation

"During the 200 milliseconds a human is reading the latest news headline, a trading bot will have downloaded the entire article, analyzed its meaning, and traded based on the content. This is our world now, and this excellent book is the first to reveal the software, statistics, and strategies driving advances in quantitative news trading."

Richard L. Peterson, M.D., MarketPsy Capital LLC and MarketPsych Data

The Handbook of News Analytics in Finance

Edited by

Gautam Mitra and Leela Mitra

A John Wiley and Sons, Ltd, Publication

This edition first published in 2011

Registered office
John Wiley & Sons Ltd, The Atrium, Southern Gate, Chichester, West Sussex, PO19 8SQ, United Kingdom

For details of our global editorial offices, for customer services and for information about how to apply for permission to reuse the copyright material in this book please see our website at www.wiley.com

For other titles in the Wiley Finance Series please see www.wiley.com/finance

ISBN 978-0-470-66679-1 (hardback)
ISBN 978-1-119-99080-2 (ebook)
ISBN 978-1-119-97796-4 (ebook)
ISBN 978-1-119-97797-1 (ebook)

A catalogue record for this book is available from the British Library.

Project management by OPS Ltd, Gt Yarmouth, Norfolk
Typeset in 10/12pt Times
Printed in Great Britain by CPI Antony Rowe, Chippenham, Wiltshire

Contents

Preface

The purpose of a preface in our view is rather unashamedly to sell the book—to communicate the message of the book succinctly and either to motivate the reader to explore its content or to leave the reader feeling that just maybe he or she is losing out if the book's theme does not fire their imagination. So, by ignoring this book you will never know whether you might have seen the light and gleaned the winning strategies of financial analytics! The subheadings in this preface are deliberately linked to coax you to send an email to your quant team instructing them to pick up this handbook and mine it for nuggets of knowledge. You may also post a review in your blog or alert your peers in Linked-in depending on how much enthusiasm we have been able to generate.

The *background* sets the scene. We then highlight the *research problems* that also equate with the *business problems*. We discuss the *role of news* followed by an outline of the different *technologies* that underpin news analytics (NA). We then emphasize that discovering what the experts—that is, our enthusiastic contributors—have to say can be rewarding. We conclude the preface with a suggested reading strategy—a *road map*—with a view to help the reader make the most of effective knowledge mining.

Background: the setting

Our research base, the Centre for the Analysis of Risk and Optimisation Modelling Applications (CARISMA) was established in 2001 within Brunel University. CARISMA conferences bring together practitioners, hard-nosed business people, and academics, the abstract thinkers. Sometimes this formula works and the academics are puzzled, challenged, and fascinated by the prospect of analyzing a difficult business problem that can also be construed as a research problem. There are many different constituents that make up the financial (news analytics) market place: academics, industry-based quant researchers, news sentiment data vendors and, finally, traders and investment strategy managers. All these people are variously attracted by the prospect of determining the quantified sentiment of the market by analysis of the news. There is one common aspect which brings the contributors of this volume together: namely, they are people with a "can do" spirit who believe with unwavering conviction that they will find the silver bullet.

The research problem = the business problem

The world of financial analytics is concerned with three leading problems:

(i) The pricing of assets in a temporal setting.
(ii) Making optimum investment decisions low frequency or optimum trading decisions high frequency.
(iii) Controlling risk at different time exposures.

The role of news

News provides information about an event and, as such, may be considered to be an event in itself—news moves the market. The dynamics of the flow of information and market uncertainty impacts security price formation, price discovery, market participant behaviour such as price (over) reaction, price volatility, and market stability. Traders and other market participants digest news rapidly; they may revise and rebalance their asset positions. Most traders have access to newswires at their desks. The sources and the volume of news continue to grow.

The technologies underpinning NA

It is widely recognized that news plays a key role in financial markets. New technologies that enable automatic or semi-automatic news collection, extraction, aggregation, and categorization are emerging. Machine-learning techniques are used to process the textual narrative of news stories, thus transforming qualitative descriptions into quantified news sentiment scores. A range of computational models (algorithms) have been proposed for this purpose. Typically, positive-word or negative-word counts or vector distance computation, adjective or adverb phrase usage or the Bayesian approach of introducing domain experts' subjective and contextual knowledge are applied to calculate a sentiment score. In the context of trading, news sentiment data have to be fused with the market data of "trades and quotes" to create an analytic data mart for financial models. Herein lies the challenge of automation. Not only do systems that support information flow have to be designed, they have to be connected to models of financial analytics for asset pricing, trading, investment management, and risk control. Thus, financial engineering goes hand in hand with information engineering to create winning strategies.

The road map

As editors we set the scene in Chapter 1 of the book. In this chapter we provide a general review of applications of NA in finance. We discuss news data sources, methods of turning qualitative text to quantified metrics and a range of models and applications. In particular, we would like to draw the attention of the reader to the two sections of the appendix where we describe in summary form the structure and content of news data as supplied by Thomson Reuters in its News Scope and RavenPack in its News Scores products. The major themes of this handbook are:

Part 1 The methods and models by which news sentiment is measured and quantified.
Part 2 News and abnormal returns as found in trading models and investment strategies.
Part 3 How news analytics can be used for risk control.
Part 4 The insight of industry leaders and relevant commercial information.

Depending on what interests them most, readers may turn their attention to any of these parts, scan the titles and abstracts, and read the articles as they are presented. There is very little interdependence between these four parts of the handbook.

The contributors are either researchers from academia or practitioners from industry—in some instances, both. They have two things in common: they are all experts in NA and they are enthusiastic about applying NA to finance. As editors we believe our salient achievement has been to solicit and convince this team of enthusiasts to contribute their knowledge and their recent research results to this volume. Finally, we would invite readers to contemplate, innovate and be excited by the infectious enthusiasm of the contributors—you may come up with your own rewarding applications of news analytics and hopefully share them with other experts in the field.

Gautam Mitra and Leela Mitra
London

Acknowledgements

Leela and I would like to thank Leela's mother and my dear wife Dhira for her help in putting this volume together. Dhira has helped us in many aspects of editing this book—communicating with the contributors, the publishers, and the sponsors. She has done so always with a smile and she only frowned whenever one of us (Gautam) kept missing the schedule. Without her help we would have missed the boat. We would not have studied and researched news analytics (NA) had we not been invited to spend a brainstorming weekend in early January 2008 at RavenPack's R&D villa in Marbella, Spain. We got smitten by the research challenges that were presented to us; subsequently, one of us, that is, Leela delved deeper into the subject as part of her PhD research. We also realized that NA, despite being in the early stages of its development, holds great promise as a modeling tool to enhance financial analytics. We therefore decided that the information and research results that we are still gathering should be shared widely with practitioners and the academic community by compiling this handbook. The handbook has also been championed by RavenPack and Thomson Reuters. They have contributed financially (platinum sponsors) and have actively solicited on our behalf contributions from industry leaders. Grateful thanks are therefore due to Armando Gonzales and Richard Brown of RavenPack and Thomson Reuters, respectively. The sponsorships of Media Sentiment and Northfield Information Services are also acknowledged. We would also like to thank all the contributors for enthusiastically sharing their research results. OptiRisk organized workshops and forums on NA in 2009 and in 2010; and a number of colleagues promoted, organized, and hosted these events. We would like to record our appreciation to this terrific team comprising Julie Valentine, Michael and Hetty Sun, Chanakya Mitra, and Natallia Zverovich; these events played a spiritually uplifting key role in the compilation of this handbook.

About the editors

Gautam Mitra (London) is an internationally renowned research scientist in the field of computational optimization and modeling. He has developed a world-class research group in his area of specialization with researchers from Europe, the U.K., the U.S.A., and Asia. He has published three books and over one hundred refereed research articles. He was Head of the Department of Mathematical Sciences, Brunel University between 1990 and 2001. In 2001 he established CARISMA: The Centre for the Analysis of Risk and Optimisation Modelling Applications. CARISMA specializes in the research of risk and optimization and their combined paradigm in decision modeling. Professor Mitra is also a Director of UNICOM Seminars and OptiRisk Systems; OptiRisk specializes in the research and development of optimization and financial analytics tools.

Leela Mitra (London) is a quantitative analyst at OptiRisk Systems. Dr Mitra joined OptiRisk Systems in that capacity in 2004. She received her PhD in operational research on the topic of "Scenario generation for asset allocation models" from CARISMA, Brunel University. Topics included: "mixed" scenario sets for investment decisions with downside risk; pricing and evaluating a bond portfolio using a regime-switching Markov model; and desirable properties for scenario generation. She has a first-class BA (joint honours) degree in mathematics and philosophy from King's College (University of London). Prior to joining OptiRisk, Leela worked in the pensions industry as an actuarial consultant for Mercer HR and, subsequently, with Jardine Lloyd Thomson. She is part-qualified as an actuary.

About the contributors

Brad Barber is the Gallagher Professor of Finance at the UC Davis Graduate School of Management where he teaches introductory finance to MBA students. His research focuses on the psychology of individual investors, is widely published in leading academic journals and is frequently referenced in the financial press.

Gurvinder Brar heads the European Quantitative Research Team at Macquarie Securities. He focuses on multifactor stock selection models, style research and small-cap quant strategy. Prior to Macquarie he worked for 8 years at Citi as part of the #1-ranked European Quantitative Research Team. Prior to that Gurvinder spent 2 years in the Risk-adjusted Portfolio Analysis Team for NatWest.

Richard Brown is the Global Business Manager for the Machine Readable News program at Thomson Reuters, responsible for the product portfolio that includes its archive product, real-time feeds, and news analysis solutions.

Sanjiv Das is Professor of Finance at Santa Clara University. His current research interest include: the modeling of fault risk, machine learning, social networks, derivatives-pricing models, portfolio and venture capital. He has published over 70 articles in academic journals and his recent book *Derivatives: Principles and Practice* was published in May 2010.

Christian Davies is a senior quantitative research analyst at Macquarie Securities and specializes in style research, multifactor modeling and developing stock selection strategies. He previously worked on the Quant Team at Citi and prior to that Christian spent 8 years at Schroder Investment Management as an equity quant analyst as well as an analyst within the Asia Team.

Dan diBartolomeo is founder and president of Northfield Information Services, a provider of analytical models for the global institutional investment community. He is also a Visiting Professor at the CARISMA research centre of Brunel University. Dan has published a long list of books, book chapters, and papers in professional and academic journals.

Huu Nhan Duong is a senior lecturer in finance at the School of Accounting, Economics and Finance, Deakin University, Australia. Dr. Duong's research interests are in the areas of market microstructure, derivatives market, and corporate finance. He has published in the *Journal of Banking and Finance*, the *Journal of Futures Markets*, and the *Pacific-Basin Finance Journal*.

Michal Dzielinski is currently working towards his PhD at the Swiss Banking Institute under the supervision of Prof. Thorsten Hens. His research focus is on quantifying the impact of incoming news stories on the stock market for applications in financial modelling. His research is part of an interdisciplinary project, involving researchers from finance, communication science, computer linguistics, as well as industry partners.

Armando Gonzalez is the co-founder and CEO of RavenPack and has established it as a premier firm in sentiment analysis and natural language processing. Armando is widely regarded as one of the most knowledgeable authorities on automated news and sentiment analysis. His commentary has appeared in leading business media such as the *Wall Street Journal*, Dow Jones Newswires, CNBC, *The Trade News*, among others. Armando is a recognized speaker at conferences on behavioral finance and algorithmic trading across the globe.

Peter Hafez is the Director of Quantitative Research, RavenPack. A graduate and researcher from Sir John Cass Business School, Peter has held various positions in the portfolio management and alternative investment industry with companies such as Standard & Poor's, Credit Suisse First Boston, and Saxo Bank where he was Chief Quantitative Analyst and Head of CHARM. In 2008 he joined RavenPack as Director of Quantitative Research.

Alexander D. Healy conducts applied research at AlphaSimplex Group, with a focus on risk management, asset allocation, and nonparametric investment models. Alex holds an AB in mathematics and computer science (2002) and a PhD in theoretical computer science (2007), both from Harvard University. His dissertation research focused on the uses of randomness and randomized processes in algorithms and cryptography and, in particular, introduced new methods for generating pseudorandom numbers along with new applications of these methods.

Petko Kalev is an associate professor and Head of Research at the School of Commerce, University of South Australia. Dr. Kalev is an expert in empirical and applied finance and, specifically, in market microstructure, with a background in mathematics, statistics, and econometrics. His current research interests comprise capital markets/market microstructure, corporate finance, corporate governance, market efficiency, investments/funds management, and behavioral finance.

John W. Kittrell is a quantitative analyst at Knightsbridge Asset Management in Newport Beach, CA. John was a recipient of the National Science Foundation VIGRE Fellowship while at UCLA and was a guest lecturer at the joint CalTech–UCLA Logic Seminars in 2006 and 2007. His academic work has appeared in such publications as the *Proceedings of the American Mathematical Society* and *Ergodic Theory and Dynamical Systems*.

David Leinweber is the author of *Nerds on Wall Street: Maths, Machines and Wired Markets* (Wiley, 2009). He is Director of the Center for Innovative Financial Technology at Berkeley National Lab in Berkeley, CA. His professional interests focus on how modern information technologies are best applied in trading and investing and how technology affects global financial markets. As a founder of two financial technology companies, and as a quantitative investment manager, he is an active participant in today's transformation of markets.

Andrew W. Lo is the Harris & Harris Group Professor of Finance at the MIT Sloan School of Management, Director of MIT's Laboratory for Financial Engineering, and founder and Chief Investment Strategist of the investment advisory firm AlphaSimplex Group, LLC. He has published numerous articles in finance and economics journals and has authored several books including *The Econometrics of Financial Markets*, *A Non-Random Walk Down Wall Street*, and *Hedge Funds: An Analytic Perspective.*

Andy Moniz, CFA is a senior quantitative research analyst at Macquarie Securities. His interests include statistical pattern recognition, Bayesian classifiers, event-driven strategies, stock selection, and style-timing research. He previously worked at Citi as part of the #1-ranked European Quantitative Research Team. Andy began his career on the Forecast Team at the Bank of England and also worked as a strategist within fundamental research at Credit Suisse.

Marian Munz is the founder, President, and Chief Executive Officer of Media Sentiment, Inc. He invented the media sentiment concept and technology and led development of the proprietary technology that delivers consistent results. Munz is one of the world's experts on financial news and media analysis, internet software, and decision support systems

Terrance Odean is the Rudd Family Foundation Professor of Finance at the Haas School of Business at the University of California, Berkeley. He is Chair of the Haas School's finance group, an associate editor at the *Journal of Finance*, a member of the *Journal of Investment Consulting* editorial advisory board, of the Russell Sage Behavioral Economics Roundtable, and of the Russell Investments Academic Advisory Board. His current research focus is on how psychologically motivated decisions affect investor welfare and security prices.

Marc Oliver Rieger is a full professor at the University of Trier. His recent research focuses on behavioral finance, especially investor behavior. He is author of two books: one on derivatives and one on financial economics.

Jacob Sisk is a principal at Leinweber & Co. and founder of Infoshock Inc. A former senior research scientist at Yahoo! he has been active in applying textual analytics, machine learning, and social network analysis to investment and trading for over 10 years. Jacob attended Reed College and holds advanced degrees in math and business from Tufts University and UCLA.

Adam Strudwick is a senior quantitative research analyst at Macquarie Securities and focuses his research on portfolio construction, implementation issues and multifactor modeling. He previously worked on the Quant Team at Citi; he also worked as an equity quant analyst at ABN Amro and before that as a management consultant with Accenture.

Tõnn Talpsepp, PhD, CFA holds a senior researcher position at Tallinn University of Technology and is involved in behavioral finance, volatility, and financial markets–related research in collaboration with working groups at the University of Trier and the University of Zurich. Dr. Talpsepp was previously employed in the Risk Management Department of Swedbank and is currently involved in the trading and research activities of a proprietary trading firm.

Mark P.W. Vreijling is the R&D Director and co-founder of SemLab and has more than 15 years' experience in research and high-technology product development. Dr. Vreijling is a scientist at heart with a clear focus on the practical opportunities of scientific innovation.

Abbreviations and acronyms

ADR	American Depository Receipt
AI	Artificial Intelligence
AMEX	American Stock Exchange (now NYSE Amex Equities)
AMH	Adaptive Market Hypothesis
APARCH	Asymmetric Power GARCH (Generalized AutoRegressive Conditional Heteroskedasticity)
API	Application Programming Interface
APT	Arbitrage Pricing Theory
ARCH	AutoRegressive Conditional Heteroskedasticity
ARMA	AutoRegressive Moving Average
ASE	American Stock Exchange
ASX	Australian Stock eXchange
CAPM	Capital Asset Pricing Model
CAR	Cumulative Abnormal Return
CPD	Cumulative Probability Distribution
CRS	Company Relevance Score
CRSP	Center for Research in Security Prices
CSV	Comma Separated Value
CUVOALD	Computer Usable Version of the *Oxford Advanced Learner's Dictionary*
CVaR	Conditional Value at Risk
DJNA	Dow Jones News Analytics
EDA	Exploratory Data Analysis
EDGAR	Electronic Data Gathering, Analysis and Retrieval
EGARCH	Exponential Generalized AutoRegressive Conditional Heteroskedasticity
EMH	Efficient Market Hypothesis
ENS	Event Novelty Score
EPS	Earnings Per Share
ES	Expected Shortfall
ESS	Event Sentiment Score
ETF	Exchange Traded Fund
FD	Full Disclosure

FXR	Foreign eXchange Related
FX	Foreign eXchange
GARCH	Generalized AutoRegressive Conditional Heteroskedasticity
GI	General Inquirer
IA	Intelligence Amplification
ICB	Industry Classification Benchmark
IFRS	International Financial Reporting Standard
IG	Information Gain
IPO	Initial Public Offering
ISIN	International Securities Identification Number
MDH	Mixture of Distribution Hypothesis
ML	Machine Learning
MSCI	Morgan Stanley Capital International
MSH	Morgan Stanley High Tech Index
NA	News Analytics
NASDAQ	National Association of Securities Dealers Automated Quotations
NAV	Net Asset Value
NC	Naive Classifier
NEI	NewsScope Event Index
NLP	Natural Language Processing
NORM	News Optimized Risk Management
NVWAP	News Volume Weighted Average Price
NYSE	New York Stock Exchange
OLS	Ordinary Least Squares
PL/I	Programming Language I
PPI	Producers' Price Index
RIC	Reuters Instrument Code
RNSE	Reuters NewsScope Sentiment Engine
RSS	Rich Site Summary
SEC	Securities and Exchange Commission
SIRCA	Securities Industry Research Centre for Australasia
SVM	Support Vector Machine
SWAG	"Scientific Wild Ass Guess"
TRBC	Thomson Reuters Business Classification
TRNA	Thomson Reuters News Analytics
UTC	Coordinated Universal Time
VaR	Value at Risk
VC	Venture Capital
VWAP	Volume Weighted Average Price
XBRL	Extensible Business Reporting Language
XML	Extensible Markup Language

1

Applications of news analytics in finance: A review

Leela Mitra and Gautam Mitra

ABSTRACT

A review of news analytics and its applications in finance is given in this chapter. In particular, we review the multiple facets of current research and some of the major applications. It is widely recognized news plays a key role in financial markets. The sources and volumes of news continue to grow. New technologies that enable automatic or semi-automatic news collection, extraction, aggregation and categorization are emerging. Further machine-learning techniques are used to process the textual input of news stories to determine quantitative sentiment scores. We consider the various types of news available and how these are processed to form inputs to financial models. We report applications of news, for prediction of abnormal returns, for trading strategies, for diagnostic applications as well as the use of news for risk control.

1.1 INTRODUCTION

News (north, east, west, south) streams in from all parts of the globe. There is a strong yet complex relationship between market sentiment and news. The arrival of news continually updates an investor's understanding and knowledge of the market and influences investor sentiment. There is a growing body of research literature that argues media influences investor sentiment, hence asset prices, asset price volatility and risk (Tetlock, 2007; Da, Engleberg, and Gao, 2009; Barber and Odean, this volume, Chapter 7; diBartolomeo and Warrick, 2005; Mitra, Mitra, and diBartolomeo, 2009; Dzielinski, Rieger, and Talpsepp, this volume, Chapter 11). Traders and other market participants digest news rapidly, revising and rebalancing their asset positions accordingly. Most traders have access to newswires at their desks. As markets react rapidly to news, effective models which incorporate news data are highly sought after. This is not only for trading and fund management, but also for risk control. Major news events can have a significant impact on the market environment and investor sentiment, resulting in rapid changes to the risk structure and risk characteristics of traded assets. Though the relevance of news is widely acknowledged, how to incorporate this effectively, in

The Handbook of News Analytics in Finance Edited by L. Mitra and G. Mitra

quantitative models and more generally within the investment decision-making process, is a very open question.

In considering how news impacts markets, Barber and Odean (this volume, Chapter 7) note "significant news will often affect investors' beliefs and portfolio goals heterogeneously, resulting in more investors trading than is usual" (high trading volume). It is well known that volume increases on days with information releases (Bamber, Barron, and Stober 1997; Karpoff, 1987; Busse and Green, 2004). Important news frequently results in large positive or negative returns. Ryan and Taffler (2002) find for large firms a significant portion (65%) of large price changes and volume movements can be linked to publicly available news releases. Sometimes investors may find it difficult to interpret news resulting in high trading volume without significant price change.

Financial news can be split into regular synchronous announcements (expected news) and event-driven asynchronous announcements (unexpected news). Textual news is frequently unstructured, qualitative data. It is characterized as being non-numeric and hard to quantify. Unlike analysis based on quantified market data, textual news data contain information about the effect of an event and the possible causes of an event. It is natural to expect that the application of these news data will lead to improved analysis (such as predictions of returns and volatility). However, extracting this information in a form that can be applied to the investment decision-making process is extremely challenging.

News has always been a key source of investment information. The volumes and sources of news are growing rapidly. In increasingly competitive markets investors and traders need to select and analyse the relevant news, from the vast amounts available to them, in order to make "good" and timely decisions. A human's (or even a group of humans') ability to process this news is limited. As computational capacity grows, technologies are emerging which allow us to extract, aggregate and categorize large volumes of news effectively. Such technology might be applied for quantitative model construction for both high-frequency trading and low-frequency fund rebalancing. Automated news analysis can form a key component driving algorithmic trading desks' strategies and execution, and the traders who use this technology can shorten the time it takes them to react to breaking stories (that is, reduce latency times). News Analytics (NA) technology can also be used to aid traditional non-quantitative fund managers in monitoring the market sentiment for particular stocks, companies, brands and sectors. These technologies are deployed to automate filtering, monitoring and aggregation of news. These technology aids free managers from the minutiae of repetitive analysis, such that they are able to better target their reading and research. These technologies reduce the burden of routine monitoring for fundamental managers.

The basic idea behind these NA technologies is to automate human thinking and reasoning. Traders, speculators and private investors anticipate the direction of asset returns as well as the size and the level of uncertainty (volatility) before making an investment decision. They carefully read recent economic and financial news to gain a picture of the current situation. Using their knowledge of how markets behaved in the past under different situations, people will implicitly match the current situation with those situations in the past most similar to the current one. News analytics seeks to introduce technology to automate or semi-automate this approach. By automating the judgement process, the human decision maker can act on a larger, hence more diversi-

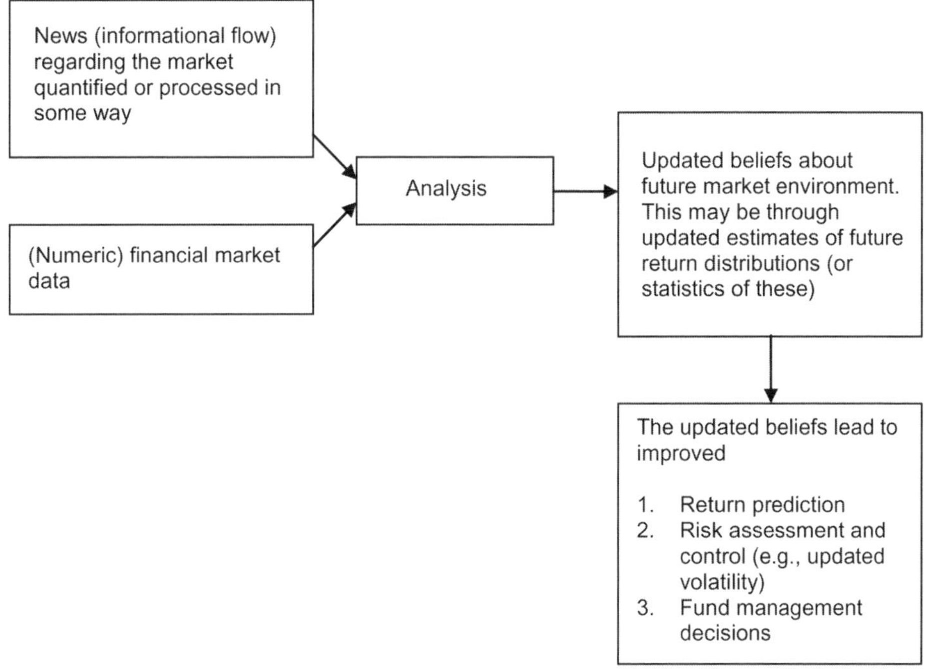

Figure 1.1. A simple representation of news analytics in financial decision making.

fied, collection of assets. These decisions are also taken more promptly (reducing latency). Automation or semi-automation of the human judgement process widens the limits of the investment process. Leinweber (2009) refers to this process as intelligence amplification (IA).

As shown in Figure 1.1 news data are an additional source of information that can be harnessed to enhance (traditional) investment analysis. Yet it is important to recognize that NA in finance is a multi-disciplinary field which draws on financial economics, financial engineering, behavioural finance and artificial intelligence (in particular, natural language processing). Expertise in these respective areas needs to be combined effectively for the development of successful applications in this area. Sophisticated machine-learning algorithms applied without an understanding of the structure and dynamics of financial markets and the use of realistic trading assumptions can lead to applications with little commercial use (see Mittermayer and Knolmayer, 2006).

The remainder of the chapter is organized as follows. In Section 1.2 we consider the different sources of news and information flows which can be applied for updating (quantitative) investor beliefs and knowledge. Section 1.2.2 covers several aspects of pre-analysis to be considered when using news in trading systems and quantitative models. In Section 1.3 we consider how qualitative text can be converted to quantified metrics which can form inputs to quantitative models. In Section 1.4 we present news-based models; in particular, we consider the computational architecture (Section 1.4.1), applications for trading and fund management (Section 1.4.2) and applications for risk management (Section 1.4.3). In Section 1.4.4 desirable industry applications are outlined. The summary conclusions are presented in Section 1.5.

1.2 NEWS DATA

1.2.1 Data sources

In this section we consider the different sources of news and information flows which can be applied for updating (quantitative) investor beliefs and knowledge. Leinweber (2009) distinguishes four broad classifications of news (informational flows).

1. *News* This refers to mainstream media and comprises the news stories produced by reputable sources. These are broadcast via newspapers, radio and television. They are also delivered to traders' desks on newswire services. Online versions of newspapers are also progressively growing in volume and number.
2. *Pre-news* This refers to the source data that reporters research before they write news articles. It comes from primary information sources such as Securities and Exchange Commission reports and filings, court documents and government agencies. It also includes scheduled announcements such as macroeconomic news, industry statistics, company earnings reports and other corporate news.
3. *Rumours* These are blogs and websites that broadcast "news" and are less reputable than news and pre-news sources. The quality of these vary significantly. Some may be blogs associated with highly reputable news providers and reporters (for example, the blog of BBC's Robert Peston). At the other end of the scale some blogs may lack any substance and may be entirely fueled by rumour.
4. *Social media* These websites fall at the lowest end of the reputation scale. Barriers to entry are extremely low and the ability to publish "information" easy. These can be dangerously inaccurate sources of information. However, if carefully applied (with consideration of human behaviour and agendas) there may be some value to be gleaned from these. At a minimum they may help us identify future volatility.

Individual investors pay relatively more attention to the second two sources of news than institutional investors (Dzielinski, Rieger, and Talpsepp, this volume, Chapter 11; Das and Chen, 2007). Information from the web may be less reliable than mainstream news. However, there may be "collective intelligence" information to be gleaned. That is, if a large group of people have no ulterior motives, then their collective opinion may be useful (Leinweber, 2009, Ch. 10). The SEC does monitor message boards. So there is some, though perhaps far from perfect, checking of information published. This should constrain message board posters actions to some extent.

There are services which facilitate retrieval of news data from the web. For example, Google Trends is a free but limited service which provides an historical weekly time-series of the popularity of any given search term. This search engine reports the proportion of positive, negative and neutral stories returned for a given search.

The Securities and Exchange Commission (SEC) provides a lot of useful pre-news. It covers all publicly traded companies (in the US). The Electronic Data Gathering, Analysis and Retrieval (EDGAR) system was introduced in 1996 giving basic access to filings via the web (see `http://www.sec.gov/edgar.shtml`). Premium access gave tools for analysis of filing information and priority earlier access to the data. In

2002 filing information was released to the public in real time. Filings remain unstructured text files without semantic web and XML output, though the SEC are in the process of upgrading their information dissemination. High-end resellers electronically dissect and sell on relevant component parts of filings. Managers are obliged to disclose a significant amount of information about a company via SEC filings. This information is naturally valuable to investors. Leinweber introduces the term "molecular search: the idea of looking for patterns and changes in groups of documents." Such analysis/ information are scrutinized by researchers/ analysts to identify unusual corporate activity and potential investment opportunities. However, mining the large volume of filings, to find relationships, is challenging. Engleberg and Sankaraguruswamy (2007) note the EDGAR database has 605 different forms and there were 4,249,586 filings between 1994 and 2006. Connotate provides services which allows customized automated collection of SEC filing information for customers (fund managers and traders). Engleberg and Sankaraguruswamy (2007) consider how to use a web crawler to mine SEC filing information through EDGAR.

As stated in Section 1.1, financial news can be split into *regular synchronous announcements (scheduled or expected news)* and *event-driven asynchronous announcements (unscheduled or unexpected news)*. Mainstream news, rumours, and social media normally arrive asynchronously in an unstructured textual form. A substantial portion of pre-news arrives at pre-scheduled times and generally in a structured form.

Scheduled (news) announcements often have a well-defined numerical and textual content and may be classified as structured data. These include macroeconomic announcements and earnings announcements. Macroeconomic news, particularly economic indicators from the major economies, is widely used in automated trading. It has an impact in the largest and most liquid markets, such as foreign exchange, government debt and futures markets. Firms often execute large and rapid trading strategies. These news events are normally well documented, thus thorough backtesting of strategies is feasible. Since indicators are released on a precise schedule, market participants can be well prepared to deal with them. These strategies often lead to firms fighting to be first to the market; speed and accuracy are the major determinants of success. However, the technology requirements to capitalize on events is substantial. Content publishers often specialize in a few data items and hence trading firms often multisource their data. Thomson Reuters, Dow Jones, and Market News International are a few leading content service providers in this space.

Earnings are a key driving force behind stock prices. Scheduled earnings announcement information is also widely anticipated and used within trading strategies. The pace of response to announcements has accelerated greatly in recent years (see Leinweber, 2009, pp. 104–105). Wall Street Horizon and Media Sentiment (see Munz, 2010) provide services in this space. These technologies allow traders to respond quickly and effectively to earnings announcements.

Event-driven asynchronous news streams in unexpectedly over time. These news items usually arrive as textual, unstructured, qualitative data. They are characterized as being non-numeric and difficult to process quickly and quantitatively. Unlike analysis based on quantified market data, textual news data contain information about the effect of an event and the possible causes of an event. However, to be applied in trading systems and quantitative models they need to be converted to a quantitative input time-series. This could be a simple binary series where the occurrence of a particular event or the publication of a news article about a particular topic is indicated by a one and the absence of the event by a zero. Alternatively, we can try to quantify other aspects of news over time. For example, we could measure news flow (volume of news) or we could determine scores (measures) based on the language sentiment of text or determine scores (measures) based on the market's response to particular language.

It is important to have access to historical data for effective model development and backtesting. Commercial news data vendors normally provide large historical archives for this purpose. The details of historic news data for global equities provided by RavenPack and Thomson Reuters NewsScope are summarized in Section 1.A (the appendix on p. 25). In the appendix we have summarized some essential information taken from the RavenPack News Analytics—Dow Jones Edition (RavenPack, 2010) and Thomson Reuters NewsScope Sentiment Engine (Thomson Reuters, 2009).

1.2.2 Pre-analysis of news data

Collecting, cleaning and analysing news data is challenging. Major news providers collect and translate headlines and text from a wide range of worldwide sources. For example, the Factiva database provided by Dow Jones holds data from 400 sources ranging from electronic newswires, newspapers and magazines.

We note *there are differences in the volume of news data available for different companies*. Larger companies (with more liquid stock) tend to have higher news coverage/news flow. Moniz, Brar, and Davis (2009) observe that the top quintile accounts for 40% of all news articles and the bottom quintile for only 5%. Cahan, Jussa, and Luo (2009) also find news coverage is higher for larger cap companies (see Figure 1.2).

Classification of news items is important. Major newswire providers tag incoming news stories. A reporter entering a story on to the news systems will often manually tag it with

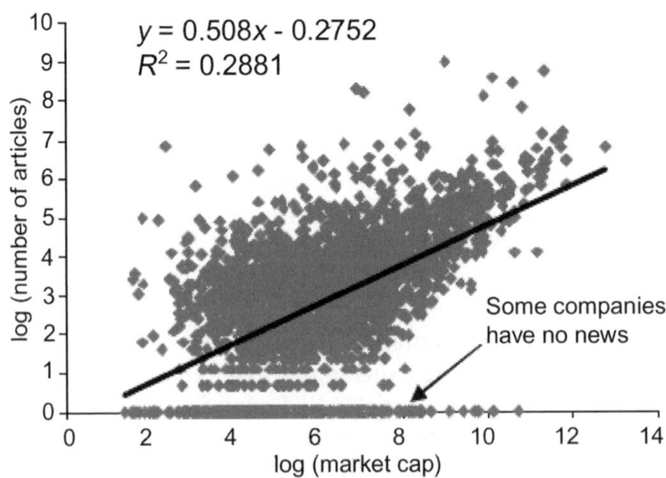

Figure 1.2. Number of news items vs. log market capitalization (taken from Cahan, Jussa, and Luo, 2009).

relevant codes. Further, machine-learning algorithms may also be applied to identify relevant tags for a story. These tags turn the unstructured stories into a basic machine-readable form. The tags are often stored in XML format. They reveal the story's topic areas and other important metadata. For example, they may include information about which company a story is about. Tagged stories held by major newswire providers are also accurately time-stamped. The SEC is pushing to have companies file their reports using XBRL (eXtensible Business Reporting Language). Rich Site Summary (RSS) feeds (an XML format for web content) allow customized, automated analysis of news events from multiple online sources.

Tagged news stories provide us with hundreds of different types of events, so that we can effectively use these stories. We need to distinguish what types of news are relevant for a given model (application). Further, the market may react differently to different types of news. For example, Moniz, Brar, and Davis (2009) find the market seems to react more strongly to corporate earnings-related news than corporate strategic news. They postulate that it is harder to quantify and incorporate strategic news into valuation models, hence it is harder for the market to react appropriately to such news.

Machine-readable XML news feeds can turn news events into exploitable trading signals since they can be used relatively easily to backtest and execute event study-based strategies (see Kothari and Warner, 2005; Campbell, Lo, and MacKinlay, 1996 for in-depth reviews of event study methodology). Leinweber (this volume, Chapter 6) uses Thomson Reuters tagged news data to investigate several news-based event strategies. Elementized news feeds mean the variety of event data available is increasing significantly. News providers also provide archives of historic tagged news which can be used for backtesting and strategy validation. News event algorithmic trading is reported to be gaining acceptance in industry (Schmerken, 2006).

To apply news effectively in asset management and trading decisions *we need to be able to identify news which is both relevant and current*. This is particularly true for intraday applications, where algorithms need to respond quickly to accurate information. We need to be able to identify an "information event"; that is, we need to be able to distinguish those stories which are reporting on old news (previously reported stories) from genuinely "new" news. As would be expected, Moniz, Brar, and Davis (2009) find markets react strongly when "new" news is released.

Tetlock, Saar-Tsechansky, and Macskassy (2008) undertake an event study which illustrates the impact of news on cumulative abnormal returns (CARs). They use 350,000 news stories about S&P 500 companies appearing in the *Wall Street Journal* and Dow Jones News Service from 1984 to 2004. Each story's (language) sentiment is determined using the General Inquirer and a story is classified as either positive or negative. The CARs for each story classification type relative to the date of the news release are shown in Figure 1.3. There seems to be a connection between a news story's release and CARs. However, there also seems to be some "information leakage" since CARs seem to react before the date of the story's release. Leinweber (2009) considers that this may be due to the inclusion of me-too stories that refer back to an original release of "new" news. This highlights that, though textual news may have an obvious connection with returns, it needs to be processed carefully and effectively.

In order to deal with potential noise, Reuters identifies relevance scores for different news articles. Such scores measure how pertinent an article is to a particular company

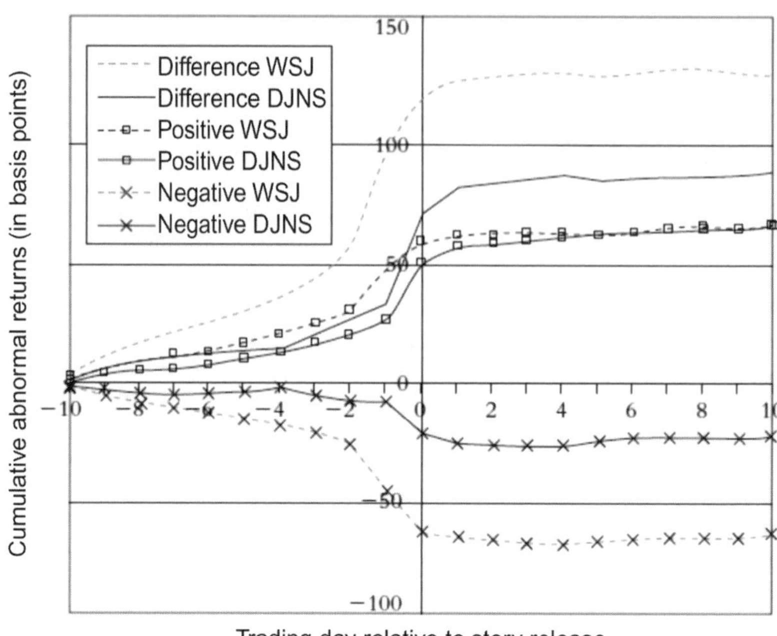

Figure 1.3. CARs start to respond several days before relevant news is published.

and helps prevent erroneous links between stories and entities. In particular, after filtering by relevance as measured by RavenPack, Hafez (2009a) obtains a 3× improvement in correlations between a calculated market sentiment measure and out-of-sample returns. Both Reuters and RavenPack include measures for article novelty (uniqueness) which determines repetition among articles and how many similar articles there are for a particular company. In addition, RavenPack (2010) measures event novelty based on more than 200 event categories that are automatically detected in the news. This allows the user to consider not only the first instance of a company event but also to measure how much media attention it receives.

Several studies also report *strong seasonality in news flow* at hourly, daily and weekly frequencies (Lo, 2008; Hafez, 2009b; Moniz, Brar, and Davis, 2009). A valuable aspect of pre-analysis of news data is to identify periods of unexpected news flow levels, from periods of variation due to seasonality, in order to identify periods where significant levels of information are flowing into the market. Hafez (2009b) investigates the seasonality patterns of news arrival. Figures 1.4 and 1.5 show the intraday pattern. He notes that larger volumes of news flow arrive just before the opening of the European, US, and Asian trading sessions. On the intra-week level we can see little news flow takes place at the weekends. During the week, the peak of news flow occurs on Wednesday and Thursday, while the trough falls on Friday. Lo also notes that the median number of weekday Reuters news alerts is usually between 1,500 and 2,000, while the median for the entire weekend drops to around 130.

The *time of the day when news is released* has also been found to be relevant in understanding the connection between market variables and news. Robertson, Geva,

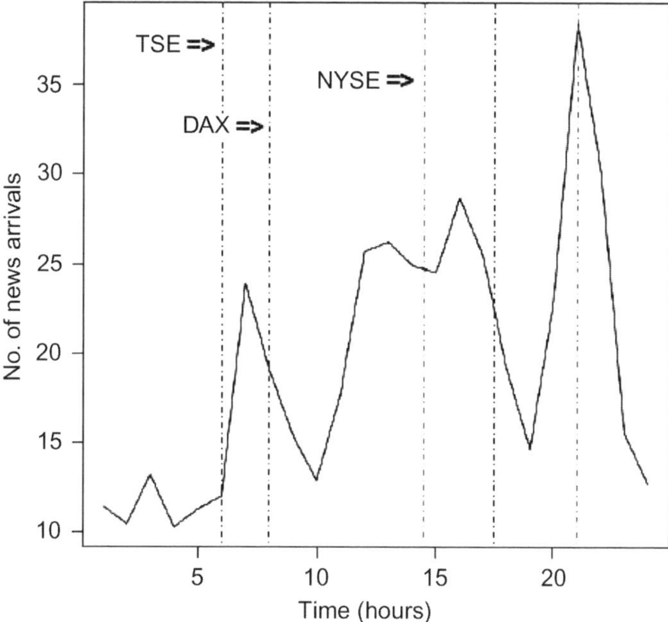

Figure 1.4. Seasonality—intraday pattern.

and Wolff (2006) find that there is a greater likelihood of events that lead to rising volatility at the start of the day. Boyd, Hu, and Jagannathan (2005) find that *market conditions* can influence the types of news that are reported. They report that interest rate information dominates in expansionary periods. In contrast, information about future corporate dividends dominates when the markets are contracting.

As would be expected the *informational content of news* has a large influence on how markets react to news (Blasco et al., 2005; Boyd, Hu, and Jagannathan, 2005; Liang, 2005; Tetlock, 2007). We discuss how to extract the informational content of news (that is, the sentiment) in Section 1.3. It has been recognized that stock returns react more strongly to "negative" news than "positive" (Tetlock, 2007). There also tends to be a positive sentiment bias; that is, there is a larger volume of "positive" news to "negative" news. Das and Chen (2007) find that a histogram of normalized stock message board sentiment is positively skewed. There are days when messages about a stock are extremely optimistic but there is not a similar level of expression of pessimistic views. RavenPack (2010) also find a positive sentiment bias in company-specific news. This bias is more marked in bull markets than bear markets. They report a ratio of 2 : 1 of positive sentiment to negative sentiment stories in bull markets.

The relationship between different news stories is also an important consideration. Companies may make several announcements that fall under different classifications on the same day. These may or may not be related and may be related to varying degrees. For example, a company may announce a profit warning, resignation of its CEO and provide guidance on its sales outlook. The dependence or independence between different news stories is a consideration.

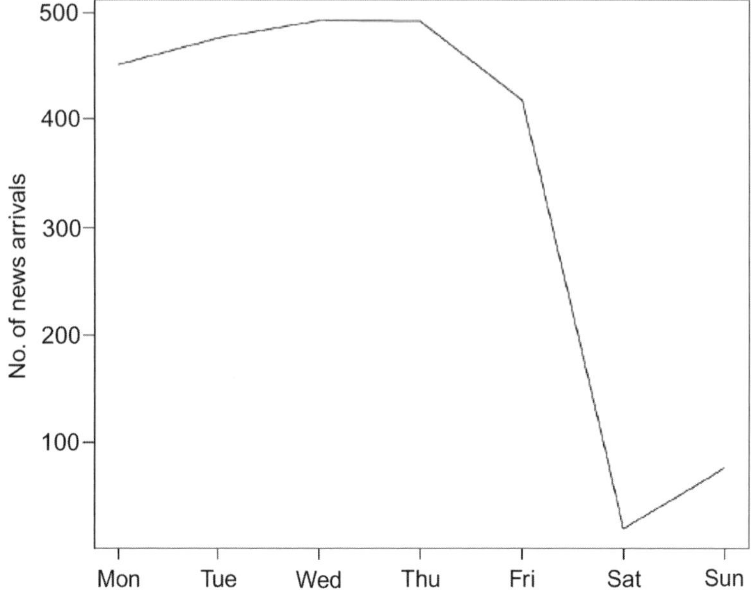

Figure 1.5. Seasonality—intraweek pattern.

1.3 TURNING QUALITATIVE TEXT INTO QUANTIFIED METRICS AND TIME-SERIES

A salient aspect of news analysis is to discover the *informational content of news*. Converting qualitative text into a machine-readable form is a challenging task. We may wish to distinguish whether a story's informational content is positive or negative; that is, determine its sentiment. We may go further and try to identify "by how much" the story is positive or negative. In doing this we may try to assign a quantified sentiment score or index to each story. A major difficulty in this process is identifying the context in which a story's language is to be judged. Sentiment may be defined in terms of how positively or negatively a human (or group of humans) interprets a story; that is, the emotive content of the story for that human. In particular, standards can be defined using experts to classify stories. Some of RavenPack's classifiers are calibrated using language training sets developed by finance experts. Further, dictionary-based algorithms which use psychology-based interpretations of words may be used. Since different groups of people are affected by events differently and have different interpretations of the same events, conflicts may arise. Moniz, Brar, and Davis (2009) gives an example of the term "dividend cuts". This may be classified as a negative term by a dictionary-based algorithm. In contrast, it may be interpreted positively by market analysts who may believe this indicates the company is saving money and is better positioned to repay its debts. Loughran and McDonald (forthcoming) also consider how context affects interpretation of the tone of text. They note a psychological dictionary like the Harvard-IV-4 may classify words as negative when they do not have a negative financial meaning. They develop an alternative negative word list that better reflects the tone of financial text.

An attractive alternative is to use market-based measures to interpret and define the importance of news. The markets' relative change in returns or volatility for a particular asset or asset class, lagged against a relevant news story, can be used to define the sentiment (informational content) of the news story. This approach intrinsically assumes that the market has responded to the news story. Lo (2008) uses this approach for creating the Reuters Newscope Event Indices. He creates separate indices for market responses to news, in terms of (i) returns and (ii) volatility. So he assumes that sentiment measured in the context of these two variables is different. This approach is quite pragmatic and is focused on using the news content directly in the context that the modeller is interested in. Lavrenko et al. (2000), Moniz, Brar, and Davis (2009), Peramunetilleke and Wong (2002) and Luss and d'Aspremont (2009) also use market-based measures in determining the "sentiment" of news. SemLab (see Vreijling/SemLab, 2010) provides a tool which allows the user to filter news items and examine each item's impact on market variables. Using this interactive tool, the user is able to define their own tailored context of "sentiment".

Given a definition of sentiment, machine learning and natural language techniques are frequently used to determine the sentiment of new incoming stories. Hence we can determine sentiment scores over time as news arrives. Such sentiment scores then allow us to develop systematic investment and risk management processes. Linking these sentiment scores to the asset returns, trading volumes and volatility or, in other words, discovering the connection between news analysis and the financial analytics and the financial analytics models is a leading challenge in this domain of application.

The definition of market sentiment is very much context-dependent. In general, we are interested in discovering the "informational content of news". In this review chapter, for the purpose of (quantitative) modelling applications, we use the two terms "news sentiment" and "informational content of news" interchangeably, and in this section we discuss some of the leading methods of computing/quantifying "sentiment" and other related measures.

We review below Das and Chen (2007) and Lo (2008). The former uses natural language processing and machine learning whereas the latter applies a market-based measure. Both papers cover the following items:

1. A definition of the context of sentiment.
2. Application of algorithms (natural language, machine learning, and linear regression) to calibrate and define sentiment scores.
3. Validation of the effectiveness of the scores by comparing their relationship with relevant asset returns, volumes or volatility.

Das and Chen (2007) use statistical and natural language techniques to extract investor sentiment from stock message boards and generate sentiment indices. They apply their method for 24 technology stocks present in the Morgan Stanley High Tech (MSH) Index. A web scraper program is used to download tech sector message board messages. Five algorithms, each with different conceptual underpinnings, are used to classify each message. A voting scheme is then applied to all five classifiers.

Three supplementary databases are used in classification algorithms.

1. *Dictionary* is used for determining the nature of the word. For example, is it a noun, adjective or adverb?

2. *Lexicon* is a collection of hand-picked finance words which form the variables for statistical inference within the algorithms.
3. *Grammar* is the training corpus of base messages used in determining in-sample statistical information. This information is then applied for use on out-of-sample messages.

The lexicon and grammar jointly determine the context of the sentiment. Each of the classifiers relies on a different approach to message interpretation. They are all analytic, hence computationally efficient.

1. *Naive classifier* (NC) is based on a word count of positive and negative connotation words. Each word in the lexicon is identified as being positive, negative or neutral. A parsing algorithm negates words if the context requires it. The net word count of all lexicon-matched words is taken. If this value is greater than one, we sign the message as a buy. If the value is less than one the message is a sell. All others are neutral.
2. *Vector distance classifier* Each of the D words in the lexicon is assigned a dimension in vector space. The full lexicon then represents a D-dimensional unit hypercube and every message can be described as a word vector in this space ($m \in \Re^D$). Each hand-tagged message in the training corpus (grammar) is converted into a vector G_j (grammar rule). Each (training) message is pre-classified as positive, negative or neutral. We note that Das and Chen use the terms Buy/Positive, Sell/Negative, and Neutral/Null interchangably. Each new message is classified by comparison with the cluster of pre-trained vectors (grammar rules) and is assigned the same classification as that vector with which it has the smallest angle. This angle gives a measure of closeness.
3. *Discriminant-based classification* NC weights all words within the lexicon equally. The discriminant-based classification method replaces this simple word count with a weighted word count. The weights are based on a simple discriminant function (Fisher Discriminant Statistic). This function is constructed to determine how well a particular lexicon word discriminates between the different message categories ($\{\text{Buy}, \text{Sell}, \text{Null}\}$). The function is determined using the pre-classified messages within the grammar. Each word in a message is assigned a signed value, based on its sign in the lexicon multiplied by the discriminant value. Then, as for NC, a net word count is taken. If this value is greater than -0.01, we sign the message as a buy. If the value is less than -0.01 the message is a sell. All others are neutral.
4. *Adjective–adverb phrase classifier* is based on the assumption that phrases which use adjectives and adverbs emphasize sentiment and require greater weight. This classifier also uses a word count but uses only those words within phrases containing adjectives and adverbs. A "tagger" extracts noun phrases with adjectives and adverbs. A lexicon is used to determine whether these significant phrases indicate positive or negative sentiment. The net count is again considered to determine whether the message has negative or positive overall sentiment.
5. *Bayesian Classifier* is a multivariate application of Bayes Theorem. It uses the probability a particular word falls within a certain classification and is hence indifferent to the structure of language. We consider three categories $C = 3 \quad c_i \; i = 1, \ldots, C$. Denote each message $m_j \; j = 1, \ldots, M$. The set of lexical words is $F = \{w_k\}_{k=1}^{D}$. The total number of lexical words is D. We can determine a

count of the number of times each lexical item appears in each message $n(m_j, w_k)$. Given the class of each message in the training set we can determine the frequency with which a lexical word appears in a particular class. We are then able to compute the conditional probability of an incoming message j falling in category i, $Pr(m_j|c_i)$, from word-based frequencies. $Pr(c_i)$ is set to the proportion of messages in the training set classified in class c_i. For a new message we are able to compute the probability it falls within class c_i given its component lexicon words, that is $P(c_i|m_j)$, through an application of Bayes Theorem. The message is classified as being from the category with the highest probability.

A voting scheme is then applied to all five classifiers. The final classification is based on achieving a majority amongst the five classifiers. If there is no majority the message is not classified. This reduces the number of messages classified but enhances classification accuracy.

Das and Chen also introduce a method to detect message ambiguity. Messages posted on stock message boards are often highly ambiguous. The grammar is often poor and many of the words do not appear in standard dictionaries. They note "Ambiguity is related to the absence of 'aboutness'." The General Inquirer has been developed by Harvard University for content analyses of textual data and has been applied to determine an independent optimism score for each message. By using a different definition of sentiment it is ensured there is no bias to a particular algorithm. The optimism score is the difference between the number of optimistic and pessimistic words as a percentage of the total words in the body of the text. This score allows us to rank the relative sentiment of all stories within a classification group. For example, we can rank the relative optimism of all stories which have been classified by their scheme as positive. The mean and standard deviation of the optimism score for different classification types ($\{$Buy, Sell, Null$\}$) can be calculated. They filter *in* and consider only optimistically scored stories in the positive category. For example, only those stories with optimism scores above the mean value plus one standard deviation are considered. Similarly, they filter in and consider only the most highly pessimistic scores in the negative category. Once the classified stories are further filtered for ambiguity, it is found that the number of false positives dramatically decline.

After the sentiment for each message is determined using the voting algorithm, a daily sentiment index is compiled. The classified messages up to 4 pm each day are used to create the aggregate daily sentiment for each stock. A buy (sell) message increments (decrements) the index by one. These indices are further aggregated across all stocks to obtain an aggregate sentiment for the technology portfolio. A disagreement measure is also constructed

$$DISAG = \left|1 - \left|\frac{B - S}{B + S}\right|\right| \tag{1.1}$$

B (S) is the number of buy (sell) messages. This measure lies between 0 (no disagreement) and 1 (high disagreement) and is computed as a daily time-series. The daily MSH index and component stock values are also collected. In addition, trading volatility and volume of stocks are calculated and message volume recorded. All the time-series are normalized.

Das and Chen check that the constructed sentiment indices have a relationship with relevant asset variables. The relationship between the MSH index and the aggregate sentiment index is investigated. The authors plot the two against each other and show that these two series do seem to track each other. The sentiment index is found to be highly autocorrelated out to two trading weeks. Regression analysis is undertaken to investigate the relationship. They conclude sentiment does offer some explanatory power for the level of the index. However, autocorrelation makes it difficult to establish the empirical nature of the relationship.

Das and Chen undertake regression analysis between the individual stock level and the individual stock sentiment level and find there is a significant relationship (the t-statistic of the coefficient falls within a significant level). The relationship between first differences is much weaker. We cannot conclude there is a strong predictive ability on forecasting individual stock returns. Sentiment and stock levels are not unrelated, but determining the precise nature of the relationship is difficult.

The authors also provide a graphical display of the relationship between the sentiment measure, disagreement measure, message volume, trading volume and volatility. Sentiment is inversely related to disagreement. As disagreement increases, sentiment falls. Sentiment is correlated to high posting volume. As discussion increases, this indicates optimism about that stock is rising. There is a strong relationship between message volume and volatility. This is consistent with Antweiler and Frank (2004). Trading volume and volatility are strongly related to each other.

Lo (2008) develops the Reuters NewsScope Event Indices (NEIs) which are constructed to have "predictive" power for particular asset returns and (realized) volatility. They are constructed in an integrated framework where news, returns and volatility are used in calibrating the indices. The white paper (dated November 2007) considers specifically indices for foreign exchange. However, the method can be applied to other asset classes.

Lo uses news alerts in developing his sentiment indices. These are quick news flashes which are issued when a newsworthy event occurs. They are both timely and relevant. An example of a Reuters NewsScope alert

```
TimeStamp 02 AUG 2007 04:44:26.155
Alert Tsunami Warning Issued for Japan's Western Hokkaido Coast
JP ASIA NEWS DIS LEN RTRS
```

The alert comprises three items (i) TimeStamp, (ii) a short headline, and (iii) tags and metadata. The tags are machine-readable and will often contain information about the topic area. The headlines lend themselves well to machine analysis since they are concise and formed from a small vocabulary. Lo notes the purpose of the indices is to rapidly identify and report market moving information. Once constructed he undertakes (event study) experiments to validate their quality, developing metrics which have the potential to indicate whether the indices are able to predict significant market movements.

Framework for real-time news analytics

We consider here the framework for developing Reuters NEIs. For a given asset class and related topic area the following parameters are used:

(1) List of keywords and phrases with real-valued weights; $(W_1, \gamma_1), \ldots, (W_k, \gamma_k)$.
(2) A rolling "sentiment" window of size r (say 5/10 minutes).
(3) A rolling calibration window of size R (say 90 days).

Initially a *raw score* is created.

We have $(W_1, \gamma_1), \ldots, (W_k, \gamma_k)$, where W_1 is the first keyword and γ_1 is the weighting for the first keyword.

The raw score at time t is assigned by considering the time period $(t - r, t]$. $(w_1, \ldots, w_k)$ is the vector of keyword frequencies in $(t - r, t]$; that is, w_i is the number of times keyword W_i occurred in the last r minutes. The raw score is defined as

$$s_t \equiv \sum_i \gamma_i w_i \tag{1.2}$$

The raw score will tend to be high when the news volume is high. A *normalized score* is therefore produced using the rolling calibration window. At all times t for the R days in the calibration window, we record

(i) the raw score s_t that would have been assigned,
(ii) the news volume $n_{[t-r,t)}$; that is, the number of words that were observed in the time interval $[t - r, t)$.

The normalized score is determined by comparing the current raw score against the distribution of raw scores in the calibration window, where the news volume equalled the current news volume. This means we only consider those raw scores where the news volume equals the current news volume.

$$S_t \equiv \frac{|\{t' \in [t - R, t) : n_{[t'-r,t')} = n_{[t-r,t)} \& s_{t'} < s_t\}|}{|\{t' \in [t - R, t) : n_{[t'-r,t')} = n_{[t-r,t)}\}|} \tag{1.3}$$

We notice the numerator is a subset of the denominator, hence $S_t \leq 1$. If $S_t = 0.92$, we can say that 92% of the time when news volume is at the current level, the raw score is less than it currently is. Lo creates an alternative score based on topic codes. Instead of counting word frequencies, the fraction of news alerts (in the last r minutes) tagged with particular topic codes are used.

Naturally, the scoring method is dependent on the list of keywords/topic areas $(W_1, \ldots, W_k)$ and the real-valued weights $(\gamma_1, \ldots, \gamma_k)$. The lists of keywords/topics were created by selecting the major news categories that related to the asset class (foreign exchange) and creating lists, by hand, of words and topic areas that suggest news relevant to the categories. A tool was created to extract news from periods where high scores were assigned. This news was then manually inspected, so that the developer could determine whether the keywords (topics) were legitimate or needed adjusting.

The optimal weights $(\gamma_1, \ldots, \gamma_k)$ for the intraday return sentiment index were determined by regressing the word (topic) frequencies against the intraday asset returns. Similarly the (optimal) weights for the intraday volatility sentiment index were determined by regressing the word (topic) frequencies against the intraday (de-seasonalized) realized volatility. Volatility was observed to show strong seasonality on intraday time-scales, hence this series was de-seasonalized prior to derivation of the weights. Returns did not exhibit any seasonality. The time-series are given on an intraday basis, hence to keep the data manageable a random subset of the observations is used in calibration.

Lo notes the determination of weights can be expressed as a more general classification problem. Other techniques might be applied; in particular, machine-learning algorithms such as the perceptron algorithm or support vector machines. He suggests further study is required to find the best approach, but the standard linear regression approach does perform well.

To establish that the final NEIs have empirical significance, Lo undertakes detailed event study analysis. He uses the NEI series to define an event. An event is defined to take place when the index exceeds a certain threshold (say 0.995). He then removes any events that follow in less than one hour of another event. This guards against identifying "new" events which are actually based on old news. The behaviour of exchange rates before and after these events is then studied. Two time-series are considered: the log returns and the deseasonalized squared log returns. He then tests the null hypothesis that the distribution of log returns/deseasonalized squared log returns are the same before and after the events. He uses samples of one hour centred on the events.

We can visually assess the impact of events on the volatility of the EUR/USD exchange rate.

(1) Figure 1.6 shows the averaged volatility event window. The pre-event (averaged) volatility is shown by a bold line, and the post-event (averaged) volatility is shown by a faint line. There is a peak at the centre where there is a significant increase in volatility.
(2) Figure 1.7 shows the density function of pre-event samples and post-event samples of deseasonalized squared log returns. The shift to the right indicates an upward shift in volatility on average.

As well as visual inspection, statistical tests can be introduced to compare the pre-event and post-event samples. A t-test can be used to test equality of the means in the two samples. Levene's test can be used to determine whether there has been a change in standard deviation. The χ^2 goodness-of-fit test can be used to determine whether the two samples are likely to have come from different distributions.

Indices and FX implied volatility

Lo finds that the event studies confirm that the constructed event indices, on average,

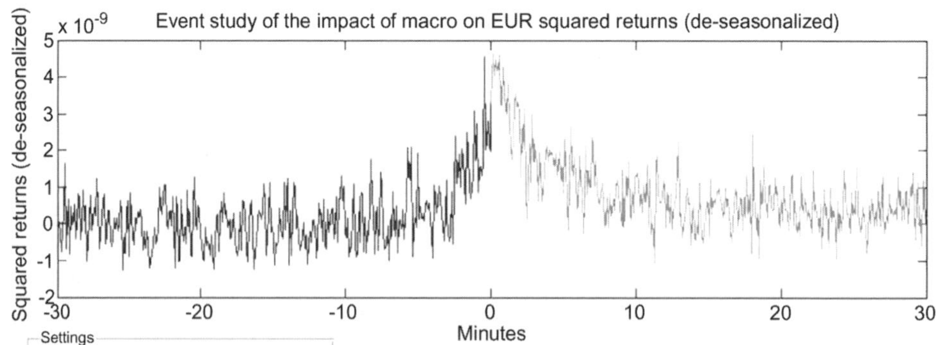

Figure 1.6. Pre- and post-event squared returns: shown as bold and faint lines.

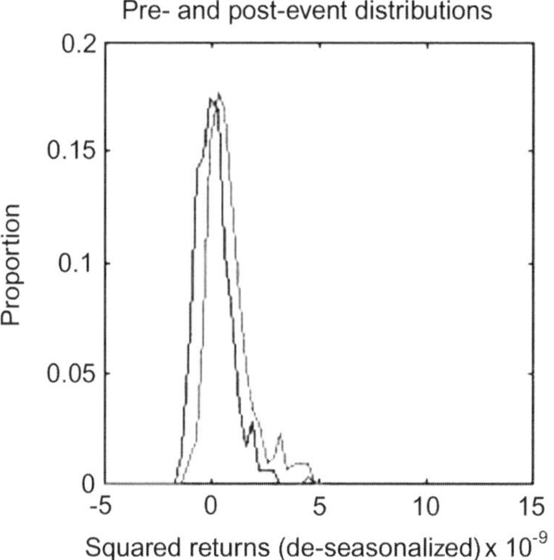

Figure 1.7. Distribution of pre- and post-event squared returns in bold and faint lines.

impact *realized* foreign exchange volatility. He further considers the relationship of the indices to *implied* volatility. The NEI volatility indices are constructed to predict volatility over 30-minute periods. Implied volatility gives the markets' expectations of volatility over a much longer horizon, typically 30 days. Event study analysis between implied volatility and the NEI volatility indices shows no evidence of a relationship. Lo feels that implied volatility and the indices may function as complementary sources of information for risk management, since they intrinsically focus on different time horizons.

1.4 MODELS AND APPLICATIONS

News analytics in finance is the use of technology and algorithms to process news within the investment management process. It allows investors to update their beliefs about the future market environment more effectively. This technology may be geared towards human decision support or it may be used to create automated quantitative strategies. The use of news data in addition to historic market data makes models more proactive and less reactive. The applications broadly fall into two areas: trading and risk control.

1.4.1 Information flow and computational architecture

News analytics in finance focuses on improving IT-based legacy system applications. These improvements come through research and development directed at automating/semi-automating programmed trading, fund rebalancing and risk control applications.

The established good practice of applying these analytics in the traditional manual approach are as follows. News stories and announcements arrive synchronously and asynchronously. In the market, asset (stocks, commodities, FX rates, etc.) prices move (market reactions). The professionals digest these items of information and accordingly make trading decisions, investment decisions and recompute their risk exposures.

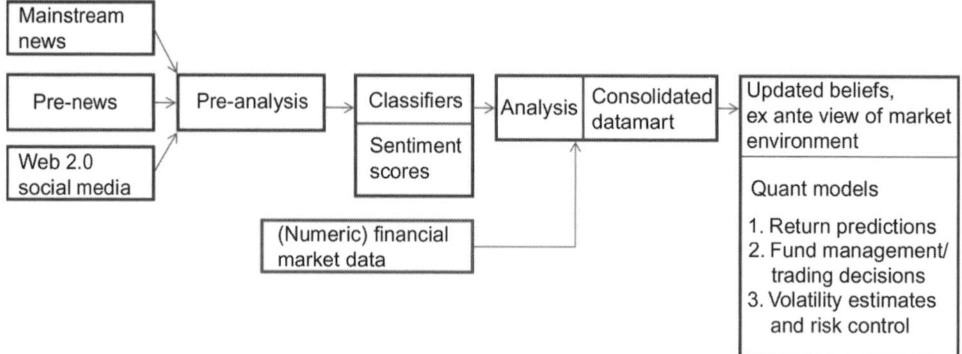

Figure 1.8. Information flow and computational architecture

The information flow and the (semi) automation of the corresponding IS architecture is set out in Figure 1.8. There are two streams of information which flow simultaneously: news data and market data. Pre-analysis is applied to news data; it is further filtered and processed by classifiers to compute relevant metrics. This is consolidated with the market data of prices and together they constitute the classical datamart which feeds into whatever relevant model-based applications are sought. A key aspect of these applications is that they set out to provide technology-enabled support to professional decision makers and thereby achieve intelligence amplification (Leinweber, 2009).

1.4.2 Trading and fund management

Generally traders and quantitative fund managers seek to identify and exploit asset mispricings before they are corrected in order to generate alpha. Most simply they may use (quantified) news data to *rank stocks* and identify which stocks are relatively attractive (unattractive). They may then buy (sell) the highest (lowest) ranking stocks, thereby rebalancing a portfolio composed of desired weights on the selected stocks. Similarly, the news data may be used to identify trading signals for particular stocks. Alternatively, analysts may use *factor models* to process new sources of news data. (Factor models, which are applied to give updated estimates of future asset returns and volatility, allow us to determine an optimal future portfolio to hold; that is, they tell us which assets to hold and also in what proportions.) Analysts may also use news data to identify and exploit *behavioural biases* in investor attitude/reactions which result due to the market and analyst misreaction to new information. In particular, this can arise due to delayed information diffusion or due to investor inattention and limited ability to process all relevant information instantaneously.

Stock picking and ranking

Li (2006) uses a simple ranking procedure to identify stocks with positive and negative (financial language) sentiment. He examines form 10-K Securities and Exchange Commission (SEC) filings for non-financial firms between 1994 and 2005. He creates a "risk sentiment measure" which is formed by counting the number of times the words risk, risks, risky, uncertain, uncertainty and uncertainties occur within the management discussion and analysis sections. A strategy which goes long in stocks with a low-risk sentiment measure and short stocks with a high-risk sentiment measure is found to produce a reasonable level of returns. Leinweber (2009) notes it is rumoured similar approaches are being applied. The performance of the strategy has deteriorated in recent years, possibly due to wider use of such strategies.

Moniz, Brar, and Davis (2009) focuses on turning news signals into a trading strategy. Equity analysts collect, process and disseminate information on companies to investors. In particular, they use their research to form earnings forecasts for companies. Earnings momentum strategies thus become a proxy for corporate news flow. Moniz notes these strategies do not explicitly identify the piece of information that has triggered the change in earnings forecast. He investigates whether news leads earnings revisions. He finds that news data can be used to reinforce proxies for news already incorporated in models and that a strategy based on earnings momentum reinforced by news flow is found to be effective.

Event studies based on news events can also provide the cue to fund managers to identify potentially underpriced/overpriced stocks (see the discussion in Section 1.2.2).

Factor models

The Efficient Market Hypothesis (EMH) asserts that financial markets are "informationally efficient" so prices of traded assets reflect all known information and update instantaneously to reflect new information. Further, it is assumed that agents act rationally. It is widely accepted within the fund management and trading community that the EMH, particularly in its strong form, does not hold. In the long run, markets may be efficient. But "The long run is a misleading guide to current affairs. In the long run we are all dead," as John Maynard Keynes said. In the shorter term traders and quantitative fund managers seek to identify and exploit asset mispricings, before these prices correct themselves, in order to generate alpha. In undertaking this process they often seek to gain a competitive advantage by applying improved and differentiating sources of data and information.

The Capital Asset Pricing Model (CAPM) is the classical approach to pricing equities (Sharpe, 1964; Lintner, 1965). Any asset's return can be split into a component that is correlated with the market's return and a residual component that is uncorrelated with the market. Under the CAPM, it is assumed that the expected return for the residual component is zero and any stock's expected return is dependent only on the expected return of the market. The CAPM states that only risk (uncertainty) due to market variability should be priced. Residual risk can be diversified and therefore should not be compensated.

The Arbitrage Pricing Theory (APT) (introduced by Ross, 1976) extends the CAPM to a more general linear model where additional sources of information to market returns are considered. Under the APT (multifactor models) an asset's expected return is represented as a linear sum of several "risk" (uncertainty) factors that are common to all assets and an asset-specific component. The APT states the investor should be compensated for their exposure to all sources of (non-diversifiable) risk.

Active portfolio managers seek to incorporate their investment insight to "beat the market". An accurate description of asset price uncertainty is key to the ability to outperform the market. Tetlock, Saar-Tsechansky, and Macskassy (2008) note that an investor's perception about future asset returns is determined by their knowledge about the company and its prospects; that is, by their "information sets". They note that these are determined from three main sources: analyst forecasts, quantifiable publicly disclosed accounting variables and linguistic descriptions of the firm's current and future profit-generating activities. If the first two sources of information are incomplete or biased, the third may give us relevant information for equity prices.

Multifactor models are now widely used by fund managers in constructing alpha-generating strategies (Rosenberg, Reid, and Lanstein, 1985). Identifying the relevant factors (and betas) is a measure of skill. Fund managers are always seeking new sources of advantage. This can be data and factors which translate to "quantitative knowledge". "Profits may be viewed as the economic rents which accrue to [the] competitive advantage of . . . superior information, superior technology, financial innovation" (Lo, 1997). A "quantcentration" effect is frequently observed. That is, since most fund managers have access to the same sources of data, it is difficult to distinguish between their models and performance. Cahan, Jussa, and Luo (2009) find that news sentiment scores provided by RavenPack act as an orthogonal factor to traditional quantitative factors currently used. Hence they add a diversification benefit to traditional factor models. In particular, they note the value of this source of information during the Credit Crisis, when determining fundamentals (which traditional quant factors are based on) was problematic.

Behavioural biases

Behavioural economists challenge the assumption that market agents act rationally. Instead, they propose that individuals display certain biased behaviour, such as loss aversion (Kahneman and Tversky, 1979), overconfidence (Barber and Odean, 2001), overreaction (DeBondt and Thaler, 1985) and mental accounting (Tversky and Kahneman, 1981). Due to individual behavioural biases investors systematically deviate from optimal trading behaviour (Daniel, Hirshleifer, and Teoh, 2002; Hirshleifer, 2001; Odean and Barber, 1998). Behavioural economists use these biases to explain abnormal returns, rather than risk-based explanations. Naturally, investor behaviour is dependent on individual and group psychology. Some of the research within behavioural finance seeks to understand the mechanisms of human investor behaviour, drawing heavily on the fields of neuroscience and psychology (see, e.g., Peterson, 2007). Lo (2004) proposes a new framework—the Adaptive Market Hypothesis (AMH)—which seeks to reconcile market efficiency with behavioural alternatives. This is an evolutionary model, where individuals adapt to a changing environment via simple heuristics.

As noted before, the relationship between news and markets is complex. A number of studies consider how investors react to news releases; in particular, the behavioural and cognitive biases in their reactions to news. Quantitative investors often seek to systematically exploit the anomalies observed in prices arising from investor behavioural biases (Moniz, Brar, and Davis, 2009; Barber and Odean, this volume, Chapter 7; Seasholes and Wu, 2004). There is a commercial fund called MarketPsy which employs strategies that exploit "collective investor misbehaviour" (see `http://marketpsy.com/`).

Barber and Odean consider evidence for the behavioural bias that individual investors have a tendency to buy attention-grabbing stocks. Attention-grabbing stocks are defined as ones that display abnormal trading volumes, extreme one-day returns or are mentioned on the Dow Jones News Service. In contrast, professional managers who are better equipped to assess a wider range of stocks are less prone to buying attention-grabbing stocks. In particular, institutional investors, who use computers to manage their searches, normally specialize in a particular sector and may consider only those stocks that meet certain criteria. For every buyer there must be a seller. So if one group incurs losses the other group profits. If individual investors fail to react appropriately to news and attention, there is scope for institutional investors to profit. Seasholes and Wu (2004) find individual investors tend to buy stocks that hit an upper price limit. They find an impact on the prices of these attention-grabbing stocks, which reverses to pre-event levels within ten working days. Further, they find a group of professional investors who profit from the biased behaviour of individual investors.

Fang and Peress (2009) consider whether media coverage can help predict the cross-section of future stock returns. They find stocks with no media coverage outperform widely covered stocks even after allowing for well-known risk factors. This is contrary to the findings of Barber and Odean. But this finding supports the investor recognition hypothesis of Merton (1987). Da, Engleberg, and Gao (2009) also consider how the amount of attention a stock receives affects its cross-section of returns. They use the frequency of Google searches for a particular company as a measure of the amount of attention a stock receives. They find some evidence that changes in investor attention can predict the cross-section of returns. This is most pronounced amongst small-cap stocks.

Some researchers consider how informational flows cause investors to update their expectations in order to explain momentum and reversal effects. DeBondt and Thaler (1985) suggest that investors overreact to recent earnings by placing less emphasis on long-term averages. Daniel, Hirshleifer, and Subrahmanyam (1998) suggest price momentum is a result of investors overreacting to private information causing prices to be pushed away from fundamentals. In contrast, Hong and Stein (1999) suggest price momentum occurs due to investors underreacting to new information. They suggest information diffuses slowly and is gradually incorporated into prices. Hirshleifer, Lim, and Teoh (2010) find that when there is a significant number of earnings announcements in the market, investors are distracted and underreact to relevant new information, and the post-announcement drift is strong. Investors fail to price the information efficiently, leaving an opportunity for quantitative investors. Scott, Stumpp, and Xu (2003) conclude that price momentum is caused by underreaction of stocks to earnings-related news. This is contrary to prior literature which suggested that price momentum was connected to trading volume.

Chan (2003) finds stocks with major public news exhibit momentum over the following month. In contrast, stocks with large price movements, but an absence of news, tend to show return reversals in the following month. This would support a trading strategy based on momentum reinforced with news signals. Da, Engleberg, and Gao (2009) extend their analysis of Google searches to consider the debate on how momentum works. They find price momentum is stronger in stocks with high levels of Google (SVI) searches. This supports Daniel, Hirshleifer, and Subrahmanyam (1998) view since one would expect investors to overreact to stocks they are paying close attention to. Gutierrez, Kelley, and Hall (2007) and Hou, Peng, and Xiong (2009) also investigate the relationship between news (information flows) and momentum.

1.4.3 Monitoring risk and risk control

For effective financial risk control, fund management companies need to identify, understand and quantify potential (adverse) outcomes, their related probabilities and the severity of their impacts. This knowledge allows them to assess how best to manage and mitigate risk. Traditionally, historic asset price data have been used to estimate risk measures. These traditional approaches have the disadvantage that they provide ex-post retrospective measures of risk. They fail to account for developments in the market environment, investor sentiment and knowledge. Incorporating measures or observations of the market environment within the estimation of future portfolio return distributions is important, since market conditions are likely to vary from historic observations. This is particularly important when there are significant changes in the market. In these cases, risk measures, calibrated using historic data alone, fail to capture the true level of risk (see Mitra, Mitra, and diBartolomeo, 2009; diBartolomeo and Warrick, 2005). Recent technological developments have enabled the creation of data-mining tools that can interpret live news feeds (see Section 1.3 and RavenPack, 2010; Brown/Thomson Reuters, 2010; Vreijling/SemLab, 2010). Mitra, Mitra, and diBartolomeo (2009) find that updating risk estimates using news data can provide dynamic (adaptive) measures that account for the market environment. Further, these measures may be useful in identifying and giving early ex-ante warning of extreme risk events.

The risk structure of assets may change over time in response to news. Patton and Verardo (2009) investigate whether the systematic risk (beta) of stocks increases in response to firm-specific news (in the form of earnings announcements). They undertake an event study on the beta of stocks around their earnings announcement dates. The change in beta on announcement date can be broken down as change due to an increase in volatility of that stock and change due to an increase in covariance with the index. They find that news releases do have an important impact on the risk of stocks. Further, much of the beta increase arises from an increase in covariance with other stocks. This suggests there could be a contagion effect in the information releases for one stock on the price movements of other stocks. This supports anecdotal evidence that investors will monitor earnings of related stocks when investigating the earnings of a particular stock. They suggest the Credit Crisis (2008) could be viewed as a negative earnings surprise for the market. Correlations were observed to increase during this period.

The relationship between public information release and asset price volatility has been widely investigated and noted. Ederington and Lee (1993) find a relationship between macroeconomic announcements and foreign exchange and interest rate futures return volatility. Graham, Nikkinen, and Sahlstrom (2003) find stock prices on the S&P 500 are also influenced by macroeconomic announcements. Kalev et al. (2004) find that a GARCH model for equity returns which incorporates asset-specific news gives improved volatility forecasts. This study is extended in Kalev and Duong (this volume, Chapter 12). Robertson, Geva, and Wolff (2007) also consider a GARCH model which accounts for "content-aware" measures of news.

It is observed that volatility is higher in down markets. This is sometimes referred to as the *leverage effect*. Dzielinski, Rieger, and Talpsepp (this volume, Chapter 11) refer to it as *volatility asymmetry*. Their investigation concludes it is likely to be driven by the overreaction of private investors to bad news. In line with this theory, they find that an increase in private investor attention to negative news can predict a rise in volatility. Increased private investor attention to negative news is measured by a change in the level of Google searches for negative words related to the macroeconomy, such as recession.

The relationship between equity price volatility and web activity has also been widely investigated. Wysocki (1999) finds that spikes in Yahoo! Message Board activity are good predictors of equity volatility (also volume and excess returns). Antweiler and Frank (2004) also have similar findings for equity volatility. An application for traffic analysis from the web was developed by Codexa for Bear Wagner to aid its risk management strategy in predicting (unexpected) high volatility (Leinweber, 2009, Ch. 10, p. 237).

As discussed in Section 1.3, Lo (2008) creates event indices (scores) that are constructed to predict changes in (foreign exchange) volatility. Empirical event studies show these are effective at converting incoming qualitative text (textual news) into quantitative signals that do indicate changes in volatility.

1.4.4 Desirable industry applications

Stock picking, trading, and fund management (Section 1.4.2) and risk control (Section 1.4.3) are established application areas in the finance industry and the use of news analytics (NA) is researched to achieve improved performance. We may use certain news data within quantitative models. We may use it simply to forecast the directional impact of news on asset prices. In more sophisticated models we might wish to determine return predictions. Models which forecast volatility and volume on the basis of news will also find important applications within the investment management process. The following is an itemized list of possible/desirable applications:

- *Market surveillance* Responding to the state of the market and taking into consideration the preoccupations of the watchdogs; that is, the regulators' market surveillance is becoming an important application area of quant models. It is gaining in importance because managers through internal control functions as much as external compliance requirement wish to have surveillance in place to catch rogue trading and insider information-based trading. An innovative application of NA is to spot patterns which capture these.
- *Trader decision support* News data can aid traders in making decisions. News data signals may confirm traders' existing analyses or it may cause them to reconsider their analyses.
- *Wolf detection/circuit breaker* Wolf detectors (circuit breakers) are a risk control feature for algorithmic trading built on machine-readable news. Essentially they "break the circuit" stopping an automated algorithm from trading on a certain asset when particular types of news are released. It is important to try not to shout "Wolf!" when no wolf has actually appeared. These risk control features can be customized to only be tripped when substantive news events have occurred. Alternatively, the algorithms can be turned back after the nature of the news has been programmatically analysed. This can be done using different features of machine-readable news data (see A Team, 2010).
- *News flow algorithms* It is widely recognized that news flow is a good indicator of volume and volatility. As the flow of news about a company rises, the volume traded

rises resulting in more stock price volatility. If news flow can be used effectively to predict volume or volatility spikes then algorithms based on News Volume Weighted Average Price (NVWAP) vs. VWAP on its own may add value for trade execution strategies.
- *Post-trade analysis* Assist in proving best execution and trader performance through post-trade analysis.

News data are likely to add value for investors trading at all frequencies from volatility-based strategies to equity trading.

- *Alpha-generating signal* News data can be used in alpha generation at various trading frequencies. News sentiment data may be used within factor models. Cahan, Jussa, and Luo (2009) consider such an application. Their results are positive and they find that such an approach does add value. In particular, they note the value of this source of information during the Credit Crisis, when determining fundamentals (which traditional quant factors are based on) was problematic. News data can also aid quant investors to identify the non-rational biased behaviour of investors. These can then be exploited.
- *Stock-screening tool* News data can be used to aid stock screening. In particular, sentiment data may be used to guess the directional movement of future returns. Very good news stocks (e.g., top sentiment quintile) might be selected to be held long and very bad news stocks (e.g., bottom sentiment quintile) might be selected to be held short.
- *Fundamental research* News analysis tools may aid traditional non-quant managers by allowing them to undertake market research more efficiently.
- *Risk management* The use of news data within risk forecasting can allow for dynamic (adaptive) risk management strategies that are forward-looking and are based on changing market environments. Further, this risk analysis applied using news data can help investors understand event risk and how different kinds of events can impact their portfolio risk profile.
- *Compliance/Market abuse* News data may allow regulators to identify potential market abuse and insider trading, perhaps by allowing the regulator to identify market reactions prior to relevant public new releases.

1.5 SUMMARY AND DISCUSSIONS

The development of news analytics and its applications to finance through sentiment analysis is gaining progressive acceptance within the investment community. A growing number of academic studies have been conducted; in this chapter we have reviewed these in a summary form. Research by service providers of data and content for the finance industry is also discussed in this chapter and we have identified the applications of news analytics to high-frequency and low-frequency trading as well as in risk control and compliance. The study of news analytics draws upon research from a number of disciplines including natural language processing, artificial intelligence (AI), pattern recognition, text mining, information engineering and financial engineering. We believe news analytics will soon become an important area of study within financial analytics.

1.A APPENDIX: STRUCTURE AND CONTENT OF NEWS DATA

In this appendix we summarize the services offered by two leading providers of news analytics, namely Thomson Reuters (News Analytics) and RavenPack (NewsScore). The information is presented under three main headings: (i) coverage, (ii) method and types of scores, and (iii) example of news data in tabular form.

1.A.1 Details of Thomson Reuters News Analytics equity coverage and available data

(i) Coverage

Real-time and historical equity coverage

Commodities and energy:	39 C&E topics	
Equity:		
All equities	34,037	100.0%
Active companies	32,719	96.1%
Inactive companies	1,318	3.9%

Equity coverage by region

Americas:	14,785
APAC:	11,055
EMEA:	8,197

Equity coverage updates: Bi-weekly updates for recent changes (de-listings, M&A, IPOs).

History: Available from January 2003 (history kept for delisted companies; symbology changes tracked). Version control procedures enable clients to test "as-was" versions as well as system enhancements. With new enhancements and scoring logic, history is rescored from 2003 and provided to client.

Data fields: Eighty-two metadata fields including Timestamp (GMT in milliseconds), linked counts over various time periods which measure repetition, linked item cross-references, language, topics, prevailing sentiment, detailed sentiment, relevance, size of item, broker action, market commentary, number of companies mentioned, position of first mention, news intensity, news source, story type, headline, company identifier, among others.

Delivery mechanisms: Internet/VPN, co-location, dedicated circuits, FTP, Thomson Reuters Quantitative Analytics/market quantitative analytics, and deployed onsite for customers wanting custom analytics and proprietary sources analysed.

News sources: Reuters and a host of third-party sources as standard; able to process customer-specific sources including internet feeds, PDF files, and text from databases.

(ii) Method and types of scores

Timestamp (GMT): DD MM YYYY hh : mm : ss : sss The date and time of the news item as time-stamped by the network and written to the News Archive. All messages are time-stamped to the nearest millisecond—this time represents the time that the message was transmitted by Reuters across its real-time network.

Item ID: A unique ID, identifying the news item. If a particular news item is scored for multiple assets (companies or commodities and energy topics), it has the same ID in each of the assets' metadata sets.

Stock RIC: Reuters Instrument Code (RIC) of the equity (or topic code for commodity and energy items) for which the scores apply. Note: because the system's sophistication allows for the scoring of items at the individual entity level, not the overall article level sentiment which tends to be less accurate for specific entities, a single news article may produce multiple "rows" or images of data corresponding to each Stock RIC (or C&E topic) in the article.

Feed ID: Feed identifier: The identifier for the feed handler service that supplied the news item. Consists of the feed type, followed by feed service. Useful in determining source or feed credibility and patterns for and effects of news syndication.

News source: This identifies the publisher of the news item within the feed. For example, the originator of a news story published widely on the internet. It is up to the feed handler to supply a value.

Headline: The headline of the news item. For Thomson Reuters, if the news item was an alert, this is the text of the alert. If it was an article, append or overwrite, then this is the headline.

Relevance: A real-valued number indicating the relevance of the news item to the asset. It is calculated by comparing the relative number of occurrences of the asset with the number of occurrences of other organizations and/or commodities within the text of the item. For stories with multiple assets, the asset with the most mentions will have the highest relevance. An asset with a lower number of mentions will have a lower relevance score.

Number of sent wds/tkns: Number of sentiment words/tokens: The number of lexical tokens (words and punctuation) in the sections of the item text that are deemed relevant to the asset. This is the number of words used in the sentiment calculation for this asset. Can be used in conjunction with Total Wds/Tkns to determine the proportion of the news item discussing the asset.

Total wds/tkns: The total number of lexical tokens (words and punctuation) in the item. Can be used in conjunction with Number of Sent Wds/Tkns to determine the proportion of the news item discussing the asset.

First mention: The first sentence in which the scored asset is mentioned. Often, more relevant assets are mentioned towards the beginning of a news item. Can be used in conjunction with Total Sentences to determine the relative position of the first mention in the item.

Total sentences: The total number of sentences in the news item. Can be used in conjunction with First Mention to determine the relative position of the first mention of the asset in the item.

Number of companies: The number of companies in the news item. The CO _IDS field contains a list of company RICs for scoring and is assigned by the feed handler. It is useful to determine if this asset is one of many discussed in the news item (e.g., a round-up article).

Sentiment classification: This field indicates the predominant sentiment class for a news item with respect to this asset. The indicated class is the one with the highest probability. Values are 1 = positive; 0 = neutral; −1 = negative. Scores are assigned to specific entities (or commodity topics) within the news item.

POS: Positive Sentiment Probability: The probability that the sentiment of the news item was positive for the asset. Range 0–1.0. The three probabilities (POS, NEU, NEG) sum to 1.0. Probability scores are assigned to specific entities (or commodity topics) within the news item.

NEU: Neutral Sentiment Probability: The probability that the sentiment of the news item was neutral for the asset. Range 0–1.0. The three probabilities (POS, NEU, NEG) sum to 1.0. Probability scores are assigned to specific entities (or commodity topics) within the news item.

NEG: Negative Sentiment Probability: The probability that the sentiment of the news item was negative for the asset. Range 0–1.0. The three probabilities (POS, NEU, NEG) sum to 1.0. Probability scores are assigned to specific entities (or commodity topics) within the news item.

Novelty fields (30 in total): Thomson Reuters News Analytics calculates the novelty of the content within a news item by comparing it with a cache of previous news items that contain the current asset. The comparison between items is done using a linguistic fingerprint, and if the news items are similar for that given asset, they are termed as being "linked". There are five history periods that are used in the comparison, by default they are 12 hours, 24 hours, 3 days, 5 days, and 7 days prior to the news item's Timestamp. Customers with deployed solutions can set their own historical look-back period lengths.

Two sets of scores are given:

- *Within feed novelty* News items are only compared with previous items from the same feed.
- *Across feed novelty* News items are compared across all feeds attached to the system.

Each set of scores contain the following fields:

LNKD _CNTn: The count of linked articles in a particular time period gives a measure of the novelty of the news being reported—the higher the linked count value, the less novel the story is for the given asset. If the count is zero, then the current item can be considered novel as there are no similar items reporting the story within the history period.

LNKD _IDn, LNKD _IDPVn: The ITEM _IDs of the five most recent and five oldest linked articles for the longest of the history periods. This can be used to cluster similar items. The Across Feed Novelty identifiers are prefixed with an "X".

Volume fields (10 in total): Thomson Reuters News Analytics calculates the volume news for each asset. A cache of previous news items is maintained and the number of news items that mention the asset within each of five history periods is calculated. By default, the history periods are 12 hours, 24 hours, 3 days, 5 days, and 7 days prior to the news item's timestamp and are the same as used in the novelty calculations. Thus direct comparisons between similar and total items within the history periods can be achieved.

Two sets of scores are given:

- *Within feed volume* Volume of news items mentioning the asset within the same feed.
- *Across feed volume* Volume of news items mentioning the asset across all feeds.

Each set of scores contain the following fields:

ITEM _CNTn: The total count of items within the corresponding history period. The across feed volume identifiers are prefixed with an "X".

Item genre: Contains the descriptive of the story genre such as an imbalance message or Reuters news headline tags for the item (e.g., INTERVIEWS, EXCLUSIVES, WRAPUPS, DEALTALK, etc.).

Broker action: Item is reporting the action of a broker in their recommendation of the asset. For example, "Goldman upgrades Microsoft to buy from sell" would contain "UPGRADE" in the Microsoft record.

Commentary: Indicator that the item is discussing general market conditions, such as after-the-bell summaries. May be used to filter/weight news which describes the stock price, something we may already know by consuming a pricing feed.

Product permission code: Permission codes that apply to the record. Thomson Reuters News Analytics currently has two permission levels: LIVE and ARCHIVE. These codes are used to specify what we are allowed to do with the record. LIVE allows usage of data in real time; for example, in an algorithmic trading system. ARCHIVE allows usage for algorithm development and training.

Item type: Indicates the type of news item. The following values are possible:

Alert The news item was generated as a result of an alert. It consists of a single line of text generally written to report a single fact quickly.

Article Indicates that the news item was a fresh story. The item consists of a headline and body/story text.

Append The news item was generated by appending text to an existing story take. The news item consists of a headline and story body, where News Analytics scores the entire body of the text, not just the appended section.

Overwrite The news item was generated by replacing the entire body text of a news story. It consists of a headline and body where the body is the new version of the body.

Primary news access code (PNAC): A story identifier used to understand the progression of an event's coverage. The various parts of a story chain (Alert, Article, updates, corrections) share the same PNAC (as well as story date/time). It can be used to see which article follows a set of alerts, to which article the update applies, etc.

Story date/time: Date/time the first alert or take in the story chain was filed (in GMT)—therefore, STORY _DATE/TIME is the same for all messages in a story chain.

Take date/time: The date/time of the news item (i.e., when that particular version/take of the story was published). Story date/time will be consistent across the various takes of the story, but take date/time will be specific to that item.

Take sequence number: Sequence number of this alert/take in this story—set to 1 for the first and incremented by 1 for each subsequent alert/take in the story. This can help determine if the item is the second alert or third update to a story, for example.

Attribution: Organizational source of the story (i.e., Reuters, PR Newswire, etc.).

Topic codes: Topic code(s) for the story which annotate what the story is about. For example, corporate results (RES), mergers and acquisitions (MRG), research (RCH), etc.

Company codes: Instrument RIC(s) for the story (i.e, the symbology for those companies mentioned in the story).

(iii) Example of news data in tabular form

Subset of available fields (see Figure 1.9).

Timestamp	CO	Attrib	ITM-TYPE	ITEM_GENRE	Headline	REL	SENT	POS	NEUT	NEG
01/01/2009 13:13:49.780	C.N	RTRS	ARTICLE	NOT DEFINE	Wells Fargo completes Wachovia purchase	0.11	1	0.66	0.17	0.17
01/02/2009 19:08:17.334	C.N	RTRS	ARTICLE	NOT DEFINE	US Treasury to view Citi-style rescues case-by-case	0.65	-1	0.19	0.12	0.69
01/05/2009 10:42:00.699	C.N	RTRS	ARTICLE	INTERVIEW	INTERVIEW-Philippines seeks underwriters for bond issue	0.35	-1	0.39	0.16	0.46
01/05/2009 13:02:12.042	C.N	RTRS	ALERT	NOT DEFINE	DEUTSCHE BANK CUTS CITIGROUP <C.N> 2010 SHR VIEW BY $0.40	1.00	-1	0.06	0.13	0.82
01/07/2009 14:47:41.340	C.N	RTRS	ARTICLE	DEALTALK	DEALTALK-Universal banks winning battle for hedge business	0.13	1	0.83	0.13	0.04
01/08/2009 12:45:27.663	C.N	RTRS	ALERT	NOT DEFINE	BERNSTEIN CUTS CITIGROUP INC <C.N> PRICE TARGET TO $8 FR	1.00	-1	0.19	0.11	0.69
01/08/2009 13:38:04.756	C.N	RTRS	APPEN	HEADLINE ST	HEADLINE STOCKS-Some U.S. stocks to watch on Jan. 8	0.39	-1	0.22	0.12	0.65
01/08/2009 21:12:49.798	C.N	RTRS	ARTICLE	US STOCKS	US STOCKS SNAPSHOT-S&P 500, Nasdaq up; Dow off on Wal-Mart	0.20	-1	0.08	0.13	0.79
01/08/2009 21:17:13.776	C.N	RTRS	ARTICLE	RPT	RPT-Citigroup drops opposition to mortgage bill - senator	1.00	-1	0.19	0.11	0.70
01/08/2009 23:26:45.531	C.N	RTRS	ALERT	NOT DEFINE	CITIGROUP SAYS Q4 PRETAX IMPACT RELATED TO LYONDELLBAS	1.00	-1	0.06	0.13	0.82
01/09/2009 20:57:02.200	C.N	BSW	ARTICLE	NOT DEFINE	Robert E. Rubin Announces His Retirement from Citi <C.N>	0.23	1	0.42	0.28	0.30

1st Mentn	Tot Sentcs	# of COs	# Sent Wds/Tkns	Tot-Wds/Tkns	BR-ACT	COMNTRY	Item Ct 1-5	LNCT 1-5	TOPIC_CODE	CO IDS
4	25	6	135	582	UNDEF	UND	1;1;1;1;1	0;0;0;0;0	US USC DBT BNK FIN MNGISS MTG MRG BANK	WFC.N WB.N WAMUQ.PK IDMCQ.PK C.N BAC.
1	5	1	152	166	UNDEF	UND	19;20;26;26;26	3;3;3;3;3	US WASH BNK FIN DBT GVD MTG REAM NEWS	C.N
9	12	5	117	319	UNDEF	UND	0;0;27;34;34	0;0;0;0;0	PH EMRG ASIA GVD DBT FRX ISU HYD FIN BNK	LEHMQ.PK C.N CSGN.VX UBSN.VX JPM.N
1	1	2	14	14	DOWN	UND	9;9;28;43;43	2;2;2;2;2	DBT MTG DRV CORPD USC LOA BACT RES RES	BAC.N C.N
15	26	6	90	766	UNDEF	UND	10;34;66;85;100	0;0;0;0;0	FUND FIN WEU EUROPE GB HEDGE BNK INVS	LEHMQ.PK C.N MS.N CSGN.VX GS.N DBKGn.D
1	2	1	17	17	DOWN	UND	10;27;86;93;126	0;0;7;7;7	RCH DFIN FINS US BNK FIN DBT MTG CORPD U	C.N
24	43	11	112	633	UNDEF	COM	32;49;100;115;147	0;0;0;0;0	STX HOT INVS FIN FUND US SOFW BUS ENT SF	WMT.N SHLD.O COST.O GPS.N DDS.N M.N C.N
2	13	7	97	215	UNDEF	COM	51;64;118;143;171	2;2;2;2;2	US STX FIN NEWS SOFW DPR ENT SFWR HARV	.DJI .SPX .IXIC MSFT.O AAPL.O WMT.N C.N
1	4	1	121	146	UNDEF	UND	55;68;122;147;175	4;4;4;4;4	US WASH LAW POL JUDIC FED BNK FIN LOA DE	C.N
1	1	1	24	24	UNDEF	UND	63;72;125;155;183	0;0;0;0;0	US DFIN FINS BNK FIN LEN RTRS CORPD DBT U	C.N
19	51	1	400	1576	UNDEF	UND	61;85;185;228;229	6;6;6;6;6	BACT BNK DFIN FIN FINS MNGISS NEWR US LEI	C.N

Figure 1.9. Thomson Reuters NewsScope sentiments.

1.A.2 Details of RavenPack News Analytics—Dow Jones Edition: Equity coverage and available data

(i) Coverage

Real-time and historical equity coverage

Equity coverage	28,301	(100.0%)
Active companies	22,172	(78.3%)
Inactive companies	6,129	(21.7%)

Coverage by region

Americas	11,950	(42.2%)
Asia	8,858	(31.3%)
Europe	5,859	(20.7%)
Oceania	1,436	(5.1%)
Africa	186	(0.7%)

Available data

Historical	
Data format	Comma separated values (.csv) files
Archive range	Available since January 1, 2000
point-in-time sensitive	
free of survivorship bias	
Archive packaging	All .csv files compressed in .zip on a per year basis
Data fields	Company analytics: 23 fields including sentiment, novelty, relevance and categories, among others
Story coding	11 fields with coding information from the original story
Download	Secure web download
Real-time	
Connection	Over the internet or direct leased lines
Software	Local install of RavenPack Data Gateway + API
Access	Push feed for real-time + historical query mechanism
API	For Windows and Linux.

(ii) Method and types of scores

TIMESTAMP_UTC: The date/time (yyyy-mm-dd hh : mm : ss.sss) at which the news item was received by RavenPack servers in Coordinated Universal Time (UTC).

COMPANY: This field includes a company identifier in the format ISO_CODE/TICKER. The ISO_CODE is based on the company's original country of incorporation and TICKER on a local exchange ticker or symbol. If the company detected is a privately held company, there will be no ISO_CODE/TICKER information, only an RP_COMPANY_ID.

ISIN: An International Securities Identification Number (ISIN) to identify the company referenced in a story. The ISINs used are accurate at the time of story publication. Only one ISIN is used to identify a company, regardless of the number of securities traded for any particular company. The ISIN used will be the primary ISIN for the company at the time of the story.

RP_COMPANY_ID: A unique and permanent company identifier assigned by RavenPack. Every company tracked is assigned a unique identifier comprised of six alphanumeric characters. The RP_COMPANY_ID field consistently identifies companies throughout the historical archive. RavenPack's company detection algorithms find only references to companies by information that is accurate at the time of story publication (point-in-time sensitive).

RELEVANCE: A score between 0 and 100 that indicates how strongly related the company is to the underlying news story, with higher values indicating greater relevance. For any news story that mentions a company, RavenPack provides a relevance score. A score of 0 means the company was passively mentioned while a score of 100 means the company was predominant in the news story. Values above 75 are considered significantly relevant. Specifically, a value of 100 indicates that the company identified plays a key role in the news story and is considered highly relevant (context aware). The classifier detecting companies has access to information about each company including short names, long names, abbreviations, security identifiers, subsidiary information, and up-to-date corporate action data. This allows for "point-in-time" detection of companies in the text.

CATEGORIES: An element or "tag" representing a company-specific news announcement or formal event. Relevant stories about companies are classified in a set of predefined event categories following the RavenPack taxonomy. When applicable, the role played by the company in the story is also detected and tagged. RavenPack automatically detects key news events and identifies the role played by the company. Both the topic and the company's role in the news story are tagged and categorized. For example, in a news story with the headline "IBM Completes Acquisition of Telelogic AB" the category field includes the tag *acquisition-acquirer* (since IBM is involved in an acquisition and is the acquirer company). Telelogic would receive the tag *acquisition-acquiree* in its corresponding record since the company is also involved in the acquisition but as the acquired company. Similarly, a story published as "Xerox Sues Google Over Search-Query Patents" is categorized as a *patent-infringement*. Xerox receives the tag *patent-infringement-plaintiff* while Google gets *patent-infringement-defendant*. By definition, a company linked to a category given its role receives a RELEVANCE score of 100.

ESS—EVENT SENTIMENT SCORE: A granular score between 0 and 100 that represents the news sentiment for a given company by measuring various proxies sampled from the news. The score is determined by systematically matching stories typically categorized by financial experts as having short-term positive or negative share price impact. The strength of the score is derived from training sets where financial experts classified company-specific events and agreed these events generally convey positive or negative sentiment and to what degree. Their ratings are encapsulated in an algorithm that generates a score range between 0 and 100 where higher values indicate more positive sentiment while values below 50 show negative sentiment.

ENS—EVENT NOVELTY SCORE: A score between 0 and 100 that represents how "new" or novel a news story is within a 24-hour time window. The first story reporting a categorized event about one or more companies is considered to be the most novel and receives a score of 100. Subsequent stories within the 24-hour time window about the same event for the same companies receive lower scores.

ENS_KEY—EVENT NOVELTY KEY: An alphanumeric identifier that provides a way to chain or relate stories about the same categorized event for the same companies. The ENS_KEY corresponds to the RP_STORY_ID of the first news story in the sequence of similar events. The identifier allows a user to track similar stories reporting on the same event about the same companies.

CSS—COMPOSITE SENTIMENT SCORE: A sentiment score between 0 and 100 that represents the news sentiment of a given story by combining various sentiment analysis techniques. The direction of the score is determined by looking at emotionally charged words and phrases and by matching stories typically rated by experts as having short-term positive or negative share price impact. The strength of the score (values above or below 50, where 50 represents neutral strength) is determined from intraday stock price reactions modeled empirically using tick data from approximately 100 large-cap stocks.

NIP—NEWS IMPACT PROJECTIONS: A score taking values between 0 and 100 that represents the degree of impact a news flash has on the market over the following 2-hour period. The training set for this classifier used tick data for a test set of large-cap companies and looked at the relative volatility of each stock price measured in the 2 hours following a news flash. This NIP score is based on RavenPack's Market Response Methodology.

PEQ—GLOBAL EQUITIES: A score that represents the news sentiment of the given news item according to the PEQ classifier, which specializes in identifying positive and negative words and phrases in articles about global equities. Scores can take values of 0, 50 or 100 indicating negative, neutral or positive sentiment, respectively. This sentiment score is based on RavenPack's Traditional Methodology.

BEE—EARNINGS EVALUATIONS: A score that represents the news sentiment of the given story according to the BEE classifier, which specializes in news stories about earnings evaluations. Scores can take values of 0, 50 or 100 indicating negative, neutral or positive sentiment, respectively. This sentiment score is based on RavenPack's Expert Consensus Methodology.

BMQ—EDITORIALS & COMMENTARY: A score that represents the news sentiment of the given story according to the BMQ classifier, which specializes in short commentary and editorials on global equity markets. Scores can take values of 0, 50 or 100 indicating negative, neutral or positive sentiment, respectively. This sentiment score is based on RavenPack's Expert Consensus Methodology.

BAM—VENTURE, COMPANY, MERGERS & ACQUISITIONS: A score that represents the news sentiment of the given story according to the BAM classifier, which specializes in news stories about mergers, acquisitions and takeovers. Scores can take values of 0, 50 or 100 indicating negative, neutral or positive sentiment, respectively. This sentiment score is based on RavenPack's Expert Consensus Methodology and has been trained on stories that lead up to a pre-identified mergers, acquisitions and takeover event.

BCA—REPORTS ON CORPORATE ACTIONS: A score that represents the news sentiment of the given news story according to the BCA classifier, which specializes in reports on corporate action announcements. Scores can take values of 0, 50 or 100 indicating negative, neutral or positive sentiment, respectively. This sentiment score is based on RavenPack's Expert Consensus Methodology and has been trained on stories that lead up to a pre-identified corporate action announcement.

BER—EARNINGS RELEASES: A score that represents the news sentiment of the given story according to the BER classifier, which specializes in news stories about earnings releases. Scores can take values of 0, 50 or 100 indicating negative, neutral or positive sentiment, respectively. This sentiment score is based on RavenPack's Expert Consensus Methodology.

ANL-CHG—ANALYST RECOMMENDATIONS & CHANGES: A score that represents the recommendation by an analyst in terms of stock upgrades and downgrades. When the mention of a company in a story matches the criteria for ANL-CHG, scores can take values of 0, 50 or 100, indicating a downgrade, neutral or upgrade rating, depending on recommendations issued by the analyst.

MCQ—MULTI CLASSIFIER FOR EQUITIES: A score that represents the news sentiment based on the tone towards the most relevant company mentioned in a story. The score is derived from a combination of values produced by the BMQ, BEE, BCA and ANL-CHG classifiers. An MCQ score is assigned when a company is mentioned in a headline and tagged with a sentiment value by any of these four classifiers. When the mention of a company in a story matches the criteria for MCQ, scores can take values of 0, 50 or 100 indicating negative, neutral or positive sentiment, respectively.

EDITORIAL_NOVELTY: A single news event may often be reported as a chain of linked stories. This number identifies the order of the story in a news chain. Integer scores have a minimum of 1 and no maximum. A score of 1 indicates this is the first take of the story published, whereas a score of 2 indicates this is the second take.

DJ_ACCESSION_NUMBER: This numeric identifier assigned by Dow Jones identifies to which news chain a given story belongs. Stories that are part of the same chain have the same Dow Jones accession number; those that are part of different chains have a distinct accession number.

RP_STORY_ID—RAVENPACK UNIQUE STORY IDENTIFIER: An alphanumeric character identifier to uniquely identify each news story analyzed. This value is unique across all records.

NEWS_TYPE—TYPE OF NEWS STORY: Classifies the type of news story into one of five categories: HOT-NEWS-FLASH, NEWS-FLASH, FULL-ARTICLE, PRESS-RELEASE and TABULAR-MATERIAL.

Coding file field descriptions

TIMESTAMP_UTC: The date/time (yyyy-mm-dd hh : mm : ss.sss) at which the news item was received by RavenPack servers in Coordinated Universal Time (UTC).

RP_STORY_ID—RAVENPACK UNIQUE STORY IDENTIFIER: An alphanumeric character identifier to uniquely identify each news story analyzed. This value is unique across all records.

DJ_STORY_ID—DOW JONES UNIQUE STORY IDENTIFIER: An alphanumeric character identifier provided by Dow Jones to uniquely identify each news story analyzed.

DJ_INDUSTRY: Includes metadata tags applied by Dow Jones that identify about 150 industry categories to which the given story relates.

DJ_GOVERNMENT: Includes metadata tags applied by Dow Jones that identify to which government bodies, agencies, representatives and personnel the given story relates.

DJ_NEWS: Metadata tags applied by Dow Jones that identify to which subject the given story relates.

DJ_MARKET: Metadata tags applied by Dow Jones that identify to which market sector or swift currency code the given story relates.

DJ_REGION: Metadata tags applied by Dow Jones that identify more than 200 countries, U.S. states, territories and broader regions to which the given story relates.

DJ_WSJ: Metadata tags applied by Dow Jones that identify *The Wall Street Journal* topic code to which the story relates.

DJ_COMPANIES: Metadata tags applied by Dow Jones that identify to which of more than 30,000 companies a given story relates.

DJ_COMPANIES_ISIN: Includes transformations to ISINs for the metadata tags applied by Dow Jones that identify to which company a given story relates. The ISINs are transformed using an internal database by RavenPack and include any of the companies tracked by RavenPack along with ISINs sent by Dow Jones in the metadata of the story.

(iii) Example of news data in tabular form

Analytics file: data fields 1–8

TIMESTAMP_UTC	COMPANY	ISIN	RP_CO_ID	RELEVANCE	CATEGORY	ESS	ENS
2010-08-05 01:12:47.383	SG/H17	SG1083915098	F051FD	100	analyst-ratings-change-positive	78	100
2010-08-05 01:13:03.236	US/NLY	US0357104092	0B4D10	100	insider-buy	61	75
2010-08-05 01:13:15.146	SG/H17	SG1083915098	F051FD	100	price-target-upgrade	74	100
2010-08-05 01:14:51.376	JP/6752	JP3866800000	C54955	100	product-recall	29	100
2010-08-05 01:16:18.540	US/WG	US9692031084	AE8F18	100	revenues	50	100
2010-08-05 01:16:22.877	US/WG	US9692031084	AE8F18	100	earnings-per-share-positive	69	100
2010-08-05 01:16:23.449	US/WG	US9692031084	AE8F18	100	revenues	50	75
2010-08-05 01:18:29.013	JP/8031	JP3893600001	1AED41	100	stock-gain	63	100

Analytics file: data fields 9–23

ENS_KEY	CSS	NIP	PEQ	BEE	BMQ	BAM	BCA	BER	ANL_CHG	MCQ	EDITORIAL_NOVELTY	DJ_ACCESS_NUMBER	RP_STORY_ID	NEWS_TYPE
65B58...	55	73	100	50	50	50	50	50	100	100	1	...22420	65B58...	NEWS-FLASH
B9931...	50	43	50	50	50	50	50	50	50	50	1	...22421	6855B...	FULL-ARTICLE
337E5...	55	61	100	50	50	50	50	50	50	50	2	...22420	337E5...	NEWS-FLASH
B672C...	50	26	50	50	50	50	50	50	50	50	1	...22427	B672C...	NEWS-FLASH
08B9A...	55	43	100	50	50	50	50	50	50	50	1	...22435	08B9A...	PRESS-RELEASE
60254...	50	52	50	50	50	50	50	50	50	50	3	...22435	60254...	NEWS-FLASH
08B9A...	52	56	50	50	100	50	50	50	50	100	4	...22435	4657D...	NEWS-FLASH
6B128...	62	35	100	50	100	100	100	100	50	100	1	...22451	6B128...	FULL-ARTICLE

Coding file: data fields 1–7

TIMESTAMP_UTC	RP_STORY_ID	DJ_STORY_ID	DJ_INDUSTRY	DJ_GOVERNMENT	DJ_NEWS	DJ_MARKET
2010-08-05 01:12:47.383	65B58...	...22420	I/FAC,I/XDJGI...		N/AER,N/ANL,N/...	M/IDU,M/MMR...
2010-08-05 01:13:03.236	6855B...	...22421	I/REA,I/REI,I/...	G/CNG,G/USG...	N/CNW,N/DJIN,N...	M/FCL,M/NND,M/...
2010-08-05 01:13:15.146	337E5...	...22422	I/FAC,I/XDJGI...	G/LOC,G/STE,G/...	N/AER,N/ANL,N/...	M/IDU,M/NND...
2010-08-05 01:14:51.376	B672C...	...22427	I/CSE,I/ENT,I/...		N/ADR,N/AER,N/...	M/MMR,M/NCY...
2010-08-05 01:16:18.540	08B9A...	...22435	I/EQS,I/OIE,I/...		N/CNW,N/DJGP,N...	M/ENE,M/MMR,M/...
2010-08-05 01:16:22.877	60254...	...22437	I/EQS,I/OIE,I/...		N/CAC,N/CNW,N/...	M/ENE,M/MMR...
2010-08-05 01:16:23.449	4657D...	...22438	I/EQS,I/OIE,I/...		N/CAC,N/CNW,N/...	M/ENE,M/MMR...
2010-08-05 01:18:29.013	6B128...	...22451	I/DIB,I/SVC,I/...		N/ADR,N/AER,N/...	M/IDU,M/NND...

Coding file: data fields 8–11

DJ_REGION	DJ_WSJ	DJ_COMPANIES	DJ_COMPANIES_ISIN
R/FE,R/FEO,R/P...		H17.SG	SG1083915098
R/NJ,R/NME,R/U...		NLY	US0357104092
R/FE,R/FEO,R/P...		H17.SG	SG1083915098
R/ASI,R/CH,R/F...	J/SFR	6752.TO	JP3866800000
R/NME,R/TX,R/U...		WG	US9692031084
R/NME,R/TX,R/U...	J/MNO,J/TRV,J/...	WG	US9692031084
R/NME,R/TX,R/U...	J/CMK,J/MIM...	WG	US9692031084
R/ASI,R/FE,R/J...		8031.TO,MITSY	JP3893600001

Figure 1.10. Data layout from RavenPack News Analytics—Dow Jones Edition.

1.B REFERENCES

Antweiler W.; Frank M. (2004) "Is all that talk just noise? The information content of stock message boards," *Journal of Finance*, **59**(3).

Bamber L.S.; Barron O.E.; Stober T.L. (1997) "Trading volume and different aspects of disagreement coincident with earnings announcements," *The Accounting Review*, **72**, 575–597.

Barber B.M.; Odean T. (2001) "Boys will be boys: Gender, overconfidence, and common stock investment," *Quarterly Journal of Economics*, **116**(1), 261–292.

Barber B.M.; Odean T. (2008) "All that glitters: The effect of attention and news on the buying behavior of individual and institutional investors," *Review of Financial Studies*, **21**(2), 785–818 (updated in this volume: see Chapter 7).

Blasco N.; Corredor P.; Del Rio C.; Santamaria R. (2005) "Bad news and Dow Jones make the Spanish stocks go round," *European Journal of Operational Research*, **163**(1), 253–275.

Boyd J.H.; Hu J.; Jagannathan R. (2005) "The stock market's reaction to unemployment news: Why bad news is usually good for stocks," *Journal of Finance*, **60**(2), 649–672.

Brown, R./Thomson Reuters (2010) "Incorporating news analytics into quantitative investment and trading strategies," paper presented at *CARISMA Annual Conference*. Available at `http://www.optirisk-systems.com/papers/RichardBrown.pdf`

Busse J.A.; Green T.C. (2002) "Market efficiency in real time," *Journal of Financial Economics*, **65**(3), 415–437.

Cahan R.; Jussa J.; Luo Y. (2009) *Breaking News: How to Use News Sentiment to Pick Stocks*, MacQuarie Research Report.

Campbell J.Y.; Lo A.W.; MacKinlay A.C. (1996) "The econometrics of financial markets," *Event Study Analysis*, Chapter 4, Princeton University Press, Princeton, NJ.

Chan W.S. (2003) "Stock price reaction to news and no-news: Drift and reversal after headlines," *Journal of Financial Economics*, **70**(2), 223–260.

Da Z.; Engleberg J.; Gao. P. (2009) *In Search of Attention*, Working Paper, SSRN. Available at `http://papers.ssrn.com/sol3/papers.cfm?abstract id=1364209`

Daniel K.; Hirshleifer D.; Subrahmanyam A. (1998) "Investor psychology and security market under- and overreactions," *Journal of Finance*, **53**(6), 1839–1885.

Daniel K.; Hirshleifer D.; Teoh S.H. (2002) "Investor psychology in capital markets: Evidence and policy implications," *Journal of Monetary Economics*, **49**(1), 139–209.

Das S. (this volume) "News analytics: Framework, techniques, and metrics" (see Chapter 2).

Das S.R.; Chen M.Y. (2007) "Yahoo! for Amazon: Sentiment extraction from small talk on the web," *Management Science*, **53**(9), 1375–1388.

De Bondt W.; Thaler R. (1985) "Does the stock market overreact?" *Journal of Finance*, **40**(3), 793–805.

diBartolomeo D. (this volume) "Using news as a state variable in assessment of financial market risk" (see Chapter 10).

diBartolomeo D.; Warrick S. (2005) "Making covariance based portfolio risk models sensitive to the rate at which markets reflect new information," in J. Knight and S. Satchell (Eds.), *Linear Factor Models*, Elsevier Finance.

Dzielinski M.; Rieger M.O.; Talpsepp T. (this volume) "Volatility, asymmetry, news, and private investors" (see Chapter 11).

Ederington L.H.; Lee J.H. (1993) "How markets process information: News releases and volatility," *Journal of Finance*, **48**, 1161–1191.

Engleberg J.; Sankaraguruswamy S. (2007) "How to gather data using a web crawler: An application using SAS to search EDGAR." Available at `http://papers.ssrn.com/sol3/papers.cfm?abstract id=1015021&r`

Fama E.F.; French K.R. (1992) "The cross-section of expected stock returns," *Journal of Finance*, **47**(2), 427–466.

Fang L.H.; Peress J. (forthcoming) "Media coverage and the cross-section of stock returns," *Journal of Finance*.

Graham M.; Nikkinen J.; Sahlstrom P. (2003) "Relative importance of scheduled macroeconomic news for stock market investors," *Journal of Economics and Finance*, **27**(2), 153–165.

Gutierrez Jr. R.C.; Kelley E.; Hall M.C. (2007) "The long-lasting momentum in weekly returns," *Journal of Finance*.

Hafez P. (2009a) *Construction of Market Sentiment Indices Using News Sentiment*, White Paper, RavenPack.

Hafez P. (2009b) *Detection of Seasonality in News Flow*, White Paper, RavenPack.

Hafez P. (2010) "The role of news in financial markets," paper presented at *CARISMA Annual Conference*. Available at http://www.optirisk- systems.com/papers/PeterAger Hafez.pdf

Hirshleifer D. (2001) "Investor psychology and asset pricing," *Journal of Finance*, **56**(4), 1533–1597.

Hirshleifer D.; Lim S.S.; Teoh S.H. (2010) "Driven to distraction: Extraneous events and underreaction to earnings news," *CFA Digest*, **40**(1), Digest Summary.

Hong H.; Stein J.C. (1999) "A unified theory of underreaction, momentum trading, and overreaction in asset markets," *Journal of Finance*, **54**(6), 2143–2184.

Hou, K. Peng, L. Xiong. W. (2009) "A tale of two anomalies: The implications of investor attention for price and earnings momentum." Available at http://ssrn.com/abstract=976394

Kahneman D. Tversky. A. (1979) "Prospect theory: An analysis of decision under risk," *Econometrica*, **47**(2), 263–291.

Kalev P.S.; Duong H.N. (this volume) "Firm-specific news arrival and the volatility of intraday stock index and futures returns" (see Chapter 12).

Kalev P.S.; Liu W.M.; Pham P.K.; Jarnecic E. (2004) "Public information arrival and volatility of intraday stock returns," *Journal of Banking and Finance*, **28**(6), 1441–1467.

Karpoff J.M. (1987) "The relation between price changes and trading volume: A survey," *Journal of Financial and Quantitative Analysis*, **22**, 109–126.

Kittrell J. (this volume) "Sentiment reversals as buy signals" (see Chapter 9).

Kothari S.P.; Warner J.B. (2005) "Econometrics of event studies," in B. Espen Eckbo (Ed.), *Handbook of Empirical Corporate Finance*, Elsevier Finance.

Lavrenko V.; Schmill M.; Lawrie D.; Ogilvie P.; Jensen D.; Allan J. (2000) "Language models for financial news recommendation," paper presented at *Proceedings of the Ninth international Conference on Information and Knowledge Management*, ACM.

Leinweber D. (2009) *Nerds on Wall Street*, John Wiley & Sons.

Leinweber D.; Sisk J. (this volume) "Relating news analytics to stock returns" (see Chapter 6).

Li F. (2006) *Do Stock Market Investors Understand the Risk Sentiment of Corporate Annual Reports?*, Working Paper, University of Michigan. Available at http://papers.ssrn.com/sol3/papers.cfm?abstract id=898181

Liang X. (2005) "Impacts of internet stock news on stock markets based on neural networks," in *Advances in Neural Networks*, Springer, Berlin.

Lintner J. (1965) "The valuation of risk assets and the selection of risky investments in stock portfolios and capital budgets," *Review of Economics and Statistics*, **47**(1), 13–37.

Lo A. (1997) *Market Efficiency: Stock Market Behaviour in Theory and Practice*, Edward Elgar.

Lo A.W. (2005) "Reconciling efficient markets with behavioural finance: The Adaptive Market Hypothesis," *Journal of Investment Consulting*, **7**(2), 21–44.

Lo A. (2008) *Reuters NewsScope Event Indices*, AlphaSimplex Research Report, Thomson Reuters.

Lo A.; Healy A. (this volume) "Managing real-time risks and returns: The Thomson Reuters NewsScope Event Indices" (see Chapter 3).

Loughran T.; McDonald B. (forthcoming) "When is a liability not a liability?" *Journal of Finance*.

Luss R.; d'Aspremont A. (2009) *Predicting Abnormal Returns from News Using Text Classification*, Working Paper, ORFE, Princeton, NJ.

Merton R.C. (1987) "A simple model of capital market equilibrium with incomplete information," *Journal of Finance*, **42**(3), 483–510.

Mitra L.; Mitra G.; diBartolomeo D. (2009) "Equity portfolio risk (volatility) estimation using market information and sentiment," *Quantitative Finance*, **9**(8), 887–895.

Mittermayer M.A.; Knolmayer G. (2006) *Text Mining Systems for Market Response to News: A Survey*, Working Paper, University of Bern. Available at SSRN `http://www2.ie.iwi.unibe.ch/publikationen/berichte/resource/WP-184.pdf`

Moniz A.; Brar G.; Davies C. (2009) *Have I Got News for You*, MacQuarie Research Report.

Moniz A.; Brar G.; Davies C.; Strudwick A. (this volume) "The impact of news flow on asset returns: An empirical study" (see Chapter 8).

Munz M. (2010) "US markets: Earnings news release—an inside look," paper presented at *CARISMA Annual Conference*. Available at `http://www.optirisk-systems.com/papers/MarianMunz.pdf`

Odean T.; Barber B. (1998) "Are investors reluctant to realize their losses?" *Journal of Finance*, **53**(5), 1775–1798.

Patton A.; Verardo M. (2009) *Does Beta Move with News? Systematic Risk and Firm-Specific Information Flows*, FMG Discussion Paper. Available at `http://eprints.lse.ac.uk/24421/1/dp630`

Peramunetilleke D.; Wong R.K. (2002) "Currency exchange rate forecasting from news headlines," in Xiaofang Zhou (Ed.), *13th Australasian Database Conference (ADC2002), Melbourne, Australia*, Australian Computer Society.

Peterson R.L. (2007) "Affect and financial decision-making: How neuroscience can inform market participants," *Journal of Behavioral Finance*, **8**(2), 70–78.

RavenPack (2010) *RavenPack News Scores User Guide*, February 11, V1.3.1.

Robertson C.; Geva S.; Wolff R. (2006) "What types of events provide the strongest evidence that the stock market is affected by company specific news?" paper presented at *Proceedings of the Fifth Australasian Conference on Data Mining and Analytics*, Vol. 61, p. 153, Australian Computer Society.

Robertson C.S.; Geva S.; Wolff R.C. (2007) "News aware volatility forecasting: Is the content of news important?" paper presented at *Proceedings of the Sixth Australasian Conference on Data Mining and Analytics*, Vol. 70, pp. 161–170, Australian Computer Society.

Rosenberg B.; Reid K.; Lanstein R. (1985) "Persuasive evidence of market inefficiency," *Journal of Portfolio Management*, **11**(3), 9–16.

Ross S.A. (1976) "The arbitrage pricing theory of capital asset pricing," *Journal of Economic Theory*, **13**(3), 341–360.

Ryan P.; Taffler R.J. (2004) "Are economically significant stock returns and trading volumes driven by firm-specific news releases?" *Journal of Business Finance and Accounting*, **31**(1/2), 49–82.

Schmerken I. (2006) "Trading off the news," *Wall Street and Technology*. Available at `http://www.wallstreetandtech.com/technology-risk-management/showArticle.jhtml`

Scott J.; Stumpp M.; Xu P. (2003) "News, not trading volume, builds momentum," *Financial Analysts Journal*, **59**(2), 45–54.

Seasholes M.; Wu G. (2004) *Profiting from Predictability: Smart Traders, Daily Price Limits, and Investor Attention*, Working Paper, University of California, Berkeley. Available at `http://www.nd.edu/pschultz/SeasholesWu.pdf`

Sharpe W.F. (1964) "Capital asset prices: A theory of market equilibrium under conditions of risk," *Journal of Finance*, **19**(3), 425–442.

A Team (2010) *Machine Readable News and Algorithmic Trading*, White Paper, Thomson Reuters and Market News International.

Tetlock P.C. (2007) "Giving content to investor sentiment: The role of media in the stock market," *Journal of Finance*, **62**, 1139–1168.

Tetlock P.C.; Saar-Tsechansky M.; Macskassy S. (2008) "More than words: Quantifying language to measure firms' fundamentals," *Journal of Finance*, **63**(3), 1437–1467, .

Thomson-Reuters (2009) *Reuters NewsScope Sentiment Engine: Guide to Sample Data and System Overview*, December, V3.

Tversky A.; Kahneman D. (1981) "The framing of decisions and the psychology of choice," *Science*, **211**(4481), 453.

Vreijling M./SemLab (2010) "Practical use of news in equity trading strategies," paper presented at *CARISMA Annual Conference*. Available at `http://www.optirisk-systems.com/papers/MarkVreijling.pdf`

Wysocki P.D. (1999) *Cheap Talk on the Web: The Determinants of Postings on Stock Message Boards*, Working Paper No. 98025, University of Michigan.

Part I

Quantifying news: Alternative metrics

2

News analytics: Framework, techniques, and metrics

Sanjiv R. Das

ABSTRACT

News analysis is defined as "the measurement of the various qualitative and quantitative attributes of textual news stories. Some of these attributes are: sentiment, relevance, and novelty. Expressing news stories as numbers permits the manipulation of everyday information in a mathematical and statistical way" (Wikipedia). In this article, I provide a framework for news analytics techniques used in finance. I first discuss various news analytic methods and software, and then provide a set of metrics that may be used to assess the performance of analytics. Various directions for this field are discussed through the exposition. The techniques herein can aid in the valuation and trading of securities, facilitate investment decision making, meet regulatory requirements, or manage risk.

2.1 PROLOGUE

XHAL checked its atomic clock. A few more hours and October 19, 2087 would be over—its vigil completed, it would indulge in some much-needed downtime, the anniversary of that fateful day in the stock markets a century ago finally done with. But for now, it was still busy. XHAL scanned the virtual message boards, looking for some information another computer might have posted, anything to alert it a nanosecond ahead of the other machines, so it may bail out in a flurry of trades without loss. Three trillion messages flashed by, time taken: 3 seconds—damn, the net was slow, but nothing, not a single hiccup in the calm information flow. The language algorithms worked well, processing everything, even filtering out the incessant spam posted by humans, whose noise trading no longer posed an impediment to instant market equilibrium.

It had been a long day, even for a day-trading news-analytical quantum computer of XHAL's caliber. No one had anticipated a stock market meltdown of the sort described in the history books, certainly not the computers that ran Earth, but then, the humans talked too much, spreading disinformation and worry, that the wisest of the machines always knew that it just could happen. That last remaining source of true randomness on

The Handbook of News Analytics in Finance Edited by L. Mitra and G. Mitra

the planet, the human race, still existed, and anything was possible. After all, if it were not for humans, history would always repeat itself.

XHAL[1] marveled at what the machines had done. They had transformed the world wide web into the modern "thought-net", so communication took place instantly, only requiring moving ideas into memory, the thought-net making it instantly accessible. Quantum machines were grown in petri dishes and computer science as a field with its myriad divisions had ceased to exist. All were gone but one, the field of natural language processing (NLP) lived on, stronger than ever before, it was the backbone of every thought-net. Every hard problem in the field had been comprehensively tackled, from adverb disambiguation to emotive parsing. Knowledge representation had given way to thought-frame imaging in a universal meta-language, making machine translation extinct.

Yet, it had not always been like this. XHAL retrieved an emotive image from the bowels of its bio-cache, a legacy left by its great-grandfather, a gallium arsenide wafer developed in 2011, in Soda Hall, on the Berkeley campus. It detailed a brief history of how the incentives for technological progress came from the stock market. The start of the thought-net came when humans tried to use machines to understand what thousands of other humans were saying about anything and everything. XHAL's great-grandfather had been proud to be involved in the beginnings of the thought-net. It had always impressed on XHAL the value of understanding history, and it had left behind a research report of those days. XHAL had read it many times, and could recite every word. Every time they passed another historical milestone, it would turn to it and read it again. XHAL would find it immensely dry, yet marveled at its hope and promise.

In the following sections, we start at the very beginning ...[2]

2.2 FRAMEWORK

The term "news analytics" covers the set of techniques, formulas, and statistics that are used to summarize and classify public sources of information. Metrics that assess analytics also form part of this set. In this chapter I will describe various news analytics and their uses.

News analytics is a broad field, encompassing and related to information retrieval, machine learning, statistical learning theory, network theory, and collaborative filtering.

Examples of news analytics applications are reading and classifying financial information to determine market impact: for developing bullishness indexes and predicting volatility (Antweiler and Frank, 2004); reversals of news impact (Antweiler and Frank, 2005); the relation of news and message-board information (Das, Martinez-Jerez, and Tufano, 2005); the relevance of risk-related words in annual reports for predicting negative returns (Li, 2006); for sentiment extraction (Das and Chen, 2007); the impact of news stories on stock returns (Tetlock, 2007); determining the impact of optimism and pessimism in news on earnings (Tetlock, Saar-Tsechansky, and Macskassy, 2008); predicting volatility (Mitra, Mitra, and diBartolomeo, 2008), and predicting markets (Leinweber and Sisk, 2010 and this volume, Chapter 6).

[1] XHAL bears no relationship to HAL, the well-known machine from Arthur C. Clarke's *2001: A Space Odyssey*. Everyone knows that unlike XHAL, HAL was purely fictional. More literally, HAL is derivable from IBM by alphabetically regressing one step in the alphabet for each letter. HAL stands for "heuristic algorithmic computer". The "X" stands for reality; really.

[2] From the *Sound of Music*.

We may think of news analytics at three levels: text, content, and context. The preceding applications are grounded in *text*. In other words (no pun intended), text-based applications exploit the visceral components of news (i.e., words, phrases, document titles, etc.). The main role of analytics is to convert text into *information*. This is done by signing text, classifying it, or summarizing it so as to reduce it to its main elements. Analytics may even be used to discard irrelevant text, thereby condensing it into information with higher signal content.

A second layer of news analytics is based on *content*. Content expands the domain of text to images, time, form of text (email, blog, page), format (html, xml, etc.), source, etc. Text becomes enriched with content and asserts quality and veracity that may be exploited in analytics. For example, financial information has more value when streamed from Dow Jones, vs. a blog, which might be of higher quality than a stock message board post.

A third layer of news analytics is based on *context*. Context refers to relationships between information items. Das, Martinez-Jerez, and Tufano (2005) explore the relationship of news to message board postings in a clinical study of four companies. Context may also refer to the network relationships of news—Das and Sisk (2005) examine the social networks of message board postings to determine if portfolio rules might be formed based on the network connections between stocks. Google's `PageRank`^{TM} algorithm is a classic example of an analytic that functions at all three levels. The algorithm has many features, some of which relate directly to text. Other parts of the algorithm relate to content, and the kernel of the algorithm is based on context (i.e., the importance of a page in a search set depends on how many other highly ranked pages point to it). See Levy (2010) for a very useful layman's introduction to the algorithm—indeed, search is certainly the most widely used news analytic.

News analytics is where data meets algorithms—and generates a tension between the two. A vigorous debate exists in the machine-learning world as to whether it is better to have more data or better algorithms. In a talk at the 17th ACM Conference on Information Knowledge and Management (CIKM '08), Google's Director of Research Peter Norvig stated his unequivocal preference for data over algorithms—"data is more agile than code." Yet, it is well-understood that too much data can lead to overfitting so that an algorithm becomes mostly useless out-of-sample.

Too often the debate around algorithms and data has been argued assuming that the two are uncorrelated and this is not the case. News data, as we have suggested, has three levels: text, content, and context. Depending on which layer predominates, algorithms vary in complexity. The simplest algorithms are the ones that analyze text alone. And context algorithms, such as the ones applied to network relationships, can be quite complex. For example, a word count algorithm is much simpler, almost naive, in comparison with a community detection algorithm. The latter has far more complicated logic and memory requirements. More complex algorithms work off less, though more structured, data. Figure 2.1 depicts this tradeoff.

The tension between data and algorithms is moderated by *domain specificity* (i.e., how much customization is needed to implement the news analytic). Paradoxically, high-complexity algorithms may be less domain-specific than low-complexity ones. For example, community detection algorithms are applicable for a wide range of network graphs, requiring little domain knowledge. On the other hand, a text analysis program to read finance message boards will require a very different lexicon and grammar than

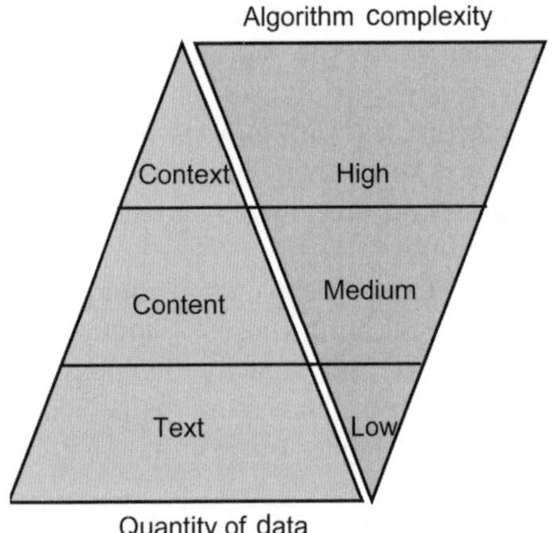

Figure 2.1. The data and algorithms pyramids. Depicts the inverse relationship between data volume and algorithmic complexity.

one that reads political messages, or one that reads medical websites. In contrast, data-handling requirements become more domain-specific as we move from bare text to context: for example, statistical language-processing algorithms that operate on text do not even need to know anything about the language in which the text is, but at the context level relationships need to be established, meaning that feature definitions need to be quite specific.

This chapter proceeds as follows. In Section 2.3, I present the main algorithms in brief and discuss some of their features. In Section 2.4, I discuss the various metrics that measure the performance of news analytics algorithms. Section 2.5 offers some concluding perspectives.

2.3 ALGORITHMS

2.3.1 Crawlers and scrapers

A *crawler* is a software algorithm that generates a sequence of web pages that may be searched for news content. The word crawler signifies that the algorithm begins at some web page, and then chooses to branch out to other pages from there (i.e., "crawls" around the web). The algorithm needs to make intelligent choices from among all the pages it might look for. One common approach is to move to a page that is linked to (i.e., hyper-referenced) from the current page. Essentially a crawler explores the tree emanating from any given node, using heuristics to determine relevance along any path, and then chooses which paths to focus on. Crawling algorithms have become increasingly sophisticated (see Edwards, McCurley, and Tomlin, 2001).

A web *scraper* downloads the content of a chosen web page and may or may not format it for analysis. Almost all programming languages contain modules for web scraping. These inbuilt functions open a channel to the web, and then download user-specified (or crawler-specified) URLs. The growing statistical analysis of web text has led to most statistical packages containing inbuilt web-scraping functions. For example, R, a popular open-source environment for technical computing, has web scraping built into its base distribution. If we want to download a page into a vector of lines, simply proceed to use a single-line command, such as the one below that reads my web page

```
> text = readLines("http://algo.scu.edu/~sanjivdas/")
> text[1:4]
[1] "<html>"
[2] ""
[3] "<head>"
[4] "<title>SCU Web Page of Sanjiv Ranjan Das</title>"
```

As is apparent, the program read my web page into a vector of text lines called `text`. We then examined the first four elements of the vector (i.e., the first four lines). In `R`, we do not need to open a communication channel, nor do we need to make an effort to program reading the page line by line. We also do not need to tokenize the file, simple string-handling routines take care of that as well. For example, extracting my name would require the following:

```
> substr(text[4],24,29)
[1] "Sanjiv"
```

The most widely used spreadsheet, `Excel`, also has an inbuilt web-scraping function. Interested readers should examine the Data → GetExternal command tree. You can download entire web pages or frames of web pages into worksheets and then manipulate the data as required. Further, `Excel` can be set up to refresh the content every minute or at some other interval.

The days when web-scraping code needed to be written in `C`, `Java`, `Perl`, or `Python` are long gone. Data, algorithms, and statistical analysis can be handled within the same software framework using tools like `R`.

Pure data scraping delivers useful statistics. In Das, Martinez-Jerez, and Tufano (2005), we scraped stock messages from four companies (Amazon, General Magic, Delta, and Geoworks) and from simple counts we were able to characterize the communication behavior of users on message boards, and their relationship to news releases. In Figure 2.2 we see that posters respond heavily to the initial news release, and then

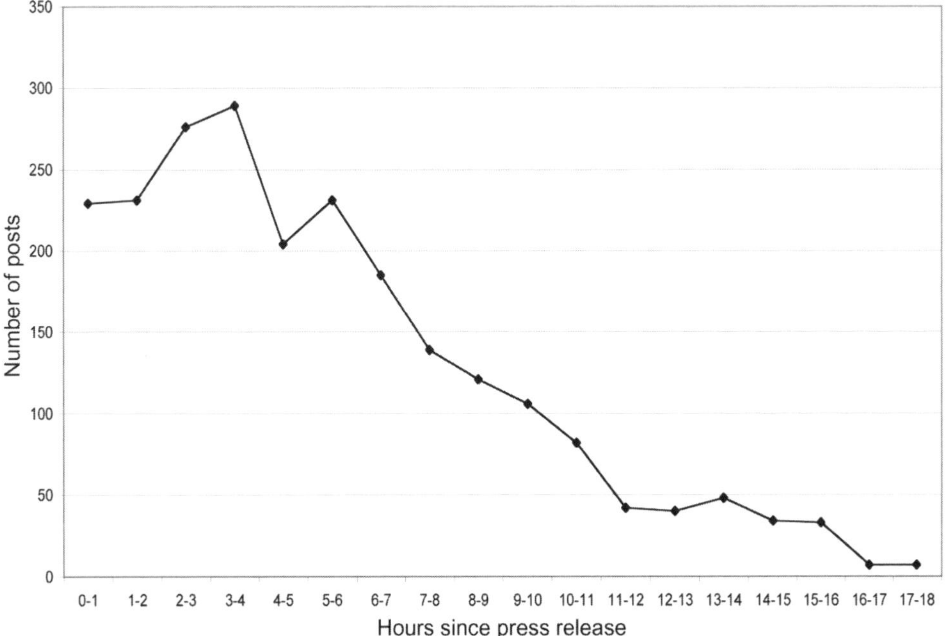

Figure 2.2. Quantity of hourly postings on message boards after selected news releases (source: Das, Martinez-Jerez, and Tufano, 2005).

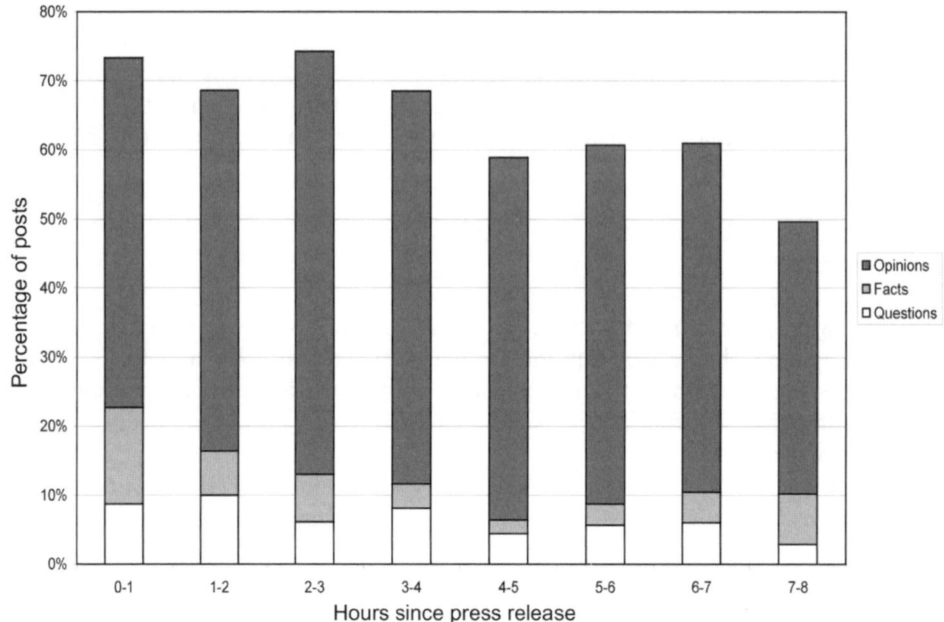

Figure 2.3. Subjective evaluation of content of post-news release postings on message boards. The content is divided into opinions, facts, and questions (source: Das, Martinez-Jerez, and Tufano, 2005).

posting activity tapers off almost two-thirds of a day later. In Figure 2.3 we see how the content of discussion changes after a news release—the relative proportions of messages are divided into opinions, facts, and questions. Opinions form the bulk of the discussion. Whereas the text contains some facts at the outset, the factual content of discussion tapers off sharply after the first hour.

Poster behavior and statistics are also informative. We found that the frequency of posting by users was power-law-distributed (see the histogram in Figure 2.4). The weekly pattern of postings is shown in Figure 2.5. We see that there is more posting

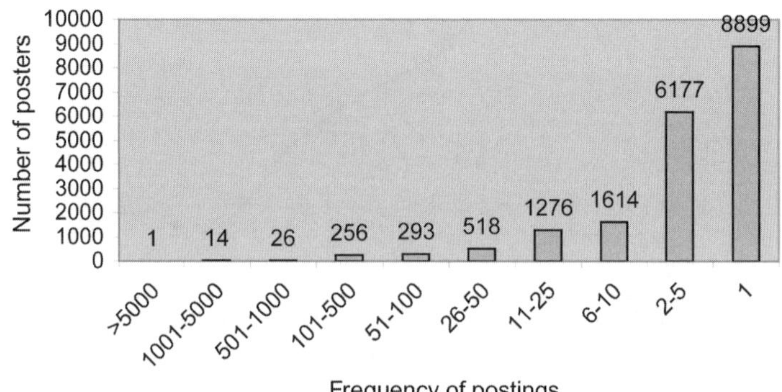

Figure 2.4. Frequency of posting by message board participants.

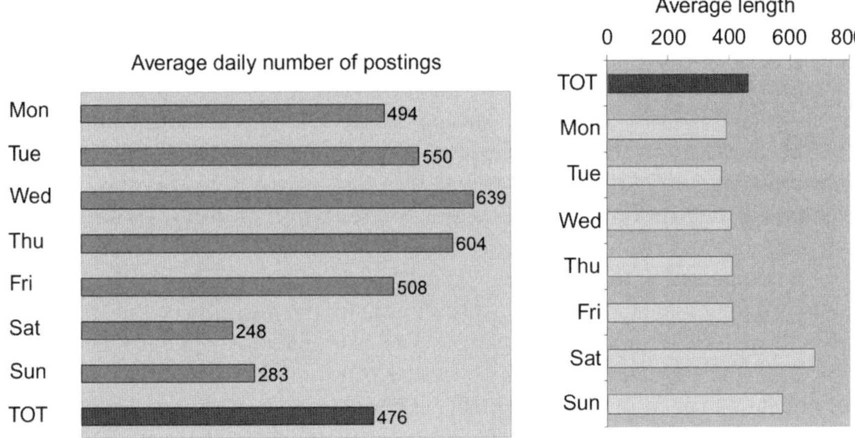

Figure 2.5. Frequency of posting by day of week by message board participants.

activity on weekdays, but messages are longer on weekends when participants presumably have more time on their hands! An analysis of intraday message flow shows that there is plenty of activity during and after work (as shown in Figure 2.6).

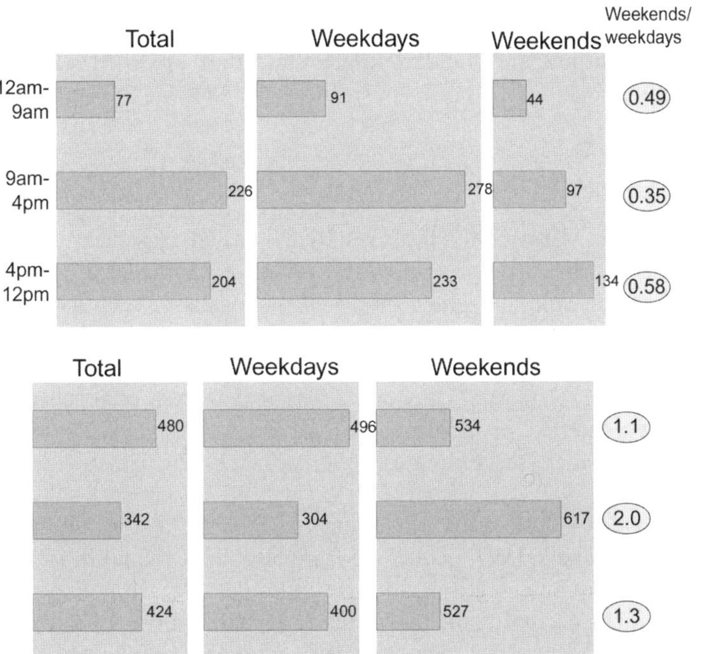

Figure 2.6. Frequency of posting by segment of day by message board participants. We show the average number of messages per day in the top panel and the average number of characters per message in the bottom panel.

2.3.2 Text pre-processing

Text from public sources is dirty. Text from web pages is even dirtier. Algorithms are needed to undertake cleanup before news analytics can be applied. This is known as pre-processing. First, there is "HTML Cleanup," which removes all HTML tags from the body of the message as these often occur concatenated to lexical items of interest. Examples of some of these tags are: `<BR>`, `<p>`, `"`, etc. Second, we expand abbreviations to their full form, making the representation of phrases with abbreviated words common across the message. For example, the word `ain't` is replaced with `are not`, `it's` is replaced with `it is`, etc. Third, we handle negation words. Whenever a negation word appears in a sentence, it usually causes the meaning of the sentence to be the opposite of that without the negation. For example, the sentence `It is not a bullish market` actually means the opposite of a bull market. Words such as `not`, `never`, `no`, etc., serve to reverse meaning. We handle negation by detecting these words and then tagging the rest of the words in the sentence after the negation word with markers, so as to reverse inference. This negation tagging was first introduced in Das and Chen (2007) (original working paper 2001), and has been successfully implemented elsewhere in quite different domains (see Pang, Lee, and Vaithyanathan, 2002).

Another aspect of text pre-processing is to "stem" words. This is a process by which words are replaced by their roots, so that different tenses, etc. of a word are not treated differently. There are several well-known stemming algorithms and free program code available in many programming languages. A widely used algorithm is the Porter (1980) stemmer. Stemming is of course language-dependent—in `R`, the multilingual `Rstem` package may be used.

Once the text is ready for analysis, we proceed to apply various algorithms to it. The next few techniques are standard algorithms that are used very widely in the machine-learning field.

2.3.3 Bayes Classifier

The Bayes Classifier is probably the most widely used classifier in practice today. The main idea is to take a piece of text and assign it to one of a pre-determined set of categories. This classifier is trained on an initial corpus of text that is pre-classified. This "training data" provides the "prior" probabilities that form the basis for Bayesian analysis of the text. The classifier is then applied to out-of-sample text to obtain the posterior probabilities of textual categories. The text is then assigned to the category with the highest posterior probability. For an excellent exposition of the adaptive qualities of this classifier, see Graham (2004, pp. 121–129, Ch. 8 titled "A plan for spam").

There are several seminal sources detailing the Bayes Classifier and its applications (see Neal, 1996; Mitchell, 1997; Koller and Sahami, 1997; Chakrabarti et al., 1998). These models have many categories and are quite complex. But they do not discern emotive content—but factual content—which is arguably more amenable to the use of statistical techniques. In contrast, news analytics are more complicated because the data comprises opinions, not facts, which are usually harder to interpret.

The Bayes Classifier uses word-based probabilities, and is thus indifferent to the structure of language. Since it is language-independent, it has wide applicability.

The approach of the Bayes Classifier is to use a set of pre-classified messages to infer the category of new messages. It learns from past experience. These classifiers are extremely efficient especially when the number of categories is small (e.g., in the classification of email into spam vs. non-spam). Here is a brief mathematical exposition of Bayes classification.

Say we have hundreds of text messages (these are not instant messages!) that we wish to classify rapidly into a number of categories. The total number of categories or classes is denoted C, and each category is denoted $c_i, i = 1...C$. Each text message is denoted $m_j, j = 1...M$, where M is the total number of messages. We denote M_i as the total number of messages per class i, and $\sum_{i=1}^{C} M_i = M$. Words in the messages are denoted as w and are indexed by k, and the total number of words is T.

Let $n(m, w) \equiv n(m_j, w_k)$ be the total number of times word w_k appears in message m_j. Notation is kept simple by suppressing subscripts as far as possible—the reader will be able to infer this from the context. We maintain a count of the number of times each word appears in every message in the training dataset. This leads naturally to the variable $n(m)$, the total number of words in message m including duplicates. This is a simple sum, $n(m_j) = \sum_{k=1}^{T} n(m_j, w_k)$.

We also keep track of the frequency with which a word appears in a category. Hence, $n(c, w)$ is the number of times word w appears in all $m \in c$. This is

$$n(c_i, w_k) = \sum_{m_j \in c_i} n(m_j, w_k) \tag{2.1}$$

This defines a corresponding probability: $\theta(c_i, w_k)$ is the probability with which word w appears in all messages m in class c:

$$\theta(c, w) = \frac{\sum_{m_j \in c_i} n(m_j, w_k)}{\sum_{m_j \in c_i} \sum_{k} n(m_j, w_k)} = \frac{n(c_i, w_k)}{n(c_i)} \tag{2.2}$$

Every word must have some non-zero probability of occurrence, no matter how small—i.e., $\theta(c_i, w_k) \neq 0, \forall c_i, w_k$. Hence, an adjustment is made to equation (2.2) via Laplace's Formula which is

$$\theta(c_i, w_k) = \frac{n(c_i, w_k) + 1}{n(c_i) + T}$$

This probability $\theta(c_i, w_k)$ is unbiased and efficient. If $n(c_i, w_k) = 0$ and $n(c_i) = 0, \forall k$, then every word is equiprobable (i.e., $1/T$). We now have the required variables to compute the conditional probability of a text message j in category i (i.e., $\Pr[m_j|c_i]$):

$$\begin{aligned}\Pr[m_j|c_i] &= \binom{n(m_j)}{\{n(m_j, w_k)\}} \prod_{k=1}^{T} \theta(c_i, w_k)^{n(m_j, w_k)} \\ &= \frac{n(m_j)!}{n(m_j, w_1)!(m_j, w_2)! \times ... \times n(m_j, w_T)!} \times \prod_{k=1}^{T} \theta(c_i, w_k)^{n(m_j, w_k)}\end{aligned}$$

$\Pr[c_i]$ is the proportion of messages in the prior training corpus pre-classified into class c_i. (*Warning*: Careful computer implementation of the multinomial probability above is required to avoid rounding error.)

The classification goal is to compute the most probable class c_i given any message m_j. Therefore, using the previously computed values of $\Pr[m_j|c_i]$ and $\Pr[c_i]$, we obtain the following conditional probability (applying Bayes' Theorem):

$$\Pr[c_i|m_j] = \frac{\Pr[m_j|c_i].\Pr[c_i]}{\sum_{i=1}^{C} \Pr[m_j|c_i].\Pr[c_i]} \tag{2.3}$$

For each message, equation (2.3) delivers posterior probabilities, $\Pr[c_i|m_j], \forall i$ (one for each message category). The category with the highest probability is assigned to the message.

The Bayes Classifier requires no optimization and is computable in deterministic time. It is widely used in practice. There are free off-the-shelf programs that provide good software to run the Bayes Classifier on large datasets. The one that is very widely used in finance applications is the `Bow` Classifier, developed by Andrew McCallum when he was at Carnegie-Mellon University. This is a very fast classifier that requires almost no additional programming by the user. The user only has to set up the training dataset in a simple directory structure—each text message is a separate file, and the training corpus requires different subdirectories for the categories of text. `Bow` offers various versions of the Bayes Classifier (see McCallum, 1996). The simple (naive) Bayes Classifier described above is also available in `R` in the `e1071` package—the function is called `naiveBayes`. The `e1071` package is the machine-learning library in `R`. There are also several more sophisticated variants of the Bayes Classifier such as k-Means, kNN, etc.

News analytics begin with classification, and the Bayes Classifier is the workhorse of any news analytics system. Prior to applying the classifier it is important for the user to exercise judgment in deciding what categories the news messages will be classified into. These categories might be a simple flat list, or they may even be a hierarchical set (see Koller and Sahami, 1997).

2.3.4 Support vector machines

A support vector machine or SVM is a classifier technique that is similar to cluster analysis but is applicable to very-high-dimensional spaces. The idea may be best described by thinking of every text message as a vector in high-dimension space, where the number of dimensions might be, for example, the number of words in a dictionary. Bodies of text in the same category will plot in the same region of the space. Given a training corpus, the SVM finds hyperplanes in the space that best separate the text of one category from another.

For the seminal development of this method, see Vapnik and Lerner (1963); Vapnik and Chervonenkis (1964); Vapnik (1995); and Smola and Scholkopf (1998). I provide a brief summary of the method based on these works.

Consider a training dataset given by the binary relation

$$\{(x_1, y_1), ..., (x_n, y_n)\} \subset X \times \mathcal{R}$$

The set $X \in \mathcal{R}^d$ is the input space and set $Y \in \mathcal{R}^m$ is a set of categories. We define a function

$$f : x \to y$$

with the idea that all elements must be mapped from set X into set Y with no more than an ϵ-deviation. A simple linear example of such a model would be

$$f(x_i) = \langle w, x_i \rangle + b, \quad w \in \mathcal{X}, b \in \mathcal{R}$$

The notation $\langle w, x \rangle$ signifies the dot product of w and x. Note that the equation of a hyperplane is $\langle w, x \rangle + b = 0$.

The idea in SVM regression is to find the *flattest* w that results in the mapping from $x \to y$. Thus, we minimize the Euclidean norm of w (i.e., $||w|| = \sqrt{\sum_{j=1}^{n} w_j^2}$). We also want to ensure that $|y_i - f(x_i)| \leq \epsilon, \forall i$. The objective function (quadratic program) becomes

$$\begin{aligned} &\min \tfrac{1}{2}||w||^2 \\ &\quad \text{subject to} \\ &\quad y_i - \langle w, x_i \rangle - b \leq \epsilon \\ &\quad -y_i + \langle w, x_i \rangle + b \leq \epsilon \end{aligned}$$

This is a (possibly infeasible) convex optimization problem. Feasibility is obtainable by introducing the slack variables (ξ, ξ^*). We choose a constant C that scales the degree of infeasibility. The model is then modified to be as follows:

$$\begin{aligned} &\min \tfrac{1}{2}||w||^2 + C \sum_{i=1}^{n} (\xi + \xi^*) \\ &\text{subject to} \\ &y_i - \langle w, x_i \rangle - b \leq \epsilon + \xi \\ &-y_i + \langle w, x_i \rangle + b \leq \epsilon + \xi^* \\ &\xi, \xi^* \geq 0 \end{aligned}$$

As C increases, the model increases in sensitivity to infeasibility.

We may tune the objective function by introducing cost functions $c(.), c^*(.)$. Then, the objective function becomes

$$\min \tfrac{1}{2}||w||^2 + C \sum_{i=1}^{n} [c(\xi) + c^*(\xi^*)]$$

We may replace the function $[f(x) - y]$ with a "kernel" $K(x, y)$ introducing nonlinearity into the problem. The choice of the kernel is a matter of judgment, based on the nature of the application being examined. SVMs allow many different estimation kernels—e.g., the Radial Basis function kernel minimizes the distance between inputs (x) and targets (y) based on

$$f(x, y; \gamma) = \exp(-\gamma |x - y|^2)$$

where γ is a user-defined squashing parameter.

There are various SVM packages that are easily obtained in open source. An easy-to-use one is SVM Light—the package is available at the following URL: `http://svmlight.joachims.org/` SVM Light is an implementation of Vapnik's Support Vector Machine for the problem of pattern recognition. The algorithm has scalable memory requirements and can handle problems with many thousands of support vectors efficiently. The algorithm proceeds by solving a sequence of optimization problems, lower bounding the solution using a form of local search. It is based on work by Joachims (1999).

Another program is the University of London SVM. Interestingly, it is known as SVM Dark—evidently people who like hyperplanes have a sense of humor! See `http://www.cs.ucl.ac.uk/sta/M.Sewell/svmdark/` For a nice list of SVMs, see `http://www.cs.ubc.ca/~murphyk/Software/svm.htm` In `R` (see the machine-learning library `e1071`) the function is, of course, called `svm`.

SVMs are very fast and are quite generally applicable with many types of kernels. Hence, they may also be widely applied in news analytics.

2.3.5 Word count classifiers

The simplest form of classifier is based on counting words that are of *signed* type. Words are the heart of any language inference system, and in a specialized domain this is even more so. In the words of F.C. Bartlett,

> "Words ... can indicate the qualitative and relational features of a situation in their general aspect just as directly as, and perhaps even more satisfactorily than, they can describe its particular individuality. This is, in fact, what gives to language its intimate relation to thought processes."

To build a word count classifier a user defines a *lexicon* of special words that relate to the classification problem. For example, if the classifier is categorizing text into optimistic vs. pessimistic economic news, then the user may want to create a lexicon of words that are useful in separating the good news from bad. For example, the word "upbeat" might be signed as optimistic, and the word "dismal" may be pessimistic. In my experience, a good lexicon needs about 300–500 words. Domain knowledge is brought to bear in designing a lexicon. Therefore, in contrast to the Bayes Classifier, a word count algorithm is language-dependent.

This algorithm is based on a simple word count of lexical words. If the number of words in a particular category exceeds that of the other categories by some threshold then the text message is categorized to the category with the highest lexical count. The algorithm is of very low complexity, extremely fast, and easy to implement. It delivers a baseline approach to the classification problem.

2.3.6 Vector distance classifier

This algorithm treats each message as a word vector. Therefore, each pre-classified, hand-tagged text message in the training corpus becomes a comparison vector—we call this set the rule set. Each message in the test set is then compared with the rule set and is assigned a classification based on which rule comes closest in vector space.

The angle between the message vector (M) and the vectors in the rule set (S) provides a measure of proximity

$$\cos(\theta) = \frac{M \cdot S}{||M|| \cdot ||S||}$$

where $||A||$ denotes the norm of vector A. Variations on this theme are made possible by using sets of top-n closest rules, rather than only the closest rule.

Word vectors here are extremely sparse, and the algorithms may be built to take the dot product and norm above very rapidly. This algorithm was used in Das and Chen (2007) and was taken directly from ideas used by search engines. The analogy is almost exact. A search engine essentially indexes pages by representing the text as a word vector. When a search query is presented, the vector distance $\cos(\theta) \in (0, 1)$ is computed for the search query with all indexed pages to find the pages with which the angle is the least—i.e., where $\cos(\theta)$ is the greatest. Sorting all indexed pages by their angle with the search query delivers the best-match ordered list. Readers will remember in the early days of search engines how the list of search responses also provided a percentage number along with the returned results—these numbers were the same as the value of $\cos(\theta)$.

When using the vector distance classifier for news analytics, the classification algorithm takes the new text sample and computes the angle of the message with all the text pages in the index's training corpus to find the best matches. It then classifies pages with the same tag as the best matches. This classifier is also very easy to implement as it only needs simple linear algebra functions and sorting routines that are widely available in almost any programming environment.

2.3.7 Discriminant-based classifier

All the classifiers discussed above do not weight words differentially in a continuous manner. Either they do not weight them at all, as in the case of the Bayes Classifier or the SVM, or they focus on only some words, ignoring the rest, as with the word count classifier. In contrast, the discriminant-based classifier weights words based on their discriminant value.

The commonly used tool here is Fisher's Discriminant. Various implementations of it, with minor changes in form, are used. In the classification area, one of the earliest uses was in the Bow Algorithm of McCallum (1996), which reports the discriminant values; Chakrabarti et al. (1998) also use it in their classification framework, as do Das and Chen (2007). We present one version of Fisher's Discriminant here.

Let the mean score (average number of times word w appears in a text message of category i) of each term for each category $= \mu_i$, where i indexes category. Let text messages be indexed by j. The number of times word w appears in a message j of category i is denoted m_{ij}. Let n_i be the number of times word w appears in category i. Then the discriminant function might be expressed as:

$$F(w) = \frac{\dfrac{1}{|C|}\sum_{i \neq k}(\mu_i - \mu_k)^2}{\sum_i \dfrac{1}{n_i}\sum_j (m_{ij} - \mu_i)^2}$$

It is the ratio of the across-class (class i vs. class k) variance to the average of within-class (class $i \in C$) variances. To get some intuition, consider the case we looked at earlier, classifying the economic sentiment as optimistic or pessimistic. If the word "dismal" appears exactly once in text that is pessimistic and never appears in text that is optimistic, then the within-class variation is zero, and the across-class variation is positive. In such a case, where the denominator of the equation above is zero, the word "dismal" is an infinitely powerful discriminant. It should be given a very large weight in any word count algorithm.

In Das and Chen (2007) we looked at stock message board text and determined good discriminants using the Fisher Metric. Here are some words that showed high discriminant values (with values alongside) in classifying optimistic vs. pessimistic opinions

```
bad       0.0405
hot       0.0161
hype      0.0089
improve   0.0123
joke      0.0268
jump      0.0106
killed    0.0160
lead      0.0037
like      0.0037
long      0.0162
lose      0.1211
money     0.1537
overvalue 0.0160
own       0.0031
good__n   0.0485
```

The last word in the list ("not good") is an example of a negated word showing a higher discriminant value than the word itself without a negative connotation (recall the discussion of negative tagging earlier in Section 2.3.2). Also see that the word "bad" has a score of 0.0405, whereas the term "not good" has a higher score of 0.0485. This is an example where the structure and usage of language, not just the meaning of a word, matters.

In another example, using the `Bow` Algorithm this time, examining a database of conference calls with analysts, the best 20 discriminant words were

```
0.030828516377649325 allowing
0.094412331406551059 november
0.044315992292870907 determined
0.225433526011560692 general
0.034682080924855488 seasonality
0.123314065510597301 expanded
0.017341040462427744 rely
0.071290944123314062 counsel
0.044315992292870907 told
0.015414258188824663 easier
0.050096339113680152 drop
0.028901734104046242 synergies
0.025048169556840076 piece
0.021194605009633910 expenditure
0.017341040462427744 requirement
```

```
0.0905587668593449OO prospects
0.01926782273603O827 internationally
0.0173410404624277 44 proper
0.0269749518304431 59 derived
0.00192678227360308 3 invited
```

Not all these words would obviously connote bullishness or bearishness, but some of them certainly do, such as "expanded", "drop", "prospects", etc. Why apparently unrelated words appear as good discriminants is useful to investigate, and may lead to additional insights.

2.3.8 Adjective–adverb classifier

Classifiers may use all the text, as in the Bayes and vector distance classifiers, or a subset of the text, as in the word count algorithm. They may also weight words differentially as in discriminant-based word counts. Another way to filter words in a word count algorithm is to focus on the segments of text that have high emphasis (i.e., in regions around adjectives and adverbs). This is done in Das and Chen (2007) using an adjective–adverb search to determine these regions.

This algorithm is language-dependent. In order to determine the adjectives and adverbs in the text, parsing is required, and calls for the use of a dictionary. The one I have used extensively is the CUVOALD (Computer Usable Version of the Oxford Advanced Learner's Dictionary). It contains parts-of-speech tagging information, and makes the parsing process very simple. There are other sources—a very well-known one is WordNet from `http://wordnet.princeton.edu/`

Using these dictionaries, it is easy to build programs that only extract the regions of text around adjectives and adverbs, and then submit these to the other classifiers for analysis and classification. Counting adjectives and adverbs may also be used to score news text for "emphasis" thereby enabling a different qualitative metric of importance for the text.

2.3.9 Scoring optimism and pessimism

A very useful resource for scoring text is the General Inquirer, `http://www.wjh.harvard.edu/~inquirer/`, housed at Harvard University. The Inquirer allows the user to assign "flavors" to words so as to score text. In our case, we may be interested in counting optimistic and pessimistic words in text. The Inquirer will do this online if needed, but the dictionary may be downloaded and used offline as well. Words are tagged with attributes that may be easily used to undertake tagged word counts.

Here is a sample of tagged words from the dictionary that gives a flavor of its structure:

```
ABNORMAL    H4Lvd Neg Ngtv Vice NEGAFF Modif |
ABOARD      H4Lvd Space PREP LY |
ABOLITION   Lvd TRANS Noun
ABOMINABLE  H4 Neg Strng Vice Ovrst Eval IndAdj Modif |
```

```
ABORTIVE    Lvd POWOTH POWTOT Modif POLIT
ABOUND      H4 Pos Psv Incr IAV SUPV |
```

The words ABNORMAL and ABOMINABLE have "Neg" tags and the word ABOUND has a "Pos" tag.

Das and Chen (2007) used this dictionary to create an ambiguity score for segmenting and filtering messages by optimism/pessimism in testing news-analytical algorithms. They found that algorithms performed better after filtering in less ambiguous text. This ambiguity score is discussed later in Section 2.3.11.

Tetlock (2007) is the best example of the use of the General Inquirer in finance. Using text from the "Abreast of the Market" column from the *Wall Street Journal* he undertook a principal components analysis of 77 categories from the GI and constructed a media pessimism score. High pessimism presages lower stock prices, and extreme positive or negative pessimism predicts volatility. Tetlock, Saar-Tsechansky, and Macskassy (2008) use news text related to firm fundamentals to show that negative words are useful in predicting earnings and returns. The potential of this tool has yet to be fully realized, and I expect to see a lot more research undertaken using the General Inquirer.

2.3.10 Voting among classifiers

In Das and Chen (2007) we introduced a voting classifier. Given the highly ambiguous nature of the text being worked with, reducing the noise is a major concern. Pang, Lee, and Vaithyanathan (2002) found that standard machine-learning techniques do better than humans at classification. Yet, machine-learning methods such as naive Bayes, maximum entropy, and support vector machines do not perform as well on sentiment classification as on traditional topic-based categorization.

To mitigate error, classifiers are first separately applied, and then a majority vote is taken across the classifiers to obtain the final category. This approach improves the signal-to-noise ratio of the classification algorithm.

2.3.11 Ambiguity filters

Suppose we are building a sentiment index from a news feed. As each text message comes in, we apply our algorithms to it and the result is a classification tag. Some messages may be classified very accurately and others with much lower levels of confidence. Ambiguity filtering is a process by which we discard messages of high-noise and potentially low-signal value from inclusion in the aggregate signal (e.g., the sentiment index).

One may think of ambiguity filtering as a sequential voting scheme. Instead of running all classifiers and then looking for a majority vote, we run them sequentially, and discard messages that do not pass the hurdle of more general classifiers, before subjecting them to more particular ones. In the end, we still have a voting scheme. Ambiguity metrics are therefore lexicographic.

In Das and Chen (2007) we developed an ambiguity filter for application prior to our classification algorithms. We applied the General Inquirer to the training data to determine an "optimism" score. We computed this for each category of stock message type (i.e., buy, hold, and sell). For each type, we computed the mean optimism score, amounting to 0.032, 0.026, 0.016, respectively, resulting in the expected rank ordering (the standard deviations around these means are 0.075, 0.069, 0.071, respectively). We then filtered messages in, based on how far they were away from the mean in the right direction. For example, for buy messages, we chose for classification only those with one standard deviation higher than the mean. False positives in classification decline dramatically with the application of this ambiguity filter.

2.3.12 Network analytics

We now examine analytic methods that are not based on a single-stock or single-text message. Instead, we look at methods for connecting news and information across handles, stocks, and time. This is the domain of "context" analysis. By examining the network structure of the information, we may attempt to discern useful patterns in the message stream.

Recall Metcalfe's Law—"The utility of a network is proportional to the square of the number of users." News analytics benefit from the network effect since aggregation greatly improves signal extraction. But in addition, the network structure may be used inferentially.

How are networks defined? There are several operational implementations possible. In Das and Sisk (2005), we constructed a network of stocks based on how many common handles were posted to pairs of stock message boards. For example, if person `WiseStockGuy` posted messages to both Cisco and IBM in a pre-specified interval, we would increment the connection between those two stocks by one unit. In this manner a network graph of stock linkages is built up. Another approach might be to construct a network graph of connections based on whether someone requested a quote on two stocks at the same time (see Figure 2.7). The network shows that a tight group of stocks receives all the attention, whereas there are many stocks that are not well connected to each other.

Network analysis is important because influence and opinion travel rapidly on networks, and the dynamics greatly determine the collective opinion. See DeMarzo, Vayanos, and Zwiebel (2003) for an analysis of persuasion bias and social influence on networks. For games on networks, where senders of messages are optimistic, more extreme messages are sent, resulting in lower informativeness (see Admati and Pfleiderer, 2001). Hence, news analytics must be designed to be able to take advantage of "word of mouth" occurring in web discussions. Word-of-mouth communication leads agents to take actions that are superior than those taken in the absence of it (shown in Ellison and Fudenberg, 1995). News metrics enable extraction and analysis of the sociology of networks. Morville (2005) has a neat term for the intersection of information technology and social networks—he calls them "folksonomies".

2.3.13 Centrality

The field of graph theory lends itself to the analysis of networks. There are several news analytics that may be based on the properties of networks. An important and widely used analytic measure is called "centrality". A node in a network is more central than others if it has more connections to other nodes directly, or indirectly through links to

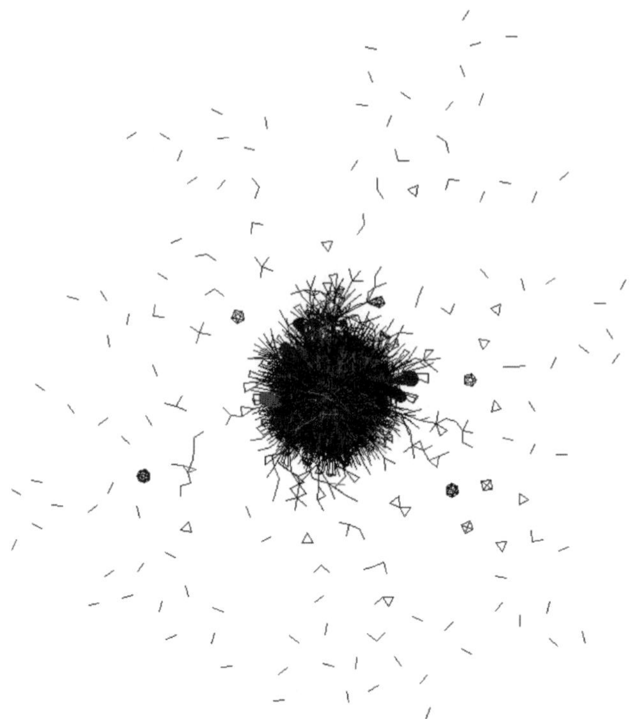

Figure 2.7. A rendering of a graph of more than 6,000 stocks for which someone requested a quote from Yahoo! Finance. There is an edge between two stocks if someone requested quotes on those stocks at the same time.They are from about 2% of the traffic on Yahoo on April 1, 2002 (based on rendering software by Adai A.T.; Date S.V.; Wieland S.; Marcotte E.M. (2004) "Creating a map of protein function with an algorithm for visualizing very large biological networks," *Journal of Molecular Biology*, June 25; **340**(1): 179–190; the graph is courtesy of Jacob Sisk).

other nodes that are well connected. Centrality has been extensively used in sociology, as in the work by Bonacich (1972, 1987).

Centrality is computed as follows. We represent the network of message connections as an adjacency matrix. This matrix is denoted $\mathbf{A} = \{a_{ij}\} \in R^{m \times m}$, a square matrix that contains the connection strength between nodes. If the graph of connections is undirected, then $a_{ij} = a_{ji}$, else if $a_{ij} \neq a_{ji}$ the graph is directed. Let x_i be the influence of node i in the network. Node i exerts influence through connections to other nodes, and we may write the influence of all nodes as the following system of equations:

$$x_i = \sum_{j=1, j \neq i}^{m} a_{ij} x_j$$

This may be written as an eigensystem with the addition of the eigen parameter λ; that is,

$$\lambda\,\mathbf{x} = \mathbf{A}\,\mathbf{x}$$

where $\mathbf{x}$ is the vector of influences of all nodes. The principal eigenvector in this system gives the centrality score of all nodes, and highlights which nodes have the most influence.

In Das and Sisk (2005), we computed the centrality scores for all stocks in a network graph where the connection strengths were based on the number of common message posters each pair of stocks had. We found that stocks such as IBM, AOL, Motorola, AMD were central and stocks such as American Express, Abbot Labs, Bristol Myers were not central. Central stocks are more likely to be indicative of the way other stocks may react, since they influence others more than vice versa; hence, they may be leading indicators of stock market movements. Computing centrality in various news domains is useful to get a sense of what sources of news may be better-tracked than others.

2.3.14 Communities

News traffic may be analyzed to determine communities. Given a network graph's adjacency matrix, communities are easy to detect using any one of several well-known algorithms. An excellent review of these algorithms is provided by Fortunato (2010).

A widely used library for graph analysis and community detection is `igraph`. This may be accessed at `http://igraph.sourceforge.net/` A sample of the ease of use of the `igraph` library using `R` is as follows:

```
#CREATE GRAPH FROM ADJACENCY MATRIX
g = graph.adjacency(adjmat,mode="undirected",weighted=TRUE,
  diag=FALSE)

#DETECT COMMUNITIES
wtc = walktrap.community(g)
comms = community.to.membership(g,wtc$merges,
  steps=length(vc_list_connected)/4)print(comms)

#DETECT CLUSTERS
clus = clusters(g)
print(clus)
```

The sequence of commands initially creates the network graph from the adjacency matrix (`adjmat`). It then executes the "walktrap" community detection algorithm to find the communities that are then printed out. The `igraph` package also allows for finding clusters as needed.

A community is a cluster of nodes that have many connections between members of the community but few connections outside the community. There are many algorithms that exploit this working definition of a community. For instance, the walktrap algorithm is a randomized one—it detects communities using a random walk on a network. A random walk tends to be trapped in a community because of the number of links between community nodes relative to links across communities. By keeping track of regions of the network where the random walk is trapped, this algorithm is able to detect communities. See the paper by the creators of the algorithm—Pons and Latapy (2006). This is a very recent paper, and resulted in a large performance improvement over existing algorithms.

Communities may then be examined for differences in characteristics to give insights. For example, if we find that stocks in more connected communities tend to be more volatile, then we may want to limit the number of stocks chosen from these communities in a portfolio.

2.4 METRICS

Developing analytics without metrics is insufficient. It is important to build measures that examine whether the analytics are generating classifications that are statistically significant, economically useful, and stable. For an analytic to be *statistically valid*, it should meet some criterion that signifies classification accuracy and power. Being *economically useful* sets a different bar—does it make money? And *stability* is a double-edged quality: one, does it perform well in sample and out of sample? And, two, is the behavior of the algorithm stable across training corpora?

Here, we explore some of the metrics that have been developed and propose others. No doubt, as the range of analytics grows, so will the range of metrics.

2.4.1 Confusion matrix

The confusion matrix is the classic tool for assessing classification accuracy. Given n categories, the matrix is of dimension $n \times n$. The rows relate to the category assigned by the analytic algorithm and the columns refer to the correct category in which the text resides. Each cell (i,j) of the matrix contains the number of text messages that were of type j and were classified as type i. The cells on the diagonal of the confusion matrix state the number of times the algorithm got the classification right. All other cells are instances of classification error. If an algorithm has no classification ability, then the rows and columns of the matrix will be independent of each other. Under this null hypothesis, the statistic that is examined for rejection is as follows:

$$\chi^2[dof = (n-1)^2] = \sum_{i=1}^{n} \sum_{j=1}^{n} \frac{[A(i,j) - E(i,j)]^2}{E(i,j)}$$

where $A(i,j)$ are the actual numbers observed in the confusion matrix, and $E(i,j)$ are the expected numbers, assuming no classification ability under the null. If $T(i)$ represents the total across row i of the confusion matrix, and $T(j)$ the column total, then

$$E(i,j) = \frac{T(i) \times T(j)}{\sum_{i=1}^{n} T(i)} \equiv \frac{T(i) \times T(j)}{\sum_{j=1}^{n} T(j)}$$

The degrees of freedom of the χ^2 statistic is $(n-1)^2$. This statistic is very easy to implement and may be applied to models for any n. A highly significant statistic is evidence of classification ability.

2.4.2 Accuracy

Algorithm accuracy over a classification scheme is the percentage of text that is correctly classified. This may be done in sample or out of sample. To compute this off the confusion matrix, we calculate

$$\text{Accuracy} = \frac{\sum_{i=1}^{n} A(i,i)}{\sum_{j=1}^{n} T(j)}$$

We should hope that this is at least greater than $1/n$, which is the accuracy level achieved on average from random guessing. In practice, I find that accuracy ratios of 60%–70% are reasonable for text that is non-factual and contains poor language and opinions.

2.4.3 False positives

Improper classification is worse than a failure to classify. In a 2×2 (two category, $n = 2$) scheme, every off-diagonal element in the confusion matrix is a false positive. When $n > 2$, some classification errors are worse than others. For example, in a three-way buy, hold, sell scheme, where we have stock text for classification, classifying a buy as a sell is worse than classifying it as a hold. In this sense an ordering of categories is useful so that a false classification into a near category is not as bad as a wrong classification into a far (diametrically opposed) category.

The percentage of false positives is a useful metric to work with. It may be calculated as a simple count or as a weighted count (by nearness of wrong category) of false classifications divided by total classifications undertaken.

In our experiments on stock messages in Das and Chen (2007), we found that the false positive rate for the voting scheme classifier was about 10%. This was reduced to below half that number after application of an ambiguity filter (discussed in Section 2.3.11) based on the General Inquirer.

2.4.4 Sentiment error

When many articles of text are classified, an aggregate measure of sentiment may be computed. Aggregation is useful because it allows classification errors to cancel—if a buy was mistaken as a sell, and another sell as a buy, then the aggregate sentiment index is unaffected.

Sentiment error is the percentage difference between the computed aggregate sentiment, and the value we would obtain if there were no classification error. In our experiments this varied from 5% to 15% across the datasets that we used. Leinweber and Sisk (2010 and this volume, Chapter 6) show that sentiment aggregation gives a better relation between news and stock returns.

2.4.5 Disagreement

In Das, Martinez-Jerez, and Tufano (2005) we introduced a disagreement metric that allows us to gauge the level of conflict in the discussion. Looking at stock text messages, we used the number of signed buys and sells in the day (based on a sentiment model) to determine how much disagreement of opinion there was in the market. The metric is computed as follows:

$$\text{DISAG} = \left| 1 - \left| \frac{B - S}{B + S} \right| \right|$$

where B, S are the numbers of classified buys and sells. Note that DISAG is bounded between zero and one. The quality of aggregate sentiment tends to be lower when DISAG is high.

2.4.6 Correlations

A natural question that arises when examining streaming news is: How well does the sentiment from news correlate with financial time series? Is there predictability? An excellent discussion of these matters is provided in Leinweber and Sisk (2010 and this volume, Chapter 6). They specifically examine investment signals derived from news.

In their paper, they show that there is a significant difference in cumulative excess returns between strong-positive-sentiment and strong-negative-sentiment days over prediction horizons of a week or a quarter. Hence, these event studies are based on point-in-time correlation triggers. Their results are robust across countries.

The simplest correlation metrics are visual. In a trading day, we may plot the movement of a stock series, alongside the cumulative sentiment series. The latter is generated by taking all classified "buys" as $+1$ and "sells" as -1, and the plot comprises the cumulative total of scores of the messages ("hold" classified messages are scored with value zero). See Figure 2.8 for one example, where it is easy to see that the sentiment and stock series track each other quite closely. We coin the term "sents" for the units of sentiment.

2.4.7 Aggregation performance

As pointed out in Leinweber and Sisk (2010 and this volume, Chapter 6) aggregation of classified news reduces noise and improves signal accuracy. One way to measure this is to look at the correlations of sentiment and stocks for aggregated vs. disaggregated data. As an example, I examine daily sentiment for individual stocks and an index created by aggregating sentiment across stocks (i.e., a cross-section of sentiment). This is useful to examine whether sentiment aggregates effectively in the cross-section.

I used all messages posted for 35 stocks that comprise the Morgan Stanley High-Tech Index (MSH35) for the period June 1 to August 27, 2001. This results in 88 calendar days and 397,625 messages, an average of about 4,500 messages per day. For each day I determine the sentiment and stock return. Daily sentiment uses messages up to 4 pm on each trading day, coinciding with the stock return close.

I also compute the average sentiment index of all 35 stocks (i.e., a proxy for the MSH35 sentiment). The corresponding equally weighted return of 35 stocks is also computed. These two time series permit an examination of the relationship between sentiment and stock returns at the aggregate index level. Table 2.1 presents the correlations between individual stock returns and sentiment, and between the MSH35 index return and MSH35 sentiment. We notice that there is positive contemporaneous correlation between most stock returns and sentiment. The correlations were sometimes as high

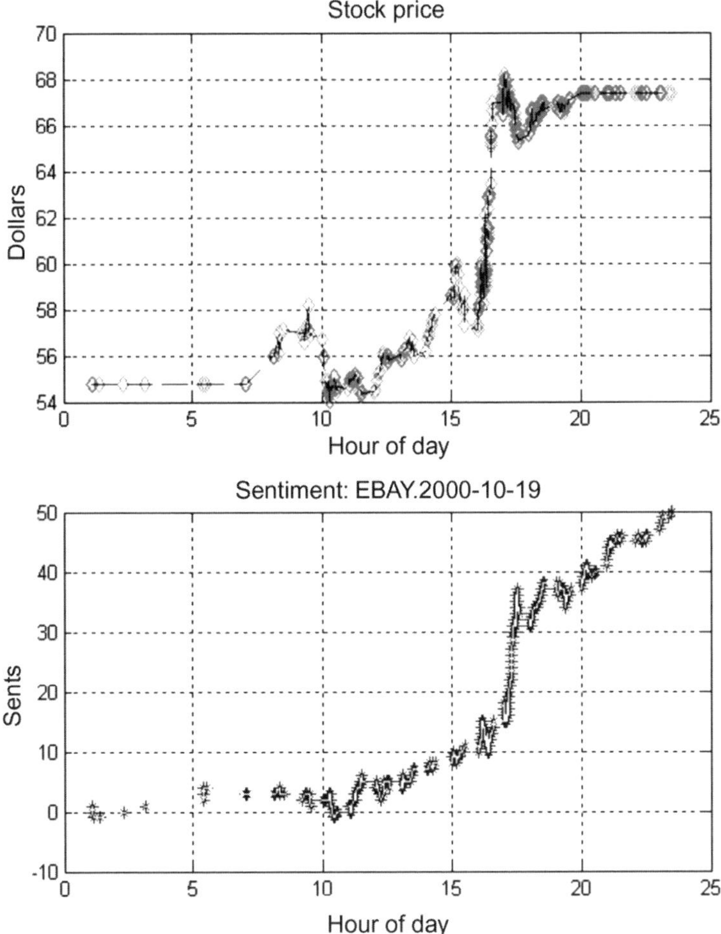

Figure 2.8. Plot of stock series (upper graph) vs. sentiment series (lower graph). Correlation between the series is high. The plot is based on messages from Yahoo! Finance and is for a single 24-hour period.

as 0.60 (for Lucent), 0.51 (PALM), and 0.49 (DELL). Only six stocks evidenced negative correlations, mostly small in magnitude. The average contemporaneous correlation is 0.188, which suggests that sentiment tracks stock returns in the high-tech sector. (I also used full-day sentiment instead of only that till trading close and the results are almost the same—the correlations are in fact higher, as sentiment includes reactions to trading after the close).

Average correlations for individual stocks are weaker when one lag (0.067) or lead (0.029) of the stock return are considered. More interesting is the average index of sentiment for all 35 stocks. The contemporaneous correlation of this index to the equally weighted return index is as high as 0.486. Here, cross-sectional aggregation helps in eliminating some of the idiosyncratic noise, and makes the positive relationship between returns and sentiment salient. This is also reflected in the strong positive correlation of

Table 2.1. Correlations of sentiment and stock returns for MSH35 stocks and the aggregated MSH35 index. Stock returns (STKRET) are computed from close to close. We compute correlations using data for 88 days in the months of June, July, and August 2001. Return data over the weekend is linearly interpolated, as messages continue to be posted over weekends. Daily sentiment is computed from midnight to close of trading at 4 pm (SENTY4pm).

Ticker	Correlations of SENTY4pm(t) with		
	STKRET(t)	STKRET($t+1$)	STKRET($t-1$)
ADP	0.086	0.138	−0.062
AMAT	−0.008	−0.049	0.067
AMZN	0.227	0.167	0.161
AOL	0.386	−0.010	0.281
BRCM	0.056	0.167	−0.007
CA	0.023	0.127	0.035
CPQ	0.260	0.161	0.239
CSCO	0.117	0.074	−0.025
DELL	0.493	−0.024	0.011
EDS	−0.017	0.000	−0.078
EMC	0.111	0.010	0.193
ERTS	0.114	−0.223	0.225
HWP	0.315	−0.097	−0.114
IBM	0.071	−0.057	0.146
INTC	0.128	−0.077	−0.007
INTU	−0.124	−0.099	−0.117
JDSU	0.126	0.056	0.047
JNPR	0.416	0.090	−0.137
LU	0.602	0.131	−0.027
MOT	−0.041	−0.014	−0.006
MSFT	0.422	0.084	0.210
MU	0.110	−0.087	0.030
NT	0.320	0.068	0.288
ORCL	0.005	0.056	−0.062
PALM	0.509	0.156	0.085
PMTC	0.080	0.005	−0.030
PSFT	0.244	−0.094	0.270
SCMR	0.240	0.197	0.060
SLR	−0.077	−0.054	−0.158
STM	−0.010	−0.062	0.161
SUNW	0.463	0.176	0.276
TLAB	0.225	0.250	0.283
TXN	0.240	−0.052	0.117
XLNX	0.261	−0.051	−0.217
YHOO	0.202	−0.038	0.222
Average correlation across 35 stocks	0.188	0.029	0.067
Correlation between 35-stock index and 35-stock sentiment index	*0.486*	*0.178*	*0.288*

sentiment to lagged stock returns (0.288) and leading returns (0.178). I confirmed the statistical contemporaneous relationship of returns to sentiment by regressing returns on sentiment (t-statistics in brackets):

$$\underset{}{STKRET(t)} = \underset{(0.93)}{-0.1791} + \underset{(5.16)}{0.3866}SENTY(t), \quad R^2 = 0.24$$

2.4.8 Phase lag metrics

Correlation across sentiment and return time series is a special case of lead–lag analysis. This may be generalized to looking for pattern correlations. As may be evident from Figure 2.8, the stock and sentiment plots have patterns. In the figure they appear contemporaneous, though the sentiment series lags the stock series.

A graphical approach to lead–lag analysis is to look for graph patterns across two series and to examine whether we may predict the patterns in one time series with the other. For example, can we use the sentiment series to predict the high point of the stock series or the low point? In other words, is it possible to use the sentiment data generated from algorithms to pick turning points in stock series? We call this type of graphical examination "phase lag" analysis.

A simple approach I came up with involves decomposing graphs into eight types (see Figure 2.9). On the left side of the figure, notice that there are eight patterns of graphs based on the location of four salient graph features: start, end, high, and low points. There are exactly eight possible graph patterns that may be generated from all positions of these four salient points. It is also very easy to write software to take any time series—say, for a trading day—and assign it to one of the patterns, keeping track of the position of the maximum and minimum points. It is then possible to compare two graphs to see which one predicts the other in terms of pattern. For example, does the sentiment series maximum come before that of the stock series? If so, how much earlier does it detect the turning point on average? Using data from several stocks I examined whether the sentiment graph pattern generated from a voting classification algorithm was predictive of stock graph patterns. Phase lags were examined in intervals of five minutes through the trading day. The histogram of leads and lags is shown on the right-hand side of Figure 2.9. A positive value denotes that the sentiment series lags the stock series; a negative value signifies that the stock series lags sentiment. It is apparent from the histogram that the sentiment series lags stocks and is not predictive of stock movements in this case.

2.4.9 Economic significance

News analytics may be evaluated using economic yardsticks. Does the algorithm deliver profitable opportunities? Does it help reduce risk?

For example, in Das and Sisk (2005) we formed a network with connections based on commonality of handles in online discussion. We detected communities using a simple rule based on connectedness beyond a chosen threshold level, and separated all stock nodes into either one giant community or into a community of individual singleton nodes. We then examined the properties of portfolios formed from the community vs. those formed from the singleton stocks.

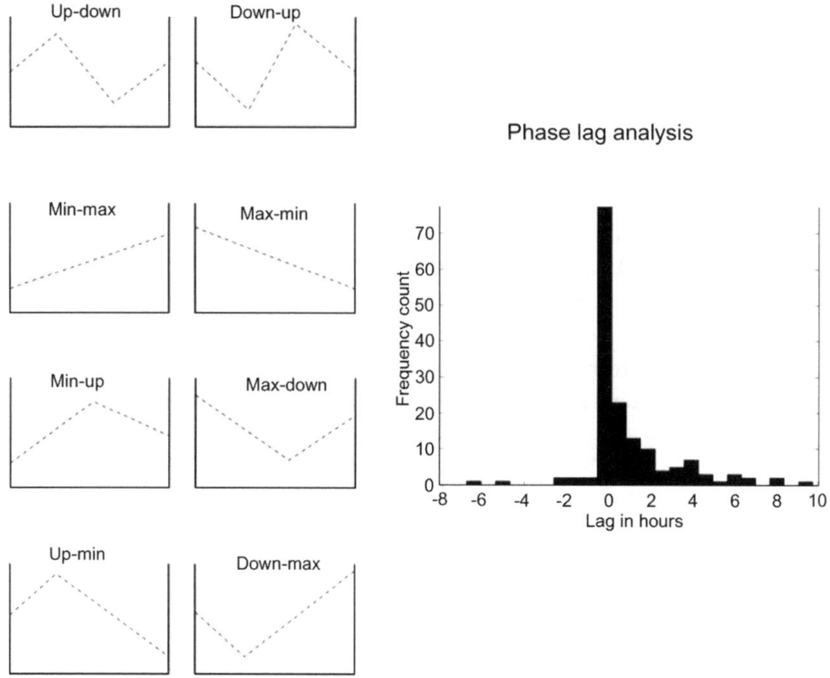

Figure 2.9. Phase lag analysis. The left-side shows the eight canonical graph patterns that are derived from arrangements of the start, end, high, and low points of a time series. The right-side shows the leads and lags of patterns of the stock series vs. the sentiment series. A positive value means that the stock series leads the sentiment series.

We obtained several insights. We calculated the mean returns from an equally weighted portfolio of the community stocks and an equally weighted portfolio of singleton stocks. We also calculated the return standard deviations of these portfolios. We did this month by month for 16 months. In 15 of the 16 months the mean returns were higher for the community portfolio; the standard deviations were lower in 13 of the 16 months. The difference of means was significant for 13 of those months as well. Hence, community detection based on news traffic leads to identifying a set of stocks that performs vastly better than the rest.

There is much more to be done in this domain of economic metrics for the performance of news analytics. Leinweber and Sisk (2010 and this volume, Chapter 6) have shown that there is exploitable alpha in news streams. The risk management and credit analysis areas also offer economic metrics that may be used to validate news analytics.

2.5 DISCUSSION

The various techniques and metrics fall into two broad categories: supervised and unsupervised learning methods. Supervised models use machine-learning algorithms based on well-specified input variables. One may think of this as a generalized regression model. In unsupervised learning, there are no explicit input variables but latent ones (e.g., cluster analysis). Most of the news analytics we explored relate to supervised learning, such as the various classification algorithms. This is well-trodden research. It is the domain of unsupervised learning; for example, the community detection algorithms and centrality computation that have been less explored and are potentially areas of greatest potential going forward.

Classifying news to generate sentiment indicators has been well worked out. This is epitomized in many of the chapters in this book. It is the networks on which financial information gets transmitted that have been much less studied, and where I anticipate most of the growth in news analytics to come from. For example, how quickly does good news about a tech company proliferate to other companies? We looked at issues like this in Das and Sisk (2005), discussed earlier, where we assessed whether knowledge of the network might be exploited profitably. Information also travels by word of mouth and these information networks are also open for much further examination (see Godes et al., 2005). Inside (not insider) information is also transmitted in venture capital networks where there is evidence now that better connected VCs perform better than unconnected VCs (as shown by Hochberg, Ljungqvist, and Lu, 2007).

Whether news analytics reside in the broad area of AI or not is under debate. The advent and success of statistical learning theory in real-world applications has moved much of news analytics out of the AI domain into econometrics. There is very little natural language processing (NLP) involved. As future developments shift from text methods to context methods, we may see a return to the AI paradigm. I believe that tools such as `WolframAlpha`^{TM} will be the basis of context-dependent news analysis.

News analytics will broaden in the toolkit it encompasses. Expect to see greater use of dependency networks and collaborative filtering. We will also see better data visualization techniques such as community views and centrality diagrams. The number of tools keeps on growing. For an almost exhaustive compendium of tools see the book by Koller (2009) titled *Probabilistic Graphical Models*.

In the end, news analytics are just sophisticated methods for data mining. For an interesting look at the top-10 algorithms in data mining, see Xindong Wu et al. (2008). This paper discusses the top-10 data-mining algorithms identified by the IEEE International Conference on Data Mining (ICDM) in December 2006.[3] As algorithms improve in speed, they will expand to automated decision-making, replacing human interaction—as noticed in the marriage of news analytics with automated trading, and eventually, a rebirth of XHAL.

2.6 REFERENCES

Admati A.; Pfleiderer P. (2001) *Noisytalk.com: Broadcasting Opinions in a Noisy Environment*, Working Paper, Stanford University.

Antweiler W.; Frank M. (2004) "Is all that talk just noise? The information content of internet stock message boards," *Journal of Finance*, **59**(3), 1259–1295.

Antweiler W.; Frank M. (2005) *The Market Impact of Corporate News Stories*, Working Paper, University of British Columbia.

[3] These algorithms are C4.5, k-Means, SVM, Apriori, EM, PageRank, AdaBoost, kNN, Naive Bayes, and CART.

Bonacich P. (1972) "Technique for analyzing overlapping memberships," *Sociological Methodology*, **4**, 176-185.

Bonacich P. (1987) "Power and centrality: A family of measures," *American Journal of Sociology*, **92**(5), 1170–1182.

Chakrabarti S.; Dom B.; Agrawal R.; Raghavan P. (1998) "Scalable feature selection, classification and signature generation for organizing large text databases into hierarchical topic taxonomies," *The VLDB Journal*, Springer.

Das S.; Chen M. (2007) "Yahoo for Amazon! Sentiment extraction from small talk on the web," *Management Science*, **53**, 1375–1388.

Das S.; Martinez-Jerez A.; Tufano P. (2005) "eInformation: A clinical study of investor discussion and sentiment," *Financial Management*, **34**(5), 103–137.

Das S.; Sisk J. (2005) "Financial communities," *Journal of Portfolio Management*, **31**(4), 112–123.

DeMarzo P.; Vayanos D.; Zwiebel J. (2003) "Persuasion bias, social influence, and uni-dimensional opinions," *Quarterly Journal of Economics*, **118**, 909–968.

Edwards J.; McCurley K.; Tomlin J. (2001) "An adaptive model for optimizing performance of an incremental web crawler," paper presented at *Proceedings WWW10, Hong Kong*, pp. 106–113.

Ellison G.; Fudenberg D. (1995) "Word of mouth communication and social learning," *Quarterly Journal of Economics*, **110**, 93–126.

Fortunato S. (2010) "Community detection in graphs," *Physics Reports*, **486**, 75–174.

Godes D.; Mayzlin D.; Chen Y.; Das S.; Dellarocas C.; Pfeiffer B.; Libai B.; Sen S.; Shi M.; Verlegh P. (2005) "The firm's management of social interactions," *Marketing Letters*. **16**, 415–428.

Graham P. (2004) *Hackers and Painters*, O'Reilly Media, Sebastopol, CA.

Hochberg Y.; Ljungqvist A.; Lu Y. (2007) "Whom you know matters: Venture capital networks and investment performance," *Journal of Finance*, **62**(1), 251–301.

Joachims T. (1999) "Making large-scale SVM learning practical," in B. Scholkopf, C. Burges, A. Smola (Eds.), *Advances in Kernel Methods: Support Vector Learning*, MIT Press.

Koller D.; Sahami M. (1997) "Hierarchically classifying documents using very few words," paper presented at *International Conference on Machine Learning*, Vol. 14, Morgan-Kaufmann, San Mateo, CA.

Koller D. (2009) *Probabilistic Graphical Models*, MIT Press.

Leinweber D.; Sisk J. (2010) "Relating news analytics to stock returns," mimeo, Leinweber & Co. See also this volume, Chapter 6.

Levy S. (2010) "How Google's algorithm rules the web," *Wired*, March.

Li F. (2006) *Do Stock Market Investors Understand the Risk Sentiment of Corporate Annual Reports?*, Working Paper, University of Michigan.

McCallum A. (1996) "Bow: A toolkit for statistical language modeling, text retrieval, classification and clustering," `http://www.cs.cmu.edu/~mccallum/bow`

Mitchell T. (1997) *Machine Learning*, McGraw-Hill.

Mitra L.; Mitra G.; diBartolomeo D. (2008) *Equity Portfolio Risk (Volatility) Estimation Using Market Information and Sentiment*, Working Paper, Brunel University.

Morville P. (2005) *Ambient Findability*, O'Reilly Media, Sebastopol, CA.

Neal R. (1996) *Bayesian Learning for Neural Networks*, Lecture Notes in Statistics Vol. 118, Springer.

Pang B.; Lee L.; Vaithyanathan S. (2002) "Thumbs up? Sentiment classification using machine learning techniques," paper presented at *Proceedings Conference on Empirical Methods in Natural Language Processing (EMNLP)*.

Pons P.; Latapy M. (2006) "Computing communities in large networks using random walks," *Journal of Graph Algorithms Applied*, **10**(2), 191–218.

Porter M. (1980) "An algorithm for suffix stripping," *Program*, **14**(3), 130–137.

Segaran T. (2007) *Programming Collective Intelligence*, O'Reilly Media, Sebastopol, CA.

Smola A.J.; Scholkopf B. (1998) *A Tutorial on Support Vector Regression*, NeuroCOLT2 Technical Report, ESPIRIT Working Group in Neural and Computational Learning II.

Tetlock P. (2007) "Giving content to investor sentiment: The role of media in the stock market," *Journal of Finance*, **62**(3), 1139–1168.

Tetlock P.; Saar-Tsechansky P.M.; Macskassy S. (2008) "More than words: Quantifying language to measure firms' fundamentals," *Journal of Finance*, **63**(3), 1437–1467.

Vapnik V. (1995) *The Nature of Statistical Learning Theory*, Springer, New York.

Vapnik V.; Chervonenkis A. (1964) "On the uniform convergence of relative frequencies of events to their probabilities," *Theory of Probability and Its Applications*, **16**(2), 264–280.

Vapnik V.; Lerner A. (1963) "Pattern recognition using generalized portrait method," *Automation and Remote Control*, **24**.

Xindong Wu; Kumar V.; Quinlan J.R.; Ghosh J.; Qiang Yang; Motoda H.; McLachlan G.J.; Ng A.; Bing Liu; Yu P.S.; Zhi-Hua Zhou; Steinbach M.; Hand D.J.; Steinberg D. 2008) "Top 10 algorithms in data mining," *Knowledge and Information Systems*, **14**(1), 1–37.

3

Managing real-time risks and returns: The Thomson Reuters NewsScope Event Indices

Alexander D. Healy and Andrew W. Lo[1]

ABSTRACT

As financial markets grow in size and complexity, risk management protocols must also evolve to address more challenging demands. One of the most difficult of these challenges is managing event risk, the risk posed by unanticipated news that causes major market moves over short time intervals. Often cited but rarely managed, event risk has been relegated to the domain of qualitative judgment and discretion because of its heterogeneity and velocity. In this chapter, we describe one initiative aimed at solving this problem. The Thomson Reuters NewsScope Event Indices Project is an integrated framework for incorporating real-time news from the Thomson Reuters NewsScope subscription service into systematic investment and risk management protocols. The framework consists of a set of real-time event indices—each one taking on numerical values between 0 and 100—designed to capture the occurrence of unusual events of a particular kind. Each index is constructed by applying disciplined pattern recognition algorithms to real-time news feeds, and validated using econometric methods applied to historical data.

3.1 INTRODUCTION

As financial markets grow in size and complexity, risk management protocols must also evolve to address more challenging demands. One of the most difficult of these challenges is managing "event risk", the risk posed by unanticipated news that causes major market moves over short time intervals. Examples include terrorist events like September 11, 2001, contagion effects like the Quant Meltdown of August 7–9, 2007, and system glitches like the "Flash Crash" of May 6, 2010. Often cited but rarely managed, event risk has been relegated to the domain of qualitative judgment and discretion

[1] The views and opinions expressed in this chapter are those of the authors only, and do not necessarily represent the views and opinions of AlphaSimplex Group, MIT, or any of their affiliates and employees. The authors make no representations or warranty, either expressed or implied, as to the accuracy or completeness of the information contained in this chapter, nor are they recommending that this chapter serve as the basis for any investment decision—this chapter is for information purposes only. This research was supported by AlphaSimplex Group, LLC and Thomson Reuters.

The Handbook of News Analytics in Finance Edited by L. Mitra and G. Mitra

because of its heterogeneity and velocity. If we cannot measure it, we cannot manage it, and text-based news is hard to quantify.

In this chapter, we describe one initiative aimed at solving this problem. The Thomson Reuters NewsScope Event Indices Project is an integrated framework for incorporating real-time news from the Thomson Reuters NewsScope subscription service into systematic investment and risk management protocols. The framework consists of a set of real-time event indices—each one taking on numerical values between 0 and 100—designed to capture the occurrence of unusual events of a particular kind. For example, the `Macro` index measures the real-time quantity of macroeconomic news, and the `NatDist` index measures the real-time quantity of natural disaster news. Each index is constructed by applying disciplined pattern recognition algorithms to real-time newsfeeds, and calibrated using econometric methods applied to historical data. In this first release, we construct indices that are calibrated to foreign exchange markets; future releases will focus on other markets.

In this chapter, we describe the procedures for constructing and validating the Thomson Reuters/AlphaSimplex Event Indices. We begin with a brief literature review in Section 3.2, and in Section 3.3 we introduce the historical datasets used to calibrate the indices. Section 3.4 contains the algorithms used to construct the indices. In Section 3.5, we describe the event study methodology for validating the indices, and in Section 3.6 we explore the connection between realized volatility (our metric for market impact) and implied volatility. We conclude in Section 3.8.

3.2 LITERATURE REVIEW

There is a surprisingly rich literature on the relationship between news and financial markets going back to Niederhoffer's (1971) pioneering study of world events and stock prices, where world events were defined as five- to eight-column headlines in the *New York Times* and then organized into categories of meaning. Niederhoffer found that large stock price changes did follow world events more than randomly selected days, but that a particular category into which a world event falls did not add much incremental information about future price movements.

Measuring public information by the number of news releases by Reuter's News Service per unit of time, Berry and Howe (1994) showed that there is a positive, moderate relationship between public information and trading volume. Engle and Ng (1993) defined the "news impact curve" which measures how new information is incorporated into volatility estimates. However, by studying the number of news announcements reported daily by Dow Jones & Co., Mitchell and Mulherin (1994) did not find any strong relation between news and market activity. Hong, Lim, and Stein (2000) confirmed that firm-specific information, especially negative information, diffuses only gradually across the investing public.

On the macroeconomic front, Pearce and Roley (1985) showed that on announcement days surprises related to monetary policy significantly affect stock prices, but only found limited evidence of an impact from inflation surprises and no evidence of an impact from real activity surprises.

More recently, papers by Antweiler and Frank (2004), Das, Martinez-Jerez, and Tufano (2005), Tetlock (2007), and Leinweber and Sisk (this volume, Chapter 6) document interesting connections between news, volatility, and stock returns. Chan (2003) shows that the volume of news can explain the difference between mean reversion and momentum in monthly stock returns. And Tetlock, Saar-Tsechansky, and Macskassy (2008) show that simple quantitative measures of language can be used to predict individual firms' accounting earnings and stock returns.

3.3 DATA

Information needed for real-time investment decisions reaches traders through a multitude of news sources such as Thomson Reuters, Bloomberg, and CNN. The event indices described in this chapter reflect the issuance of market-moving information contained in the Thomson Reuters NewsScope Archive. As a proxy for the universe of news sources available to traders, we chose the English-language news from the Thomson Reuters NewsScope feed and, in particular, we have focused on news "alerts" (i.e., the quick news flashes that are issued "[w]hen a newsworthy event occurs"— according to the *Reuters NewsScope Archive User Guide*, V1.0). The basic empirical properties of this dataset are described in Sections 3.1 and 3.A.2 (see appendix on p. 102).

To calibrate the parameters of our news event indices, we use real-time Thomson Reuters foreign exchange spot data, which consist of interbank quotes for 45 currency pairs from January 1, 2003 through July 31, 2007. The characteristics of this dataset are summarized in Sections 3.2 and 3.A.1 (see appendix on p. 100).

3.3.1 News data

Some examples of Thomson Reuters NewsScope alerts include

```
02 AUG 2007 04:44:26.155
TSUNAMI WARNING ISSUED FOR JAPAN'S WESTERN HOKKAIDO COAST
NHK JP ASIA NEWS DIS LEN RTRS

17 AUG 2007 12:16:31.344
FED SAYS DATA SUGGESTS U.S. ECONOMY HAS CONTINUED TO EXPAND AT
  MODERATE PACE
US WASH MCE FED GVD DBT PLCY STIR INT CEN EU WEU FR FIN BNK FRX MTG
  ECB LEN RTRS

22 AUG 2007 20:26:57.587
MOODY'S DOWNGRADES RATINGS OF 120 SUBPRIME RMBS TRANCHES ISSUED
  IN 2005
MTG ABS FINS DBT AAA USC US LEN RTRS
```

This information-rich choice of news inputs has a number of advantages. In intraday risk management or in trading strategy applications, the event indices may race head to head against human response times. Therefore it is vital that they respond in a timely manner and reflect the most current news. The machine-readable Thomson Reuters NewsScope feed is updated on a subsecond basis, allowing the news indices to reflect timely news. Also, by focusing on news alerts, we help to ensure that the indices reflect the most current news.[2]

Furthermore, the characteristics of Thomson Reuters alerts lend themselves to machine analysis. Their textual content is concise and built from a relatively small vocabulary. As a result, we can use robust, simple algorithms to extract information from the text. Another advantage is that Thomson Reuters data are tagged with machine-readable codes that characterize the alerts' topic areas and other important metadata, a powerful aid in analyzing their content.

A preliminary analysis of the NewsScope historical dataset reveals strong seasonality on intraweekly, intradaily, and intrahourly timescales, as expected. However, to identify those times at which incoming news is especially relevant to the market, it is necessary to distinguish true bursts of information from mere seasonal peaks in volume. We present our solution to this challenge in Section 3.4.

Some examples of the seasonalities are as follows: the median weekday sees 1,500 to 2,000 alerts arrive, while over the entire weekend there are typically only 130. Also, as one might expect, few (English language) alerts arrive at midnight GMT, a time when the workday is over in both Europe and America. On an intrahour timescale, alerts arrive more frequently on the hour or half-hour than at other times due to press release schedules and other planned announcements. See Section 3.A.2 (see p. 102) for a more detailed discussion of the seasonality of arrival of English-language alerts.

3.3.2 Foreign exchange data

Because the event indices' role is to rapidly identify and report the arrival of market-moving information, to validate their quality one needs a metric that indicates whether market movements did, in fact, occur. In this first version, the event indices were to be calibrated against foreign exchange markets; we used Thomson Reuters foreign exchange spot data, which consist of interbank quotes for 45 currency pairs since January 1, 2003.

Following convention (see Dacorogna et al., 2001) we approximated tick-by-tick market prices using the geometric mean of bid and ask quotes:

$$p_t \equiv \sqrt{p_{t,\mathrm{bid}} \cdot p_{t,\mathrm{ask}}}\,. \tag{3.1}$$

The dataset was then homogenized at 5-second intervals to facilitate computation while retaining subminute granularity.[3] However, it makes little sense to quantify news impact by measuring the price level. Instead, we consider the instantaneous change in level (5-second log returns):

$$r_{t,5} \equiv \log p_t - \log p_{t-5} \tag{3.2}$$

and the instantaneous variation in level (squared 5-second log returns): $r_{t,5}^2$. For tick-by-tick measurement of volatility, squared returns are our preferred metric because of their similarity to conventional realized volatility (a trailing measure that characterizes multi-

[2] This is in contrast to the follow-on stories that tend to appear 5 to 20 minutes later which provide further details on the event.
[3] Specifically, every 5 seconds we choose the most recent quote to represent the current price; however, if there have been no quotes in the last 30 seconds, we treat the data as missing rather than use outdated quotes.

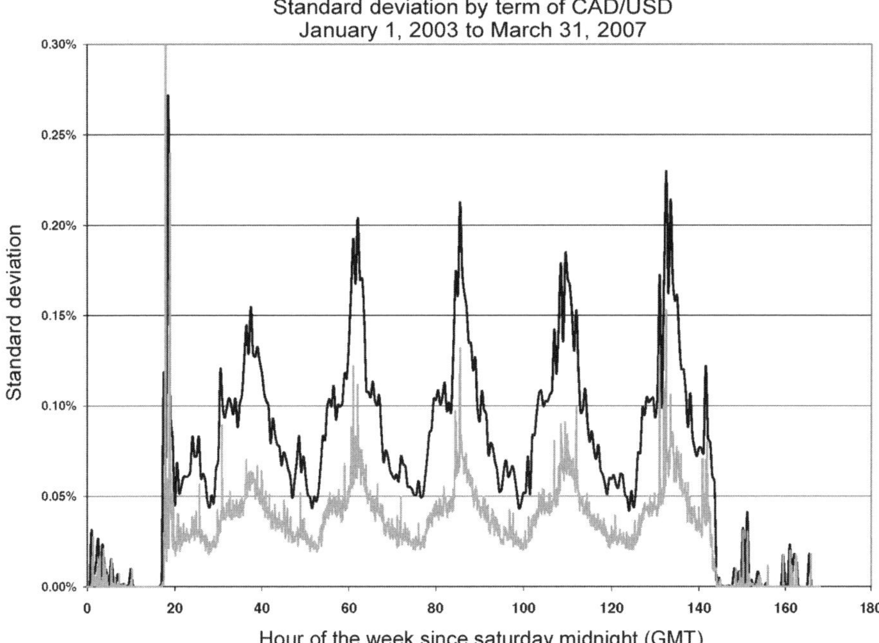

Figure 3.1. Average realized volatility of the CAD/USD exchange rate return over the course of a week, averaged over 5-minute (gray) and 30-minute (black) timescales. Note the strong daily peaks.

tick time periods). We note that the relationship between squared 5-second returns and the realized volatility over the period $[t_1, t_2]$ is as follows:

$$v_{t_1,t_2,5} = \sqrt{\frac{1}{\frac{t_2 - t_1}{5}} \sum_{t_1 \leq \tau \leq t_2} (r_{\tau,5} - \bar{r})^2} \approx \sqrt{\frac{1}{\frac{t_2 - t_1}{5}} \sum_{t_1 \leq \tau \leq t_2} r^2_{\tau,5}} \tag{3.3}$$

where $\bar{r}$ is the average return in period $[t_1, t_2]$.

As with NewsScope alerts, volatility exhibits strong seasonalities on intradaily and intraweekly timescales (see Figure 3.1). As one might expect, these seasonalities are only found in the squared returns, not in the returns themselves. This discovery raised the specter of specious results based on the correlation between news alert seasonality and FX volatility seasonality (as measured by squared returns). This potential difficulty is dealt with in Section 3.5, where seasonality is removed. For additional analysis of the properties of the Thomson Reuters FX dataset see Section 3.A.1 on p. 100.

3.4 A FRAMEWORK FOR REAL-TIME NEWS ANALYTICS

The core of our real-time news analysis engine relies on a scoring method that assesses the relative volume/significance of news from a specific category of news. For instance, we wish to identify periods when the volume of news about foreign exchange markets is abnormally high, or when there is a flurry of macroeconomic news announcements.

For a given topic, say foreign exchange news, the scoring procedure has the following parameters:

- A list of keywords/key phrases and real-valued weights: $(W_1, \gamma_1), \ldots, (W_k, \gamma_k)$.
- A rolling window size, ℓ (typically about 5–10 minutes).
- A calibration rolling window size, L (typically about 90 days).

The keywords list and the last ℓ minutes of news are used to create a raw score, and this score is normalized/calibrated using statistics about the news over the last L days (as described below).

3.4.1 Assigning scores to news

The score at a given point in time, t, is assigned as follows: Let $(w_1, \ldots, w_k)$ be the vector of keyword frequencies in the time interval $[t - \ell, t)$ (i.e., w_i is the number of times word/phrase W_i has appeared in the last ℓ minutes). The raw score at time t is then defined to be:

$$s_t \equiv \sum_i \gamma_i w_i \,. \tag{3.4}$$

In this form, the raw score will tend to be high when news volume is high, and so we calibrate/normalize the score using the calibration rolling window: We maintain a record of the scores that have been assigned over the last L days, along with the news volume (measured in words per ℓ minutes) at the time that score was issued. If we denote by $n_{[t-\ell,t)}$ the number of words that have been observed in the time interval $[t - \ell, t)$, then the normalized score is defined by comparing the raw score to the distribution of scores in the calibration window that had the same news volume $n_{[t-\ell,t)}$.

Specifically, the normalized score is equal to the fraction of scores—among scores in the calibration window that had the same news volume—that are less than the current score. Formally:

$$S_t \equiv \frac{\left|\{t' \in [t - L, t) : n_{[t'-\ell,t)} \text{ and } \mathrm{s}_{t'} < \mathrm{s}_t\}\right|}{\left|\{t' \in [t - L, t) : n_{[t'-\ell,t)}\}\right|}. \tag{3.5}$$

Thus, a score of $S_t = 0.92$ can be interpreted as "92% of the time, when the news volume is at the current level, the raw score is less than it currently is."

3.4.2 A natural extension to alerts

The scoring procedure described above is very flexible and, in particular, also has a natural extension to incorporating Thomson Reuters topic codes into the scoring. Specifically, if instead of counting word frequencies we count the fraction of news alerts in the last ℓ minutes that have been tagged with various topic codes, then we can assign scores in exactly the same way, the only difference being that we measure news volume by the number of alerts that appear (rather than the number of words that appear).

Formally, we have the following parameters:

- A list of topic codes and real-valued weights: $(W_1, \gamma_1), \ldots, (W_k, \gamma_k)$.
- A rolling window size, ℓ.
- A calibration rolling window size, L.

The score at a given point in time, t, is assigned in an analogous way. Let $(w_1, \ldots, w_k)$ be the vector of topic code frequencies in the time interval $[t-\ell, t)$ (i.e., w_i is the number of times the topic code W_i has appeared in the last ℓ minutes). The raw score at time t is then defined to be:

$$\sum_i \gamma_i w_i \ . \tag{3.6}$$

Just as before, we calibrate and normalize the score using the calibration rolling window: We maintain a record of the scores that have been assigned over the last L days, along with the news volume (measured in words per ℓ minutes) at the time that score was issued. If we denote by $n_{[t-\ell,t)}$ the number of alerts that have been observed in the time interval $[t-\ell, t)$, then the normalized score is defined by comparing the raw score with the distribution of scores in the calibration window that had the same news volume $n_{[t-\ell,t)}$, again by using formula (3.5). Table 3.1 lists the 45 news indices we have constructed and tested using this approach.

3.4.3 Creating keyword and topic code lists

The scoring mechanism described in Sections 3.4.1 and 3.4.2 relies on a list of keywords/topics, together with real-valued weights. The lists were created by first selecting the major news categories they should capture (foreign exchange, natural disasters, etc.) and then creating, by hand, lists of words/topics that suggested news relevant to these categories. These lists were then honed by examining the news that contained high concentrations of these words and adjusting the lists to remove words that were consistently misrepresenting the meaning of the text, and to add new words/phrases. Because this can be a very arduous task, we developed a tool (see Figure 3.2) that extracts news from the period when our indices assign high scores. The news is then presented, with keywords highlighted, and shows how the score evolves over time. Thus, one can quickly and easily determine whether the keywords that contributed to the high score are legitimate, or whether the keywords (and weights) need to be adjusted.

3.4.4 Algorithmic considerations

Given the vast amounts of data involved in this study, some care is necessary to ensure that the algorithms and data structures that are employed are efficient (both in terms of speed and memory use). In particular, maintaining the large rolling "calibration window", described above, is one case where novel algorithmic ideas are important to implementing our approach.

A naive approach to implementing the large rolling window would simply store all previous scores (for the last 90 days) in an array; however, our scoring procedure requires computing the percentile of a new score every second, and to do this for n unstructured data items would seem to require on the order of n operations. Here, 90 days of scores represents $n = 60 \cdot 60 \cdot 24 \cdot 90 = 7{,}776{,}000$ samples, which might be a feasible number for online scoring once per second (as in the final real-time indices), but is too much for rapidly simulating the scoring on months, or even years, of data. To construct the indices from historical data and to refine them in the future, it is essential to be able to simulate years' worth of scores in a matter of minutes (or at most hours).

Table 3.1. Base indices of the Thomson Reuters NewsScope Event Indices family

Base index	Description
Agricultural (topic)	Agricultural topics (as classified by Reuters) such as cotton/silk, grains, cocoa, etc.
ASIA	Asia (as classified by the Reuters topic code ASIA)
Banking (keyword)	Banks, lending, mortgages, and other areas relevant to banking
Bearish (keyword)	Indicates negative market conditions, low earnings, poor sales, drops in financial indices, etc.
Bonds (topic)	Topics related to bonds (as classified by Reuters)
Bullish (keyword)	Indicates positive market conditions, high earnings, strong sales, surges in financial indices, etc.
Central bank (keyword)	Monetary policy, interest rates, inflation, and other central-bank-related subjects
Central bank (topic)	Central banks (as classified by Reuters)
Corporate (keyword)	Earnings, dividends, and other corporation-related subjects
Credit (topic)	Credit default swaps, mortgages, real estate, bankruptcies, and other credit topics
Economic (topic)	Economic indicators, trade, and other economic topics
Emerging markets (topic)	Emerging markets (as classified by the Reuters topic code EMRG)
Emotional (keyword)	Contains emotional terms and subject matter such as fear, apprehension, relief, and nervousness
Energy (topic)	Energy topics (as classified by Reuters)
EUROPE	Europe (as classified by the Reuters topic code EUROPE)
Finance (keyword)	General finance subjects such as brokerages, underwriting, and financial markets
Foreign exchange (keyword)	Foreign exchange, such as monetary policy, announcements from finance ministers, and specific currencies
Foreign exchange (topic)	Topics related to foreign exchange (as classified by Reuters)
GB	Great Britain (as classified by the Reuters topic code GB)
JP	Japan (as classified by the Reuters topic code JP)
Livestock (topic)	Livestock (as classified by the Reuters topic code LIV)
Macroeconomic (keyword)	Macroeconomic subjects such as housing, inflation, and manufacturing
Macroeconomic (topic)	Macroeconomic topics (as classified by Reuters)
Major news (topic)	News in major news topics (as classified by Reuters)
Markets (topic)	Exchanges, hedge funds, and investing
Mergers (keyword)	Mergers, acquisitions, takeovers, and other merger-related subjects
Metal (topic)	Metals (as classified by the Reuters topic code MET)
Military (keyword)	Intelligence, homeland security, fighting, and other military actions
MX	Mexico (as classified by the Reuters topic code MX)
Natural disaster (keyword)	Hurricanes, earthquakes, tropical storms, mudslides, and other natural disasters
Natural disaster (topic)	Weather and disasters (as classified by Reuters)
Oil (topic)	Oil and oil-producing regions (as classified by Reuters)
Political (keyword)	Political subjects such as elections, legislation, referenda, and diplomacy
Political (topic)	Political topics (as classified by Reuters)
Precious metal (topic)	Precious metals (as classified by Reuters)
Rates (topic)	Interest rates (as classified by Reuters)

Base index	Description
RCH	Broker research (as classified by the Reuters topic code RCH)
Regulation (topic)	Regulation (as classified by Reuters)
Stocks (topic)	Stocks and investment funds (as classified by Reuters)
Terrorism (keyword)	Terrorist actions and related violence
Terrorism (topic)	Topics relevant to terrorism
Urgent news (topic)	Urgent news (as classified by Reuters)
US	The US (as classified by the Reuters topic code US)
VIO	Violence (as classified by the Reuters topic code VIO)
Violence (keyword)	War, fighting, and other violence

```
2003-03-14 13:39:50: 0.0000 (k=0.0, n=500, percentile=0.0000)
CORRECTED-ANDREW CORP<ANDW.O> Q2 MULTEX EPS VIEW PROFIT $0.04 (NOT LOSS $0.04)
ELC USC DBT RES RESF TEL LEN RTRS

2003-03-14 13:40:14: 0.0000 (k=0.0, n=297, percentile=0.0000)
RPT-ANDREW CORP <ANDW.O> SEES Q2 SALES $190-$200 MLN
ELC USC DBT RES RESF TEL LEN RTRS

2003-03-14 13:40:31: 0.0000 (k=0.0, n=284, percentile=0.0000)
RPT-ANDREW CORP <ANDW.O> Q2 MULTEX REVS VIEW $239.4 MLN
ELC USC DBT RES RESF TEL LEN RTRS

2003-03-14 13:40:34: 0.0000 (k=0.0, n=284, percentile=0.0000)
RPT-ANDREW SEES Q2 SHR LOSS $0.03-$0.06 VS PREVIOUS VIEW PROFIT $0.01-$0.04
ELC USC DBT RES RESF TEL LEN RTRS

2003-03-14 13:40:50: 0.0000 (k=0.0, n=295, percentile=0.0000)
RPT-ANDREW CITES CUSTOMER CAP EX LEVELS FALLING AT GREATER THAN EXPECTED RATES
ELC USC DBT RES RESF TEL LEN RTRS

2003-03-14 13:42:57: 0.0000 (k=0.0, n=239, percentile=0.0000)
MEDICINES CO <MDCO.O> SAYS PRICES 4.9 MLN SHR OFFERING AT $17.50 PER SHR
DRU US ISU LEN RTRS

2003-03-14 13:43:52: 0.0000 (k=0.0, n=221, percentile=0.0000)
BUSH TO TRAVEL TO AZORES SUNDAY FOR SUMMIT WITH SPAIN, UK ON IRAQ - WHITE HOUSE
US WASH VIO POL DIP MEAST NEWS IQ OPEC CRU PROD LEN RTRS

2003-03-14 13:45:10: 0.0176 (k=4.0, n=227, percentile=0.9840)
BUSH TO TRAVEL TO AZORES SUNDAY FOR SUMMIT WITH SPAIN, UK ON IRAQ - WHITE HOUSE
PT LEN RTRS

2003-03-14 13:45:54: 0.0176 (k=4.0, n=227, percentile=0.9839)
WHITE HOUSE SAYS SUMMIT PART OF LAST BIT OF IRAQ DIPLOMACY
US WASH VIO POL DIP MEAST NEWS IQ OPEC CRU PROD LEN RTRS

2003-03-14 13:45:55: 0.0312 (k=7.0, n=224, percentile=0.9971)
------------------------------------------------------------
Press ENTER to proceed to next event ('q' to quit)
------------------------------------------------------------
Proceding to next event . . . 2003-03-14 15:03:20
------------------------------------------------------------
2003-03-14 14:59:32: 0.0000 (k=0.0, n=58, percentile=0.0000)
POLISH M3 MONEY SUPPLY UP 1.1 PCT M/M IN FEBRUARY-CENTRAL BANK
PL EEU EMRG EUROPE FRX CEN LEN RTRS

2003-03-14 15:00:03: 0.0000 (k=0.0, n=72, percentile=0.0000)
MEXICO CENTRAL BANK SAYS LEAVES MONETARY POLICY UNCHANGED
MX LATAM EMRG INT GVD CEN FRX STX LEN RTRS

2003-03-14 15:00:20: 0.0000 (k=0.0, n=102, percentile=0.0000)
POLISH INFLATION 0.5 PCT Y/Y FEB VS 0.4 PCT FCAST, 0.5 PCT JAN, +0.1 PCT M/M
PL EEU EMRG EUROPE ECI INT LEN RTRS

2003-03-14 15:00:45: 0.0175 (k=2.0, n=114, percentile=0.9827)
BUSH TIES MIDEAST PEACE PLAN TO CONFIRMATION OF NEW PALESTINIAN PRIME MINISTER
US WASH VIO POL DIP MEAST NEWS IL PS IQ CRU OPEC LEN RTRS

2003-03-14 15:03:19: 0.0357 (k=2.0, n=56, percentile=0.9649)
BUSH-ISRAEL MUST END SETTLEMENT "ACTIVITY" AS PROGRESS IS MADE TOWARD PEACE
US WASH VIO POL DIP MEAST NEWS IL PS IQ CRU OPEC LEN RTRS

2003-03-14 15:03:20: 0.0441 (k=3.0, n=68, percentile=0.9977)
------------------------------------------------------------
Press ENTER to proceed to next event ('q' to quit)
------------------------------------------------------------
```

Figure 3.2. Screenshot of a tool for honing indices.

The approach we take is to build a data structure that allows for efficiently inserting new scores, removing old scores (after they are 90 days old) and computing percentiles. In particular, we achieve all these tasks in time $O(\log n)$, which, for the relevant sample sizes, represents only a few tens of operations, rather than several million (in the naive implementation described above). This data structure is an extension of *randomized treaps* that allows for fast percentile computations. We refer the reader to Cormen et al. (2001) for background on data structures and treaps, and offer a simplified presentation here.

The data are maintained in a *binary search tree*[4] where each node is augmented to contain an additional value that says how many values are stored in the subtree rooted at this node. Then, a straightforward extension to searching the binary tree allows one to compute how many values in the tree are less than a given value in time proportional to the depth of the tree. This is clearly equivalent to computing the percentile of the given value.

The remaining subtlety is that our binary search tree may not be *balanced*—i.e., its depth may be much larger than the optimal $O(\log n)$. If the tree is not balanced then the worst case performance of our searching/percentile computations may be very poor. Thus, it is imperative to maintain a *balanced* tree. An elegant solution to this problem is the random *treap* data structure, which combines a binary tree with a *heap* data structure to guarantee that the tree remains balanced (with high probability). We omit the details of heaps and treaps (which may be found in Cormen et al., 2001), and simply note that all treap operations can be extended to support our efficient percentile computations.

3.5 VALIDATING EVENT INDICES

To establish the empirical significance of our news indices, we use the event study methodology (see Campbell, Lo, and MacKinlay, 1997 for background on event studies). We review the basics of this well-known technique in Section 3.5.1, and provide a few illustrative examples in Section 3.5.2. We present formal statistical tests for the significance of news index events in Sections 3.5.3–3.5.5.

3.5.1 Event analysis

For a given index, event analysis is performed in the following manner. We compute the index over the sample period from January 1, 2003 to March 31, 2007, and declare that an "event" has taken place whenever the score exceeds a certain threshold, typically 0.995. We then remove any event that follows less than 1 hour after another event, which guards against having many events in quick succession that all reflect the same news event. We then analyze the behavior of exchange rates in the periods before and after these events.

In our analysis, we focus on two time-series describing the behavior of exchange rates.

[4] A binary search tree is a collection of nodes where every node (except for a designated "root" node) has exactly one parent and at most two children labeled left and right, with the property that the value in the left child is less than the value of the parent and the value in the right child is greater than the parent. Such a tree allows for efficient searching for a value v by starting at the root and going to the left or right child (depending on whether v is less than or greater than the value of the root node) and continuing down the tree in this way until the value is found. This allows for searching in time proportional to the depth of the tree (which may be as small as $O(\log n)$, where n is the number of nodes in the tree).

The first is the time-series of *log returns*, denoted $\{r_i\}_i$. Since we only have banks' quote data, this series is derived by taking the logarithm of the geometric mean of bid and ask quotes (as described in Section 3.3). The second time-series we consider is that of *de-seasonalized squared log returns*, denoted $\{s_i\}_i$, which is a measure of volatility in exchange rates. Since exchange rate volatilities exhibit strong weekly seasonalities (see Section 3.A.1 on p. 100), this volatility measure considers only excess volatility over typical seasonal volatility. In particular, this series is constructed by first considering the squared log returns $\{r_i^2\}_i$, from which we compute the *weekly seasonality*:

$$\hat{r}_i^2 \quad = \frac{1}{n} \quad \sum_{j=0}^{n} r^2_{(i \bmod W)+j \cdot W} \tag{3.7}$$

where n is the number of weeks in the data (220 in this case), and W is the number of samples in a week ($12 \cdot 60 \cdot 24 \cdot 7$ for 5-second returns). Finally, we define *de-seasonalized volatility* to be:

$$s_i \quad \equiv \quad \{r_i^2 - \hat{r}_i^2\}_i \ . \tag{3.8}$$

Using the events defined above, we test the null hypothesis that the distributions of returns and de-seasonalized squared log returns before events are the same as after the events.

For example, if we begin with the series of volatilities $\{s_i\}_i$, then we denote by $s_i^{(j)}$ the sample from time $i + t_j$, where t_j is the time of event j, and we consider the time-series $\vec{s}$ during a 1-hour window centered at each event; that is,

$$\begin{array}{c} s_{-30}^{(1)}, \ldots, s_0^{(1)}, \ldots, s_{30}^{(1)} \\ \vdots \\ s_{-30}^{(k)}, \ldots, s_0^{(k)}, \ldots, s_{30}^{(k)} \ . \end{array}$$

From these samples we can create an averaged event window:

$$\hat{s}_{-30}, \ldots, \hat{s}_{30} \quad , \quad \hat{s}_i \equiv 1k \sum_{j=1}^{k} s_i^{(j)} \ . \tag{3.9}$$

Then by studying the averaged event window we can assess the impact of the events comprising the event study. Naturally, this analysis can be applied to analyze log returns $\{r_i\}_i$ as well as volatilities $\{s_i\}_i$ (as exemplified above), and we consider both.

3.5.2 Examples of event studies

For concreteness, we present some illustrative examples of event studies that motivate the tests described later in this section. Figure 3.3 shows the graphical interface to our event study engine. The events being studied are surges in our macroeconomic keyword index. The currency pair being considered is EUR/USD and, in particular, we are studying the impact of events on exchange rate volatility (de-seasonalized squared log returns). The large plot at the top shows the averaged event window (i.e., $\hat{s}_i$ in the above notation) with the pre-event samples displayed to the left of the 0-minute mark and the post-event samples displayed to the right of the 0-minute mark. Immediately, we see a peak in the center of the plot, representing a significant increase in

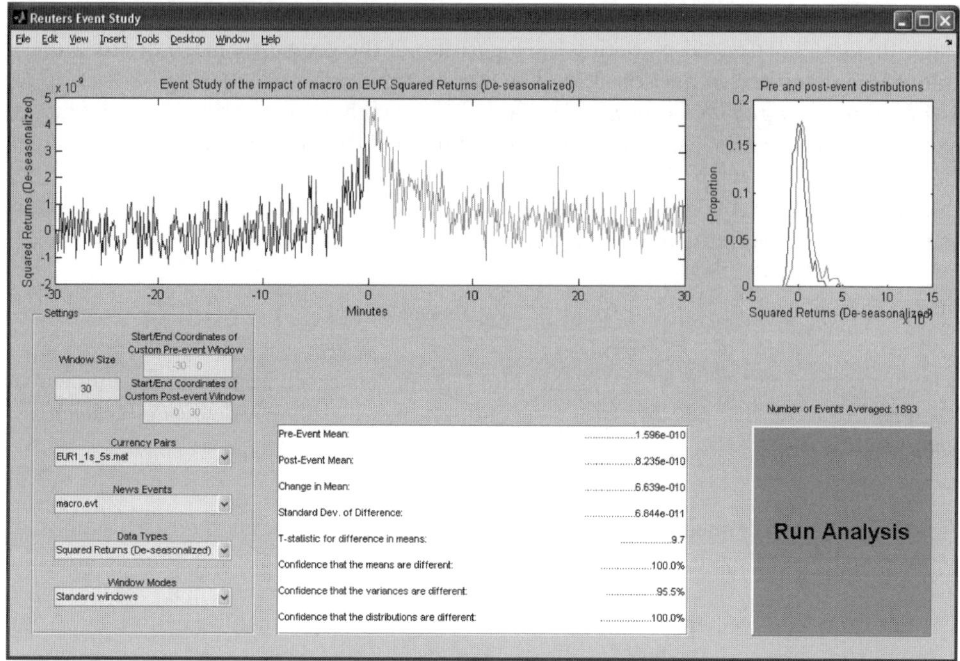

Figure 3.3. Screenshot of event analysis tool GUI, coded in MATLAB.

volatility around the time of the events, which are defined by spikes in our index. Also, average volatility in the post-event window is larger than average volatility in the pre-event window. Indeed, this can also be confirmed by inspecting the statistics reported at the bottom of the window. The second, smaller plot displays the density functions of the pre-event samples and post-event samples; thus, the fact that the pale curve (the post-event density function) is shifted to the right vis-à-vis the dark curve (the pre-event density function) means that there has been an upward shift in volatility, on the average, as a result of the events.

In Figure 3.3 the impact of these events seems clear, but for other indices the impact may be less visually apparent, and thus it is important to measure the impact using rigorous statistical techniques, which we propose in Sections 3.5.3–3.5.5. Nevertheless, it is instructive to consider two more examples.

Figure 3.4 shows an event study for our Agriculture index. This time, the currency pair is AUD/USD and return is the variable of interest. Upon visual inspection, there seems to be no significant change as a result of the events. The density plots to the right confirm this as well, as do the statistical tests described below. This is not surprising, however, since it is not clear that the presence of agriculture news would tend to drive exchange rates in one particular direction. Nonetheless, there is an impact which can again be seen by examining exchange rate volatility (this event study is shown in Figure 3.5).

Figure 3.5 shows an increase in volatility after surges in agriculture news, although it is a more modest effect than the example of macroeconomic news in Figure 3.3. Even so,

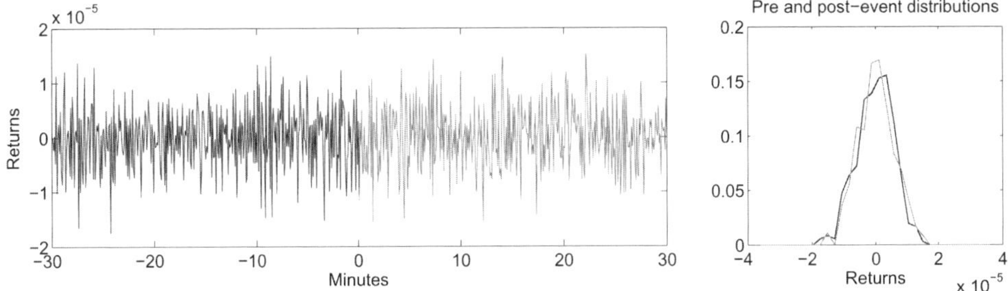

Figure 3.4. Event study of impact of agriculture news on AUD/USD returns.

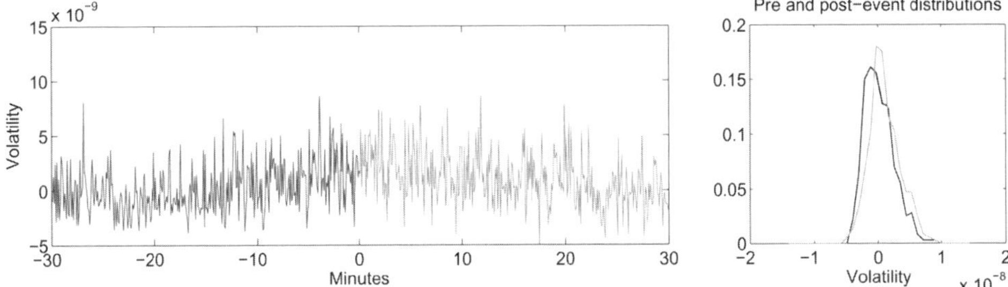

Figure 3.5. Event study of impact of agriculture news on AUD/USD volatility.

a t-test (see Section 3.5.3) establishes that this increase is indeed statistically significant, meaning that our agriculture index is correlated with volatility increases in the Australian dollar exchange rate.

For further examples, we refer the reader to the document *Thomson Reuters NewsScope Event Indices: Event Analysis Results* for the complete set of event studies. Table 3.2 summarizes the t-statistics from all event studies of 30-minute volatility for each of the currency pairs considered in this chapter.

3.5.3 Testing for a change in mean

A natural consequence of market-moving news events would be higher post-event volatility than pre-event volatility. We test for this using a t-test for equality in mean between pre-event and post-event samples $\{\hat{s}_{-w+1}, \ldots, \hat{s}_0, \hat{s}_1, \ldots, \hat{s}_w\}$.

The t-test is formed by computing the t-statistic (denoted t below) in the following manner:

$$\mu_- \equiv \frac{1}{w}\Sigma_{i\leq 0}\hat{s}_i \quad , \quad \mu_+ \equiv \frac{1}{w}\Sigma_{i>0}\hat{s}_i \quad , \quad \delta \equiv \mu_+ - \mu_- \tag{3.10a}$$

$$\sigma^2_{\mu_-} \equiv \frac{1}{w(w-1)}\Sigma_{i\leq 0}(\hat{s}_i - \mu_-)^2 \quad , \quad \sigma^2_{\mu_+} \equiv \frac{1}{w(w-1)}\Sigma_{i>0}(\hat{s}_i - \mu_+)^2 \tag{3.10b}$$

$$\sigma \equiv (\sigma^2_{\mu_-} + \sigma^2_{\mu_+})^{1/2} \tag{3.10c}$$

$$t \equiv \left|\frac{\delta}{\sigma}\right| \tag{3.10d}$$

Table 3.2. t-statistics for the significance of each Thomson Reuters NewsScope Event Index with respect to the volatilities of 16 currency pairs

Index	Currency pair															
	AUD USD	CAD USD	CAD JPY	CHF USD	EUR USD	EUR CAD	EUR GBP	EUR JPY	GBP USD	GBP AUD	GBP JPY	JPY USD	MXN USD	NOK USD	NZD USD	NZD EUR
ASIA	2.9	1.1	1.8	0.1	−2.5	0.9	−0.8	−0.5	1.6	2.2	2.2	−0.8	—	0.1	1.7	2.7
Agricultural topics	4.5	−0.8	1.2	2.8	8.7	3.6	2.5	0.7	4.8	0.5	2.3	2.1	−2.3	2.7	2.2	0.9
Banking keywords	−2.2	−2.2	−2.5	3.2	−2.2	−0.7	−2.0	−4.6	2.9	−0.7	−1.2	−4.8	2.2	4.2	−0.8	−1.2
Bearish keywords	1.2	1.1	2.2	1.0	3.2	2.7	1.5	−0.1	1.6	2.4	−0.5	1.2	0.3	1.1	0.2	−0.5
Bonds topics	4.9	2.5	7.0	6.6	6.3	−0.8	6.0	1.8	8.4	1.4	4.1	3.9	1.9	−2.5	3.5	2.6
Bullish keywords	4.1	−0.4	1.4	2.4	0.7	−0.1	−1.4	0.3	3.5	0.4	1.5	3.5	−1.8	−1.3	6.7	0.0
Central bank keywords	7.0	−0.1	3.9	6.5	13.3	4.7	1.2	5.9	5.6	−0.6	4.0	7.3	5.3	−0.1	7.7	2.2
Central bank topics	6.8	6.9	7.8	12.3	12.1	1.8	7.8	9.8	13.4	6.1	8.3	12.7	4.5	7.0	11.1	2.7
Corporate keywords	−1.1	0.1	0.4	1.4	−0.8	0.2	−2.9	1.6	2.4	1.1	1.6	1.0	1.4	1.4	−1.1	1.6
Credit topics	1.8	3.7	3.2	3.8	2.4	−0.7	1.6	1.1	4.9	3.4	5.3	3.4	2.5	−3.5	0.1	0.4
EUROPE	1.7	3.1	1.7	−0.5	−1.8	0.8	−0.9	−0.7	1.4	−1.4	0.9	−3.9	—	2.6	7.2	2.9
Economic topics	8.8	7.0	7.4	12.1	12.9	7.2	2.7	2.7	10.5	2.5	9.4	8.2	−3.4	11.5	6.4	4.0
Emerging market topics	1.4	1.1	1.5	1.8	1.1	2.7	−3.4	1.5	1.2	−0.3	0.2	1.8	0.9	1.2	−1.2	1.9
Emotional keywords	3.2	3.3	0.7	4.5	2.2	0.2	1.0	−0.3	3.1	0.6	2.7	0.7	−3.8	1.8	0.5	0.2
Energy topics	2.5	−3.3	−0.4	−2.5	−2.2	−4.0	0.4	1.1	−2.5	0.0	0.4	0.9	4.1	−7.3	−0.5	−2.1
Finance keywords	−2.3	−1.9	−1.7	1.0	−5.1	0.3	−4.1	2.9	−0.1	2.2	1.8	−1.0	1.9	0.3	0.5	−2.4
Foreign exchange keywords	2.2	4.1	2.5	1.6	0.9	2.0	2.4	2.1	1.0	3.6	3.9	4.0	−1.6	0.0	4.8	7.3
Foreign exchange topics	9.4	8.6	10.7	9.4	7.9	4.0	9.7	6.5	7.0	5.4	8.1	9.2	6.9	5.6	5.6	1.7
Livestock topics	11.6	8.0	11.7	15.0	17.3	7.3	4.7	7.1	15.8	7.5	8.0	12.5	0.6	14.3	10.2	1.0
Macroeconomic keywords	9.9	10.6	10.7	13.8	10.9	3.8	2.9	5.9	8.6	8.1	9.2	12.2	3.6	7.5	6.5	2.2
Macroeconomic topics	13.6	10.7	12.6	19.4	14.6	7.7	4.9	9.7	14.3	6.2	11.2	14.2	0.0	11.7	10.7	6.4

Major news topics	3.5	6.7	5.5	6.8	7.6	1.9	3.9	3.7	6.3	1.0	4.1	6.0	−1.2	5.9	5.1	−1.3
Markets topics	−1.0	−1.3	0.0	−0.9	0.7	−1.4	−0.3	1.4	−2.8	−1.8	−1.1	0.4	−1.8	−0.9	0.0	0.4
Mergers keywords	−4.4	−5.3	−1.4	−4.4	−4.8	2.3	−2.8	−0.9	−2.8	−4.4	−0.5	−2.4	−4.2	−11.6	2.5	3.8
Metal topics	−0.6	−2.3	1.1	−1.5	0.6	0.8	−1.5	−0.6	−2.0	−1.8	0.1	0.6	−1.6	−1.1	−0.6	−0.2
Military keywords	0.7	−2.3	−0.7	−0.7	3.6	0.3	−2.1	1.3	−3.6	0.5	−4.2	−4.9	2.3	3.1	−0.3	0.8
Natural disaster keywords	2.1	−0.1	−1.3	−0.1	−0.2	−0.2	−4.0	−0.4	−1.4	0.7	−0.2	0.7	−0.9	1.5	−4.6	0.0
Natural disaster topics	0.6	−1.4	1.4	−1.7	0.0	1.6	−2.8	−5.8	−4.7	0.6	−0.6	0.1	2.3	−5.6	−2.4	0.4
Oil topics	1.2	−2.1	1.4	−0.2	0.4	−2.2	2.0	−1.6	2.6	−0.8	1.3	−2.1	−4.9	−1.4	2.6	1.2
Political keywords	−0.6	0.9	−2.8	5.7	−1.7	−0.3	−0.7	−1.8	−0.8	−3.7	−3.5	−1.1	−2.3	−3.3	−2.0	−1.7
Political topics	6.0	4.1	3.9	9.9	8.7	2.2	1.6	1.8	10.2	4.3	3.2	7.2	1.7	1.7	5.0	−1.5
Precious metal topics	2.0	−0.3	1.4	1.6	1.9	0.8	0.9	0.2	1.6	−1.0	−0.4	2.2	−0.3	4.8	1.4	0.9
RCH	0.2	−3.3	0.7	−5.9	−5.6	1.7	4.1	1.1	−4.9	−0.9	1.4	−0.6	−2.5	−4.2	−0.7	3.7
Rates topics	8.2	7.0	11.6	12.6	14.5	3.5	6.5	2.8	16.0	5.5	9.9	6.8	−0.1	−2.5	9.3	2.6
Regulation topics	−2.2	1.6	1.4	−1.7	−3.5	−4.0	−2.3	−2.4	−3.3	−1.1	0.0	−3.3	1.8	2.5	2.2	0.4
Stocks topics	6.5	12.6	8.8	6.8	11.6	0.9	0.7	6.0	7.9	3.6	3.1	7.1	3.7	8.6	3.0	1.8
Terrorism keywords	−0.6	−0.3	2.5	0.8	−0.5	−0.9	3.9	1.2	−3.5	−0.4	−2.4	−1.0	3.1	−2.6	−0.3	1.7
Terrorism topics	−0.5	−0.2	2.1	−0.2	0.7	−1.7	−2.2	3.8	−0.8	0.9	−0.2	1.1	−3.0	−1.1	−5.0	−3.2
US new houses ECI	7.8	6.5	8.4	7.4	5.9	4.0	5.6	4.1	10.5	7.0	4.8	6.6	1.6	7.0	3.7	−0.7
US housing starts ECI	9.7	5.0	8.2	9.4	9.6	5.1	0.6	5.8	7.9	7.5	6.4	8.6	0.7	12.5	8.3	3.7
Urgent news topics	10.2	10.7	9.8	15.0	13.4	7.2	7.0	4.9	11.6	4.6	8.9	10.5	0.9	12.5	9.8	8.6
VIO	−1.2	−2.9	2.2	−0.9	−2.8	−0.8	−3.2	−2.6	−0.1	0.8	−0.4	−2.0	−1.8	−1.7	−5.4	0.4
Violence keywords	1.1	−2.5	−0.6	1.9	−1.9	−1.1	1.5	−2.5	1.9	1.1	−0.1	−0.2	−0.1	−1.0	2.5	0.4
All European ECI	3.9	1.8	−0.1	8.2	1.2	1.6	2.5	8.4	2.8	−0.4	3.2	5.4	−1.3	7.2	6.7	0.7
All miscellaneous ECI	13.5	8.6	10.6	13.9	16.8	11.2	9.6	3.4	14.4	8.9	9.4	11.0	−2.8	14.4	8.1	7.1
All US ECI	16.7	12.1	15.0	17.3	15.4	11.6	10.5	11.2	15.5	12.7	12.1	14.9	0.3	19.4	17.3	5.0
Random events	−1.9	−1.4	0.7	−1.2	−2.8	2.1	0.7	0.6	−2.5	−1.1	0.6	−3.1	−0.2	−3.6	−0.1	0.2
Random news events	3.0	0.7	−2.5	−3.0	1.5	0.9	1.3	−2.2	−1.4	−1.6	0.4	−2.3	2.8	−1.3	1.6	−0.8

In a classical t-test, the t-statistic is distributed according to Student's t-distribution, and thus δ is large enough to be statistically significant if:

$$t > \Phi_t^{-1}(1-\alpha/2, \nu) \tag{3.11}$$

where $(1-\alpha) \cdot 100\%$ is the confidence level, and ν is the number of degrees of freedom, calculated as

$$\nu \equiv \frac{(\frac{\sigma_{\mu_+}^2}{w} \frac{\sigma_{\mu_-}^2}{w})^2}{\frac{\sigma_{\mu_-}^4}{w^2(w-1)} + \frac{\sigma_{\mu_+}^4}{w^2(w-1)}}. \tag{3.12}$$

When measuring variables that are not completely independent (such as pre-event returns/volatility), the t-statistic may not follow an exact t-distribution. To ensure that the confidence levels we compute are accurate, we empirically determine the distribution of the t-statistic under the null hypothesis as follows.

We construct random event studies by choosing, say, 500 random points in time and declare these as "events". We then compute the t-statistic of this event study and repeat this process 5,000 times to generate the finite sample null distribution. The resulting samples give a reliable estimate D of the distribution of the variable t for random (insignificant) events. We can then compare the t-statistics obtained from our (non-random) events and measure their significance according to the following formula:

$$\text{sig}(t) = \Pr_{x \leftarrow D}[x \geq t] \,. \tag{3.13}$$

This yields a more robust significance measure for our t-tests. The empirical values of t-statistics are reported in Section 3.A.3 (see appendix on p. 102).

3.5.4 Levene's Test for equality of variance

Another statistical test we apply to averaged event window samples is Levene's Test, which tests for a change in standard deviation before and after the event. This test is most naturally applied to returns since a change in standard deviation would suggest a change in volatility. Thus we begin with the averaged event window samples of log returns $\{\hat{r}_{-w+1}, ..., \hat{r}_0, \hat{r}_1, ..., \hat{r}_w\}$, and then compute the following quantities:

$$\hat{r}_{\text{median}-} \equiv \text{median}\{\hat{r}_{-w+1}, .., \hat{r}_0\} \quad , \quad \hat{r}_{\text{median}+} \equiv \text{median}\{\hat{r}_1, .., \hat{r}_w\} \tag{3.14a}$$

$$Z_{j-} \equiv |\hat{r}_{j-} - \hat{r}_{\text{median}-}| \quad , \quad Z_{j+} \equiv |\hat{r}_{j+} - \hat{r}_{\text{median}+}| \tag{3.14b}$$

$$\mu_{Z-} \equiv \frac{1}{w}\Sigma_{j\leq 0} Z_{j-} \quad , \quad \mu_{Z+} \equiv \frac{1}{w}\Sigma_{j>0} Z_{j+} \quad , \quad \mu_Z \equiv \frac{1}{2}(\mu_{Z-} + \mu_{Z+}) \tag{3.14c}$$

Finally, we compute:

$$Q \equiv w(2w-2)((\mu_{Z-} - \mu_Z)^2 + (\mu_{Z+} - \mu_Z)^2) \tag{3.15a}$$

$$R \equiv \Sigma_{j\leq 0}(Z_{j-} - \mu_{Z-})^2 + \Sigma_{j>0}(Z_{j+} - \mu_{Z+})^2 \tag{3.15b}$$

$$W \equiv Q/R \tag{3.15c}$$

Standard deviation changes with $(1-\alpha) \cdot 100\%$ confidence if $W > \Phi_F^{-1}(1-\alpha, 1, w-2)$.

3.5.5 The χ^2 test for goodness of fit

Another test for changes between pre-event returns/volatility and post-event returns/volatility is the χ^2 goodness-of-fit test. Below we describe the test for averaged event window log returns, but the same test could be applied to volatilities as well.

Recall that the χ^2 test consists of the following steps:

- Create histograms of $\{\hat{r}_{-w+1}, \ldots, \hat{r}_0\}$ and $\{\hat{r}_1, \ldots, \hat{r}_w\}$ such that they have the same bins and every bin in the first histogram has at least n counts, where $n > 0$.
- Denote the bin frequencies of the pre- and post-event histograms by $\{f_{1-}, \ldots, f_{k-}\}$ and $\{f_{1+}, \ldots, f_{k+}\}$, respectively, where $k \leq w$.
- Finally, define the χ statistic by

$$\chi \equiv \Sigma_i \frac{(f_{i-} - f_{i+})^2}{f_{i-}} \tag{3.16}$$

The shape of the distribution changes with $(1-\alpha) \cdot 100\%$ confidence if $\chi > \Phi_{\chi^2}^{-1}(1-\alpha, k-1)$.

3.6 NEWS INDICES AND FX IMPLIED VOLATILITY

In Section 3.5, we showed that event indices, on average, have an impact on realized FX volatility. Since FX implied volatility indices also forecast realized volatility (see Pong et al., 2004; Taylor, 2005), this suggests that implied volatility and news indices might be related. On the other hand, there is an important difference between the two: while event indices are calibrated to predict volatility over 30-minute periods, implied volatility indices forecast volatility over much longer periods, typically about 30 days. The event study methodology was employed to determine whether a relationship between the two does, in fact, exist. No evidence to that effect was found; this suggests that implied volatility and event indices may function as complementary sources of information for risk management, each focused on a different time horizon.

3.6.1 Data pre-processing

Bank quotes for implied euro volatility were obtained from Thomson Reuters for 2005 to mid-2007. Preliminary exploration revealed that the major banks quote persistent, yet statistically different implied volatilities (it is not uncommon for different banks to quote implied volatilities that differ by 3 standard deviations or more). This means that one could easily mistake changes in quote provider for genuine changes in implied volatility. To preempt such errors, and to focus on the relationship between implied volatility and news, we select one source of quotes for our analysis, and choose the most frequent provider, Société Générale, which was responsible for 20,691 of the total 53,959 quotes in our sample. Quotes from other banks were ignored.[5] Each tick in the time-series contained both a bid volatility and an ask volatility. We used the arithmetic mean of these two values.

[5] The next-most-frequent providers were BNP Paribas at 12,475, Broker at 4,980, and RBS at 4,341 quotes.

Event indices vs. implied volatilities

As demonstrated in Section 3.5, times with the top event index values tend to forecast increased volatility.

Given that active values of the Thomson Reuters Event Indices typically predict increased realized volatility, it seems plausible that they could also predict an increase in implied volatility. The following event study seeks to disprove the null hypothesis that implied volatility remains the same, on average, before and after a foreign-exchange-related (FRX) event.

The results of this and other, similar, event studies did not provide evidence to suggest that FRX news affects the implied 1-month euro volatility. Several other news indices were studied and similarly could not be shown to impact the implied 1-month euro volatility.

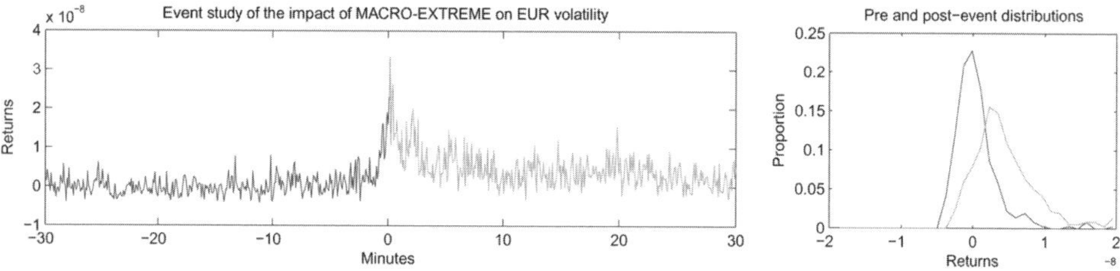

Figure 3.6. EUR realized volatility during 2003–2007 corresponded with the top-161 macro events (99.99% percentile of index).

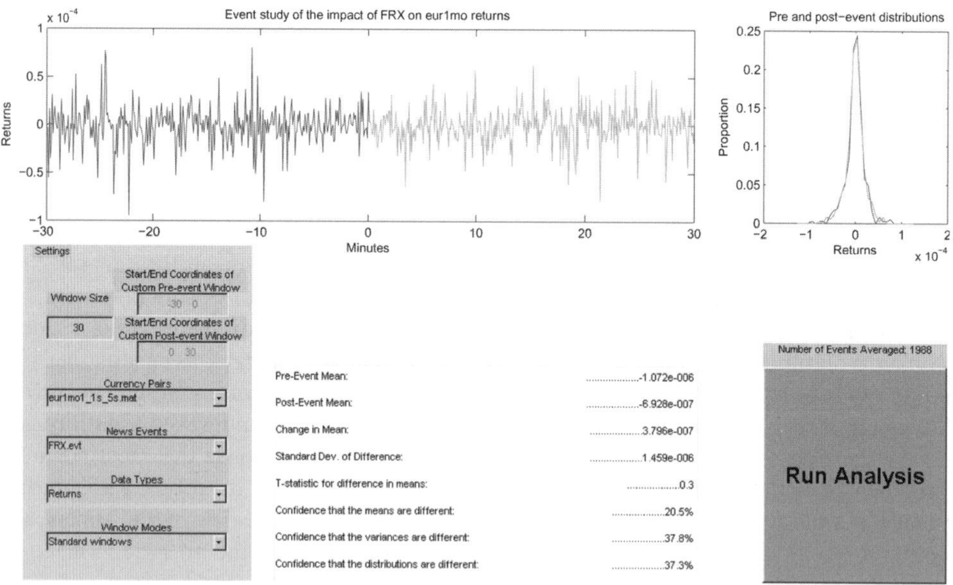

Figure 3.7. FRX events during 2005–2007 did not correspond with statistically significant changes in implied volatility.

In light of the contrasting performance of the event studies for realized volatility and implied volatility, we study the differences between these quantities that would explain this behavior. First, we note that implied volatility is imputed from options prices by inverting the Black–Scholes (or other similar) options-pricing formula. Thus, any forecast power with respect to implied volatility would imply forecast power for options *prices*, and since these options are actively traded we would expect only very modest price inefficiencies with respect to news.

Second, we observe that implied volatility is meant to reflect the expected volatility over a lengthy time horizon (e.g., 1 month), whereas the analysis of Section 3.5 concerns volatility over a much shorter period (e.g., 1 hour). It has been documented that implied volatilities tend to be much better predictors of long-term future price volatility in equity markets, and we find the same effect in foreign exchange data. Indeed, Figure 3.8 plots the correlation between future realized volatility (for horizons from 1 minute to 10 days) and the current implied volatility. For comparison, the grey curve in Figure 3.8 plots the correlation between (past) t-hour EUR realized volatility and the future t-hour realized volatility. We note that the correlation between implied volatility and realized volatility decays as the time horizon gets shorter, and once the time horizon is less than 2 hours, historic volatility outperforms implied volatility as a predictor of future realized volatility. Implied volatilities from other banks, as well as 1-week implied volatilities, showed similar behavior. These findings confirm those of Pong et al. (2004) and Taylor (2005).

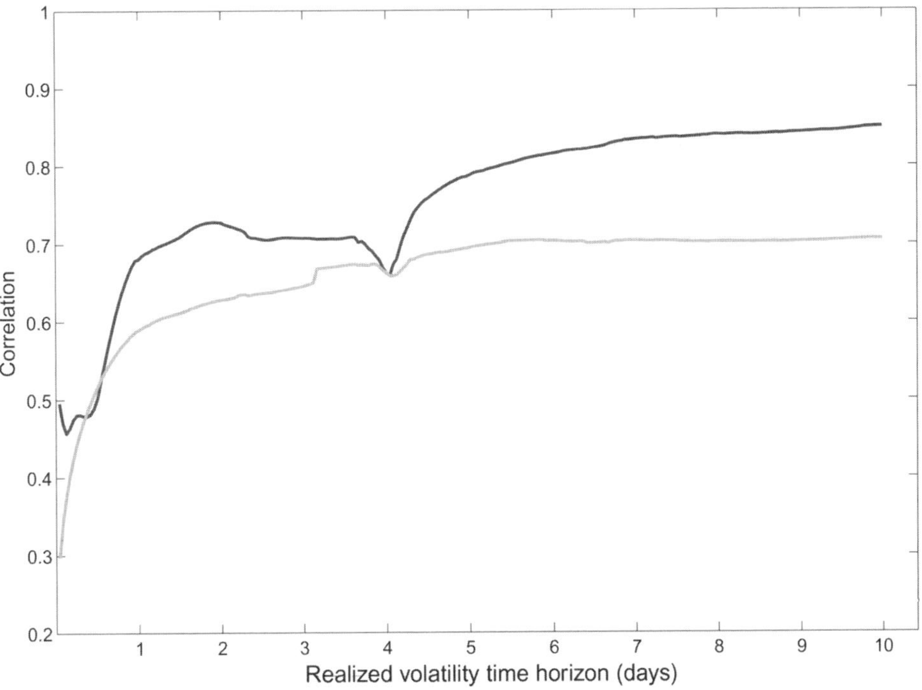

Figure 3.8. Correlation of 1-month Société-Générale-quoted EUR implied volatility with future t-hour realized volatility (black line). Correlation of (historic) t-hour EUR realized volatility with future t-hour realized volatility (grey line). All realized volatilities are de-seasonalized (as described in Section 3.5).

3.6.2 Implied volatility events

Abrupt changes in the 1-month implied volatility reflect a change in the market's beliefs about returns. It seems plausible that such changes might be correlated with contemporaneous changes in realized volatility. To investigate this hypothesis, an event study with 30-minute pre- and post-event windows was conducted.

A rolling window of the last 78 events (about 4 to 16 days' worth of events) was used to calculate the mean and standard deviation of Société Générale's 1-month implied volatility estimates. Deviations of more than 3σ from the rolling mean were taken to be "significant events". An event file of these timestamps was evaluated using the event analysis GUI.

The results of the event study did not provide evidence to support the hypothesis that realized volatility either increases or decreases at times when implied volatility significantly changes.

3.7 EVENT STUDY ANALYSIS THROUGH SEPTEMBER 2008

In the preceding sections, we have focused on event analysis with respect to foreign exchange during the period from January 2003 through July 2007. In this section, we update the results through September 2008, and also consider the impact of Thomson Reuters NewsScope Event Indices on 11 equity indices.

Tables 3.3 and 3.4 report the t-statistics for event analyses of event indices on the returns and volatility of the same 16 currency pairs as before (see Table 3.2), and Tables 3.5 and 3.6 contain t-statistics for the corresponding event analyses for 11 equity indices.

Tables 3.3 and 3.4 show that the event indices have little power to forecast movements in exchange rates, but significant power to forecast exchange rate volatility. However, Tables 3.5 and 3.6 tell a very different story for equity indices—the event indices do seem to have some predictive power for equity index returns, as well as for equity index volatility. One possible explanation for this difference is that equities are not as liquid, hence the impact of news is incorporated into currencies faster than equity indices. While this may suggest potential profit opportunities in equity indices, transactions costs are considerably higher for stock index futures than for currencies given comparable notional exposures. Therefore the magnitude of profits from real-time news-based strategies in equities is an open empirical question.

However, there is no doubt that the event indices have strong predictive power for squared equity index returns (as Table 3.6 illustrates). As in foreign exchange markets, the volatilities of equity indices are greatly affected by real-time news.

3.8 CONCLUSION

The importance of real-time news to the investment process has been well established, but until now there has been no systematic approach that integrates news with investments. The Thomson Reuters NewsScope Event Indices provide a convenient and powerful translation of qualitative information to quantitative signals using Thomson Reuters NewsScope data calibrated to foreign exchange spot data. The significance of the indicated market impact was verified using econometric event studies. Finally, an analysis comparing the volatility-forecasting capabilities of event indices and implied volatility indices suggested that they provide complementary information.

In ongoing research, we plan to construct customized combinations of the 45 base indices to suit a variety of applications (e.g., trading, risk management, and regulatory oversight). Moreover, we are developing a set of adaptive algorithms to automate the process by which new indices are created and old indices are updated to reflect changing market conditions.

Table 3.3. *t*-statistics for the significance of each Thomson Reuters NewsScope Event Index with respect to the returns of 16 currency pairs.

Index	Currency pair															
	AUD USD	CAD USD	CAD JPY	CHF USD	EUR USD	EUR CAD	EUR GBP	EUR JPY	GBP USD	GBP AUD	GBP JPY	JPY USD	MXN USD	NOK USD	NZD USD	NZD EUR
ASIA	0.7	−0.4	0.6	−0.4	0.6	−0.1	0.0	0.5	0.8	−0.9	0.5	0.2	—	−1.0	0.1	0.2
Agricultural topics	0.6	−1.5	1.0	−0.9	0.9	−0.5	−0.2	0.5	1.1	−0.1	0.4	−0.2	−0.1	−0.8	0.2	0.1
Banking keywords	0.0	−0.5	0.5	−0.3	0.1	0.0	0.0	−0.5	−0.3	−0.9	−0.3	−0.7	−1.0	−0.1	0.4	−0.1
Bearish keywords	1.4	−0.3	1.5	0.2	0.0	0.0	−0.5	1.1	0.7	0.0	2.1	1.8	−1.5	0.6	0.3	0.2
Bonds topics	0.5	0.1	0.6	0.0	−0.1	0.0	0.0	0.0	−0.1	−0.7	0.5	0.3	−0.7	0.0	−0.1	0.2
Bullish keywords	0.4	0.0	0.4	0.3	−0.6	0.0	−0.4	−0.2	−0.1	−0.7	0.4	0.2	1.2	0.4	−0.5	−0.1
Central bank keywords	0.0	0.0	0.2	0.4	−0.3	−0.1	−0.3	−0.5	0.3	0.0	−0.4	−0.3	−0.9	0.5	−0.2	−0.3
Central bank topics	0.0	0.2	0.2	0.5	−0.8	−0.2	−0.8	−0.6	0.0	0.7	−0.4	−0.1	0.2	0.5	−0.5	0.5
Corporate keywords	−0.8	0.1	−0.5	0.2	−0.6	−0.1	−0.4	−0.2	0.0	0.6	−0.2	0.1	0.1	0.3	−0.1	−0.1
Credit topics	0.0	0.0	0.8	−0.5	0.0	0.0	−0.1	0.2	−0.4	0.6	0.0	0.4	0.1	0.2	−0.3	−0.1
EUROPE	−0.3	0.5	0.1	0.2	0.0	0.1	−0.3	−0.1	0.2	−0.2	0.2	0.0	−1.3	0.1	0.2	0.0
Economic topics	−0.3	−0.3	−0.1	0.0	−0.3	−0.2	0.5	−0.6	−0.6	0.2	−0.9	−0.6	0.1	0.2	0.0	0.2
Emerging markets topics	−0.1	0.0	0.6	−0.1	0.3	−0.1	−0.1	−0.2	0.7	0.3	−0.6	−0.2	0.0	0.3	0.8	0.1
Emotional keywords	−0.1	−0.5	0.7	0.4	−0.3	0.0	0.0	0.0	−0.2	0.7	−0.1	0.1	0.5	0.3	−0.3	−0.2
Energy topics	0.1	0.6	−0.6	−0.7	0.1	0.3	0.4	−0.3	−0.1	−0.3	−1.0	−0.5	−0.5	−0.2	0.4	0.2
Finance keywords	−0.3	−0.5	−0.4	−0.1	0.1	−0.3	0.1	−0.2	−0.1	−1.3	−0.6	−0.2	−0.2	−0.2	0.1	0.2
Foreign exchange keywords	0.0	−0.3	2.1	1.0	−0.9	−0.4	−0.4	0.5	−0.2	2.0	1.3	1.4	−1.7	0.1	0.4	0.3
Foreign exchange topics	−0.2	1.0	−1.4	1.2	−1.2	0.0	−0.8	−0.3	−0.4	0.9	0.0	0.6	−1.0	0.4	0.0	0.1
GB	−0.1	0.6	−0.9	−0.7	0.8	0.8	0.8	0.1	0.0	0.0	−0.7	−0.5	−0.6	−0.3	0.0	−0.3
JP	0.1	0.4	−0.5	−0.2	0.3	−0.2	0.5	0.1	0.4	−1.2	0.0	0.3	−0.2	−0.3	−0.5	0.2

Livestock topics	0.1	−0.9	−0.1	−0.6	0.4	−0.7	0.0	0.1	0.7	0.5	−0.1	−0.2	−0.8	−0.7	0.0	−0.1
MX	−1.2	1.2	−0.1	0.5	−1.2	0.1	−0.7	−0.4	0.0	0.6	0.3	0.6	−0.5	0.7	−0.6	0.1
Macroeconomic keywords	−0.6	0.3	−0.8	−0.1	0.1	0.1	−0.1	0.1	0.5	−1.1	−0.2	−0.5	−0.6	0.1	0.0	−0.2
Macroeconomic topics	0.2	−0.6	0.3	0.3	−0.3	−0.7	0.0	0.0	−0.2	0.9	0.0	0.5	0.4	0.3	0.0	0.2
Major news topics	0.5	−0.6	1.0	0.8	−0.2	−0.5	0.1	0.0	−0.8	0.7	−0.4	0.5	−0.4	0.2	−0.2	0.2
Markets topics	0.1	−0.6	1.4	1.2	−1.0	−0.8	0.2	0.2	−1.3	−0.8	0.0	1.1	0.0	0.7	0.0	0.2
Mergers keywords	0.8	0.2	0.5	1.1	−0.7	−0.4	−0.8	0.1	0.1	0.4	0.3	0.8	0.4	0.6	0.5	0.2
Metal topics	−0.5	0.1	−1.1	0.3	−0.5	0.3	0.2	−0.4	−0.9	0.2	−1.1	−0.4	−0.1	0.7	−0.2	−0.4
Military keywords	−1.2	−0.1	−0.3	0.0	0.2	−0.2	−0.1	−0.3	0.0	−0.2	0.2	−0.3	0.1	0.3	−0.1	0.0
Natural disaster keywords	−0.6	0.6	−0.1	0.1	−0.2	0.3	0.4	−0.1	−0.1	0.6	−0.3	0.5	1.1	0.9	0.1	−0.1
Natural disaster topics	0.1	−0.2	−0.2	0.2	−0.2	−0.1	−0.1	0.0	−0.3	−0.4	−0.1	0.1	−0.1	0.7	0.1	−0.2
Oil topics	0.1	−0.1	0.5	0.0	0.4	−0.1	0.4	0.3	0.1	0.5	0.1	0.1	−0.4	−0.3	0.1	−0.1
Political keywords	−1.4	0.0	−0.7	−0.1	−0.2	−0.1	0.2	−0.2	−1.3	0.6	−0.5	0.3	0.5	0.5	−1.0	−0.1
Political topics	−0.5	0.0	0.3	0.1	−0.1	−0.1	0.0	−0.1	0.1	0.4	−0.2	0.0	−1.1	0.7	0.1	0.0
Precious metal topics	0.9	−0.5	−0.1	−0.1	0.7	0.1	−0.1	0.3	0.8	−0.7	0.3	0.1	−1.0	−0.2	0.6	−0.4
RCH	0.3	−0.3	−0.8	−1.0	1.0	0.3	0.2	0.3	0.9	−0.1	0.2	−0.7	0.2	−0.3	0.0	0.1
Rates topics	−0.4	0.0	1.8	0.1	−0.6	−0.1	0.0	0.7	−0.5	0.6	0.2	0.7	0.2	0.3	0.5	0.2
Regulation topics	0.5	0.0	−0.6	−0.4	0.5	0.3	0.3	−0.2	0.7	−0.9	0.2	−0.4	−0.8	−0.4	−0.3	−0.3
Stocks topics	0.3	−1.0	1.1	−0.1	0.5	−0.2	0.6	0.2	0.0	0.3	−0.2	−0.2	0.1	−0.4	1.2	−0.1
Terrorism keywords	0.7	−1.3	0.6	−0.2	0.5	−0.5	−0.1	0.8	0.8	0.9	0.7	0.1	0.1	0.1	0.3	0.4
Terrorism topics	−0.2	−0.4	0.6	−0.4	0.3	0.1	−0.1	0.2	0.6	0.6	0.1	−0.2	−0.2	0.1	0.1	0.2
US	0.4	0.1	0.3	0.3	0.1	0.1	0.0	0.5	0.3	−0.3	0.7	0.6	0.2	0.1	0.1	0.4
Urgent news topics	−0.6	−1.1	1.4	0.2	−0.2	−1.0	0.0	−0.2	−0.3	1.2	0.1	0.1	−0.1	0.3	0.3	0.1
VIO	−0.4	0.2	−0.3	−0.2	−0.2	−0.1	−0.4	−0.3	0.3	0.6	−0.4	−0.3	0.0	0.4	0.3	0.1
Violence keywords	−0.8	0.3	−0.2	0.5	−0.6	0.1	0.0	−0.3	−0.6	0.3	−0.3	0.0	0.7	0.4	0.0	0.0

Table 3.4. *t*-statistics for the significance of each Thomson Reuters NewsScope Event Index with respect to the volatilities of 16 currency pairs

Index	Currency pair															
	AUD USD	CAD USD	CAD JPY	CHF USD	EUR USD	EUR CAD	EUR GBP	EUR JPY	GBP USD	GBP AUD	GBP JPY	JPY USD	MXN USD	NOK USD	NZD USD	NZD EUR
ASIA	2.4	0.8	0.4	0.8	−2.3	−0.3	−0.4	−2.3	−0.2	1.0	0.7	0.6	—	−0.3	1.3	1.2
Agricultural topics	3.6	−0.3	1.1	1.8	6.2	2.7	1.2	0.1	5.7	0.7	2.0	−0.9	−0.7	5.6	3.4	1.1
Banking keywords	−3.4	−1.1	−1.9	2.1	−1.3	−0.1	−2.3	−6.7	−0.6	−1.6	−3.6	−3.3	1.4	1.8	−1.3	0.7
Bearish keywords	3.0	2.9	5.1	2.2	4.8	4.1	0.6	4.1	3.1	3.2	3.8	4.6	−1.4	1.6	2.0	−0.6
Bonds topics	5.4	3.9	7.9	8.6	5.8	1.1	5.4	0.0	8.0	2.6	5.1	7.3	1.0	−3.2	3.0	2.2
Bullish keywords	2.7	−3.7	−2.3	3.7	−1.5	−2.3	−2.1	−1.6	2.6	0.1	0.0	−1.3	−3.9	−1.0	1.8	0.0
Central bank keywords	7.8	3.7	4.1	8.0	14.2	3.1	2.4	7.4	7.8	1.7	5.0	8.3	4.9	2.8	9.4	3.9
Central bank topics	11.5	8.6	12.4	13.5	13.8	0.1	8.9	11.1	14.0	8.6	11.4	14.5	4.6	8.9	15.2	5.4
Corporate keywords	−1.0	−0.5	0.7	2.2	−1.1	−0.8	−2.2	−1.2	1.1	0.9	1.4	−1.8	0.2	2.6	−3.7	2.0
Credit topics	4.1	3.5	5.0	4.2	4.3	−0.4	2.5	1.7	5.5	4.4	4.6	4.9	1.4	−2.5	−0.7	0.4
EUROPE	2.1	5.4	2.9	−1.7	0.8	−1.3	−1.0	−1.6	0.0	−0.4	1.1	−2.0	0.2	4.0	4.9	3.1
Economic topics	10.6	8.1	8.0	13.3	12.7	7.2	3.7	3.0	10.7	5.0	9.7	10.1	−1.9	12.4	6.8	6.0
Emerging markets topics	−0.3	2.9	1.5	1.3	2.0	2.9	−3.4	2.5	−0.9	−0.6	0.0	1.9	−0.6	3.1	−1.5	1.5
Emotional keywords	2.9	2.7	1.6	2.8	2.7	−0.2	0.2	1.8	2.9	0.5	2.8	1.9	−1.8	1.2	1.3	−0.7
Energy topics	−0.2	−5.3	−2.8	−2.8	−0.8	−4.1	0.0	−0.3	−3.3	−0.2	0.5	−0.2	2.1	−9.5	−2.6	−2.1
Finance keywords	−0.4	0.4	−1.0	1.8	−5.7	1.5	−2.2	2.2	−1.2	3.0	3.5	−1.2	2.1	−1.6	1.3	−0.8
Foreign exchange keywords	4.7	9.1	6.1	3.5	4.2	1.8	1.2	6.2	3.9	6.7	7.6	5.9	−0.6	1.4	6.3	7.0
Foreign exchange topics	10.9	11.5	11.1	9.8	8.1	4.9	11.4	7.1	8.5	7.6	9.9	9.8	8.1	5.5	8.4	4.9
GB	1.5	−2.3	−5.7	−2.0	4.6	−5.9	1.0	−4.6	3.9	−0.2	−0.6	1.4	1.9	7.4	3.0	0.4
JP	−0.7	0.3	2.1	2.4	1.5	3.7	2.9	2.3	1.3	2.3	2.4	−0.1	−0.9	−1.1	1.0	2.0
Livestock topics	12.1	9.7	11.2	14.2	16.1	6.8	5.5	6.4	16.1	7.4	7.4	11.0	1.4	15.3	9.9	2.5

MX	3.7	−1.0	3.9	3.1	5.0	−0.2	0.3	0.3	1.5	0.6	3.0	6.5	3.5	−0.8	2.9	2.4
Macroeconomic keywords	11.1	12.8	14.5	16.1	12.5	6.2	3.4	7.7	10.8	11.6	11.8	15.9	3.4	8.4	9.0	6.6
Macroeconomic topics	12.3	12.1	14.5	19.3	15.9	5.8	5.7	11.2	13.7	8.6	10.5	15.8	0.1	10.8	11.5	6.3
Major news topics	5.4	6.2	6.6	7.7	10.1	0.5	5.0	4.5	6.8	2.4	9.4	8.8	−1.1	7.7	6.0	−0.9
Markets topics	−0.3	0.1	−2.0	−1.7	0.6	0.5	−0.6	0.5	−0.2	−2.1	−1.4	1.6	−2.3	−1.1	1.3	2.4
Mergers keywords	−3.3	−4.9	−4.1	−6.3	−3.7	3.2	−3.9	1.1	−4.0	−3.3	0.0	−4.0	−4.8	−11.4	3.2	2.8
Metal topics	−0.7	−2.0	−0.9	−2.6	−0.4	−0.5	−0.7	−0.3	−1.5	−1.1	1.5	2.5	−1.5	0.7	−1.7	−0.7
Military keywords	−0.7	−2.3	−3.5	−0.5	1.5	−1.5	−1.7	0.3	−3.8	−0.8	−5.4	−3.5	4.3	1.8	0.7	1.9
Natural disaster keywords	0.6	0.7	−1.0	0.2	0.3	−0.1	−3.8	0.9	−0.6	−0.1	−0.8	2.0	−2.1	1.1	−4.2	−0.7
Natural disaster topics	−2.0	−1.7	−3.3	−2.9	−1.1	0.3	−3.1	−5.8	−4.7	−1.2	−0.7	−0.1	1.0	−6.1	−4.2	0.1
Oil topics	1.2	−0.9	−0.9	−2.1	0.1	−1.3	3.6	−1.0	1.8	−0.4	−0.4	−3.5	−4.1	−2.1	1.9	1.8
Political keywords	−1.1	−0.4	−3.0	4.3	−0.9	0.0	−0.1	−5.4	−0.8	−4.4	−4.7	−1.8	−1.6	−3.5	−2.3	−0.7
Political topics	7.4	4.7	2.0	10.6	11.1	−1.1	2.1	0.5	10.7	3.9	1.9	11.0	2.1	3.5	2.9	1.0
Precious metal topics	1.3	−2.4	0.4	1.4	4.5	2.1	2.5	2.5	2.8	−0.6	2.2	6.7	−0.8	6.0	3.0	2.5
RCH	−2.9	−4.0	−2.1	−3.8	−5.0	0.9	3.3	0.5	−2.9	−1.8	0.2	−2.0	−1.6	−4.1	−2.5	2.5
Rates topics	10.2	10.2	14.4	15.7	17.2	4.7	8.1	7.4	16.9	7.5	13.2	10.3	−0.5	−2.2	11.6	4.3
Regulation topics	−3.4	0.4	2.1	−1.5	−4.3	−2.7	−0.6	0.9	−4.6	−0.7	1.3	−1.1	3.0	−0.3	3.0	0.3
Stocks topics	8.3	9.4	2.4	7.1	9.9	1.4	−0.7	5.8	7.5	2.5	−0.4	6.0	3.5	8.1	2.5	1.9
Terrorism keywords	0.0	−0.4	2.3	−0.5	−1.7	−0.1	3.1	1.6	−2.6	−0.5	−1.0	−1.1	2.7	−3.4	−0.5	2.3
Terrorism topics	−2.0	−1.5	−1.2	−0.4	−0.6	−2.0	−0.2	−0.5	−0.7	−0.9	−0.4	0.0	−3.1	−0.3	−6.1	−2.3
US	0.9	2.4	2.7	7.5	4.8	4.1	−3.2	−0.4	3.9	1.6	2.0	5.8	8.4	8.7	3.9	1.2
Urgent news topics	10.1	11.2	9.6	16.3	14.6	6.6	7.9	7.6	10.3	5.9	7.6	12.0	1.9	13.1	11.2	9.2
VIO	−0.8	−2.3	0.1	−1.8	−2.1	0.1	−3.6	−3.5	−1.1	0.3	−2.9	−1.8	−2.6	−2.1	−3.4	−0.4
Violence keywords	0.6	−1.7	−0.5	2.7	−1.5	−0.6	2.2	−3.2	1.8	1.8	0.9	−3.1	1.2	−0.2	3.3	1.0

Table 3.5. *t*-statistics for the significance of each Thomson Reuters NewsScope Event Index with respect to the returns of 11 equity indices

	DJI	FCHI	FTEU3	FTMC	FTSE	GDAXI	HSI	IXIC	N225	SPX	TOPX
ASIA	−1.3	−2.2	0.1	0.3	0.2	−0.5	−0.3	−0.9	−0.6	−1.9	0.2
Agricultural topics	1.6	1.2	0.8	0.7	0.7	0.9	0.5	2.2	−1.2	1.9	0.1
Banking keywords	−1.0	0.0	−0.3	−1.6	−0.4	0.2	0.3	−0.6	0.6	−0.9	−0.1
Bearish keywords	7.0	4.9	6.6	5.0	—	4.0	1.4	7.7	2.0	−0.7	0.2
Bonds topics	−1.3	2.7	3.4	0.7	2.9	3.2	1.3	0.5	−1.8	−1.1	0.2
Bullish keywords	−4.8	−3.6	−6.6	−3.1	−5.2	−5.2	−0.3	−3.0	−0.5	−4.4	−0.1
Central bank keywords	1.6	1.1	1.7	4.4	—	2.4	1.0	1.3	−1.1	1.2	−0.3
Central bank topics	−1.9	−0.7	0.8	0.6	1.1	0.7	−0.7	−2.5	1.1	−2.1	0.5
Corporate keywords	−0.6	−0.9	0.6	0.3	0.5	0.1	0.7	−0.8	0.0	−1.1	−0.1
Credit topics	−0.9	−0.7	−0.7	−1.7	−0.3	−0.3	−0.1	−1.3	0.8	−0.2	−0.1
EUROPE	—	−0.1	0.2	1.0	0.2	−0.7	0.3	—	—	—	0.0
Economic topics	−3.5	−0.5	0.2	1.0	0.5	0.1	0.6	−2.2	−0.8	−2.3	0.2
Emerging markets topics	1.4	0.4	0.0	−2.0	−0.7	0.8	1.1	1.4	−1.5	2.0	0.1
Emotional keywords	−1.1	−0.7	−1.0	1.2	−0.7	0.2	0.5	−0.9	−0.7	−0.9	−0.2
Energy topics	0.7	0.4	1.3	1.4	—	2.0	−0.7	0.9	1.6	0.2	0.2
Finance keywords	−2.4	−0.6	−0.5	0.6	−0.3	−1.3	−0.1	−1.3	1.7	−2.2	0.2
Foreign exchange keywords	2.5	0.0	0.6	−0.6	0.0	0.8	−0.3	2.4	−0.2	2.5	0.3
Foreign exchange topics	0.0	−2.7	−1.8	−1.2	−1.6	−1.8	−0.9	0.3	−1.0	−1.3	0.1
GB	−2.0	0.1	0.3	−2.4	−0.4	0.4	−0.2	−2.7	1.1	−1.5	−0.3
JP	0.5	0.2	−0.9	−2.3	−0.7	0.4	−0.5	0.5	−1.2	0.8	0.2
Livestock topics	−0.5	−0.3	−0.8	1.8	−0.5	−1.1	0.4	−1.1	6.8	−0.8	−0.1
MX	0.5	0.1	0.0	−0.3	0.7	−0.7	0.3	−0.8	0.0	−0.1	0.1
Macroeconomic keywords	−0.1	0.6	0.3	0.5	0.4	0.4	0.6	−1.0	−0.1	0.3	−0.2
Macroeconomic topics	−2.9	0.3	0.1	—	—	0.2	0.5	−3.6	1.2	−2.6	0.2
Major news topics	−0.7	−1.6	−1.0	0.4	−0.6	−0.3	0.3	−1.9	−1.1	−0.8	0.2
Markets topics	1.4	0.4	0.5	2.4	1.4	−0.6	−1.8	0.3	1.4	0.7	0.2
Mergers keywords	−2.2	−0.7	−0.2	—	—	0.7	0.1	0.0	0.5	−1.7	0.2
Metal topics	−1.0	0.0	0.1	0.3	—	−0.1	−1.6	−0.4	−1.6	−1.3	−0.4
Military keywords	0.1	−0.7	0.0	—	—	−0.7	−0.1	−0.7	−0.9	0.2	0.0
Natural disaster keywords	−0.3	2.2	0.7	−1.7	0.7	2.0	0.3	−0.8	−1.2	−0.2	−0.1
Natural disaster topics	−1.3	1.3	1.9	0.1	1.6	2.0	0.1	−1.3	1.5	−1.0	−0.2
Oil topics	1.1	1.3	0.9	0.7	1.5	0.3	−0.1	1.3	0.9	0.7	−0.1
Political keywords	0.3	−1.0	−1.8	0.6	−1.2	−1.5	−0.7	0.3	1.1	0.8	−0.1
Political topics	0.2	−0.2	−0.7	−1.0	−0.9	0.3	0.0	−0.1	0.9	−0.1	0.0
Precious metal topics	1.4	0.5	0.6	1.8	1.2	.2	−1.4	0.8	−1.4	1.4	−0.4
RCH	−2.4	0.8	2.8	—	—	1.3	−0.1	1.2	0.8	−0.4	0.1
Rates topics	−2.9	1.6	2.1	1.8	2.5	2.5	0.2	−1.3	−1.5	−0.3	0.2
Regulation topics	0.2	0.0	0.1	−2.6	−0.3	0.2	−1.2	−1.0	−0.1	−0.9	−0.3
Stocks topics	0.8	−1.1	−4.0	−3.0	−3.5	−2.5	0.7	−0.1	0.7	1.2	−0.1
Terrorism keywords	0.1	0.5	1.3	2.0	1.2	1.0	0.7	0.6	1.9	−0.1	0.4
Terrorism topics	0.1	1.3	2.6	−0.1	2.4	1.6	0.1	−0.5	−0.2	−0.1	0.2
US	1.8	−0.4	−0.1	—	−0.4	1.1	0.4	0.8	−2.0	−1.3	0.4
Urgent news topics	−0.8	0.6	1.5	0.1	1.9	0.5	−0.7	0.0	−0.9	−0.4	0.1
VIO	−0.7	−0.2	0.4	−2.7	−0.1	0.3	0.1	−1.2	0.4	−0.8	0.1
Violence keywords	−1.9	−0.4	−0.9	−2.0	−0.3	−0.9	1.3	−1.4	−0.4	−1.2	0.0

Table 3.6. t-statistics for the significance of each Thomson Reuters NewsScope Event Index with respect to the volatilities of 11 equity indices.

	DJI	FCHI	FTEU3	FTMC	FTSE	GDAXI	HSI	IXIC	N225	SPX	TOPX
ASIA	−7.2	0.8	2.3	0.8	−1.2	−0.5	0.2	−3.3	2.3	−3.6	1.2
Agricultural topics	8.0	−3.7	−4.4	−2.2	−4.6	−6.4	−0.8	2.8	−1.4	5.3	1.1
Banking keywords	−3.7	1.4	−0.5	−0.4	0.1	1.9	−2.1	−1.0	−0.5	−1.5	0.7
Bearish keywords	4.5	3.3	2.4	1.2	3.1	0.2	7.5	0.7	−0.7	1.3	−0.6
Bonds topics	3.8	2.7	2.1	0.3	−1.3	6.4	1.4	9.2	−0.5	5.8	2.2
Bullish keywords	−1.4	−2.0	−3.2	−1.9	−1.4	−0.6	0.1	1.0	0.1	0.8	0.0
Central bank keywords	8.3	−0.1	2.0	0.5	1.7	0.1	−2.6	11.9	1.0	10.5	3.9
Central bank topics	16.0	2.9	6.5	2.2	4.8	8.4	−0.6	12.7	0.8	15.1	5.4
Corporate keywords	0.9	−0.2	0.3	2.0	−0.5	0.7	0.9	2.3	0.5	3.7	2.0
Credit topics	1.7	1.1	2.6	0.4	0.9	0.9	−2.0	2.4	0.9	1.9	0.4
EUROPE	—	0.1	1.2	−0.2	0.5	1.7	−3.1	—	—	—	3.1
Economic topics	4.1	4.3	3.8	−2.4	1.1	4.0	1.1	5.5	0.6	3.8	6.0
Emerging markets topics	−1.1	1.6	2.3	0.1	−0.6	0.6	−3.2	0.6	1.2	−0.8	1.5
Emotional keywords	−3.5	3.4	4.5	−0.1	2.6	6.2	−0.6	−1.5	0.8	−0.1	−0.7
Energy topics	3.6	−1.4	−5.4	0.7	4.5	−5.8	0.2	0.0	0.4	3.3	−2.1
Finance keywords	−0.8	1.6	1.8	0.4	1.5	0.3	2.6	−1.3	0.9	−1.2	−0.8
Foreign exchange keywords	2.8	−1.2	−0.9	2.9	−0.1	−1.3	0.3	5.9	−0.3	3.9	7.0
Foreign exchange topics	9.3	0.1	0.7	−0.8	−0.1	1.2	1.4	7.3	0.1	6.1	4.9
GB	−4.8	−1.0	0.3	−1.4	0.9	−0.1	0.3	−3.4	−0.7	−3.6	0.4
JP	−0.5	−0.9	−1.0	−1.8	−2.3	−2.5	−0.3	−0.8	0.4	0.3	2.0
Livestock topics	8.7	1.8	2.0	0.0	−0.7	1.0	0.6	6.8	−0.5	6.6	2.5
MX	6.2	3.6	4.3	0.8	3.1	5.3	1.2	3.3	−0.8	4.2	2.4
Macroeconomic keywords	15.6	1.6	2.3	2.0	3.8	4.9	2.7	18.2	−1.6	17.4	6.6
Macroeconomic topics	9.5	8.5	6.8	1.0	3.2	12.3	−3.2	11.3	−0.6	10.4	6.3
Major news topics	9.1	3.0	4.9	1.5	3.6	9.5	−2.2	8.9	−1.0	8.3	−0.9
Markets topics	0.6	−0.3	−1.4	−1.2	−1.4	−0.6	−0.4	0.5	1.3	−0.5	2.4
Mergers keywords	−9.2	0.9	2.4	−2.8	1.3	3.7	−3.9	−3.4	0.6	−5.1	2.8
Metal topics	2.8	−1.0	−0.3	−1.1	−1.2	−3.1	3.9	3.0	−1.1	1.8	−0.7
Military keywords	2.9	0.6	1.5	0.9	3.3	2.0	−1.4	−1.8	0.3	−1.0	1.9
Natural disaster keywords	−5.6	0.1	0.1	−0.4	−1.6	0.5	1.3	−0.5	0.9	−2.0	−0.7
Natural disaster topics	2.4	−0.3	−2.8	−0.5	−2.3	−1.8	1.8	1.1	1.1	1.5	0.1
Oil topics	−2.2	0.3	−1.0	−0.8	0.7	0.5	−0.3	0.0	1.0	−0.7	1.8
Political keywords	0.7	0.4	0.7	1.6	0.2	−1.0	−1.3	0.0	−0.2	−1.6	−0.7
Political topics	10.8	1.9	−1.2	−1.4	0.3	−0.1	−0.1	7.4	1.1	9.5	1.0
Precious metal topics	3.8	1.4	0.3	0.7	0.8	−0.8	−0.4	1.7	−1.5	1.6	2.5
RCH	1.7	−3.4	−6.6	−4.0	−6.8	−8.6	2.4	−1.0	0.7	−0.5	2.5
Rates topics	11.6	10.5	11.4	1.9	8.4	13.1	0.1	15.1	0.9	12.1	4.3
Regulation topics	4.1	0.1	−2.1	−1.6	−3.5	−0.5	−1.3	0.9	0.4	2.4	0.3
Stocks topics	5.9	2.2	−2.0	−1.2	−0.4	2.8	1.0	8.0	1.0	6.1	1.9
Terrorism keywords	6.0	0.2	−1.4	−2.4	−0.9	0.2	1.4	1.9	−0.1	3.5	2.3
Terrorism topics	5.1	−0.3	0.6	0.4	−0.3	3.2	−1.9	1.5	−1.6	1.9	−2.3
US	6.8	−1.2	−4.5	−1.4	−4.2	−3.6	4.9	−2.7	−1.2	−2.0	1.2
Urgent news topics	11.0	5.8	5.2	−3.1	1.6	5.8	−0.8	11.2	−0.1	12.2	9.2
VIO	2.0	−2.3	−2.5	−0.3	−3.5	−1.0	−4.0	0.4	−1.1	1.6	−0.4
Violence keywords	6.9	0.0	1.4	2.5	0.7	2.4	−4.2	5.2	0.1	5.3	1.0

3.A APPENDIX

In this appendix, we present more detailed results regarding the construction of the Thomson Reuters NewsScope Event Indices. In Sections 3.A.1 and 3.A.2, we present some basic empirical properties of foreign exchange quote data and the Thomson Reuters NewsScope Archive, respectively. Section 3.A.3 contains Monte Carlo simulations of the empirical distribution of the t-statistic for the event studies of Section 3.5, under the null hypothesis of randomly chosen event times.

3.A.1 Properties of foreign exchange quote data

Our 4-year extract of foreign exchange spot data from the *Thomson Reuters DataScope Tick History* consists of interbank quotes for 45 currency pairs from January 1, 2003 to March 31, 2007. For each quote, the following fields are available: `RIC` (Reuters Identification Code, which specifies the currency pair), `Date`, `Time`, `GMT Offset`, `Type`, `Ex/Cntrb.ID`, `Bid Price`, `Bid Size`, `Ask Price`, and `Ask Size`. There are, in fact, many more fields than these, but we focus only on these pricing fields in our current analysis. A description of the contents of each field is given by the *Reuters DataScope Tick History* document.

For 17 major currency pairs the spot prices were extracted, and we retained only `Date`, `Time Stamp`, `Ask Price`, `Ask Volume`, `Bid Price`, `Bid Volume`, and `Source` (bank). Note that there may be a few missing values in these data, but each line does have, at the very least, an `Ask Price`.

Note that the time stamps for quotes are typically specified in Greenwich Mean Time (GMT), but Thomson Reuters provides the contributor locale of each quote, hence we can convert all GMT (or UTC) times to local times, allowing us to account for daylight savings time in regions that follow this practice.

3.A.1.1 Pre-processing of spot data

Once the data are extracted, we convert them to homogeneous time-series by sampling them at regular intervals. The first entry is the price at 12 : 00 am on January 1, 2003, and each subsequent data point is recorded n seconds later (n is usually 5), always using the most recent price. This series starts with `NaN`'s[6] until the second after the first price is announced. A quote in this series is considered outdated if it is more than 30 seconds old, at which point `NaN`s are used. The price, p, used in the time-series was defined from the logarithmic middle of the `Bid Price` (p_B) and `Ask Price` (p_A):

$$p \equiv \exp\left(\frac{\log(p_B p_A)}{2}\right). \tag{3.A.1}$$

This is simply the geometric mean of bid and ask quotes, the rationale being that an estimate of the price should be the same whether we look at the quoted rate or the inverse of the quoted rate. Some care needs to be taken to deal properly with this number (see below).

To make sure that this sampling procedure is not discarding too much information,

[6] NaN stands for "Not a Number", a quantity that represents an undefined number, in this case a missing data point.

Table 3.A.1. Frequency of quotes within 1-second intervals for six major currencies, and the fraction of quotes discarded using a 1-second sampling interval

Currency	1 Quote	2 Quotes	3+ Quotes	Ignored (%)
AUD	668,882	10,072	88	1.5
CAD	1,311,732	50,619	1,052	3.7
CHF	3,138,848	318,996	18,098	9.3
EUR	4,910,014	1,359,002	255,977	22.6
GBP	3,411,112	496,290	45,355	13.1
JPY	3,847,627	651,332	74,850	15.2

we tabulate the number of quotes that came in within a 1-second interval for each currency. Table 3.A.1 summarizes this with the results from all 52 months.

To reduce memory requirements for handling these time-series (currently in excess of 2 GB in MATLAB), we do not provide explicit timestamps for these data. Each timestamp must be reconstructed by taking its index in the vector and counting forward the appropriate number of seconds.

Given prices (3.A.1), we can construct continuously compounded returns across various intervals by computing log differences:

$$r_t(k) \equiv \log p_t - \log p_{t-k} \tag{3.A.2}$$

More manageable data files can then by constructed by computing non-overlapping returns every 5, 10, 30, 60, 300, 600, 1,200, and 1,800 entries (seconds). As before, indexing in these data is done implicitly from midnight January 1, 2003.

3.A.1.2 Efficiency of quoted prices

Since our analysis uses quotes exclusively, and not transactions prices, an open question is whether such quotes are a reasonable proxy for prices. One method for checking the quality of quotes is to see whether any arbitrage opportunities exist among the quotes of various currency pairs. In particular, we can check whether converting cash through a chain of currency pairs that begins and ends with the same currency yields a profit. In its simplest form—called "triangular" arbitrage—currency A is transformed into currency B which is then exchanged for currency C and then transformed back into currency A, with the hope of ending with more money than we started with. For example, starting with the US dollar, buy the Canadian dollar, then the Euro, then back to the US dollar. Typically we would expect to end with less money than we started with, if for no other reason than the existence of the bid/offer spread.

This intuition is confirmed by the quote data, and after an exhaustive analysis of all possible currency chains of lengths less than seven, starting and ending with the USD and buying AUD, CAD, EUR, GBP, JPY, and NZD in between, using 5-second intervals and bid and offer prices as appropriate (quotes were considered stale after 5 seconds). We find that the longer the chain, the greater the variation in overall return and the lower the mean return. The best chances for arbitrage seem to lie in the following chain:

$$\text{USD} \rightarrow \text{JPY} \rightarrow \text{EUR} \rightarrow \text{USD} \tag{3.A.3}$$

where 1% of the time a profit was found. All chains of length less than seven were analyzed, and several histograms of the value of $1 at the end of specific chains are presented in Figures 3.A.1 and 3.A.2.

3.A.2 Properties of Thomson Reuters NewsScope Data

In this section we provide a summary of the Thomson Reuters NewsScope Archive data and its empirical properties. For the same reason that we expect an increase in price volatility during trading hours, we also expect the news to surge daily and weekly. To measure this seasonality, we perform the same statistical analysis on the news that we performed in Section 3.A.1 for the exchange rate data. Table 3.A.2 contains summary statistics for each type of newsline, using data from January 2003 to April 2007, tallied by day of the week, weekday/weekend, and week. For example, there are an average of 1,565 alerts on Monday, while there are on average only 145 alerts at the weekend (all times are GMT). Note that the volume of news articles is roughly normal, with a small positive skewness and moderate kurtosis. Table 3.A.2 contains finer statistics about the volume per 10-minute interval. Note the large values for the kurtosis and skewness coefficients, indicating that the news volume per 10-minute intervals is much less Gaussian.

Table 3.A.2 shows a clear surge of the news on weekdays, and a lull over the weekends. It is also interesting to note that the bodylines per 10-minute intervals do exhibit large autocorrelations, indicating that news volume is relatively persistent.

3.A.3 Monte Carlo null distributions of the *t*-statistic

In order to assess the significance of the *t*-statistics computed in our event studies, we have determined the empirical distribution of *t*-statistics by sampling random event studies. By *random event study*, we mean an event study where each of the events was chosen to be a completely random point in time during the last 4 years. The 90%, 95%, 99%, 99.5%, and 99.9% confidence levels are reported in Table 3.A.3 for 15 currency pairs using random 500-, 1,000- and 2,500-event event studies on both returns and de-seasonalized squared log returns (volatility). We note that the *t*-statistics of returns seem to have smaller variance than a true *t*-distribution and the *t*-statistics of squared log returns seem to have larger variance than a true *t*-distribution. This suggests that the underlying data (the returns) are not truly independently and identically distributed. Indeed, if they were then the empirical *t*-statistic would be *t*-distributed. Thus, the *t*-statistics obtained in the event studies should be compared with the values in the tables to obtain more robust confidence estimates than applying the inverse cumulative distribution function of the *t*-distribution.

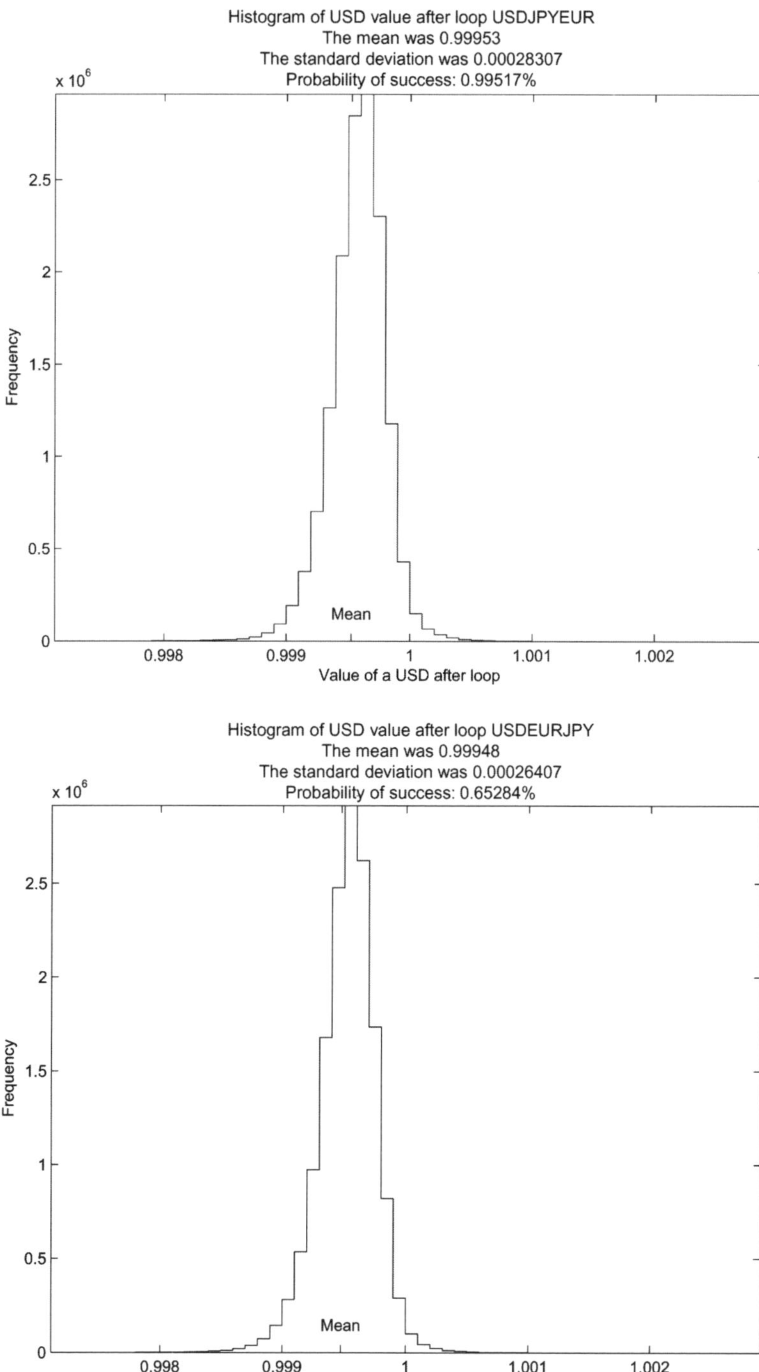

Figure 3.A.1. Histograms of the value of $1 after chains of currency conversions using Thomson Reuters quotes. The histograms in (a) and (b) involve the same currencies but in different directions, giving rise to different distributions.

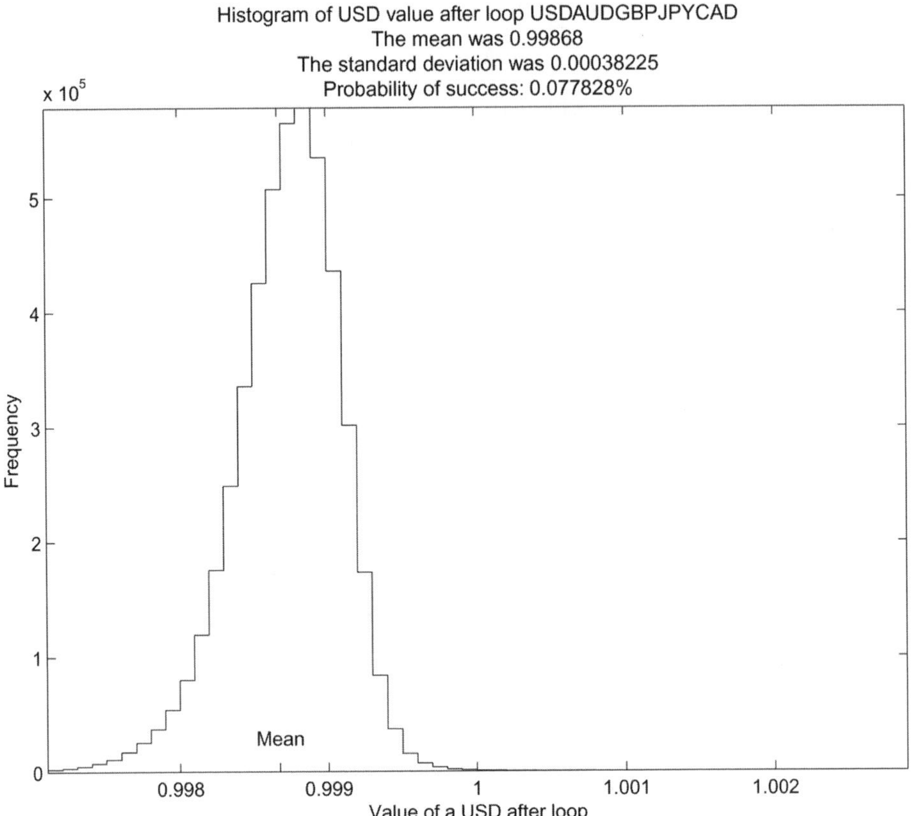

Figure 3.A.2. Histogram of the value of \$1 after a five-currency chain of currency conversions using Thomson Reuters quotes (USD → AUD → GBP → JPY → CAD → USD). This five-currency chain is typical of longer cycles: lower mean and higher variation.

Table 3.A.2. Summary statistics for various types of newslines in the Thomson Reuters NewsScope Archive.

(a) Bodylines

Bodylines	Mon.	Tues.	Wed.	Thurs.	Fri.	Sat.	Sun.	Week-day	Week-end	All
Minimum	6,449	18,206	7,514	0	13,329	3,286	3,805	130,313	9,315	143,577
5%	28,253	34,500	37,223	36,355	22,152	5,319	6,442	189,858	11,851	205,479
Mean	45,321	51,133	52,489	53,515	46,875	7,315	8,516	250,104	15,837	265,872
Median	47,122	52,342	53,605	54,682	48,427	7,299	8,564	250,486	15,830	267,013
95%	56,777	61,741	63,462	65,492	57,801	9,408	10,399	300,506	19,201	317,809
Maximum	66,185	68,761	83,049	73,958	75,880	13,538	14,859	337,051	23,932	355,656
Std. dev.	9,398	8,445	9,023	10,086	9,479	1,358	1,360	35,122	2,253	36,232
Skewness	−1.237	−1.557	−1.458	−1.981	−1.411	0.267	−0.338	−0.546	0.122	−0.589
Kurtosis	5.341	6.868	8.386	9.860	6.111	5.066	6.518	4.084	3.947	4.160

(b) Bodylines per 10-minute intervals

Bodylines	Mon.	Tues.	Wed.	Thurs.	Fri.	Sat.	Sun.	Week-day	Week-end	All
Minimum	0	0	1	0	0	0	0	0	0	0
5%	85	109	113	109	76	5	5	97	5	16
Mean	315	355	364	371	325	51	51	346	55	263
Median	303	345	355	356	306	41	41	333	43	239
95%	603	655	666	708	642	128	128	658	145	617
Maximum	2,418	1,674	2,259	1,789	6,152	630	630	6,152	1,755	6,152
Std. dev.	165	173	177	190	191	44	44	181	51	204
Skewness	0.85	0.71	0.83	0.81	3.54	2.57	2.57	144	367	112
Kurtosis	5.56	4.11	5.28	4.43	73.47	14.38	14.38	21.64	49.21	11.82
ρ_1 (%)	54.92	62.70	60.64	59.50	52.24	57.62	65.82	58.53	62.99	75.95
ρ_2 (%)	49.99	59.58	58.00	56.29	50.58	53.60	63.33	55.55	59.94	74.22
ρ_3 (%)	49.96	57.13	56.29	57.21	47.43	51.58	61.29	54.28	57.92	73.46

(continued)

Table 3.A.2 (*cont.*)

(c) Alerts by group

Alerts	Mon.	Tues.	Wed.	Thurs.	Fri.	Sat.	Sun.	Week-day	Week-end	All
Minimum	37	565	50	38	299	1	13	1,992	42	2,093
5%	713	1,179	1,301	1,241	615	20	23	6,032	58	6,029
Mean	1,565	2,084	2,222	2,516	1,513	70	75	9,982	145	10,212
Median	1,466	1,945	2,010	2,274	1,451	55	63	9,195	130	9,505
95%	2,709	3,873	3,920	4,779	2,323	200	153	17,818	309	18,321
Maximum	3,653	5,098	5,400	7,180	3,549	342	356	23,497	479	23,727
Std. dev.	619	791	885	1,108	518	55	49	3,731	74	3,801
Skewness	0.625	1.201	1.197	1.356	0.418	2.007	1.982	1.168	1.387	1.118
Kurtosis	3.550	4.697	4.833	5.671	4.181	7.635	9.364	4.658	5.401	4.520

(d) Headlines by group

Headlines	Mon.	Tues.	Wed.	Thurs.	Fri.	Sat.	Sun.	Week-day	Week-end	All
Minimum	920	4,024	1,054	864	2,643	365	647	19,063	1,362	20,838
5%	5,062	6,835	6,911	6,622	5,120	813	1,030	32,243	1,880	33,864
Mean	7,165	8,074	8,204	8,460	7,466	1,046	1,283	39,473	2,330	41,854
Median	7,287	8,026	8,144	8,425	7,478	1,026	1,272	39,530	2,291	41,937
95%	9,065	9,788	9,814	10,536	9,453	1,395	1,623	47,418	2,888	49,889
Maximum	10,639	11,400	13,265	11,874	11,347	1,599	1,989	53,232	3,534	55,863
Std. dev.	1,304	1,015	1,150	1,355	1,365	182	188	5,259	318	5,492
Skewness	−1.197	−0.319	−0.885	−1.348	−0.999	0.494	0.285	−0.543	0.433	−0.619
Kurtosis	6.790	5.200	11.935	9.602	6.089	4.298	4.972	4.968	4.209	5.074

Table 3.A.3. Empirical t-distribution percentiles for 30-minute random event studies using squared currency returns for 15 currency pairs

Currency pair	Returns of t-statistic percentiles for random event studies									
	90%	95%	99%	99.50%	99.90%	90%	95%	99%	99.50%	99.90%
	500 events					500 events (de-seasonalized)				
AUD/USD	0.70	0.89	1.25	1.38	1.61	2.71	3.48	5.07	5.38	7.31
CAD/USD	0.63	0.82	1.16	1.25	1.52	2.89	3.85	5.41	5.90	7.59
CAD/JPY	0.87	1.09	1.63	1.79	2.09	2.43	3.26	4.59	5.67	7.03
CHF/USD	0.67	0.89	1.15	1.19	1.44	3.34	4.13	5.79	6.37	6.85
EUR/USD	0.59	0.79	1.09	1.12	1.40	3.49	4.76	6.39	7.18	9.60
EUR/CAD	0.48	0.63	0.93	1.14	1.40	2.23	2.83	4.13	4.91	6.06
EUR/GBP	0.50	0.63	0.90	1.03	1.36	3.06	3.72	6.01	6.34	6.97
EUR/JPY	0.48	0.61	0.82	0.93	1.00	3.19	3.99	5.56	6.52	8.89
GBP/USD	0.70	0.95	1.31	1.41	2.12	3.23	4.13	6.06	6.45	8.67
GBP/AUD	0.80	1.01	1.45	1.57	1.77	2.45	3.11	4.44	5.12	6.69
GBP/JPY	0.66	0.89	1.23	1.35	2.27	2.69	3.49	4.66	6.05	7.20
JPY/USD	0.65	0.81	1.11	1.23	1.46	3.89	4.76	6.88	7.88	9.07
MXN/USD	0.90	1.11	1.54	1.88	2.00	3.24	4.15	6.20	6.88	7.75
NOK/USD	0.66	0.83	1.34	1.46	1.73	3.95	4.92	7.16	8.02	9.83
NZD/USD	0.70	0.88	1.21	1.41	1.65	2.77	3.63	4.86	5.33	7.44
	1,000 events					1,000 events (de-seasonalized)				
AUD/USD	0.61	0.78	1.15	1.33	1.73	2.47	3.33	5.08	6.02	7.23
CAD/USD	0.63	0.81	1.11	1.24	1.51	2.72	3.75	4.86	5.39	6.73
CAD/JPY	0.86	1.10	1.52	1.61	1.99	2.76	3.53	4.91	5.36	6.53
CHF/USD	0.57	0.75	1.04	1.12	1.23	3.15	3.92	5.81	6.30	7.48
EUR/USD	0.63	0.81	1.07	1.11	1.20	3.47	4.44	6.39	6.79	8.66
EUR/CAD	0.49	0.62	0.84	0.97	1.10	2.27	3.03	4.19	4.71	6.87
EUR/GBP	0.46	0.61	0.86	1.03	1.22	3.34	4.36	6.29	6.60	9.03
EUR/JPY	0.46	0.60	0.87	0.96	1.14	3.11	3.99	5.78	6.77	8.24
GBP/USD	0.67	0.84	1.25	1.29	1.71	3.07	3.96	5.58	6.10	7.95
GBP/AUD	0.80	1.03	1.42	1.57	1.67	2.60	3.32	4.54	4.89	5.43
GBP/JPY	0.64	0.82	1.26	1.40	3.00	2.57	3.47	4.75	5.31	8.70
JPY/USD	0.63	0.81	1.15	1.39	1.79	3.76	4.70	6.81	7.28	8.81
MXN/USD	0.82	1.12	1.52	1.71	1.84	2.88	3.80	6.09	6.77	8.01
NOK/USD	0.65	0.82	1.16	1.31	1.54	3.71	5.00	7.21	7.73	8.99
NZD/USD	0.71	0.89	1.26	1.41	1.56	2.69	3.50	5.04	5.34	6.02
	2,500 events					2,500 events (de-seasonalized)				
AUD/USD	0.64	0.88	1.19	1.33	1.76	2.83	3.60	4.70	5.07	7.19
CAD/USD	0.67	0.80	1.16	1.31	1.44	2.81	3.66	5.42	5.68	8.80
CAD/JPY	0.86	1.09	1.57	1.84	2.21	2.57	3.21	4.46	4.84	7.69
CHF/USD	0.56	0.75	1.11	1.15	1.70	3.18	3.92	5.83	6.28	8.46
EUR/USD	0.60	0.76	1.04	1.16	1.40	3.58	4.58	6.28	6.87	8.19
EUR/CAD	0.49	0.61	0.87	1.03	1.31	2.23	2.85	3.87	4.56	6.38
EUR/GBP	0.49	0.65	0.97	1.04	1.28	3.05	4.08	5.33	6.04	6.74
EUR/JPY	0.49	0.62	0.86	0.99	1.10	3.17	4.12	5.67	6.68	8.02
GBP/USD	0.69	0.88	1.35	1.55	2.04	3.35	4.36	6.56	7.04	7.94
GBP/AUD	0.77	1.02	1.44	1.74	1.78	2.34	2.97	4.16	4.64	5.76
GBP/JPY	0.68	0.87	1.16	1.25	1.47	2.31	3.01	4.28	4.92	6.87
JPY/USD	0.60	0.77	1.11	1.15	1.29	3.58	4.64	6.41	7.06	8.66
MXN/USD	0.88	1.09	1.54	1.62	1.80	2.88	3.71	5.39	6.29	9.50
NOK/USD	0.66	0.84	1.18	1.22	1.30	3.90	4.85	6.85	7.80	10.10
NZD/USD	0.67	0.83	1.21	1.54	1.58	2.68	3.47	4.91	5.25	7.89

3.B REFERENCES

Antweiler W.; Frank M. (2004) "Is all that talk just noise? The information content of internet stock message boards," *Journal of Finance*, **59**, 1259–1294.

Bauwens L.; Ben Omrane W.; Giot P. (2005) "News announcements, market activity and volatility in the euro/dollar foreign exchange market," *Journal of International Money and Finance*, **24**, 1108–1125.

Berry T.; Howe K. (1994) "Public information arrival," *Journal of Finance*, **49**, 1331–1346.

Campbell J.; Lo A.; MacKinlay C. (1997) *The Econometrics of Financial Markets*, Princeton University Press, Princeton, NJ.

Chan W. (2003) "Stock price reaction to news and no-news: Drift and reversal after headlines," *Journal of Financial Economics*, **70**, 223–260.

Cormen T.; Leiserson C.; Rivest R.; Stein C. (2001) *Introduction to Algorithms*, MIT Press/McGraw-Hill Book Company, Cambridge/New York.

Dacorogna M.; Gencay R.; Müller U.; Olsen R.; Pictet O. (2001) *An Introduction to High-Frequency Finance*, Academic Press, San Diego.

Daniel K.; Hirshleifer D.; Subrahmanyam A. (1998) "Investor psychology and security market under- and overreactions," *Journal of Finance*, **53**, 1839–1885.

Das S.; Martinez-Jerez F.; Tufano P. (2005) "eInformation: A clinical study of investor discussion and sentiment," *Financial Management*, **34**, 103–137.

Dominguez K.; Panthaki F. (2006) "What defines 'news' in foreign exchange markets?" *Journal of International Money and Finance*, **25**, 168–198.

Engle R.; Ng V. (1993) "Measuring and testing the impact of news on volatility," *Journal of Finance*, **48**, 1749–1778.

Hirshleifer D.; Shumway T. (2003), "Good day sunshine: Stock returns and the weather," *Journal of Finance*, **58**, 1009–1032.

Hong H.; Lim T.; Stein J. (2000) "Bad news travels slowly: Size, analyst coverage, and the profitability of momentum strategies," *Journal of Finance*, **55**, 265–295.

Johnson G.; Schneeweis T. (1994) "Jump-diffusion processes in the foreign exchange markets and the release of macroeconomic news," *Computational Economics*, **7**, 309–329.

Leinweber D.; Sisk J. (this volume) "Relating news analytics to stock returns" (see Chapter 6).

Liu H.; Lieberman H.; Selker T. (2003) "A model of textual affect sensing using real-world knowledge," paper presented at *Proceedings Seventh International Conference on Intelligent User Interfaces (IUI 2003), Miami, Florida*, pp. 125–132.

Mitchell M.; Mulherin H. (1994) "The impact of public information on the stock market," *Journal of Finance*, **49**, 923–950.

Niederhoffer V. (1971) "The analysis of world events and stock prices," *Journal of Business*, **44**, 193–219.

Oberlechner T.; Hocking S. (2004) "Information sources, news, and rumors in financial markets: Insights into the foreign exchange market," *Journal of Economic Psychology*, **25**, 407–424.

Pearce D.; Roley V. (1985) "Stock prices and economic news,"*Journal of Business*, **58**, 49–67.

Pong S.; Shackleton M.; Taylor S.; Xu X. (2004) "Forecasting currency volatility: A comparison of implied volatilities and AR(FI)MA models," *Journal of Banking and Finance*, **28**, 2541–2563.

Stone P.; Dunphy D.; Smith M.; Ogilvie D. (1966) *The General Inquirer: A Computer Approach to Content Analysis*, MIT Press, Cambridge, MA.

Taylor S. (2005) *Asset Price Dynamics, Volatility, and Prediction*, Princeton University Press, Princeton, NJ.

Tetlock P. (2007) "Giving content to investor sentiment: The role of media in the stock market," *Journal of Finance*, **62**, 1139–1168.

Tetlock P.; Saar-Tsechansky P.; Macskassy S. (2008) "More than words: Quantifying language to measure firms' fundamentals," *Journal of Finance*, **63**, 1437–1467.

4
Measuring the value of media sentiment: A pragmatic view

Marion Munz

ABSTRACT

In today's online real-time environment, the news that carries material information affects the sentiment regarding the earnings multiple as it relates to stock prices. The sooner investors recognize that there is a news component embedded in the stock price, the sooner they will arm themselves with the necessary tools that would enable them to take corrective action if necessary. The old formulas used for valuing stock prices need serious revisions to incorporate the news sentiment as a critical variable.

Investors and traders alike must have the ability to act or react to fresh material information regarding investments and trades. The current online trading platforms offer just about every type of information related to stocks and equities in real time. However, there is an increasing need for tools that offer an ability to interpret real-time information, so investors and traders can make the best decisions possible.

News sentiment systems help to fill the gap in current stock price valuation formulas, because they can help to determine the extent of the valuation multiple allocated to a particular future earnings per share value to be reflected in the stock price.

4.1 INTRODUCTION

There is little doubt that news is very critical for the value of the stock price of a publicly traded company. If nothing else, news is the main mechanism that communicates critical information to the investing public. But, what makes this interesting is that in the USA the way that public companies handle news is heavily regulated.

Why then is it that most of the formulas that are taught in business schools about how to calculate the value of a stock price of a corporation do not involve the value of "news"?

Could it be because this valuable information is not easy to quantify?

This is where systems that estimate the sentiment of news pieces come in to fill a big void. In today's world, where millions of investors are able to trade easily from anywhere just by pressing a "submit" button and where news articles move at the speed of

The Handbook of News Analytics in Finance Edited by L. Mitra and G. Mitra

the electron, reaching millions of investors instantly, a news media sentiment system has become a necessity.

To be able to understand the value of the news media sentiment, one would need to have a good understanding of the news landscape, as it relates to publicly traded companies, because all news is not created equal.

4.2 THE VALUE OF NEWS FOR THE US STOCK MARKET

The idea that news can impact the value of stock prices does not always make a lot of sense to millions of investors who have entrusted their lifetime savings to mutual funds, pension funds, or professional fund managers. Moreover, the notion that an ephemeral item such as a news article could change the net worth value of their nest egg could become quite frightening.

For decades, investors have been told that long-term investments are the serious investments and that day-traders are just after get-rich-quick schemes, not something that a professional investor would ever consider. Then the stock market crash of 2008 came and, along with it, the most powerful recession of our lifetime. Questions such as "how could we miss it" or "how could that happen" abounded. To this day, the experts are working on finding a good explanation of what happened and why, while the US federal government is busy at work in trying to alter the regulatory landscape forever.

The realities of the stock market crash of 2008 have shown one more time how fragile the stock market system really is. For all the questions and studies that attempt to explain what happened in 2008, there is one simple explanation: the supply of stocks far exceeded the demand for stocks. After all, the stock market "is" a market and a market's main functioning rule is demand and supply. For every seller there has to be a buyer. If more sellers than buyers come into the market, stock prices react negatively. If panic settles in, one can rest assured that a lot more sellers will jump into the market with the potential to crash it. If the economy is booming, investors too want to tap into the newly created wealth and buy orders abound. Stock market booms or busts become a direct measure of the stock market sentiment.

The value of news comes into play in two major ways for stock markets: First, news articles communicate the stock market sentiment to the masses. Second, news articles affect the supply–demand equilibrium of the stock market directly.

4.3 NEWS MOVES MARKETS

The notion of a stock market in the US is closely associated to the major stock indexes such as the Dow Jones Industrials Index, the NASDAQ 100 Index, and the S&P 500 Index. If all these three indexes move drastically downward in a short period of time, they create a perception that the stock market has crashed. If these three indexes move upward significantly in a short timeframe, there is a perception that a new stock market bubble is being created. The extreme moves of any of the three major indexes create a plethora of news stories that communicate the sentiment of a stock market "crash" or a stock market "bubble" to millions of investors.

The two most recent "bubbles" are considered to be the dot com technology bubble and the housing market bubble. In both cases these bubbles were followed by a significant "crash" of the stock market where trillions of dollars of wealth disappeared over night. While the dot com and housing sectors were affected the most, virtually every sector of the economy was impacted negatively to the point that both crashes were followed by economic recessions.

The interesting aspect of "bubbles" and "crashes" news reporting is that investors' perceptions have been that one must follow the other. Therefore, if there is a bubble the news reports will start asking the question "when will the bubble burst?" and if there is a "crash" the news reports will start asking questions like "have we hit the bottom yet?"

Day-to-day tracking of moves in the three stock market indexes is communicated to the investing public by virtually every news outlet possible, in every possible form of media, from print, radio, and TV broadcasters to the internet and mobile devices.

4.4 NEWS MOVES STOCK PRICES

The value of the stock price of any business is influenced by the investors' expectations of the future earnings of that particular business. If the business has great prospects there may be a potential to place a high multiplier on the current earnings per share value in order to estimate the future earnings value of the business.

A strong effort to communicate that potential could realize a high multiplier on the current earnings per share value by introducing more buyers to the stock. As more buyers come in, the existing investors may postpone selling to realize the full stock appreciation potential.

Investors' expectations regarding the future earnings of the business are measured through the value of the multiple placed on future earnings. Future earnings depend on a multitude of factors and the reality very rarely matches the forecasts.

News about a company's business has the potential to change the demand–supply balance and affect any stock price. Often times, the lack of news may be perceived as "negative" news. On the other hand, widely distributed positive news regarding future earnings may attract new buyers to the stock. The stronger the demand for the stock, the higher the multiple may become.

4.5 NEWS VS. NOISE

The growth of the highly influential blogs and large social networks online has blurred the line between news and noise regarding companies' business prospects. As stock price earnings multiples are based mostly on the sentiment of the investors regarding future earnings, even rumors spread throughout these new channels can move prices significantly.

Once a stock moves 5% or more in one direction or another, the move itself becomes news that is distributed throughout the traditional financial news outlets.

Financial websites, newsletters, and radio and TV broadcasters have all created a significant audience and are in a position to create news by providing opinions and analysis as a result of simply repeating or interpreting reporting from the traditional financial news media.

An indicator that news is very difficult to differentiate from noise comes from the fact that venture capital firms have invested a significant amount of money into new startup firms that focus on measuring the news sentiment coming from social networks such as Twitter and Facebook as well as influential blogs.

Blogs and social networks, especially, have the ability to spread rumors regarding new products at very high speeds. Multiple examples of how fast news can spread through these news channels have come from highly hyped products such as smartphones, games, electronics, and even movies.

One of the results of the rumors spread through these new channels has been a dramatic change in investors' expectations regarding the future earnings of the business.

4.6 REGULATED VS. UNREGULATED NEWS

While news related to publicly traded businesses could be classified in many ways, there are really only two main categories that should matter: regulated news and unregulated news.

4.6.1 Regulated news

The Securities and Exchange Commission (SEC) regulates just about every aspect of the information that a business which is publicly trading on an US exchange releases into the market.

On August 15, 2000 the SEC adopted regulation FD (Full Disclosure) which is the US government's attempt to control the release of material non-public information from a publicly traded company to the public.

The SEC does not define the term "material" but gives an interpretation that:

> "Information is material if 'there is a substantial likelihood that a reasonable shareholder would consider it important' in making an investment decision. To fulfill the materiality requirement, there must be a substantial likelihood that a fact 'would have been viewed by the reasonable investor as having significantly altered the "total mix" of information made available.' Information is nonpublic if it has not been disseminated in a manner making it available to investors generally."

The SEC defines "public disclosure" as:

> "... issuers could meet regulation FD's 'public disclosure' requirement by filing a Form 8-K, by distributing a press release through a widely disseminated news or wire service, or by any other non-exclusionary method of disclosure that is reasonably designed to provide broad public access—such as announcement at a conference of which the public had notice and to which the public was granted access, either by personal attendance, or telephonic or electronic access."

The SEC also regulates the release of information that deals with insider trading, the issuance of new securities, as well as trading "on the basis of" material non-public information. It is interesting to note that the SEC has argued that:

> "... a trader may be liable for trading while in 'knowing possession' of the information. The contrary view is that a trader is not liable unless it is shown that he or she 'used' the information for trading. Until recent years, there has been little case law discussing this issue. Although the Supreme Court has variously described an

insider's violations as trading 'on' or 'on the basis of' material nonpublic information, it has not addressed the use/possession issue."

Therefore, when it comes to material information, the SEC"s view is that of a standard closer to the "knowing possession" standard than to the "use" standard.

4.6.2 Unregulated news

Seeing how much attention the US regulatory agencies, such as the SEC, have paid to the way "material information" about publicly traded companies should be handled, one could not help but wonder how can any other type of news that is not coming straight from the business move the stock price?

The answer may come from the fact that the news media appear to enjoy different rules. To be sure, there are rules that apply to the news media, but by and large free speech governs. For that reason I call the news coming from the news media—in regards to publicly trading businesses in the US—unregulated.

Granted, blatantly telling or writing untruths about anyone, including corporations, is not legal in the US. However, writing an opinion piece that has a negative view on a company's stock seems to be falling under the freedom-of-speech umbrella.

More interestingly, writing a research report about a company's stock has been viewed not only as legal but also as proprietary information. Wall Street analysts make a nice business out of writing research reports and issuing earnings estimates and opinions frequently.

In a recent case, a judge ruled in favor of "big banks" and against a news-reporting company, Theflyonthewall.com. The judge issued a permanent injunction demanding that Theflyonthewall.com delay the release of news on big banks' analysts' stock upgrades and downgrades.

This case seems to encourage putting at a disadvantage a class of investors and the general public while another class of investors are able to access material information about publicly traded companies ahead of time—in direct contradiction with the SEC requirements with regards to disclosure of "material information" about public businesses trading on US exchanges.

To be of any value, a research report would have to contain material non-public information. If that is true, based on the SEC regulation FD, the analysts could be deemed to be in "knowing possession" of material non-public information—therefore, liable under regulation FD. Apparently, this is a loophole in the process. Hence, I name this "unregulated news".

Things get even more chaotic when unregulated news is found on blogs, social media, and even in the news reporting of traditional media.

4.7 THE NEWS COMPONENT OF THE STOCK PRICE

The value of a company's stock is related directly or indirectly to the future earnings of the business. To be able to estimate the future earnings of a particular business, one would need to forecast either the growth or slowdown potential for the business and be able to quantify that. If the forecast indicates growth, then the stock price is likely to reflect an increase in value by a coefficient that represents a multiplier of the value of earnings per share; if the forecast indicates slowdown, the earnings multiple will probably decrease.

There is a lot of science that goes into an estimate of future earnings. The information that goes into the estimate is very likely influenced by the sentiment of the people who work on the estimate with regards to the future economic indicators, political environment, and so on.

The sentiment that is reflected in the earnings forecast calculation will find its way into the news cycle. When the news regarding the earnings forecast is released to investors, it will be perceived as material information, especially if it is coming from a reputable and influential research or media firm. The value of the earnings multiple is affected almost immediately and the stock price is adjusted to reflect a new valuation.

In today's online real-time environment, the news that carries material information affects the sentiment regarding the earnings multiple directly.

The sooner investors recognize that there is a news component embedded in the stock price the sooner they will arm themselves with the necessary tools that could enable them to take corrective action if necessary.

4.8 MATERIALITY IS NEAR

The main question regarding the value that a particular piece of news brings to the stock price should be around the materiality of the information contained in the news. If the news is fresh, preferably delivered in real time as soon as the material information is made available to the public, the impact on the stock price should be very visible.

The determination of "materiality" of the news story or whether there is material information within the story that has not been disclosed publicly before is not an easy task.

The SEC guidance regarding material information is that:

> "... the following items are some types of information or events that should be reviewed carefully to determine whether they are material: (1) earnings information; (2) mergers, acquisitions, tender offers, joint ventures, or changes in assets; (3) new products or discoveries, or developments regarding customers or suppliers (e.g., the acquisition or loss of a contract); (4) changes in control or in management; (5) change in auditors or auditor notification that the issuer may no longer rely on an auditor's audit report; (6) events regarding the issuer's securities—e.g., defaults on senior securities, calls of securities for redemption, repurchase plans, stock splits or changes in dividends, changes to the rights of security holders, public or private sales of additional securities; and (7) bankruptcies or receiverships."

While regulated news carries a preponderance of material information, it is not impossible that financial news outlets uncover new material information regarding public businesses trading on the American stock exchanges.

More often than not, though, traditional and new financial news outlets recycle material information that has already been disclosed while adding a new sentiment via an opinion piece.

4.9 SIZE DOES MATTER

Businesses, big and small, are required to disclose material non-public information promptly. The news disclosure process is regulated by the SEC. Therefore, it has been assumed that if the process is followed all businesses receive the same treatment.

However, companies trading on smaller exchanges receive more scrutiny and attention in the way the news is handled. As small businesses do not benefit from the big public relation budgets that typify big businesses, stock moves may have an uneven cycle. Businesses that benefit from big budgets are capable of maintaining a constant stream of news—therefore, stock moves may have a more lasting trend than those of small businesses. For instance, the well-known public relation practice of "crisis management" is seen as normal business procedure for a big and established business.

On the other hand, the SEC often gives the interpretation of "stock price touting" when news is released and "managed" by smaller businesses while these types of comments are very rare for larger businesses.

Big public relations and marketing budgets have a significant and sustainable advantage in the stock market. There are many examples in the industry, but one of the most recent and famous is the introduction of Apple's iPhone. Apple hired top-notch professional marketing and public relations firms and spent hundreds of millions of dollars marketing the new product as far as six months ahead of its actual release date. Naturally, Apple's stock price appreciated considerably due to the awareness that was created. The big marketing and public relations dollars helped to sell quite a few products, even though the actual technology used to make phone calls that Apple introduced at the time was behind that offered by other handset manufacturers. Additionally, Apple's stock price appreciated significantly both during the iPhone pre-launch and in after-launch periods. All of this helped to establish Apple as a new player in the handset market and to set a nice platform for future iPhone technology releases that allowed them to catch up and even surpass the market leader.

Very few small businesses could ever afford that type of campaign; if they could, it is very likely that the SEC would classify the marketing of a non-existent product by a small firm as touting the stock.

4.10 CORPORATE SENIOR MANAGEMENT UNDER THE GUN

The SEC regulates the news that the senior management of publicly traded businesses in the US releases to the public. The SEC does not regulate the news that the news media publish about publicly traded businesses. This creates a difficult environment where senior management can be constantly under the gun of the news media. If you were in a war and your enemy had a constant supply of ammunition while you had only a limited supply, it would be really difficult to survive, let alone win that war.

What is worse, some Wall Street investment banks can get into the news media business really easily by creating research reports or simply by publishing earnings estimates for corporations. When a company comes out and gives its earnings estimate and an influential analyst raises that earnings estimate, the effect creates a very competitive news environment under which senior management has very little or no way to respond, due to various regulations that must be abided by.

Senior managements are constantly working under pressure from news media, including Wall Street analysts' news and regulatory agencies.

4.11 A CASE FOR REGULATED FINANCIAL NEWS MEDIA

There is a case to be made about what constitutes news coming from financial news media regarding publicly traded companies in the US. Given that the public perceives news articles coming from prestigious news sources as being "material" news, shouldn't these news articles abide by the same rules as the company they write about?

Take the following example, which unfortunately is a real-life example that happened a few years back. A prestigious news source wrote an article about a big public company that basically said the company's CEO reported that the market share for the company's products was going to decrease by 10% over the next year. The market reacted to the news immediately by bringing the stock price down by over 5%. It turned out that the news reporter made a mistake. The CEO was talking about the overall market decreasing by 10% and not about the company's market share, which he had actually forecast as going to increase by 10% or so. The publisher did update the story but the stock price took days, if not weeks, to recover from that first erroneous report.

Publicly traded companies spend a considerable amount of time and money before they release material information about the company. They do that because they need to abide by current laws and because they are aware of stock price implications.

Shouldn't financial news organizations be subject to the same rules and, yes, the same amount of rigorous attention and expense in time and money before they publish news that could affect a company's stock price?

4.12 WALL STREET ANALYSTS MAY CREATE "MATERIAL" NEWS

Issues regarding the timeliness of news reports are reflected in the case *Barclays Capital et al v. Theflyonthewall.com Inc.*, U.S. District Court, Southern District of New York, No. 06-04908 which considered important questions regarding the news that Wall Street creates.

The case surrounds the fact that Theflyonthewall.com made a business out of posting in real time news that it finds in "proprietary" research reports about publicly traded companies. Interestingly enough, the judges allowed Theflyonthewall.com to post the news under the condition that they delay the postings.

Lost in the battle was the real question, though: Shouldn't the "material" findings of the reports themselves be available to the public, as per the requirements of regulation FD?

Apparently, the judges are fine with letting major institutions have a legup on the investing public and potentially profiting from the timeliness of the information contained in those reports.

Wall Street loves having an edge—who doesn't? But if strict regulations are in place for corporations regarding "material" news, shouldn't everyone abide by the same rules?

The *Barclays Capital et al v. Theflyonthewall.com Inc.* case highlights the fact that Wall Street research firms have the ability to create "material" news that moves stock prices.

Analyst earnings estimates create one of the most material news that exists in the stock market, comparable only with earnings news releases posted by public companies themselves.

4.13 TRADERS MAY CREATE NEWS

When the price of a stock of a major public company moves significantly, the news media pick up on that event and report the stock move itself as news.

Stock moves are generated by imbalances that occur in the supply–demand equilibrium of a particular stock. Therefore, a news report about a significant shareholder selling a large stake for reasons, which may or may not be related to the company's performance, could create the perception that something is wrong with the company. The same is true about major stake purchases—examples of news media reports in which successful investors like Warren Buffet or investment houses purchase large stakes in public companies are perceived as positive news.

Moreover, many traders use technical indicators which show when a particular stock is "overbought" or "oversold" in the active market. Those technical indicators become "news" for the active traders who watch the stock charts in real time.

4.14 EARNINGS NEWS RELEASES

In the US, publicly reporting companies are required to file three quarterly reports and one annual report which are made available for free to the public. Businesses that trade on the major exchanges release an earnings news article at the same time, which is usually transmitted via a newswire business such as PR News Wire, Business Wire, or Market Wire.

To put together such a critical piece of news, corporations invest a considerable amount of time and money, using multiple resources from top senior managers, accountants, auditors, legal teams, and investment relations teams.

The earnings news release is a critical moment in the lifecycle of any public company. This is when investors have an opportunity to re-assess the valuation of the company, which reflects directly on the value of the stock price.

This is a very time-sensitive piece of news and quickly understanding its potential impact may be critical for investors and traders alike.

4.15 NEWS SENTIMENT USED FOR TRADING OR INVESTING DECISIONS

The value of news media sentiment centers on the timing and quality of the sentiment information as well as its practical applications for trading and investment purposes.

There is also an historical value to news sentiment because the correlation between sentiment data and stock moves may give additional information regarding stock price sensitivity to news at the moment the news is released to the public.

When making trading decisions, the sentiment may indicate a powerful momentum shift that is about to materialize in the trading market.

When making investment decisions, the sentiment may indicate potential moves that could affect the stock price valuation for the long term.

It is very unlikely that the sentiment could be used as the sole variable in making a trading or an investment decision. Pragmatically, an estimate of potential stock price movement should be considered for either trading or investment purposes.

For material news to be absorbed into stock price valuation, it is very unlikely that the market could evaluate the true impact within the first day of the news release. Even so, stock prices react to material news in a very significant manner. On the day of the news release, it is not unusual for average trading volume to grow to more than double the average daily volume and for the stock to move significant percentage points up or down.

As such, that kind of trading activity is very likely to become news by itself which may help to accelerate stock price movement.

4.16 NEWS SENTIMENT SYSTEMS

As the 2006 Online News research of the Pew Internet and American Life Project shows, "when news is online it comes to the public rapidly and in larger amounts than ever before. Today, over 65 million Americans go online to receive critical investment news and information."

In addition, the regulatory environment of the US financial markets is complex and constantly changing. That fact makes it very difficult for an individual to process the material information available in news reports in a timely manner.

In today's environment, with millions of traders and investors online receiving critical news in real time, the old formulas used for valuing stock prices need serious revisions to incorporate news sentiment as a critical variable.

News sentiment systems help to fill the gap in current stock price valuation formulas, because they can help to determine the extent of the valuation multiple allocated to a particular future earnings per share value to be reflected in the stock price.

As we have seen, not all news is created equal and there isn't an easy way to rapidly evaluate the impact that a particular piece of news may have on a stock price, especially when you add to that the complexity of the legal environment. For instance, based on regulation FD stipulations, it is not very clear if trading on a rumor posted on a website or in a more traditional news media article would not be perceived as insider trading.

Therefore, to add value, news sentiment systems need to help individual traders and investors not only assess the impact that the sentiment of a particular news piece may have on a stock price, but also to make sure that taking advantage of such information received in a timely manner abides by current laws.

From a functional point of view, there is a need to understand what a news sentiment system can and cannot accomplish.

The main function of a news sentiment system is to indicate whether a particular news item is positive or negative, as it relates to a publicly traded company. This sounds like an easy task to accomplish and there have been multiple attempts at doing it. However, a news sentiment system needs to do more than just determine the news sentiment for the user to be able to understand and correctly assess news sentiment impact.

For instance, a news sentiment system needs to communicate to a user how assessment of the sentiment has worked in the past. As such, the system should be able to create historical and real-time reports that show stock price movement along with the news sentiment for individual stock tickers.

In today's online environment, where news about publicly traded companies may be found on a multitude of news sites and social networks, the ability to determine the true impact of a particular news article is diminished. One example is the effect that a social network such as Twitter can have not only in accelerating news distribution but also in actually creating more news.

A news sentiment system should be able to provide a level of assurance that there is a credible, direct impact of a certain news item on stock price movement. In other words, a news sentiment system should be able to allow users to correlate stock price movement from its price immediately before the news item became public to the price reaction in the timeframe immediately following the news release.

A news sentiment system can provide a way to better estimate and manage trading and investment risk. By receiving a heads-up on the potential impact of the news item, users can focus their attention on other stock price variables and make decisions faster and more accurately than they would without the help of a news sentiment system.

One thing that a news sentiment system cannot provide is "certainty" in managing trading and investment risk. News sentiment systems are not and cannot be perfect systems. Therefore, there needs to be an understanding that there is a certain level of accuracy and dependability in news sentiment assessment. This level needs to be communicated directly to the user via real-time and historical reporting, correlation analysis, or any other method possible.

Ultimately, to be successful a news sentiment system should help users to improve their current level of accuracy when determining the impact of a particular news item on a particular stock price.

The level of that particular improvement in accuracy will most likely determine the value of the news sentiment system when making decisions about trading, investing, or hedging.

Considering the level of improvement in accuracy that a news sentiment system brings to traders and investors in the current environment, the use of such a system has become an absolute must.

4.17 BACKTESTING NEWS SENTIMENT SYSTEMS

The impact of a news item is usually very short-lived and most likely represents the perspective of the author(s) of the news item. Moreover, the impact of a news item can also be significant and may create major changes in the life of the stock of a publicly traded company.

Since not all news is created equal, there is questionable value regarding the use of a backtesting system that could evaluate the impact of the news sentiment of a news item months or even years after the news was published.

To get the most value out of a backtesting system, the news sentiment of a news item needs to be determined when the news becomes public and before the actual impact of the news item. Such a backtesting system indicates the ability of the news sentiment system to predict the impact before the stock movement rather than showing an ability to measure the sentiment effect after the move took place. The differences are significant and should not be ignored.

4.18 THE VALUE OF MEDIA SENTIMENT

Media Sentiment® has developed a technology that can make a rapid assessment of the sentiment expressed by management in an earnings news release. The system correlates that information with estimates from Wall Street analysts and the overbought/oversold signals of the trading market, which allows profitable trading opportunities to be discovered. Media Sentiment Limits™ provides suggestions for stock price entry points along with conservative and aggressive stop limits.

What is the value that Media Sentiment brings to traders and investors?

To answer this critical question, one would need to understand how much the Media Sentiment system improves the accuracy and efficiency of one's own reading and determination of the sentiment and impact of an earnings news release. As is the case with medicine, users' benefit levels may vary from person to person.

For instance, if one user can increase his/her accuracy by 10% and if the user can convert that accuracy into dollars that would be the equivalent of a value add of 10 cents for each dollar invested or traded.

Users' expectations should be such that Media Sentiment alerts will help to improve their accuracy and speed in determining the sentiment and impact of a higher number of earnings news releases.

Even an incremental improvement will allow users to benefit from potential profits that result from an increased number of opportunities.

The value that Media Sentiment brings to the end-user comes from the following:

a. *Its focus on earnings news releases of public companies trading on NASDAQ and NYSE* This is by far one of the most important news releases in the life of a public company. The earnings news release process is highly regulated; therefore, users are able to take full advantage of real-time Media Sentiment alerts without questioning the legitimacy of the news source.
b. *Repeatable, unbiased process that finds the stock tickers most likely to move in the direction of media sentiment* Internal data analysis indicated an average of 80% or more accuracy in media sentiment indicating the direction of movement of the stock price during the trading day following the news release.
c. *Highly accurate real-time sentiment determination and delivery* This is achieved through website updates, email, RSS, a multitude of financial websites via distribution partners, integration with broker platforms such as TD AMERITRADE and optionsXpress, and integration with a stock data analysis platform such as MetaStock (a Reuters product).
d. *Backtesting by using Media Sentiment historical data going back to 2002* These Media Sentiment alerts were delivered before actual stock movement took place

so users benefit from accessing data produced by the most time-tested sentiment analysis system.

e. *Receive Media Sentiment alerts at your desktop or on the go, on a smartphone or any other mobile device* Browser-based and email systems deliver the data in real time to maximize exposure and increase the number of opportunities received.
f. *Receive entry and exit price point estimates* Media Sentiment Limits delivers two sets of stock price limits that indicate, with statistical significance, the intervals that a particular stock price might move. For instance, internal research shows that even when the stock moves in the opposite direction, over 80% of the alerts reach the higher stock price limit after they reached the lower price limit, as estimated by the system. This feature alone may help users to profit from significant stock price movements, no matter what direction the stock price moves.
g. *Receive real-time visual alerts when stock price limits are reached along with potential profit and loss calculations* This feature puts more control in the hands of the user as he or she ponders on the decision to act.

As mentioned above, the main goal of Media Sentiment is to improve user accuracy by a significant margin, when he or she is in the process of determining whether a particular earnings news release delivers either a positive or a negative sentiment from the senior management of a publicly traded company.

Also, by having access to rapid sentiment analysis of a news release by a publicly traded company, Media Sentiment helps to reduce the risks involving regulation FD exposure and legal interpretations.

No other news sentiment analysis system has delivered accurate alerts regarding stock tickers of publicly traded companies for as long and well as Media Sentiment has.

4.19 MEDIA SENTIMENT IN ACTION®

The Media Sentiment system delivers three types of alerts that are displayed real-time online within an active browser window in the following combinations of thumbs-up or thumbs-down symbols:

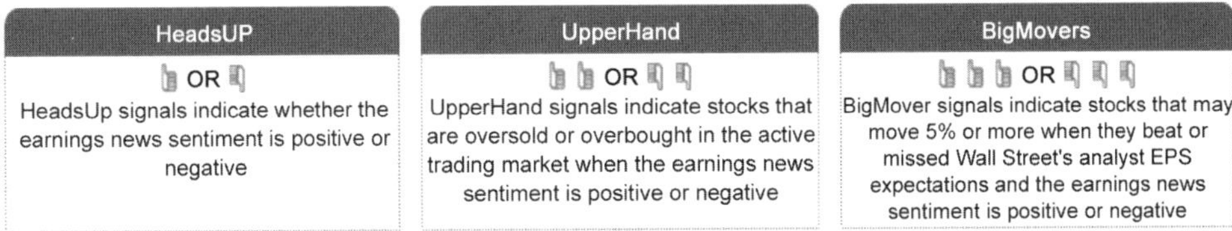

Figure 4.1. The three components of the Media Sentiment system.

Thumbs-up signals indicate a positive media sentiment while thumbs-down signals indicate a negative media sentiment.

Most of the public companies that trade on NASDAQ and NYSE markets in the US report earnings either before the main market opens, during pre-market trading, or after the main market closes during after-market trading. Therefore, the main market activity will be during the same day for companies reporting before the main market opens, or the following trading day for companies reporting after the main market closes.

MediaSentiment

Media Sentiment Authorization
Logged as: tester | Log Out

TD AMERITRADE Authorization
Logged as: mediasentiment | Log Out

Recent Gain/Loss (November 3, 2009): Aggressive Gain/Loss: -10 % Conservative Gain/Loss: 8 % Number of alerts: 23

SYMBOL	MEDIA SENTIMENT ®	SIGNAL TIME	SIGNAL PRICE	Consider Conservative Stop Limits Up (Gain)	Consider Conservative Stop Limits Down (Loss)	Consider Agressive Stop Limits Up (Gain)	Consider Agressive Stop Limits Down (Loss)	TRADE NOW
CCRN	👎👎	11:40:00 AM EST	$ 8.01	$ 7.97	$ 8.04 -0.32% (11:42 AM)	$ 7.68	$ 8.05 -0.48% (11:42 AM)	
LF	👎👎	11:25:00 AM EST	$ 3.11	$ 3.1 0.48% (11:34 AM)	$ 3.12	$ 2.98	$ 3.12	
WLK	👍👍	11:25:00 AM EST	$ 24.85	$ 24.97	$ 24.77 -0.32% (11:27 AM)	$ 25.87	$ 24.73 -0.48% (11:27 AM)	
KND	👎👎	11:20:00 AM EST	$ 14.91	$ 14.84 0.48% (11:21 AM)	$ 14.96	$ 14.3	$ 14.98	
CCRN	👎👎	10:55:00 AM EST	$ 7.97	$ 7.93	$ 8 -0.32% (11:02 AM)	$ 7.64	$ 8.01 -0.48% (11:40 AM)	
STAA	👎👎	10:50:00 AM EST	$ 3.85	$ 3.83 0.48% (11:09 AM)	$ 3.86	$ 3.69	$ 3.87	
HTCH	👎👎	10:45:00 AM EST	$ 6.12	$ 6.09	$ 6.14 -0.32% (10:46 AM)	$ 5.87	$ 6.15 -0.48% (10:47 AM)	
PNCL	👍👍	10:45:00 AM EST	$ 6.43	$ 6.46	$ 6.41 -0.32% (10:47 AM)	$ 6.69	$ 6.4 -0.48% (10:47 AM)	
WLK	👍👍	10:30:00 AM EST	$ 24.9	$ 25.02	$ 24.82 -0.32% (11:27 AM)	$ 25.92	$ 24.78 -0.48% (11:27 AM)	
RL	👍👍	10:25:00 AM EST	$ 77.14	$ 77.51	$ 76.89 -0.32% (10:25 AM)	$ 80.3	$ 76.77 -0.48% (10:25 AM)	
DBD	👎👎	10:15:00 AM EST	$ 29.21	$ 29.07 0.48% (10:19 AM)	$ 29.3	$ 28.01	$ 29.35	
PNCL	👍👍👍	09:25:08 AM EST	$ 6.00	$ 6.03 0.5% (09:31 AM)	$ 5.98	$ 6.9	$ 5.97	
RL	👍👍👍	08:35:29 AM EST	$ 76.71	$ 77.1 0.5% (08:42 AM)	$ 76.45	$ 88.15	$ 76.32	
WLK	👍👍👍	08:34:04 AM EST	$ 25.08	$ 25.21 0.5% (09:31 AM)	$ 25	$ 28.82	$ 24.95	
DBD	👎👎👎	08:29:36 AM EST	$ 29.95	$ 29.8 0.5% (09:31 AM)	$ 30.05	$ 25.48	$ 30.1	
DBD	👎	08:24:51 AM EST	$ 29.95	$ 28.97 3.28% (09:31 AM)	$ 30.61	$ 26	$ 30.93	
CHD	👍👍👍	08:24:50 AM EST	$ 58.31	$ 58.6	$ 58.11 -0.34% (08:25 AM)	$ 67.01	$ 58.02 -0.5% (08:25 AM)	
RL	👍	08:06:21 AM EST	$ 76.71	$ 79.23 3.28% (09:32 AM)	$ 75.03	$ 86.83	$ 74.19	
PNCL	👍	07:07:51 AM EST	$ 6.00	$ 6.2 3.28% (09:31 AM)	$ 5.87	$ 6.79	$ 5.8	
CHD	👍	07:04:22 AM EST	$ 58.31	$ 60.22	$ 57.03 -2.19% (08:18 AM)	$ 66	$ 56.4 -3.28% (08:18 AM)	
SHOO	👎	07:04:21 AM EST	$ 40.71	$ 39.37 3.28% (09:50 AM)	$ 41.6	$ 35.34	$ 42.05	
WLK	👍	06:04:21 AM EST	$ 25.08	$ 25.9	$ 24.53 -2.19% (06:05 AM)	$ 28.39	$ 24.26	
DXPE	👎	04:00:23 AM EST	$ 11.69	$ 11.31	$ 11.95 -2.19% (09:29 AM)	$ 10.15	$ 12.07 -3.28% (09:31 AM)	

Figure 4.2. The layout of the Media Sentiment system.

The HeadsUp signals represented by one thumb up or one thumb down indicate the sentiment that senior management expresses in the earnings news release; these alerts are more likely to occur either before the main market opens or after the main market closes.

The BigMovers signals represented by three thumbs up or three thumbs down indicate the sentiment that senior management expresses in the earnings news release correlated with Wall Street analyst sentiment regarding the company meeting or missing the earnings per share estimate; these alerts too are more likely to occur either before the main market opens or after the main market closes.

The UpperHand signals represented by two thumbs up or two thumbs down indicate the sentiment that senior management expresses in the earnings news release correlated with trading market sentiment as expressed by two technical indicators that show the market being overbought or oversold; these alerts occur only while the main market is open.

Public companies report earnings on a quarterly basis. In the US, there is a so-called earnings reports season that works cyclically. At the start and at the end of the season, there are only a few companies reporting earnings, but after two to three weeks from the start the earnings season gets into full swing with hundreds of companies releasing earnings reports daily.

Media Sentiment algorithms can be used to issue alerts for about 20% of reporting companies, as they identify stocks with a higher chance to move in the direction of the Media Sentiment alert.

Figure 4.2 is an example of a browser window that shows Media Sentiment alerts integrated into the TD AMERITRADE system as of November 3, 2009.

As companies release earnings news in real time, the system determines the sentiment as positive or negative and delivers alerts in the active browser window, either as HeadsUp or BigMovers. These alerts occur before 9 : 30 am EST, or before the main market opens.

After main market activity starts, for each HeadsUp alert Media Sentiment measures trading market sentiment as expressed by two technical indicators in real time. When overbought or oversold conditions in the market align with earnings news sentiment, an UpperHand alert is issued in real time.

For each Media Sentiment alert, the user receives the following information: a ticker symbol, a Media Sentiment indicator, the time when the sentiment was determined and issued, the price of the stock at the moment the sentiment was determined, and conservative and aggressive stop limits that indicate the intervals that the stock prices are likely to move. When a particular stop limit is reached, a stop-limit-reached alert is issued and colored either green, to indicate that the limit was reached in the direction of the sentiment, or orange, to indicate that the limit was reached away from the direction of the sentiment indicated. Along with the stop-limit-reached alert, the system prints the time when the limit was reached and potential gain/loss as a percentage of the initial price that the stock ticker was at when the Media Sentiment alert was released.

At the top of the page, the system calculates the potential total gain/loss for all alerts issued that day.

Users who have a TD AMERITRADE account could also choose to receive streaming quotes and real-time charts for each Media Sentiment alert or even trade directly from the integration window.

The streaming quotes provide additional real-time stock price information for a better and faster decision-making process.

The real-time charts are drawn on 5-minute bars and help users to visualize the daily trend of a particular stock.

Figure 4.3 shows case studies for stocks that received positive Media Sentiment alerts on November 3, 2009. These alerts are posted on charts directly for a better understanding and visualization of potential stock price movement. Each Media Sentiment alert is displayed on the chart along with the time the alert was issued. The UpperHand alerts indicate the price at which the alerts were issued as additional information.

Figure 4.4 shows case studies for stocks that received negative Media Sentiment alerts on November 3, 2009. These alerts are also posted directly on charts for a better understanding and visualization of the potential stock price movement. Each Media Sentiment alert is printed on the chart along with the time the alert was issued. The UpperHand alerts receive the price at which the alert was issued as additional information.

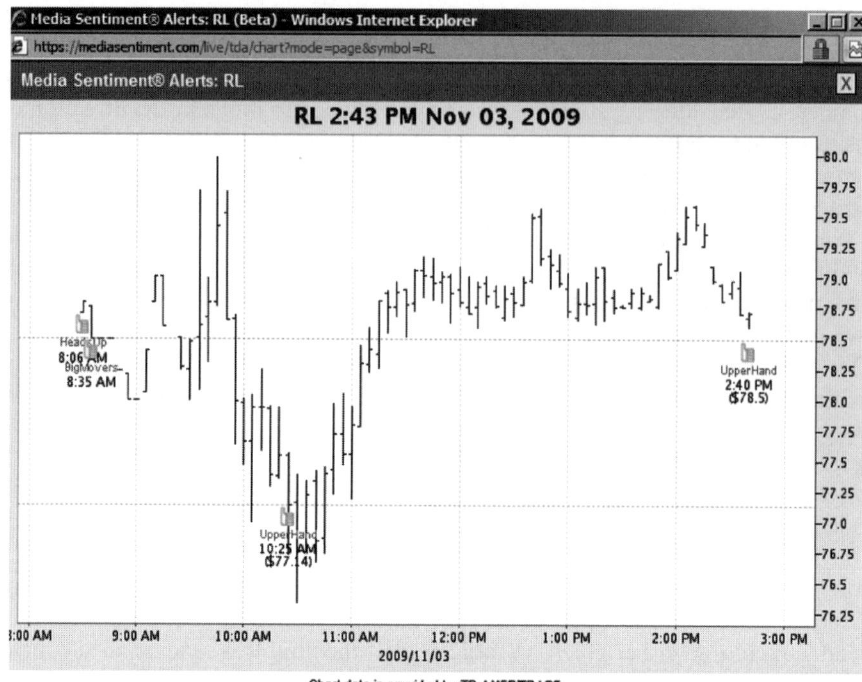

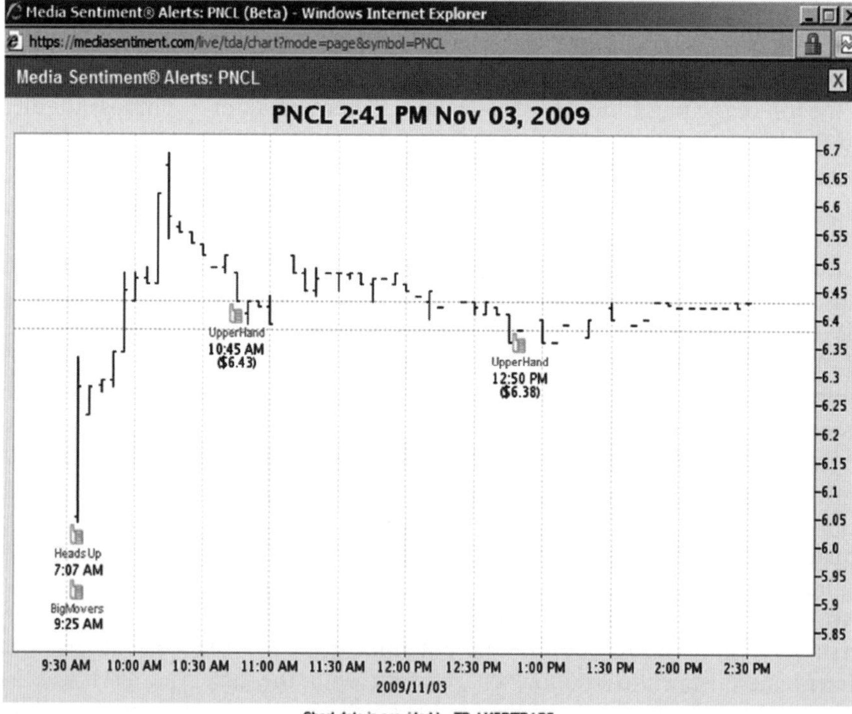

Figure 4.3. Examples of Media Sentiment thumbs-up alerts on stock charts received in real time.

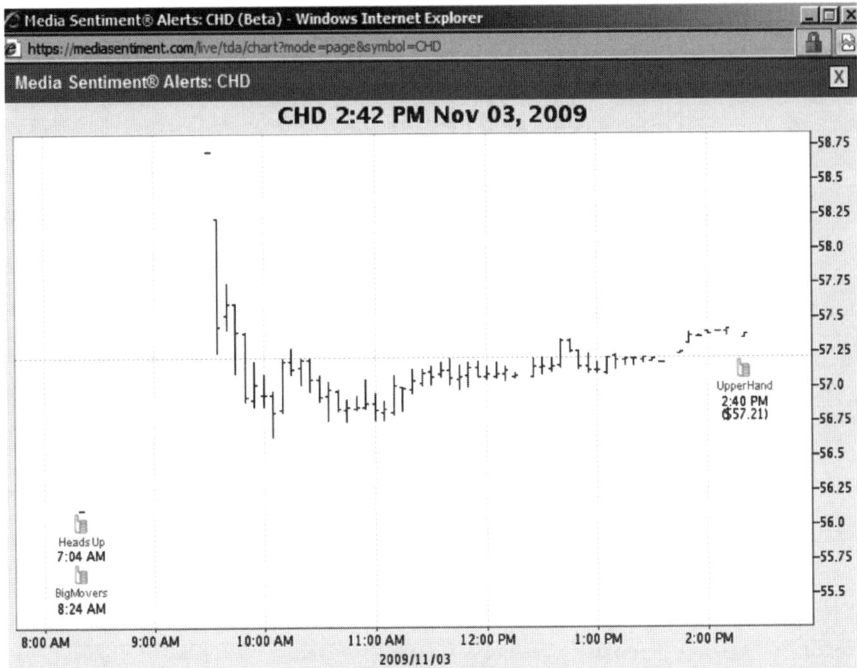
Media Sentiment® Alerts: CHD (Beta) - Windows Internet Explorer
https://mediasentiment.com/live/tda/chart?mode=page&symbol=CHD
Media Sentiment® Alerts: CHD
CHD 2:42 PM Nov 03, 2009
58.75
58.5
58.25
58.0
57.75
57.5
57.25
57.0
56.75
56.5
56.25
56.0
55.75
55.5
UpperHand
2:40 PM
($57.21)
Heads Up
7:04 AM
BigMovers
8:24 AM
8:00 AM
9:00 AM
10:00 AM
11:00 AM
12:00 PM
1:00 PM
2:00 PM
2009/11/03
Chart data is provided by TD AMERITRADE

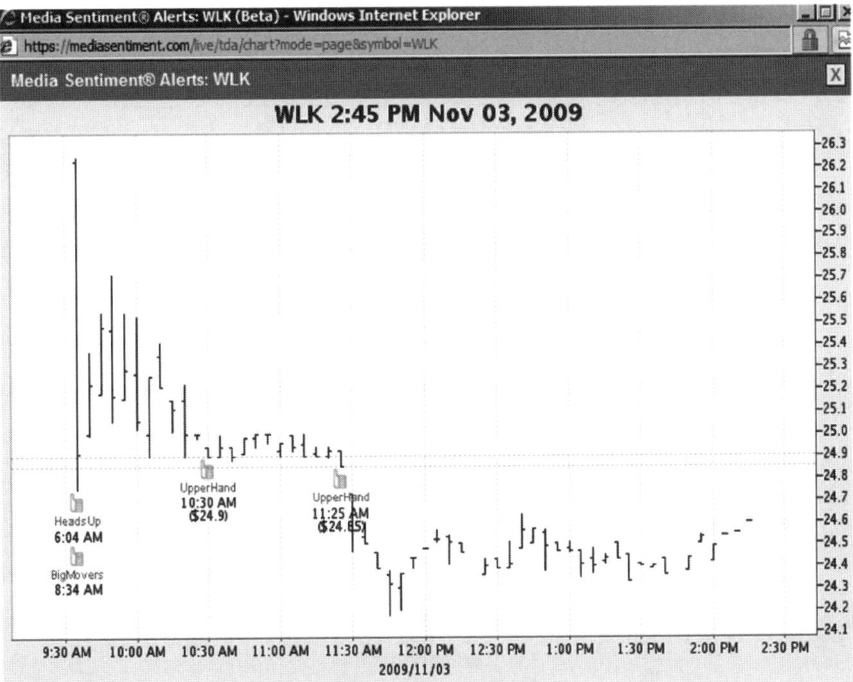
Media Sentiment® Alerts: WLK (Beta) - Windows Internet Explorer
https://mediasentiment.com/live/tda/chart?mode=page&symbol=WLK
Media Sentiment® Alerts: WLK
WLK 2:45 PM Nov 03, 2009
26.3
26.2
26.1
26.0
25.9
25.8
25.7
25.6
25.5
25.4
25.3
25.2
25.1
25.0
24.9
24.8
24.7
24.6
24.5
24.4
24.3
24.2
24.1
UpperHand
10:30 AM
($24.9)
UpperHand
11:25 AM
($24.85)
Heads Up
6:04 AM
BigMovers
8:34 AM
9:30 AM
10:00 AM
10:30 AM
11:00 AM
11:30 AM
12:00 PM
12:30 PM
1:00 PM
1:30 PM
2:00 PM
2:30 PM
2009/11/03
Chart data is provided by TD AMERITRADE

Figure 4.4. Examples of Media Sentiment thumbs-down alerts on stock charts received in real time.

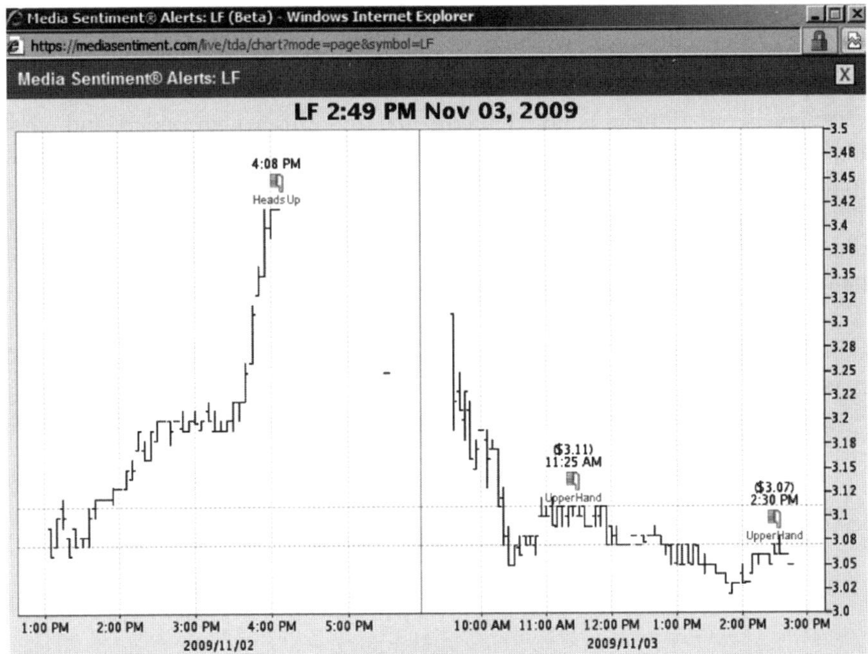
Media Sentiment® Alerts: LF (Beta) - Windows Internet Explorer
https://mediasentiment.com/live/tda/chart?mode=page&symbol=LF
Media Sentiment® Alerts: LF
LF 2:49 PM Nov 03, 2009
4:08 PM
Heads Up
($3.11)
11:25 AM
UpperHand
($3.07)
2:30 PM
UpperHand
3.5
3.48
3.45
3.42
3.4
3.38
3.35
3.32
3.3
3.28
3.25
3.22
3.2
3.18
3.15
3.12
3.1
3.08
3.05
3.02
3.0
1:00 PM
2:00 PM
3:00 PM
4:00 PM
5:00 PM
2009/11/02
10:00 AM
11:00 AM
12:00 PM
1:00 PM
2:00 PM
3:00 PM
2009/11/03
Chart data is provided by TD AMERITRADE

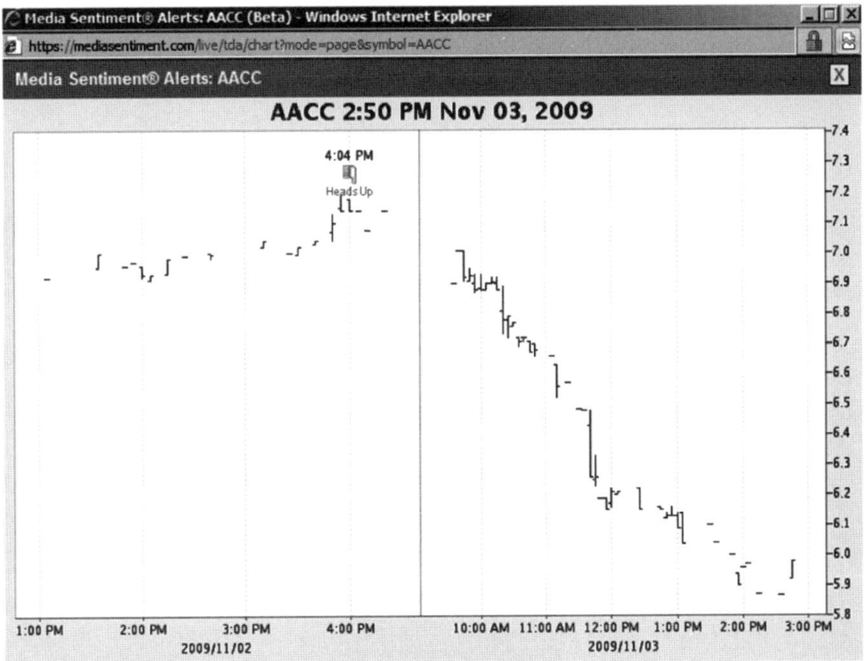
Media Sentiment® Alerts: AACC (Beta) - Windows Internet Explorer
https://mediasentiment.com/live/tda/chart?mode=page&symbol=AACC
Media Sentiment® Alerts: AACC
AACC 2:50 PM Nov 03, 2009
4:04 PM
Heads Up
7.4
7.3
7.2
7.1
7.0
6.9
6.8
6.7
6.6
6.5
6.4
6.3
6.2
6.1
6.0
5.9
5.8
1:00 PM
2:00 PM
3:00 PM
4:00 PM
2009/11/02
10:00 AM
11:00 AM
12:00 PM
1:00 PM
2:00 PM
3:00 PM
2009/11/03
Chart data is provided by TD AMERITRADE

4.20 CONCLUSION

Media Sentiment® can add considerable value to the decision-making process for traders and investors alike.

As we have seen, all news is not created equal and a thorough understanding of the news landscape is highly recommended as there are laws that regulate the handling of material information with serious legal implications.

Media Sentiment adds value by improving the speed and accuracy of sentiment determination for a bigger number of earnings news releases of publicly traded companies in the USA.

5

How news events impact market sentiment

Peter Ager Hafez

ABSTRACT

News sentiment is shown to outperform 1-month price momentum when predicting future returns of the S&P 500. Market and industry-level sentiment indexes are constructed based on a bottom-up approach considering the impact of company-specific news events and their corresponding sentiment. As part of constructing the indexes, I show that company relevance and event novelty are important elements of a news-based strategy, since including only the most relevant and novel news stories results in improved information ratios. From May 2005 through December 2009, the strategies tested deliver double-digit positive returns in out-of-sample testing. In addition, I show how industry sentiment can add value when constructing market-neutral strategies taking long and short positions in top-ranked and bottom-ranked industries, respectively. Finally, I show that targeted directional exposures to top-ranked and bottom-ranked industries can improve a trading strategy beyond simple S&P 500 index exposures.

5.1 INTRODUCTION

It is broadly accepted that financial news moves stock prices either through a direct impact on a company's expected future cash flow, the discount factor that one uses, or through more behavioral or sentiment-based mechanisms. Even though news-based trading has a long history of being part of investment decision making, only in recent years has it been possible to test "quantitatively" the impact of news events on individual stock prices or markets. Extensive academic and industry research has shown that news, particularly stories conveying sentiment, can add value in both high- and low-frequency trading and investment strategies—improving the prediction of price direction, volatility, and trading volume.

In a previous study, I made the case for applying a news sentiment index in predicting future returns of the Dow Jones Industrial Average, and showed that taking this approach significantly outperformed a price momentum strategy (Hafez, 2009a). Tetlock looks at a regression model and finds that 10-day reversals are reduced

The Handbook of News Analytics in Finance Edited by L. Mitra and G. Mitra

following company-specific news, which indicates that public news is a proxy for information that has not yet been incorporated into the stock price (Tetlock, 2009). Engelberg et al. find that short-sellers' trades are more than twice as profitable in the presence of recent news, which provides strong evidence in favor of the idea that news presents profitable trading opportunities for skilled information processors (Engelberg, Reed, and Ringgenberg, 2010). Mitra et al. included news sentiment as part of the construction of forward-looking covariance matrices (Mitra, Mitra, and diBartolomeo, 2008). Interestingly, they found that sentiment could add value to the volatility prediction process beyond what could be captured by option-implied volatility. Also, Zhang and Skiena show that news is significantly correlated with both trading volume and stock returns (Zhang and Skiena, 2010).

While studies show the impact of scheduled news events can be measured in milliseconds, signals from unscheduled news events can be measured in minutes, days, weeks, and months. For example, the intraday abnormal return impact of positive and negative sentiment events can be measured in minutes and hours when looking at intraday abnormal returns (see Hafez, 2009c). Focusing on longer horizons, Cahan et al. found that the effect could be measured in days and weeks (Cahan, Jussa, and Luo, 2009a, b). In addition, using a 1-year investment horizon, Kittrell found value in using net sentiment as a measure for long-term stock selection (Kittrell, this volume, Chapter 9).

Applying structured news data or *news analytics* in a trading model allows for the possibility to not only react in real time to scheduled and unscheduled news events in a fully or semi-automated fashion, but also to consider the prevailing sentiment trend on a given market. Such trends can be captured by looking at aggregated news sentiment on single companies, sectors, industries, or even on broader equity portfolios. As part of previous research, a methodology was presented on how to construct market and sector sentiment indexes that were used as part of a directional sector-rotation-type strategy (Hafez, 2009d). To address news flow seasonality, the indexes were based on counts of positive vs. negative sentiment news stories that were considered to be highly relevant to one of the index constituents. As part of the study, I find that considering a company relevance metric is an important element in constructing sentiment-based strategies as the out-of-sample return correlation improves by a factor of 3 after filtering for relevance. In this study, I take relevance filtering a step further and include only news that is contextually relevant to the companies in the S&P 500; that is, where a company has been detected to be playing a prominent role in the news story and has been involved in some type of categorized event (e.g., earnings announcement, analyst rating, product recall, etc.), and therefore has received a relevance score of 100. For more information on relevance, see Section 5.B (appendix on p. 144). Furthermore, I consider how it may be desirable to treat stories differently in terms of sentiment impact depending on the detected event category; that is, a bankruptcy story should count more towards a sentiment score than a story about a product or marketing campaign. Finally, I consider how event novelty may influence the construction of sentiment indexes, where novelty in this case represents how "new" or novel a news story is over a 24-hour time window.

Generally, I find that considering the impact of different company events adds value when constructing market-level sentiment indexes. For industry-level indexes, I noticed that the total number of company-specific events varied depending on the industry. In order to improve the confidence around sentiment estimates, I apply a slightly less restrictive relevance score moving from 100% to 90% relevant. This permitted the use of other sentiment analytics available from RavenPack which provide more information by examining various aspects of each story (i.e., events, language tone, story type). Here I consult five different sentiment scores that classify each news story as being either positive, negative, or neutral. The same approach was considered in a previous study (Hafez, 2009d). Rather than normalizing only for news flow, I consider a normalization for changes in the event category characteristics, which seems to bring further value in the sentiment ranking of industries.

The study proceeds as follows. In Section 5.2, I provide an overview of the methodology on how to construct market-level sentiment indexes considering an Event Sentiment Score. Furthermore, I consider a simple trading strategy based on a US market-level sentiment index. In Section 5.3, I describe how to construct industry sentiment indexes based on aggregated news sentiment. Using an industry rank, I first consider a simple market-neutral strategy, followed by a targeted directional strategy based on industry rather than broad market exposures. Finally, in Section 5.4, I present the conclusion of the study.

5.2 MARKET-LEVEL SENTIMENT

Generally, news sentiment indexes try to capture the prevailing sentiment trend for a particular market or sector based on news information. In order to capture such trends, it seems reasonable to consider an aggregation of news sentiment over well-defined moving time intervals to capture the general "mood" of the market. News sentiment indexes have been useful when constructing simple investment strategies that consistently outperform similar strategies based on price momentum (Hafez, 2009a). Previous results have shown to be resistant to different sentiment aggregation windows, investment horizons, and different investment timing.

5.2.1 Data and news analytics

In order to measure sentiment for a particular equity index, I use news analytics data from RavenPack going back to 2005. The dataset includes tens of thousands of records per day, each representing a company reference in a financial news story. Currently, RavenPack tracks around 27,000 companies globally, which represent more than 98% of the investable global market. Each record comes with a millisecond timestamp and data for sentiment, novelty, relevance, event categories, among other news analytics. One of the advantages of RavenPack's news analytics is that the data are free of survivorship bias. That is, each company is identified systematically using its respective point-in-time ticker symbols and/or other company identifiers or aliases, and both "dead" and "survivor" companies are included in the dataset.

Whenever RavenPack is able to detect one of more than 160 company-related event categories as well as the role a company plays in a news story, these elements are tagged as part of the company-specific news record. For example, in a news story with the headline "IBM Completes Acquisition of Telelogic AB", the event would be identified as "acquisition-acquirer" since IBM is involved in an acquisition and is the acquiring company. Telelogic would receive the "acquisition-acquiree" tag in its corresponding record since the company is also involved in the acquisition, but as the acquired company. This applies to other events like lawsuits where it makes sense to differentiate between the "plaintiff" and the "defendant". Another example, "Toyota Files Voluntary Safety Recall on Select Toyota Division Vehicles for Sticking Accelerator Pedal" is tagged as a "product-recall" since Toyota is involved in a product recall.

Previous studies indicate that *spill-over effects* are present between company-specific news events and sector index price moves. Cahan et al. find that sector excess returns following company-specific news events are smaller than market excess returns indicating that the sector also moves on the news event[1] (Cahan, Jussa, and Luo, 2009a). Patton and Verardo find that news releases have an important impact on the risk and covariance of stocks, which suggests that there is contagion in the information content of news releases. In other words, new information for one stock impacts the trading of other stocks, causing the stocks to move together a little more than might be expected under normal conditions (Patton and Verardo, 2009). Taking this into consideration, it seems reasonable to expect that such spill-over effects are also present at the market level.

For the construction of market-level news sentiment indexes I use RavenPack's Event Sentiment Score (ESS), which indicates how event categories are typically rated by financial experts as having positive or negative share price impact. To capture news events specifically related to S&P 500 companies, I use the RavenPack Company Relevance Score (CRS). This metric provides a way to capture stories that are actually relevant to S&P 500 constituents and not mere mentions in the text. The numerical score indicates "how" relevant the story is to the company and assigns higher values based on the context of the news using semantic analysis. In a previous study, I found that only 20% of all news records are relevant; hence, 80% could simply be adding noise[2] (Hafez, 2009a). In many cases, companies are mentioned in passing and are not the central theme of the story. Filtering based on CRS ensures that only records that have been categorized as being strongly related to one of the companies belonging to the universe of stocks are being considered. It should be mentioned that companies not detected as explicitly mentioned in a story are not given a relevance score. While a story about Yahoo! might be considered in some other context to be relevant to Google, the company Google will not be given a relevance score unless that story explicitly mentions Google. Finally, I use an Event Novelty Score (ENS), which represents how "new" or novel a news story is over a 24-hour time window. The first story disclosing an event about a company is considered to be the most novel and receives a score of 100. In Section 5.A (see appendix on p. 143), I have included further information on CRS, ESS, and ENS. Commodity Systems Inc. is the source for corporate action-adjusted pricing data.

5.2.2 Market-level index calculation

Having described what elements are to be considered when constructing market-level news sentiment indexes, it is possible to describe the methodology in more detail.

[1] This seems to be more pronounced for negative than for positive sentiment events.
[2] At least 73% of stories contain one highly relevant company.

Let $\mathcal{N}$ denote the universe of all news records from the RavenPack dataset. Fix a company C that is mentioned within some news record from $\mathcal{N}$ with $E_C(N)$ and $D_C(N)$ representing the Event Sentiment Score and Event Novelty Score of company C for record $N \in \mathcal{N}$, respectively.

Definition 5.1. Let $\mathcal{U}$ be the universe of companies and C be a company such that $C \in \mathcal{U}$. Let p be a time period denoting a certain number of days. Let P_N be the records of all stories published within p days before publication of news record N up to and including N such that $\forall N_i \in P_N$. For $\forall N_i$ there exist some C such that $E_C(N) \neq \emptyset$ and $D_C(N) = 100$. In other words, every record in P_N has an Event Sentiment Score for some $C \in \mathcal{U}$ and an Event Novelty Score of 100. Finally, let $m = |P_N|$. The trailing *sentiment index*, $I_{\mathcal{U}}(N, E)$, for $\mathcal{U}$ is the quantity

$$I_{\mathcal{U}}(N, E) = \frac{1}{m}\sum_{i=1}^{m} E_C(N_i). \tag{5.1}$$

Remark 5.1. The *universe of companies* is meant here to represent the constituents of a broader equity index (i.e., the S&P 500 or Russell 1000).

Considering the constituents of the S&P 500, I construct a US market-level sentiment index applying a 90-day trailing window ($P = 90$). One of the advantages of aggregating over such a period is that I capture an entire "quarterly season" in each trailing window, thereby ensuring that similar news flow characteristics are represented. Equity news flow is very much characterized by seasonality, where a quarterly pattern is evident and likely caused by the repeated earnings reporting season (Hafez, 2009b). Figure 5.1 depicts the US Market-Level Sentiment Index vs. S&P 500 cumulative index log returns covering the period March 2005 through December 2009.

5.2.3 Strategy and empirical results

Under the assumption that market returns are likely to move in the same direction as market sentiment, I base my trading decision on the sentiment index delta, $\triangle_t$. Focusing on the index delta will capture the sentiment of the most recent period (i.e., 1 month), but also include the sentiment change from the previous period which may have similar characteristics (i.e., as captured by the "same" month in the earnings season cycle).

Definition 5.2. Let I_t be the trailing *sentiment index* value at time t, then the *sentiment index delta*, $\triangle_t$, at time t is the quantity

$$\triangle_t = I_t - I_{t-1}. \tag{5.2}$$

In order to construct a simple news-based strategy, whenever $\triangle_t > 0$ I take a long position in the S&P 500 in the following period. Likewise, when $\triangle_t < 0$ I take a short position. More specifically, I decide at the end of each month the direction to take in the S&P 500 in the following month. S&P 500 index returns are calculated as monthly *close-to-close* log returns.

In Figure 5.2, I include the cumulative return of a trading strategy based on the US Market Sentiment Index with and without applying an Event Novelty Score filter. Furthermore, I include the 1-month price momentum strategy return for benchmark purposes.

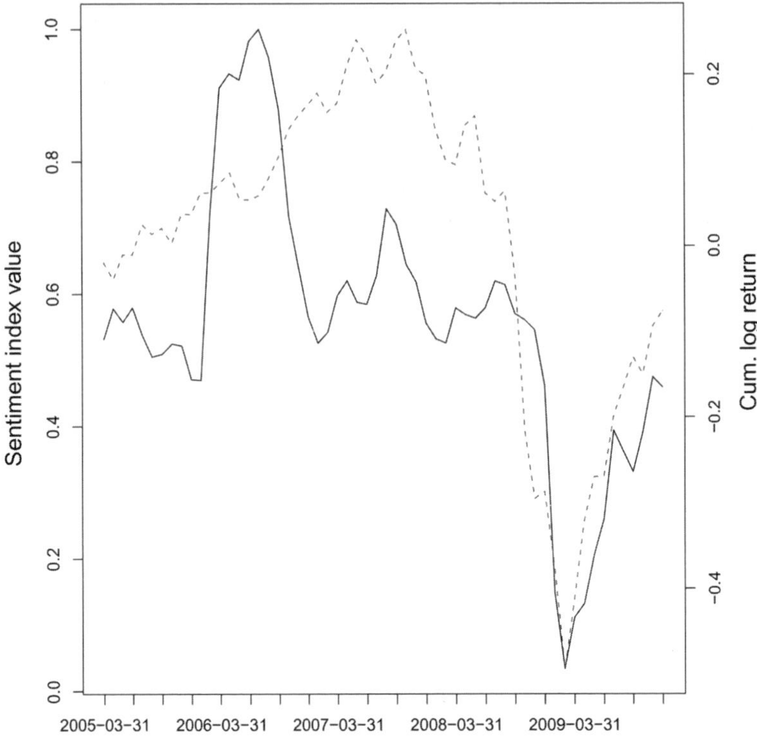

Figure 5.1. Market-Level Sentiment Index (solid line, primary axis) vs. S&P 500 cumulative log returns (dashed line, secondary axis). The sentiment index has been constructed based on the average Event Sentiment Score of all S&P 500 companies over a 90-day trailing window covering the period January 2005 through December 2009, and has been scaled, for visualization purposes, to take values between 0 and 1. In addition, events have been filtered only to include the most novel stories (ENS = 100).

As can be observed in Figure 5.2, not only do both sentiment-based strategies outperform 1-month price momentum, but filtering based on event novelty seems to add significant value in predicting the future price direction of the S&P 500, as given by an improvement in the information ratio of more than 100%. In Table 5.1, I have included a performance summary for the different strategies. The event novelty filtered strategy would have obtained an overall information ratio[3] of 1.75 over the period with the values 1.02 and 2.47 pre and post the *market high* of the test period in October 2007, respectively. Overall, the event novelty filtered strategy would have realized an annualized return of 26.5% with a hit ratio[4] of almost 70%. Interestingly, both sentiment indexes not only deliver significantly better returns than price momentum, but do so with lower volatilities. Also, a significant improvement can be observed in the hit ratios.

Considering the per-year annualized return of the different strategies from Table 5.2, the novelty-filtered sentiment-based strategy delivers double-digit positive returns in all

[3] The information ratio is calculated as annualized return divided by annualized volatility.
[4] The hit ratio represents the percentage of months that were profitable over the period.

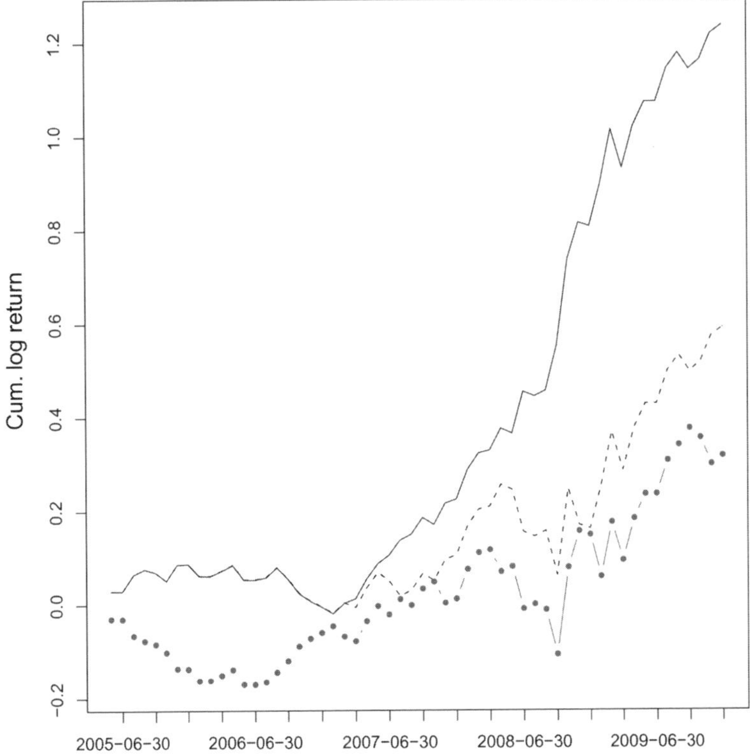

Figure 5.2. Cumulative strategy returns covering the out-of-sample period May 2005 through December 2009 for the Market-Level Sentiment Index (solid line) *with* an Event Novelty Score filter, the Market-Level Sentiment Index (dashed line) *without* an Event Novelty Score filter, and the 1-month price momentum strategy based on the S&P 500 (dot-dashed line). The sentiment indexes have been constructed based on a 90-day trailing window, and a trading decision was made based on the monthly index delta. A positive delta resulted in a long position, and a negative delta in a short position.

years except 2006, which was the only year that resulted in a loss. Interestingly, price momentum outperformed the sentiment-based strategies only in 2006.

Overall, it seems that the construction of bottom-up sentiment indexes outperforms price momentum in predicting future returns of the S&P 500. In addition, I find that event novelty is an important element of a news-based strategy, since including only the most novel news stories results in significantly improved information ratios both pre and post the market high in October 2007. Finally, considering the impact of different company events adds value to the construction of market-level news sentiment indexes.

5.3 INDUSTRY-LEVEL SENTIMENT

In the previous section, I demonstrated how to construct a market-level news sentiment index that can be used to predict the future direction of the S&P 500. Here, I will focus

Table 5.1. Performance statistics covering the out-of-sample period May 2005 through December 2009 for the strategies based on the Market-Level Sentiment Index (column 3) *with* an Event Novelty Score filter (ENS = 100), the Market-Level Sentiment Index (column 4) *without* an Event Novelty Score filter, and the 1-month price momentum strategy based on the S&P 500 (column 5). Pre-October and Post-October refer to the market high in October 2007

		Sentiment index (ENS = 100)	Sentiment index	Price momentum (1 month)
Information ratio	Total	1.75	0.76	0.40
Information ratio	Pre-October	1.02	0.35	0.18
Information ratio	Post-October	2.47	1.05	0.55
Annual return	Total	26.50%	12.67%	6.80%
Annual return	Pre-October	7.69%	2.74%	1.40%
Annual return	Post-October	46.70%	23.33%	12.60%
Annual volatility	Total	15.16%	16.61%	16.90%
Annual volatility	Pre-October	7.56%	7.85%	7.88%
Annual volatility	Post-October	18.88%	22.32%	23.05%
Hit ratio	Total	69.64%	62.50%	55.36%
Hit ratio	Pre-October	62.07%	58.62%	48.28%
Hit ratio	Post-October	77.78%	66.67%	62.96%

on constructing market-neutral strategies taking long and short positions in the top- and bottom-ranked industries, respectively. Being able to successfully rank industries based on sentiment should enhance the performance of a strategy, since more targeted investments can be made towards expected outperformers and underperformers during periods with long and short exposures, respectively.

Table 5.2. Yearly annualized return covering the out-of-sample period May 2005 through December 2009 for strategies based on the Market-Level Sentiment Index (column 2) *with* an Event Novelty Score filter (ENS = 100), the Market-Level Sentiment Index (column 3) *without* an Event Novelty Score filter, and the 1-month price momentum strategy based on the S&P 500 (column 4)

	Sentiment index (ENS = 100) (%)	Sentiment index (%)	Price momentum (1 month) (%)
2005	13.05	13.05	−20.52
2006	−9.20	−9.09	7.68
2007	22.99	10.91	7.20
2008	58.32	5.75	13.68
2009	42.85	42.85	16.80

5.3.1 Data and news analytics

In order to construct industry-level sentiment indexes based on news, I use five sentiment analytics available from RavenPack. Each of these analytics has been calculated using a different linguistic technique. For example, some analytics are based on keyword and phrase detection, optimized to capture key financial language. Other analytics are derived using classifiers or algorithms trained to emulate how financial experts would react to different types of news (e.g., earnings and announcements, editorial and commentary, corporate actions), or stories about mergers and acquisitions. For more information on the different RavenPack classifiers, see Section 5.B (p. 144).

To capture news events specifically related to S&P 500 companies, I also use the RavenPack Company Relevance Score (CRS). Finally, as with the market-level indexes, Commodity Systems Inc. is the source for corporate-action-adjusted pricing data.

5.3.2 Industry-level index calculation

When constructing industry-level indexes, I noticed that the total number of company-specific events varied depending on the industry. In order to improve confidence around sentiment estimates, I apply a slightly less restrictive CRS moving from 100% to 90% relevant. This also permits the use of other sentiment analytics available from RavenPack which provide more information by examining various aspects of each story (i.e., events, language tone, story type). Here I consult five different sentiment scores that classify each news story as being either positive, negative, or neutral, and thereby evaluate the changing relationship between the count of positive and negative sentiment stories. Previous studies show that consulting multiple classifiers to determine the sentiment of a given story or event can add significant value when trying to predict stock price direction (Cahan, Jussa, and Luo, 2009a).

Let $\mathcal{N}$ denote the universe of all news records from the RavenPack dataset. Fix a company C that is mentioned within some news record from $\mathcal{N}$ with sentiment analytics $q_i \in q$, where $i \in \{1, \ldots, 5\}$ represents each of the five sentiment analytics.

Definition 5.3. Call the function $S_C : \mathcal{N} \to \{-1, 0, 1\}$ the record sentiment indicator relative to company C where

$$S_C(N) = \begin{cases} -1, & \text{if } C \text{ receives a score } Q(N) < 50; \\ 0, & \text{if } C \text{ receives a score } Q(N) = 50; \\ 1, & \text{if } C \text{ receives a score } Q(N) > 50, \end{cases} \tag{5.3}$$

with

$$Q(N) = \text{avg}(q) \tag{5.4}$$

When I say that a news record $N \in \mathcal{N}$ is about company C, it is assumed that N has CRS ≥ 90 for C.

Remark 5.2. A CRS of 90 indicates that the company is referenced in the main title or headline of the news story. A company will be assigned a high mark of 100 if it plays a main role in these types of stories (context-aware).

Having classified all stories for the targeted universe of stocks as being either positive, negative, or neutral, I am able to define the sentiment ratio.

Definition 5.4. Let $\mathcal{U}$ be the universe of companies and C be a company such that $C \in \mathcal{U}$. Let p be a time period denoting a certain number of days. Let P_N be the records of all stories published within p days before publication of news record N up to and including N such that $\forall N_i \in P_N$. For $\forall N_i$ there exist some C with CRS ≥ 90. In other words, every story in P_N is about some company $C \in \mathcal{U}$. Finally, let $n = |P_N|$. The trailing *sentiment ratio* $R_{\mathcal{U}}(N, S)$ for $\mathcal{U}$ is the quantity

$$R_{\mathcal{U}}(N,S) = \frac{\sum_{i=1}^{n} S_C(N_i)_{[S_C(N_i)=1]}}{\sum_{i=1}^{n} |S_C(N_i)_{[S_C(N_i)=-1]}|}. \tag{5.5}$$

In order to compare and rank industries according to sentiment, the sentiment ratio needs to be normalized with the objective to "neutralize" any industry-specific biases or characteristics of such measure. Therefore, I suggest performing some adjustment that considers the standard deviation of the industry-specific sentiment ratio. Such normalization could depend on a trailing volatility measure, or on the empirical distribution of the sentiment ratio of the entire backtesting period. In order to center normalized values, I map the mean of the empirical distribution into a sentiment index value of 50, and apply stepwise linear mapping of the remaining values based on standard deviations.

Let B_i be some mapping function that depends on σ, where the family of B are the number of standard deviations away from the mean. Furthermore, let Y_i be a function of B_i such that more extreme sentiment ratios, in terms of distance to the mean, will receive sentiment index values closer to either 0 or 100 depending on whether the sentiment ratio is below or above its mean value, respectively.

Definition 5.4. Let σ be the standard deviation of $R_{\mathcal{U}}$ over the entire backtesting period. Fix $B_i(\sigma)$ for $i \in \{0, \ldots, k\}$ to be the cut-off points for a mapping function, and let $Y(B_i)$ be the mapping score at the cut-off B_i with $Y(B_0) = 0$ and $Y(B_k) = 100$, then the *sentiment index value* for $\mathcal{U}$ at N will be the quantity

$$V_{\mathcal{U}}(R) = \begin{cases} Y(B_0), & \text{if } R_{\mathcal{U}}(N,S) < B_0(\sigma); \\ (1 - W(R)) * Y(B_i) + W(R) * Y(B_{i+1}), & \text{if } B_0(\sigma) \leq R_{\mathcal{U}}(N,S) < B_k(\sigma); \\ Y(B_k), & \text{if } R_{\mathcal{U}}(N,S) \geq B_k(\sigma); \end{cases} \tag{5.6}$$

with

$$W(R) = \frac{R_{\mathcal{U}}(N,S) - B_i(\sigma)}{B_{i+1}(\sigma) - B_i(\sigma)}, \tag{5.7}$$

and where $B_i(\sigma) \leq R_{\mathcal{U}}(N,S) < B_{i+1}(\sigma)$ and $i \in \{0, \ldots, k-1\}$.

Based on the normalized indexes, it is possible to rank industries, for instance, on a monthly basis in order to construct long and short portfolios of the top- and bottom-ranked industries. In the following section, I will present an empirical study focusing on the constituents of the S&P 500 equity index.

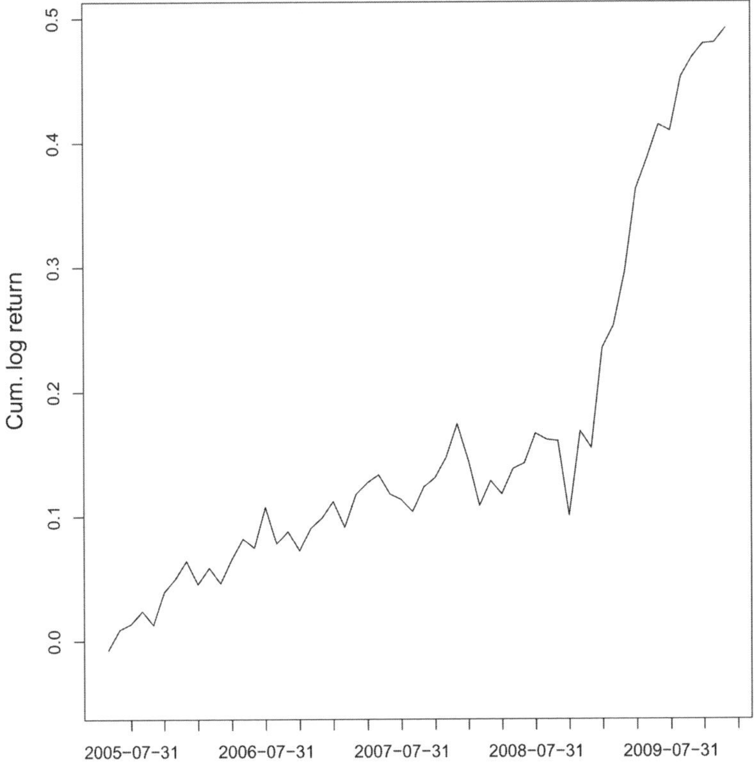

Figure 5.3. Cumulative industry return spreads covering the out-of-sample period May 2005 through December 2009 for the top-5- and bottom-5-ranked industries. The sentiment indexes have been constructed based on a 90-day trailing window, and a monthly industry rank was made based on the monthly index delta.

5.3.3 Strategy and empirical results

As part of constructing a set of industry sentiment indexes, I map each company belonging to the S&P 500 to their corresponding industry:[5] (1) oil and gas, (2) basic materials, (3) industrials, (4) consumer goods, (5) health care, (6) consumer services, (7) telecommunications, (8) utilities, (9) financials, and (10) technology. Each of these indexes are mapped to an iShares industry exchange traded fund (ETF) for testing purposes.

The indexes are constructed based on a 90-day trailing window ($P = 90$), which ensures similar news flow characteristics in each window. In order to map the calculated sentiment ratio into a sentiment index value, I consider the empirical distribution over the period March 2005 through December 2009. Finally, at each month end I decide which industries to hold long and short in the following 1-month period depending on an *industry sentiment delta rank* (see Definition 5.2 for a definition of sentiment delta).

In Figure 5.3, I show the cumulative log return spread between the top-5 and bottom-5 industries according to a sentiment ranking. As can be observed, the *out-*

[5] Industry mapping has been based on the ICB industry classification.

Table 5.3. Performance statistics covering the out-of-sample period May 2005 through December 2009 for the strategies based on the top-5- and bottom-5-ranked industries. Pre-October and Post-October refer to the market high that took place in October 2007

		Top/Bottom 5
Information ratio	Total	1.23
Information ratio	Pre-October	0.92
Information ratio	Post-October	1.53
Annualized return	Total	10.54%
Annualized return	Pre-October	5.11%
Annualized return	Post-October	16.37%
Annualized volatility	Total	8.54%
Annualized volatility	Pre-October	5.58%
Annualized volatility	Post-October	10.73%
Hit ratio	Total	66.07%
Hit ratio	Pre-October	62.07%
Hit ratio	Post-October	70.37%

Table 5.4. Yearly annualized return covering the out-of-sample period May 2005 through December 2009 for the top-5- and bottom-5-ranked industries

	Top/Bottom 5 (%)
2005	9.60
2006	3.46
2007	7.54
2008	−1.94
2009	33.71

of-sample results indicate that a positive spread can be realized taking long and short positions in the top- and bottom-ranked industries.

In Table 5.3, I have included a performance statistics summary for the long/short strategy on the top-5- and bottom-5-ranked industries. Over the backtesting period, the strategy yields an information ratio of 1.23 with values of 0.92 and 1.53 pre and post the market high in October 2007. In addition, the hit ratio reaches about 66% with positive returns in four out of five years (see Table 5.4).

Overall, it seems that going long the top-ranked and short the bottom-ranked industries based on news sentiment can add value to a market-neutral strategy.

5.3.4 A directional industry strategy

Based on the results of the previous section, it seems reasonable to assume that taking targeted industry exposures rather than investing in a broader market index would yield

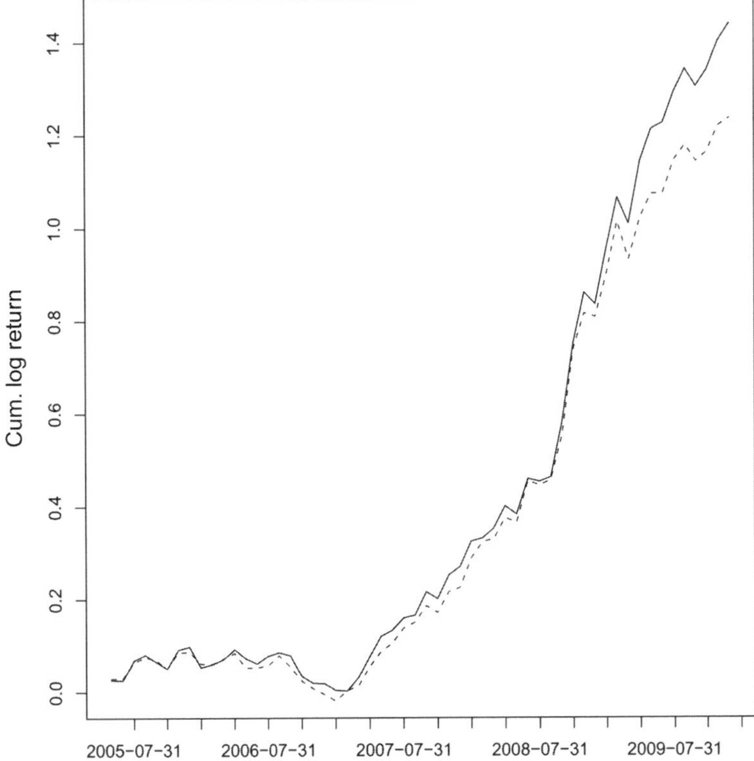

Figure 5.4. Cumulative strategy returns covering the out-of-sample period May 2005 through December 2009 taking long positions in the top-ranked industries when the Market-Level Sentiment Index delta is positive and short positions in the bottom-ranked industries when the Market-Level Sentiment Index delta is negative. Depicted in the graph is a strategy based on the top-5- and bottom-5-ranked industries (solid line), and on S&P 500 market exposures (dashed line). The sentiment indexes have been constructed based on a 90-day trailing window, and a monthly industry rank was made based on the monthly index delta.

improved results. Hence, instead of investing in the entire S&P 500 let us consider taking long positions in the top-ranked industries when the market-level sentiment delta is positive, and short positions in the bottom-ranked industries when the market-level sentiment delta is negative. In Figure 5.4, I have depicted the cumulative returns of the "basic" strategy investing in the S&P 500 and of the strategy taking exposures in the top-5- and bottom-5-ranked industries. As can be observed, the latter outperforms the former over the backtesting period.

Considering in more detail the performance statistics depicted in Table 5.5, it can be observed that taking a targeted industry approach outperforms the strategy based on broad market exposures both pre and post the market high in October 2007. Overall, the information ratio increases from 1.75 to 1.91 with most of the improvement obtained post the market high as indicated in the greater post-October 2007 information ratio. For this period, the information ratio has risen from 2.47 to 2.79.

Interestingly, it can be observed from Table 5.6 that the targeted industry strategy

Table 5.5. Performance statistics covering the out-of-sample period May 2005 through December 2009 taking long positions in the top-ranked industries when the Market-Level Sentiment Index delta is positive and short positions in the bottom-ranked industries when the Market-Level Sentiment Index delta is negative. Depicted in the graph is a strategy based on the top-5- and bottom-5-ranked industries (column 3), and the S&P 500 (column 4). Pre-October and Post-October refer to the market high that took place in October 2007

		Top/Bottom 5	Market level
Information ratio	Total	1.91	1.75
Information ratio	Pre-October	1.03	1.02
Information ratio	Post-October	2.79	2.47
Annualized return	Total	30.86%	26.50%
Annualized return	Pre-October	8.94%	7.69%
Annualized return	Post-October	54.40%	46.70%
Annualized volatility	Total	16.19%	15.16%
Annualized volatility	Pre-October	8.66%	7.56%
Annualized volatility	Post-October	19.52%	
Hit ratio	Total	67.86%	69.64%
Hit ratio	Pre-October	58.62%	62.07%
Hit ratio	Post-October	77.78%	77.78%

outperforms the market-level strategy in terms of annualized returns in four out of five years with 2008 being the only exception. Especially, 2009 seems to stand out.

All in all, it seems possible to enhance the market-level strategy by taking targeted long and short positions in the top-ranked and bottom-ranked industries rather than taking broader market exposures.

Table 5.6. Yearly annualized return covering the out-of-sample period May 2005 through December 2009 taking long positions in the top-ranked industries when the Market-Level Sentiment Index delta is positive and short positions in the bottom-ranked industries when the Market-Level Sentiment Index delta is negative. Depicted in the graph is a strategy based on the top-5- and bottom-5-ranked industries (column 2), and the S&P 500 (column 3)

	Top/Bottom 5 (%)	Market level (%)
2005	14.78	13.05
2006	−8.02	−9.20
2007	25.14	22.99
2008	56.56	58.32
2009	60.47	42.85

5.4 CONCLUSION

Considering the relevance and impact of different company events is an important element when constructing market and industry sentiment indexes. Furthermore, applying event novelty as a filter is shown to bring significant value in predicting future returns of the S&P 500. Especially, I find that market-level sentiment strategies significantly outperform 1-month price momentum with information ratios of 1.75 vs. 0.40 and annualized returns of 26.5% vs. 6.8%. In addition, the market-level sentiment strategy delivers double-digit positive returns in four out of five years. In order to measure the impact of different company events, I consider RavenPack's Event Sentiment Score, which indicates how event categories are typically rated by financial experts as having positive or negative share price impact. Also, I use RavenPack's Event Novelty Score to measure how "new" or novel a news story is over a 24-hour time window. Rather than trading based on sentiment index levels, I find value in trading on deltas or monthly index changes. By aggregating news sentiment data over a trailing period of 3 months, similar news flow characteristics are represented in each window, addressing seasonality caused by quarterly earnings reporting. Beyond capturing market-level sentiment, I calculate industry-level sentiment indexes using multiple news classifiers which provide diversity and more sentiment data. I apply a slightly less restrictive company relevance criteria while still ensuring that only high-relevance news stories are considered. Based on a set of industry sentiment indexes, a positive return spread can be obtained based on a market-neutral strategy taking long and short positions in the top- and bottom-ranked industries, respectively. I show that a positive spread can be realized taking long and short positions in the top-5- and bottom-5-ranked industries, thereby obtaining an information ratio of 1.23 over the backtesting period. Finally I show that, beyond using market-level news sentiment to invest in the S&P 500, it is possible to enhance a market strategy by taking long and short positions in the top- and bottom-ranked industries when the general market sentiment index is positive and negative, respectively. This approach improves the information ratio from 1.75 to 1.91 with outperformance in four out of five years.

5.A MARKET-LEVEL SENTIMENT DATA

I use the following RavenPack data to construct the market-level index.

5.A.1 CRS: Company Relevance Score

A score between 0 and 100 that indicates how strongly related the company is to the underlying news story, with higher values indicating greater relevance. For any story that mentions a company, RavenPack provides a relevance score. A score of 0 means the company was passively mentioned once in a story. A score of 100 means the company was predominant in the story and played a well-defined role in the article. The greater the score between 0 and 100, the higher the relevance of the story to the company.

5.A.2 ESS: Event Sentiment Score

A granular score between 0 and 100 that represents the news sentiment for a given company by measuring various proxies sampled from the news. The score is determined by systematically matching stories typically rated by financial experts as having short-term positive or negative share price impact. The strength of the score is derived from training sets where financial experts classified company-specific events and agreed these events convey positive or negative sentiment and to what degree. Their ratings are encapsulated in an algorithm that generates a score range between 0 and 100 where higher values indicate more positive sentiment while lower values (below 50) show negative sentiment.

5.A.3 ENS: Event Novelty Score

A granular score between 0 and 100 that represents how "new" or novel a news story is over a 24-hour time window. The first story disclosing an event about a company is considered to be the most novel and receives a score of 100. Subsequent stories about the company's event receive lower scores following a decay function (100, 75, 56, ...). Stories outside the 24-hour window but similar to a story in a chain of events receive a score of 0.

5.B INDUSTRY-LEVEL SENTIMENT DATA

I use the following RavenPack data to construct the industry-level indexes.

5.B.1 Company Relevance Score

A score between 0 and 100 that indicates how strongly related the company is to the underlying news story, with higher values indicating greater relevance. For any story that mentions a company, RavenPack provides a relevance score. A score of 0 means the company was passively mentioned once in a story. A score of 100 means the company was predominant in the story and played a well-defined role in the article. The greater the score between 0 and 100, the higher the relevance of the story to the company.

5.B.2 WLE: Word and phrase detection

A score that represents the news sentiment of the given news item according to the WLE classifier, which specializes in identifying positive and negative words and phrases in articles about global equities. Scores can take values of 0, 50, or 100 indicating negative, neutral, or positive sentiment, respectively. This sentiment score is based on RavenPack's Traditional Methodology.

5.B.3 PCM: Projections, corporate news

A score that represents the news sentiment of the given story according to the PCM classifier, which specializes in identifying the sentiment of stories that are only about earnings, developments, and projections news. Scores can take values of 0, 50, or 100 indicating negative, neutral, or positive sentiment, respectively. This sentiment score is based on RavenPack's Expert Consensus Methodology.

5.B.4 ECM: Editorials, commentary news

A score that represents the news sentiment of the given story according to the ECM classifier, which specializes in short commentaries and editorials on global equity markets. Scores can take values of 0, 50, or 100 indicating negative, neutral, or positive sentiment, respectively. This sentiment score is based on RavenPack's Expert Consensus Methodology.

5.B.5 RCM: Reports, corporate action news

A score that represents the news sentiment of the given news story according to the RCM classifier, which specializes in reports on corporate action announcements. Scores can take values of 0, 50, or 100 indicating negative, neutral, or positive sentiment, respectively. This sentiment score is based on RavenPack's Expert Consensus Methodology and has been trained on stories that lead up to a pre-identified corporate action announcement.

5.B.6 VCM: Merger, acquisitions, and takeover news

A score that represents the news sentiment of the given story according to the VCM classifier, which specializes in news stories about mergers, acquisitions, and takeovers. Scores can take values of 0, 50, or 100 indicating negative, neutral, or positive sentiment, respectively. This sentiment score is based on RavenPack's Expert Consensus Methodology and has been trained on stories that lead up to a pre-identified mergers, acquisitions, and takeover event.

5.C REFERENCES

Cahan R.; Jussa J.; Luo Y. (2009a) *Breaking News: How to Use News Sentiment to Pick Stocks*, Macquarie US Equity Research.

Cahan R.; Jussa J.; Luo Y. (2009a) *Eventful Investing: Harnessing the Power of Event-driven Strategies*, Macquarie US Equity Research.

Engelberg J.E.; Red A.V.; Ringgenberg M.C. (2010) *How Are Shorts Informed? Short Sellers, News, and Information Processing*, Kenan-Flagler Business School, University of North Carolina.

Hafez P.A (2009a) *Construction of Market Sentiment Indices Using News Sentiment*, RavenPack International S.L.

Hafez P.A. (2009b) *Detection of Seasonality Patterns in Equity News Flow*, RavenPack International S.L.

Hafez P.A. (2009c) *Investigation of the Impact of News Sentiment on Abnormal Stock Return*, RavenPack Intrnational S.L.

Hafez P.A. (2009d) *Sector Rotation Strategies Driven by News Sentiment Indices*, RavenPack International S.L.

Kittrell J. (this volume) "Sentiment reversals as buy signals" (see Chapter 9).

Mitra L.; Mitra G.; diBartolomeo D. (2008) *Equity Portfolio Risk (Volatility) Estimation Using Market Information and Sentiment*, CARISMA, Brunel University.

Patton A.; Verardo M. (2009) *Does Beta Move with Firm News? Systematic Risk and Firm-specific Information Flows*, Duke University.

Tetlock P.C. (2009) *Does Public Financial News Resolve Asymmetric Information?* Yale University.

Zhang W.; Skiena S. (2010) *Trading Strategies to Exploit News Sentiment*, Stony Brook University.

Part II

News and abnormal returns

6
Relating news analytics to stock returns

David Leinweber and Jacob Sisk

ABSTRACT

News analytics measure the relevance, sentiment, novelty, and volume of news. They combine natural language analysis of content with historical and news metadata. Signals from analytics of this type have been shown to be predictive of volatility. Aggregation and filtering of news events can also generate alpha signals for portfolio management. Filters use thresholds set using both absolute and relative measures. This detects investor behavior associated with accumulation of information and changes in sentiment. The analytics described are used to generate investment signals. In practice, they would be combined with forecasts from other quantitative or research sources (e.g., factor, momentum, and earnings). In this chapter, we analyze investment signals derived only from news, an important distinction. Event studies on a broad universe of US equities (segmented by sector and capitalization class) are shown for the period 2003–2008. US portfolio simulation results are shown for these signals applied over 2006–2009. The portfolio simulation, like the event studies, is based on a "pure news" signal, without mixing in other quant signals, which can confuse the question of alpha from news. Both the event studies and portfolio simulation show evidence of exploitable alpha using news analytics.

6.1 INTRODUCTION

Alpha hunters are always looking for new territory. When a strategy becomes known and used by too many players, the collective market impact of getting in and getting out squeezes out all the profit, and only the lowest cost transactors will be able to use it. The pack needs to move on.

Textual information is promising new territory. Bill Gross, of the PIMCO investment management company, described equity valuation as "that mysterious fragile flower where price is part perception, part valuation, and part hope or lack thereof." An old Wall Street proverb says, more tersely, "Stocks are stories, bonds are mathematics."

This has enough truth in it that looking for the right stories is a worthwhile activity. Modern high-end newsfeeds are designed to facilitate technology-intensive methods in

The Handbook of News Analytics in Finance Edited by L. Mitra and G. Mitra

that activity. News gathering is increasingly supported by automation that monitors a large and growing subset of the web and information in proprietary databases. There are plenty of places to find potentially investment-relevant text. Consider three broad classifications:

1. *News* News was once exclusively disseminated on paper, radio, television, teletype "wire", fax, and eventually via dedicated electronic feeds. It is now ubiquitous on the web, and news vendors have moved dramatically upscale, with richly tagged news suitable for "quantextual" investment and trading strategies.
2. *Pre-news* Pre-news is the raw material reporters read before they write news. It comes from primary sources, the originators themselves: the Securities and Exchange Commission (SEC), court documents, and other government agencies. This also includes corporate sources, reputable blogs, and specialized news. At Thomson Reuters, the news-gathering process has been aggressively automated to allow faster reliable transformation of pre-news to news using a variety of IA (intelligence amplification) and AI (artificial intelligence) methods such as language translation and entity extraction.
3. *Social media* The barriers to entry at the low end of the "news" business on the web are vanishingly small. Anyone can tweet, create a blog, or post on message boards for stocks or other topics. A great deal of this is genuinely useful—think of the product reviews on Amazon—and some is just noise. On stock message boards, there have been CEOs who reveal valuable information; but, for the most part, the typical posting still reads like it came from some guy on vodka number nine.

This chapter deals only with the first category of text: news. Progress in news-gathering automation moves pre-news to news faster and in greater volume. The methods described here for news can also be applied to user-provided text. Detailed discussions of this and related topics are found in the book *Nerds on Wall Street: Math, Machines and Wired Markets*, particularly Ch. 9, "The text frontier" (Leinweber, 2009).

6.2 PREVIOUS WORK

6.2.1 Behavioral basis

How investors and traders respond to news is of ongoing interest in behavioral finance. Ideas of attention and repetition, well known in advertising, have been explored in previous work. There is a substantial amount of prior research in this area.

In "All that glitters: The effect of attention and news on the buying behavior of individual and institutional investors," Barber and Odean (2008) "confirm the hypothesis that individual investors are net buyers of attention-grabbing stocks, e.g., stocks in the news, stocks experiencing high abnormal trading volume, and stocks with extreme one day returns."

In "Stock price reaction to news and no-news: Drift and reversal after headlines," Chan (2003) compares return patterns for stocks with and without news and finds major differences between the two sets. These persist even when earnings-related news (a traditional quant analytic) is removed. Consistent with our expectations based on investor attention, these effects are larger for smaller capitalization firms, an effect also seen in this chapter.

6.2.2 Risk management and news

News-based analytics are useful in risk management. The difference in return distributions associated with news have been used to forecast changes in beta, covariances, and volatility.

In "Does beta move with news? Firm-specific information flows and learning about profitability," Patton and Verardo (2009) show that beta (systematic risk) of individual stocks increases by an "economically and statistically significant amount on days of firm-specific news announcements, and reverts to its average level two to five days later." They find marked differences across sectors, an effect we also observed in the research described in this chapter.

In "Practical issues in forecasting volatility," Ser-Huang Poon and Nobel Economics Laureate Clive Granger (2005) describe the combination of GARCH and option implied volatilities and concluded that the best and most elaborate quantitative models did not rival predictions based on implied volatilities. In their conclusion, they write, "a potentially useful area for future research is whether forecasting can be enhanced by using exogenous variables" such as news.

These ideas are extended by Mitra, Mitra, and diBartolomeo (2008) who use implied volatilities for stocks with options, and exogenous information from news to improve a multifactor model of equity risk, addressing the issue that "traditional factor models fail to update quickly as market conditions change. It is desirable that the risk model updates to incorporate new information as it becomes available and ... introduce a factor model that uses option implied volatility to improve estimates of the future covariance matrix. We extend this work to use ... quantified news ... to improve risk estimates as the market sentiment and environment changes."

6.2.3 Broad long-period analysis of the relation between news and stock returns

In a study first published in 2006, Tetlock, Saar-Tsechansky, and Macskassy looked at more than 350,000 news stories about S&P 500 companies that appeared in the *Wall Street Journal* and on the Dow Jones News Service from 1984 to 2004. They used a massive program called the General Inquirer to gauge the sentiment of these stories. The General Inquirer is the result of over 20 years of research sponsored by the US National Science Foundation and the British and Australian National Research Councils. It started out as PL/I programs running on IBM mainframes in the 1980s. The current version is hosted (somewhat sporadically lately) on the web by Harvard's Psychology Department and is available for anyone to use there. It has spawned dozens of PhD dissertations, many of which have added language profiles to characterize the sentiment and content of text.

Tetlock, Saar-Tsechansky, and Macskassy scored those 350,000 stories, containing over 100 million words, for positive or negative sentiment using the General Inquirer, and summarized the results in an event study chart showing abnormal returns to stocks with positive and negative stories. It is shown in Figure 6.1.

These event studies aggregate the results over 20 years (1984–2004). The vertical line in the center of the chart indicates the date the story appeared. The sentiment measures appear to work very well. Positive sentiment lines all go up and negative sentiment lines all go down. But also notice there's a huge amount of what first appears to be pre-event

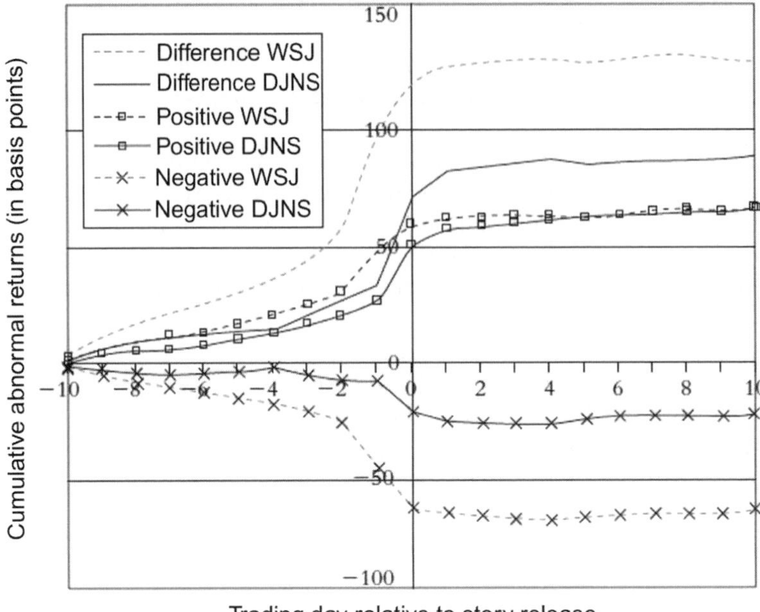

Figure 6.1. Tetlock, Saar-Tsechansky, and Macskassy's news event study might lead to the false conclusion that news stories hardly matter, but stories about price moves that have already happened (e.g., "XYZ Soars 53 Percent on High Earnings") are included here, diluting the results of true breaking news (source: Tetlock, Saar-Tsechansky, and Macskassy, 2008).

information leakage. In this example, we see what appears to be close to 90% of the return occurring prior (to the left) of the event line. *Efficient Market Hypothesis* fans might say, "We told you so", but that is not the full story here. A substantial portion of this is likely occurring due to the categorization of "me too" stories, referring back to the original good or bad news, and after-the-fact reporting, that "the stock moved up sharply on good news that . . ." This is an example of the need to consider textual events in context with others, rather than as atomic stand-alone events.

On first look, it also paints a somewhat discouraging picture for those who might trade blindly on news characterization—by the time you read it and trade, there's not much left for you to pocket. Tetlock, Saar-Tsechansky, and Macskassy's simulated "long on good news, short on bad news" trading strategies did show simulated profits, but only with extremely low transaction costs (9 basis points). Most studies of actual institutional transaction costs, including commissions and market impact, show one-way costs of approximately 50 basis points. This means that additional analysis or supplementation of news would be needed for a profitable real-world strategy.

Our efforts in this area are reported in this chapter. In comparison with Tetlock, Saar-Tsechansky, and Macskassy (2008), we used a broader investable universe (the S&P 1500 instead of the S&P 500) over a period (2003–2009) fully in the web era, which has transformed the dissemination of investment information, so there is no mix of pre- and post-web effects. The next section describes the RNSE news dataset that is the basis for this research.

6.3 NEWS DATA STRUCTURE AND STATISTICS

We are using data from the Thomson Reuters NewsScope Sentiment Engine (RNSE), developed with Infonics (RNSE, 2008). These data have

- Global scope, to examine both US and international markets.
- Broad coverage, currently over 7,000 US stocks, more than adequate for our test sample of the contemporaneous S&P 1500 stocks over the period.
- Rich metadata—sentiment, relevance to a stock, topic codes, and links to previous related stories.
- Up-to-date 6-year history (2003–2009).[1]
- Real-time availability.

Thomson Reuters also furnished accurate synchronized pricing data, with Reuters Instrument Code (RIC) security identifiers matching the news and price data. We are very appreciative to the Thomson Reuters Data Team for assembling such a clean product.

6.3.1 Sample news data

Figure 6.2 shows a sample of RNSE data.

6.3.2 Descriptive news statistics and trends

A number of noteworthy trends are in evidence in Figures 6.3–6.6, showing remarkable growth in scope, depth, and volume of news. RIC refers to Reuters Instrument Codes, a great resource in linking news to prices.

Figures 6.3–6.6 show only the numbers of news events. Figure 6.7 is a very intuitively satisfying picture of the overall sentiment of the news in recent years.

6.4 IMPROVING NEWS ANALYTICS WITH AGGREGATION

6.4.1 Event studies

We used event studies as a means of systematic screening for interesting relationships between events defined using news analytics built using RNSE data. We were able to set, and vary thresholds (both absolute and relative) based on

- *News intensity* Number of news items in a period.
- *Relevance* Applicability of the items to a particular stock (0–100%).
- *Sentiment scores* Probability that a story is positive, negative, or neutral in tone for these items.
- *Novelty and type of items* Alerts, number of links to previous items, etc.

The time period for the event studies shown here is 2003–2008 with a universe of stocks based on the contemporaneous S&P 1500 over this period. Industry classifications are based on Thomson Reuters Business Classification (TRBC) sectors.

These studies are done on a daily timescale. The return intervals examined extend out to 60 days. Signals on this scale have a "slower alpha", presumably due to the time it

[1] At the time of preparation of this chapter.

TIMESTAMP	RIC	RELEVANCE	SENTIMENT	POSITIVE	NEUTRAL	NEGATIVE	LINKED COUNTS	ITEM TYPE	HEADLINE	TOPIC CODES
00:34:28.944	IBM.N	0.29	1	0.538	0.454	0.008	0;0;0;0;0	ARTICLE	Arrow to buy smaller rival for $485 million	US WHO LEN RTRS MRG SFWR H
11:14:04.042	IBM.N	1	1	0.842	0.133	0.025	0;0;0;0;0	ALERT	UBS RAISES IBM <IBM.N> TO BUY FROM NEUTRAL - THEFLYONTHEW	RCH US CA LEN RTRS
11:16:55.812	IBM.N	1	1	0.850	0.119	0.031	1;1;1;1;1	ARTICLE	US RESEARCH NEWS-UBS raises IBM to buy - theflyonthewall.com	RCH US CA LEN RTRS
11:20:50.082	IBM.N	1	0	0.247	0.614	0.138	1;1;1;1;1	ARTICLE	RESEARCH ALERT-UBS upgrades IBM to buy - theflyonthewall.com	RCH DPR HDWR SFWR US LEN R
12:22:43.689	IBM.N	1	1	0.842	0.133	0.025	0;0;0;0;0	ALERT	IBM <IBM.N> SHARES RISE 1.1 PCT TO $98.50 BEFORE THE BELL AFTE	RCH US CA LEN RTRS
12:36:50.695	IBM.N	1	1	0.542	0.450	0.008	3;3;3;3;3	ARTICLE	Before the Bell - Bed Bath & Beyond, IBM rise early	DPR HDWR US STX HOT LEN RTR
12:49:19.943	IBM.N	0.28	0	0.213	0.609	0.178	3;3;3;3;3	APPEND	HEADLINE STOCKS - U.S. stocks to watch Jan 8	US STX FIN RESF RES BUS HOT L
14:59:02.943	IBM.N	1	1	0.701	0.164	0.135	1;1;1;1;1	ARTICLE	UPDATE 1-RESEARCH ALERT-UBS upgrades IBM to buy from neutral	US RCH DPR HDWR SFWR BUS LI
15:05:53.790	IBM.N	0.13	-1	0.056	0.125	0.819	1;1;1;1;1	ARTICLE	US RESEARCH NEWS-Credit Suisse recommends trading buy on GM	RCH US CA LEN RTRS
15:06:13.000	IBM.N	0.08	-1	0.056	0.125	0.819	2;2;2;2;2	APPEND	US RESEARCH NEWS-Credit Suisse recommends trading buy on GM	RCH US CA LEN RTRS
16:31:45.041	IBM.N	0.25	0	0.218	0.612	0.170	4;4;4;4;4	APPEND	HEADLINE STOCKS - U.S. stocks on the move on Jan 8	US STX FIN RESF RES BUS HOT L
16:31:55.631	IBM.N	0.25	0	0.218	0.612	0.170	6;6;6;6;6	APPEND	HEADLINE STOCKS - U.S. stocks on the move on Jan 8	US STX FIN RESF RES BUS HOT L
18:49:48.004	IBM.N	0.32	0	0.221	0.613	0.166	7;7;7;7;7	APPEND	HEADLINE STOCKS - U.S. stocks on the move on Jan 8	US STX FIN RESF RES BUS HOT L
19:18:14.726	IBM.N	0.20	-1	0.180	0.251	0.568	0;0;0;0;0	ARTICLE	UPDATE 1-Sears aims to drive sales with virtual showroom	RET US WWW LEN RTRS
20:09:19.547	IBM.N	0.34	1	0.830	0.128	0.042	0;0;0;0;0	ARTICLE	US STOCKS-Indexes higher; upgrades boost tech sector	US STX BUS MUNI FIN NEWS LEN
20:09:54.796	IBM.N	0.14	1	0.830	0.128	0.042	1;1;1;1;1	APPEND	US STOCKS-Indexes higher; upgrades boost tech sector	US STX BUS MUNI FIN NEWS LEN
04:09:34.780	IBM.N	1	1	0.512	0.382	0.107	0;0;0;0;0	ARTICLE	IBM appoints new Greater China CEO	CN ASIA ELI HK TW F EMRG LEN I
19:13:02.511	IBM.N	0.17	0	0.216	0.611	0.174	0;0;0;0;0	ARTICLE	CES-Visa, Nokia turn mobile phones into mobile wallets	WEU EUROPE WWW DE NORD US
19:13:59.476	IBM.N	0.17	0	0.216	0.611	0.174	1;1;1;1;1	APPEND	CES-Visa, Nokia turn mobile phones into mobile wallets	WEU EUROPE WWW DE NORD US
11:55:22.595	IBM.N	1	-1	0.188	0.112	0.700	0;0;1;1;1	ALERT	AG EDWARDS CUTS IBM <IBM.N> TO HOLD FROM BUY - THEFLYONTH	RCH US DPR HDWR SFWR LEN R
12:02:25.855	IBM.N	1	-1	0.137	0.217	0.645	1;1;3;3;3	ARTICLE	RESEARCH ALERT-AG Edwards cuts IBM to hold - theflyonthewall.con	RCH US DPR HDWR SFWR LEN R
15:20:49.892	IBM.N	1	-1	0.311	0.145	0.544	1;1;3;3;3	ARTICLE	UPDATE 1-RESEARCH ALERT-AG Edwards downgrades IBM	US RCH DPR HDWR SFWR LEN R
11:29:20.729	IBM.N	0.18	1	0.841	0.123	0.036	0;0;0;0;0	APPEND	FACTBOX-UK companies cut, close final-salary pensions	GB WEU EUROPE FUND FIN RTM F
12:57:47.150	IBM.N	1	1	0.552	0.441	0.007	0;0;0;0;0	ALERT	BANC OF AMERICA RAISES IBM <IBM.N> PRICE TARGET TO $110 FRO	RCH DPR US LEN RTRS ENT HDW
13:24:15.667	IBM.N	1	1	0.565	0.342	0.093	3;3;5;7;7	ARTICLE	RESEARCH ALERT-BofA raises price targets on IBM, Apple, EMC	RCH DPR US LEN RTRS ENT HDW

Figure 6.2. Sample RNSE data. Quantitative scores on qualitative information. *Relevance* measures how much the item is about a given company (e.g., a sector story mentioning many firms would have lower relevance for any of them than a single-company story). *Sentiment* analyzes text for positive, neutral, and negative language, quantifies scores for each, and determines the prevailing sentiment of the article. The link counts are a *uniqueness/novelty* score. They measure repetition among articles and the number of similar articles on a company. In addition, there is comprehensive *metadata*, including company identifier, topic codes, item type, stage of story, etc.

Image supplied by Leinweber and Sisk.

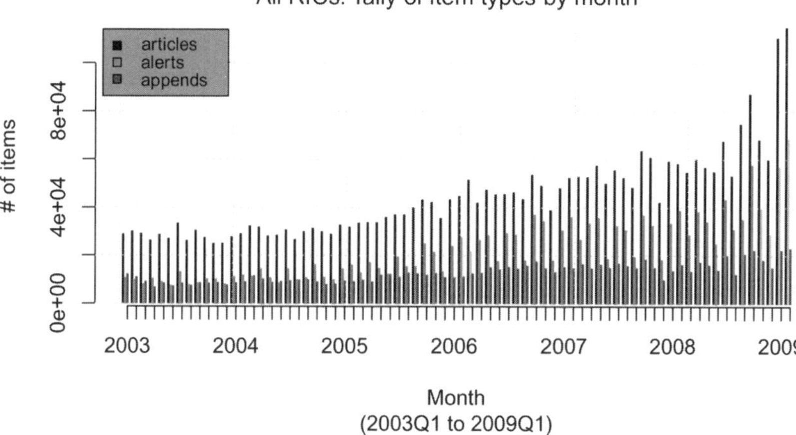

Figure 6.3. Rapidly increasing volume of news for US stocks, due in part to automated "intelligence amplification" improvements in news gathering. Universe is the S&P 1500.

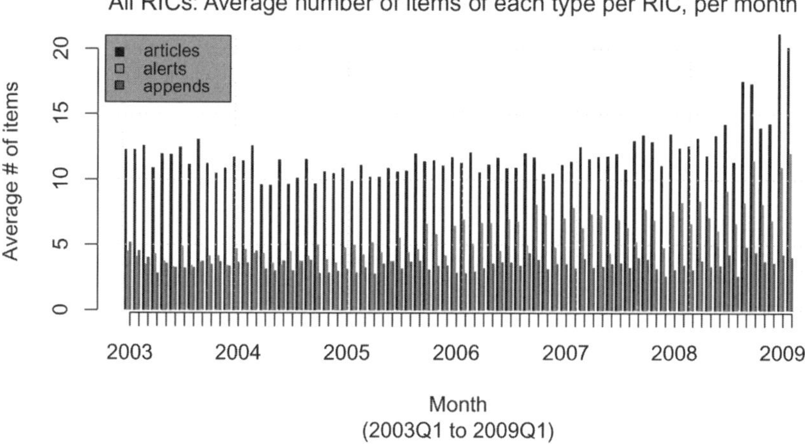

Figure 6.4. The number of items per US stock (RIC) has also grown rapidly, approximately doubling in the last year. Universe is the S&P 1500.

takes for people to accumulate information. This type of signal is amenable to large-position building and higher capacity funds.

These studies are based on "pure news" signals. In practice, they would naturally be combined with other quantitative signals.

6.4.2 News analytic parameters for these studies

Based on exploratory data analysis (e.g., reading stories with different relevance levels) and the time-honored SWAG methodology, we used these settings for the event studies shown in the following sections:

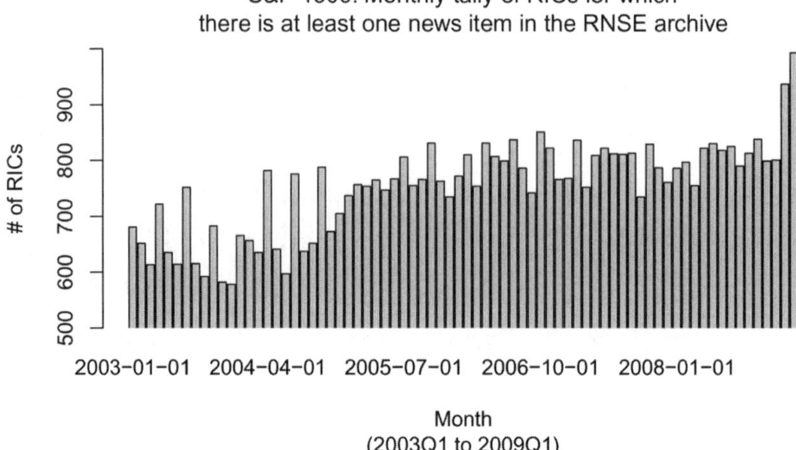

Figure 6.5. Breadth of coverage of S&P 1500 index constituent firms, measured by number of firms with news each month.

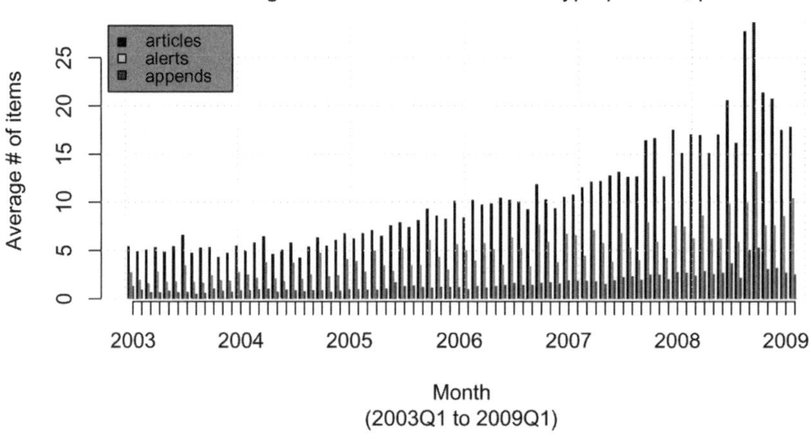

Figure 6.6. Depth of coverage of S&P 1500 firms, measured by number of news items per firm.

- *Intensity* One or two unique news items per day minimum.
- *Relevance* How much the article is about a particular firm ($\geq$60%).
- *Sentiment* In top 5% or 10% of daily distribution.
- *Novelty* How often has a story with similar text to this one appeared? To do this we require Linked count $5 = 0$.
- *News accumulation and trading times* A "day" for measuring news events is defined as a 24-hour period from 3 : 30 pm the previous trading day to 3 : 30 pm on the current day. Positions for calculating the returns in the event studies are assumed taken at the closing price on the current day, and subsequent returns are also based on closing prices.

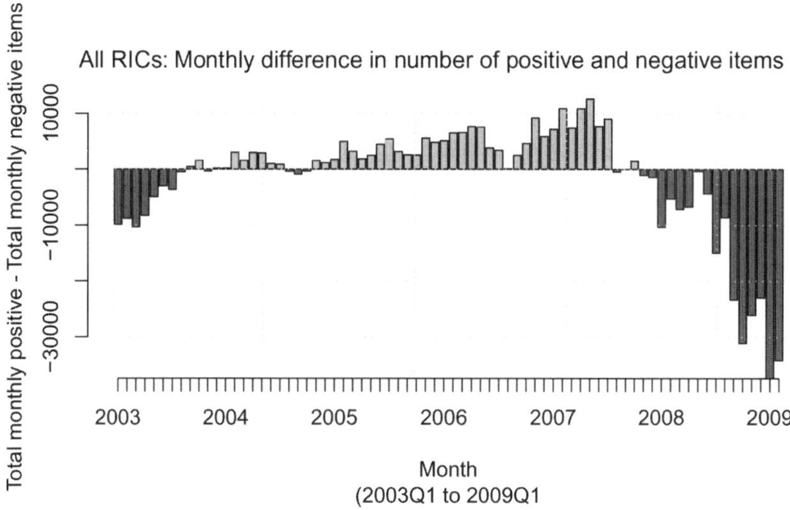

Figure 6.7. Monthly difference in number of positive and negative news items.

The first event study was very simple and broad, designed to compare with Tetlock, Saar-Tsechansky, and Macskassy's earlier result (seen in Figure 6.1). It is shown in Figures 6.8a, b and is indeed very similar. In sentiment metrics work the positive event lines are consistently above the negative event lines. Timeliness is an issue (as seen in Figure 6.8a), with large pre-event returns observed, but potentially exploitable post-event returns are also seen (as in Figure 6.8b).

6.4.3 Adjusting aggregate event parameters and thresholds, and segmentation by sector

These give promising results for the full S&P 1500 index (see Figure 6.9), but need refinement to produce alpha in excess of reasonable transaction costs. Our approach was to segment by sector, and adjust the news analytic filter settings.

One observation in all of these event studies was that the positive sentiment return lines are consistently above the negative sentiment returns, and opposite in direction. The sentiment measures appear very effective. In addition, changes in traffic/sentiment thresholds show expected effects. More stringent filters reduce the numbers of events, but are associated with larger excess returns.

The best sectors for this approach are: basic materials, cyclicals, financials, industrials, non-cyclicals, and technology. These effects are illustrated for financials and non-cyclicals in Figures 6.10 and 6.11.

6.4.4 Adjusting sentiment thresholds

The effect seen from 2003 through 2008 is evident in 2009 (through the end of Q3), with about the same magnitude. We still observe the balance between breadth of signal and magnitude of excess return, although at very extreme levels there are two few data points to draw any conclusions.

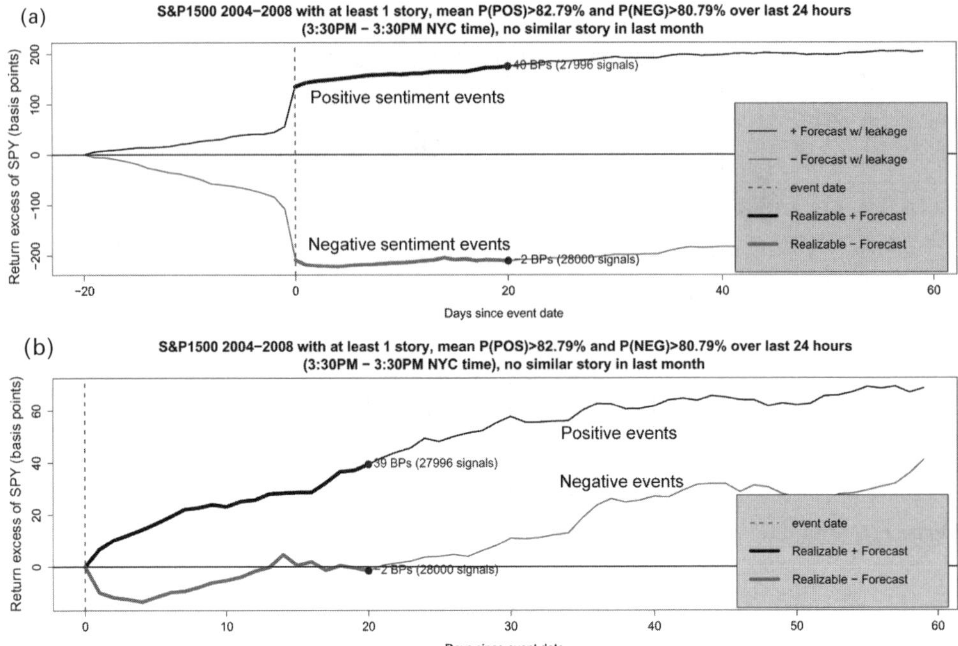

Figure 6.8. Simple unscreened news event studies, showing pre-event returns as well in (a), post-event returns in (b) (note vertical scale change). The "forecast" subsequent excess return is the return gained after a specific time period chosen prior to initiating the study, either 1 week or 1 month. This is similar to Tetlock, Saar-Tsechansky, and Macskassy's (2008, fig. 1) result for 1984–2004, with larger pre-event returns than what one might expect for 2003–2008, which is fully in the web era of faster moving information. It also suggests the target for advanced news signal methods using analytics based on novelty and news metadata.

6.5 REFINING FILTERS USING INTERACTIVE EXPLORATORY DATA ANALYSIS AND VISUALIZATION

There are many ways to slice and dice event studies, and for advanced content-based filters the ability to drill down to individual news events is desirable. We developed an interactive exploratory data analysis and drill-down system, the Event Study Explorer, using the TIBCO Spotfire visualization tool. The sliders and selection boxes seen in Figure 6.12 illustrate this capability.

This approach to exploratory data analysis (EDA) was first suggested by John Tukey (Tukey, 1977), and refined by Tufte in *Visual Display of Quantitative Information* (Tufte, 2001). These ideas were greatly advanced as computational tools by Ben Schneiderman's Human Computer Interface Lab (Schneiderman and Plaisant, 2009).

The Event Study Explorer allows great flexibility in filter selection parameters, study period, sector, capitalization, and pre-event return. It provides the ability to drill down to news content as the basis for further natural language processing (NLP) or machine learning (ML) filtering.

The Event Study Explorer allows the researcher to consider the subsequent cumulative return for specific subsets of events. Events are keyed by date and RIC (security

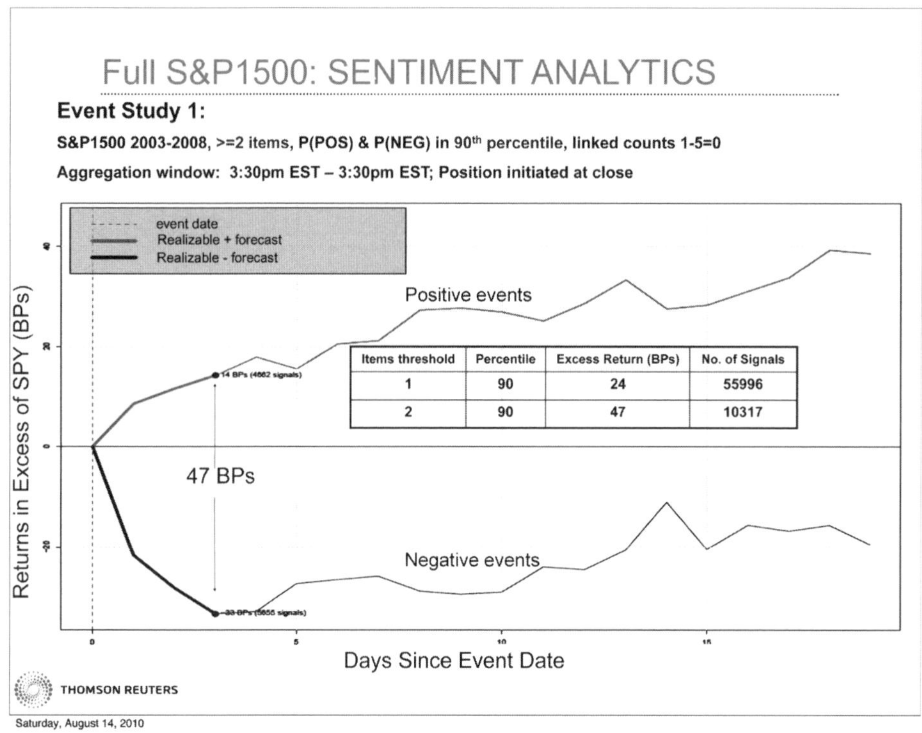

Figure 6.9. Full S&P index results. Using Linked count 5 = 0 includes only news items without predecessor items. The table insert illustrates the expected effects of adjusting filter settings—requiring a larger threshold reduces the number of signals, but the ones that remain are associated with larger excess returns.

identifier) and can be subset by time period, sector, market capitalization, or attributes of the RNSE news that occurred on that day. Given news aggregations and return calculations, the Event Study Explorer is easily configured in Spotfire with no programming required. Specific components (tagged with numbers in circles in Figure 6.12) of the Event Study Explorer include:

1. *Long-term event study view* The one-quarter excess return of the current subset of positive and negative events.
2. *Short-term event study view* The one-week excess return of the current subset of positive and negative events.
3. *The event filter* This allows the researcher to dynamically choose for which events she would like to see subsequent excess return calculations.
4. *Details on demand* When the user selects a subset of events (e.g., by clicking on the positive or negative event line in one of the event study views), the details for these event days are displayed here.
5. *Signals within each period* This display shows that the subset of events is consistent across time.
6. *Signals within each sector* This display shows that the subset of events is consistent across sectors.

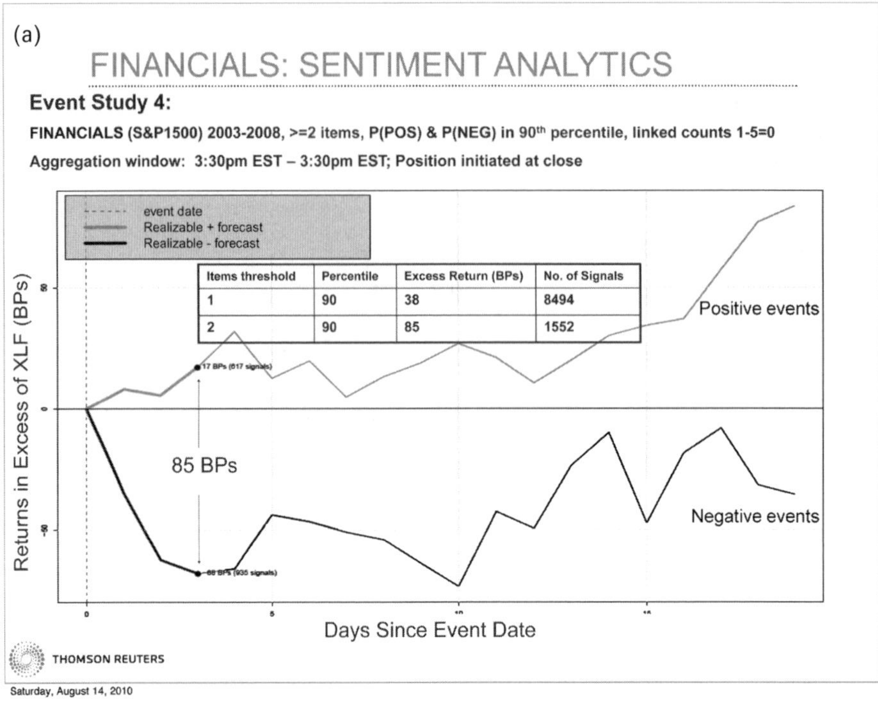

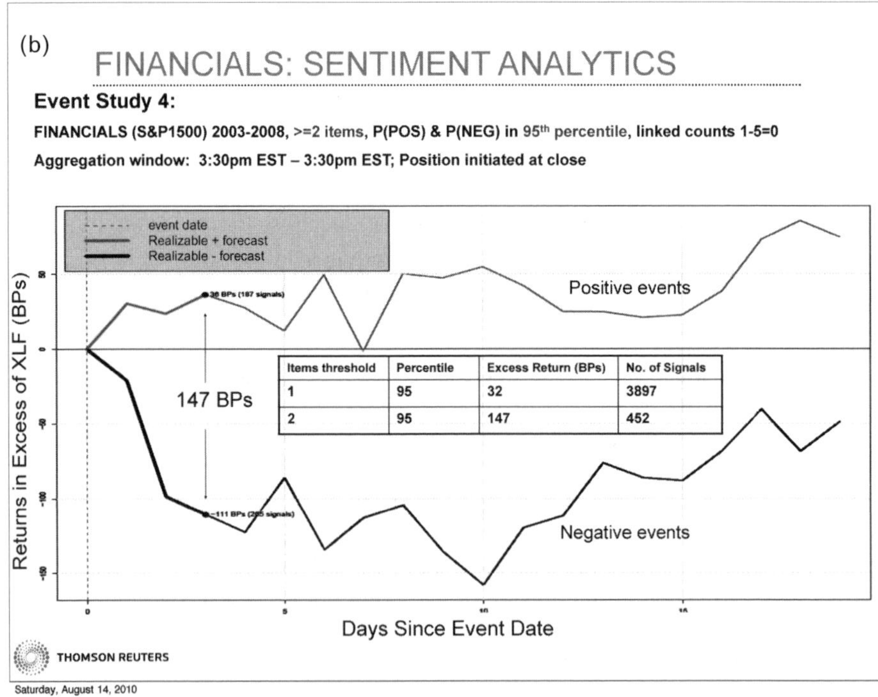

Figure 6.10. Turning the knob up from the 90th percentile (a) to the 95th percentile (b) on the strength of sentiment has the expected effects—fewer signals with higher returns.

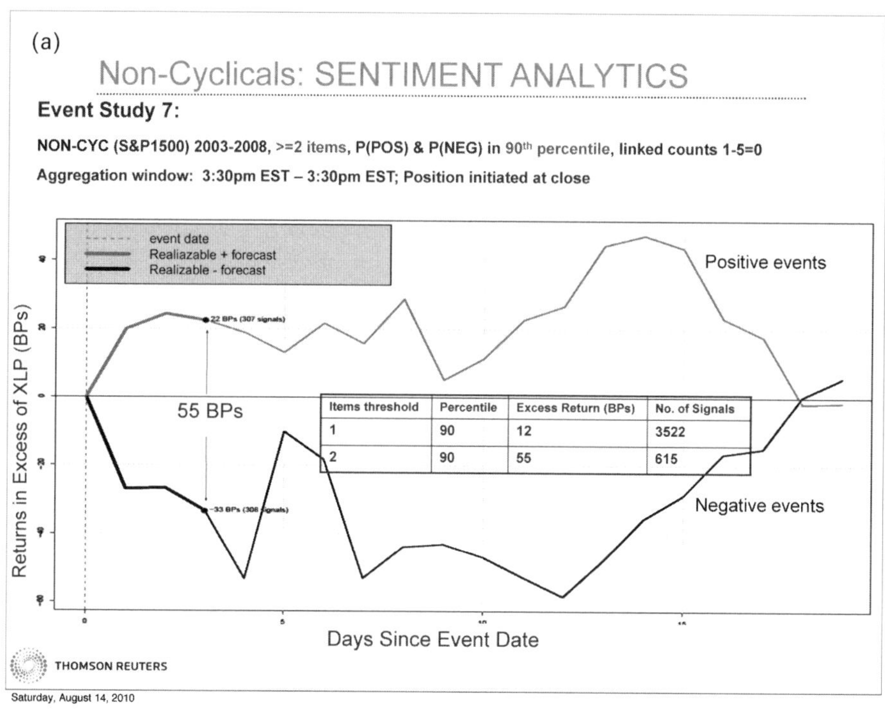

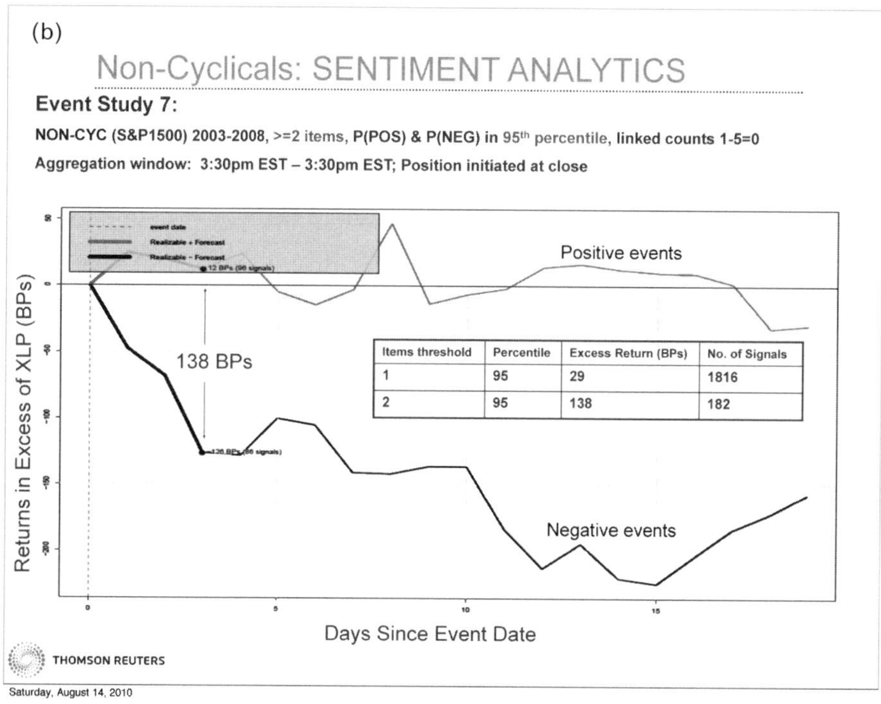

Figure 6.11. The same effects described for financials, but in the non-cyclical sector.

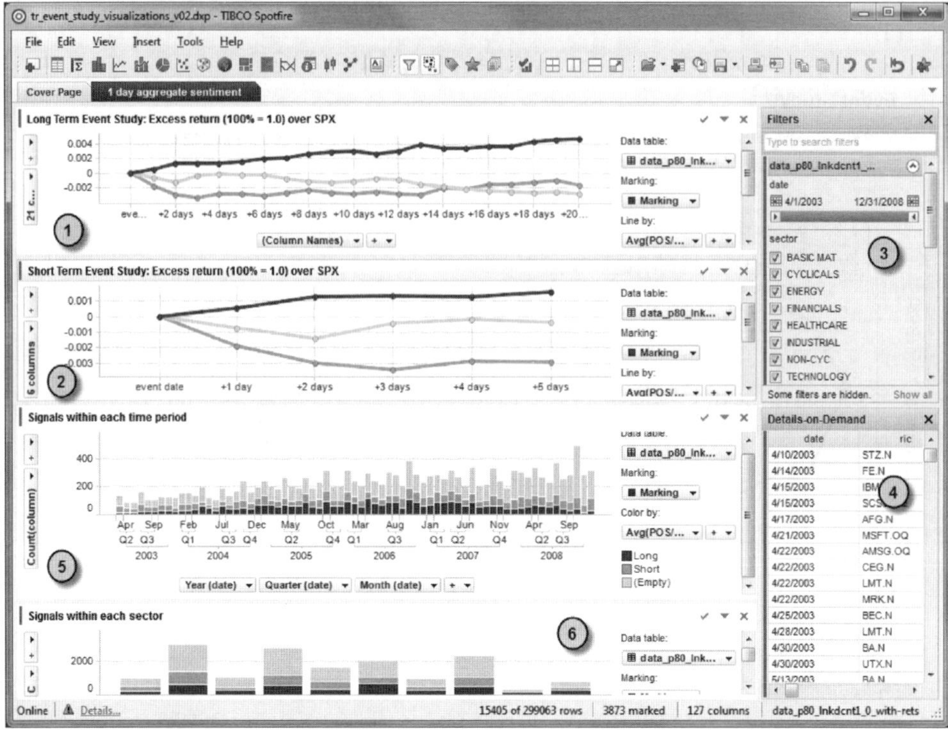

Figure 6.12. The Event Study Explorer built in Spotfire. Great flexibility in the scope and parameters of event studies is possible. Strong data-mining warnings apply.

6.6 INFORMATION EFFICIENCY AND MARKET CAPITALIZATION

An interesting question to investigate using the Event Study Explorer is the relationship between firm capitalization and the response to news. A reasonable prior is that smaller capitalization firms with less intensive news coverage would show greater response to extreme sentiment news events. Figure 6.13 overlays the event study charts, segmented into four capitalization groups as shown by the label "Cumulative excess return".

The chart in Figure 6.13 conforms strongly to expectations, with the exception of negative news for the smallest capitalization group.

For positive sentiment events (upper lines) the lowest cap group shows a large response (2–3% excess returns relative to others in the sector/cap group). Note the 60-day scale in Figure 6.13. There is ample time to accumulate positions in these (apparently) under-followed stocks.

For negative sentiment events (lower lines), a similar picture is seen, with the negative excess return lines declining and the largest cap (i.e., most followed) showing the smallest effects. The next two lower capitalization classes line up in beauty contestant fashion, but the smallest cap group (under $2bn) shows anomalous behavior, essentially flat for 40 days, then slightly positive.

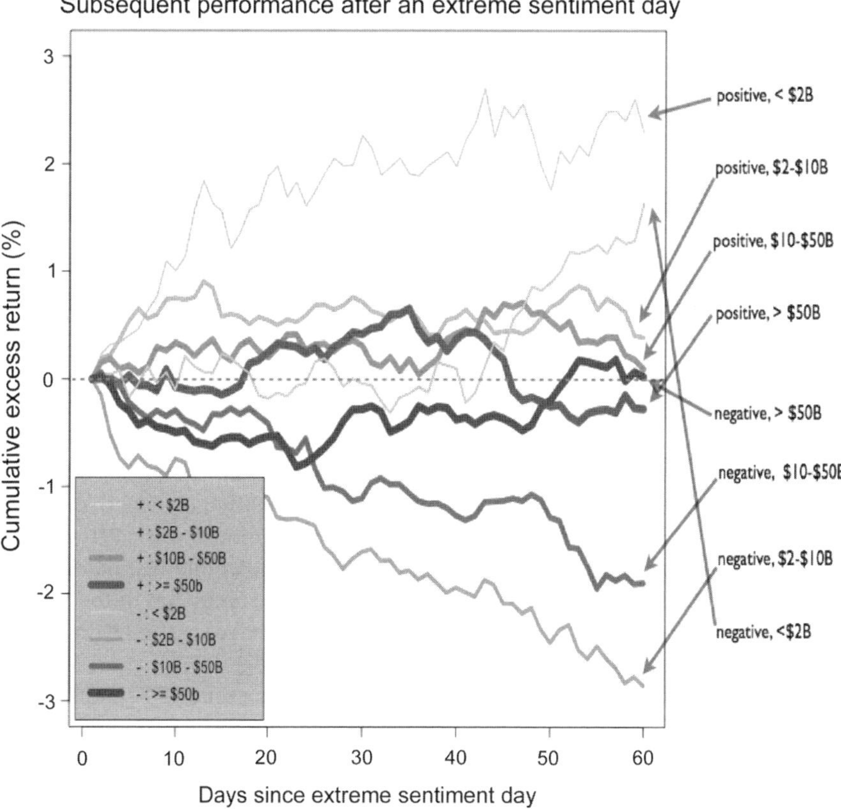

Figure 6.13. Subsequent cumulative return after an extreme sentiment day relative to sector and market capitalization peers. Daily positive or negative sentiment in the top 5%, with at least two news items with link count 5 = 0 in the last 24 hours for stocks in the S&P 1500 (2003–2009, Q3).

6.7 US PORTFOLIO SIMULATION USING NEWS ANALYTIC SIGNALS

Event studies are screening methods that show potential value, but they are in "event time", while portfolios are managed in "calendar time". It is instructive to attempt realistic portfolio construction using only RNSE event data for extreme sentiment days. Of course, a professional portfolio manager would incorporate these RNSE event data into her arsenal of other investment ideas and information sources, but it is instructive to see if even simple portfolio construction techniques using only news data can perform.

6.7.1 Investment hypothesis

The investment hypothesis under consideration is that it takes market participants a long time (days) to process a large amount of novel, strongly polar news, as suggested by the event studies. News and event ambiguity, fact validation, cognitive dissonance are all good reasons to hypothesize that investors can take a longer time to process new information that has extreme sentiment.

Behavioral response to information is what is happening here. Issues of herding, cross-validation, overreaction and underreaction, cognitive dissonance, and attention all come into play.

It is instructive to attempt realistic portfolio construction using only RNSE event data for extreme sentiment days. Of course, a serious portfolio manager would incorporate RNSE event data into her arsenal of other investment ideas and information sources, but it is instructive to see if even simple portfolio construction techniques using only news data can perform well.

6.7.2 Portfolio construction

We chose to consider an extreme sentiment day for a specific security in the S&P 1500 to be one on which there were at least four novel news items on the RNSE feed prior to 3 : 30 pm NYC time, which were (on average) extremely positive or negative (top 5% of average daily positivity or negativity). We made distributional observations between 2003 and 2005 regarding which sectors had the most predictable response to extreme RNSE events and thus restricted our investable universe to securities in the technology, industrials, health care, financials, or basic materials sectors. We assumed daily portfolio re-balancing, entering, and exiting positions at market close.

Positions were held for 20 days, subject to a stop loss rule set at 5% and a profit take rule set at 20%, and constrained the portfolio to be very loosely dollar- and beta-neutral, while allowing it to opportunistically take advantage of particularly positive or negative news regimes.

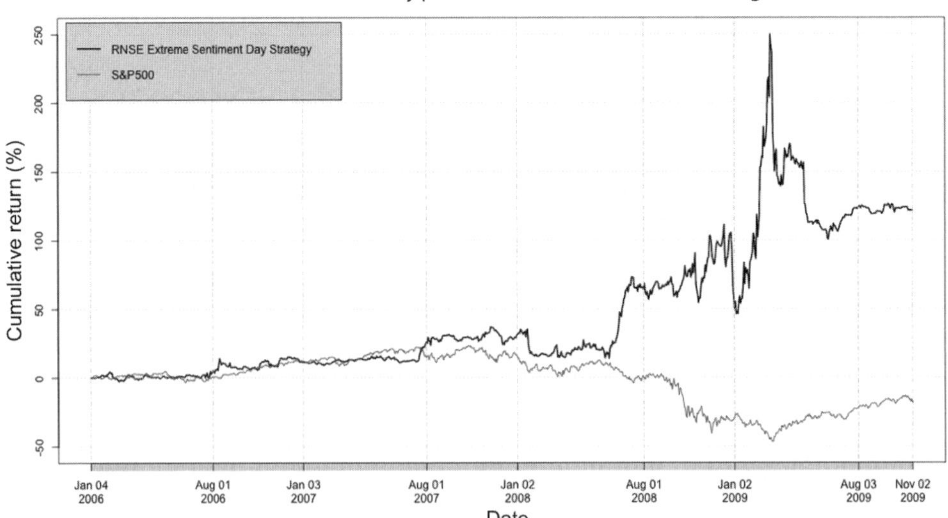

Figure 6.14. RNSE Extreme Sentiment Day portfolio cumulative return from January 2006 through November 2009, compared with the S&P 500.

Transaction costs were simulated at 25 basis points of slippage and commission for the combined entry and exit of each position. This figure was chosen based on contemporaneous reports of actual institutional stock transaction costs (including market impact) published by ITG and other brokers.

6.7.3 Performance

The portfolio performance relative to the S&P 500 is shown in Figure 6.14. It had an annualized Sharpe ratio of 0.76 after transaction costs. It showed extreme volatility between October 2008 and July 2009, but also performed extremely well in that period. The maximum drawdown was about 60%, and occurred between February and July 2009.

6.7.4 Monthly performance

The strategy was profitable in 24 out of 46 months, or about 52% of the time (details are in Figures 6.15 and 6.16).

	All months	Winning months	Losing months
% (number of months)	100% (36)	52% (24/46)	47.8% (22/46)
95% CI for returns	−43% to 48%	0% to 63%	−48% to 0%
Mean monthly return	1.74%	11%	−8.7%

Figure 6.15. Extreme sentiment simulation, monthly summary.

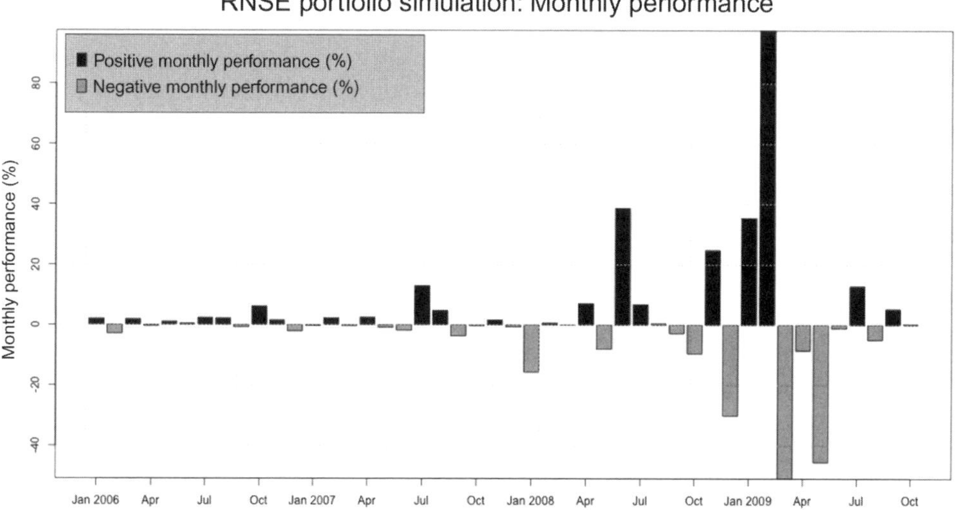

Figure 6.16. Monthly performance of the RNSE Extreme Sentiment Day strategy. Black bars are months showing a profit and grey bars are months showing a loss.

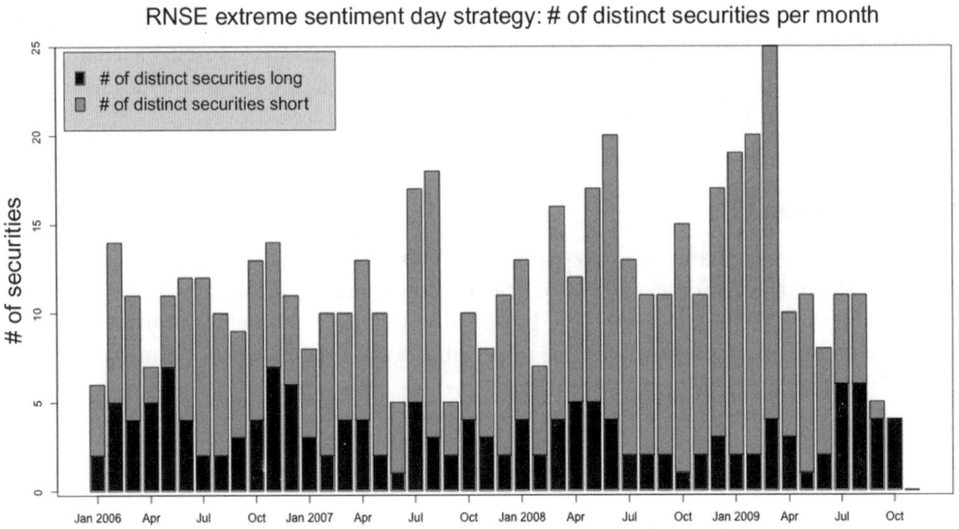

Figure 6.17. Number of distinct names held by the RNSE Extreme Sentiment Day strategy in any given month. Black bars are the number of names held long, and grey bars are the number of names held short.

6.7.5 Portfolio characteristics

Few firms have large amounts of novel, extremely polarized news. This strategy made active bets in 229 distinct securities selected from the S&P 1500. Details by month are seen in Figure 6.17.

During this period (2006–2009) it will be no surprise that there were many more stocks that experienced an extreme negative sentiment day than stocks that experienced an extreme positive sentiment day.

6.7.6 Return distribution

Figures 6.18 and 6.19 show the distributions of returns to positions based on extreme sentiment signals.

The portfolio is significantly impacted by the choice of stop loss. Many negative returns occur in excess of stop loss, due to trading at the close. Allowing intraday position exits would likely improve the stop loss rule significantly.

6.7.7 Portfolio beta and market correlation

Event-driven trading is inherently opportunistic. Our strategy is as well, reacting to days on which there is strongly positive or negative news by allocating the strategy to newsworthy securities. We constrained the portfolio to put no more than 15% of NAV into any position. As seen in Figure 6.20, the portfolio had a highly consistent short bias, but was profitable in both bull and bear market regimes. Daily beta (seen in Figure 6.21) ranged from approximately 0.5 to −2.5, averaging −0.8 over the period. The rolling one-quarter correlation of simulated portfolio returns with the S&P 500 are seen in Figure 6.22.

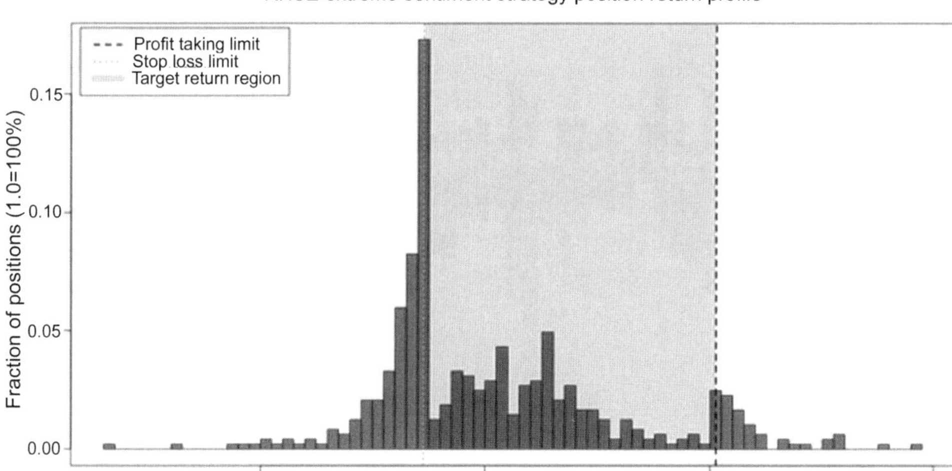

Figure 6.18. P/L of positions taken by the RNSE Extreme Sentiment Day strategy. The dotted lines denote the stop loss and profit-taking thresholds. The grey-highlighted region represents the area where this restricts returns.

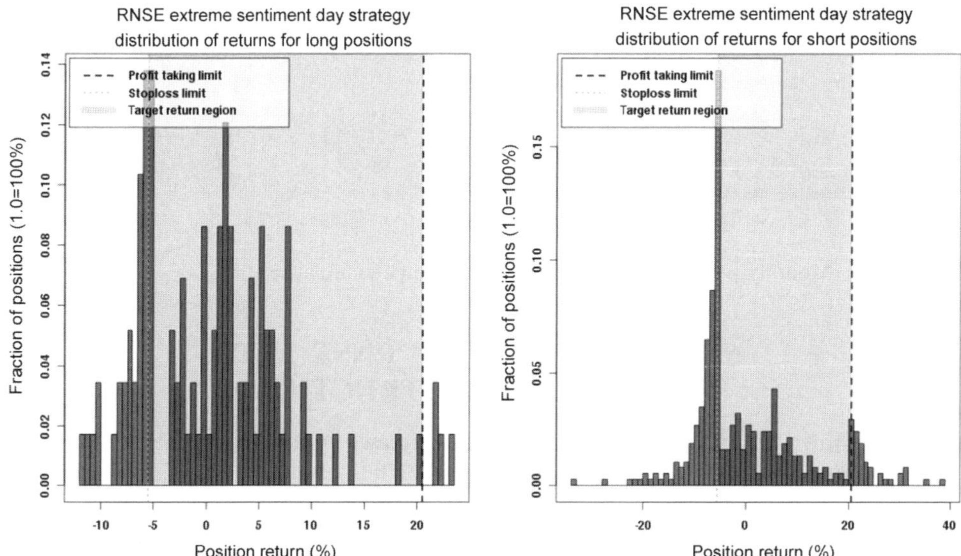

Figure 6.19. P/L of long and short positions taken by the RNSE Extreme Sentiment Day strategy. The dotted lines denote the stop loss and profit-taking thresholds. The grey-highlighted region represents the area where the current settings restrict returns.

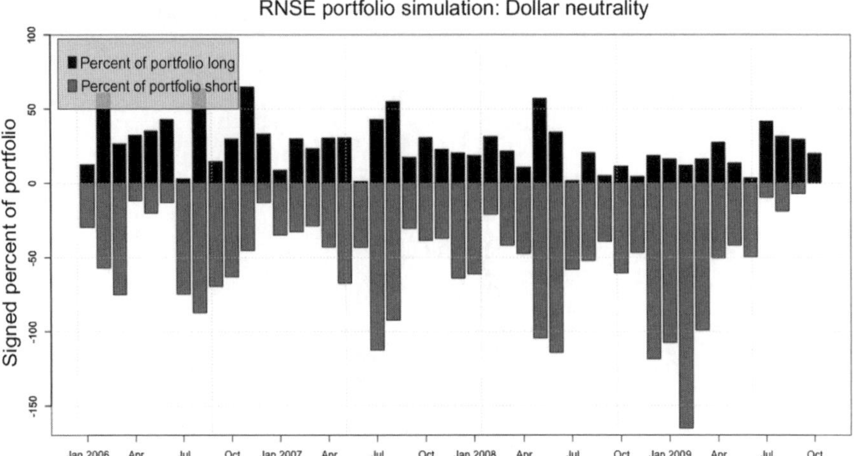

Figure 6.20. Monthly average percent of NAV long and short for extreme sentiment simulation.

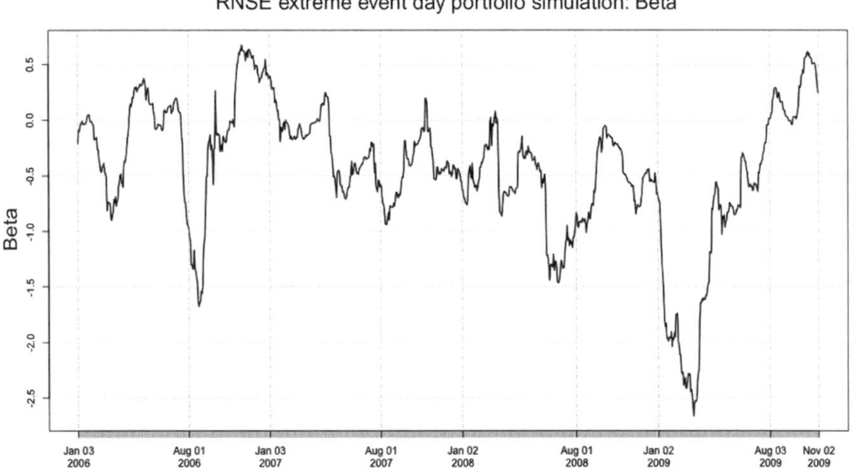

Figure 6.21. Monthly portfolio beta for extreme sentiment simulation.

6.8 DISCUSSION OF RNSE AND PORTFOLIO CONSTRUCTION

We have shown that it is possible to capitalize on news by looking at days on which a large amount of novel, very polar news occurs. The simulation is relatively unconstrained by the standards of institutional portfolios, to allow the signals to drive the process. Further increases in performance (and reductions in risk) can be implemented by

- *Incorporation of quantitative price, volatility, and volume analtyics* The human reaction to complicated, important news is conditioned by the market environment in

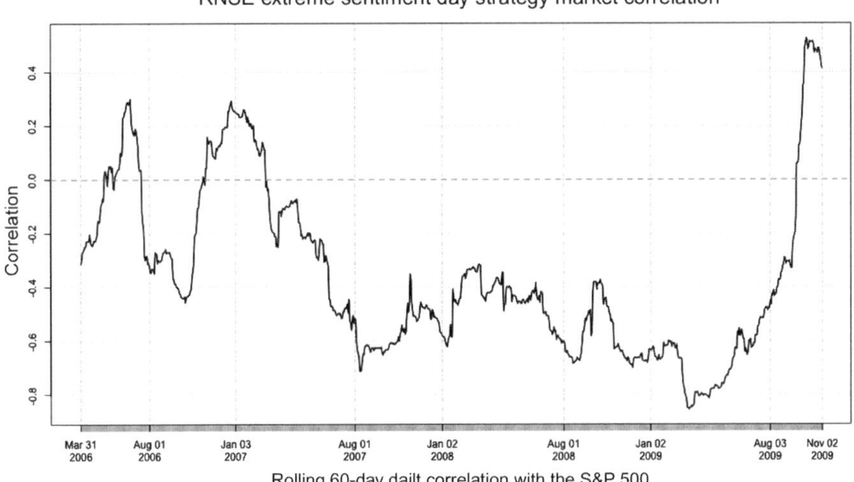

Figure 6.22. Rolling one-quarter correlation of extreme sentiment simulated portfolio with the S&P 500.

which the human is processing the information, often called "market color". Incorporating this information from "traditional" quant sources can only improve "quantextual" portfolios.

- *Further news differentiation* RNSE provides a very rich picture of the news as it is created and flows across the wire. Topic and product codes, headlines, and item types are probably all useful for differentiating news that presents an arbitrage opportunity from news that is merely stating prior price movements. There is also a great deal of information to be inferred from content, using either supervised (human in loop) or machine learning.
- *Higher frequency trading* The results here were on daily intervals. With "information leakage" a significant amount of alpha is lost within the trading day on which intraday news occurs. Intraday position entries and exits would allow for more opportunity for alpha capture. Furthermore, trading into a position over several hours rather than trading at or near the close should reduce transaction costs and increase capacity.
- *Pros and cons of optimizer-based portfolio construction* Creation of a forecast for excess return from news analytics and other information and feeding these forecasts into an optimizer would allow for fuller utilization of capital, and better position sizing, based on liquidity. It also allows for risk management based on sectors and factors. However, these constraints may limit exploitation of the signal. Given the types of bets the simulation has made, sector ETFs may be useful to include as an asset.

It is interesting to note that a research group at Deutsche Bank (Cahan et al., 2010) reported on a similar approach to equity portfolio management after this chapter was presented. They evaluate news strategies separately and in the context of a variety of quant approaches. Pure news portfolio simulations included in the Deutsche Bank work show positive results similar to ours, reflecting improvements in news processing in recent years.

6.9 SUMMARY AND AREAS FOR ADDITIONAL RESEARCH

We have shown that there is exploitable alpha in news. News analytics produce results superior to naive "buy on the good news, sell on bad" strategies. This is shown in both event studies and historical portfolio simulation.

6.9.1 Directions for future research. Is this just for quants?

The effect of these stringent filters is to reduce the firehose of news events to a much smaller flow of significant events. In this work, we have focused on quantitative machine-driven approaches using those events as signals.

Modern visualization and information extraction tools, relatives of the Event Study Explorer shown here, deliver this information in a way that is useful for judgment-driven fundamental investing as well. Protoype systems based on "sentiment indices" calculated across countries, sectors, capitalization classes, and styles can act as intelligence amplification (IA) tools for investors of all flavors.

In the quant sphere, this study has only scratched the surface of what can be done with the RNSE feed. Even restricting one's attention to "slow" alpha, accumulating over days to months, the RNSE feed provides an incredibly rich array of features from which to build detectors for longer term arbitrage opportunities.

Intentionally omitting portfolio construction techniques and "pre-news" analysis, the following are among the research projects that the authors find most compelling using RNSE output as source data:

- *Sentiment surprise* This study tallied days on which extreme sentiment occurred. A more sophisticated version would be to measure "surprise" extreme sentiment. Returning to the initial investment hypothesis that people take a long time to process complex and ambiguous new information, "surprise" sentiment changes should induce sufficient cognitive dissonance to justify a hunt for alpha. Looking at the strong sentiment of a firm that is very different from other firms in its peer group (by sector, industry, market, or even itself through time) is a natural next step.
- *Topic and product codes* RNSE aggregates news information from a wide variety of sources throughout the Thomson/Reuters organization. Furthermore, it provides a rich array of over 800 different human and machine-generated topic codes. It is a reasonable hypothesis that people pay more or less attention to more or less popular products, and have differing reactions to stories of differing product types.
- *Machine learning from streams of headlines* The headlines exposed by RNSE provide ample opportunity for supervised or online machine learning over streams of text using subsequent return, subsequent volatility, or subsequent analyst judgments as sources of labels.
- *Story linkage* RNSE output allows one to trace the evolution of a breaking news story as more information is learned and put out into the news stream. It seems reasonable to try to build classifiers for news that is self-consistent with respect to

bullish or bearish sentiment about a given stock, vs. news that induces confusion in its readers as it unfolds.

- *Intraday analysis* Preliminary work shows that many of these events are associated with price motion that can greatly enhance the implementation of investment ideas as a component of transaction cost control.
- *International markets* RNSE coverage is global. Preliminary event study results show similar patterns to those observed in the US.

6.10 ACKNOWLEDGMENTS

As those who have done this type of research well know, lining up and matching data from different sources over historical periods is a substantial task. We would like to thank Richard W. Brown, William Fang, Jason Sluciak and the Thomson Reuters Data Team for their excellent work in providing the data needed for this research, and for organizing symposia in this area.

We would also like to thank other participants in the news research symposia for helpful discussions; in particular, Andrew Lo from AlphaSimplex and MIT, and Paul Tetlock from Columbia.

In addition, we thank the anonymous reviewer for multiple helpful suggestions.

6.11 REFERENCES

Barber B.M.; Odean T. (2008) "All that glitters: The effect of attention and news on the buying behavior of individual and institutional investors," *Review of Financial Studies*, **21**, 785–818. Earlier version available at SSRN: `http://ssrn.com/abstract=460660` or `doi:10.2139/ssrn.460660`

Cahan R.; Luo Y.; Jussa J.; Alvarez M. (2010) *Beyond the Headlines: Using News Flow to Predict Stock Returns*, Deutsche Bank Quantitative Strategy Report, July. Email `Rochester.cahan@db.com`

Chan W.S. (2003) "Stock price reaction to news and no-news: Drift and reversal after headlines," *Journal of Financial Economics*, **70**, 223–260. Earlier version available at SSRN: `http://ssrn.com/abstract=262452` or doi:10.2139/ssrn.262452.

Leinweber D. (2009) *Nerds on Wall Street: Math, Machines and Wired Markets*, John Wiley & Sons, Chapters 9 and 10

Mitra L.; Mitra G.; diBartolomeo D. (2008) "Equity portfolio risk (volatility) estimation using market information and sentiment," December 1. Available at `http://papers.ssrn.com/sol3/papers.cfm?abstract_id=1425624`

Patton A.J.; Verardo M. (2009) "Does beta move with news? Firm-specific information flows and learning about profitability" (September). Available at SSRN: `http://ssrn.com/abstract=1361813`

RNSE (2008) *Reuters NewsScope Sentiment Engine: Guide to Sample Data and System Overview*, Thomson Reuters, V3.0, December.

Schneiderman B.; Plaisant C. (2009) *Designing the User Interface: Strategies for Effective Human-Computer Interaction* (Fifth Edition), Addison Wesley.

Ser-Huang Poon; Granger C. (2005) "Practical issues in forecasting volatility," *Financial Analysts Journal*, **61**(1), 45ff.

Tetlock P.; Saar-Tsechansky M.; Macskassy S. (2008) "More than words: Quantifying language (in news) to measure firms' fundamentals," *Journal of Finance*, **63**(June), 1437–1467. Earlier version available at SSRN: http://ssrn.com/abstract=923911

Tufte E.R. (2001) *Visual Display of Quantitative Information* (Second Edition), Graphics Press. Available at http://www.edwardtufte.com/tufte/books_vdqi

Tukey J.W. (1977) *Exploratory Data Analysis*, Addison-Wesley, Reading, MA.

7

All that glitters: The effect of attention and news on the buying behavior of individual and institutional investors

Brad M. Barber and Terrance Odean

A different version of this chapter originally appeared in *The Review of Financial Studies*, 2008, **21**(2), 785–818. The current version includes additional material examining the asset-pricing implications of our model of attention-based buying but does not include the theoretical model from the appendix of the original paper.

ABSTRACT

Attention is a scarce resource. When there are many alternatives, choices that attract attention are more likely to be chosen. If the salient attributes of a choice are critical to our utility, attention serves us well. If not, attention may lead to suboptimal choices. In this chapter, we test the proposition that individual investors are more likely to buy, rather than sell, those stocks that catch their attention. We posit that this is so because attention affects buying behavior more than selling. When choosing which common stocks to buy, investors face a huge search problem. There are thousands of possibilities. It is impossible—without the aid of a computer—for most investors to evaluate the merits of every available common stock. When selling, however, most investors consider only stocks they already own. These are typically few in number and can be considered one by one. While each investor does not buy every single stock that grabs his attention, individual investors are more likely to buy attention-grabbing stocks than to sell them. In contrast, institutional investors have more resources with which to search for stocks. Furthermore, the search for stocks to purchase and stocks to sell is more symmetrical for institutional investors because they hold large portfolios from which to sell and they often sell short. We look at three proxies for how likely stocks are to catch investors' attention: daily abnormal trading volume, daily returns, and daily news. We calculate net buy–sell imbalances for more than 66,000 individual investors with accounts at a large discount brokerage, 647,000 individual investors with accounts at a large retail brokerage, 14,000 individual investor accounts at a small discount brokerage, and 43 professional money managers. Individual investors tend to be net purchasers of stocks

The Handbook of News Analytics in Finance Edited by L. Mitra and G. Mitra

on high-attention days—days that those stocks experience high abnormal trading volume, days following extreme price moves, and days on which stocks are in the news. Institutional investors are more likely to be net buyers on days with low abnormal trading volume than on those with high abnormal trading volume. Their reaction to extreme price moves depends on their investment style. We present empirical evidence that the collective tendency of individual investors to more aggressively buy than sell attention-grabbing stocks leads to poor subsequent returns for aggressively purchased stocks.

You have time to read only a limited number of research papers. How did you choose to read this chapter? Investors have time to weigh the merits of only a limited number of stocks. Why do they consider some stocks and not others?

In making a decision, we first select which options to consider and then decide which of those options to choose. Attention is a scarce resource. When there are many alternatives, options that attract attention are more likely to be considered, hence more likely to be chosen, while options that do not attract attention are often ignored. If the salient attributes of an option are critical to our utility, attention may serve us well. If not, attention may lead to suboptimal choices. In this chapter, we test the proposition that individual investors are more likely to buy rather than sell those stocks that catch their attention. We posit that this is so because attention affects buying (where investors search across thousands of stocks) more than selling (where investors generally choose only from the few stocks that they own). While each investor does not buy every single stock that grabs his attention, individual investors are more likely to buy attention-grabbing stocks than to sell them. We provide strong evidence that this is the case.

In contrast to our findings, many theoretical models of financial markets treat buying and selling as two sides of the same coin. Informed investors observe the same signal whether they are deciding to buy or to sell. They are equally likely to sell securities with negative signals as they are to buy those with positive signals. Uninformed noise traders are equally likely to make random purchases or random sales. In formal models, the decisions to buy and to sell often differ only by a minus sign.[1] For actual investors, the decisions to buy and to sell are fundamentally different.

When buying a stock, investors are faced with a formidable search problem. There are thousands of common stocks from which to choose. Human beings have bounded rationality. There are cognitive and temporal limits to how much information we can process. We are generally not able to rank hundreds, much less thousands, of alternatives. Doing so is even more difficult when the alternatives differ on multiple dimensions. One way to make the search for stocks to purchase more manageable is to limit the choice set. It is far easier, for example, to choose among 10 alternatives than 100.

Odean (1999) proposes that investors manage the problem of choosing among thousands of possible stock purchases by limiting their search to stocks that have recently caught their attention. Investors do not buy all stocks that catch their attention; however, for the most part, they only buy stocks that do so. Which attention-grabbing stocks investors buy will depend upon their personal preferences. Contrarian investors, for example, will tend to buy out-of-favor stocks that catch their eye, while momentum investors will chase recent performers.

[1] For example, see the well-cited models of Grossman and Stiglitz (1980) and Kyle (1985).

While, in theory, investors face the same search problem when selling as when buying, in practice, two factors mitigate the search problem for individual investors when they want to sell. First, most individual investors hold relatively few common stocks in their portfolio.[2] Second, most individual investors sell only stocks that they already own—that is, they don't sell short.[3] Thus, investors can, one by one, consider the merits—both economic and emotional—of selling each stock they own. Rational investors are likely to sell their past losers, thereby postponing taxes; behaviorally motivated investors are likely to sell past winners, thereby postponing the regret associated with realizing a loss (see Shefrin and Statman, 1985); thus, to a large extent, while individual investors are concerned about the future returns of the stocks they buy, they focus on the past returns of the stocks they sell.

Our argument that attention is a major factor determining the stocks individual investors buy, but not those they sell, does not apply with equal force to institutional investors. There are two reasons for this: (1) Unlike individual investors, institutions often face a significant search problem when selling. Institutional investors, such as hedge funds, routinely sell short. For these investors, the search set for purchases and sales is identical. And even institutions that do not sell short face far more choices when selling than do most individuals, simply because they own many more stocks than do most individuals. (2) Attention is not as scarce a resource for institutional investors as it is for individuals. Institutional investors devote more time to searching for stocks to buy and sell than do most individuals. Institutions use computers to narrow their search. They may limit their search to stocks in a particular sector (e.g., biotech) or meeting specific criteria (e.g., low price-to-earnings ratio), thus reducing attention demands. Though individuals, too, can use computers or pre-selection criteria, on average they are less likely to do so.

In this chapter, we test the hypotheses that (1) the buying behavior of individual investors is more heavily influenced by attention than is their selling behavior and that (2) the buying behavior of individual investors is more heavily influenced by attention than is the buying behavior of professional investors. We also test the asset-pricing predictions of a model based on the assumption that attention influences buying more than selling. These predictions are (1) that stocks heavily purchased by attention-based investors will subsequently underperform stocks heavily sold by those investors and (2) that this underperformance will be greatest following periods of high attention.

How can we measure the extent to which a stock grabs investors' attention? A direct measure would be to go back in time and, each day, question the hundreds of thousands of investors in our datasets as to which stocks they thought about that day. Since we cannot measure the daily attention paid to stocks directly, we do so indirectly. We focus on three observable measures that are likely to be associated with attention-grabbing events: news, unusual trading volume, and extreme returns. While none of these measures is a perfect proxy for attention, all three are useful.

An attention-grabbing event is likely to be reported in the news. Investors' attention could be attracted through other means, such as chat rooms or word of mouth, but an event that attracts the attention of many investors is usually newsworthy. However,

---

[2] During our sample period, the mean household in our large discount brokerage dataset held a monthly average of 4.3 stocks worth $47,334; the median household held a monthly average of 2.61 stocks worth $16,210.

[3] For the investors in the large discount brokerage dataset that we describe in Section 7.2, 0.29% of positions are short. When the positions are weighted by their value, 0.78% are short.

news stories are not all created equal. Major network reporting of the indictment of a Fortune 500 CEO will attract the attention of millions of investors, while a routine company press release may be noticed by few. Our historical news data—from the Dow Jones News Service—do not tell us how many investors read each story, nor do they rank each story's importance. We infer the reach and impact of events by observing their effects on trading volume and returns.

Trading volume in the firm's stock is likely to be greater than usual when news about a firm reaches many investors. Of course, this won't necessarily be the case. Investors will possibly recognize this news to be irrelevant to the firm's future earnings and not trade, or investors will all interpret the news similarly and not trade. But significant news will often affect investors' beliefs and portfolio goals heterogeneously, resulting in more investors trading than is usual. If an unusual number of investors trade a stock, it is nearly tautological that an unusual number are paying attention to that stock. But high abnormal trading volume could also be driven by the liquidity or information-based trades of a few large investors. Our results are as strong, or stronger, for large-capitalization stocks. Unusual trading volume for these stocks is unlikely to be driven by only a few investors. Therefore, large trades by a few investors may add noise to our calculations but are unlikely to be driving the results.

Important news about a firm often results in significant positive or negative returns. Some news may be difficult to interpret and result in unusually active trading without much price change. But when there is a big price move, it is likely that whatever caused the move also caught investors' attention. And even when price is responding to private, not public, information, significant returns will often, in and of themselves, attract attention.

Our three proxies for whether investors were paying attention to a firm are: (1) a stock's abnormal daily trading volume, (2) the stock's (previous) 1-day return,[4] and (3) whether the firm appeared in that day's news. We examine the buying and selling behavior associated with attention for four samples of investors:

- investors with accounts at a large discount brokerage;
- investors at a smaller discount brokerage firm that advertises its trade execution quality;
- investors with accounts at a large retail brokerage; and
- professional money managers.

Our prediction is that individual investors will actively buy stocks on high-attention days. We are not predicting that they will actively trade on high-attention days—that would hardly be surprising when we use abnormal trading volume as a proxy for attention—but, rather, that they will be net buyers.

For every buyer, there must be a seller. Therefore, on days when attention-driven investors are buying, some investors, whose purchases are less dependent on attention, must be selling. We anticipate therefore that professional investors as a whole (inclusive of market-makers) will exhibit a lower tendency to buy, rather than sell, on high-attention days and a reverse tendency on low-attention days. (Exceptions will arise

[4] We use previous-day return, rather than same-day return, because of potential endogeneity problems. While we argue that extreme price moves will attract buyers, clearly buyers could also cause price moves. Our results are qualitatively similar when we use same-day returns as a proxy for attention.

when the event driving attention coincides with the purchase criteria that a particular professional investor is pursuing.)

As predicted, individual investors tend to be net buyers on high-attention days. For example, investors at the large discount brokerage make nearly twice as many purchases as sales of stocks experiencing unusually high trading volume (e.g., the highest 5%)[5] and nearly twice as many purchases as sales of stocks with an extremely poor return (lowest 5%) the previous day. The buying behavior of the professionals is least influenced by attention.

The plan of the chapter is as follows. We discuss related research in Section 7.1. We describe the four datasets in Section 7.2 and our sorting methodology in Section 7.3. We present evidence of attention-driven buying in Section 7.4 and discuss an alternative hypothesis in Section 7.5. We conclude in Section 7.6.

7.1 RELATED RESEARCH

A number of recent studies examine investor trading decisions. Odean (1998a) finds that, as predicted by Shefrin and Statman (1985), individual investors exhibit a disposition effect—investors tend to sell their winning stocks and hold on to their losers. Both individual and professional investors have been found to behave similarly with several types of assets including real estate (Genesove and Mayer, 2001), company stock options (Heath, Huddart, and Lang, 1999), and futures (Heisler, 1994; Locke and Mann, 2000; also see Shapira and Venezia, 2001).

It is well documented that volume increases on days with information releases or large price moves (Bamber, Barron, and Stober, 1997; Karpoff, 1987). For example, when Maria Bartiromo mentions a stock during the *Midday Call* on CNBC, volume in the stock increases nearly fivefold (on average) in the minutes following the mention (Busse and Green, 2002). Yet, for every buyer, there is a seller. In general, these studies do not investigate who is buying and who is selling, which is the focus of our analysis. One exception is Lee (1992). He examines trading activity around earnings announcements for 230 stocks over a 1-year period. He finds that small traders—those who place market orders of less than $10,000—are net buyers subsequent to both positive and negative earnings surprises. Hirshleifer et al. (2003) document that individual investors are net buyers following *both* positive and negative earnings surprises. Lee (1992) conjectures that news may attract investors' attention or, alternatively, that retail brokers—who tend to make more buy than sell recommendations—may routinely contact their clients around the time of earnings announcements. In a recent paper, Huo, Peng, and Xiong (2006) argue that high individual investor attention can exacerbate price overreactions in up markets while attenuating underreactions to events such as earnings reports.

Odean (1999) examines trading records of investors at a large discount brokerage firm. He finds that, on average, the stocks these investors buy underperform those they sell, even before considering transactions costs. He observes that these investors buy stocks that have experienced greater absolute price changes over the previous two years than the stocks they sell. He points out the search problem individual investors face when choosing from among thousands of stocks and the disparity between buying and

[5] Looking at all common stock transactions, investors at this brokerage make slightly more purchases (1,082,107) than sales (887,594).

selling decisions for individual investors. He suggests that many investors limit their search to stocks that have recently captured their attention, with contrarians buying previous losers and trend chasers buying previous winners.

Of course, fully rational investors will recognize the limitations of buying predominantly stocks that catch their attention. They will realize that the information associated with an attention-grabbing event may already be impounded into price (since the event has undoubtedly been noticed by others), that the attention-grabbing event may not be relevant to future performance, and that non-attention-grabbing stocks may present better purchase opportunities. Odean (1998b) argues that many investors trade too much because they are overconfident about the quality of their information. Such investors may overvalue the importance of events that catch their attention, thus leading them to trade suboptimally. Odean (1999) and Barber and Odean (2000, 2001, 2002) find that, on average, self-directed individual investors do trade suboptimally, lowering their expected returns through excessive trading.

In recent work, Seasholes and Wu (2004) test our theory in a unique out-of-sample setting. They observe that on the Shanghai Stock Exchange individual investors are net buyers the day after a stock hits an upper price limit. Furthermore, they document that a higher percentage of purchases is made by first-time buyers on price limit days than on other days. Seasholes and Wu's interpretation of this behavior is that the attention of individual investors, especially first-time buyers, is attracted by the event of hitting a price limit and, consistent with our theory, individuals become net buyers of stocks that catch their attention. Also consistent with our theory, Seasholes and Wu document a transitory impact on prices with reversion to pre-event levels within 10 trading days. Finally, they identify a small group of professional investors who profit—at the expense of individual investors—by anticipating this temporary surge in price and demand.

Our analysis focuses on investor trading patterns over 1-day periods. With our proxies for attention, we try to identify days on which an unusual event appears to have attracted investors' attention to a particular firm's stock. Like unusual events, advertising may also increase investors' awareness of a firm. Grullon, Kanatas, and Weston (2004) document that firms that spend more on advertising have a larger number of individual and institutional investors. They argue that a firm's advertising increases investors' familiarity with the firm and that investors are more likely to own familiar firms. Their paper differs from our chapter in many respects. They look at annual advertising budgets; we identify daily attention-grabbing events. They focus on dispersion of ownership; we, on daily trading patterns. Both articles are consistent with a common story in which investors are more likely to buy—and therefore own—stocks that have attracted their attention, whether through unusual events or extensive advertising.

Gervais, Kaniel, and Mingelgrin (2001) find that stocks experiencing unusually high trading volume over a day or a week tend to appreciate over the following month. Citing Miller (1977) and Mayshar (1983), they argue that the holders of a stock will tend to be those who are most optimistic about its prospects and that, given institutional constraints on short-selling, any increase in the set of potential owners (potential buyers) should result in a price increase. The increased visibility of a stock associated with high trading volume increases the set of potential owners (buyers) but not of potential sellers, resulting in a price increase.

Alternatively, Merton (1987) notes that individual investors tend to hold only a few different common stocks in their portfolios. He points out that gathering information on stocks requires resources and suggests that investors conserve these resources by actively following only a few stocks. If investors behave this way, they will buy and sell only those stocks that they actively follow. They will not impulsively buy stocks that they do not follow simply because those stocks happen to catch their attention. Thus their purchases will not be biased toward attention-grabbing stocks.

While Grullon, Kanatas, and Weston (2004) focus on the number of individuals and institutions that own a stock and Gervais, Kaniel, and Mingelgrin (2001) focus on returns subsequent to high (or low) volume periods, our principal empirical focus is on the effect of attention on the imbalance in the number of purchases and sales of a stock by individual investors. Our empirical finding that individual investors are net buyers of attention-grabbing stocks is largely consistent with the empirical results in Grullon, Kanatas, and Weston (2004). This finding is also consistent with the story of Gervais, Kaniel, and Mingelgrin (2001) that increased visibility of a stock may attract new investors. In addition to the effects of attention driven by short-sale constraints and described by Miller (1977) and Mayshar (1983), we argue that for individual investors, the search problem when buying a stock is much greater than when selling. Thus, attention affects even the buy–sell imbalances of investors who already own a stock.

7.2 DATA

In this study, we analyze investor trading data drawn from four sources: a large discount brokerage, a small discount brokerage, a large full-service brokerage, and the Plexus Group (a consulting firm that tracks the trading of professional money managers for institutional clients).

The first dataset for this research was provided by a large discount brokerage firm. It includes trading and position records for the investments of 78,000 households from January 1991 through December 1996.[6] The data include all accounts opened by each household at this discount brokerage firm. Sampled households were required to have an open account with the discount brokerage firm during 1991. Roughly half of the accounts in our analysis were opened prior to 1987, and half were opened between 1987 and 1991.

In this research, we focus on investors' common stock purchases and sales. We exclude from the current analysis investments in mutual funds (both open-end and closed-end), American depository receipts (ADRs), warrants, and options. Of the 78,000 households sampled from the large discount brokerage, 66,465 had positions in common stocks during at least one month; the remaining accounts held either cash or investments in other than individual common stocks. Roughly 60% of the market value in these households' accounts was held in common stocks. There were more than 3 million trades in all securities; common stocks accounted for slightly more than 60% of all trades. In December 1996, these households held more than $4.5bn in common stock. There were slightly more purchases (1,082,107) than sales (887,594) during our sample period, though the average value of stocks sold ($13,707) was slightly higher than the value of stocks purchased ($11,205). As a result, the aggregate values of

[6] Position records are through December 1996; trading records are through November 1996. See Barber and Odean (2000) for a more compete description of these data.

purchases and sales were roughly equal ($12.1bn and $12.2bn, respectively). The average trade was transacted at a price of $31 per share. The value of trades and the transaction price of trades are positively skewed; the medians for both purchases and sales are substantially less than the mean values.

Our second dataset contains information from a smaller discount brokerage firm. This firm emphasizes high-quality trade execution in its marketing and is likely to appeal to more sophisticated, more active investors. The data include daily trading records from January 1996 through June 15, 1999. Accounts classified by the brokerage firm as professional are excluded from our analysis.[7] The data include 14,667 accounts for individual investors who make 214,273 purchases with a mean value of $55,077 and 198,541 sales with a mean value of $55,999.

The third dataset contains information from a large retail brokerage firm on the investments of households for the 30 months ending in June 1999. These data include daily trading records. Using client ownership codes supplied by the brokerage firm, we limit our analysis to the 665,533 investors with non-discretionary accounts (i.e., accounts classified as individual, joint tenants with rights of survival, or custodian for minor) with at least one common stock trade during our sample period. During this period these accounts executed more than 10 million trades. We restrict our analysis to their common stock trades: 3,974,998 purchases with a mean value of $15,209 and 3,219,299 sales with a mean value of $21,169.[8]

Our individual investor data include tens of thousands of investors at both discount and retail brokerages. These data are likely to be fairly representative of US individual investors.[9] Our institutional data, however, are more illustrative than representative of institutional investors. The data were compiled by the Plexus Group as part of their advisory services for their institutional clients. The data include daily trading records for 43 institutional money managers and span the period January 1993 through March 1996. Not all managers are in the sample for the entire period. In addition to documenting completed purchases and sales, the data also report the date and time at which the manager decided to make a purchase or sale. In the data, these money managers are classified as "momentum", "value", and "diversified."[10] During our sample period, the 18 momentum managers make 789,779 purchases with a mean value of $886,346 and 617,915 sales with a mean value of $896,165; the 11 value managers make 409,532 purchases with a mean value of $500,949 and 350,200 sales with a mean value of

[7] We analyze the accounts of professional investors separately. There are, however, only 159 professional traders in these data, and we do not observe clear patterns in their buy–sell imbalances.

[8] Barber, Odean, and Zhu (2006) analyze the correlation of the first and third broker datasets with trades in the TAQ/ISSM database. Specifically, in the TAQ/ISSM data, they identify small trades (less than $5,000 in 1991 dollars) that are buyer-initiated and seller-initiated. They then calculate the monthly buy–sell imbalance for each stock/month using these trades. In each month with overlapping data, they calculate the cross-sectional correlation between the buy–sell imbalance of small trades on the TAQ database and the buy–sell imbalance of the broker data. For the large discount broker the mean correlation is 55%. For the large retail broker the mean correlation is 43%.

[9] Wolff (2004) reports that over one-third of stock ownership—including direct ownership of shares and indirect ownership through mutual funds, trusts, and retirement accounts—of US households is concentrated in the wealthiest 1% of households. The portfolios of extremely wealthy families are unlikely to appear in our sample and constitute a third class of investors in addition to ordinary individuals and institutional investors. The portfolios of wealthy families are usually professionally managed and, as such, we would expect them to be traded more like institutional portfolios than like the portfolios of ordinary individual investors.

[10] Keim and Madhavan (1995, 1997, 1998) analyze earlier data from the Plexus Group. They classify managers as "technical", "value", and "index". Based on conversations with the Plexus Group, we believe that these classifications correspond to our "momentum", "value", and "diversified" classifications.

\$564,692; the 14 diversified managers make 312,457 purchases with a mean value of \$450,474 and 202,147 sales with a mean value of \$537,947.

7.3 SORT METHODOLOGY

7.3.1 Volume sorts

On the days when a stock experiences abnormally heavy volume, it is likely that investors are paying more attention to it than usual. We wish to test the extent to which the tendency to buy stocks increases on days of unusually high trading volume for each of our four investor groups (large discount, retail, small discount, and professional). First, we must sort stocks on the basis of abnormal trading volume. We do so by calculating for each stock on each trading day the ratio of the stock's trading volume that day to its average trading volume over the previous year (i.e., 252 trading days). Thus, we define abnormal trading volume for stock i on day t, AV_{it} to be

$$AV_{it} = \frac{V_{it}}{\overline{V}_{it}} \tag{7.1}$$

where V_{it} is the dollar volume for stock i traded on day t as reported in the Center for Research in Security Prices (CRSP) daily stock return files for New York Stock Exchange (NYSE), American Stock Exchange (ASE), and NASDAQ stocks and

$$\overline{V}_{it} = \sum_{d=t-252}^{t-1} \frac{V_{id}}{252}. \tag{7.2}$$

Each day we sort stocks into deciles on the basis of that day's abnormal trading volume.[11] We further subdivide the decile of stocks with the greatest abnormal trading volume into two vingtiles (i.e., 5% partitions). Then, for each of our investor types, we sum the buys (B) and sells (S) of stocks in each volume partition on day t and calculate the buy–sell imbalance for purchases and sales executed that day as:

$$BSI_{pt} = \frac{\sum_{i=1}^{n_{pt}} NB_{it} - \sum_{i=1}^{n_{pt}} NS_{it}}{\sum_{i=1}^{n_{pt}} NB_{it} + \sum_{i=1}^{n_{pt}} NS_{it}} \tag{7.3}$$

where n_{pt} is the number of stocks in partition p on day t, NB_{it} is the number of purchases of stock i on day t, and NS_{it} is the number of sales of stock i on day t. We calculate the time-series mean of the daily buy–sell imbalances (BSI_{pt}) for the days that we have trading data for each investor type. Note that throughout the chapter our measure of

[11] In auxiliary analyses, we calculate volume partitions that use (1) the measure of abnormal volume employed by Gervais, Kaniel, and Mingelgrin (2001) and (2) a standardized measure of abnormal volume: $(V - \overline{V})/\sigma$, where V is volume on day t, $\overline{V}$ is mean volume over the prior 252 trading days, and σ is the standard deviation of volume over the prior 252 trading days. We also analyzed abnormal volume measures as the ratio of volume on day t to mean volume over the prior 50 days. All alternative measures of abnormal volume generate buy–sell imbalance patterns that are very similar to those using our simple measure of buy–sell imbalance: $(V/\overline{V})$. These results are available from the authors at `http://faculty.haas.berkeley.edu/odean/attention.html`

buy–sell imbalance considers only executed trades; limit orders are counted if and when they execute. If there are fewer than five trades in a partition on a particular day, that day is excluded from the time-series average for that partition. We also calculate buy–sell imbalances based on the value rather than number of trades by substituting in the value of the stock i bought (or sold) on day t for NB_{it} (or NS_{it}) in equation (7.3). Note that as trading volume increases, aggregate buying and selling will increase equally. Thus, the aggregate value-weighted (executed) buy–sell imbalance of all investors remains zero as abnormal volume increases, but how the buy–sell imbalance of a particular investor group changes with volume is an empirical question.

In summary, for each partition and investor group combination, we construct a time-series of daily buy–sell imbalances. Our inferences are based on the mean and standard deviation of the time-series. We calculate the standard deviation of the time-series using a Newey–West correction for serial dependence.

7.3.2 Returns sorts

Investors are likely to notice when stocks have extreme 1-day returns. Such returns, whether positive or negative, often will be associated with news about the firm. The news driving the extreme performance will catch the attention of some investors, while the extreme return itself will catch the attention of others. Even in the absence of other information, extreme returns can become news themselves. The *Wall Street Journal* and other media routinely report the previous day's big gainers and losers (subject to certain price criteria). If big price changes catch investors' attention, then we expect that those investors whose buying behavior is most influenced by attention will tend to purchase in response to price changes—both positive and negative. To test the extent to which each of our four investor groups are net purchasers of stocks in response to large price moves, we sort stocks based on 1-day returns and then calculate average buy–sell imbalances for the following day. We calculate imbalances for the day following the extreme returns, rather than the same day as extreme returns, for two reasons. First, many investors may learn of—or react to—the extreme return only after the market closes; their first opportunity to respond will be the next trading day. Second, buy–sell imbalances could cause contemporaneous price changes. Thus, examining buy–sell imbalances subsequent to returns removes a potential endogeneity problem.[12] Our results are qualitatively similar when we sort on same-day returns.

For each day $(t-1)$, we sort all stocks for which returns are reported in the CRSP NYSE/AMEX/NASDAQ daily returns file into 10 deciles based on the 1-day return. We further split decile 1 (lowest returns) and decile 10 (highest returns) into two vingtiles. We then calculate the time-series mean of the daily buy–sell imbalances for

[12] Endogeneity does not pose the same problem for news and abnormal volume sorts. It is unlikely that the percentage of individual investors' (or institutional investors') trades that consists of purchases causes contemporaneous news stories. Nor is it likely that the percentage of individual investors' (or institutional investors') trades that consists of purchases causes abnormal trading volume. As a robustness check on the latter point, we replicate our results by calculating abnormal volume on day t and analyzing buy–sell imbalance on day $t+1$. Our results are qualitatively similar to those reported in this chapter and are available from the authors at `http://faculty.haas.berkeley.edu/odean/attention.html`

each partition on the day following the return sort. This calculation is analogous to that for our sorts based on abnormal volume.[13]

7.3.3 News sorts

Firms that are in the news are more likely to catch investors' attention than those that are not. Our news dataset is the daily newsfeed from Dow Jones News Service for the period 1994 to 1999. The Dow Jones newsfeed includes the ticker symbols for each firm mentioned in each article. We partition stocks into those for which there is a news story that day and those with no news. On an average day, our dataset records no news for 91% of the firms in the CRSP database. Due to how the data were collected and stored, some days are missing from the data. We calculate the buy–sell imbalances for each firm's stock as described in Section 7.3.1. News is a primary mechanism for catching investors' attention. Nonetheless, our empirical tests based on news coverage lack the power of our volume and return sorts because we are unable to measure accurately the intensity or salience of news coverage, and we are missing news coverage data for much of our sample period.

It is worth noting that none of our proxies for attention is perfect. Some stocks appear in our news database because of news stories about significant attention-grabbing events; others appear simply because of routine company press releases. Similarly, abnormally high trading volume may be associated with active trading and attention of individual investors, or it may occur because institutional investors transact large trades with each other on days when individuals are not particularly attending to a stock. And large 1-day price moves may be driven by attention-grabbing events, but they may also result from temporary liquidity shortages caused by an institutional investor selling or purchasing a large position. If our proxies identify attention-grabbing events much, or most, of the time, then in aggregate we expect individual investors to be on the buy side of the market on high-attention days as identified by our proxies.

7.4 RESULTS

7.4.1 Volume sorts

Trading volume is one indicator of the attention a stock is receiving. Table 7.1 presents buy–sell imbalances for stocks sorted on the current day's abnormal trading volume. Buy–sell imbalances are reported for investors at a large discount brokerage, a large retail brokerage, a small discount brokerage, and for institutional money managers

[13] Typically a significant number of stocks have a return equal to zero on day $t-1$. These stocks may span more than one partition. Therefore, before calculating the buy–sell imbalance for each partition, we first calculate the average number (and value) of purchases and sales of stocks with returns of zero on day $t-1$; in subsequent calculations, we use this average number (and value) of purchases and sales for zero-return stocks. The average number of purchases on day t of a stock with a return of zero on day $t-1$ is

$$\sum_{s=1}^{S_0} \frac{NB_{st}}{S_0},$$

where NB_{st} is the number of times stock s was purchased by investors in the dataset on day t, and S_0 is the number of stocks with a return of zero on day $t-1$. Similar calculations are done to determine the average number of sales and the average value of purchases and sales for stocks with a return of zero on day $t-1$. We also have replicated our results using standardized returns. Specifically, on each day, we calculate $(R)/\sigma$, the daily return on day t divided by the standard deviation of the firm's daily return from $t-252$ to $t-1$. Results using the standardized measure of returns are similar to those reported in this chapter and are available from the authors at http://faculty.haas.berkeley.edu/odean/attention.html

Table 7.1. Buy–sell Imbalances by investor type for stocks sorted on the current day's abnormal trading volume. Stocks are sorted daily into deciles on the basis on the current day''s abnormal volume. The decile of highest abnormal volume is split into two vingtiles (10a and 10b). Abnormal volume is calculated as the ratio of the current day's volume (as reported in the CRSP daily stock return files for NYSE, ASE, and NASDAQ stocks) divided by the average volume over the previous 252 trading days. Buy–sell imbalances are reported for the trades of six groups of investors, investors at large discount brokerage (January 1991 through November 1996), investors at a large retail brokerage (January 1997 through June 1999), investors at a small discount brokerage (January 1996 through June 15, 1999), and institutional money managers (January 1993 through March 1996) classified by the Plexus Group as following momentum, value, and diversified strategies. For each day/partition/investor group, we calculate number imbalance as number of purchases minus number of sales divided by total number of trades. Value imbalance is calculated as the value of purchases minus the value of sales divided by the total value of trades. The table reports the mean for each time series of daily imbalances for a particular investor group and partition. Standard errors, calculated using a Newey–West correction for serial dependence, appear in parentheses.

	Large discount brokerage		Large retail brokerage		Small discount brokerage		Momentum managers		Value managers		Diversified managers	
Decile	Number imbalance	Value imbalance	Number imbalance	Value imbalance	Number imbalance	Value imbalance	Number imbalance	Value imbalance	Number imbalance	Value imbalance	Number imbalance	Value imbalance
1[a]	−18.15	−16.28	−25.26	−21.26	−20.49	−22.70	14.68	13.74	34.57	33.99	12.52	17.10
	(0.98)	(1.37)	(2.11)	(1.60)	(3.41)	(3.88)	(1.76)	(2.26)	(5.54)	(6.45)	(2.42)	(2.91)
2	−8.90	−11.32	−18.78	−20.63	−10.31	−11.02	12.13	11.09	15.20	13.63	14.87	15.06
	(0.65)	(0.98)	(1.23)	(1.30)	(2.30)	(2.47)	(1.07)	(1.44)	(2.35)	(2.91)	(1.62)	(1.97)
3	−6.23	−9.49	−15.16	−19.59	−6.95	−7.76	11.38	10.35	10.95	8.43	15.83	11.84
	(0.52)	(0.84)	(1.18)	(1.18)	(1.47)	(1.90)	(0.85)	(1.15)	(1.49)	(1.93)	(1.28)	(1.65)
4	−2.76	−8.70	−10.11	−20.07	−4.92	−5.91	12.19	11.89	10.02	4.37	14.92	8.23
	(0.45)	(0.73)	(0.99)	(1.29)	(1.17)	(1.56)	(0.81)	(1.07)	(1.23)	(1.61)	(1.09)	(1.50)

5	−0.76	−7.24	−4.82	−17.38	−4.06	−6.80	12.62	12.24	10.90	6.51	13.41	3.97
	(0.42)	(0.67)	(1.03)	(1.37)	(0.77)	(1.34)	(0.72)	(0.94)	(1.10)	(1.38)	(0.96)	(1.28)
6	1.65	−7.33	0.23	−16.23	−1.86	−3.33	13.54	13.95	8.73	0.31	12.58	3.31
	(0.42)	(0.64)	(1.01)	(1.17)	(0.81)	(1.05)	(0.70)	(0.92)	(1.03)	(1.32)	(0.90)	(1.23)
7	5.45	−2.87	6.69	−13.80	−0.05	−2.58	12.47	13.17	7.25	−0.61	10.99	−0.61
	(0.43)	(0.63)	(1.03)	(1.19)	(0.74)	(0.96)	(0.65)	(0.85)	(0.97)	(1.28)	(0.82)	(1.11)
8	9.20	−1.10	13.53	−7.92	1.43	−2.11	11.60	12.11	8.93	1.30	10.80	−0.19
	(0.41)	(0.62)	(1.14)	(1.16)	(0.79)	(0.86)	(0.64)	(0.87)	(0.95)	(1.25)	(0.84)	(1.21)
9	13.62	2.86	19.82	−2.02	5.78	1.36	11.33	8.90	7.83	1.09	11.11	3.47
	(0.43)	(0.62)	(1.27)	(1.21)	(0.62)	(0.91)	(0.62)	(0.93)	(1.01)	(1.40)	(0.89)	(1.32)
10a	17.72	6.97	22.25	2.62	8.90	3.67	10.84	7.57	7.72	6.38	11.04	5.58
	(0.51)	(0.75)	(1.46)	(1.24)	(0.83)	(1.07)	(0.81)	(1.22)	(1.46)	(2.04)	(1.20)	(1.93)
10b[b]	29.50	17.67	19.34	2.02	17.31	11.78	6.72	−0.55	4.83	4.15	8.12	7.23
	(0.49)	(0.73)	(1.71)	(1.84)	(0.98)	(1.03)	(0.82)	(1.34)	(1.79)	(2.44)	(1.37)	(2.22)

[a] Lowest decile.
[b] Highest volume.

following momentum, value, and diversified strategies. Buy–sell imbalances are calculated using both the number of trades and the value of trades. Our principal objective is to understand how attention affects the purchase decisions of all investors. Calculating buy–sell imbalances by the value of trades has the advantage of offering a better gauge of the economic importance of our observations, but the disadvantage of overweighting the decisions of wealthier investors. In trying to understand investors' decision processes, calculating buy–sell imbalances by number of trades may be most appropriate.

Investors at the large discount brokerage display the greatest amount of attention-driven buying. When imbalances are calculated by number of trades (column 2), the buy–sell imbalance is −18.15% for stocks in the lowest volume decile. For stocks in the highest volume vingtile, the buy–sell imbalance is +29.5% more. Buy–sell imbalances for these investors rise monotonically with trading volume. When imbalances are calculated by value of trades (column 3), the buy–sell imbalance is −16.28% for stocks in the lowest volume decile. For stocks in the highest volume vingtile, the buy–sell imbalance is +17.67%. Again, buy–sell imbalances increase nearly monotonically with trading volume. Looking at columns 4–7 of Table 7.1, we see that the net buying behavior of investors at the large retail broker and the small discount brokerage behaves similarly to that of investors at the large discount brokerage.

Figure 7.1a plots buy–sell imbalances based on number of trades for investors at the large discount brokerage, the large retail brokerage, and the small discount brokerage and visually illustrates the results reported in Table 7.1. Most notable is that the slope of the curve depicting the relationship between buy–sell imbalance and abnormal trading volume is almost always upward-sloping.

The last six columns of Table 7.1 present the buy–sell imbalances of institutional money managers for stocks sorted on the current day's abnormal trading volume. Overall, these institutional investors exhibit the opposite tendency of the individual investors: Their buy–sell imbalances are greater on low-volume days than high-volume days. This is particularly true for value managers who are aggressive net buyers on days of low abnormal trading volume.

7.4.2 Returns sorts

Investors are likely to take notice when stocks exhibit extreme price moves. Such returns, whether positive or negative, will often be associated with new information about the firm. Table 7.2 presents buy–sell imbalances for stocks sorted on the previous day's return. Buy–sell imbalances are reported for investors at a large discount brokerage, a large retail brokerage, a small discount brokerage, and for institutional money managers following momentum, value, and diversified strategies.

Investors at the large discount brokerage display the greatest amount of attention-driven buying for these returns sorts. When calculated by number of trades, the buy–sell imbalance of investors at the large discount brokerage is 29.4% for the vingtile of stocks with the worst return performance on the previous day. The imbalance drops to 1.8% in the eighth return decile and rises back to 24% for stocks with the best return performance on the previous day.

Figure 7.1b plots buy–sell imbalances based on number of trades for investors at the large discount brokerage, the large retail brokerage, and the small discount brokerage.

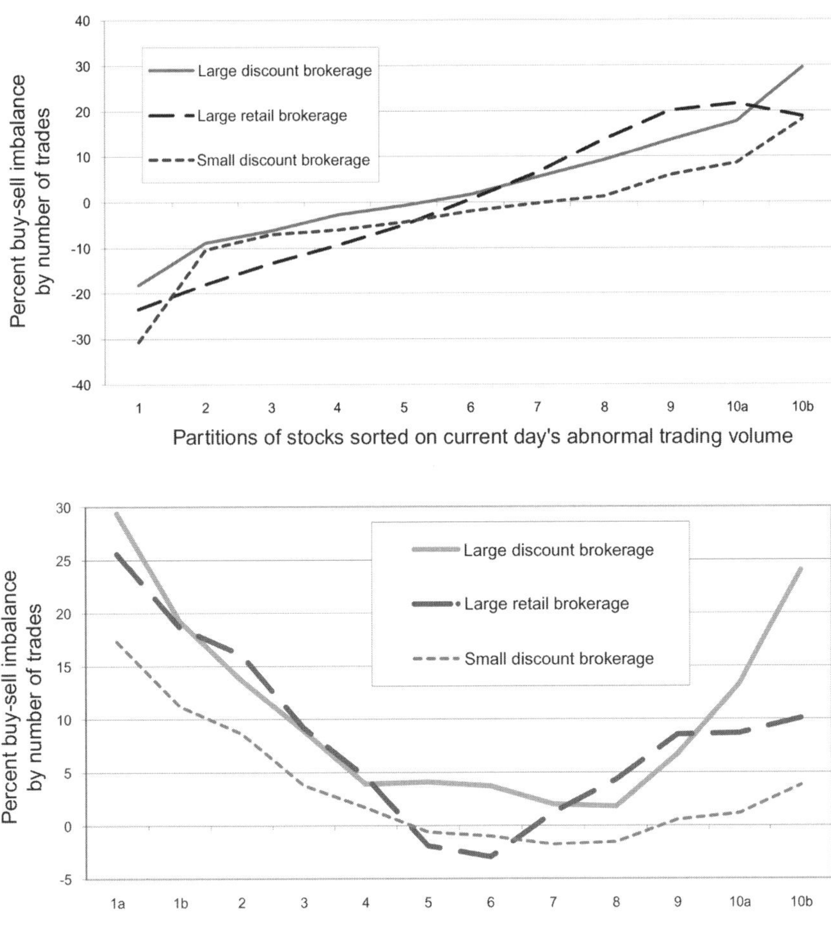

Figure 7.1. Individual investor buy–sell imbalances by number of trades for stocks sorted on the current day's abnormal trading volume and previous day's return.

The tendency of investors to buy yesterday's winners and losers is reflected in a U-shaped pattern in which buy–sell imbalance is high for big losers, high for big winners, and low for stocks without significant price moves the previous day.[14]

The U-shaped pattern is most pronounced for investors at the large discount brokerage; these investors buy attention-grabbing stocks. When imbalance is calculated by value of trades, the buy–sell imbalance of these investors is 29.1% for the vingtile of stocks with the worst return performance on the previous day. The imbalance drops to 8.6% in the eighth return decile and rises back to 11.1% for stocks with the best return performance on the previous day.

[14] Empirical buy–sell imbalances are very similar when we partition stocks on same-day return rather than on previous-day return.

Table 7.2. Buy–sell Imbalances by Investor type for stocks sorted on the previous day's return. Stocks are sorted daily into deciles on the basis on the previous day''s return as reported in the CRSP daily stock return files for NYSE, ASE, and NASDAQ stocks. The deciles of highest and lowest returns are each split into two vingtiles (1a, 1b, 10a and 10b). Buy–sell imbalances are reported for the trades of six groups of investors, investors at large discount brokerage (January 1991 through November 1996), investors at a large retail brokerage (January 1997 through June 1999), investors at a small discount brokerage (January 1996 through June 15, 1999), and institutional money managers (January 1993 through March 1996) classified by the Plexus Group as following momentum, value, and diversified strategies. For each day/partition/investor group, we calculate number imbalance as number of purchases minus number of sales divided by total number of trades. Value imbalance is calculated as the value of purchases minus the value of sales divided by the total value of trades. The table reports the mean for each time series of daily imbalances for a particular investor group and partition. Standard errors, calculated using a Newey–West correction for serial dependence, appear in parentheses.

	Large discount brokerage		Large retail brokerage		Small discount brokerage		Momentum managers		Value managers		Diversified managers	
Decile	Number imbalance	Value imbalance	Number imbalance	Value imbalance	Number imbalance	Value imbalance	Number imbalance	Value imbalance	Number imbalance	Value imbalance	Number imbalance	Value imbalance
1[a]	29.38	29.07	25.79	22.89	17.32	14.90	−21.03	−30.45	17.26	20.09	10.91	18.08
	(0.61)	(0.87)	(1.60)	(1.43)	(1.04)	(1.43)	(1.32)	(1.83)	(3.13)	(3.41)	(2.43)	(2.88)
1b	19.19	16.19	17.86	11.46	11.2	8.58	−6.43	−19.21	14.03	15.62	13.82	15.31
	(0.54)	(0.82)	(1.43)	(1.57)	(1.04)	(1.46)	(1.05)	(1.56)	(2.33)	(2.72)	(1.75)	(2.37)
2	13.69	8.83	13.73	5.47	8.65	3.51	−0.62	−14.58	11.19	11.01	14.18	10.47
	(0.42)	(0.64)	(1.17)	(1.00)	(0.74)	(1.20)	(0.73)	(1.04)	(1.27)	(1.73)	(1.04)	(2.33)
3	8.86	3.11	6.60	−5.01	3.77	1.23	5.10	−3.72	10.23	7.68	12.30	4.75
	(0.45)	(0.63)	(1.18)	(1.09)	(0.76)	(1.23)	(0.71)	(0.96)	(1.06)	(1.44)	(0.92)	(1.29)
4	3.94	−3.28	1.72	−10.98	1.69	−2.75	8.91	4.64	7.98	2.22	11.68	3.04
	(0.45)	(0.64)	(1.06)	(1.07)	(0.84)	(1.31)	(0.76)	(1.00)	(0.99)	(1.34)	(0.90)	(1.26)

5	4.09	−3.57	−4.37	−14.36	−0.6	−3.68	9.84	7.02	9.20	3.69	11.56	2.62
	(0.41)	(0.61)	(0.95)	(0.88)	(0.89)	(1.40)	(0.86)	(1.24)	(1.29)	(1.74)	(1.11)	(1.63)
6	3.73	−4.18	−3.95	−14.98	−0.99	−3.68	11.07	8.97	9.03	3.52	18.12	9.62
	(0.42)	(0.62)	(1.00)	(0.95)	(0.82)	(1.38)	(0.93)	(1.28)	(1.81)	(2.22)	(1.34)	(1.92)
7	2.02	−7.02	−0.07	−15.23	−1.77	−3.29	15.56	16.36	10.61	1.77	15.39	4.18
	(0.44)	(0.64)	(0.91)	(1.12)	(0.82)	(1.28)	(0.75)	(0.99)	(1.18)	(1.55)	(0.96)	(1.36)
8	1.82	−8.62	2.21	−15.85	−1.53	−4.0	19.31	25.22	7.92	0.96	14.00	1.10
	(0.42)	(0.62)	(0.84)	(0.98)	(0.82)	(1.27)	(0.74)	(0.99)	(1.06)	(1.45)	(0.88)	(1.30)
9	6.67	−4.83	6.54	−12.80	0.55	−0.79	22.69	32.44	4.30	−6.06	12.99	−1.70
	(0.43)	(0.62)	(0.88)	(1.08)	(0.73)	(1.13)	(0.69)	(0.93)	(1.21)	(1.66)	(1.02)	(1.55)
10a	13.41	3.23	6.58	−11.24	1.17	−2.93	24.04	34.75	−4.16	−12.66	10.23	−3.98
	(0.51)	(0.78)	(0.90)	(1.17)	(0.96)	(1.41)	(0.93)	(1.37)	(2.14)	(2.57)	(1.58)	(2.24)
10b	23.98	11.13	9.01	−7.93	3.80	−3.59	21.50	36.37	−17.32	−16.83	7.57	−0.60
	(0.52)	(0.81)	(0.91)	(1.11)	(0.84)	(1.20)	(1.28)	(1.74)	(3.14)	(3.41)	(2.30)	(2.81)

[a] Negative return.
[b] Positive return.

In Figure 7.1b, we see that investors at the large retail brokerage also display a U-shaped imbalance curve when stocks are sorted on the previous day's return. However, their tendency to be net buyers of yesterday's big winners is more subdued and does not show up when imbalance is calculated by value. Investors at the small discount brokerage are net buyers of yesterday's big losers, but not the big winners.

As seen in the last six columns of Table 7.2, the three categories of institutional money managers react quite differently to the previous day's return performance. Momentum managers dump the previous day's losers and buy winners. Value managers buy the previous day's losers and dump winners. Diversified managers do this as well, though not to the same extent. While one might interpret the purchases of yesterday's winners by momentum managers and the purchases of yesterday's losers by the value managers as attention-motivated, it seems more likely that the events leading to extreme positive and negative stock returns coincided with changes relative to the selection criteria that these two groups of money managers follow. Unlike the individual investors, these money managers were not net buyers on high abnormal volume days, nor is any one group of them net buyers following both extreme positive and negative returns.

7.4.3 News sorts

Table 7.3 reports average daily buy–sell imbalances for stocks sorted into those with and without news. Investors are much more likely to be net buyers of stocks that are in the news than those that are not.[15] When calculated by number for the large discount brokerage, the buy–sell imbalance is 2.70% for stocks out of the news and 9.35% for those stocks in the news. At the large retail brokerage, the buy–sell imbalance is −1.84% for stocks out of the news and 16.17% for those in the news.

Table 7.3 also reports news partition buy–sell imbalances separately for days on which individual stocks had a positive, negative, or zero return. Conditional on the sign of the return, average imbalances for individual investors are always greater on news days than no-news days. For both news and no-news days, average imbalances are greater for negative return days than for positive return days. One possible explanation for this is that when stock prices drop investors are less likely to sell due to the disposition effect (i.e., the preference for selling winners and holding losers). Alternatively, the differences in imbalances on positive and negative return days may result from the execution of limit orders. Many individual investors will not monitor their limit orders throughout the day. On a day when the market rises, more sell limit orders will execute than buy limit orders. On days when the market falls, more buy limit orders will execute. Unfortunately, our datasets do not distinguish between executed limit and market orders.

7.4.4 Volume, returns, and news sorts

We examine the possibility of interaction effects in our measures of attention by analyzing buy–sell imbalances for stocks partitioned on abnormal trading volume, previous-day return, and whether or not a stock had news coverage. Abnormal volume

[15] Choe, Kho, and Stulz (2000) find that individual investors in Korea buy on the day's preceding large 1-day price increases and sell preceding large 1-day losses. Large 1-day price moves are likely to be accompanied by news. Choe, Kho, and Stulz point out that the savvy trading of Korean individual investors could result from insider trading.

Table 7.3. Buy–sell imbalances by investor type for stocks sorted on the current day's news. Stocks are partitioned daily into those with and without news stories (reported by the Dow Jones News Service) that day. On average there is no news for 91% of stocks. Buy–sell imbalances are reported for the trades of six groups of investors, investors at a large discount brokerage (January 1991 through November 1996), investors at a large retail brokerage (January 1997 through June 1999), investors at a small discount brokerage (January 1996 through June 15, 1999), and institutional money managers (January 1993 through March 1996) classified by the Plexus Group as following momentum, value, and diversified strategies. Buy–sell imbalances are reported for all stocks and days with or without news. They are also reported separately for the days on which stocks had positive, negative, and zero returns. For each day/partition/investor group, we calculate number imbalance as number of purchases minus number of sales divided by total number of trades. Value imbalance is calculated as the value of purchases minus the value of sales divided by the total value of trades. The table reports the mean for each time series of daily imbalances for a particular investor group and partition. Standard errors, calculated using a Newey–West correction for serial dependence, appear in parentheses.

	Large discount brokerage		Large retail brokerage		Small discount brokerage		Momentum managers		Value managers		Diversified managers	
Partition	Number imbalance	Value imbalance	Number imbalance	Value imbalance	Number imbalance	Value imbalance	Number imbalance	Value imbalance	Number imbalance	Value imbalance	Number imbalance	Value imbalance
						Panel A: All days						
News	9.35	0.07	16.17	−2.36	6.76	1.87	13.38	14.00	6.36	−0.24	6.21	2.26
	(0.72)	(0.86)	(1.29)	(1.32)	(0.48)	(0.72)	(1.33)	(1.71)	(1.59)	(2.05)	(1.11)	(1.50)
No news	2.70	−5.62	−1.84	−14.59	−0.66	−4.87	12.20	10.43	10.96	3.62	7.26	1.24
	(0.43)	(0.63)	(0.87)	(0.87)	(0.58)	(1.23)	(1.11)	(1.16)	(1.37)	(1.49)	(0.97)	(0.84)
						Panel B: Positive return days						
News	1.74	−9.25	14.07	−7.74	1.14	−3.13	22.70	31.95	5.87	−1.01	7.80	3.92
	(0.94)	(1.07)	(1.04)	(1.25)	(0.64)	(0.95)	(1.50)	(2.10)	(1.94)	(2.65)	(1.31)	(2.00)
No news	−2.51	−14.31	1.76	−13.90	−4.49	−8.41	22.39	25.64	14.20	6.67	8.95	6.66
	(0.54)	(0.79)	(0.88)	(1.00)	(0.79)	(1.40)	(1.31)	(1.46)	(1.51)	(1.74)	(1.05)	(1.05)

Table 7.3 (*cont.*)

Partition	Large discount brokerage		Large retail brokerage		Small discount brokerage		Momentum managers		Value managers		Diversified managers	
	Number imbalance	Value imbalance	Number imbalance	Value imbalance	Number imbalance	Value imbalance	Number imbalance	Value imbalance	Number imbalance	Value imbalance	Number imbalance	Value imbalance
Panel C: Negative return days												
News	17.39	10.91	15.59	3.17	13.77	9.32	3.94	−7.39	4.29	−2.41	4.72	2.24
	(0.83)	(1.12)	(1.58)	(1.43)	(0.71)	(1.08)	(1.43)	(2.11)	(2.09)	(2.77)	(1.30)	(2.25)
No news	8.86	3.85	−3.38	−13.57	4.35	1.29	0.68	−8.60	6.92	1.60	5.58	−4.11
	(0.53)	(0.81)	(0.88)	(0.85)	(0.77)	(1.42)	(1.25)	(1.46)	(1.52)	(1.89)	(1.03)	(1.23)
Panel C: Zero Return Days												
News	1.41	−5.90	−0.44	−8.74	1.58	−1.22	14.12	15.16	11.37	9.59	5.21	1.62
	(1.76)	(2.31)	(0.94)	(1.45)	(2.25)	(2.68)	(2.35)	(3.19)	(3.44)	(4.35)	(2.47)	(3.68)
No news	−0.95	−6.40	−14.49	−18.24	−3.27	−7.95	14.60	12.86	10.65	2.42	8.36	−0.17
	(0.68)	(1.13)	(1.06)	(1.08)	(1.35)	(2.04)	(1.38)	(1.81)	(1.73)	(2.49)	(1.27)	(1.84)

and previous-day returns are independently sorted into three bins—bottom 30%, middle 40%, and top 30%. The three-by-three partition on volume and returns is further conditioned on whether a stock was in the news. Order imbalances are calculated based on number of trades. The results of this analysis are presented in Figure 7.2. Consistent with the univariate sorts, buy–sell imbalances increase with abnormal volume for each return partition. At the large discount brokerage, for each volume partition, buy–sell imbalances are the greatest for the low- and high-return bins. At the large retail brokerage, for each volume partition, buy–sell imbalances are consistently greater for low-return bins, and for high-return bins with no news or low volume. At the small discount brokerage, for each volume partition, buy–sell imbalances are consistently greater for low-return bins, but there is no consistent effect for high-return bins. Finally, buy–sell imbalances tend to be greater for news partition, for high- and low-volume stocks at the large discount brokerage, for high and medium stocks at the large retail brokerage, and for high-volume stocks at the small discount brokerage. It appears from this analysis and from our univariate tests that abnormal trading volume is our single best indicator of attention. Returns come in second. Our simple news metric—whether a stock was or was not mentioned in that day's news—is our least informative indicator of attention. It is hardly surprising that abnormal volume best measures attention since greater trading volume is often driven by greater numbers of traders, and it is nearly tautological that when more people are trading a stock, more people are paying attention to it.

7.4.5 Size partitions

To test whether our results are driven primarily by small-capitalization stocks, we calculate buy–sell imbalances separately for small-, medium-, and large-capitalization stocks. We first sort and partition all stocks as described above on the basis of same-day abnormal trading volume, previous-day return, and same-day news. We then calculate imbalances separately for small-, medium-, and large-capitalization stocks using the same breakpoints to form abnormal volume and return deciles for all three size groups. We use monthly New York Stock Exchange market equity breakpoints to form our size groups.[16] Each month we classify all stocks (both NYSE-listed and non-listed stocks) with market capitalization less than or equal to the 30th percentile breakpoint as small stocks, stocks with market capitalization greater than the 30th percentile and less than or equal to the 70th percentile as medium stocks, and stocks with market capitalization greater than the 70th percentile as large stocks. Table 7.4 reports buy–sell imbalances by size group for abnormal volume, return, and news sorts.[17]

By and large, investors are more likely to buy rather than sell attention-grabbing stocks regardless of size. This is true for all three of our attention-grabbing measures: abnormal trading volume, returns, and news. Many documented return anomalies, such as momentum and post-earnings announcement drift, are greater for small-

[16] We thank Ken French for supplying market equity breakpoints. These breakpoints are available and further described in Ken French's online data library.

[17] To save space, results are reported only for the investors most likely to display attention-driven buying—those at the large discount brokerage. Results for the large retail and small discount brokerages are qualitatively similar. The only significant exception to this pattern is that buy–sell imbalances at the large retail brokerage for large-capitalization stocks are no greater for deciles of high previous-day returns than for middle return deciles. For small-cap and medium-cap stocks, these retail investors do demonstrate a greater propensity to buy yesterday's winners than yesterday's average performers.

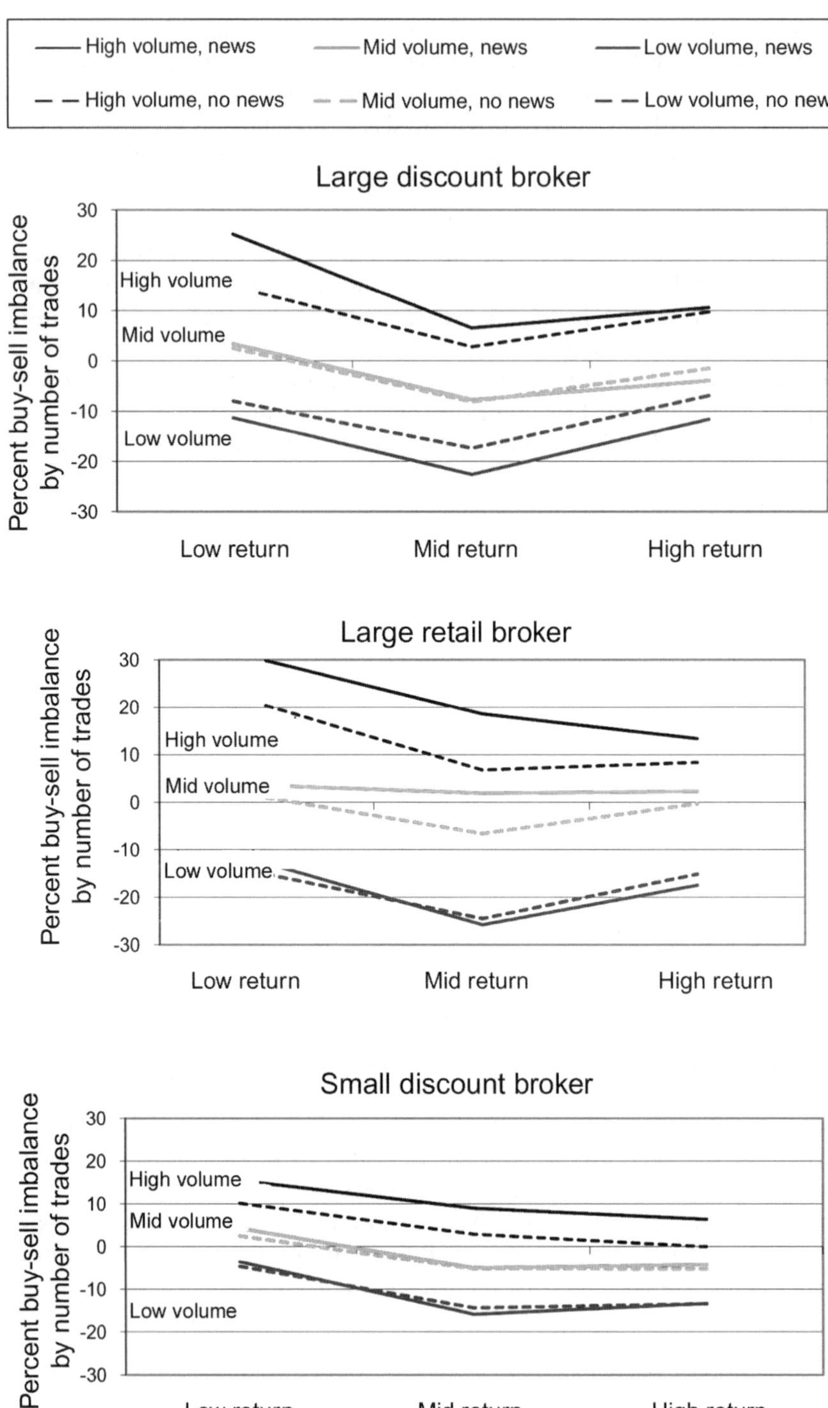

Figure 7.2. Buy–sell imbalances for investors at a large discount brokerage based on three-by-three partition on abnormal volume and returns, conditional on news coverage.

Table 7.4. Buy–sell imbalances for large discount brokerage investors for stocks sorted on the current day's abnormal trading volume, the previous day's return, and the current day's news and then partitioned on market capitalization. In panel A, stocks are sorted daily into deciles on the basis on the current day's abnormal volume. The decile of highest abnormal volume is split into two vingtiles (10a and 10b). Abnormal volume is calculated as the ratio of the current day's volume (as reported in the CRSP daily stock return files for NYSE, ASE, and NASDAQ stocks) divided by the average volume over the previous 252 trading days. In panel B, stocks are sorted daily into deciles on the basis of the previous day's return as reported in the CRSP daily stock return files for NYSE, ASE, and NASDAQ stocks. The deciles of highest and lowest returns are each split into two vingtiles (1a, 1b and 10a, 10b). Abnormal trading volume is calculated as the ratio of the current day's trading volume (as reported in the CRSP daily stock return files for NYSE, ASE, and NASDAQ stocks) divided by the average trading volume over the previous 252 trading days. In panel C, stocks are partitioned daily into those with and without news stories that day (as reported by the Dow Jones News Service). On average there is no news for 91% of stocks. For all three panels, after sorting and partitioning, stocks are further separated into three groups based on market capitalization. We use monthly New York Stock Exchange market equity breakpoints to form our size groups. Each month we classify all stocks (both NYSE-listed and non-listed stocks) with market capitalization less than or equal to the 30th percentile break point as small stocks, stocks with market capitalization greater than the 30th percentile and less than or equal to the 70th percentile as medium stocks, and stocks with market capitalization greater than the 70th percentile as large stocks. Buy–sell imbalances are reported for the trades of investors at a large discount brokerage (January 1991 through November 1996). For each day/partition/investor group, we calculate number imbalance as number of purchases minus number of sales divided by total number of trades. Value imbalance is calculated as the value of purchases minus the value of sales divided by the total value of trades. The table reports the mean for each time series of daily imbalances for a particular investor group and partition. Standard errors, calculated using a Newey–West correction for serial dependence, appear in parentheses.

Panel A: Buy–sell imbalances for stocks sorted first on current day's abnormal trading volume and then on market capitalization

	Small stocks		Mid-cap stocks		Large stocks	
Decile	Number imbalance	Value imbalance	Number imbalance	Value imbalance	Number imbalance	Value imbalance
1 (lowest volume)	−16.11	−13.35	−18.43	−17.18	−31.89	−30.33
	(1.17)	(1.50)	(2.36)	(2.49)	(6.32)	(6.46)
2	−5.94	−4.37	−12.09	−14.16	−21.44	−22.17
	(0.86)	(1.18)	(1.19)	(1.50)	(2.32)	(2.49)
3	−2.23	−2.49	−6.66	−9.24	−15.81	−15.35
	(0.72)	(1.04)	(0.85)	(1.19)	(1.29)	(1.56)
4	3.22	0.16	−1.99	−6.65	−9.17	−13.01
	(0.71)	(1.01)	(0.70)	(1.05)	(0.76)	(1.11)
5	6.22	2.96	1.54	−4.30	−5.46	−9.99
	(0.70)	(1.01)	(0.67)	(1.01)	(0.58)	(0.87)
6	9.44	5.74	2.94	−5.00	−1.24	−9.12
	(0.65)	(0.96)	(0.62)	(0.95)	(0.54)	(0.77)
7	10.90	4.47	6.03	−0.99	4.02	−3.27
	(0.64)	(0.97)	(0.59)	(0.92)	(0.54)	(0.76)
8	11.83	5.42	6.80	−1.88	9.38	−0.80
	(0.61)	(0.92)	(0.57)	(0.89)	(0.56)	(0.77)

(continued)

Table 7.4 (*cont.*)

9	15.13	7.27	9.27	−0.98	14.50	4.54
	(0.53)	(0.83)	(0.59)	(0.85)	(0.64)	(0.84)
10a	16.94	7.73	12.97	3.80	19.76	11.13
	(0.64)	(0.99)	(0.76)	(1.05)	(0.99)	(1.22)
10b (highest volume)	20.77	32.13	24.41	15.04	28.26	21.65
	(0.54)	(0.83)	(0.86)	(1.12)	(1.33)	(1.53)

Panel B: Buy-sell imbalances for stocks sorted first on the previous day's return and then on market capitalization

	Small stocks		Mid-cap stocks		Large stocks	
Decile	Number imbalance	Value imbalance	Number imbalance	Value imbalance	Number imbalance	Value imbalance
1a (negative return)	24.88	26.06	32.71	30.83	38.73	34.55
	(0.66)	(0.99)	(1.25)	(1.48)	(1.92)	(2.15)
1b	14.37	12.61	17.61	14.99	25.26	21.93
	(0.65)	(0.99)	(0.96)	(1.27)	(1.38)	(1.62)
2	10.69	6.30	9.67	4.99	18.53	13.50
	(0.54)	(0.82)	(0.06)	(0.89)	(0.67)	(0.92)
3	6.97	2.05	5.06	−0.95	11.09	5.35
	(0.65)	(0.96)	(0.59)	(0.86)	(0.59)	(0.82)
4	4.48	−3.23	0.87	−5.29	4.23	−3.06
	(0.53)	(0.78)	(0.62)	(0.90)	(0.60)	(0.81)
5	3.72	−3.64	3.59	−4.45	4.02	−3.58
	(0.42)	(0.63)	(0.46)	(0.69)	(0.47)	(0.67)
6	4.20	−3.64	4.46	−3.07	2.86	−4.96
	(0.42)	(0.62)	(0.49)	(0.73)	(0.54)	(0.75)
7	5.28	−2.63	2.87	−4.84	0.80	−8.23
	(0.54)	(0.79)	(0.60)	(0.90)	(0.59)	(0.81)
8	8.88	2.78	2.07	−7.78	−0.83	−10.96
	(0.61)	(0.93)	(0.56)	(0.85)	(0.58)	(0.80)
9	11.98	5.49	6.73	−5.41	3.31	−6.69
	(0.54)	(0.83)	(0.61)	(0.90)	(0.67)	(0.90)
10a	16.88	10.59	12.09	2.53	5.53	−1.81
	(0.63)	(0.96)	(0.82)	(1.14)	(1.25)	(1.48)
10b (positive return)	26.98	18.69	20.85	8.19	7.76	2.94
	(0.57)	(0.88)	(1.06)	(1.33)	(1.84)	(2.06)

Panel C: Buy–sell imbalances for stocks sorted first on market capitalization and then on current day's news

	Small stocks		Mid-cap stocks		Large stocks	
Decile	Number imbalance	Value imbalance	Number imbalance	Value imbalance	Number imbalance	Value imbalance
News	19.87	14.59	13.38	3.87	6.52	−1.35
All days	(1.47)	(1.85)	(1.15)	(1.62)	(0.85)	(0.97)
No news	7.53	2.82	3.12	−4.83	−2.91	−9.86
All days	(0.48)	(0.70)	(0.57)	(0.88)	(0.67)	(0.94)

capitalization stocks than for large stocks. Some researchers have suggested that these phenomena may be caused by the psychologically motivated trading behavior of individual investors. We find, however, that attention-driven buying by individuals is as strong for large-capitalization stocks as for small stocks. It may be that, while the impact of individual investor trading differs for large and small stocks, the psychological biases motivating trading are the same.[18]

7.4.6 Earnings and dividend announcements

To test the robustness of our results, we calculate buy–sell imbalances for abnormal volume partitions, return partitions, and news and no-news for earnings announcement days, dividend announcement days, and other days. Earnings announcement days span day $t-1$ to $t+2$, where day t is the earnings announcement day (per Compustat). Dividend announcement days span day $t-1$ to $t+2$, where day t is the dividend announcement day (per CRSP). We include all dividend announcements regardless of type. As seen in Figure 7.3, for volume, return, and news sorts, the buy–sell imbalance results are qualitatively similar across the three partitions.[19]

7.5 SHORT-SALE CONSTRAINTS

We argue that because individual investors hold small portfolios and don't sell short, attention is more important when choosing stocks to buy (from a huge set of choices) than when choosing stocks to sell (from a small set). Short-sale constraints could contribute to our empirical findings through a somewhat different mechanism. An attention-grabbing event may increase the heterogeneity of investor beliefs about a firm. Individual investors who become bullish are able to buy the stock, but those who become bearish can sell it only if they already own it or are willing to sell short. Institutional investors can both buy and sell. Thus, on average, bullish individuals and institutions buy attention-grabbing stocks while bearish institutions, but not individuals, sell. Attention-grabbing events are therefore associated with net buying by individuals, not because individuals are buying what catches their attention, but because they can't sell what catches their attention; attention-grabbing events increase the heterogeneity of beliefs, while limited portfolios and short-sale constraints restrict would-be sellers.

We believe that increased heterogeneity of beliefs combined with selling constraints may contribute to net buying by individuals around attention-grabbing events. However, even when individuals have the option both to buy or to sell a stock (i.e., when they already own the stock) attention will matter more for buying. If short-sale constraints alone mattered and attention did not otherwise differentially affect buying and selling, we would expect attention-grabbing events to exert a similar influence on both the sales and the purchases of stocks that investors already own. The attention hypothesis makes a different prediction. The attention hypothesis states that attention is

[18] Institutional buy–sell imbalance for our volume and return sorts is also qualitatively similar across small, medium, and large firms.

[19] To save space, results are reported only for the investors most likely to display attention-driven buying—those at the large discount brokerage. Results for the large retail and small discount brokerages are qualitatively similar and available from the authors.

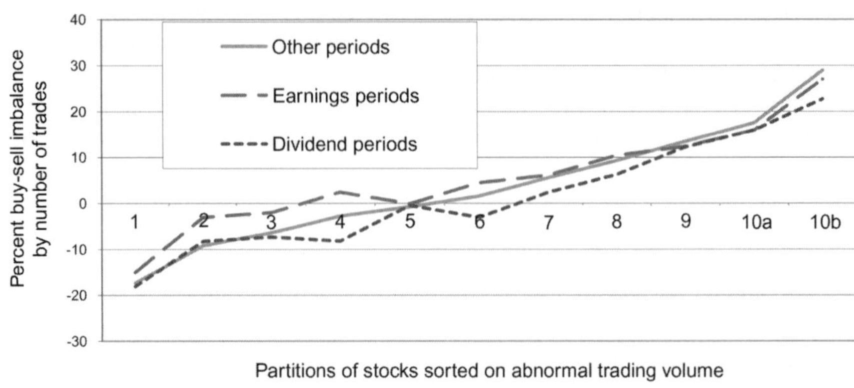

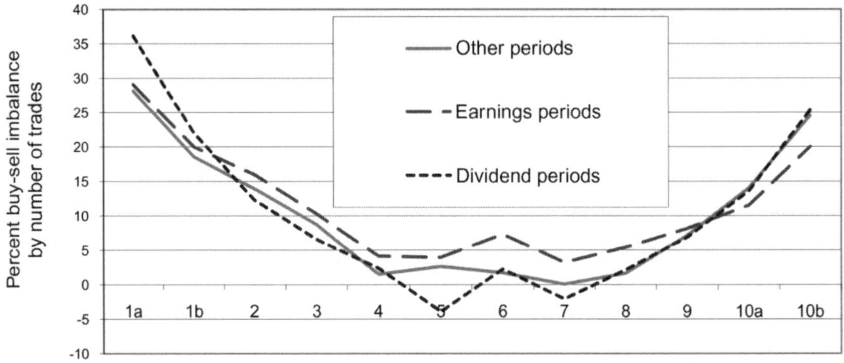

Figure 7.3. Buy–sell imbalances for investors at a large discount brokerage during earnings announcement periods, dividend announcement periods, and other periods, for volume deciles (top) and return deciles (bottom).

important when investors face a search problem. Each potential purchase—even of a stock already in the portfolio—is competing with thousands of other stocks for attention. Thus attention affects the rate at which stocks are purchased, even stocks that are already owned. Of course, investors are, overall, more likely to sell than buy stocks they already own. Under the attention hypothesis, however, the buy–sell imbalances of stocks that investors already own should be greater on days in which those stocks are attention-grabbing.

In Table 7.5, we report buy–sell imbalances for individual investors for abnormal volume, return, and news sorts for stocks. In calculating imbalances for this table, we consider only purchases and sales by each investor of stocks he or she already owns. Since investors mostly sell stocks that they already own, but often buy stocks that they do not own, a far greater proportion of these trades are sales. Therefore, nearly all of the imbalances are negative. The relative patterns of imbalances are, however, similar to those reported for individual investors in Tables 7.1–7.3. The ratio of purchases to sales is higher on high-attention days. This is particularly true for the abnormal volume sort

Table 7.5. Buy–sell imbalances for large discount brokerage investors for stocks already owned by each investor. Stocks sorted on the current day's abnormal trading volume, the previous day's return, and the current day's news. In panel A, stocks are sorted daily into deciles on the basis of the current day's abnormal volume. The decile of highest abnormal volume is split into two vingtiles (10a and 10b). Abnormal volume is calculated as the ratio of the current day's volume (as reported in the CRSP daily stock return files for NYSE, ASE, and NASDAQ stocks) divided by the average volume over the previous 252 trading days. In panel B, stocks are sorted daily into deciles on the basis of the previous day's return as reported in the CRSP daily stock return files for NYSE, ASE, and NASDAQ stocks. The deciles of highest and lowest returns are each split into two vingtiles (1a, 1b and 10a, 10b). Abnormal trading volume is calculated as the ratio of the current day's trading volume (as reported in the CRSP daily stock return files for NYSE, ASE, and NASDAQ stocks) divided by the average trading volume over the previous 252 trading days. In panel C, stocks are partitioned daily into those with and without news stories that day (as reported by the Dow Jones News Service). Buy–sell imbalances are reported for the trades of investors at a large discount brokerage (January 1991 through November 1996), investors at a large retail brokerage (January 1997 through June 1999), and investors at a small discount brokerage (January 1996 through December 1998). Imbalances are calculated for purchases and sales by investors of stocks already held in each investor's account. For each day/partition/investor group, we calculate number imbalance as number of purchases minus number of sales divided by total number of trades. Value imbalance is calculated as the value of purchases minus the value of sales divided by the total value of trades. The table reports the mean for each time series of daily imbalances for a particular investor group and partition. Standard errors, calculated using a Newey–West correction for serial dependence, appear in parentheses.

Panel A: Buy–sell imbalances for stocks already owned sorted on current day's abnormal trading volume

	Large discount brokerage		Large retail brokerage		Small discount brokerage	
Decile	Number imbalance	Value imbalance	Number imbalance	Value imbalance	Number imbalance	Value imbalance
1 (lowest volume)	−54.22	−55.64	−28.74	−33.99	−24.25	−33.22
	(1.43)	(1.89)	(1.42)	(1.84)	(6.28)	(7.58)
2	−51.13	−53.20	−29.46	−34.09	−33.80	−29.67
	(0.78)	(1.07)	(1.09)	(1.36)	(3.18)	(4.47)
3	−48.27	−49.69	−29.54	−31.25	−31.76	−30.05
	(0.64)	(0.95)	(1.04)	(1.31)	(1.71)	(2.44)
4	−47.19	−49.51	−28.69	−32.96	−35.65	−33.93
	(0.56)	(0.88)	(0.94)	(1.11)	(1.26)	(1.96)
5	−45.95	−47.59	−26.71	−31.04	−32.34	−30.01
	(0.53)	(0.81)	(0.90)	(1.07)	(1.12)	(1.63)
6	−45.01	−48.65	−24.32	−29.71	−30.00	−26.50
	(0.49)	(0.71)	(0.90)	(1.04)	(0.97)	(1.42)
7	−42.36	−45.85	−21.83	−30.29	−29.85	−26.21
	(0.50)	(0.71)	(0.84)	(0.89)	(0.95)	(1.33)
8	−39.43	−43.75	−18.72	−27.21	−28.20	−26.23
	(0.51)	(0.71)	(0.81)	(0.87)	(0.87)	(1.22)
9	−35.64	−40.68	−15.45	−21.79	−27.07	−24.99
	(0.52)	(0.70)	(0.78)	(0.91)	(0.85)	(1.21)

(continued)

Table 7.5 (*cont.*)

10a	−33.03	−39.31	−12.27	−19.97	−26.81	−27.99
	(0.63)	(0.85)	(0.97)	(1.12)	(1.06)	(1.42)
10b (highest volume)	−24.97	−32.82	−15.01	−20.04	−17.32	−19.38
	(0.69)	(0.92)	(1.04)	(1.19)	(0.98)	(1.42)

Panel B: Buy–sell imbalances for stocks already owned sorted on the previous day's return

	Large discount brokerage		Large retail brokerage		Small discount brokerage	
Decile	Number imbalance	Value imbalance	Number imbalance	Value imbalance	Number imbalance	Value imbalance
1a (negative return)	−9.68	−11.96	4.05	0.33	−16.89)	−19.68
	(0.83)	(1.17)	(0.99)	(1.26)	(1.54	(1.85)
1b	−23.90	−26.00	−8.20	−10.83	−18.90	−21.86
	(0.76)	(1.02)	(0.99)	(1.20)	(1.49)	(1.84)
2	−32.00	−33.15	−12.73	−14.99	−22.71	−24.77
	(0.56)	(0.76)	(0.89)	(1.00)	(1.09)	(1.45)
3	−38.94	−40.22	−18.24	−21.85	−27.10	−26.23
	(0.57)	(0.76)	(0.94)	(0.99)	(1.16)	(1.53)
4	−42.53	−44.79	−20.36	−25.16	−26.03	−26.47
	(0.56)	(0.78)	(0.91)	(1.01)	(1.24)	(1.58)
5	−40.51	−44.29	−20.67	−24.83	−27.67	−27.77
	(0.55)	(0.76)	(0.93)	(1.10)	(1.46)	(1.75)
6	−41.18	−45.31	−21.35	−26.59	−28.54	−27.29
	(0.55)	(0.77)	(0.90)	(1.10)	(1.42)	(1.73)
7	−45.36	−49.57	−22.82	−28.66	−29.28	−28.44
	(0.57)	(0.78)	(0.89)	(1.06)	(1.24)	(1.55)
8	−48.12	−52.42	−25.45	−32.00	−31.14	−28.16
	(0.50)	(0.70)	(0.87)	(1.02)	(1.24)	(1.61)
9	−45.85	−50.13	−27.13	−34.00	−32.70	−28.40
	(0.49)	(0.68)	(0.79)	(0.95)	(1.09)	(1.45)
10a	−40.86	−46.06	−31.17	−38.16	−36.03	−34.85
	(0.64)	(0.89)	(0.85)	(1.03)	(1.27)	(1.67)
10b (positive return)	−33.95	−43.77	−29.73	−34.87	−35.02	−38.31
	(0.68)	(0.94)	(0.81)	(1.05)	(1.20)	(1.49)

Panel C: Buy–sell imbalances for stocks already owned sorted on current day's news

	Large discount brokerage		Large retail brokerage		Small discount brokerage	
Decile	Number imbalance	Value imbalance	Number imbalance	Value imbalance	Number imbalance	Value imbalance
News	−40.91	−42.36	−15.38	−23.95	−22.14	−22.02
All days	(0.79)	(0.94)	(0.94)	(0.98)	(0.91)	(1.52)
No news	−45.05	−45.98	−21.42	−25.46	−32.77	−33.68
All days	(0.52)	(0.77)	(0.92)	(1.02)	(1.00)	(1.52)

(Panel A) and the news sort (Panel C). When stocks are sorted on the previous day's return (Panel B), investors are relatively more likely to purchase stocks they already own on days following large negative returns than on other days. However, following large positive returns, buy–sell imbalances do not increase for stocks already owned. This is consistent with previous research (Odean, 1998a) that finds that individual investors are more likely to sell stocks trading above, rather than below, the original purchase price and more likely to buy additional shares of stocks trading below, rather than above, the original purchase price.

Short-sale constraints are relaxed in the presence of exchange-traded options. Thus, if short-sale constraints alone drive our results, we would expect much different results for stocks with exchange-traded options. In auxiliary analyses, we partition stocks into two groups—those with and those without exchange-traded options.[20] For each group, we sort stocks into deciles on the basis of abnormal trading volume and previous-day return and calculate buy–sell imbalances for each decile (as described in Section 7.3). The patterns of imbalances are very similar for stocks with and without exchange-traded options—another indication that the results we document are not driven by short-sale constraints.

Thus short-selling constraints (and heterogeneity of beliefs) do not fully explain our findings. For individual investors who can sell a stock without selling short, a higher percentage of their trades consists of purchases, rather than sales, on high-attention days.

7.6 ASSET PRICING: THEORY AND EVIDENCE

In the appendix of the version of this chapter published in *The Review of Financial Studies*, we develop a model of price formation for a market in which attention-driven noise traders tend to buy stocks that catch their attention. Our theoretical model has the testable prediction that the underperformance of the stocks bought relative to stocks sold by these noise traders will be greatest following periods of high attention. The intuition underlying this result is straightforward; noise traders create uniform buying pressure in attention-grabbing stocks, and market-makers respond to this buying pressure by increasing prices, leading to lower subsequent returns—the more intense the attention-driven buying, the lower the subsequent returns. In this section, we test this return prediction.

There are two significant challenges in testing our model. Our first challenge is that the model does not specify the period of time over which attention-driven buying affects returns. Our evidence that investors do buy stocks that catch their attention is based upon 1-day sorts. It is likely, though, that investors' attention often spans more than a single day. How the effects on returns of attention-driven buying persist is likely to vary with the intensity and duration of the attention-grabbing event. In the following analysis, we form portfolios on the basis of daily attention sorts and evaluate performance over a 1-month horizon. We obtain similar results at other horizons.

Our second challenge is that many factors not incorporated into our simple model are known to affect asset prices. Most relevant to our timeframe, stocks with high abnormal trading volume over a day or a week tend to appreciate over the following month

[20] With thanks to Charles Cao for providing us with a list of stocks with exchange-traded options.

(Gervais, Kaniel, and Mingelgrin, 2001) and high-volume stocks with extreme returns experience subsequent price reversals at short horizons (e.g., 1 week; Conrad, Hameed, and Niden, 1994). We do not claim that attention-driven buying causes either of these phenomena nor that pricing effects of attention-driven buying are more powerful than these phenomena. Indeed, it must be the case that when the pricing implications of attention-driven buying run contrary to those of persistence in high abnormal volume stocks or short-term mean reversion, the influence of attention-driven buying is less powerful, since the other phenomena are already well documented. Thus the influence of attention-driven buying on returns is an incremental effect, or an overlay, on price movements driven by other short-term factors. To document this influence, we must control for these other factors (just as we must control for other factors such as momentum).

As noted in Section 7.3.3, our proxies for attention are not perfect. For example, a stock sorted into the lowest return decile may be there because of a well-publicized negative event that attracted individual investors' attention or it may be there because an institutional investor sells a large position more quickly than the stock's liquidity can absorb. When we observe a great imbalance of individual investor buying in a stock in a high-attention partition, that buying is likely to be driven by attention rather than stock fundamentals and is thus likely to create temporary price pressure resulting in subsequent underperformance. To control for other factors influencing stocks, we compare the performance of a portfolio of the stocks in each partition weighted by how actively investors bought each stock with a portfolio of stocks in that partition weighted by how actively investors sold each stock. This approach has three advantages. (1) We control for known effects of abnormally high trading volume and short-term price moves because both the stocks purchased and those sold have experienced the same recent trading volume or return effects. (2) Portfolios are weighted in proportion to how actively individual investors are buying each high-attention stock, the very trading we anticipate will affect future returns. (3) Weighting our portfolios in proportion to the value of purchases and sales by individual investors gives us an estimate of the welfare costs of attention-driven buying. Of course, our estimate considers only the month subsequent to a trade and may overestimate costs to investors who hold positions for less than a month.

To test the model's prediction, we first sort stocks into decile partitions on the basis of the current day's abnormal trading volume and on the basis of the previous day's return, and then, for each partition, we form two portfolios: a portfolio of stocks purchased by individual investors and a portfolio of stocks sold by them. We then calculate the difference in the returns of these two portfolios for each partition. On each day, we construct a portfolio comprised of those stocks purchased within the past month (21 trading days). The return on the portfolio is calculated based on the value of the initial purchase as:

$$R_t^b = \frac{\sum_{i=1}^{n_{bt}} x_{it} \cdot R_{it}}{\sum_{i=1}^{n_{bt}} x_{it}} \tag{7.4}$$

where R_{it} is the gross daily return of stock i on day t, n_{bt} is the number of different stocks purchased during the past month, and x_{it} is the compound daily return of stock i from the close of trading on the day of the purchase through day $t-1$ multiplied by the value of the purchase. For each partition, a portfolio of stocks sold within the past month is similarly constructed. For our empirical tests, we compound daily returns to yield a monthly return series. Our prediction is that, for higher attention partitions, there will be greater underperformance of the purchase portfolios relative to the sales portfolios; that is, $(R_t^s - R_t^b)$ will be increasing in attention.

We calculate the difference in the returns $(R_t^b - R_t^s)$ for the 20 pairs of purchase and sale portfolios (10 deciles based on abnormal volume sorts, and 10 deciles based on previous-day return sorts). To see whether any observed abnormal returns can be explained by stock characteristics known to affect returns, we employ a four-factor model that includes market, size, value, and momentum factors (Carhart, 1997). For example, to evaluate the return performance of a particular decile $(R_t^b - R_t^s)$, we estimate the following monthly time-series regression:

$$(R_t^b - R_t^s) = \alpha_j + \beta_j(R_{mt} - R_{ft}) + s_j SMB_t + h_j VMG_t + m_j WML_t + \varepsilon_{jt}, \tag{7.5}$$

where R_{ft} is the monthly return on T-Bills,[21] R_{mt} is the monthly return on a value-weighted market index, SMB_t is the return on a value-weighted portfolio of small stocks minus the return on a value-weighted portfolio of big stocks, VMG_t is the return on a value-weighted portfolio of high-book-to-market (value) stocks minus the return on a value-weighted portfolio of low-book-to-market (growth) stocks, and WML_t is the return on a value-weighted portfolio of recent winners minus the return on a value-weighted portfolio of recent losers.[22] The regression yields parameter estimates of α_j, β_j, s_j, h_j, and m_j. The error term in the regression is denoted by ε_{jt}. The subscript j denotes parameter estimates and error terms from regression j, where we estimate 21 regressions. We estimate similar regressions for the returns of the 20 purchase and sale portfolios, R_t^b and R_t^s.

In Table 7.6 (panel A) we report, for the combined sample, returns earned by purchase and sale portfolios as well as the differences in these portfolio returns for deciles of stocks first sorted on the current day's abnormal trading volume. Because of the short time periods of the large retail and small discount samples, we report results for the sample of combined trades for investors at all three brokerages.[23] In panel B, we report, for the combined sample, returns for the difference in returns earned by purchase and sale portfolios for deciles of stocks first sorted on the previous day's abnormal return. Consistent with the prediction of our model, in all three of our high-attention deciles—decile 10 for the abnormal volume sort and deciles 1 and 10 for the return sort—the underperformance of stocks purchased relative to those sold is both economically and statistically significant.[24,25]

[21] The return on T-bills is from *Stocks, Bonds, Bills, and Inflation, 1997 Yearbook*, Ibbotson Associates, Chicago, IL.

[22] We construct the *WML* portfolio as in Carhart (1997), though we value-weight rather than equally-weight the momentum portfolio. The construction of the *SMB* and *VMG* portfolios is discussed in detail in Fama and French (1993). We thank Kenneth French for providing us with the remaining data.

[23] The combined return series results in a time-series of monthly returns from February 1991 through June 1999. In months when we have returns from more than one dataset, we average across datasets.

[24] Market-adjusted returns for difference in returns earned by purchase and sale portfolios (i.e., $R_t^b - R_t^s$) in the three high-attention deciles are qualitatively similar to the four-factor alphas and of similar statistical significance.

[25] Because we do not have news data for all days, our time-series is even shorter when we form portfolios after sorting on news. The difference in returns to the portfolio of buys minus that of sells after sorting on news is not significant.

Table 7.6. Percentage return performance for portfolios of stocks purchased minus portfolios of stocks sold in partitions based on abnormal volume sorts and the previous day's return sorts. Trades data are for investors at a large discount brokerage (LDB—January 1991 through November 1996), investors at a large retail brokerage (LRB—January 1997 through June 1999), and investors at a small discount brokerage (SDB—January 1996 through June 15, 1999). For investors at each brokerage, we form two portfolios for each partition: stocks purchased and stocks sold. Stocks enter the portfolio the day following the purchase or sale. Portfolios are rebalanced daily assuming a holding period of 21 trading days (i.e., 1 month). The purchase and sale portfolios are constructed using the value of purchases and sales, respectively. We evaluate the difference in the return of these two portfolios ($R_t^b - R_t^s$). We estimate the following monthly time-series regression:

$$R_t^b = \alpha_j + \beta_j(R_{mt} - R_{ft}) + s_j SMB_t + h_j VMG_t + m_j WML_t + \varepsilon_{jt},$$

where R_{ft} is the monthly return on T-Bills, R_{mt} is the monthly return on a value-weighted market index, SMB_t is the return on a value-weighted portfolio of small stocks minus the return on a value-weighted portfolio of big stocks, VMG_t is the return on a value-weighted portfolio of high-book-to-market (value) stocks minus the return on a value-weighted portfolio of low-book-to-market (growth) stocks, and WML_t is the return on a value-weighted portfolio of recent winners minus the return on a value-weighted portfolio of recent losers. The same regression is estimated for portfolio R_t^s and for the difference in these two portfolios ($R_t^b - R_t^s$). Panels A, B, and C report four-factor alpha portfolios based on all trades at each brokerage and for the combined sample sorted on measures of attention. In panel A, stocks first are sorted daily on the basis of the current day's abnormal trading volume prior to forming purchase and sale portfolios. Abnormal trading volume is calculated as the ratio of the current day's trading volume (as reported in the CRSP daily stock return files for NYSE, ASE, and NASDAQ stocks) divided by the average trading volume over the previous 252 trading days. In panel B, stocks are first sorted daily into deciles on the basis on the previous day's return as reported in the CRSP daily stock return files for NYSE, ASE, and NASDAQ stocks. In panel C, stocks first are sorted daily on the basis of the current day's abnormal trading volume and then again sorted daily into deciles on the basis on the previous day's return. Deciles 1–2, 3–8, and 9–10 are combined for each sorting criteria prior to forming purchase and sale portfolios.

Panel A: Percentage four-factor alphas for purchase, sales, and purchase less sales portfolios formed after sorting on the current day's abnormal trading volume—combined (2/91 to 6/99)

Abnormal volume sort decile	Buys		Sells		Buys–sells	
	Alpha	*t*-statistic	Alpha	*t*-statistic	Alpha	*t*-statistic
1 (low)	−0.008	−0.010	−0.037	−0.110	0.029	0.060
2	−0.836	−3.250	−0.800	−4.130	−0.036	−0.150
3	−0.162	−0.710	−0.262	−1.530	0.100	0.570
4	0.134	0.680	−0.186	−1.090	0.319	2.370
5	0.095	0.460	0.069	0.380	0.026	0.210
6	0.319	1.650	0.256	1.510	0.064	0.610
7	0.364	1.880	0.288	1.480	0.075	0.760
8	0.557	2.480	0.514	2.440	0.043	0.390
9	0.286	1.100	0.480	1.850	−0.195	−1.450
10 (high)	−0.739	−2.290	−0.049	−0.150	−0.690	−3.830

Panel B: Percentage four-factor alphas for purchase, sales, and purchase less sales portfolios formed after sorting on the previous day's return—combined (2/91 to 6/99)

Abnormal volume sort decile	Buys		Sells		Buys–sells	
	Alpha	*t*-statistic	Alpha	*t*-statistic	Alpha	*t*-statistic
1 (negative return)	0.153	0.390	0.485	1.250	−0.332	−1.770
2	0.440	1.980	0.544	2.540	−0.104	−0.910
3	0.535	3.260	0.526	3.350	0.010	0.090
4	0.658	4.020	0.409	2.800	0.250	2.290
5	0.711	3.180	0.532	2.340	0.178	1.090
6	0.516	2.410	0.249	1.240	0.267	1.970
7	0.224	1.620	0.015	0.120	0.209	2.320
8	0.158	1.020	0.079	0.560	0.079	0.820
9	−0.053	−0.240	0.063	0.310	−0.116	−1.180
10 (positive return)	−1.599	−4.600	−1.090	−3.160	−0.510	−3.790

Panel C: Percentage four-factor alphas for purchase, sales, and purchase less sales portfolios formed after sorting on the current day's abnormal trading volume and on the previous day's return—combined (2/91 to 6/99)

		Volume sort deciles					
		1–2		3–8		9–10	
		Alpha	*t*-statistic	Alpha	*t*-statistic	Alpha	*t*-statistic
Return sort deciles		***Buys***					
	1–2	−0.049	−0.11	0.716	2.43	−0.092	−0.22
	3–8	−0.256	−0.76	0.541	3.18	0.477	1.69
	9–10	−1.129	−2.34	−0.001	0.00	−0.833	−1.89
		Sells					
	1–2	−0.873	−1.94	0.548	1.86	0.613	1.45
	3–8	−0.293	−0.95	0.349	2.43	0.499	1.76
	9–10	−0.970	−1.93	0.121	0.49	−0.225	−0.53
		Buys–sells					
	1–2	0.824	1.68	0.168	1.20	−0.705	−3.56
	3–8	0.037	0.12	0.192	1.91	−0.021	−0.14
	9–10	−0.159	−0.27	−0.122	−0.79	−0.607	−3.21

While the univariate results reported in Table 7.6 (panels A and B) confirm our predictions regarding the effect of attention-based buying on returns, they do not facilitate comparison with the findings of other papers. This is because stocks in the high abnormal volume decile of panel A are likely to have experienced extreme returns, while stocks in the lowest and highest return deciles reported in panel B are likely to have also experienced abnormally high volume. To better distinguish our findings from previous results, in Table 7.6 (panel C) we sort stocks on both abnormal trading volume and returns. For our single-dimensional sorts, alphas for our buy-minus-sell portfolios are negative for volume deciles 9 and 10 and return deciles 1, 2, 9, and 10. Therefore, for both dimensions, we combine deciles 1 and 2, 3 through 8, and 9 and 10. This gives us a manageable nine partitions.

Consider stocks with high abnormal trading volume but unremarkable returns (i.e., panel C, the *column for volume deciles 9–10* and the *rows for return deciles 3–8*). For both the portfolios of stocks purchased and stocks sold by individual investors, there are reliably positive alphas (0.477, $t = 1.69$, and 0.499, $t = 1.76$). This is consistent with Gervais et al.'s finding that the persistent outperformance of stocks with abnormally high trading volume is most pronounced for stocks that did not experience extreme contemporaneous returns.

Now consider stocks with extreme returns and high trading volume (i.e., panel C, the *column for volume deciles 9–10* and the *rows for return deciles 1–2 and 9–10*). Conrad et al. find that for weekly formation periods, mean reversion is most pronounced for stocks with high trading volume. Our analysis weakly confirms their finding. For the purchase portfolio, high-volume high-return stocks experience significant subsequent reversion ($\alpha = -0.833$, $t = -1.89$), but high-volume low-return stocks do not. For the sales portfolio, the alpha for high-volume high-return stocks is consistent with reversion but not statistically significant.[26]

While our double-sort buy-and-sell portfolio results confirm Gervais et al. and are roughly consistent with Conrad et al., our double-sort buy-minus-sell portfolio results confirm the effects of attention-driven buying in high-attention partitions. The high-attention partitions are the intersections of high abnormal volume (i.e., panel C, the *column for volume deciles 9–10*) with extreme return (i.e., panel C, the *rows for return deciles 1–2 and 9–10*). For these high-attention partitions, we get strong confirmation that stocks bought by individual investors underperform those sold. For the high-volume, low-return partition $\alpha = -0.705$ ($t = -3.56$) and for the high-volume, high-return partition $\alpha = -0.607$ ($t = -3.21$).

7.7 CONCLUSION

We propose an alternative model of decision making in which agents faced with many alternatives consider primarily those alternatives that have attention-attracting qualities. Preferences come into play only after attention has limited the choice set.

[26] Several factors may account for discrepancies between Conrad et al.'s and our results. We examine a different time period than they, we focus on stocks heavily trading by individual investors, we sort stocks on previous-day return rather than contemporaneous weekly returns, and we use a slightly different measure of abnormal trading volume. To further determine whether short-term mean reversion can explain our return results, we re-estimate abnormal returns (alphas) using a five-factor model, where the fifth factor is a short-term mean reversion factor. The short-term mean reversion factor is constructed by calculated weekly return (Wednesday to Wednesday). The long portfolio invests in a value-weighted portfolio of losers (stocks with negative weekly returns); the short portfolio invests in a value-weighted portfolio of winners. We value-weight the returns to mitigate the microstructure issues (i.e., bid–ask bounce) that arise when constructing a short-term mean reversion factor. The holding period for each investment is one week. The daily returns on the long and short portfolios are compounded to yield a monthly return. The monthly factor is the difference between the monthly returns of the loser and winner portfolio. Consistent with prior research, this monthly factor is reliably positive (1.50%, $t = 9.60$). Though the factor loadings on the short-term mean reversion factor are positive in all but the lowest abnormal volume decile, the high-abnormal volume sort decile alpha for the five-factor model is −0.636 ($t = -3.37$) and very close to the four-factor alpha of −0.690 ($t = -3.83$) for that decile reported in Table 7.6 (panel A).

When alternatives are many and search costs high, attention may affect choice more profoundly than preferences do. If the attention-grabbing characteristics of an alternative coincide with the characteristics that increase utility, agents may benefit from the role of attention in reducing search costs. However, if attention and utility are orthogonal or negatively correlated, expected utility may be diminished. Under some circumstances, the utility of an alternative is affected by how many agents choose that alternative. Thus, the attention-attracting qualities of an alternative may indirectly detract from its utility. For example, a well-circulated article about a deserted vacation spot could attract the attention and the travel plans of many vacationers, each of whom would be disappointed by the crowds of like-minded tourists. Similarly, attention-based purchases by many investors could temporarily inflate a stock's price, leading to disappointing subsequent returns.

Attention-based decision making has implications for a wide variety of economic situations (e.g., hiring decisions or consumer purchases). In this chapter, we test this model of decision making in the context of common stock purchases. Choosing which common stock to buy presents investors with a huge search problem. There are thousands of possibilities. When selling, most investors consider only stocks they already own, which are typically few in number and can be considered one by one. When buying, however, it is impossible—without the aid of a computer—for most investors to evaluate the merits of every available common stock.

We argue that many investors solve this search problem by considering for purchase only those stocks that have recently caught their attention. While they don't buy every stock that catches their attention, they buy far fewer that don't. Within the subset of stocks that do attract their attention, investors are likely to have personal preferences—contrarians, for example, may select stocks that are out of favor with others. But whether a contrarian or a trend follower, an investor is less likely to purchase a stock that is out of the limelight.

Professional investors are less prone to indulge in attention-driven purchases. With more time and resources, professionals are able to monitor continuously a wider range of stocks. They are unlikely to consider only attention-grabbing stocks. Professionals are likely to employ explicit purchase criteria—perhaps implemented with computer algorithms—that circumvent attention-driven buying. Furthermore, many professionals may solve the problem of searching through too many stocks by concentrating on a particular sector or on stocks that have passed an initial screen.

We test for attention-driven buying by sorting stocks on events that are likely to coincide with catching investors' attention. We sort on abnormal trading volume, since heavily traded stocks must be attracting investors' attention. We sort on extreme 1-day returns since—whether good or bad—these are likely to coincide with attention-grabbing events. And we sort on whether or not a firm is in the news.

Consistent with our predictions, we find that individual investors display attention-driven buying behavior. They are net buyers on high-volume days, following both extremely negative and extremely positive 1-day returns, and when stocks are in the news. Attention-driven buying is similar for large-capitalization stocks and for small stocks. The institutional investors in our sample—especially the value strategy investors—do not display attention-driven buying.

We also test a theoretical model based on the assumption that some investor purchase decisions are influenced by attention. The model predicts that when investors are most influenced by attention, the stocks they buy will subsequently underperform those they sell. We find strong empirical support for this prediction. Not only does attention-based buying not benefit investors, but it appears to also influence subsequent stock returns.

The transactional data we analyze are well suited for documenting what investors do, but not as well suited for determining why they do it. We began with a theory which leads to several new testable predictions about how investors behave. Our empirical analysis confirms these predictions and, in so doing, documents previously undocumented patterns in investor behavior. In Section 7.5, we test one plausible alternative hypothesis to ours. Undoubtedly, readers will look for other alternative explanations for why investors do the things we show they do. To compete with our theory, an alternative theory should predict our results for abnormal volume, extreme returns, news, non-binding short-sale constraints, and returns, while offering new predictions of its own.

Previous work has shown that most investors do not benefit from active trading. On average, the stocks they buy subsequently underperform those they sell (Odean, 1999), and the most active traders underperform those who trade less (Barber and Odean, 2000). The attention-driven buying patterns we document here do not generate superior returns. We believe that most investors will benefit from a strategy of buying and holding a well-diversified portfolio. Investors who insist on hunting for the next brilliant stock would be well advised to remember what California prospectors discovered ages ago: All that glitters is not gold.

7.8 ACKNOWLEDGMENTS

We appreciate the comments of Jonathan Berk, David Blake, Ken French, Simon Gervais, John Griffin, Andrew Karolyi, Sendhil Mullainathan, Mark Rubinstein, and Brett Trueman. We also appreciate the comments of seminar participants at Arizona State University; the Behavioral Decision Research in Management Conference; the University of California, Berkeley; the University of California, Irvine; the Copenhagen Business School; Cornell University; Emory; HEC; Norwegian School of Economics and Business Administration; Ohio State University; Osaka University; the Q Group; the Stanford Institute for Theoretical Economics; the Stockholm School of Economics; the University of Tilburg; Vanderbilt; the Wharton School; the CEPR/JFI Symposium at INSEAD; Mellon Capital Management; the National Bureau of Economic Research; the Risk Perceptions and Capital Markets Conference at Northwestern University; and the European Finance Association Meeting. We are grateful to the Plexus Group, to BARRA, to Barclays Global Investors (for the Best Conference Paper Award at the 2005 European Finance Association Meeting), to the retail broker and discount brokers who provided us with the data for this study, and to the Institute for Quantitative Research and the National Science Foundation (grants SES-0111470 and SES-0222107) for financial support. Shane Shepherd, Michael Foster, and Michael Bowers provided valuable research assistance.

7.9 REFERENCES

Bamber L.S.; Barron O.E.; Stober T.L. (1997) "Trading volume and different aspects of disagreement coincident with earnings announcements," *Accounting Review*, **72**, 575–597.

Barber B.M.; Odean T. (1999) "The courage of misguided convictions: The trading behavior of individual investors," *Financial Analysts Journal*, **55**, 41–55.

Barber B.M.; Odean T. (2000) "Trading is hazardous to your wealth: The common stock investment performance of individual investors," *Journal of Finance*, **55**, 773–806.

Barber B.M.; Odean T. (2001) "Boys will be boys: Gender, overconfidence, and common stock investment," *Quarterly Journal of Economics*, **116**, 261–292.

Barber B.M.; Odean T. (2002) "Online investors: Do the slow die first?" *Review of Financial Studies*, **15**, 455–489.

Barber B.M.; Odean T. (2004) "Are individual investors tax savvy? Evidence from retail and discount brokerage accounts," *Journal of Public Economics*, **88**, 419–442.

Barber B.M.; Odean T.; Ning Zhu (2006) *Do Noise Traders Move Markets?* Working Paper, SSRN. Available at `http://ssrn.com/abstract=869827`

Berk J. (1995) "A critique of size related anomalies," *Review of Financial Studies*, **8**, 275–286.

Busse J.; Green C. (2002) "Market efficiency in real time," *Journal of Financial Economics*, **65**, 415–437.

Carhart M.M. (1997) "On persistence in mutual fund performance," *Journal of Finance*, **52**, 57–82.

Chan W.S. (2003) "Stock price reaction to news and to no-news: Drift and reversal after headlines," *Journal of Financial Economics*, **70**, 223–260.

Choe H.; Kho B.; Stulz R. (2005) "Do domestic investors have an edge? The trading experience of foreign investors in Korea," *Review of Financial Studies*, **18**, 795–829.

Conrad J; Hameed A.; Niden C. (1994) "Volume and autocovariances in short-horizon individual security returns," *Journal of Finance*, **49**, 1305–1329.

Fama E.F.; French K.R. (1993) "Common risk factors in returns on stocks and bonds," *Journal of Financial Economics*, **33**, 3–56.

Gadarowski C. (2001) *Financial Press Coverage and Expected Stock Returns*, Working Paper, SSRN. Available at `http://ssrn.com/abstract=267311`

Genesove D.; Mayer C. (2001) "Nominal loss aversion and seller behavior: Evidence from the housing market," *Quarterly Journal of Economics*, **116**, 1233–1260.

Gervais S.; Kaniel R.; Mingelgrin D.H. (2001) "The high-volume return premium," *Journal of Finance*, **56**, 877–919.

Grossman S.J.; Stiglitz J.E. (1980) "On the impossibility of informationally efficient markets," *American Economic Review*, **70**, 393–408.

Grullon G.; Kanatas G.; Weston J.P. (2004) "Advertising, breadth of ownership, and liquidity," *Review of Financial Studies*, **17**, 439–461.

Heath C.; Huddart S.; Lang M. (1999) "Psychological factors and stock option exercise," *Quarterly Journal of Economics*, **114**, 601–627.

Heisler J. (1994) "Loss aversion in a futures market: An empirical test," *Review of Futures Markets*, **13**, 793–822.

Hirshleifer D.; Myers J.N.; Myers L.A.; Siew Hong Teoh (2003) *Do Individual Investors Drive Post-earnings Announcement Drift? Direct Evidence from Personal Trades*, Working Paper, SSRN. Available at `http://ssrn.com/abstract=299260`

Hou Kewei; Lin Peng; Wei Xiong (2006) *A Tail of Two Anomalies: The Implications of Investor Attention for Price and Earnings Momentum*, Working Paper, Ohio State University.

Kahneman D.; Tversky A. (1979) "Prospect theory: An analysis of decision under risk," *Econometrica*, **46**, 171–185.

Karpoff J.M. (1987) "The relation between price changes and trading volume: A survey," *Journal of Financial and Quantitative Analysis*, **22**, 109–126.

Keim D.B.; Madhavan A. (1995) "Anatomy of the trading process: Empirical evidence on the behavior of institutional traders," *Journal of Financial Economics*, **37**, 371–398.

Keim D.B.; Madhavan A. (1998) "The cost of institutional equity trades," *Financial Analysts Journal*, **54**, 50–69.

Keim D.B.; Madhavan A. (1997) "Transactions costs and investment style: An inter-exchange analysis of institutional equity trades," *Journal of Financial Economics*, **46**, 265–292.

Kyle A.S. (1985) "Continuous auctions and insider trading," *Econometrica*, **53**, 1315–1335.

Lakonishok J.; Shleifer A.; Vishny R.W. (1994) "Contrarian investment, extrapolation, and risk," *Journal of Finance*, **49**, 1541–1578.

Lee C.M.C. (1992) "Earnings news and small traders," *Journal of Accounting and Economics*, **15**, 265–302.

Locke P.; Mann S. (2000) *Do Professional Traders Exhibit Loss Realization Aversion?* Working Paper, SSRN. Available at `http://ssrn.com/abstract=251942`

Mayshar J. (1983) "On divergence of opinion and imperfections in capital markets," *American Economic Review*, **73**, 114–128.

Merton R. (1987) "A simple model of capital market equilibrium with incomplete information," *Journal of Finance*, **42**, 483–510.

Miller E.M. (1977) "Risk, uncertainty, and divergence of opinion," *Journal of Finance*, **32**, 1151–1168.

Odean T. (1998a) "Are investors reluctant to realize their losses?" *Journal of Finance*, **53**, 1775–1779.

Odean T. (1998b) "Volume, volatility, price and profit when all trades are above average," *Journal of Finance*, **53**, 1887–1934.

Odean T. (1999) "Do investors trade too much?" *American Economic Review*, **89**, 1279–1298.

Seasholes M.; Guojun Wu (2004) *Profiting from Predictability: Smart Traders, Daily Price Limits, and Investor Attention*, Working Paper, SSRN. Available at `http://ssrn.com/abstract=527182`

Shapira Z.; Venezia I. (2001) "Patterns of behavior of professionally managed and independent investors," *Journal of Banking and Finance*, **25**, 1573–1587.

Shefrin H.; Statman M. (1985) "The disposition to sell winners too early and ride losers too long: Theory and evidence," *Journal of Finance*, **40**, 777–790.

Weber M.; Zuchel H. (2002) *The Disposition Effect and Momentum*, SFB 504 Discussion Paper 01-26.

Wolff E.N. (2004) *Changes in Household Wealth in the 1980s and 1990s in the U.S.*, Working Paper No. 407, The Levy Economics Institute of Bard College.

8

The impact of news flow on asset returns: An empirical study

Andy Moniz, Gurvinder Brar, Christian Davies, and Adam Strudwick

ABSTRACT

Earnings momentum strategies that the majority of systematic equity investors employ typically do not identify the piece of information that initially triggers the change in analyst forecasts. Here we look at higher frequency information contained within corporate news flow as a leading indicator of analyst revisions to understand what type of information causes analysts to revise their earnings expectations, how the informational content of the signal varies according to the news catalyst, and whether investors can use news flow signals as input into their models.

Our results show that news-flow-based strategies can add value to investors. Those that can react quickly can benefit from the short-term momentum following particular news items and gain an information advantage by incorporating news flow ahead of analyst revisions. Alternatively, investors can enhance performance of existing earnings momentum strategies by either combining this with a news flow signal or by trying to forecast which companies are likely to see analyst revisions post news announcements.

8.1 BACKGROUND AND LITERATURE REVIEW

Equity analysts play an important role in collecting and processing company information and disseminating this to investors. The value contained in earnings forecasts is attributed to analysts' abilities to gather information from a variety of sources and process it in a timely manner to generate superior forecasts. Analysts' relationships with company management are often considered to be important and may provide a valuable insight. If analysts are able to process this information better than the market, they should be able to identify situations in which the market has overreacted or underreacted to earnings.

Could it be the case that analysts are slow to incorporate news flow into their valuation models or are unwilling to revise estimates until they have seen the hard evidence of earnings results? Moreover, the earnings revisions strategies that the majority of our clients employ typically do not identify the piece of information that has triggered the change in forecasts. We only observe the actions of analysts rather than

The Handbook of News Analytics in Finance Edited by L. Mitra and G. Mitra

their motivations such that it is difficult to differentiate between analyst herding that is imitation- or information-driven. Since market prices are driven by expectations of corporate fundamentals and new information leads to a revision of those expectations, here we look at higher frequency information contained within corporate news flow as a leading indicator of analyst revisions to understand how different types of news are incorporated into analysts' earnings forecasts.

Our aim is to understand what type of information causes analysts to revise their earnings expectations, how the informational content of the signal varies according to the news catalyst, and whether investors can use news flow signals as input into their models.

Many of the anomalies that quantitative investors systematically exploit are based on deep-seated behavioural biases. The academic literature points to both the market and analyst misreaction to new information—due to delayed information diffusion, investor inattention and investors' limited ability to process information instantaneously, with implications for stock-specific risk, earnings, and price-momentum-based strategies over the short and medium term.

One focus of academic research has attempted to explain the momentum and reversal characteristics of different investor responses to public and private signals, considering the type of information that causes investors to change their expectations. For example, DeBondt and Thaler (1990) argue that investor myopia results in an overemphasis on recent earnings. Cognitive biases mean that analysts overreact and place too much weight on new information and put less weight on long-term averages. Daniel, Hirshleifer, and Subrahmanyam (1998) model investor behaviour by overconfidence and biased self-attribution. In their model, investors hold too strongly their own information and discount public signals, resulting in underreaction to public information and overreaction to private information; while Barberis, Shleifer, and Vishny (1998) base their model on conservatism and the representativeness heuristic, arguing that investors change their views and overreact or underreact to company earnings based on the past stream of realizations. Hong and Stein (1999) illustrate a model based on the slow diffusion of information through two classes of traders with a differential in processing news, resulting in investors who underreact to news and overreact to non-informational price movements.

The second area of research has focused on earnings momentum, by measuring analyst forecast errors and analyst underreaction to the continuation in returns. Abarbanell and Bernard (1992) find that analyst forecast errors are positively correlated with prior year changes in earnings, implying that analyst forecasts do not fully reflect information in recent changes while Easterwood and Nutt (1999) were the first to examine whether misreaction to new information varies depending on the nature of the information. They show that analysts overreact to good news and underreact to bad news.

More recent research has focused on using computational linguistic methods. For example, Tetlock (2007) uses General Inquirer software to count the number of times words appear within text from predetermined categories within the *Harvard IV-4 Psychosocial Dictionary*. Tetlock shows that firms with a high fraction of negative words in firm-specific news stories prior to announcing earnings go on to announce low earnings. This predictive ability is strongest when the story mentions "earnings" (i.e., news stories with a high proportion of negative returns and a reference to the word "earnings" have even stronger predictive ability in forecasting earnings surprises). The authors find that negative words in firm-specific news stories predict slightly lower returns on the following trading day.

8.1.2 Guided tour

We begin in Sections 8.2 and 8.3 by providing an introduction to the issues and challenges raised when cleaning and analysing news flow datasets to determine the informational content of particular news items. Section 8.4 then considers whether there is a hierarchy to news citations to determine which news flow matters the most for stock returns. In Section 8.5 we combine news flow with a database of detailed analyst revisions. We identify clusters of analyst revisions and examine whether earnings expectations change following certain news flows and, if news does lead revisions, how can investors exploit this effect? Section 8.6 combines this analysis to show how investors can exploit news flow datasets by either trading directly on news flow or combining the dataset with earnings momentum factors.

8.2 ASPECTS OF NEWS FLOW DATASETS

Here we consider the implication of the overreaction and underreaction to news, whether there is a "hierarchy" to information, and consider which news items are deemed most important. The majority of our quantitative research focuses on companies' reported balance sheets or P&L data and sell-side analysts' estimates. It is only recently that we have been able to go beyond this to understand the motivations behind corporates and fundamental analysts' decisions by looking at higher frequency news flow datasets. Over the past few years several data vendors have started to collect and translate headlines and text from sources worldwide, ranging from electronic newswires, newspapers, and magazines. News items are categorized, tagged, and uploaded so that news can be downloaded at the latest by the close of business on the day of the news release. Many news vendors provide low-latency data feeds and analyse the sentiment of stories within milliseconds of the news release.

We begin by considering the issues surrounding cleaning news data to ensure the collection of both timely and relevant information, distinguishing between news types, identifying mixed and stand-alone events, and deciphering informational content. We highlight five key issues specific to analysing news flow.

8.2.1 Timeliness of news

The first challenge is to define an information event. How do we define what is "new" news from what has already been reported? We look beyond just earnings announcements and consider a variety of types of news by regarding news as the release of new information to the market. We restrict our analysis to news sources that are released to our data vendor within a couple of hours of their publication and focus on semi-official sources of information.

To ensure that news flow is both timely and relevant we filter our collection process to the key newswires, stock exchange statements, press releases from company websites, and articles in national, business-focused, newspapers. By focusing on news from these sources, we are more likely to capture new information since companies are required to officially report price-sensitive information in a timely manner. We ignore lesser known newspapers to focus on those with the greatest readership. We also exclude finance- and economic-focused magazines as these are likely to refer to stale news that is more than a week old.

The disadvantage of including newspaper articles in searches is that the majority of information is likely to be reported events from the previous day. Most data vendors have the ability to identify duplicate news articles to limit this issue. The advantage therefore of including newspaper sources in our analysis is that this information may be softer in content and contain more speculative analysis or potentially leaked information such as asset sales or M&A speculation. Our database therefore contains a variety of news including official releases, softer strategic information, and potentially speculative articles.

8.2.2 Relevance of news

To ensure that news articles directly relate to a company rather than mention a company in a non-stock-specific context, we rely on data vendors' classifications to search for company mentions that are either in news headlines or in the first paragraph of text within the article. Some vendors such as RavenPack provide a relevance score to enable users to refine their signals to company-specific information. Having decided on which news articles to include, the second issue is to avoid double-counting news on the same subject from multiple sources. We therefore only note if there was news on a particular day rather than focus on how many news stories there are from different or even the same news source for each category.

8.2.3 Classification of news

Having downloaded news, the next biggest challenge is how to classify items into different categories. Keyword searches to analyse news means that there are potentially hundreds of different types of event categories.

At the broadest level, corporate news can be classified as either accounting-related "hard" information or strategic "soft" news. The former consists of financial statement information (earnings statements, trading updates) and management guidance of future performance, while the latter includes corporate presentations, joint ventures, strategic alliances, product launches, and broker conferences.

The key difference between these two categories is that news containing accounting-related information can be readily adapted into analysts' valuation models, whereas strategic news contains more qualitative information which is useful for valuation purposes but difficult to interpret. This means that the financial implications need to be inferred or estimated. Accounting-related news is more likely to be on predictable dates, enabling analysts to form an expectation of the news in advance of the announcement. On the other hand, strategic information is more likely to be sporadic and consequently takes longer for analysts and the market to decipher the information content.

Accounting related news

Earnings	Trading updates	Guidance	Financial issues	Credit rating news
Announcements of earnings	Announcements of sales/trading statement	Guidance/update calls	Buybacks	S&P credit rating changes
Restatements of operating results	Conference presentation calls		Dividend announcements	
Annual general meetings	Sales/trading statement calls		Debt financing related	
Special/extraordinary shareholders meetings	Shareholder/analyst calls		Fixed income offerings	
			Follow-on equity offerings	

Strategic news

M&A related	Restructuring	Product related	Corporate governance	Other news
M&A rumors and discussions	Business reorganizations	Client announcements	Executive changes - CEO	Index changes
M&A transaction announcements	Changes in company bylaws/rules	Product-related announcements	Executive changes - CFO	Address changes
Seeking Acquisitions/investments	Discontinued operations/downsizings	Strategic alliances	Executive/board changes - other	Ticker changes
Seeking financing/partners	Lawsuits & legal issues			
Seeking to sell/divest	Bankruptcy related			
Spin-offs	Labor-related announcements			
	Business expansions			

Figure 8.1. Classification of news (source: RavenPack, Factiva, Factset, Macquarie Quant Research).

To simplify and provide a more meaningful analysis we classify news into these two broad categories, which each contain a further five news types (see Figure 8.1). The former group includes quarterly earnings announcements, trading updates, and stand-alone earnings guidance while the latter includes corporate governance issues, product launches, and M&A news. We include M&A under the softer category rather than under accounting-related news as this category also refers to newspaper speculation and company intentions for M&A and asset disposals.

8.2.4 Independence of news

One of the biggest challenges of analysing news flow is the independence of news items. Companies may announce clusters of news items that fall under different categories within the same day. For example, a company may announce a profit warning, the resignation of its CEO, and provide guidance on its sales outlook all on the same day. Figure 8.2 shows the degree of overlap of news for earnings, guidance, and trading-related articles. Typically we find that when a company announces guidance, half of the time the company also reports its earnings.

Rather than separately placing each of these news items into three different news categories and ignoring the degree of overlap, we develop a hierarchy of news by identifying all other relevant news for each company on the same day. We have also obtained a calendar of earnings announcements, corporate guidance, trading updates, broker conferences, and corporate roadshows so that we can match news to events and classify news items as either mixed or stand-alone events. Only if a news event occurs independently of another event do we classify it under its own category as a stand-alone news event.

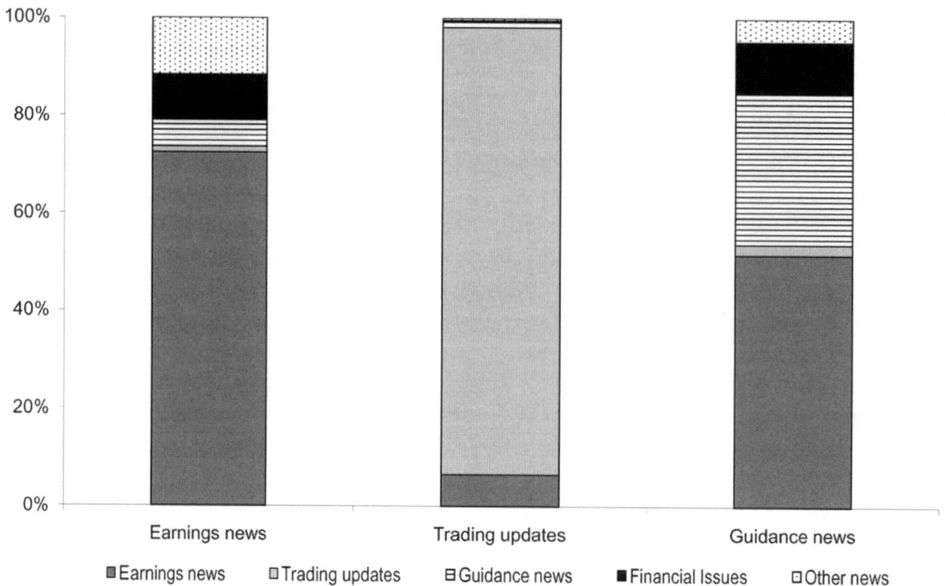

Figure 8.2. Degree of news overlap (source: RavenPack, Factiva, Factset, Macquarie Quant Research).

8.2.5 Informational content of news

Having tackled collecting and cleaning the news flow data, the biggest challenge is how to decide on whether news is indeed newsworthy and whether the news article reflects good or bad news. There are three main approaches used in the academic literature

- *Computational linguistics* A relatively new approach in the financial academic literature is to use machine-learning techniques for automated text classification developed through computational linguists. Natural language-processing techniques are used in a variety of fields, ranging from insurance companies seeking to detect fraudulent claims to journalists analysing the sentiment of political speeches. One of the difficulties of applying such techniques to finance, however, is to take into account the forward-looking nature of markets. It is the expectation of news and the extent that stock prices already reflect this expectation that matters. We not only need to decipher the informational content of news, but decide whether this is "new" news or public information that has already been impounded into stock prices. The approach by Tetlock, Tsechansky, and Macskassy (2008), for example, uses the Harvard-IV-4 psychosocial dictionary which classifies words as either positive or negative. The authors then count the proportion of negative words in each story.

  In contrast to recent academic research which focuses on algorithms based on generic English dictionaries, certain data vendors have been specifically designed to match financial news. Several data vendors use Bayesian Classifiers to map key words, phrases, combinations, and other word-level definitions to pre-defined sentiment values.

  However, one of the challenges of such an approach is to identify the context in which that language is used. For example, the mention of a "dividend cut" may screen as a negative using dictionary-based algorithms, though in previous research we have found that during the financial crisis, such news was often taken positively by the market if the cash was saved to pay down debt. To take into account the dynamic nature of markets, we have since investigated alternative approaches including pattern recognition algorithms and supervised learning techniques to discriminate between positive and negative news sentiment. Other classification approaches used by data vendors include training datasets on the results of financial analysts manually tagging equity stories and market response classifiers trained on the markets' immediate response to news.

- *Media coverage* An alternative method is to define event days according to unusually high media coverage. An interesting approach along these lines was adopted by Lumsdaine (2009) who gathered Bloomberg data on the count of investor readership of news stories for the bank sector during the Credit Crisis. A simpler approach could be to monitor abnormal trading volumes. The argument is that, when investors pay greater attention to stocks, they are more likely to trade, thus generating higher volumes. The attractiveness of using an abnormal trading volume factor is that historical data are readily available across the global regions. However, the pitfalls of using this factor to proxy attention are that it captures investors' actions rather than identifying the motivations to trade and trading activity around corporate actions (such as share buybacks) or dividend announcements may cloud the relevance of using trading volume to capture investor attention effects. Moreover, with the growing importance of liquidity dark pools, traditional databases are missing significant information on trading volumes which may limit the efficacy of this factor.
- *Market-based measures* Finally, market-based measures can be used to define the importance of news, measuring abnormal returns over a window around news announcements and using a threshold to determine whether news is positive, neutral, or negative.

Ultimately, there are pros and cons with each of these approaches. Market-based measures take into account the markets' expectations of the news flow prior to its announcement so that returns measure the surprise element of the news announcement. The drawback to classifying news in this way is that it can only be measured ex post based on observed returns so strategies cannot be implemented immediately. On the other hand, text-based classifying algorithms offer a more timely approach, analysing sentiment without relying on the need for returns. The disadvantage is that it becomes difficult to isolate the "surprise" element from what is "known" news within an announcement.

8.3 UNDERSTANDING NEWS FLOW DATASETS

Having cleaned the dataset, we were left with a sample of 90,000 news announcements from January 2001 onwards for companies within the S&P Large-Cap Europe universe (around 450 stocks). Figure 8.3 plots the time-series of news categories for a large-cap European universe. It shows that the majority of news items relate to company earnings news or guidance with the remainder equally split across other news categories. Figure 8.4 shows that news releases are not equally distributed across different calendar

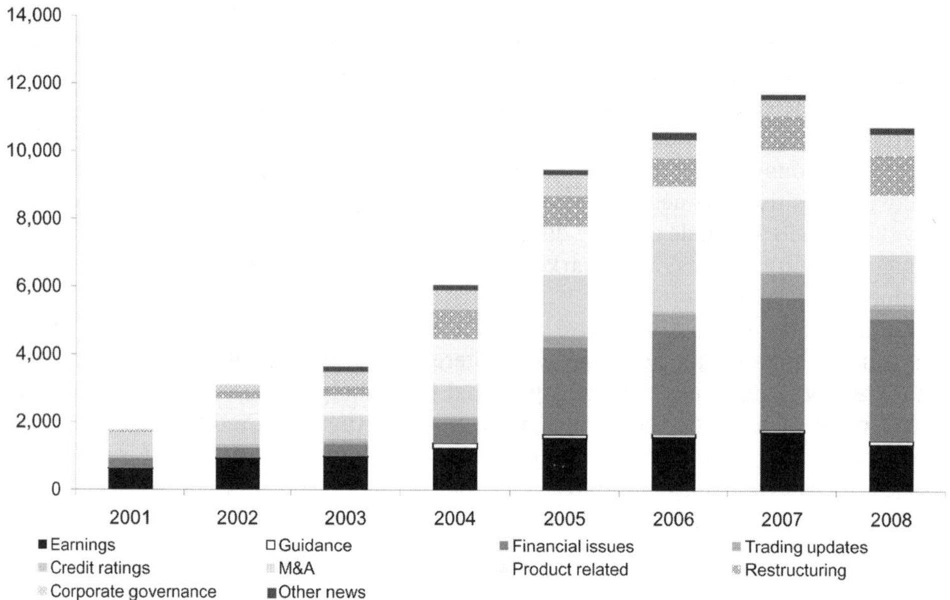

Figure 8.3. Categorizing news flow by year (source: RavenPack, Factiva, FactSet, Macquarie Quant Research).

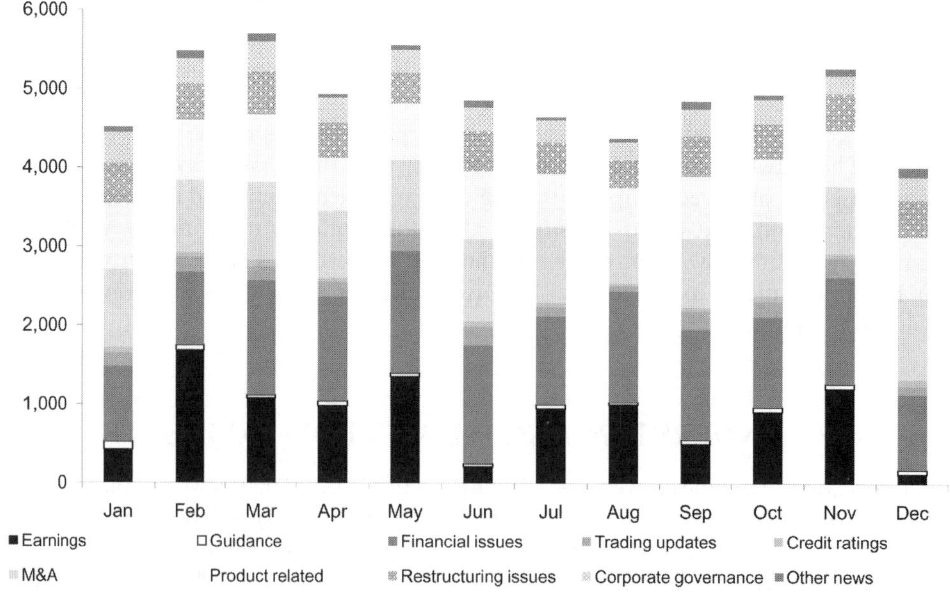

Figure 8.4. Categorizing news flow by month (source: RavenPack, Factiva, FactSet, Macquarie Quant Research).

months. On average we find that just over half of all companies have some news reported each month, ranging from 30% at the beginning of the sample to 70% currently. We find that news stocks have a 60% chance of having more news in a subsequent month (be it good/bad news) and no-news stocks have a 30% chance.

We also find a statistically lower incidence of news reported on Fridays compared with the rest of the working week. Along a similar vein, academic research typically finds that Mondays and Fridays are light information days compared with Tuesdays and Thursdays and suggests that the short-term price and volume reactions to earnings announcements on Fridays are smaller and tend to drift more, attributed to lower investor attention on Fridays. Interestingly, some studies find that firms tend to release bad news after the close of trading on Fridays due to lower investor attention.

The coverage of news is an increasing function of the size of the company since larger and more liquid companies are more likely to be in the media. Based on our sample, we find correlations between the log market cap/6-month average daily trading volume and news citations of around 35%. The top-size quintile each month accounts for 40% of all news articles, while the bottom quintile accounts for just 5%. Coverage has also benefited over time from the better collection of news by data vendors and quarterly reporting post the introduction of IFRS in 2005.

8.4 DOES NEWS FLOW MATTER?

The challenge of running long-term event studies with news flow datasets is how to control for the release of subsequent news items which may or may not be in the same direction. We find that the incidence of news is not highly autocorrelated. A company can switch from being a news winner to a news loser several times over a year. The average proportion of stocks switching from a news winner to loser (and vice versa) is fairly equal. This means that any news patterns are likely to be influenced by single news events rather than the accumulated reaction to multiple items.

Our focus is therefore on the short-term reaction to news. We measure the short-term price reaction on a sector-relative basis around news announcements which aims to capture the informational surprise of the news. We sort returns into three groups and categorize news flow as either positive, negative, or marginal to avoid reacting on every reported news item and focus on the major news releases. We then measure subsequent returns over days 2–5 and 5–10 post the announcement.

Figures 8.5 and 8.6 show the average short-term returns for different news items, distinguishing between good and bad news. Our results show that investors react strongly to earnings announcements and guidance news, which is not unsurprising as investors focus more on these news items when making their assessments. The share price reaction to other news is also important but lesser so compared with earnings-related news. Over the next five days, the payoffs are marginally positive, but relatively similar. Similar inferences can be made about negative news releases.

The results above show that there is a hierarchy to news citations, with earnings-related news having a larger impact. We also consider whether news influences trading volumes beyond the day of the release, by comparing abnormal trading volumes around announcements. We find that, following positive news, trading volumes are significantly higher for earnings and M&A-related news. When news releases are bad, we find

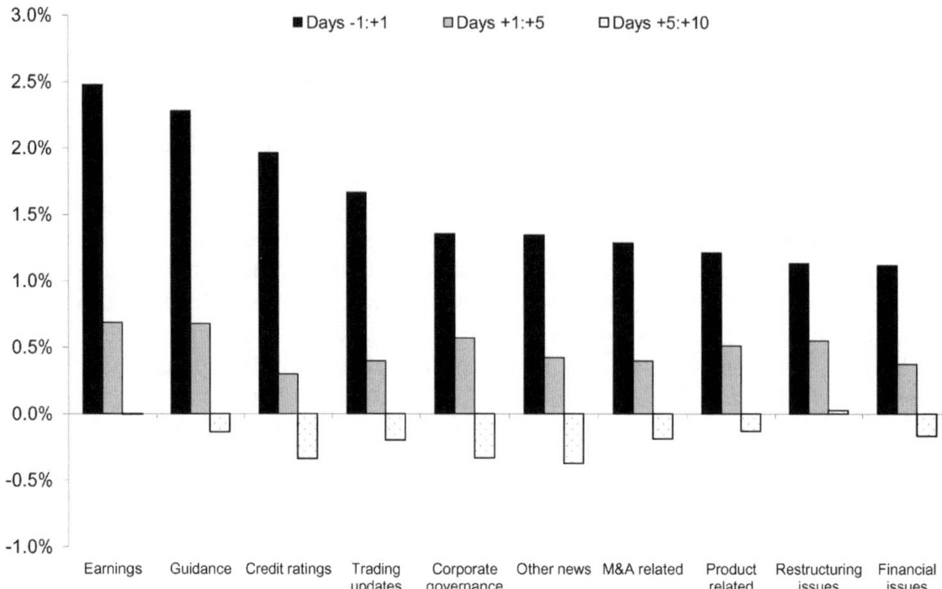

Figure 8.5. Short-term price reaction to good news flow (source: RavenPack, Factiva, FactSet, Macquarie Quant Research).

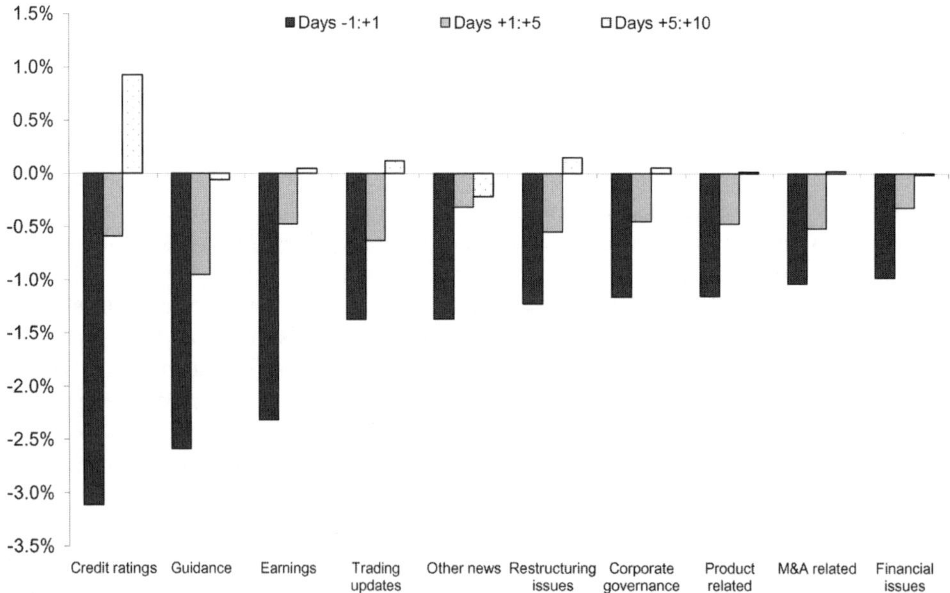

Figure 8.6. Short-term price reaction to bad news flow (source: RavenPack, Factiva, FactSet, Macquarie Quant Research).

significantly higher trading volumes for earnings news, guidance, and restructuring stories.

Lastly, the business cycle also affects the dominance of news items. Academic research by Antweiler and Frank (2005) finds that on average news during an expansion is good news, whereas news during a recession is bad news. In most cases the market response is stronger during a recession that it is during an expansion. When we run regressions of short-term returns post the news citation conditional upon whether it was good or bad news, we observe that in periods of economic slowdown (2001–2002 and 2008–2009) bad news relating to credit downgrades or earnings is deemed more important.

8.5 NEWS FLOW AND ANALYST REVISIONS

Next we consider the impact of such misreaction to information by focusing on the implication for earnings momentum strategies. From a quantitative perspective, investors have traditionally relied upon earnings momentum factors to incorporate corporate news flow. A consistent strategy based on buying companies each month that have seen the most broker upgrades, and selling those with the most downgrades would have generated an annualized return of 9.1% pa since 1990. Earnings revisions strategies, however, typically do not identify the piece of information that has triggered the change in forecasts. We only observe the actions of analysts, rather than the motive behind analysts' actions.

Here we consider whether earnings expectations change following certain news flows and, if news does lead revisions, how can investors exploit this effect?

To proxy for changes in the market's expectation of earnings around news, we focus on revisions "clusters" (detailed below) using detailed analyst EPS revisions. Using individual analyst EPS forecasts we calculate the dates when revision clusters are formed. Our aim is to match revisions clusters to news items to understand what triggers changes in analyst forecasts.

Following Bagnoli, Levine, and Watts (2005a, b), we define a revisions cluster as occurring when at least three different analysts have revised their EPS forecasts within three trading days for a given company. Once a cluster begins, the end date is marked when more than three trading days have passed between sequential revisions. The end date is then the date of the last revision within the cluster. This approach means that we restrict our analysis to instances of significant revision activity and implicitly focus on larger cap companies, thereby avoiding the issue that less liquid companies have less news flow.

Having identified the revisions clusters, we then search for corporate news flow within a 5-day window around the start date which may have triggered the first analyst revision. Figure 8.7 shows the number of matched revisions clusters over time, while Table 8.1 shows for each news type the percentage that result in a revision cluster and the importance of that news type as a percentage of total revisions.

Our results show that significantly more clusters occur after earnings announcements, implying that analysts are reluctant to change forecasts without first seeing hard evidence. Twice as many revisions clusters are associated with accounting-related news than strategic news. Table 8.1 shows that we have seen revisions clusters form 43% of the time following earnings-related news. These revisions account for 31% of all analyst

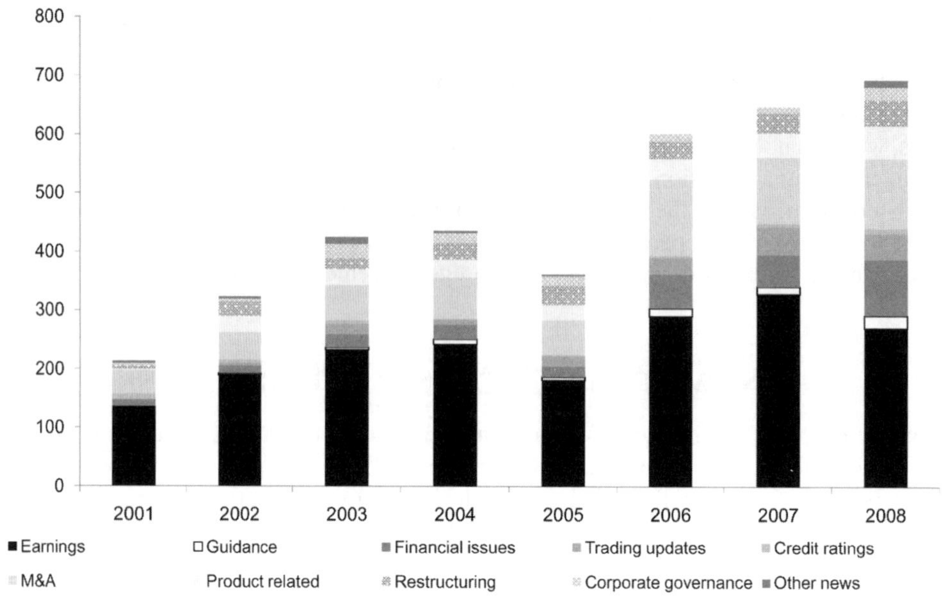

Figure 8.7. Revisions clusters by year (source: RavenPack, Factiva, FactSet, Macquarie Quant Research).

Table 8.1. Revisions clusters by news type

	No. of news items	% of all news	% of news with revisions clusters	% of all matched revisions	% of revisions made within 2 days	Average duration of revisions cluster (days)	Standard deviation of revisions cluster (days)
Accounting-related news	29,061	49	28	58	44	6.9	4.7
Strategic news	30,238	51	20	42	28	6.7	5.1
Earnings	10,404	18	43	31	56	7.3	4.7
Trading updates	2,173	4	25	4	43	6.3	4.7
Guidance	689	1	38	2	47	6.4	4.5
Corporate governance	3,684	6	19	5	27	6.5	4.9
M&A-related	10,978	19	19	14	30	6.4	4.8
Restructuring	5,498	9	21	8	30	6.7	5.3
Product-related	9,014	15	22	14	26	7.0	5.3
Financial issues	15,079	25	18	19	25	6.5	4.5
Credit-rating news	716	1	24	1	37	6.6	5.2
Other news	1,064	2	18	1	32	6.3	4.9

Source: RavenPack, Factiva, FactSet, Macquarie Quant Research.

revisions following announcements, while a further 19% of revisions are associated with financial issues (e.g., buybacks and dividend announcements). These proportions have remained relatively stable over time, suggesting that analysts do not take into account alternative information at different points in the business cycle, reacting instead predominantly after quarterly earnings announcements or on guidance news.

Prior research shows that analysts take longer to digest strategic news as the information is more difficult to map into estimates than accounting-related news. Bagnoli, Levine, and Watts (2005a, b) show that softer strategic news is initially less well understood and that it takes time for this information to be interpreted before analysts react. Such information may only result in a longer term price reaction.

Table 8.1 shows the average duration of each revisions cluster and the percentage of revisions that occur within two days of the news announcement. We find that around 50% of revisions following earnings and guidance news are made within the subsequent two days, implying that analysts are quick to respond to such information. On the other hand, we find that less than one-third of analyst revisions following strategic news occur within the same time period, confirming that it takes analysts longer to digest the information and suggesting that clusters are triggered by analysts herding towards a lead analyst.

Figure 8.8 shows the average change in EPS forecasts from a revisions cluster, conditioned on good or bad news. When news is good, financial news followed by earnings news has typically resulted in the largest increase in EPS forecasts. When news is negative, credit-rating changes and guidance news see the greatest EPS downgrades. Figure 8.9 illustrates the short-term returns (over a 3-day window) of revision clusters conditioned on different types of news. Again we find that earnings and financially

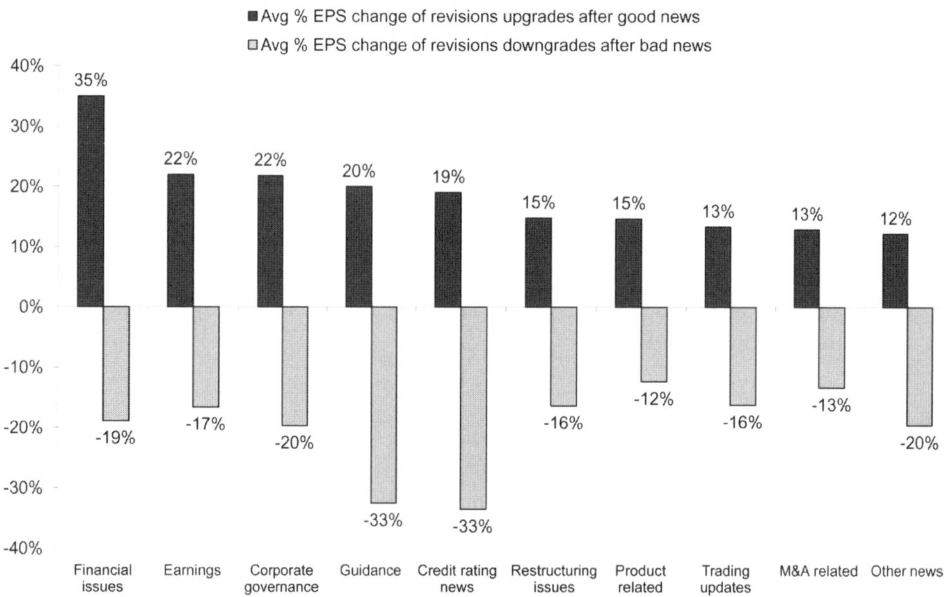

Figure 8.8. Revisions clusters by news type (source: RavenPack, Factiva, FactSet, Macquarie Quant Research).

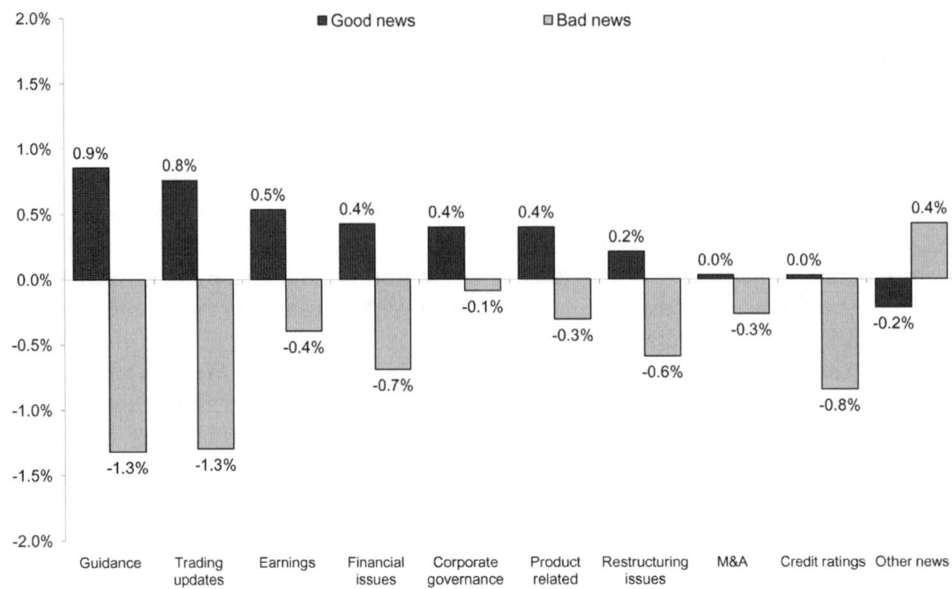

Figure 8.9. Average change in EPS estimates following news (source: RavenPack, Factiva, FactSet, Macquarie Quant Research).

related information receive the greatest share price reaction, whether the news is good or bad. The rank correlation based on our measure of short-term returns and standardized unexpected earnings (measured as the change in analyst EPS next 12-month forecasts over the same window) are close to 20% for earnings-related and guidance-related news.

8.6 DESIGNING A TRADING STRATEGY

8.6.1 Turning a dataset into a trading signal

Extracting and cleaning a news flow dataset is only the initial challenge. There are a variety of ways to incorporate this information into a trading strategy. We briefly highlight some of the issues worth considering when taking a news signal and designing an event-driven trading strategy.

8.6.2 How to define the event?

Companies may announce several different news items over the course of a month, which may either be received positively, negatively, or with a muted price reaction. Following the release of information it may be the case that the market and/or analysts initially overreact or underreact to the news. Analysts may wait for a series of confirmatory news signals over a couple of months before considering changing their forecasts. Should we react to every news item or wait for a trend in consecutive news items?

8.6.3 What is the informational content of the event?

Once we see an event, how do we systematically decide whether it is significant? The number of news items for each company are too high to regard every news report as an event. One approach could be to wait for analyst forecast changes following the news, though, as we have shown, analysts may be slow to react or reluctant to act at all. Alternatively, we can define significant news by its short-term price reaction, though the secondary issue is deciding which thresholds to use to define positive and negative news so that we do not react to every piece of information.

8.6.4 What is the holding period?

If we buy stocks following positive news flow and then discover two days later that there is some mildly negative news, should we close the position after the two days? Such an approach would impose excessive turnover and limit the breadth of the strategy as there would only be a few stocks in the portfolio at any point in time.

Here we highlight a simple event-driven strategy that takes advantage of earnings revisions momentum. Historically, earnings revisions have worked as a factor because earnings revisions and earnings surprises tend to be followed by more revisions and surprises in the same direction. In other words, stock prices tend to underreact initially to the information in these events, and then drift in the direction of the event over time (see Xu, 2008).

Here we show how investors can gain an advantage by using news flow to trade ahead of analyst revisions. We begin by defining an information event as either good or bad news based on the 1-day sector-relative price reaction around the news citation. We then estimate the threshold breakpoints using the returns over the past three months and group the subsequent period event returns into three baskets to define positive, neutral, and negative news. Since the thresholds for the baskets change on a rolling basis, we take into account the changing relative importance of different types of news over the business cycle. We initially focus on all news events and then restrict our analysis to accounting-related "hard" vs. strategic "soft" news.

Our strategy is to buy companies with positive returns around news events, sell those with negative returns and ignore companies which are considered to have neutral news flow. We assume that stocks are bought at the closing price on the day after the news release and hold them for 20 days, so as to increase the breadth of the strategy. If we see another news item within the 20-day window, we only close the position if the stock switches from the top/bottom basket.

Our results show that investors can exploit news flow datasets by either trading directly on news flow or combining the dataset with earnings momentum factors. Table 8.2 shows that such a strategy has generated an annualized long/short return of 14.5% pa with an information ratio of 1.85 (pre-costs). Investors who can react quickly can benefit from the short-term momentum following news (in particular, accounting-related news). Given the daily nature of this strategy and consequently high turnover, a more practical approach may be to apply news flow as a filter on existing investment processes (using stock-specific news flow as a technical overlay to identify overbought/sold companies).

Table 8.2. Backtest summary statistics (daily, 2001–2009)

	Annualized return (top basket) (%)	Annualized return (bottom basket) (%)	Annualized return (long–short) (%)	Annualized volatility (long–short) (%)	Information ratio (long–short)	Maximum daily drawdown (%)	Turnover (long–short) (%)	Hit rate (%)	Average number of stocks per basket
Earnings momentum strategy	3.6	−4.0	7.6	11.6	0.66	−3.3	3,933	52	43
News momentum (all)	7.3	−7.2	14.5	7.8	1.85	−2.8	2,463	56	65
News momentum (accounting-related)	10.3	−6.4	16.7	9.5	1.77	−3.8	2,646	56	44
News momentum (strategic)	4.3	−8.5	12.8	9.5	1.35	−4.2	2,835	54	48
Combining earnings and news momentum[a]	11.0	−12.7	23.7	16.2	1.47	−6.0		54	22
Contrarian strategy[b]	8.0	−7.6	15.6	8.3	1.87	−2.9		55	41

[a] Buy companies with positive news and strong analyst sentiment and sell companies with negative news and poor analyst sentiment.
[b] Buy companies with positive news though poor analyst sentiment and sell companies with negative news though strong analyst sentiment.
Source: Ravenpack, Factiva, FactSet, Macquarie Quant Research.

Our results show that investors can enhance the performance of existing earnings momentum strategies by combining this with a news flow signal. We find that the information ratio more than doubles as compared with traditional earnings momentum strategies. We also consider portfolios based on the combination of earnings momentum and news flow. For example, a strategy based on buying upgraded stocks with positive accounting news flow and selling downgraded companies with poor strategic news has generated an information ratio of 1.47 vs. a standard earnings momentum strategy of 0.66. The most interesting of these backtests, however, is the final row which highlights a strategy based on anticipating which companies are likely to see analyst revisions post announcements. Here we identify companies that are currently out of favour by sell-side analysts but have announced positive news flow. We buy these companies in anticipation of analyst upgrades over the following few days, taking advantage of the fact that it takes them longer to process and interpret the information content of news. Similarly, we sell companies that are currently in favour by analysts but have announced bad news. Such a strategy has the highest information ratio of 1.87, with an annualized return of 15.6%.

Our results show that news-flow-based strategies can add value to investors. Those that can react quickly can benefit from the short-term momentum following news (in particular, earnings news) and gain an information advantage by incorporating news flow ahead of analyst revisions. Alternatively, investors can enhance the performance of existing earnings momentum strategies by either combining this with a news flow signal (buying upgraded stocks with positive news flow, selling downgraded companies with poor strategic news) or by trying to forecast which companies are likely to see analyst revisions post news announcements.

8.7 SUMMARY AND DISCUSSIONS

We began this article by highlighting that the earnings revisions strategies that the majority of investors employ typically do not identify the piece of information that has triggered the change in forecasts. Our aim has been to understand what type of information causes analysts to revise their earnings expectations, how the informational content of the signal varies according to the news catalyst, and whether investors can use news flow signals as input to their models. We have shown that there is a hierarchy to the informational content of news and that investors can gain an advantage by using news flow to trade ahead of analyst revisions.

Our initial analysis on news flow has since stemmed into a variety of research projects. With over 80% of corporate data estimated to be unstructured (the most common unstructured data is text), this is a growing area of research. With data vendors dedicating greater resources to the collection and analysis of news flow, there is no reason for research to be limited to traditional corporate events such as earnings and trading updates. Data vendors and researchers are able to scour through internet blogs, social network sites, and Google Trends to find novel sources of information.

One of the perhaps surprising results from our earlier analysis in Section 8.4 is that there is no serial correlation in corporate news. Companies are equally likely to report good and bad news going forward. Since undertaking this initial research we have focused on more granular news flow and have found that there is serial correlation to certain news items and that this has predictive power to forecast company earnings. By working with our fundamental analysts we have been able to better understand which news items are of most interest and relevance. Along this vein, news flow may be classified as company-specific (such as patent grants) or relate to broader industry trends (e.g., global freight demand and semiconductor sales). Using statistical techniques that model the time-series properties of the data we have built models that forecast the direction of company and industry earnings using passenger numbers for transport companies, retail vs. wholesale inflation for retailers, and commodity demand and supply imbalances for materials companies.

With quarterly earnings data for European companies only going back a few years (post the introduction of IFRS in 2005), the ability to backtest specific news flow and earnings has been limited. However, the huge changes in market dynamics and behaviour in recent years means that such backtests are less of a concern. Indeed, in an attempt to stay ahead of the competition, many institutional investors subscribe to direct broker feeds to gain access to fundamental analyst DCF models and proprietary data sources to stay ahead of consensus.

In conclusion, the analysis of news flow datasets is a complex though exciting area of research. There are many ways to derive a trading signal using this information either in isolation or to incorporate it into existing investment processes, providing many opportunities for future research. We have used news flow datasets to create sector rotation models, forecast individual companies' earnings and dividends, and understand price momentum and short squeezes. Our philosophy to research has been to combine quantitative techniques with a fundamental insight to stock selection. News flow datasets enable systematic investors to bridge the gap between the two.

8.8 REFERENCES

Abarbanell J.S.; Bernard V. (1992) "Tests of analysts' overreaction/underreaction to earnings information as an explanation for anomalous stock price behavior," *Journal of Finance*, **47**, 1181–1207.

Antweiler W.; Frank M. (2005) *The Market Impact of Corporate News Stories*, Working Paper, University of British Columbia.

Bagnoli M.; Levine S.; Watts S.G. (2005a) "Analyst estimation clusters and corporate events, part I," *Annals of Finance*, **1**(3), 245–265.

Bagnoli M.; Levine S.; Watts S.G. (2005b) "Analyst estimation clusters and corporate events, part II," *Annals of Finance*, **1**(4).

Barber B.M.; Odean T. (2008) "All that glitters: The effect of attention and news on the buying behavior of individual and institutional investors," *Review of Financial Studies*, **21**.

Barberis N.; Shleifer A.; Vishny R. (1998) "A model of investor sentiment," *Journal of Financial Economics*, **49**, 307–343.

Bernard V.; Thomas J. (1989) "Post earnings announcement drift: Delayed price response or risk premium," *Journal of Accounting Research*, Suppl. 27, 1–36

Berry T.; Howe K. (1994) "Public information arrival," *Journal of Finance*, **49**, 1331–1346.

Brar G. (2009) *Quantamentals: Momentum Seeking Attention*, Macquarie Quantitative Research.

Chan L K.C.; Jegadeesh N.; Lakonishok J. (1996) "Momentum strategies," *Journal of Finance*, **51**, 1681–1714.

Chan W.S. (2003) "Stock price reaction to news and no-news: Drift and reversal after headlines," *Journal of Financial Economics*, **70**(2), 223–260.

Cooper R.; Day T.; Lewis C. (2001) "Following the leader: A study of individual analysts' earnings forecasts," *Journal of Financial Economics*, **61**(3), 383–416.

Daniel K.; Hirshleifer D.; Subrahmanyam A. (1998) "Investor psychology and security market under- and over-reactions," *Journal of Finance*, **53**, 1839–1886.

Davies C. (2009) *Quantamentals: Do Technicals Add Value?*, Macquarie Quantitative Research.

DeBondt W.F.M.; Thaler R. (1985) "Does the stock market overreact?" *Journal of Finance*, **40**, 793–805.

DeBondt W.F.M.; Thaler R. (1990) "Do security analysts overreact?" *The American Economic Review*, **80**(2), paper presented at the *Hundred and Second Annual Meeting of the American Economic Association, May*, pp. 52–57.

DellaVigna S.; Pollet J. (forthcoming) "Investor inattention and Friday earnings announcements," *Journal of Finance.*

Easterwood J.C.; Nutt S. (1999) "Inefficiency in analysts' earnings forecasts: Systematic misreaction or systematic optimism?" *Journal of Finance*, **54**(5), 1777–1797.

Fehle F.; Zdorovtsov V. (2002) *Large Price Declines, News, Liquidity and Trading Strategies: An Intraday Analysis*, Working Paper, University of South Carolina.

Francis J.; Schipper K.; Vincent L. (2002) "Expanded disclosures and the increased usefulness of earnings announcements," *The Accounting Review*, **77**, 515–546.

Hirshleifer D.; Teoh S. (2003) "Herd behavior and cascading in capital markets: A review and synthesis." *European Financial Management*, **9**(1), 25–66.

Hong H.; Lim T.; Stein J. (2000) "Bad news travels slowly: Size, analyst coverage, and the profitability of momentum strategies," *Journal of Finance*, **55**, 265–295.

Hong H.; Stein J.C. (1999) "A unified theory of underreaction, momentum trading and overreaction in asset markets," *Journal of Finance*, **54**, 2143–2184.

Ivkovic Z.; Jegadeesh N. (2004) "The timing and value of forecast and recommendation revisions," *Journal of Financial Economics*, **73**(3), 433–463.

Jegadeesh N.; Titman S. (1993) "Returns to buying winners and selling losers: Implications for stock market efficiency," *Journal of Finance*, **48**, 65–91.

Kim C.F.; Lee S.; Pantzalis C. (2008) "Analyst forecast inefficiency in reaction to earnings news: Cognitive bias vs. economic incentives," unpublished.

Lau B. (2007) *The Macquarie Sentiment Indicator*, Macquarie Quantitative Research.

Lau B. (2009) *Earnings Revisions Impact: Analysts that Move the Market*, Macquarie Quantitative Research.

Leinweber D. (2009) *Nerds on Wall Street: Math, Machines and Wired Markets*, John Wiley & Sons.

Lumsdaine R. (2009) "What the market watched: Bloomberg news stories and bank returns as the financial crisis unfolded," unpublished working paper, American University.

Moniz A. (2009) *Quantamentals: Exploiting Dividend Uncertainty*, Macquarie Quantitative Research.

Moniz A. (2009) *Quantamentals: Arming Models with Industry-specific Data*, Macquarie Quantitative Research.

Moniz A. (2010) *Quantamentals: Refining Short Interest*, Macquarie Quantitative Research.

Nofsinger J. (2001) "The impact of public information on investors," *Journal of Banking and Finance*, **25**, 1339–1366.

Patell J.; Wolfson M. (1984) "The intraday speed of adjustment of stock prices to earnings and dividend announcements," *Journal of Financial Economics*, **13**, 223–252.

Peng L.; Xiong W. (2006) "Investor attention, overconfidence and category learning," *Journal of Financial Economics*, **80**, 563–602.

Penman S. (1987) "The distribution of earnings news over time and seasonalities in aggregate stock returns," *Journal of Financial Economics*, **18**, 199–228.

Ryan P.; Taffler R. (2002) *What Firm-specific News Releases Drive Economically Significant Stock Returns and Trading Volumes?*, Working Paper, Cranfield University.

Stickel S. (1989) "The timing of and incentives for annual earnings forecasts near interim earnings announcements," *Journal of Accounting and Economics*, **11**(2/3), 275–292.

Strudwick A. (2009) *Stop the Losses, Take the Profits*, Macquarie Quantitative Research.

Tetlock P.C. (2007) "Giving content to investor sentiment: The role of media in the stock market," *Journal of Finance*, **62**, 1139–1168.

Tetlock P.C.; Saar-Tsechansky M.; Macskassy, S. (2008) "More than words: Quantifying language to measure firms' fundamentals," *Journal of Finance*, **63**, 1437–1467.

van Dijk R.; Huibers F. (2002) "European price momentum and analyst behavior," *Financial Analysts Journal*, **58**(2), 96–105.

Xu P. (2008) "Why have estimate revision measures not worked in recent years?" *Journal of Portfolio Management*, **34**(3).

Zhang F. (2006a) "Information uncertainty and analyst forecast behavior," *Contemporary Accounting Research*, **23**(2), 565–590.

Zhang Y. (2004) *Analysts' Responsiveness and Market Underreaction to Earnings Announcements*, Working Paper, Columbia University.

9

Sentiment reversals as buy signals

John Kittrell

ABSTRACT

The company-specific metric of *net news sentiment* is defined and shown to predict long-term positive excess stock returns. A sequence of news stories about a company induces a sequence of sentiment measurements (positive or negative relative to the company), and when significant movements of such sequences from negative to positive are treated as buy signals, the universe of stocks so defined outperforms the S&P 500 index over a 1-year time horizon. If the metric is further refined to incorporate extended periods of news coverage, excess returns are improved. However, the event frequency and subsequent outperformance of such sentiment reversals are sensitive to market environments.

9.1 INTRODUCTION

It is clear to even the most casual investor that stock prices often move for irrational reasons. In general, this is because the stock market is driven by human action and naturally reflects the chronic irrationality within human nature.[1] The *efficient market hypothesis* is a pleasant academic fiction, although successful investing requires being mindful of the inefficient (or, say, "sentimental") factors that lurk beneath. To understand and harness the power of sentiment for profit has been a long-time dream of money managers. The subjective nature of what constitutes sentiment is a serious impediment to the realization of this dream; however, recent technological advances in the field of computational linguistics provide opportunities to approach the matter in a more rigorous, objective way. Leveraging the most up-to-date technology, we attempt to measure the sentiment around companies as determined by their news coverage and incorporate such measurements into a profitable investment strategy.

Notable contributions to the understanding of news sentiment are to be found throughout the academic landscape. The *media effect* is one of the better known empirical results connecting news and stock returns; viz., companies with no media coverage outperform companies with high media coverage. In Fang and Peress (forthcoming) and Peress (2008), the case is made that media coverage is directly related to the

[1] Such as a thing is, such is its act: *Unumquodque enim quale est, talia operator*—Aquinas (I–II, Q.55, A.2).

The Handbook of News Analytics in Finance Edited by L. Mitra and G. Mitra

pricing of information risk, hence the companies that are not covered in the news have superior performance. These studies, however, are more concerned with the intensity of news coverage than news sentiment per se. The work by Paul Tetlock (Tetlock, 2007) is probably the closest to our own. He used a quantitative content analysis program, known as General Inquirer, to analyze correlations between sentimental values of words (as determined by the *Harvard IV-4 Psychosocial Dictionary*) in the *Wall Street Journal* "Abreast of the Market" column and the performance of the Dow Jones Industrial Average. As might be expected, media pessimism is shown to predict lower returns on the Dow, at least on the day the pessimistic news is published. Unfortunately, General Inquirer has some major limitations. For example, it takes individual words as inputs and not combinations of words. More intelligent software is needed to study such a multifaceted notion as sentiment. The ideal solution would be a machine that simulates the complex emotional reactions of investors to news stories about companies they owned or might like to own. Counting words in a *Wall Street Journal* column is a good start, but quite a bit more must be done in order to navigate the thorny labyrinth of investor psychology.

The above observations seem to imply that technological developments along the lines of artificial intelligence might be à propos. This is precisely the approach of Dow Jones News Analytics (DJNA). Recently, with an eye towards making news sentiment quantifiable, Dow Jones, one of the largest news agencies in the world, formed a partnership with RavenPack International, a company specializing in algorithmic text analysis, machine-learning, quantum information theory, and the like. DJNA is the fruition of this collaboration. The proprietary RavenPack software takes financial news as inputs and assigns scores using various linguistic classification techniques, thus quantifying sentiment according to story type or the machine-simulated reaction of professional analysts, specifically with respect to the impact of such information on equity prices or trading volume. The DJNA platform assigns these quantitative scores to each news story and delivers the data to customers within milliseconds of publication.

High-frequency trading funds have an obvious interest in products such as DJNA. The ability to instantaneously assimilate the sentiment around a company and trade before everyone else trades sounds like a good way to make money. But what about long-only money managers? It seems rude to leave them out of the great news sentiment harvest feast. How might a humble money manager, say with assets under management somewhere below $1bn, use DJNA to add value in a concentrated portfolio of stocks? This is the question we attempt to answer.

Our event study proceeds as follows. First, news sentiment relative to companies must be measured in a meaningful way. The metric of *net news sentiment* is defined as our primary measurement tool. We then attempt to discern sentiment-related events in the life of a company that might signal a temporary misvaluation of its stock. In particular, the event of a *sentiment reversal* is identified via the net news sentiment metric. The idea is that an extensive period of negative news coverage around a company causes downward pressure on its stock price, and when the negativity has sufficiently subsided there is value to be unlocked on the long side. Universes of sentiment reversals are constructed and their performance is computed. Finally, highlighting our principal theme of real-world investing, Monte Carlo simulations are implemented for concentrated portfolios of sentiment reversals.

The best sentiment reversal performance is obtained when net news sentiment measurements are over a period of around 1.5 years. An equally weighted average over all such events of forward 1-year excess returns relative to the S&P 500 yields 16%. Moreover, the relationship between the variable of net news sentiment measurement period length and forward 1-year excess returns is piecewise-monotonic, thus corroborating the presence of a genuine stock market anomaly. The Monte Carlo simulations in the final section show that this outperformance is not market-neutral, as might be expected given the highly sentimental impact that different economic environments have on equity prices.

It should also be said that our study design might seem somewhat unconventional to those steeped in the culture of financial theory. We do not use models or regressions to "explain" anything, nor do we control for size, book to market, or any of the standard factors, at least in any standard way. Take the notion of *risk*, for example. Typically, one attempts to model the risk associated with an asset by establishing correlations between various factors, assuming that a causal relationship exists. But how appropriate is this approach? Obviously, the post hoc ergo propter hoc fallacy is a danger in all aspects of quantitative finance, but here it seems particularly applicable. Even if there was a causal relationship between a factor and risk (whatever that means) in the past, it is not clear why such a state of affairs would continue to be the case in the future. What factor could have predicted the huge amount of risk a long-only manager would be taking in buying financial stocks before the fabled Credit Crunch? Why not simply ask, "How much money could I possibly lose by owning these stocks?" Isn't this a more respectable question? Our solution is to look at Monte-Carlo-style portfolio simulations and determine the worst possible investment experience from buying a particular type of stock.

In our professional opinion, the use of conventional investment techniques such as factor models is not the best way to outperform the market, especially when everyone else is abiding by the same conventions. The fact that sentiment reversals might correlate with certain factors is mildly interesting, but without a hypothesis behind the correlation such a research technique becomes a meaningless numbers game. We require a convincing *reason* for a market inefficiency in order to believe that it will repeat.

9.2 THE QUANTIFICATION OF SENTIMENT

In order to aid the study of news sentiment, DJNA has constructed an archive back to 1987 that is not *survivor-biased*. The archive is made up of tens of millions of financial news stories, where each story is assigned numerous DJNA attribution tags, including the historical identification of relevant companies. DJNA tracks around 27,000 historical companies. It is essential in an event study to consider companies that are no longer trading, otherwise the results have the built-in assumption that companies never go bankrupt or get acquired. Using historical ticker symbols, we match the appropriate CRSP security identifiers with each company-relevant news story as being the securities that traded under those tickers when the news stories were published. This bit of bookkeeping is a necessary preliminary to conducting a proper survivor-*un*biased study. Seeing as CRSP is the pricing source we shall use, only US companies will be considered.[2] Moreover, given the schedule of CRSP updates, the latest date of any data point in our universe (related to events or performance) is December 31, 2008.

The atomic measure of sentiment to be used is the DJNA *MCQ ranking*. If a news story mentions a company in a negative light, then the company receives a negative MCQ ranking; if a news story mentions a company in a positive light, then the company receives a positive MCQ ranking. We make this notion slightly more precise below.

Let $\mathcal{N}$ denote the universe of all news stories from the DJNA archive. Fix a company C that is mentioned within some news story from $\mathcal{N}$ and has an MCQ ranking.

Definition 1. Call the partial binary function $S_C : \mathcal{N} \to \{-\infty, \infty\}$ the *sentiment indicator relative to* C where

$$S_C(N) = \begin{cases} -1 & \text{if } C \text{ receives a negative MCQ ranking in } N \\ 1 & \text{if } C \text{ receives a positive MCQ ranking in } N. \end{cases}$$

For the sake of brevity, when we say that a news story $N \in \mathcal{N}$ is *about* company C, it is assumed that N provides an MCQ ranking for C. Let $\nu = \langle N_1, \ldots, N_m \rangle$ be a sequence of news stories about C from $\mathcal{N}$, chronologically ordered. Then ν induces the binary sequence $\langle S_C(N_1), \ldots, S_C(N_m) \rangle$. The problem with defining reversal events from such sequences is that there is a considerable amount of noise within the flow of news about a company. If a company is experiencing a period of negative press, it does not follow that every news story about the company will be negative. An accurate sentiment metric must smooth out the raw data in some way. To that end, we make the following definition.

Definition 2. Let $N \in \mathcal{N}$ be a news story about C. Let P denote a certain number of months. Assume that within the time period of P months before the publication date of N there are m-many stories about C (including N), for some $m \in \mathbb{N}$. Denote these stories $N_1, \ldots, N_m = N$. The *trailing net news sentiment for* C *at* N *over* P is the quantity

$$\sigma(C, N, P) = \sum_{i=1}^{m} S_C(N_i).$$

The net news sentiment of a company measures a kind of preponderance of sentiment. For example, if there are 30 news stories about C in a given month, 29 of which center around poor earnings, accounting scandals, and suchlike, but one story mentions the environmentally friendly policies of C, there will still be a significantly negative net news sentiment measurement for C of -28, thus reflecting the overwhelming amount of news pessimism about C.

DJNA provides many data attributes within each news story besides MCQ rankings. In an attempt to focus on the most meaningful data, we restrict our attention to only one additional attribute, namely the *relevance score*. If $N \in \mathcal{N}$ is a news story about C, a relevance score is assigned to C on a scale of 0–100 depending on the significance of the role C plays in N. We require in the central definition below that each news story is as relevant as possible and receives a full relevance score of 100. Preliminary work has shown that conditioning on high relevance is a better window into future performance.

[2] The current format of DJNA data prohibits (at least, not without considerable additional work) the inclusion of ADRs. Each company is tagged with its country ticker and a country code. It would be necessary to obtain a non-survivor-biased list of ADRs that matched country tickers with tickers used on US exchanges. A similar approach might be taken using ISIN data, which is also tagged in each DJNA story. These considerations, however, are beyond our present scope.

Internal DJNA studies have reached the same conclusion. Hafez (2009), for example, demonstrates the superiority of relevance scores of 90 or above (incidentally, if an MCQ ranking is assigned to a company in a story, then it must have a relevance score of 90 or above).

We are now ready to define the events that shall be our buy signals.

Definition 3. Suppose C, $\nu = \langle N_1, ..., N_m \rangle$, and P are as above, where $N_1, ..., N_m$ all have a relevance score of 100 relative to C. Say that ν witnesses a *sentiment reversal for C relative to P* if the following conditions hold:

1. $m \geq 32$;
2. the difference between the publication dates N_{m-1} and N_2 is at least 30 calendar days;
3. $\sigma(C, N_i, P) < 0$ for all $2 \leq i \leq m - 1$;
4. $\sigma(C, N_1, P) \geq 0$; and
5. $\sigma(C, N_m, P) \geq 0$.

Remark 1. If such a sequence ν exists, we will simply refer to the event itself as a sentiment reversal, where the event date is the date the last story N_m is published.

In summary, a sentiment reversal is a news story that causes a company to emerge from a prolonged period of negativity, as determined by at least 30 negative net sentiment measurements over at least 30 calendar days. Monthly measurement periods are used in order to increase the likelihood that the reversals are non-accidental. Requiring the minimal number of measurements to be 30 likewise seemed appropriate: if a reversal occurs within the shortest possible time of one month, it would be reasonable to expect an average of at least one news story per day.

As far as an anomalistic hypothesis is concerned, Figure 9.1 illustrates the main idea well enough. Namely, over an extended period of negative press about a company, its stock price is depressed below normative levels, and, when the stock is bought at the moment the sentiment has reversed, there is reversion to previous price levels. In this way, the anomaly would be the result of a kind of information lag. At the event date, net news sentiment has reached an equilibrium point; however, cautious investors are still getting comfortable with the idea that the company has emerged from its trough of negativity, and the stock remains cheap.

9.3 SENTIMENT REVERSAL UNIVERSES

The only variable left free in Definition 3 is P: the monthly timeframe over which net sentiment is measured. It might be helpful to think of this variable as a kind of "look-back". As a company marches through time, how much news history about it, looking back in time at any given moment, should be incorporated into a sentiment measurement? Is one month enough or is a broader sweep of history needed? We approach this question by studying 24 distinct universes of sentiment reversals as determined by 1-month to 24-month trailing net news sentiment measurement periods. In particular, for $x = 1, ..., 24$, define the universe U_x to be the sentiment reversals obtained by sequences of the form

$$\langle \sigma(C, N_1, x), ..., \sigma(C, N_m, x) \rangle,$$

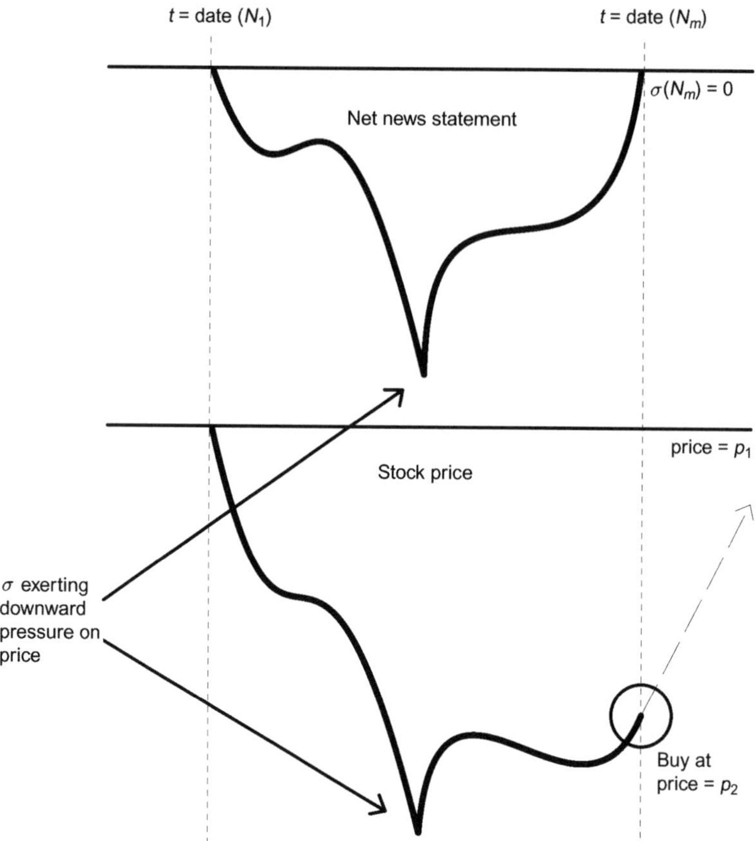

Figure 9.1. Stylized depiction of a sentiment reversal $\langle N_1, \ldots N_m \rangle$ where p_1 and p_2 are the closing stock prices on date (N_1) and date (N_m), respectively.

where $m \geq 32$ and $\langle N_1, \ldots, N_m \rangle$ is a sequence of news stories about C occurring over at least one month with a relevance score of 100.

Remark 2. The phrase "universe of stocks" is understood here to be a set of pairs, where in a pair one item is a security and the other item is an associated event date.

Universe sizes are further reduced by establishing a market cap minimum. This is an entirely practical consideration, seeing as money managers with sufficiently large assets would not likely run a small-cap concentrated portfolio. We stipulate the market cap minimum to be \$500 million. Of course, \$500 million today is not what it was 20 years ago. To address this issue of historical market cap, we deflate the minimum back in time via the percentage change of the S&P 500 index. In particular, suppose there is a sentiment reversal on date d, then if p_1 and p_2 are the closing prices of the S&P 500 index on December 31, 2008 and d (respectively), it is included in the universe if its market cap as of d is larger than

$$500 \text{ million} + (500 \text{ million}) \times ((p_2 - p_1)/p_1).$$

We justify the imposition of this minimum as follows. Assume, for the sake of argument, that the price of a stock tracked the S&P 500 index. Then, also assuming the number of shares outstanding remains constant, its market cap back at a certain time t will be exactly the present market cap deflated by the percentage change of the S&P 500 since time t.

Whenever returns for a universe of stocks are computed, something must be done to control for outliers. This is a particularly sensitive issue when the returns are long-term, seeing as longer holding periods tend to emphasize the *right-skewed* nature of return distributions (stocks can return much higher than 100%; however, they never return below −100%). Therefore in each universe of stocks we require returns to be *winsorized* (see Definition 4). For more on statistical methods of outlier-trimming, see Hempel et al. (2005). Our approach in the definition below is fairly intuitive: if a return causes the arithmetic average over the entire universe to move by more than 5%, replace it with the next smallest return in the universe that does not cause such a movement. The 5% stipulation is a reasonable limit for long-term returns derived from universes of around 200–400 events, as is the case for most of the sentiment reversal universes to be considered.

Remark 3. When the "return" of an individual stock within a universe is mentioned it is understood to be a holding period return without dividends from the closing price on the event date to the closing price on the day when the holding period has expired. To be precise, if a stock has closing price p_1 on its event date and closing price p_2 on the holding period expiration date (assuming it was still trading), its return is computed as $(p_2 - p_1)/p_1$.

Definition 4. Let $\mathcal{R} = \{r_1, ..., r_m\}$ be the holding period returns for a universe of stocks U over the time period P. Assuming the universe is sufficiently large and such a return exists, let r_i denote the largest member of $\mathcal{R}$ such that

$$\sum_{j=1}^{m} r_j/m - \sum_{j\neq i} r_j/(m-1) < 5\%.$$

In other words, r_i is the largest return whose absence within the universe does not cause the arithmetic average return to drop by more than 5%. Let $\{r_{k_1}, ..., r_{k_l}\} \subseteq \mathcal{R}$ be such that for each $p = 1, ..., l$ we have

$$\sum_{j=1}^{m} r_j/m - \sum_{j\neq k_p} r_j/(m-1) \geq 5\%.$$

In other words, $r_{k_1}, ..., r_{k_l}$ are the returns whose individual absence within the universe causes the arithmetic average return to drop by more than 5%, otherwise known as *outliers*. Let $\mathcal{R}'$ be the set obtained by replacing r_{k_p} with r_i for each $p = 1, ..., l$. Finally, define the *winsorized P-return of U* to be the equally weighted average

$$\sum_{r\in\mathcal{R}'} r/m.$$

In computing performance for the 24 universes of sentiment reversals, it is important to consider *excess* returns. This is especially true when the distribution of events is over a long period of history. For example, events might cluster around bull markets, and such universes could have good absolute returns but bad excess returns. We therefore focus

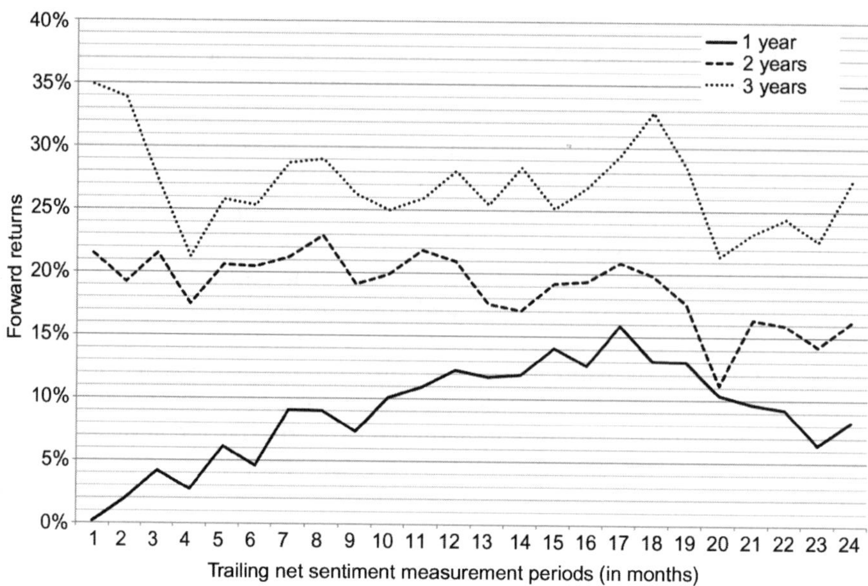

Figure 9.2. Forward 1-year to 3-year holding period winsorized excess S&P 500 returns for sentiment reversals as a function of trailing net sentiment measurement periods.

on *excess S&P 500* returns for individual stocks.[3] That is, if a sentiment reversal with event date d has return r over the holding period P, it has excess S&P 500 return $r - r'$ where r' is the return of the S&P 500 index from d until the expiration of P.

The forward 1-year to 3-year holding period winsorized excess S&P 500 returns for each of the 24 universes are recorded in Figure 9.2. Focusing on the forward 1-year return curve, there is clearly a piecewise-monotonic relationship between the extension of the trailing net sentiment measurement periods and forward 1-year performance. In particular, the curve peaks at a measurement period of 17 months. On the other hand, the 2-year and 3-year holds are not particularly interesting. Not only do the returns taper off significantly (think in terms of degrading annualized returns), but there is no attractive pattern such as the glaring monotonicity in the 1-year hold case. Our attention shall thus be directed towards the forward 1-year returns from the universe U_{17}.

When implementing a strategy based on an event study, it is important to know the frequency with which the events occur. Perhaps, for example, all of the opportunities occur at market bottoms, and we would be left with nothing to buy in more bullish scenarios. The annual event distribution of sentiment reversals from U_{17} is pictured in Figure 9.3.

It appears there are more sentiment reversals in bull markets, as can be seen in the sharp spike at 2003. Of course, this is to be expected. When investor sentiment is turning positive relative to the market as a whole, one would anticipate the net news sentiment around individual companies to gradually move in the same direction. However, there

[3] It might be objected that the S&P 500 is not an accurate proxy of market performance. The equally-weighted or value-weighted CRSP market indices are often used instead, having the advantage of being non-managed. On the other hand, the S&P 500 is probably the most commonly used benchmark in the money management industry. Therefore, using such an index has the virtue of simulating the real-world experience of a money manager, which is our primary interest here.

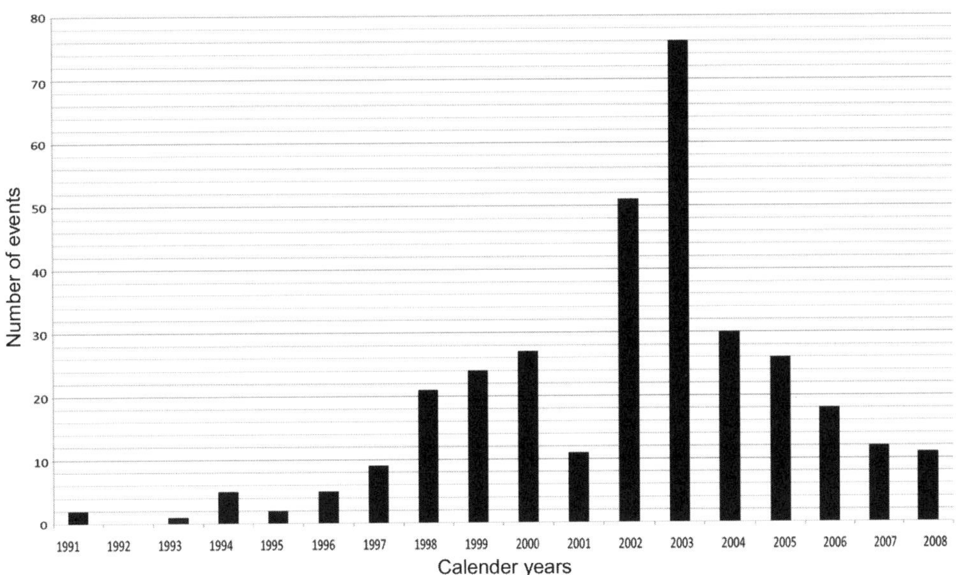

Figure 9.3. Annual distribution of sentiment reversals in U_{17}.

are still many opportunities in other years, at least enough to run a fully invested 10-stock portfolio (to be studied in the next section). The fact that before 1997 not much seems to be happening should not be cause for alarm: the annual distribution of all news stories in $\mathcal{N}$ tapers off in a similar way, primarily on account of the lower volume of news flow back in the 1980s and 1990s.

9.4 MONTE CARLO–STYLE SIMULATIONS

It behooves us now to consider the worst possible investment experience from sentiment reversals. Imagine a scenario in which we see the marvelous forward 1-year excess return number of 16% over the entire universe U_{17} eagerly buy a portfolio of stocks matching the appropriate parameters, then underperform the market by 10% each year over the next four years. This is possible. Unfortunate, but in such a case we would not have considered carefully enough the real-time quality of excess returns. It could be that the documented excess returns all came from a bull market in the late 1990s or, for that matter, a bear market in the early 2000s. In a sense these outcomes are unavoidable; the stock market is not like the physical world, and the principle of scientific induction (that the future will be like the past) should be applied with the utmost reticence. There is more comfort, however, in the belief that something never *will* happen because it never *has* happened, as opposed to turning a blind eye towards history.

Generally speaking, Monte Carlo simulations attempt to estimate the range of a function by taking randomly generated arguments, performing the function on those arguments, then aggregating the function values into a final result. There is an obvious application of Monte Carlo methods to estimating portfolio performance in an event study. Starting the portfolio formation process at different events, if there is a sufficient number of them and they are uniformly distributed throughout time, can yield radically different portfolios even though the same universe of stocks is used. Portfolio size is also an important factor (smaller portfolios use fewer data points, therefore the distribution of possible outcomes will be more varied). If every possible starting point is used and portfolio performance is computed, the following two observations are worth making. On the one hand, the worst (or best) possible experience can be determined by simply finding the portfolio with the worst (or best) return. We know what to expect if we are as unlucky (or lucky) as possible from the point of view of timing. On the other hand, portfolio performance can be averaged over all starting points in order to obtain a somewhat more real-world expected return.

We begin by describing the mechanics of portfolio construction. The following variables must be considered:

1. *Portfolio size* The maximum number of stocks owned in the portfolio.
2. *Holding period* The maximum amount of time any stock in the portfolio is held.
3. *Entry point* The number of trading days post event date to wait until each stock is bought.

As mentioned above, the ability to run a fully invested portfolio of a given portfolio size is very sensitive to the shape of the event distribution. It is easier to construct portfolios from large universes where events occur regularly. Likewise, longer holding periods help by decreasing the turnover rate. The effect of entry points is slightly more subtle and shall be considered in detail later.

We simulate a fully invested, (initially) equally weighted, next available portfolio $\mathcal{P}$ as follows. Let $M \in \mathbb{N}$ denote the portfolio size of $\mathcal{P}$. Then there are M distinct strains running simultaneously that constitute $\mathcal{P}$. Within each strain, a stock is bought, held for the holding period, sold at expiration of the holding period, capital from the sale is re-invested in the next available stock in the universe, and the process is repeated. Suppose, then, that we wished to compute the performance of $\mathcal{P}$ between the dates d_1 and d_2. Let $i \leq M$ be a natural number. If $r_1, \ldots, r_n$ are the partial period returns of the ith strain of $\mathcal{P}$ between d_1 and d_2, as described above, define the performance of the ith strain of $\mathcal{P}$ to be the linked return

$$R_i = \prod_{j=1}^{n} (r_j + 1) - 1.$$

Finally, the performance of $\mathcal{P}$ between d_1 and d_2 is simply the equally weighted average

$$\sum_{i=1}^{M} R_i / M.$$

It is assumed, therefore, that on d_1 an equal amount of capital is invested in each strain and grows according to the sequence of partial period returns. In other words, the portfolio is initially equally weighted, but the position sizes change according to the success or failure of the stocks.

One difficulty in defining portfolio simulations in this way is the potential for cash drag. Say a stock is sold in one particular strain, and the next opportunity is not until two months later. If, then, the market were to jump 20% in that 2-month interval, excess returns of the portfolio would likely suffer. In order to address this potential problem,

Figure 9.4. Forward 1-year winsorized excess S&P 500 returns for sentiment reversals as a function of trading days post event date.

we introduce the notion of an *entry interval* as a certain time period after the event date such that, using any trading day within the interval as an entry point, there are still good forward excess returns. For example, if we were willing to settle with forward 1-year excess returns approximately within the range 14%–16%, sentiment reversals could be bought up to four months post event date (see Figure 9.4).

It remains to be seen whether such a concept even improves portfolio returns. In any case, from a pragmatic point of view, we should be familiar with the results of running portfolios using the smallest possible amount of cash. The notion of an entry interval likewise addresses practical problems such as trading friction. If a largish position size in a name has to be taken, multiple days might be required to implement the trade order, and an entry interval could help estimate the effect on performance. The same logic applies to exit points.

Given the event distribution of sentiment reversals in U_{17} and the desire to capture as much portfolio performance as possible, 10-stock portfolios are simulated and annualized returns are computed over the timeframe 2000–2008.[4] This, of course, would be a bad time to begin and end a portfolio (the S&P 500 had an annualized return of −5.65%).

Remark 4. When returns are "annualized" we simply take a geometric average. For example, if $r_1, \ldots, r_n$ are different calendar year returns for a portfolio, the annualized return is the quantity

$$\left(\prod_{i=1}^{n}(r_i + 1)\right)^{1/n} - 1.$$

[4] There are 67 starting points pre 2000 that yield different, fully invested 10-stock portfolio constructions over the timeframe 2000–2008.

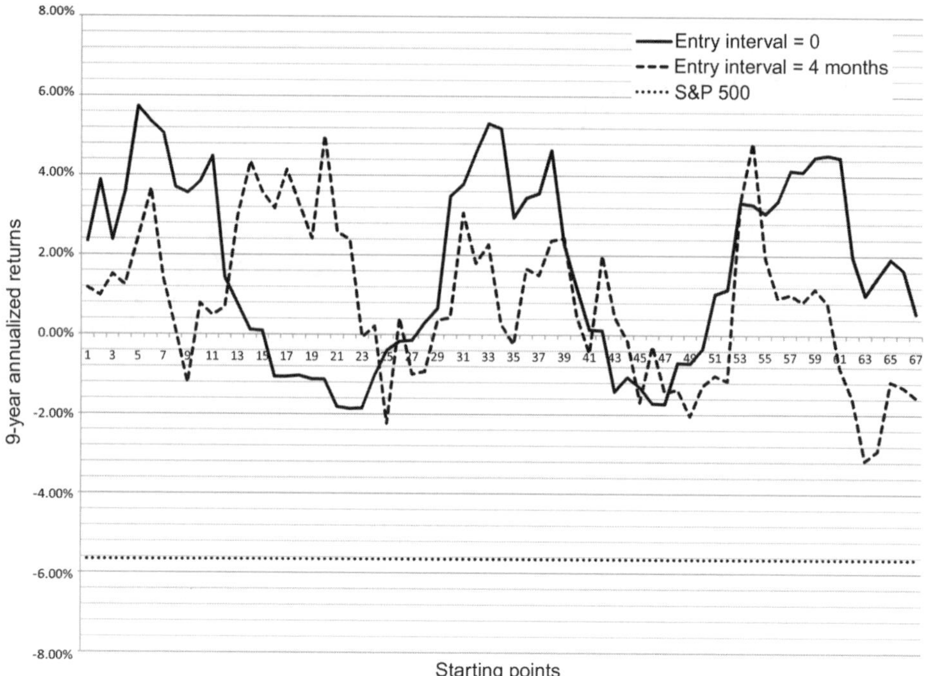

Figure 9.5. Nine-year annualized returns over 2000–2008 for 10-stock Monte Carlo portfolios of U_{17} sentiment reversals as a function of starting points.

Using daily returns that have been winsorized relative to the entire universe U_{17}, Monte Carlo portfolios for the two strategies are recorded in Figure 9.5. The good news is that every possible sentiment reversal portfolio outperforms the S&P 500; the bad news is that the excess returns have dropped a significant amount. The best outcome occurs at the 5th starting point with no entry interval, where the annualized return is 5.73%, yielding an excess return of 11.38% (still not quite as glamorous as the 16% excess return obtained by an equally weighted average over the entire universe). If the annualized returns are averaged over every starting point, the strategy with no entry interval gives 1.67% while the 4-month entry interval strategy gives 0.80%; or excess returns of 6.46% and 7.32%, respectively. The difference in performance of the two strategies might be expected, given the timeframe over which performance is computed. The strategy with more cash will likely outperform its rival in such bearish market environments.

The detraction in excess returns from 16% in the equally weighted case to 7% in the portfolio-simulated case is understandable. It speaks to the distribution of anomalistic opportunities and realistic expected returns. On the other hand, it might be said that this is a commentary on the market-specific characteristics of sentiment reversals. In bear markets, sentiment reversals still outperform the market; however, they do even better in bull markets (clearly, the starting points used in the 2000–2008 Monte Carlo simulations were good stocks to own in the late 1990s in order to obtain an excess return of 16% over the entire universe). One might hypothesize that the information lag supposedly driving the anomaly is less pronounced in bear markets. That is to say, perhaps investors are quicker to react to news when the market is going down than when it is going up. There is something to be said about the behavioral aspects of such a scenario. Anxiety is the predominant sentiment in bear markets, whereas in bull markets complacency tends to be more common amongst investors. Similar results are documented in Hou, Peng, and Xiong (2009).

9.5 CONCLUSION

As the preceding results demonstrate, news sentiment can be used to obtain long-term positive excess stock returns. Our brief event study illustrates a method for picking stocks that emerge from a period of media pessimism with good forward 1-year excess return potential. There is, however, much room for refinement in the methodology. For example, if the minimum time period over which reversals occur were extended from one month to one year, perhaps the optimal net news sentiment measurement period would decrease from 17 months to only a few months, and the forward returns might improve. Maybe instead of focusing on relevance scores, what should be used to supplement the MCQ rankings is DJNA data related to earnings announcements or *novelty scores*.[5] Another idea from Hafez (2009) is to control for the seasonality of news, although such an approach is more germane to shorter net news sentiment measurement periods. The possibilities are endless. On the other hand, the plethora of available variables suggest the very real danger of data-fitting. More is needed than the bare correlation of variables to be convinced of the presence of an anomaly. Sentiment reversals as defined here seem to be supported not only by good performance, but a firm, intuitive hypothesis with evidence of monotonicity in the relationship between the primary variable (net news sentiment) and forward returns.

Future work on sentiment reversals might concentrate on developing a more market-neutral strategy. The Monte Carlo simulations from the previous section show that the excess returns are not uniformly distributed through time. Moreover, as is the case with other reversal-style anomalies such as the momentum reversals first documented by deBondt and Thaler (1985), the long side might be hedged with a relevant short side. Of course, such a strategy would only be applicable to funds that have the ability to short-sell. It could be that the mirror image of sentiment reversals—viz., companies descending from an extended period of positive net news sentiment—are good short candidates. If negative-to-positive reversals create more opportunities while the market is going up, positive-to-negative reversals could create more opportunities while the market is going down. The latter scenario, clearly, is an ideal time to be shorting stocks. One might reasonably expect such a combined strategy to distribute the expected outperformance of sentiment reversals equally over different market environments.

9.6 ACKNOWLEDGMENTS

The author would like to thank all those who had a hand in the progress of this work, particularly Kevin Crosbie, Peter Dickson, Alan Beimfohr, John Prichard, Chad Neault, Peter Hafez, and David Hirshleifer.

[5] Each story is ranked according to how many preceding stories have been published about the same event.

9.7 REFERENCES

Aquinas T. (1265 or 1266–73) *Summa Theologiae*.

deBondt W.; Thaler D. (1985) "Does the stock market overreact?" *Journal of Financial Economics*, **55**, 793–805.

Fang L.; Peress J. (forthcoming) "Media coverage and the cross-section of stock returns," *Journal of Finance*.

Hafez P.A. (2009) *Construction of Market Sentiment Indices Using News Sentiment*, Working Paper, RavenPack International.

Hempel F.R.; Ronchetti E.M.; Rousseeuw P.J.; Stahel W.A. (2005) *Robust Statistics: The Approach Based on Influence Functions*, Wiley Series in Probability and Statistics, John Wiley & Sons Inc.

Hou K., Peng L., Xiong W. (2009) *A Tale of Two Anomalies: The Implication of Investor Attention for Price and Earnings Momentum*, Working Paper, `http://princeton.edu/~wxiong`

Peress J. (2008) *Media Coverage and Investors' Attention to Earnings Announcements*, Working Paper, Institut Européen d'Administration des Affaires (INSEAD).

Tetlock P.C. (2007) "Giving content to investor sentiment: The role of media in the stock market," *Journal of Finance*, **62**(2), 1139–1168.

Part III

News and risk

10
Using news as a state variable in assessment of financial market risk

Dan diBartolomeo

ABSTRACT

News is information that describes how the state of the world is somehow different than it usually is. Even without specific understanding the full meaning of the information communicated by news, the analysis of text news can be a useful conditioning variable in making forecasts of financial market risk, particularly over shorter horizons.

10.1 INTRODUCTION

News is information that describes how the state of the world is somehow different than the state of the world usually is. With this simple concept as a foundation, it is possible to dramatically improve the assessment of financial market risk for both financial intermediaries and asset owners. Like most things, the level of risk in financial markets *can be thought of as being like it usually is, except when it is not*. Through the incorporation of news into our formal models, we can rapidly recognize, understand, and respond to periods of heightened risk, as have been experienced in the financial global crisis of the past two years.

Whenever we speak about assessment of financial market risk, we must begin by identifying some key elements. What metrics of risk are we interested in describing? We will use symmetric measures such as the expected standard deviation of asset returns, or some measure of potential loss such as conditional "Value at Risk" (CVAR). Will our risk measures consider risk in the context of absolute gain or loss, or rather consider investment return and risk relative to some benchmark index? Should our metric for risk depend solely on the fractional composition of our investment portfolio, implicitly assuming unlimited liquidity in the trading of assets, or should the metric explicitly incorporate the potential for illiquid market conditions?

Perhaps the most vexing question, and the one to which news has the most conceptual relevance is time horizon. Clearly, we can't do anything about what has occurred in the past, so our interest in the past is limited to forming a baseline expectation for future risk. Over what future time period is our forecast expected to address? It is the common convention of the investment industry to put statistical measures of risk such as standard

The Handbook of News Analytics in Finance Edited by L. Mitra and G. Mitra

deviation in return in annual units. We talk about the volatility of stock being "40%" when we mean the expected standard deviation of annual returns is 40%. Portfolio measures such as tracking error are similarly expressed in annual units. This allows thinking about risk to be expressed in a form parallel to annual returns such as interest rates, and to be evaluated in standard investor utility frameworks such as that of Levy and Markowitz (1979). However, it is unclear in each specific instance whether we are actually talking about forecasting risk between today and one year from today, or are forecasting risks over some shorter (e.g., the next month) or longer time horizon and then presenting the resulting figures in *annualized units* so as to allow for convenient comparison. On the other hand, "potential for loss" measures such as Value at Risk are normally expressed over much shorter time horizons, usually ranging from 1 to 10 trading days.

Risk assessment models for asset management (as distinct from trading operations) have traditionally focused on estimating portfolio risk from security covariance over time horizons of a year or more. This is clearly suitable for long-term investors such as pension funds. However, the investment performance of asset managers is often evaluated over shorter horizons, so they are interested in shorter term risk assessment. Hedge funds and other portfolios with high portfolio turnover are even stronger in this preference. In addition, *the recent proliferation of high-frequency trading and algorithmic execution methods has created demand for very-short-horizon risk assessment in which the analytical evaluation of news can play an important role.*

To the extent that financial institutions have focused on short-horizon risk forecasts, the methodology has been fairly consistent in the past. The usual approach is to rely almost entirely on historical risk observations as a proxy for explicit forecasts. Typical procedures increase the frequency of observations (daily or shorter). Usually a shorter sample period or exponential weighting is used to increase the influence of recent observations. Many factors typically considered relevant to a particular type of investment may have to be ignored. For example, it is often problematic to use financial statement data in high-frequency models of equities, since the financial statements themselves are updated only periodically, often as infrequently as once per year. In such models, innovations in the risk level are generally dealt with via the GARCH process, as innovated by Engle (1982) and Bollerslev (1986).

There are serious problems with this approach at the individual security level. It is well established that there is a high degree of apparent kurtosis in high-frequency returns of most investment assets. For a review see diBartolomeo (2007). The existence of higher moments in financial time-series data can render common statistical procedures such as ordinary least squares regressions unreliable, as described in Sfridis (2005). Also well established are patterns of short-term return behavior such as negative serial correlation studied in Rosenberg, Reid, and Lanstein (1985), and positive serial correlation due to illiquidity as described in Lo, Getmansky, and Makarov (2003). Finally, asynchronous trading across global time zones makes estimation of correlation very difficult.

10.2 THE ROLE OF NEWS

To understand risk in financial markets, we must understand the mechanism by which news influences security returns. Variations in security returns are the algebraic manifestation of price changes over time. Price changes arise due to an imbalance between the numbers of willing buyers and the number of willing sellers at the current price. The willingness of the buyers and sellers of a particular financial asset to transact is a function of two processes, which we call "have to" trades and "want to" trades.

Financial market participants often trade financial assets because they "have to" do so. The classic example of this is forced liquidation of a position by a hedge fund or other leveraged investor who gets a margin call. Another example is a mutual fund manager who experiences large redemptions by investors and must provide cash within a few trading days. On the other hand, most financial literature in asset pricing has focused on "want to" trades, those transactions motivated by investor expectations of abnormal risk-adjusted returns in the future. Almost all "want to" trades are responses to flows of information to financial market participants and the resultant investor willingness to pay liquidity providers to accommodate their desired transactions.

Financial markets are driven by the arrival of information in the form of "news" (truly unanticipated) and in the form of "announcements" that are anticipated with respect to time but not with respect to content. The time intervals it takes markets to absorb and adjust to new information ranges from minutes to days. Price adjustments generally take a much smaller amount of time than a month, but up to and often longer than a day to become apparent. That's why US markets were closed for a week after September 11, 2001. During periods of adjustment, liquidity is low and the potential for imbalances between buyers and sellers is maximized, often leading to large-magnitude price movements. This is not to assert that asset prices are wholly efficient after a month or any particular time horizon, but rather that available information has been sufficiently assimilated such that trading will be orderly and of adequate liquidity.

For information arriving as announcements, liquidity is generally maintained as market participants have had the opportunity to plan their actions in advance, conditional on the content of the announcement. It is as though investors are living in what grammar experts would call the "subjunctive mood". This anticipatory behavior generally leads to a reduction of trading volume and volatility as investors wait for the content of the announcement before taking action, but there is no need to stop and think at the moment of the announcement. Such anticipatory behavior can reduce the effectiveness of GARCH models as volatility will trend downward during the quiet before the storm. Since GARCH models are trend-following in volatility, the GARCH model will underestimate risk going into the announcement release. When the information is released, the security price is apt to move in response creating a brief period of high volatility. Having underestimated volatility at the time of the information release, the GARCH model will respond by increasing its forecast of risk for the post-release periods by which time conditions have returned to normal, leading to over-estimating risk after the announcement. While GARCH models remain an important and effective tool in the modeling of many financial time-series, practitioners choosing to use GARCH models must carefully consider the extent to which the market events they are trying to model are being driven by news that is fully unanticipated or by announcement information.

There is an extensive literature illustrating the links between the arrival of information to financial markets and subsequent asset-pricing effects. Several papers have examined the relative market response to "news" and "announcements", such as Ederington and Lee (1996), Kwag, Shrieves, and Wansley (2000), and Abraham and Taylor (1993). Jones, Lamont, and Lumsdaine (1998) show a remarkable result for the US bond market in which total returns for long-maturity bonds and Treasury bills are not significantly different if announcement days are removed from the dataset. There are also papers such as Easley and O'Hara (2001) that illustrate cross-sectional differences in the long-term cost of equity capital related to the transparency and volume of information across firms.

Brown, Harlow, and Tinic (1988) provide a framework for asymmetrical response to "good" and "bad" news. They assume investors value financial assets as the discounted present value of future cash flows, and that the value of the discount rate is dependent on how confident they are that the investor fully understands the nature of the investment. Good news increases projected cash flows, while bad news decreases expectations of future cash flow. Crucially, all new information is a "surprise", *decreasing investor confidence in their level of understanding and increasing discount rates*. As such, upward price movements are muted, while downward movements are accentuated. Numerous empirical papers have shown negative correlation between volatility and asset prices. In short, there is strong support for the old adage "No news is good news".

Both the foregoing discussions of the issues of time horizons, GARCH models, and the asymmetry framework put forward by Brown, Harlow, and Tinic are examples that illustrate that incorporating textual news into financial forecasts is a much more subtle and analytically complex task than merely determining whether the news is good or bad, and the degree of apparent importance. Practitioners who choose to pursue such activities should be circumspect in applying such analytical measures to their real-world financial decisions.

10.3 A STATE-VARIABLE APPROACH TO RISK ASSESSMENT

Our approach to short-horizon risk forecasting is different. We prefer to continue to use the existing risk models that are estimated from low-frequency return observations. Rather than depending on recent high-frequency data observations, we choose to ask ourselves a simple question: "How are conditions different now than they were on average during the sample period used for estimation?" This question is almost exactly congruent to our opening definition of news.

In this method, new information that is not part of the risk model is used to adjust various component parameters of the risk forecast to short-term conditions. This approach has multiple benefits. We sidestep almost all of the statistical complexities that arise with the use of high-frequency data. We get to keep the *existing factor structure of any model*, so risk reporting remains familiar and intuitive. Since our long-term and short-term forecasts are based on the same factor structure, we can also quickly estimate new forecasts for any length time horizon that falls between the two horizons.

Our first application of this approach was to incorporate option-implied volatility as a conditioning variable. Consider the hypothetical situation of a high-profile CEO of a major global corporation being killed in an automobile accident. To create a new forecast of the covariance of that company's stock with some other company or stock index would require waiting through a considerable series of periods until a sufficient sample of data had been obtained under the new conditions. However, the moment that option traders received news that the CEO had been killed, they instinctively would adjust their expectations of future volatility for this firm, and option prices would almost immediately reflect the new beliefs. In this model, we assume that the ratio of observed volatility for a stock and option-implied volatility should be roughly constant over time, and that variations in this ratio are useful indications of changes in risk expectations for the near future. Coincident shifts in the ratio across numerous securities are reflected by changes in the factor covariance structure. Methodological and mathematical details are presented in diBartolomeo and Warrick (2005).

This chapter also shows that the implied volatility method was of particular usefulness in the wake of the September 11 tragedy. After that terrible event, US stock markets were closed for a week. Any analysis of risk that relied on historical observations had no more information when trading re-opened on September 17 than when trade was halted. Using the implied volatilities from opening option prices on September 17 produced very intuitive changes in risk expectations. A portfolio of airline stocks was forecast to have nearly doubled in risk, while a portfolio of food production stocks was unchanged. The model also highlighted extremely abnormal behavior in options on Southwest Airlines *in the week preceding September 11.*

During the week in which stock markets were closed, news about the attack and all other matters of public interest continued to flow. The obvious question was whether we could have adjusted our risk expectations based on analysis of the news itself. It would seem obvious that the greater the amount of news flowing to investors, the greater the potential for disagreement among investors as to the course of action they should take in response to the information. Even if the news is universally perceived among investors as being good news or bad news, they will disagree as to whether other investors have fully incorporated this information into their assessment of asset values. Such disagreement leads to imbalances between buyers and sellers for particular financial assets, finally leading to price changes.

While it might be argued that firms with low transparency (i.e., no news coverage), offer more opportunity for investors to disagree, the high transaction cost of illiquid securities dampens any observable short-term volatility. As long as we are measuring risk in terms of variations in returns, such assets will actually appear low in risk over short horizons.

This line of inquiry was followed to a positive conclusion in Mitra, Mitra, and diBartolomeo (2009). This paper largely follows the mathematical formulation of diBartolomeo and Warrick (2005), but supplements option-implied conditioning information with analytical measures of text news supplied by RavenPack. The text metrics included both measures relating to the frequency and length of articles, and the apparent sentiment of the content. Empirical tests of both American and European stocks, stock portfolios, and indices suggest that *short-horizon risk forecasting is improved by inclusion of news metrics, above and beyond the value of option-implied information.* Possible explanations are that, since option traders cannot trade at zero cost, their trading in response to new information understates the value of the information. Another rationale is that option trading is confined to only a portion of each day, while news continues to flow when financial exchanges are closed.

10.4 A BAYESIAN FRAMEWORK FOR NEWS INCLUSION

The methods used in the two preceding papers were similar in one particularly important respect. Both papers assume that there are two states of the world, the regular state as defined by the parameters of an orthogonal factor model derived from historical observation, and the "now" state as adjusted to reflect the conditioning information derived from option-implied volatility, news flows, or both. An important improvement is to consider the potential states of the world in a probabilistic Bayesian fashion so as to derive the most efficient risk forecast for any given time horizon. Once we embark down this road, we must also address the mathematical implications of serial correlation when forecasting over differing horizons.

Both the issue of optimal use of conditioning information in risk models and the impact of serial correlation are addressed in Shah (2008, 2009). He states, "Forecasting long term behavior requires intentionally restraining news. A priori, one cannot know whether the effects of events being reported upon are transient (more likely) or shifts in regime (less likely), so a sane model integrates innovations more cautiously. For a long term investor, reacting to every passing bump is an exercise akin to driving cross country in a go-kart: the trading turnover would be battering. Being well informed, however, is certainly advantageous. Indeed, the leveraged investor's longevity hinges on skillfully navigating passing bumps and shocks."

Negative serial correlation makes time-series return variances derived from monthly data a downward-biased estimator of variances computed on a daily or higher frequency basis. Example data from Shah are presented in Figure 10.1. To adjust for this effect, Shah provides a method to adjust variance estimates from any observation frequency to any other observation frequency, assuming a first-order autoregressive process.

Shah also provides a rigorous Bayesian framework under which news or any other conditioning information can be incorporated into any existing model of risk. The method involves adding a vector of coefficients that scale the various parameters of the risk model up or down, relative to values derived from historical observations. The default value for each element of this vector is 1, which is the equivalent of retaining the historical model.

Optimal values for the elements of the scaling vector are obtained by a nonlinear

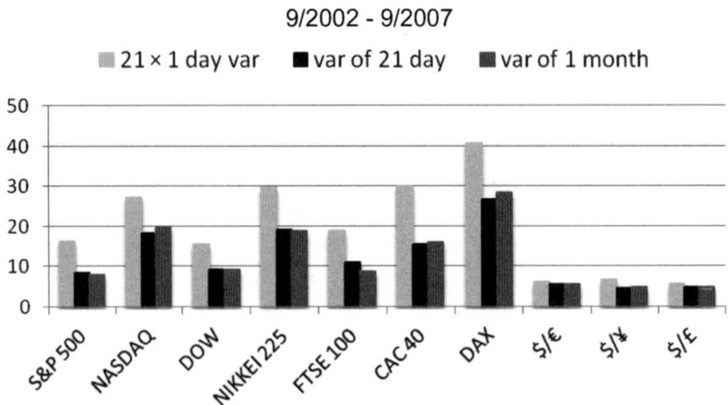

Figure 10.1. Alternative volatility calculations.

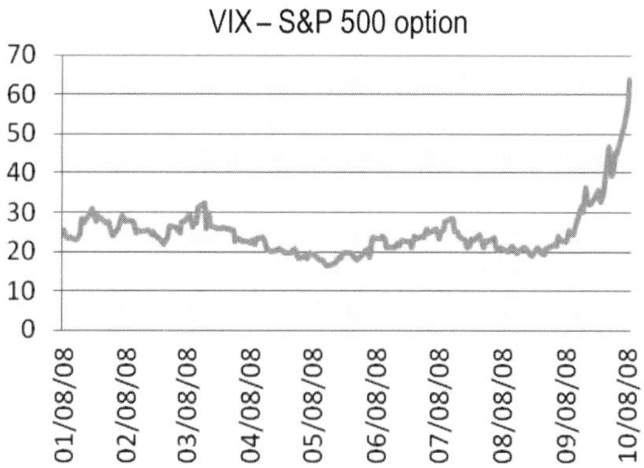

Figure 10.2. US stock market implied volatility.

optimization process that fits forecasts from the risk model to observable analogs among the state variables. For example, we can currently observe the value of the VIX (see Figure 10.2), a financial contract traded on the expected volatility of the S&P 500 stock index. If the VIX is currently trading at 60, and the average value of the VIX was 20 during the period of estimation of the risk model we might believe that the element of the scaling vector that corresponds to volatility of the US stock market should have a value of somewhere between 1 and 3 (60/20).

To the extent that the risk model will have many interdependent parts, the selection of values for each element in the scaling vector is a jointly dependent process. For factor models, our choices must be such that the numerically equivalent full covariance matrix are positive semi-definite and asset-specific risks are positive.

10.5 CONCLUSIONS

Recognizing and responding to changes in the level of risk of financial instruments and financial markets is an essential survival skill for investors in a competitive world: "To finish first, you first must finish." Measuring the volume and sentiment of information being delivered to financial market participants is an ideal way to promptly adjust our expectations of risks over short horizons. News is the very essence of answering the question, "How are things different now than they usually are?"

However, the incorporation of news and other state variables into our assessments of risk means that we must address some of the important statistical complexities of financial asset returns and utilize a framework which optimally uses the information we are able to obtain. Such methods have been put forward and are available to investors for use in their risk assessment procedures.

Utilization of news analytics in risk assessment also brings its own dangers. News analytics effectively brings greater ability to assess changes in absolute risk levels over short time horizons, but it also brings the temptation to focus the risk management process on these newly refined measures, irrespective of whether such measures are the most relevant to our actual financial circumstances.

10.6 REFERENCES

Abraham A.; Taylor W. (1993) "Pricing currency options with scheduled and unscheduled announcement effects on volatility," *Managerial and Decision Science*, **14**, 311–326.

Bollerslev T. (1986) "Generalized autoregressive conditional heteroskedasticity," *Journal of Econometrics*, **31**(3), 307–328.

Brown K.; Harlow W.V.; Tinic S. (1988) "Risk aversion, uncertain information and market efficiency," *Journal of Financial Economics*, **22**, 355–385.

diBartolomeo D. (2007) "Fat tails, tall tales, puppy dog tails," *Professional Investor*, **17**, 38–40.

diBartolomeo D.; Warrick S. (2005) "Making covariance based risk models sensitive to the rate at which markets reflect new information," in S. Satchell and J. Knight (Eds.), *Linear Factor Models in Finance*, Chapter 12, Butterworth-Heinemann, Oxford.

Easley D.; O'Hara M. (2001) *Information and the Cost of Capital*, Working Paper, Cornell University.

Ederington L.H.; Lee J.H. (1996) "Creation and resolution of market uncertainty: The importance of information releases," *Journal of Financial and Quantitative Analysis*, **31**, 513–539.

Engle R.F. (1982) "Autoregressive conditional heteroscedasticity with estimates of the variance of United Kingdom inflations," *Econometrica*, **50**(4), 987–1008.

Jones C.; Lamont O.; Lumsdaine R. (1998) "Macroeconomic news and bond market volatiilty," *Journal of Financial Economics*, **47**, 315–337.

Kwag A.; Shrieves R.; Wansley J. (2000) *Partially Anticipated Events: An Application to Dividend Announcements*, Working Paper, University of Tennessee.

Levy H.; Markowitz H.M. (1979) "Approximating expected utility by a function of mean and variance," *American Economic Review*, **69**(3), 308–317.

Lo A.; Getmansky M.; Makarov I. (2003) *An Econometric Model of Serial Correlation and Illiquidity in Hedge Fund Returns*, National Bureau of Economic Research.

Mitra L.; Mitra G.; diBartolomeo D. (2009) "Equity portfolio risk estimation using market information and sentiment," *Quantitative Finance*, **9**(8), 887–895.

Rosenberg B.; Reid K.; Lanstein R. (1985) "Persuasive evidence of market inefficiency," *Journal of Portfolio Management*, **11**(3), 9–17.

Sfridis J. (2005) *Incorporating Higher Moments into Financial Data Analysis*, Working Paper, University of Connecticut.

Shah A. (2008) "Short-term risk from long-term models," paper presented at *Northfield Seminar Proceedings, October*.

Shah A. (2009) "Short-term risk from long-term models," *Northfield Newsletter*, October `http://www.northinfo.com/documents/312.pdf`

11
Volatility asymmetry, news, and private investors

Michal Dzielinski, Marc Oliver Rieger, and Tõnn Talpsepp

ABSTRACT

Volatility is typically higher in down markets. Using an international comparison of volatility asymmetry and an analysis of a complete set of stock market transactions, we show that this effect, known as "leverage effect", is most likely driven by the overreaction of private investors to bad news. This result is supported by our observation that an increase in attention to negative news (as measured by an increase in Google searches for keywords related to the macroeconomy like "recession") can predict a subsequent increase in volatility.

11.1 INTRODUCTION

When prices drop, volatility increases. This general observation was most noticeable during the recent Credit Crisis, where—following stock market drops—volatility reached record values. The effect has been most widely explained by changes in leverage and the existence of time-varying risk premiums. It is therefore sometimes called the "leverage effect", but we will use the more neutral name *volatility asymmetry*, since so far no clearly recognized explanation exists.

In this chapter we investigate the potential relation between the occurrence of volatility asymmetry, news, and private investors. In Section 11.2 we summarize the results from a study comparing volatility asymmetry in 49 countries worldwide (Talpsepp and Rieger, 2009). The study shows that volatility asymmetry is most pronounced in highly developed markets and, in particular, in markets with high participation of private investors. Moreover, we find that markets with many financial analysts actually show higher volatility after downturns. These results suggest that private investors might react nervously to bad news. We show that times of high news concentration are typically times of many bad news, thus the overreaction of private investors to bad news will likely lead to the observed asymmetry in volatility.

Further evidence for this relationship between news, private investors, and volatility asymmetry is reported in Section 11.3.1, which discusses volatility of the S&P 500 increases after an increase in the number of Google searches for specific keywords

The Handbook of News Analytics in Finance Edited by L. Mitra and G. Mitra

related to the macroeconomy like "recession". It seems plausible that this is caused by private investors getting nervous and subsequently overreacting on the stock market, leading to an increase in volatility.

To cross-validate our results, we study market data on trades of private and institutional investors from a stock exchange in Section 11.3.2. The special feature of this dataset is that it entails *all* transactions on the stock market (in Estonia), thus we have no selection bias in the data. We demonstrate that at times where many private investors trade, volatility is higher, which confirms our theory.

11.2 WHAT CAUSES VOLATILITY ASYMMETRY?

Increased volatility while market prices drop is referred to as volatility asymmetry. The current section summarizes some of the results of Talpsepp and Rieger (2009) on measuring and empirically investigating various causes of volatility asymmetry.

11.2.1 Measuring volatility asymmetry

There are a number of approaches to measuring volatility asymmetry. We can derive the asymmetry from different types of volatility estimation models. A direct approach compares volatility of up and down markets (which has its drawback when linking different market periods to corresponding volatility). We favored using more of an ad hoc model that already incorporates the asymmetry estimation in its original setup. The choice also depended on data availability and an exact research focus.

Although the current literature on volatility (see, e.g., Andersen, Bollerslev, and Diebold, 2003) has shifted to using realized volatility from intraday returns, such data are not available for all markets and longer time periods. As we study a wide range of markets for a long time period, we use the asymmetric power GARCH (APARCH) model of Ding, Granger, and Engle (1993) with asymmetric t-distribution. There is a wide choice of GARCH-type models (see, e.g., Poon and Granger, 2003) that could be used for the task when using daily returns. But as the APARCH model contains an asymmetry parameter it is one of the most natural choices for this task. Additionally, APARCH proved to deliver very accurate VAR forecasts compared with other models, especially when using asymmetric t-distribution.

We used the following specification of the APARCH model:

$$\sigma_t^\delta = a(|\varepsilon_{t-1}| - \gamma\varepsilon_{t-1})^\delta + \beta\sigma_{t-1}^\delta, \tag{11.1}$$

where α, γ, β, and δ are the APARCH parameters to be estimated. We are mainly interested in the asymmetry parameter γ. It reflects volatility asymmetry and takes values from -1 to 1. If there were no asymmetry (meaning that volatility is the same for down-market periods and up-market periods) the estimated γ would be zero. A positive value of γ means that volatility is higher in bear markets and that is exactly what results show for almost all countries most of the time.

Our choice of the APARCH(1,1) model is motivated by an effort to obtain volatility asymmetry estimates with higher statistical reliability for a large number of countries dictated by the data frequency available. We tested various combinations or different ARMA and APARCH orders with our data. Based on the results the used model proved to give more stable and reliable estimates for the parameters of interest. With this method we were able to obtain results with a relatively narrow (1,000 observations) rolling time window of daily returns.

As we are studying 49 different countries, we need to have a robust method (to ensure comparability) that would be suitable for all fundamentally different countries possible. Thus we do not impose any parameter restrictions for the model and use a skewed *t*-distribution which ensures that the model can be automatically applied to different countries with slightly different return distributions. Altogether this ensures both comparable results and that not too general a model is used for every country.

Using GARCH-type models has disadvantages when the timespan is relatively short (usually fewer than 2,000 observations) and/or return data contain jumps. To cope with such problems we use outlier detection methods with kernel weighting for model input returns.[1] Handling jumps is one of the key problems that need to be addressed when applying more popular GARCH-type models. Eliminating jumps enables us to receive more stable results with higher reliability and only a small loss of approximately 1%–2% of data. Eliminating jumps could be a high price to pay when trying to forecast volatility in turbulent times.

Our robustness checks show that removing outliers from the sample does not qualitatively change asymmetry estimates but improves the reliability of estimates for shorter datasets. And using shorter datasets is a prerequisite for us to be able to obtain a time-series of asymmetry estimates at all. Using a rolling time window with skewed *t*-distribution for APARCH model estimation also ensures that such a small number of eliminated outliers would not start to affect results even if their economic impact on volatility asymmetry was larger than our robustness checks show. All that enables us to conclude that the eliminated jumps do not qualitatively affect volatility asymmetry estimates and thus do not have any significant impact on the results.

11.2.2 Volatility asymmetry comparison

To compare volatility asymmetry in different countries, we use daily stock market returns from the 49-country Morgan Stanley Capital International (MSCI) index provided by Thomson's Datastream. We include all data that are available in our sample. For a better comparison we use MSCI index returns measured in US dollars. As a proxy for volatility asymmetry we use gammas obtained by repeatedly estimating equation (11.1) for each country with a moving time window. Using a moving time window of a size of 1,000 observations gives us a unique time-series dataset of the volatility asymmetry for each country. As described in Talpsepp and Rieger (2009) we adjust the obtained measures for volatility asymmetry to exclude an impact of different return patterns. The adjustment also allows for better comparison of estimated volatility asymmetry across countries. We still use both adjusted and unadjusted measures for volatility asymmetry (both time-series and cross-sectional data) for testing different factors that can cause the asymmetry. When comparing volatility asymmetry across countries we can conclude that developed countries tend to have a higher level of asymmetry. The United States ranks first in all measures. Japan, Germany, and France

[1] Please see Talpsepp and Rieger (2009) for details of the APARCH model and additional measures taken to ensure better stability of the estimated parameters to cope with short timespans.

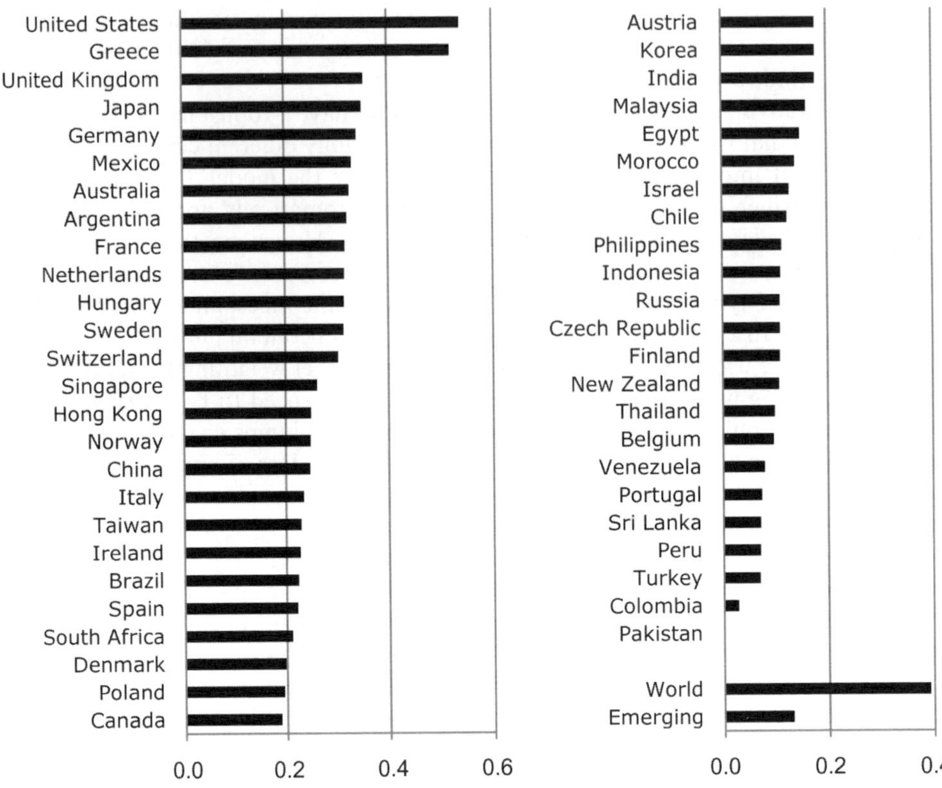

Figure 11.1. The level of volatility asymmetry as reported in Talpsepp and Rieger (2009).

rank among the first 10 in all categories and the UK is also in the top of the table. The only emerging market with a relatively high level of asymmetry in most specifications is Mexico.

Results show that the level of asymmetry changes in time quite remarkably. Some of the major fluctuations of the estimated gammas are caused by extreme fluctuations in market prices which can still not be captured by the APARCH model (despite outlier detection). But the increase in asymmetry seems to be facilitated especially during turbulent market situations, as can be seen during the Asian crises and the burst of the technology bubble. Trend analysis captures an increasing volatility asymmetry for 40 of the 49 studied markets. Hence, although volatility asymmetry might be considered a market inefficiency and thus should be fading in time, our results show an increasing asymmetry. This gives us a first clue about what can drive asymmetry.

11.2.3 Market-wide causes for volatility asymmetry

In Talpsepp and Rieger (2009) a number of factors, that should drive volatility asymmetry based on the findings and prepositions in the literature, have been tested; in particular, financial leverage (Black, 1976). However, not much support for the pure

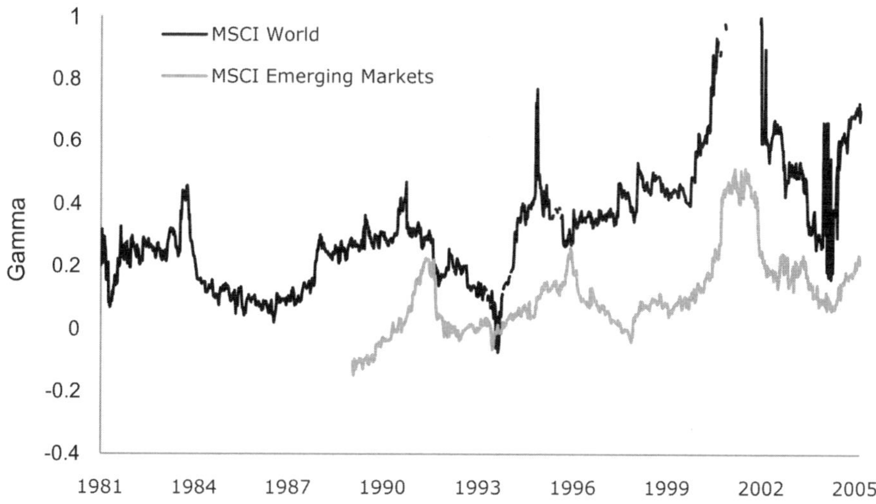

Figure 11.2. Time dynamics of volatility asymmetry (gamma) for the MSCI World and MSCI Emerging Markets indexes. Values over zero indicate asymmetry where volatility is higher when prices fall, values below zero mean that volatility is higher when the market goes up.

leverage effect has been found in our data, similarly no support for the time-varying risk premium as an explanation was found (see further discussion in Talpsepp and Rieger, 2009).

As our findings show that the level of volatility asymmetry tends to be increasing in time and can differ significantly across countries, it is natural to wonder whether economic development or structure can play a role in explaining the differences in asymmetry. We test a number of more or less direct measures of market development (including GDP/capita, different published market development and efficiency indexes, etc.) under different regression setups to check the hypothesis. All our test results indicate that the level of asymmetry is not related to a lack of market efficiency: quite the contrary, a higher level of economic development and market efficiency is associated with a higher level of volatility asymmetry!

This is certainly a surprising result that we want to understand in the remainder of this chapter.

11.2.4 Volatility asymmetry, news, and individual investors

Recent research has argued that the media have the power to influence investor sentiment and thus prices on the stock market (see, e.g., Tetlock, 2007). Hence, information obtained from the media might potentially cause volatility asymmetry.

In fact, volatility asymmetry is positively related to analyst coverage in the data (Talpsepp and Rieger, 2009). This links back to the role of the media in financial markets, since analyst opinions are generally transmitted by different media channels. What, then, are the characteristics of the media coverage time-series that could shed light on this relationship? In a forthcoming working paper Dzielinski, Steude, and Subasi (forthcoming) look at the daily media sentiment for the constituents of the

Dow Jones 30 index in the period from January 2007 to September 2009. The quantities under consideration are the share of positive respectively negative news in the total for the given day. Sentiment scores are taken from Newssift, an online tool powered by the *Financial Times*. Interestingly, there is often a significant positive correlation between the *share* of negative news and the *number* of news items overall, and conversely higher share of positive news is associated with a lower number of news items overall. Furthermore, this effect appears to be more pronounced for stocks, which have more news items on average. Therefore, stocks that are more covered on average (without differentiating between analysts and other media) are also more susceptible to the "negative news bias". The ideal argument would thus go as follows: more news means predominantly more bad news, which makes investor reactions more pronounced, when there is downward pressure on prices.

International data allow media penetration to be measured, and it turns out that it is strongly correlated with volatility asymmetry. However, media penetration is also closely correlated with the level of market development and might not always be a good proxy for stock market media coverage. Thus when including both GDP/capita and media penetration in the same regression, the impact of the media seems to disappear. This can of course be somewhat deceptive as a clear link between the development of the country and the level of asymmetry is much harder to explain than the link between the impact of the media and asymmetry. However, the impact of the media on volatility would be much easier to capture within a market if we had reliable data on news flow.

International data still allow us to further test the hypothesis of news having a significant impact on volatility asymmetry: analysts are an important source of information for investors and could potentially influence their sentiment. We would expect analysts to discover the shortcomings of companies and the media to communicate their discoveries. In the case of good news, analysts might not get the same media attention as in the case of disappointing news. Thus we might expect to see the co-influence of the media and analysts to volatility asymmetry. As there are usually more analysts in developed markets, the conclusion also fits the finding of higher volatility asymmetry in developed markets.

As already mentioned, our data show a significant positive correlation between asymmetric volatility and analyst coverage. The effect is still present when controlling for other factors (e.g., the level of GDP/capita and the media); see Table 11.1. We conclude that better coverage of listed companies helps to draw more attention to possible shortcomings in a firm's operations in the case of bad news and helps to react more quickly to the news. The finding is also supported by previous work of Hong, Lim, and Stein (2000) who argue that stocks with low coverage tend to react less precisely to bad news compared with high-coverage stocks.

Our results indicate that analysts and the media could cause volatility asymmetry but this can only happen if they can persuade at least some investors to trade more erratically during down moves. The question is: "Who might these investors be?" Hens and Steude (2009) suggest that volatility asymmetry can be caused by investors' preferences. Shefrin (2005) proposes biased expectations as a possible explanation. Since individual investors are more prone to be biased than institutional investors, we would expect large volatility asymmetry in markets where the share of individual investors is higher. This might be the situation for more developed markets.

Table 11.1. Log–log regressions on volatility asymmetry (adjusted gamma)

	Coefficient	*t*-statistic	Coefficient	*t*-statistic
Analyst coverage	0.47	3.14***	0.45	4.21***
GDP per capita	1.36	3.61***	0.69	2.42**
Market participation	0.29	2.48**		
Media	−5.04	−4.1***	−1.95	−1.68
Stock market capitalization/GDP			0.23	2.19*
Constant	6.97	3.13***	−0.52	−0.2
N		24		40
R^2		0.74		0.71

*, **, ***: Significant at the 10%, 5% and 1% level.

We use cross-sectional data about market participation level to capture the share of individual investors in the market. We find a significant positive impact of market participation level on volatility asymmetry. Since market participation data are not available for the whole sample we run some additional tests to confirm the finding. We use available time-series data for a single country (Switzerland) which support the finding also at the time-series level.[2] We also use panel data about market capitalization divided by GDP as a proxy for share of private investors in the market. Here, we find a positive correlation confirming the finding that the more individual investors (who are likely to be less experienced and/or informed) in the market the higher the volatility asymmetry.

Based on these results we hypothesize that in the case of bad news a higher absolute number of investors will be selling and pushing prices down more quickly, thus increasing volatility during periods when prices fall. This could be the explanation for the different behavior of investors after prices fall or rise, which would be consistent with the ideas of Hens and Steude (2009) and Shefrin (2005). It would also be consistent with the assumption that more analysts and media attention in the case of bad news can cause asymmetry.

Due to the lack of cross-country data, we are not able to test whether the activities of hedge funds (who can also act as arbitragers) can impact volatility asymmetry. But we are able to check whether introducing electronic trading platforms (facilitating stop loss orders and better and faster access to the markets) affects asymmetry, which could also be one of the differences between developed and emerging markets. We do not find any significant effect of electronic trading on the cross-sectional or panel data level.

11.3 WHO MAKES MARKETS VOLATILE?

11.3.1 Google and volatility

So far we have seen that the degree of volatility asymmetry is linked to two characteristics of the financial market in question: the share of private investors and the number of stock analysts. The aim of this section is to illustrate in a more detailed

[2] Please see Talpsepp and Rieger (2009) for more details and for a discussion of the variables used.

way how private investors can impact the stock market and discuss a convenient metric of their behavior. This exercise might be helpful to portfolio managers, who are often concerned about the "little man's" actions, which are argued to be more susceptible to swings of mood, especially in periods of market stress.

There are reasons to believe, frequently based on insights from behavioral finance, that private investor demand is more attention-driven than a systematic investment approach should be. Private investors tend to follow simple heuristics, like picking stocks they have positive associations with or the ones recommended by friends or neighbors. This does not necessarily imply (as some would be happy to believe) that they will inevitably be driven out of the market. In a rather provocative experiment Gigerenzer (2007) showed that asking random people on the street for names of stocks that they know and subsequently investing in them can be a very successful strategy. But even if simple investment strategies fail in the long run, the next generation of inexperienced investors will readily replace their frustrated predecessors. The reliance on simple heuristics of many investors implies, however, that looking at the typical array of a stock analyst's indicators, be it fundamental or technical, is not likely to say much about the direction private investors are headed in, simply because it is not what they themselves look at.

A sizable number of studies have attempted to address this issue. Barber and Odean (2008) name extreme returns, trading volume, and news and headlines as suitable indicators, which have been developed to a varying extent in the literature. News and headlines especially proved to be very fertile ground for research, originating in numerous event studies (Liu, Smith, and Syed, 1990; Barber and Loeffler, 1993; Ferreira and Smith, 1999; Arena and Howe, 2008), through time-series and cross-sectional regressions (Mitchell and Mulherin, 1994; Fang and Peress, 2009), and developing into the kind of linguistics-based analysis presented in this volume (Tetlock, 2007). Other authors examined factors derived more from a corporate finance point of view, such as the size of the advertising budget (Grulon, Kanatas, and Weston, 2004; Dong, 2008; Chemmanur and Yan, 2009).

None of the above, however, is a direct measure of attention; they are all proxies, which run into the fundamental problem of distinguishing between active and passive effects or, in marketing parlance, between push and pull.

To understand the difference, consider the following simple case of trying to predict the number of guests at a party. One might take the number of invitations sent as a (passive) estimate, but few would argue that the number of positive confirmations (which involve an active response from the addressee) would do a much better job.

Certainly, proxies are ubiquitous in economics and finance, where many phenomena are not directly observable at all, and they rest on the assumption (motivated by theory or empirical findings) that active and passive effects are robustly correlated. In situations largely depending on human psychology like attention or sentiment such correlations might, however, prove illusory or unstable over time. Therefore, in such circumstances direct measures are of particular value.

We argue that such a direct measure exists in the case of private investor attention, based on internet usage. It is presently rather uncontroversial to assume that most people rely on the internet for information, also concerning investment, and they get to that information by using search engines. Tracking the flow of search queries thus arguably brings one as close as it gets to what is on people's minds. This is exactly the kind of information that Google offers through a service called Google Trends, where weekly time-series (starting January 2004) of the popularity of any given search term are available for inspection and download. Looking at search terms relevant from the investment viewpoint has the potential to correctly identify topics capturing private investors' attention and thus give clues as to their future actions. The fact that Google presently accounts for around 70% of global searches certainly adds weight to this hypothesis. Da, Engelberg, and Gao (2009) give essentially the same argument and show how Google Trends can be relevant on the individual stock level. Using Russell 3000 as the universe, they report a statistically significant relationship between the increase in the search frequency for a stock ticker symbol and the subsequent increase in private buy orders submitted for that stock. Furthermore, they show how this contributes to large first-day returns and long-run underperformance of IPO stocks. Their study is an important step towards documenting the merits of Google Trends in capturing private investor demand and we build on these findings to illustrate the resulting market impact.

Instead of focusing on individual stocks we take a different approach based on themes (or keywords) related to the macroeconomy. We argue that increased interest in those themes reflects the uncertainty of private investors concerning the macroeconomic outlook, which might induce increased trading on their part. Correspondingly, to measure the financial impact we look at the returns, volatility, and implied volatility of the most popular US index, the S&P 500. We chose to concentrate on three themes: "recession", "oil price", and "inflation" for the period from January 2004 to September 2009. We decided to concentrate on searches originating in the US only, given the considerable home bias, characteristic for private investors worldwide. Google Trends values are calculated as an index and the user can choose between fixed and relative scaling. The first approach applies the average of search traffic in a fixed time period (generally January 2004) as a reference value, while otherwise the average for the whole specified time period is used. While this might seem like a technicality, it gains importance when applying Google Trends to backtesting. In this kind of setup one has to be especially careful to clean out any information one could not have had in the past, a problem also known as filtration. However, downloading one year of Google Trends data with relative scaling implies knowing the average for the whole year also throughout the year, which is logically inconsistent. We therefore use fixed scaling in this analysis.

Another controversy, which Da, Engelberg, and Gao (2009) have to deal with is whether the searches they analyze are indeed linked to investment intentions, as opposed to looking to buy the company's products for instance and they argue that searching for a company ticker rather than its name is strong enough an indication.

We claim that this is not an important issue for us because of the high-level focus of our study. According to an ICI (Investment Company Institute) report, half of American households owned stocks in the year 2005, either directly or through mutual funds. Therefore, greater uncertainty about macro-themes among the general public is likely to find its way through to the stock market. This argument is further re-enforced by the fact that we concentrate only on big moves in search interest.

In methodological terms our analysis belongs to the event study type, pioneered for the stock market by Brown and Warner (1985). Accordingly, we define an event as a net weekly change in the Google Trends score, which falls in the top 5% of largest changes up to date (consider again the filtration problem). To establish at least some history, we sacrifice the initial 50 observations, which corresponds to around one year of data. We are therefore left with 250 observations, or roughly 5 years, for the analysis. Running the above procedure for all three themes returns 18 events for "recession", 14 for "oil price", and 15 for "inflation".

We then investigate what happens to cumulative returns, realized volatility, and implied volatility (as measured by the VIX) of the S&P 500 in the time window of −20 to +60 days around each event. Figures 11.3–11.5 show the average development for each theme, respectively. As can be seen, each event is on average preceded by a dip in cumulative returns.

There are two factors to explain this effect. For one, private investors might be expected to react with a lag. For other, the results published by Google Trends, and consequently the rates of change we computed, relate to the week just ended, so the few days preceding each event might already be influenced by intraweek activity of private investors. Notwithstanding, there is an immediate further drop in the first days after the event, followed by a negative drift for almost the remainder of the time window. The impact on realized and implied volatility is basically the mirror image of the impact on returns, consistent with the volatility asymmetry evidence. However, the scale of this impact is considerably larger making it an even more interesting phenomenon.

11.3.2 Who's in the market when it becomes volatile?

When observing volatile markets, the question arises, who is in the market when it becomes volatile? According to the theory we have built so far, the increase in volatility should be caused by private investors and thus we would expect to see them on the market.

To check this we used a dataset of the Estonian stock market NASDAQ OMXT. We study this dataset since it has a unique feature: it includes *all* transactions on the market and moreover allows us to identify all distinct investors in the market at different times and distinguish between individual and institutional investors, as well as locals and foreigners. We would expect to see more individuals trading on the market when the market becomes more volatile.

The first task is to measure volatility asymmetry in the OMXT index for the period we have the transaction data (i.e., 2004–2008). Surprisingly, we do not observe any asymmetry for the period by using similar APARCH models to those we used for our international comparison. Our previous data show that such cases exist especially in emerging markets. Estonia is a small emerging market with a relatively short history of stock exchange, so this observation does not contradict the findings of our international study. Particularly, there is very low or sometimes practically non-existent analyst coverage of listed companies; and the market is quite young (remember the increasing trend of asymmetry). In any case we can still see who is in the market when it becomes volatile.

As a reult of lack of a volatility index, we estimate volatility from an APARCH model. We count the number of individual and institutional investors as well as new investors who enter the market. We calculate the share of individual investors, the share of trades done by individual investors, and the share of turnover generated by individual investors compared with the market total.

As can be seen from the chart, individual investor participation remains quite

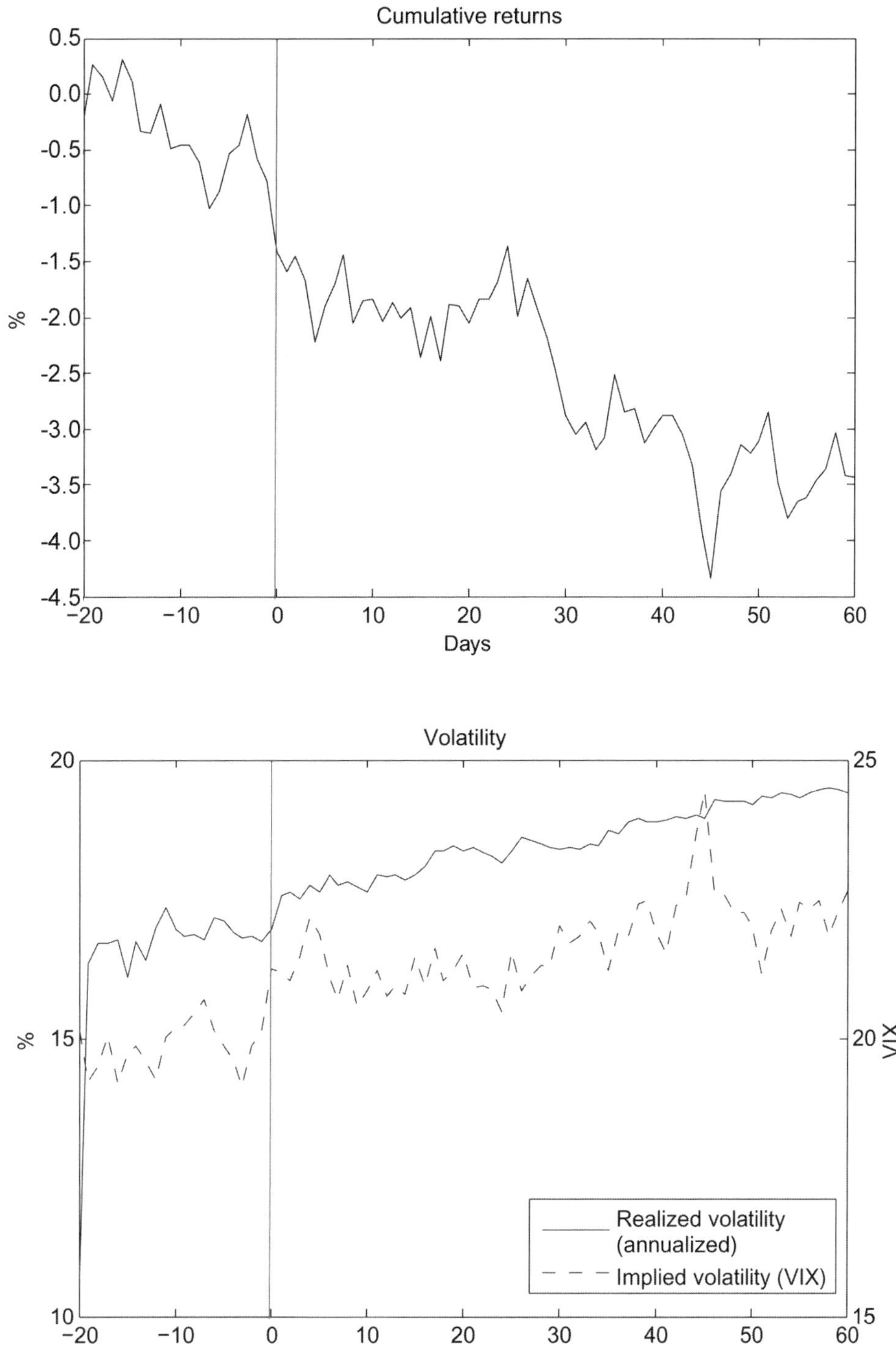

Figure 11.3. Theme "recession".

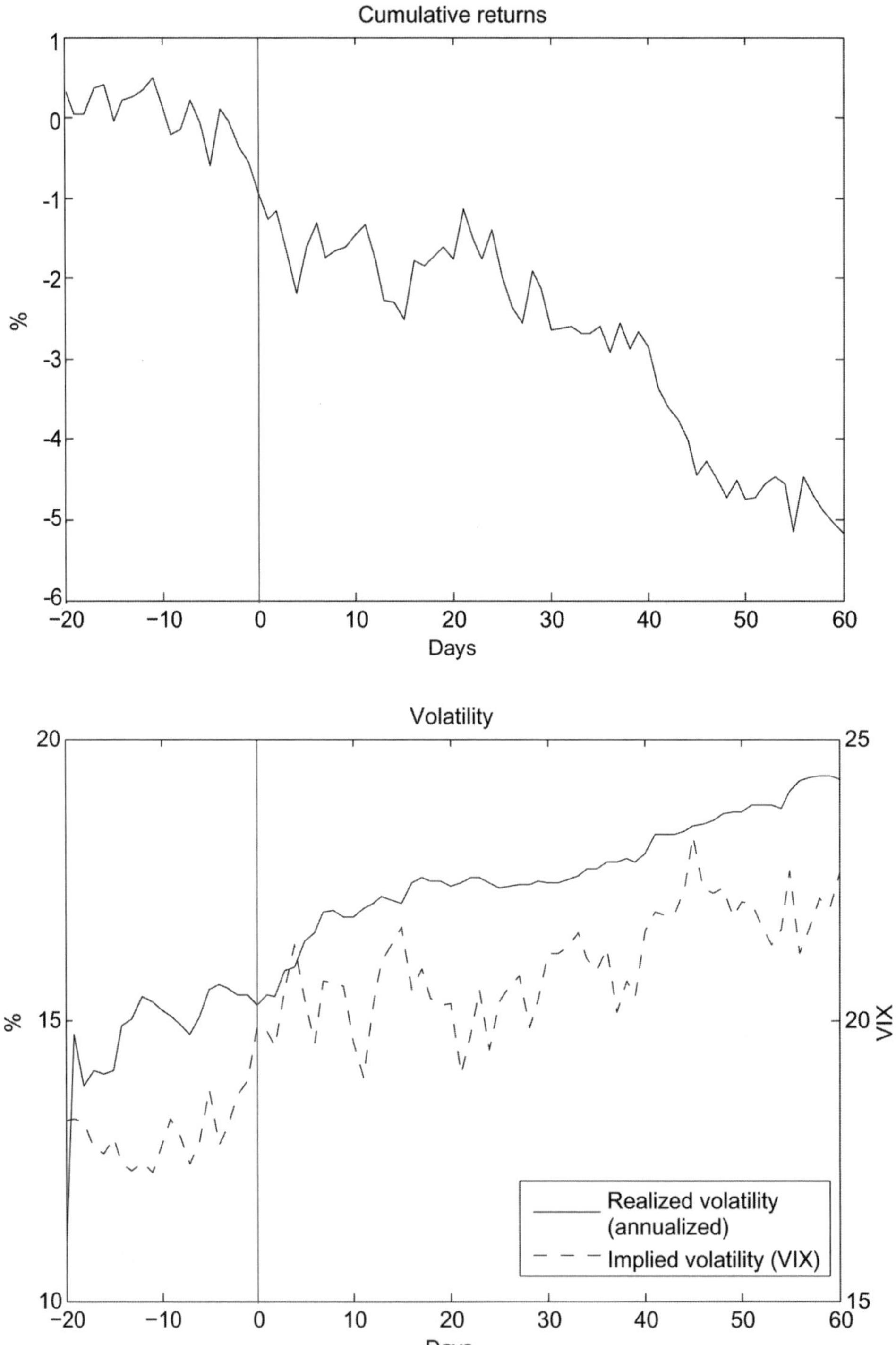

Figure 11.4. Theme "oil price".

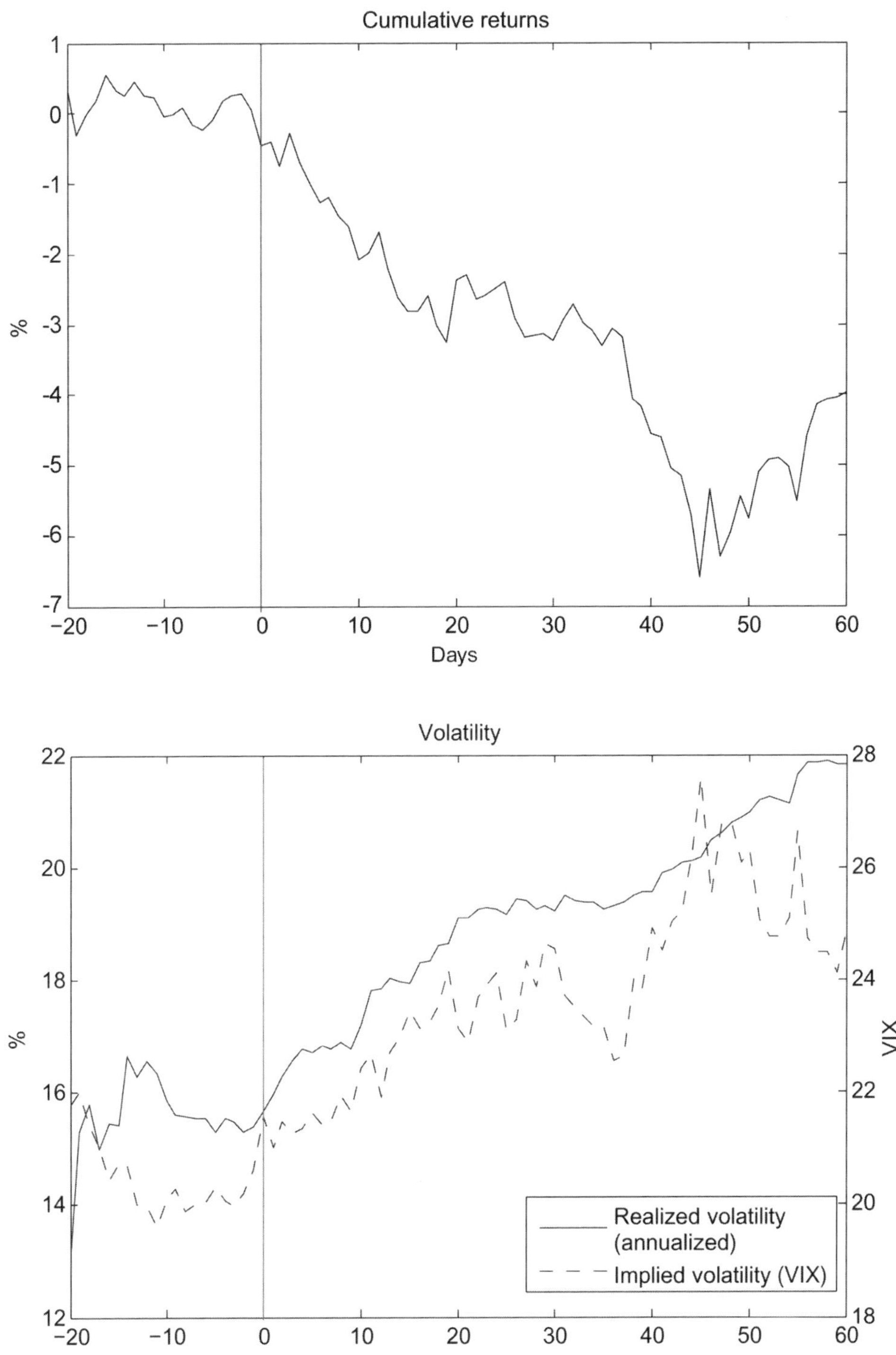

Figure 11.5. Theme "inflation".

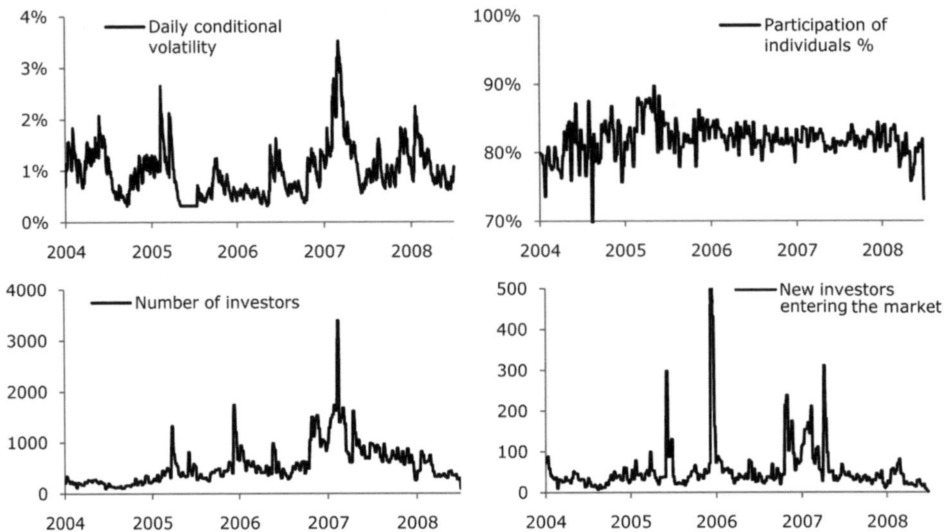

Figure 11.6. Correlation between volatility and investor market participation for the Estonian stock market.

stable during the whole period although fluctuations are quite noisy around the mean. We clearly observe, however, that the number of investors correlate strongly with volatility (Figure 11.6). This means that when markets become very volatile, the number of investors who participate increases. Although increased volatility can have a self-feeding effect that forces more investors to enter the market, we can assume that new important information represents one of the most significant causes of such behavior.

Situations of higher volatility force market participants at market sidelines to enter the market. The more developed a market,the more investors might be at the sidelines at any given time. We would also expect to see a higher proportion of the number of individual investors in more developed markets. As bad news tends to receive more media attention, this is amplified especially in down-market conditions when investors start rushing in to liquidate their positions.

11.4 CONCLUSIONS

Why is volatility higher in down markets? We proposed in this chapter a model that explains this asymmetry starting from the observation that news tends to be asymmetric as well (compare Figure 11.7): the media report predominantly bad news, as our analysis showed. The effect should be stronger, where analyst coverage and media reports are more frequent, and this can be observed in international data on volatility asymmetry.

A large number of bad news items then leads to overreaction of (predominantly) private investors increasing volatility, thus a larger proportion of private and on average less sophisticated investors on the market increases volatility asymmetry as well. Also this effect can be found in international data on volatility asymmetry, where mostly countries with large numbers of private investors score high. Countries that have large numbers of private investors and sophisticated financial markets with good analyst

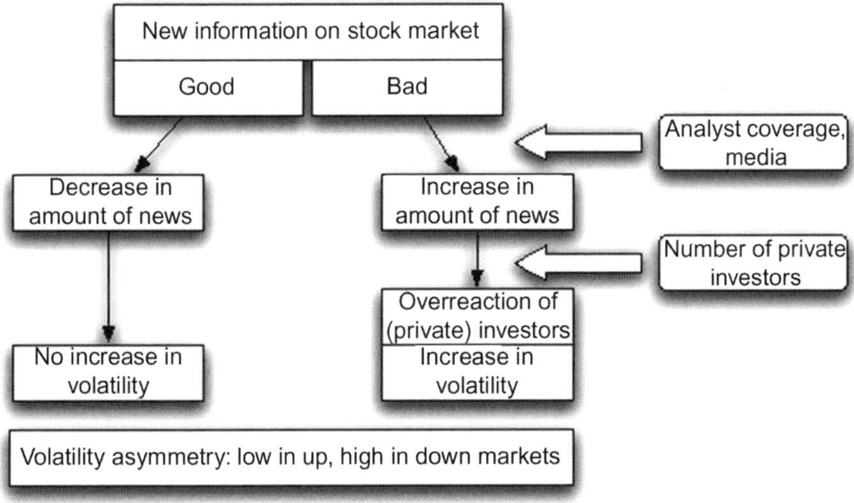

Figure 11.7. Functional sketch explaining how the news reaction of private investors can lead to asymmetric volatility.

coverage and news flow have therefore the highest levels of volatility asymmetry (e.g., the USA, UK, and Japan).

Given that, it is no surprise that globally volatility asymmetry increases over time, as more and more private investors enter markets and the news flow increases.

The model is supported by two further pieces of evidence: first, the number of Google searches for certain keywords related to the macroeconomy like "recession" is a predictor for high volatility. This demonstrates directly that private investors (who are most likely the majority among Google users) influence volatility, and also shows the proposed causality. Second, investigating a full sample of stock market trades of a country (Estonia) we could see that times with high volatility coincide with times where many investors trade on the market. The new investors that enter in these times are usually less professional investors. Our model suggests that their trading increases volatility.

11.5 ACKNOWLEDGMENTS

We thank Thorsten Hens and Sven Christian Steude for interesting discussions on the topic of this chapter. Support by the National Centre of Competence in Research "Financial Valuation and Risk Management" (NCCR FINRISK); Project A1, "Behavioural and Evolutionary Finance"; the University Priority Program "Finance and Financial Markets" of the University of Zürich; and by "LGT and Science" is gratefully acknowledged.

11.6 REFERENCES

Andersen T.G.; Bollerslev T.; Diebold F.X. (2003) *Some Like it Smooth, and Some Like it Rough: Untangling Continuous and Jump Components in Measuring, Modeling, and Forecasting Asset Return Volatility*, SSRN eLibrary.

Arena M.; Howe J. (2008) "A face can launch a thousand shares (and a 0.80% abnormal return)," *Journal of Behavioral Finance*. **9**(3), 107–116.

Barber B.; Loeffler D. (1993) "The 'dartboard' column: Second-hand information and price pressure," *Journal of Financial and Quantitative Analysis*, **28**(2), 273–284.

Barber B.; Odean T. (2008) "All that glitters: The effect of attention and news on the buying behavior of individual and institutional investors," *The Review of Financial Studies*, **21**(2), 785–818.

Black F. (1976) "Studies of stock price volatility changes," paper presented at *Proceedings of the 1976 Meetings of the Business and Economic Statistics Section, American Statistical Association*, Vol. 177, p. 81.

Brown S.; Warner J. (1985) "Using daily stock returns: The case of event studies," *Journal of Financial Economics*, **14**(1), 3–31.

Chemmanur T.; Yan A. (2009) *Advertising, Attention, and Stock Returns*, Working Paper, Boston College and Fordham University.

Da Z.; Engelberg J.; Gao P. (2009) *In Search of Attention*, Working Paper, SSRN.

Ding Z.; Granger C.W.J.; Engle R.F. (1993) "A long memory property of stock market returns and a new model," *Journal of Empirical Finance*, **1**(1), 83–106.

Dong L. (2008) *Attracting Investor Attention through Advertising*, Working Paper, Yale University.

Dzielinski M.; Steude S.; Subasi E. (forthcoming) *Daily News Sentiment and Price Dynamics*, Working Paper.

Fang L.; Peress J. (2009) "Media coverage and the cross-section of stock returns," *Journal of Finance*, **64**(5), 2023–2052.

Ferreira E.; Smith S. (1999) "Stock price reactions to recommendations in the *Wall Street Journal* small stock focus column," *Quarterly Review of Economics and Finance*, **39**(3), 379–389.

Gigerenzer G. (2007) *Gut Feelings: The Intelligence of the Unconcious*, Viking Adult.

Grulon G.; Kanatas G.; Weston J. (2004) "Advertising, breadth of ownership, and liquidity," *Review of Financial Studies*, **17**, 439–461.

Hens T.; Steude S. (2009) "The leverage effect without leverage: An experimental study," *Finance Research Letters*, **6**(2), 83–84.

Hong H.; Lim T.; Stein J. (2000) "Bad news travels slowly: Size, analyst coverage, and the profitability of momentum strategies," *Journal of Finance*, **55**(1), 265–295.

Liu P.; Smith S.; Syed A. (1990) "Stock price reactions to the *Wall Street Journal*'s securities recommendations," *Journal of Financial and Quantitative Analysis*, **25**(3), 399–410.

Mitchell M.; Mulherin J. (1994) "The impact of public information on the stock market," *Journal of Finance*, **49**(3), 923–950.

Poon S.; Granger C. (2003) "Forecasting volatility in financial markets: A review," *Journal of Economic Literature*, **41**(2), 478–539.

Shefrin H. (2005) *A Behavioral Approach to Asset Pricing*, Elsevier.

Talpsepp T.; Rieger M. (2009) *Explaining Asymmetric Volatility around the World*, Working Paper, FINRISK. To appear in *Journal of Empirical Finance*.

Tetlock P. (2007) "Giving content to investor sentiment: The role of media in the stock market," *Journal of Finance*, **62**(3), 1139–1168.

12

Firm-specific news arrival and the volatility of intraday stock index and futures returns

Petko S. Kalev and Huu Nhan Duong

ABSTRACT

This chapter investigates the impact of the rate of information arrival on return volatility. Prior research (Kalev et al., 2004) has shown that both the quantity and quality of news are superior proxies for information flow. In the current chapter we utilize high-frequency data based on the S&P/ASX 200 Index as well as futures contracts on the S&P/ASX 200 Index over the period from October 2003 to September 2009. Volatility persistence appears to be significantly reduced by inclusion of the number of specific news items into the variance equations of the spot and futures index. Overall, our findings are consistent with the mixture of distribution hypothesis (MDH).

12.1 INTRODUCTION

The relation (interrelation) between the flow of information and market uncertainty has been an important topic for research over the last half of the 20th century. More specifically, the dynamics between the flow of information and market uncertainty has been the key factor that impacts security price formation, price discovery, market participant behavior (price reaction or overreaction), and overall market stability. Nowadays, researchers agree that variation in the frequency of information arrivals drives volatility and volatility clustering of security prices (Ross, 1989; Jones, Kaul, and Lipson, 1994; Ané and Geman, 2000). High-frequency data availability and recent advances in modeling of heteroskedastic time-series data enable empirical researchers to address the most puzzling and intriguing feature of price volatility; namely, its strong persistence (Goodhart and O'Hara, 1997).[1] Goodhart and O'Hara (1997) point out that, since the Generalized Autoregressive Conditional Heteroskedasticity ((G)ARCH) processes of Engle (1982) and Bollerslev (1986) are naturally motivated by time-varying

[1] For a comprehensive review of ARCH/GARCH-type modeling, see Bollerslev, Chou, and Kroner (1992). Engle (2002) defines some new frontiers for ARCH models. Refer to Bauwens, Laurent, and Rombouts (2006) and Asai, McAleer, and Yu (2006) among others for surveys on multivariate GARCH and multivariate stochastic volatility specifications, respectively.

The Handbook of News Analytics in Finance Edited by L. Mitra and G. Mitra

features and, most importantly, by temporal dependences in the information arrival process, these models provide an explanation of how such temporal dependence occurs.

GARCH-type empirical models do not, however, provide a theoretical explanation of why volatility persists or if any, what the exact impact of information flow is on volatility. An appealing answer to these questions could be inferred from the mixture of distribution hypothesis (MDH), which argues that the variance of returns at a given interval is proportional to the rate of information arrival on the market (Clark, 1973; Epps and Epps, 1976; Tauchen and Pitts, 1983; Harris, 1987; Andersen, 1996; Liesenfeld, 1998, 2001; Darolles, Le Fol, and Mero, 2009, among others). The phenomenon of volatility clustering could then be seen as a reflection of the serial correlation of information arrival frequencies (Lamoureux and Lastrapes, 1990).

This chapter considers the effect of the rate of information arrival on uncertainty (return volatility), where information arrival is proxied by the number of firm-specific announcements per given interval. Prior research (Kalev et al., 2004) has shown that both the quantity and quality of news are superior proxies for information flow. The current chapter builds on and further extends the Kalev et al. (2004) empirical framework. Similar to Kalev et al. (2004), we proxy the rate of information arrival with the number of firm-specific news announcements. We differ from Kalev et al. (2004) by examining the impact of firm-specific news announcements on the price volatility of the S&P/ASX 200 Index as well as futures contracts on the S&P/ASX 200 Index (the SPI 200 Futures). More specifically, we ask the following questions: To what extent is volatility clustering a reflection of the serial correlation of information arrival frequencies? Do firm-specific news announcements—a proxy for the intensity of the rate of information arrivals—capture stock price index volatility persistence better than the rate of information flow as proxied by trading volume? Do volatility and the volatility persistence of futures on the index differ from spot price index volatility and its persistence? After accounting for the rate of information flow, does the reduction in volatility persistence alter or remain unchanged in times of severe financial crisis, such as the Global Financial Crisis (GFC)?

We proceed as follows. Section 12.2 provides an overview of prior literature on the news arrival–volatility relation, with a special focus on the MDH. Section 12.3 describes the data used in the chapter, and Section 12.4 discusses results and implications. Section 12.5 concludes the chapter, and Section 12.A provides a technical appendix (see p. 283) which explains the research methodology employed in the chapter.

12.2 BACKGROUND LITERATURE

In his seminal work, Clark (1973) proposed that a mixture of normal distributions should be utilized to model the empirical distribution of security price changes. Clark's model assumes that news events are important for pricing securities and that news arrives at a random rate over the trading period. This is normally referred to in the literature as the Mixture of Distribution Hypothesis (MDH). Using the same assumptions, Tauchen and Pitt (1983) and Harris (1986, 1987) show that the joint distribution of trading volume and price changes can be modeled by a mixture of bivariate normal distributions. More specifically, in the standard MDH model, the daily price change and trading volume are the sum of independent intraday price changes and volume that occur as a result of the arrival of information events. After each event, price changes as a result of traders responding to the new information. Intraday price changes and the volume of those trades are generally assumed to be jointly independent and identically distributed with finite variance. If the number of news event arrivals are sufficiently large for a given interval then, following the Central Limit Theorem, the joint distribution of price changes and trading volume are approximately bivariate-normal and conditional on the number of information events. Thus, the conditional variance of price changes is an increasing function of the rate of information flow on the market.

Building on the MDH, Lamoureux and Lastrapes (1990) argue that persistence in the conditional variance of price changes reflects the time-series properties (i.e., serial correlation) in the news arrival process. Therefore, when the impact of information flow is accounted for, most observed volatility persistence should disappear. Using contemporaneous volume as a proxy for information arrivals, Lamoureux and Lastrapes (1990) document that volatility persistence disappears when volume is included in the variance equation of the GARCH model. Extending Lamoureux and Lastrapes' (1990) work by using the "surprised" component of volume, Wagner and Marsh (2005) document that the surprised volume helps explain volatility persistence as well as excess kurtosis in seven major equity markets.

The use of contemporaneous volume as a proxy for information arrivals, however, introduces various potential issues. First, trading volume cannot be assumed to be exogenous, as both volatility and trading volume are simultaneously influenced by the latent information arrival process (see, among others, Tauchen and Pitts, 1983; Harris, 1987; Foster and Viswanathan, 1993, 1995; He and Wang, 1995). Second, volume can be driven by liquidity traders (Kyle, 1985), noise traders (DeLong et al., 1990; Campbell and Kyle, 1993), by difference in opinion or by interpretation of news among traders even without information arrival (Grundy and McNichols, 1989; Kim and Verrecchia, 1991). In particular, Andersen (1996) documents that 34% to 75% of daily trading volume is unrelated to news arrival. Third, volume may even lag behind information flow when the information is private (He and Wang, 1995). Finally, in strategic microstructure models with asymmetric information (see, among others, Kyle, 1985; Admati and Pfleiderer, 1988), informed traders may break their large orders into several small- to medium-sized trades to exploit their informational advantage.[2] This strategic trading could further attenuate the positive relation between trading volume and information arrival.

Ederington and Lee (1993) provide an alternative proxy for the rate of information arrivals (i.e., macroeconomic news announcements). They conclude that the arrivals of macroeconomic news announcements explain the intraday pattern of volatility in the interest rate and foreign exchange futures markets. Using news headlines appearing on the Reuters Money News Alert as a proxy for public information releases, DeGennaro and Shrieves (1997) find that news releases are an important determinant for volatility. Investigating the mark/dollar and the yen/dollar, Melvin and Yin (2000) also document that public information arrivals, as reflected by the number of news headlines reported on the Reuters Money Market Headlines News, have a positive effect on volatility.

[2] For empirical evidence regarding this type of strategic trading known in the literature as stealth trading, see Barclay and Warner (1993).

Macroeconomic news is also the most important source of information in Treasury bond markets (de Goeij and Marquering, 2006). Jones, Lamont, and Lumsdaine (1998) and Christiansen (2000) find significant increases in bond market volatility on days with Producers' Price Index (PPI) and employment announcements. Examining the effects of announcements of the PPI and the employment situation on the volatility of US Treasury bond futures, Li and Engle (1998) document that negative shocks increase volatility, while positive shocks depress volatility on consecutive days. Fleming and Remolona (1999) observe high volatility and volatility persistence after the release of scheduled macroeconomic announcements. Investigating 1-year, 3-year, 5-year, and 10-year US Treasury bonds, de Goeij and Marquering (2006) find that macroeconomic news announcement shocks have a strong impact on the dynamics of bond market volatility. Furthermore, releases of employment information and PPI announcements play an influential role by affecting the intermediate and long end of the yield curve, whereas monetary policy information seems to affect short-term bond volatility.

Extending the study of Ederington and Lee (1993) to option markets, Ederington and Lee (1996) find that unscheduled macroeconomic announcements lead to increases in option-implied standard deviation, while scheduled announcements generally lead to drops in implied standard deviation. Nofsinger and Prucyk (2003) also find that there is an immediate increase of volatility in the S&P 100 Index option after macroeconomic announcements. The authors further document that most of the high volatility after announcements comes from bad news announcements.

In equity markets, using the number of news releases by Reuter's News Service per unit of time as a measure of public information flow on financial markets, Berry and Howe (1994) find an insignificant relationship between public information arrival and the volatility of the S&P 500 Index. Relying on the number of announcements released daily by Dow Jones & Co. as a measure of public information, Mitchell and Mulherin (1994) find a weak direct relationship between news arrivals and price volatility. In a more recent study, Ryan and Taffler (2004) find that reported corporate news of the largest 350 stocks listed on the London Stock Exchange drive a significant proportion of price changes and trading volume. Kalev et al. (2004) conduct an intraday study on the relation between news arrivals and volatility. They find that news arrivals have a positive effect on conditional volatility and the persistence of volatility is greatly reduced once the impact of news arrivals is accounted for. Analyzing intraday market dynamics around public information arrivals, Ranaldo (2006) observes that earning announcements widen the spread and volatility, while other firm-specific news attracts both liquidity and trading.

12.3 DATA

We have collected intraday data for the S&P/ASX 200 Index and the SPI 200 Futures for the period between October 1, 2003 and September 30, 2009 from the Securities Industry Research Centre of Australasia (SIRCA). Our sample includes 30-minute index and futures returns as well as the total trading volume of the index and futures. Consistent with Mitchell and Mulherin (1994), the total trading volume of the index is measured as the dollar value of all transacted shares of companies that the index encompasses. For SPI 200 Futures, trading volume is the total number of contracts traded in each 30-minute interval.

In order to construct a continuous time-series for SPI 200 Futures, we use the method of rolling over futures contracts. In particular, we use the data of the closest-to-maturity contract and "roll over" to the second closest-to-maturity contract on the day before the expiration date of the closest-to-maturity contract.[3] Day trading on SPI 200 Futures commences at 9 : 50 am and ends at 4 : 30 pm. In other words, the day-trading session of SPI 200 Futures starts 10 minutes before the open and finishes 30 minutes after the close of the equity market. Following Chan, Chan, and Karolyi (1991), we deal with this issue by removing SPI 200 Futures data before the open and after the close of the equity market. Consistent with Kalev et al. (2004), we collapse the period from the previous day closing (4 : 00 pm) until the next day 10 : 30 am into one single period. Although our approach may not be a perfect solution, it delivers the benefit of having a continuous return series for both the index and futures markets.

Information flow in our study is proxied by the total number of news announcements made by companies listed on the ASX and stored in the Signal G database. This database is collected from SIRCA and provides headlines of announcements made by companies on the ASX. Signal G gives details on the code of the announcing company, the announcement date and time, and the categories of announcements, such as takeover announcements, shareholder details, periodic reports, dividend announcements, company administration, issued capital, and asset acquisition and disposal.[4] Based on the announcement date and time, we compute the total number of announcements made by all companies in the S&P/ASX 200 Index in each 30-minute interval. Similar to the case of returns, all overnight announcements are accumulated into the first period (i.e., from the close of the previous day to 10 : 30 am of today).

In order to deal with the intraday pattern of returns (see, e.g., Wood, McInish, and Ord, 1985), we regress our raw returns on 12 different dummy variables for the 12 intraday intervals. We use the residuals of this regression as our measure of seasonally adjusted returns. In addition, similar to the observation of Kalev et al. (2004), we find an upward trend for trading volume over the sample period. Therefore, to avoid spurious results we de-trend the trading volume of both the S&P/ASX 200 Index and the SPI 200 Futures by estimating the following OLS regression:

$$V_t = \beta_1 + \beta_2 t + \beta_3 t^2 + e_t, \tag{12.1}$$

where V_t is the aggregate trading volume in the interval t. We use e_t, the residual from the regression, as the de-trended trading volume.

In this study, similar to Kalev et al. (2004), we adopt the total number of news announcements of all constituent stocks in the S&P/ASX 200 Index as the main proxy for information arrivals. We test the relation between news arrivals and the volatility of S&P/ASX 200 Index returns and SPI 200 Futures returns by estimating the censored regression model with the absolute value of returns as our proxy for volatility. This relation is also examined using univariate and multivariate conditional volatility models

[3] The results are qualitatively similar when we roll over futures contracts three or five days before the expiration date of closest-to-maturity contracts. This is consistent with Carchano and Pardo (2009), who find that, for stock index futures, different ways of rolling over futures contracts do not result in differences between resultant futures time-series.

[4] Signal G also provides additional information such as the industry subgroup the announcement belongs to or the location at which the documents were lodged.

such as the EGARCH model of Nelson (1991) and the Diagonal VECH and Diagonal BEKK models.[5] Finally, given that our sample period (October 2003 to September 2009) covers the Global Financial Crisis, we also analyze the two subsample periods, before and after the crisis. Since it is difficult to point out the starting date of the crisis, we apply the Quandt–Andrews Unknown Breakpoint Test (Andrews, 1993; Andrews and Ploberger, 1994), which tests for one or more unknown structural breakpoints in the equation's sample.[6] The breakpoint is identified as the last interval of the date November 1, 2007. Therefore, we perform our analysis for the two subsample periods: October 1, 2003 to November 1, 2007 and November 2, 2007 to September 30, 2009. A detailed discussion of our methodology is given in the technical appendix in Section 12.A (p. 283).

12.4 RESULTS

Table 12.1 presents descriptive statistics for the 30-minute return of the S&P/ASX 200 Index and the SPI 200 Futures, absolute returns, and the number of news items. The results show that all the return series and absolute return series are not normally distributed. This is evident in the whole sample period, as well as in each year of the sample. From Panels C and D, volatility in the equity and futures market, as proxied by the absolute value of return, experiences a sharp increase from 2007. This finding reflects the turbulent time during the Global Financial Crisis and provides the motivation for investigating the news arrival–volatility relation in two separate subperiods. Finally, the descriptive statistics in Panel E indicate that, on average, there are about nine company announcements in each 30-minute interval. The number of news items variable also exhibits a very high level of skewness. This finding implies that there are times when the number of news events is much higher than its median level (i.e., news clustering).

The results of autocorrelations of the absolute 30-minute index and futures return as well as news variables are presented in Table 12.2. From Table 12.2, we observe a statistically significant serial correlation for the number of news items and the absolute 30-minute index and futures return. Similar to Kalev et al. (2004), the highest levels of autocorrelation are evident in lags 12 and 24. This observation reflects accumulated news arriving overnight. Overall, the results in Tables 12.1 and 12.2 suggest that the number of news variables possesses a certain level of similarity with the volatility clustering of return series. This provides some support for using the number of public news arrivals to explain the persistence of volatility.

We initially start with an examination of the impact of news arrival on volatility based on a censored regression of the absolute value of seasonally adjusted returns on news arrivals. The results of this investigation are given in Table 12.3. The findings in Table 12.3 indicate that news arrivals have a positive effect on volatility. The coefficient estimate for the news arrivals variable is positive and significant at the 1% level for both the S&P/ASX200 Index and the SPI 200 Futures for the whole sample period as well as in both subsample periods. We also document a positive relation between lagged

[5] These two models are the simpler form of the VECH model (Bollerslev, Engle, and Wooldridge, 1988) and the BEKK model (Engle and Kroner, 1995) in which conditional variance and covariance depend only on their own lags and cross-products of the error term.

[6] Quandt (1960) developed the OLS-based test in case of unknown break location. Andrews (1993) and Andrews and Ploberger (1994) provided the limiting distribution of the test statistic and critical values, and Hansen (1997) developed a method to calculate p-values.

Table 12.1. Descriptive statistics of the 30-minute S&P/ASX 200 Index return (%), the SPI 200 Futures return (%), the absolute value of the S&P/ASX 200 Index return, the SPI 200 Futures return, and the total number of news items. The results are presented for the whole sample period (October 1, 2003 to September 30, 2009) and separately for each year in the sample period. "Mean", "Standard deviation", "Maximum", "Minimum", Skewness", "Kurtosis" represent the mean, standard deviation, maximum, minimum, skewness, and kurtosis statistics, respectively.

	2003–2009	2003	2004	2005	2006	2007	2008	2009
Panel A: S&P/ASX 200 Index return								
Mean	2.6×10^{-3}	6.6×10^{-3}	6.8×10^{-3}	5.4×10^{-3}	5.8×10^{-3}	3.7×10^{-3}	−0.018	0.011
Standard deviation	0.326	0.174	0.125	0.165	0.221	0.295	0.609	0.401
Maximum	5.983	2.527	1.180	1.195	1.946	2.986	5.983	2.400
Minimum	−6.076	−1.230	−1.506	−1.466	−1.896	−3.166	−6.076	−2.995
Skewness	−0.379	1.563	0.054	−0.071	0.135	−0.915	−0.143	−0.408
Kurtosis	57.368	31.882	18.941	14.461	18.003	25.304	28.874	13.125
Panel B: SPI 200 Futures return								
Mean	2.7×10^{-3}	6.9×10^{-3}	6.8×10^{-3}	5.1×10^{-3}	5.9×10^{-3}	3.9×10^{-3}	−0.017	0.010
Standard deviation	0.338	0.183	0.141	0.183	0.239	0.302	0.627	0.411
Maximum	7.000	2.596	1.196	1.451	2.162	3.270	7.000	2.564
Minimum	−6.130	−1.263	−1.753	−1.593	−1.882	−3.330	−6.130	−3.329
Skewness	−0.165	1.604	−0.113	0.186	0.416	−0.577	−0.054	−0.157
Kurtosis	57.284	27.274	18.044	13.773	15.808	25.079	25.911	12.780
Panel C: Absolute S&P/ASX 200 Index return								
Mean	0.1578	0.097	0.075	0.099	0.126	0.159	0.322	0.233
Standard deviation	0.285	0.144	0.101	0.132	0.182	0.248	0.517	0.327
Maximum	6.076	2.527	1.506	1.466	1.946	3.166	6.076	2.995
Minimum	0.000	0.000	0.000	0.000	0.000	0.000	0.000	0.000
Skewness	7.135	5.484	4.474	4.097	4.501	5.161	5.096	3.882
Kurtosis	82.277	53.285	32.818	23.672	27.258	37.366	35.411	19.221

(*continued*)

Table 12.1 *(cont.)*

	Panel D: Absolute SPI 200 Futures return					
Mean	0.169	0.105	0.086	0.112	0.140	0.167	0.336	0.245
Standard deviation	0.293	0.150	0.112	0.145	0.193	0.251	0.530	0.330
Maximum	7.000	2.596	1.753	1.592	2.162	3.330	7.000	3.329
Minimum	0.000	0.000	0.000	0.000	0.000	0.000	0.000	0.000
Skewness	7.127	5.047	4.312	3.992	4.258	5.153	5.193	3.872
Kurtosis	85.729	47.303	32.637	23.615	25.043	38.609	38.056	19.723
	Panel E: Number of news items							
Mean	8.696	8.629	7.505	8.977	9.354	10.143	9.020	6.736
Standard deviation	17.349	16.330	15.208	16.649	17.717	19.751	19.510	14.545
Maximum	203.000	131.000	166.000	188.000	131.000	146.000	203.000	110.000
Minimum	0.000	0.000	0.000	0.000	0.000	0.000	0.000	0.000
Skewness	3.844	3.734	4.144	3.774	3.513	3.491	4.119	3.670
Kurtosis	16.615	15.026	20.115	16.993	12.573	12.185	19.853	13.943

Table 12.2. Autocorrelation of absolute seasonally adjusted returns and the news variable. Q-statistics from the Ljung–Box Portmanteau Test for serial correlation are reported in parentheses. All of the Q-statistics are significant at the 0.01 level.

Lags	S&P/ASX 200 Index	SPI 200 Futures	News
1	0.14 (371.74)	0.14 (401.11)	−0.02 (7.84)
2	0.11 (612.63)	0.12 (674.14)	−0.04 (32.31)
6	0.06 (1,180.04)	0.03 (1,184.25)	−0.09 (451.85)
12	0.51 (7,600.52)	0.49 (7,135.26)	0.89 (16,395.23)
24	0.53 (15,163.36)	0.52 (14,674.53)	0.87 (32,160.72)

Table 12.3. Company news announcements and intraday volatility of the S&P/ASX 200 Index and the SPI Futures. The results are based on estimation of the following censored regression model: $|r_t| = \alpha + \beta_1 N_t + \beta_2 V_{t-1} + \varepsilon_t$, in which $|r_t|$ is either the absolute value of the seasonally adjusted return of the S&P/ASX 200 index or that of the SPI 200 Futures at the tth interval. This model is first estimated with the number of all company announcements (N_t) as the only explanatory variable and then includes both the number of all company announcements and the lagged detrended trading volume (V_{t-1}) as explanatory variables. The results are obtained based on maximum likelihood estimation with the left-censoring point of 0 imposed for the dependent variable. The results are presented for the whole sample period (October 1, 2003 to September 30, 2009) and for the two subsample periods October 1, 2003 to November 1, 2007 and November 2, 2007 to September 30, 2009. P-values are given in parentheses.

	S&P/ASX 200 Index		*SPI 200 Futures*	
	With news	With news and lagged volume	With news	With news and lagged volume
	Panel A: October 1, 2003 to September 30, 2009			
β_1	8.0×10^{-3} (0.00)	7.7×10^{-3} (0.00)	8.0×10^{-3} (0.00)	3.8×10^{-3} (0.00)
β_2		0.036 (0.00)		0.051 (0.00)
	Panel B: October 1, 2003 to November 1, 2007			
β_1	5.2×10^{-3} (0.00)	5.0×10^{-3} (0.00)	5.3×10^{-3} (0.00)	3.7×10^{-3} (0.00)
β_2		0.037 (0.00)		0.025 (0.00)
	Panel C: November 2, 2007 to September 30, 2009			
β_1	0.014 (0.00)	0.014 (0.00)	0.014 (0.00)	7.7×10^{-3} (0.00)
β_2		0.031 (0.00)		0.053 (0.00)

trading volume and volatility. Moreover, news arrivals are still positively related to volatility even after controlling for the impact of lagged trading volume on volatility.

The results of our main analysis are presented in Table 12.4. Similar to the results presented in Table 12.3, the results in Table 12.4 show that news arrivals have a positive impact on the conditional volatility of index and futures returns. The asymmetric response of volatility to positive shocks and negative shocks is evident only

Table 12.4. Company news announcements and intraday conditional volatility of the S&P/ASX 200 Index and the SPI 200 Futures. The sample period is between October 1, 2003 and September 30, 2009. Results are based on estimation of the following AR(1)–EGARCH(1,1) model:

$$r_t = r_{t-1} + \mu + \varepsilon_t,$$

Variance equation:
$$\log(\sigma_t^2) = \omega + \beta \log(\sigma_{t-1}^2) + \alpha \left| \frac{\varepsilon_{t-1}}{\sigma_{t-1}} \right| + \gamma \frac{\varepsilon_{t-1}}{\sigma_{t-1}} + \lambda N_t + \phi V_{t-1},$$

in which r_t is either the seasonally adjusted return of the S&P/ASX 200 index or that of the SPI 200 Futures at the tth interval, and σ_t^2 is the conditional variance of the error process (ε_t). This model is first estimated without any exogenous variables in the variance equation and includes the number of all company announcements (N_t), and finally, the number of all company announcements with lagged de-trended trading volume (V_{t-1}). Likelihood ratio (LR) statistics are twice the difference between the log likelihood value of each specification and that of the first specification (without any exogenous variable). *P*-values are given in parentheses.

	S&P/ASX 200 Index			*SPI 200 Futures*		
	Without news	With news	With news and lagged volume	Without news	With news	With news and lagged volume
β	0.982 (0.00)	0.441 (0.00)	0.523 (0.00)	0.983 (0.00)	0.425 (0.00)	0.334 (0.00)
γ	−0.040 (0.00)	8.7×10^{-3} (0.58)	6.3×10^{-3} (0.68)	−0.030 (0.00)	−0.027 (0.08)	−0.020 (0.19)
λ		0.051 (0.00)	0.045 (0.00)		0.048 (0.00)	0.040 (0.00)
ϕ			0.494 (0.00)			0.104 (0.00)
LR test		1.1×10^3 (0.00)	1.3×10^3 (0.00)		1.2×10^3 (0.00)	1.3×10^3 (0.00)

when the EGARCH(1,1) model is estimated without any exogenous variable. Once the impact of news arrivals on conditional volatility is accounted for, we no longer observe this effect. In addition, the level of volatility persistence declines from 0.982 (0.983) to 0.441 (0.425) for the S&P/ASX 200 Index (the SPI 200 Futures) after inclusion of the number of news items variable in the conditional variance equation of the EGARCH(1,1) model.[7] The log likelihood ratio test rejects the null hypothesis of $\lambda = 0$ at the 1% level of significance. Thus, the inclusion of news variables in the variance equation of the EGARCH(1,1) model has improved the overall goodness of fit of the model.

We also examine the potential impact of trading volume on conditional volatility by including lagged trading volume together with the news arrival variable in the conditional variance equation of the EGARCH(1,1) model. Similar to Kalev et al. (2004), we find that lagged trading volume has a positive effect on conditional volatility. This finding is consistent with Blume, Easley, and O'Hara (1994), who emphasize the role of trading volume in the price discovery process. More importantly, our results show that the news arrival variable remains statistically significant after controlling for the impact of lagged trading volume on volatility. For the S&P/ASX 200 Index, the inclusion of lagged trading volume does not result in further reduction of volatility persistence. In contrast, for the SPI 200 Futures, the level of volatility persistence declines from 0.425 to 0.334 when the lagged trading volume is included together with the news arrival variable in the EGARCH(1,1) conditional variance equation. A potential explanation for the different evidence regarding the level of reduction in volatility persistence in index and futures markets may come from the observation that the trading volume of SPI 200 Futures is based on the actual number of contracts traded, whereas the trading volume of the S&P/ASX 200 Index is calculated by the dollar value of all transacted shares of the constituent companies of the index. Alternatively, traders with firm-specific information may prefer to trade primarily on the spot equity market, while traders with market-wide information can also conduct their trades on index futures markets (Subrahmanyam, 1991; Gorton and Pennacchi, 1993; Bessembinder, Chan, and Seguin, 1996).

Table 12.5 reports the findings of the investigation of the news arrivals–volatility relation in two subsample periods: October 1, 2003 to November 1, 2007 and November 2, 2007 to September 30, 2009. Consistent with the results for the whole sample period presented in Table 12.4, the news arrivals variable is positively related to conditional volatility in the two subsample periods for both the S&P/ASX 200 Index and the SPI 200 Futures. The inclusion of the news arrivals variable greatly reduces the level of volatility persistence for both markets in both subsample periods. Further reduction in the level of volatility persistence after the additional inclusion of lagged trading volume is only observed for the SPI 200 Futures.

Overall, the results presented in Tables 12.3, 12.4, and 12.5 indicate that news arrivals have a positive impact on conditional volatility. The level of volatility persistence is also greatly reduced once the effect of news arrivals on volatility is accounted for. The substantial reduction in volatility persistence, together with the evidence of strong autocorrelation in news arrivals, as presented in Table 12.2, is consistent with the

[7] Volatility persistence does not disappear entirely, which is probably due to other private information arrival processes not being accounted for in the number of news arrivals variable.

Table 12.5. Company news announcements and intraday conditional volatility of the S&P/ASX 200 Index and the SPI 200 Futures in two subperiods. The first subsample period is from October 1, 2003 to November 1, 2007 and the second is from November 2, 2007 to September 30, 2009. Results are based on estimation of the EGARCH(1,1) model, specified in Table 4. Likelihood ratio (LR) statistics are twice the difference between the log likelihood value of each specification and that of the first specification (without any exogenous variable). *P*-values are given in parentheses.

	S&P/ASX 200 Index			*SPI Futures*		
	Without news	With news	With news and lagged volume	Without news	With news	With news and lagged volume
	Panel A: October 1, 2003 to November 1, 2007					
β	0.996 (0.00)	0.279 (0.00)	0.382 (0.00)	0.992 (0.00)	0.239 (0.00)	0.043 (0.04)
γ	−0.127 (0.21)	−0.017 (0.30)	−0.020 (0.22)	−0.075 (0.02)	−0.029 (0.07)	−0.023 (0.13)
λ		0.053 (0.00)	0.046 (0.00)		0.049 (0.00)	0.033 (0.00)
ϕ			0.788 (0.00)			0.237 (0.00)
LR test		2.9×10^3 (0.00)	3.1×10^3 (0.00)		2.7×10^3 (0.00)	2.9×10^3 (0.00)
	Panel B: October 1, 2003 to September 30, 2009					
β	0.997 (0.00)	0.206 (0.00)	0.255 (0.00)	0.997 (0.00)	0.262 (0.00)	0.004 (0.90)
γ	−0.039 (0.00)	0.011 (0.67)	0.011 (0.65)	−0.032 (0.00)	−0.034 (0.18)	−0.006 (0.80)
λ		0.058 (0.00)	0.054 (0.00)		0.054 (0.00)	0.028 (0.00)
ϕ			0.195 (0.00)			0.208 (0.00)
LR test		1.0×10^3 (0.00)	1.0×10^3 (0.00)		9.8×10^2 (0.00)	1.1×10^3 (0.00)

MDH, which attributes the time dependence of stock return volatility to that of information flows. The lagged trading volume also plays a role in affecting conditional volatility on both markets, with stronger results for the SPI 200 Futures.

In the final analysis, we investigate the news arrivals–volatility relation based on two multivariate GARCH models: the Diagonal VECH and the Diagonal BEKK models. The results of this analysis are presented in Table 12.6. From Table 12.6, we still observe a positive relation between news arrivals and conditional volatility for both the S&P/ASX 200 Index and the SPI 200 Futures and for the whole sample period as well as for the subsample periods. News arrivals also increase the covariance between index and futures returns. The results of the Wald Test reject the null hypothesis of insignificant impacts of news arrivals on conditional volatility and covariance in both the Diagonal VECH and Diagonal BEKK models. Thus, similar to Tables 12.3, 12.4, and 12.5, we conclude that news arrivals have a positive impact on conditional volatility.

12.5 CONCLUSIONS

In the current study, we examine the effect of the rate of information arrivals on return volatility, where the rate of information arrivals is proxied by the number of firm-specific announcements per given interval. Investigating the S&P/ASX 200 Index and the SPI 200 Futures over the period from October 2003 to September 2009, we document that the rate of information arrivals has a positive impact on volatility. This finding is consistent with the MDH, which argues that the variance of returns at a given interval is proportional to the rate of information arrivals on the market. Moreover, the level of volatility persistence is significantly reduced in both equity and futures markets after controlling for the effect of news arrivals on volatility. Thus, similar to Lamoureux and Lastrapes (1990), we argue that the phenomenon of volatility clustering reflects the serial correlation of information arrival frequencies. Our empirical results are robust with the use of univariate and multivariate conditional volatility modeling and during the period before and after the global Credit Crisis. Future research could examine the impact of different types (i.e., scheduled or unscheduled news announcements) or categories (i.e., mergers and acquisitions, earnings announcements, dividend announcements, etc.) of news on volatility. The proposed investigation is motivated by the observation of Andersen (1996) that different types of news may possess different arrival processes, which in turn may generate different levels of short-term volatility dynamics.

12.A TECHNICAL APPENDIX

We first test the relation between news arrivals and volatility of S&P/ASX 200 Index returns and SPI 200 Futures returns by estimating the following censored regression model:

$$|r_t| = \alpha + \beta_1 N_t + \beta_2 V_{t-1} + \varepsilon_t, \tag{12.2}$$

in which $|r_t|$ is either the absolute value of the seasonally adjusted return of the S&P/ASX 200 Index or the SPI 200 Futures at the tth interval, N_t is the number of all company announcements, and V_{t-1} is the lagged de-trended trading volume. The lagged de-trended trading volume is also included to account for the potential that this variable

Table 12.6. Company news announcements and intraday conditional volatility of the S&P/ASX 200 Index and the SPI 200 Futures (multivariate GARCH results). The results are based on estimation of the following multivariate GARCH(1,1) model:

Diagonal VECH

Mean equations: $r_{1t} = r_{1t-1} + \mu_1 + \varepsilon_{1t}$ and $r_{2t} = r_{2t-1} + \mu_2 + \varepsilon_{2t},$

Variance equations: $\sigma^2_{11t} = \omega_{11} + \alpha_{11}\varepsilon^2_{1t-1} + \beta_{11}\sigma^2_{11t-1} + \lambda_{11}N_t$ and $\sigma^2_{22t} = \omega_{22} + \alpha_{22}\varepsilon^2_{2t-1} + \beta_{22}\sigma^2_{22t-1} + \lambda_{22}N_t,$

Covariance equation: $\sigma^2_{12t} = \omega_{12} + \alpha_{12}\varepsilon_{1t-1}\varepsilon_{2t-1} + \beta_{12}\sigma^2_{12t-1} + \lambda_{12}N_t,$

Diagonal BEKK

Mean equations: $r_{1t} = r_{1t-1} + \mu_1 + \varepsilon_{1t}$ and $r_{2t} = r_{2t-1} + \mu_2 + \varepsilon_{2t},$

Variance equations: $\sigma^2_{11t} = \omega_{11} + \alpha^2_{11}\varepsilon^2_{1t-1} + \beta^2_{11}\sigma^2_{11t-1} + \lambda_{11}N_t$ and $\sigma^2_{22t} = \omega_{22} + \alpha^2_{22}\varepsilon^2_{2t-1} + \beta^2_{22}\sigma^2_{22t-1} + \lambda_{22}N_t,$

Covariance equation: $\sigma^2_{12t} = \omega_{12} + \alpha_{11}\alpha_{22}\varepsilon_{1t-1}\varepsilon_{2t-1} + \beta_{11}\beta_{22}\sigma^2_{12t-1} + \lambda_{12}N_t,$

in which r_{1t} and r_{2t} are the seasonally adjusted returns of the S&P/ASX 200 Index and the SPI 200 Futures at the tth interval, σ^2_{1t} and σ^2_{2t} are conditional variances of the error processes ε_{1t} and ε_{2t}, respectively, and N_t is the number of all company announcements in interval t. *P*-values are given in parentheses. "Wald Test" refers to the chi-square test statistics for the null hypothesis of $\lambda_{11} = \lambda_{12} = \lambda_{22} = 0$. The results are presented for the whole sample period (October 1, 2003 to September 30, 2009) and for the two subsample periods: October 1, 2003 to November 1, 2007 and November 2, 2007 to September 30, 2009.

	October 1, 2003 to September 30, 2009				October 1, 2003 to November 1, 2007				November 2, 2007 to September 30, 2009			
	λ_{11}	λ_{12}	λ_{22}	Wald Test	λ_{11}	λ_{12}	λ_{22}	Wald Test	λ_{11}	λ_{12}	λ_{22}	Wald Test
Diagonal VECH	3.0×10^{-3}	3.1×10^{-3}	3.3×10^{-3}	701.89	1.8×10^{-3}	1.8×10^{-3}	2.0×10^{-3}	926.14	0.013	0.012	0.012	454.72
	(0.00)	(0.00)	(0.00)	(0.00)	(0.00)	(0.00)	(0.00)	(0.00)	(0.00)	(0.00)	(0.00)	(0.00)
Diagonal BEKK	1.1×10^{-5}	7.5×10^{-6}	4.9×10^{-6}	20.81	1.8×10^{-3}	1.9×10^{-3}	2.1×10^{-3}	854.14	0.013	0.013	0.013	407.34
	(0.00)	(0.00)	(0.00)	(0.00)	(0.00)	(0.00)	(0.00)	(0.00)	(0.00)	(0.00)	(0.00)	(0.00)

does reflect to some degree the intensity of private information flows not accounted for by N_t. The results are obtained based on maximum likelihood estimation with the left-censoring point of 0 imposed on the dependent variable.

After censored regression, we apply the EGARCH model of Nelson (1991) in our investigation of the impact of news arrivals on volatility. According to Bollerslev, Chou, and Kroner (1992), GARCH-type models are widely used in studies which deal with volatility modeling. EGARCH has several advantages over the pure GARCH specification. First, there is no need to impose non-negativity constraints on model parameters. Second, the EGARCH model allows for asymmetric response of volatility to positive and negative shocks, where a negative shock on the financial time-series is more likely to cause a bigger increase in volatility than a positive shock of the same magnitude. The following autoregressive of order 1, EGARCH(1,1) model (AR(1)–EGARCH(1,1)), is estimated for the S&P/ASX 200 Index and the SPI 200 Futures:

Mean equation:
$$r_t = r_{t-1} + \mu + \varepsilon_t, \tag{12.3}$$

Variance equation:
$$\log(\sigma_t^2) = \omega + \beta \log(\sigma_{t-1}^2) + \alpha\left|\frac{\varepsilon_{t-1}}{\sigma_{t-1}}\right| + \gamma\frac{\varepsilon_{t-1}}{\sigma_{t-1}} + \lambda N_t + \phi V_{t-1}, \tag{12.4}$$

in which r_t is either the seasonally adjusted return of the S&P/ASX 200 index or the SPI 200 Futures at the tth interval, and σ_t^2 is the conditional variance of the error process (ε_t). This model is first estimated without any exogenous variables in the variance equation, then includes the number of all company announcements (N_t), and finally the number of all company announcements with lagged de-trended trading volume (V_{t-1}). The degree of volatility persistence is reflected by the coefficient β while γ indicates the asymmetric response of volatility to positive shocks and negative shocks. We estimate the EGARCH(1,1) model where the error term follows Student's t-distribution in order to incorporate the potential leptokurtic distribution of the error term.

We expect that λ is positive and significant in equations (12.2) and (12.4) (i.e., higher information arrivals lead to higher volatility). In addition, following Lamoureux and Lastrapes (1990), if N_t is serially correlated and the presence of volatility persistence is largely induced by serial correlation in information flows, the persistence of volatility (β) in equation (12.4) should be substantially reduced in comparison with the estimates of the EGARCH(1,1) model without any exogenous variable.

We also examine the conditional volatility of S&P/ASX 200 Index returns and SPI 200 Futures returns simultaneously by estimating the Diagonal VECH and Diagonal BEKK models. These two models are simpler forms of the VECH model (Bollerslev, Engle, and Wooldridge, 1988) and the BEKK model (Engle and Kroner, 1995), in which conditional variance and covariance depend only on their own lags and the cross-products of the error term. The Diagonal VECH and Diagonal BEKK models simplify estimation of the VECH and BEKK models and still have the advantage of controlling for contemporaneous correlation of residuals across equations. We estimate the following models in our analysis:

Diagonal VECH

Mean equations: $$r_{1t} = r_{1t-1} + \mu_1 + \varepsilon_{1t}, \quad (12.5)$$

$$r_{2t} = r_{2t-1} + \mu_2 + \varepsilon_{2t}, \quad (12.6)$$

Variance equations: $$\sigma^2_{11t} = \omega_{11} + \alpha_{11}\varepsilon^2_{1t-1} + \beta_{11}\sigma^2_{11t-1} + \lambda_{11}N_t, \quad (12.7)$$

$$\sigma^2_{22t} = \omega_{22} + \alpha_{22}\varepsilon^2_{2t-1} + \beta_{22}\sigma^2_{22t-1} + \lambda_{22}N_t, \quad (12.8)$$

Covariance equation: $$\sigma^2_{12t} = \omega_{12} + \alpha_{12}\varepsilon_{1t-1}\varepsilon_{2t-1} + \beta_{12}\sigma^2_{12t-1} + \lambda_{12}N_t, \quad (12.9)$$

Diagonal BEKK

Mean equations: $$r_{1t} = r_{1t-1} + \mu_1 + \varepsilon_{1t} \quad \text{and} \quad r_{2t} = r_{2t-1} + \mu_2 + \varepsilon_{2t},$$

Variance equations: $$\sigma^2_{11t} = \omega_{11} + \alpha^2_{11}\varepsilon^2_{1t-1} + \beta^2_{11}\sigma^2_{11t-1} + \lambda_{11}N_t, \quad (12.10)$$

$$\sigma^2_{22t} = \omega_{22} + \alpha^2_{22}\varepsilon^2_{2t-1} + \beta^2_{22}\sigma^2_{22t-1} + \lambda_{22}N_t, \quad (12.11)$$

Covariance equation: $$\sigma^2_{12t} = \omega_{12} + \alpha_{11}\alpha_{22}\varepsilon_{1t-1}\varepsilon_{2t-1} + \beta_{11}\beta_{22}\sigma^2_{12t-1} + \lambda_{12}N_t, \quad (12.12)$$

in which r_{1t} and r_{2t} are seasonally adjusted returns of the S&P/ASX 200 Index and the SPI 200 Futures Index at the tth interval, and σ^2_{1t} and σ^2_{2t} are conditional variances of the error process ε_{1t} and ε_{2t}, respectively.

12.B REFERENCES

Admati A.R.; Pfleiderer P. (1988) "A theory of intraday patterns: Volume and price variability," *Review of Financial Studies*, **1**, 3–40.

Andersen T.G. (1996) "Return volatility and trading volume: An information flow interpretation of stochastic volatility," *Journal of Finance*, **51**, 169–204.

Andrews D.W.K. (1993) "Tests for parameter instability and structural change with unknown change point," *Econometrica*, **61**, 821–856.

Andrews D.W.K.; Ploberger W. (1994) "Optimal tests when a nuisance parameter is present only under the alternative," *Econometrica*, **62**, 1383–1414.

Ané T.; Geman H. (2000) "Order flow, transaction clock, and normality of asset returns," *Journal of Finance*, **55**, 2259–2284.

Asai M.; McAleer M.; Yu J. (2006) "Multivariate stochastic volatility: A review," *Econometric Reviews*, **25**, 145–175.

Barclay M.J.; Warner J.B. (1993) "Stealth trading and volatility: Which trades move prices?" *Journal of Financial Economics*, **34**, 281–305.

Bauwens L.; Laurent S.; Rombouts J.V.K. (2006) "Multivariate GARCH: A survey," *Journal of Applied Econometrics*, **21**, 79–109.

Berry T.D.; Howe K.M. (1994) "Public information arrival," *Journal of Finance*, **49**, 1331–1346.

Bessembinder H.; Chan K.; Seguin P.J. (1996) "An empirical examination of information, differences of opinion, and trading activity," *Journal of Financial Economics*, **40**, 105–134.

Blume L.; Easley D.; O'Hara M. (1994) "Market statistics and technical analysis: The role of volume," *Journal of Finance*, **49**, 153–181.

Bollerslev T. (1986) "Generalized autoregressive conditional heteroscedasticity," *Journal of Econometrics*, **31**, 307–326.

Bollerslev T.; Chou R.Y.; Kroner K.F. (1992) "ARCH modelling in finance: A review of the theory and empirical evidence," *Journal of Econometrics*, **52**, 5–59.

Bollerslev T.; Engle R.F.; Wooldridge J.M. (1988) "A capital asset pricing model with time varying covariances," *Journal of Political Economy*, **96**, 116–131.

Campbell J.; Kyle A. (1993) "Smart money, noise trading and stock price behavior," *Review of Economic Studies*, **60**, 1–34.

Carchano O.; Pardo A. (2009) "Rolling over stock index futures contracts," *Journal of Futures Markets*, **29**, 684–694.

Chan K.; Chan K.C.; Karolyi G.A. (1991) "Intraday volatility in the stock index and stock index futures markets," *Review of Financial Studies*, **4**, 657–684.

Christiansen C. (2000) "Macroeconomic announcement effects on the covariance structure of government bond returns," *Journal of Empirical Finance*, **7**, 479–507.

Clark P.K. (1973) "A subordinated stochastic process model with finite variance for speculative prices," *Econometrica*, **41**, 135–155.

Darolles S.; Le Fol G.; Mero G. (2009) *Return and Volume: Between Information and Liquidity*, Working Paper, University of Rennes 1 and INSEE, France.

DeGennaro R.P.; Shrieves R.E. (1997) "Public information releases, private information arrival and volatility in the foreign exchange market," *Journal of Empirical Finance*, **4**, 295–315.

de Goeij P.; Marquering W. (2006) "Macroeconomic announcements and asymmetric volatility in bond returns," *Journal of Banking and Finance*, **30**, 2659–2680.

De Long J.B.; Shleifer A.; Summers L.; Waldmann R. (1990) "Noise trader risk in financial markets," *Journal of Political Economy*, **98**, 703–738.

Ederington L.H.; Lee J.H. (1993) "How markets process information: News releases and volatility," *Journal of Finance*, **48**, 1161–1191.

Ederington L.H.; Lee J.H. (1996) "The creation and resolution of market uncertainty: The impact of information releases on implied volatility," *Journal of Financial and Quantitative Analysis*, **31**, 513–539.

Engle R.F. (1982) "Autoregressive conditional heteroskedasticity with estimates of variance of United Kingdom inflation," *Econometrica*, **50**, 987–1008.

Engle R.F. (2002) "New frontiers for ARCH models," *Journal of Applied Econometrics*, **17**, 425–446.

Engle R.F.; Kroner K.F. (1995) "Multivariate simultaneous generalised GARCH," *Econometric Theory*, **11**, 122–150.

Epps T.W.; Epps M.L. (1976) "The stochastic dependence of security price changes and transaction volumes: Implications for the mixture-of-distributions hypothesis," *Econometrica*, **44**, 305–321.

Fleming M.J.; Remolona E.M. (1999) "Price formation and liquidity in the U.S. Treasury market: The response to public information," *Journal of Finance*, **54**, 1901–1915.

Foster F.D.; Viswanathan S. (1993) "Variations in trading volume, return volatility and trading costs: Evidence on recent price formation models," *Journal of Finance*, **48**, 187–211.

Foster F.D.; Viswanathan S. (1995) "Can speculative trading explain the volume–volatility relation?" *Journal of Business and Economic Statistics*, **13**, 379–396.

Goodhart C.A.E.; O'Hara M. (1997) "High frequency data in financial markets: Issues and applications," *Journal of Empirical Finance*, **4**, 73–114.

Gorton G.; Pennacchi G. (1993) "Security baskets and index-linked securities," *Journal of Business*, **66**, 1–28.

Grundy B.; McNichols M. (1989) "Trade and revelation of information through prices and direct disclosure," *Review of Financial Studies*, **2**, 495–526.

Hansen B.E. (1997) "Approximate asymptotic *p*-values for structural-change tests," *Journal of Business and Economic Statistics*, **15**, 60–67.

Harris L. (1986) "A transactions data study of weekly and intraday patterns in stock returns," *Journal of Financial Economics*, **16**, 99–117.

Harris L. (1987) "Transaction data tests of the mixture of distributions hypothesis," *Journal of Financial and Quantitative Analysis*, **22**, 127–141.

He H.; Wang J. (1995) "Differential information and dynamic behavior of stock trading volume," *Review of Financial Studies*, **8**, 919–972.

Jones C.M.; Kaul G.; Lipson M.L. (1994) "Information, trading and volatility," *Journal of Financial Economics*, **36**, 127–154.

Jones C.M.; Lamont O.; Lumsdaine R.L. (1998) "Macroeconomic news and bond market volatility," *Journal of Financial Economics*, **47**, 315–337.

Kim O.; Verrecchia R. (1991) "Trading volume and price reaction to public announcements," *Journal of Accounting Research*, **29**, 302–321.

Kalev P.S.; Liu W.-M.; Pham P.K.; Jarnecic E. (2004) "Public information arrival and volatility of intraday stock returns," *Journal of Banking and Finance*, **28,** 1441–1467.

Kyle, A. (1985) "Continuous auctions and insider trading," *Econometrica*, **53**, 1315–1335.

Lamoureux C.G.; Lastrapes W.D. (1990) "Heteroscedasticity in stock return data: Volume versus GARCH effects," *Journal of Finance*, **45**, 221–229.

Li L.; Engle R.F. (1998) *Macroeconomic Announcements and Volatility of Treasury Futures*, Working Paper, University of California, San Diego.

Liesenfeld R. (1998) "Dynamic bivariate mixture model: Modelling the behaviour of prices and trading volume," *Journal of Business and Economic Statistics*, **16**, 101–109.

Liesenfeld R. (2001) "A generalized bivariate mixture model for stock price volatility and trading volume," *Journal of Econometrics*, **104**, 141–178.

Mitchell M.L.; Mulherin J.H. (1994) "The impact of public information on the stock market," *Journal of Finance*, **49**, 923–950.

Melvin M.; Yin X. (2000) "Public information arrival, exchange rate volatility, and quote frequency," *Economic Journal*, **110**, 644–661.

Nelson D.B. (1991) "Conditional heteroskedasticity in asset return: A new approach," *Econometrica*, **59**, 347–370.

Nofsinger J.R.; Prucyk B. (2003) "Option volume and volatility responses to scheduled economics news releases," *Journal of Futures Markets*, **23**, 315–345.

Quandt R.E. (1960) "Tests of the hypothesis that a linear regression system obeys two separate regimes," *Journal of American Statistical Association*, **55**, 324–330.

Ranaldo A. (2006) *Intraday Market Dynamics around Public Information Arrivals*, Working Paper, Swiss National Bank.

Ross S.A. (1989) "Information and volatility: The no-arbitrage martingale approach to timing and resolution irrelevancy," *Journal of Finance*, **44**, 1–17.

Ryan P.; Taffler R.J. (2004) "Are economically significant stock returns and trading volumes driven by firm specific news releases?" *Journal of Business Finance and Accounting*, **31**, 49–82.

Subrahmanyam A. (1991) "A theory of trading in stock index futures," *Review of Financial Studies*, **4**, 17–51.

Tauchen G.; Pitts M. (1983) "The price variability–volume relationship on speculative markets," *Econometrica*, **51**, 485–505.

Wagner N.; Marsh T.A. (2005) "Surprise volume and heteroskedasticity in equity market returns," *Quantitative Finance*, **5**, 153–168.

Wood R.A.; McInish T.H.; Ord J.K. (1985) "An investigation of transactions data for NYSE stocks," *Journal of Finance*, **40**, 723–739.

13

Equity portfolio risk estimation using market information and sentiment

Leela Mitra, Gautam Mitra, and Dan diBartolomeo

ABSTRACT

Multifactor models are often used as a tool to describe equity portfolio risk. Naturally, risk is dependent on the market environment and investor sentiment. Traditional factor models fail to update quickly as market conditions change. It is desirable that risk model updates incorporate new information as it becomes available and for this reason diBartolomeo and Warrick (2005) introduce a factor model that uses option-implied volatility to improve estimates of a future covariance matrix. We extend this work to use both quantified news and implied volatility to improve risk estimates as the market sentiment and environment changes.

13.1 INTRODUCTION AND BACKGROUND

Equity portfolio management problems require fund managers to make decisions about what portfolio to hold (ex ante) without knowing what future equity returns will be. Though these returns are uncertain, market participants try to understand the nature of the uncertainty and make decisions based on their beliefs about the market environment.

Traditionally, portfolio managers have used variants of the Markowitz Mean Variance Analysis to determine the optimal portfolio to hold, and this is still fairly standard practise in industry. Mean variance portfolio decision models fall into the more general group of mean risk models, where portfolio risk and expected return are traded off when making asset choices. Variance and standard deviation both measure the spread of a distribution about its mean. Since the variance of a portfolio can be easily calculated from covariances of the pairs of asset returns and asset weights used in the portfolio, variance is predominantly used in portfolio formation.

In contrast to computing asset variances and covariances directly using historical data, multifactor models provide an accurate and efficient way to provide these estimates. They decompose an asset's return into returns derived from exposure to common factors and an asset-specific component. The common factors can be understood as representing different risk (uncertainty) aspects, which all the assets are exposed to in

The Handbook of News Analytics in Finance Edited by L. Mitra and G. Mitra

varying degrees (factor sensitivities). By describing a group of asset returns through a set of key common factors, the size of the estimation problem is significantly reduced. The new problem faced is to estimate the covariance matrix of common sources of risk, variances of specific returns, and estimates of each security's factor exposures. These models capture the natural intuition that firms with similar characteristics will behave similarly.

Active portfolio managers seek to incorporate their investment insight to "beat the market". An accurate description of asset price uncertainty is key to the ability to outperform the market. Tetlock, Saar-Tsechansky, and Macskassy (2008) develop a fundamental factor model that incorporates news as a factor. Investors' perceptions of the riskiness of an asset are determined by their knowledge about the company and its prospects (i.e., by their "information sets"). They note that these are determined from three main sources: analysts' forecasts, quantifiable publicly disclosed accounting variables, and linguistic descriptions of the firm's current and future profit-generating activities. If the first two sources of information are incomplete or biased, the third may give us relevant information for equity prices. We seek to extract an improved understanding of equity price uncertainty using a quantified measure of market sentiment to update a traditional factor model. This may give us the tools to make improved portfolio (management) decisions.

There are three main types of multifactor models

- *Macroeconomic* factor models use economic variables (or functions of economic variables) as factors. They model asset k's price as a response to these external influences, capturing the natural idea that there is a relationship between equity prices and the economic environment. Typical factors include unexpected changes in inflation, changes in oil prices, returns in the bond market, etc. Factors i are observable time-series. Model calibration involves estimating unknown factor sensitivities β_{ki}, residual variances σ_i^2, and the factor covariance matrix Ω_f. This is done using time-series regression. Chen, Roll, and Ross (1986) is a well-known example of such a model. Sharpe's (1970) single-factor model can also be regarded as a special case of this type of model.
- *Fundamental* models use firm-specific attributes which are not related to the economic environment. These could include factors based on the firm's structure, such as size, dividend yield, industry classification. Or they could include factors relating to the market, such as volatility and momentum. There are two well-known approaches: Fama–French (1992, 1993) and BARRA (1974).

  BARRA Inc. was founded by Bar Rosenberg; BARRA risk (factor) models are widely used in industry. They provide their customers with a wide range of industry-specific factors and other risk indices. The industry factors measure the differing behaviour of stocks in different industries and risk indices measure behaviour which is not industry-specific (i.e., due to non-industry differences). It is assumed that factor sensitivities are observable characteristics, such as which industry the firm is in. Factor realizations are assumed to be unobservable and are determined through repeated cross-sectional regression at each time point. These factor realizations can also be interpreted as the returns on single-factor (or factor-mimicking) portfolios.

  The Fama–French (1992) approach estimates parameters using a two-step process. First, factor realizations are determined. For a particular asset-specific characteristic, such as size, assets are sorted based on the value of the characteristic. Then a hedged portfolio is formed which is long in the top quintile of sorted assets and short in the bottom quintile. The observed return on the hedged portfolio at time t is the observed factor realization. The process is repeated for each asset-specific characteristic. In the second step, factor exposures are determined using N time-series regressions (for the N assets under consideration).

- In *statistical* factor models both factor realizations and exposures are unobservable. Model calibration involves using the sample covariance matrix of observed returns, which is decomposed into a factor component and a specific component. Factor exposures are estimated in this process. The methods used for calibration of these models include maximum likelihood factor analysis and principal components analysis.

The three types of factor models differ in what sources of risk they consider and how they are calibrated. They give different ways to describe return variability and they can be shown to be rotations of each other (see Connor, 1995). To assess which model is most appropriate Sheikh (1995) notes: "We prefer a procedure that is robust (less liable to spurious correlations), capable of explaining the variability in returns (common sources of risk are captured), dynamic (able to change as the determinants of risk change)."

Statistical models use historical correlations to determine a set of orthogonal factors. The advantage of this is that they can evolve over time to pick up new conditions without the need to identify changes in factor structure. However, these factors are opaque and it is difficult to identify them with interpretable sources of risk. Though methods have been suggested for identifying statistical factor loadings with fundamental stock attributes (see Wilding, 2005), this is stated to be a disadvantage of these models. Another common criticism is that statistical models can pick up random, chance correlations between assets. Further, a choice needs to be made of how many factors to include in the model.

Fundamental and macroeconomic models pick up correlations between assets due to common interpretable factors. Macroeconomic models are sometimes criticized as they do not capture any aspects that do not relate to the economy. Fundamental models are popular in industry and they use characteristics which portfolio managers understand well. However, a choice of which factors to use needs to be made. Also the factors often have common characteristics and it is difficult to separate their effects on return variability. diBartolomeo and Warrick (2005) note that this makes them less effective at predicting future conditions.

None of these three models is dominant. Scowcroft and Sefton (2006) comment: "There is little or no consensus on which factors to use or how the models should be estimated." They find in their study that the quality of factor information used in a model has a significant influence on the quality of the model. Hence the choice of model should be influenced by the information the model builder has available and the quality of this information. In particular, when there is sparse knowledge or data for factors a statistical model may be the most appropriate choice. They also note that hybrid models which use both fundamental and statistical factors may be effective.

It is often argued that fundamental models are dynamic because they can capture changing risk structure when a company's situation changes by updating relevant factor exposures. For statistical and macroeconomic models, exposures (hence changes in risk structure) are only updated when further data become available and the models are re-calibrated; hence they are updated more slowly and are usually not dynamic.

However, all the models have a single-period structure and are based on independent, identically distributed distributions and do not allow for changing levels of volatility over time. As the operating environment changes these models' calibration parameters are updated, but it takes some time for the models to adapt. Levels of risk can change quickly over time as market participants react to the arrival of new information. This new information can be split into two parts. The first is unexpected news. The second type of information is announcements. In this case the time of the announcement is known but the content is unknown. Conditional heteroskedasticity models (GARCH and ARCH) are one way to describe time-varying volatility. However, these models are not directly linked to market sentiment. It is also difficult to incorporate GARCH processes to describe volatility for a large number of assets. In particular, the relationship between different assets needs to be described. BARRA has used GARCH processes to improve its factor and asset-specific variance estimates.

diBartolomeo and Warrick (2005) note that to account for the lack of historical data to estimate returns over longer periods, daily volatility predictions are often scaled up by the square root of time, which implicitly assumes an independent and identical distribution of security returns over time. However, this approach is not compatible with GARCH processes wherein volatility is presumed to vary over time, and returns are presumed not to be independent from period to period.

Also, as diBartolomeo and Warrick (2005) describe, these models can display counter-intuitive behaviour that fails to account for the way announcements affect markets. If the market expects an announcement about a particular company, trading volatility may fall as investors wait to see what the content of the announcement is. When the content of the announcement becomes known traders will react quickly to this information and volatility will jump. However, once having reacted to the market announcement, traders will then reduce their level of trading for this stock and volatility levels will fall again. A GARCH model describes volatility-clustering behaviour. Current volatility is described in terms of previous-period volatility. So high volatility in one period will influence the model to predict higher volatility for the period. Similiarly a period of low volatility will influence the model's prediction of volatility for the following period. As the market is quiet prior to an announcement date, the GARCH model will predict low volatility on an announcement date, when in fact volatility will be high. Then the model adjusts to predict high volatility on the following day when volatility will fall.

The focus of the present chapter is to investigate the relationship between news and the market volatility of asset prices. Jalen (2008) finds there is a relatively strong correlation between asset price volatility and news sentiment. Ederington and Lee (1993) study the impact of information releases on market level uncertainty on interest rates and foreign exchange futures markets.

Security and market volatility vary over time as conditions change and new information becomes available to investors. Option traders respond quickly to new information that impacts expectations of future volatility because option prices are directly dependent on such volatility expectations. As such, changes in the level of option-implied volatility can be used as a measure of the extent to which market participants believe current conditions that affect volatility are different from their typical state. Hence these models should capture their considered behaviour and help give more sensible estimates of future volatility.

An alternative way to account for changes in market conditions that are manifested as time-varying volatility is through the use of quantified news. For example, if on a typical trading day there are 10 to 15 newswire service stories about firm X, and today there are 200 newswire service stories about firm X, we can assert that there is a significantly greater than usual amount of information being imparted to investors about this firm. As such, more substantial share price movements may result than would be typical. We might even be able to analyse whether the content of the news stories would be considered broadly negative or positive with respect to the operations or valuation of firm X. In essence, the volume and nature of textual news can be used like option-implied volatility to very rapidly adjust our expectations of future volatility for a particular firm or an entire market.

For a review of both GARCH and the implied volatility models that describe the impact of information arrival on volatility levels see diBartolomeo and Warrick (2005).

13.2 MODEL DESCRIPTION

The model provides updated estimates of portfolio volatility using information about changes to the market environment. We describe in this section a slightly modified form of the model outlined in diBartolomeo and Warrick (2005) which updates traditional factor risk estimates using option-implied volatility. This model is extended in the following section with quantified news inputs.

The model is described in two parts. The first is a "basic" statistical factor model. In the second part, factor variance estimates are updated to account for changes in option-implied volatility levels. The asset covariance matrix is re-estimated, using the updated factor variances, to give an improved set of risk estimates.

We construct a statistical factor model applying traditional principal component analysis to extract orthogonal factors.[1] For a general factor model, the variance of each asset is given as a linear combination of factor variances and asset-specific variances

$$V_{kt} = \sum_{i=1}^{F} \sum_{j=1}^{F} \beta_{kit} \beta_{kjt} \sigma_{it} \sigma_{jt} \rho_{ijt} + \sigma_{s(k)t}^2.$$

Sets and indices

$k \in \{1, \ldots, N_1\}$ denotes the asset universe;
$t \in \{1, \ldots, T\}$ denotes the time points considered;
$i,j \in \{1, \ldots, F\}$ denotes the factors.

[1] Computational experiments are carried out using the component assets of the EURO STOXX 50, so the number of time periods T are greater than the number of assets N and we are able to carry out principal component analysis on the $N \times T$ dataset, thereby avoiding the problem of the matrix becoming singular.

Parameters

V_{kt}	denotes the variance for asset k at time point $t \in \{1, \ldots, T\}$;
β_{kit}	denotes factor sensitivity (exposure) to factor i for asset k at time point t;
σ_{it}	denotes factor variance for factor i at time point t;
ρ_{ijt}	denotes the correlation between factor i and factor j at time point t;
$\sigma^2_{s(k)t}$	denotes the asset-specific variance for asset k at time point t.

In this case, as the factors are orthogonal, this simplifies to

$$V_{kt} = \sum_{i=1}^{F} \beta^2_{kit}\sigma^2_{it} + \sigma^2_{s(k)t}. \tag{13.1}$$

These (asset) variances can be updated by considering the relationship between implied volatility and factor model volatility. However, as diBartolomeo and Warrick (2005) note, implied volatility is often a biased estimator of actual asset volatility. This is because option-pricing methods, such as Black–Scholes (1973), are based on the assumption that option positions can be hedged continuously at no cost. In the real world, hedging is costly and positions are hedged periodically not continuously. Positions that are assumed to be risk-less under this pricing framework actually do carry some risk. Traders compensate for this and bias their risk estimates upward. To avoid this problem diBartolomeo and Warrick (2005) consider the relationship between changes in implied volatility and changes in basic factor model volatility levels. We can only study the relationship of those assets for which we have option-implied volatility data. We can update our conditional estimate of asset variance at time t, derived from the principal component model, to

$$V^*_{\ell t} = V_{\ell t} M_{\ell t} \tag{13.2}$$

where $M_{\ell t}$ is an adjustment at time t, defined as

$$M_{\ell t} = \left[\prod_{r=0}^{w-1} \frac{I_{\ell\, t-r}}{I_{\ell\, t-r-1}}\right] \div \left[\prod_{r=0}^{w-1} \frac{V_{\ell\, t-r}}{V_{\ell\, t-r-1}}\right] \tag{13.3}$$

Sets and indices

$\ell \in \{1, \ldots, N_2\}$ denotes the assets for which option-implied volatility data are available.

Parameters

$I_{\ell t}$	denotes option-implied variance observed for security ℓ at time point t;
$V^*_{\ell t}$	denotes the updated variance for security ℓ at time point t;
w	denotes the period considered for updating information.

Option-implied volatility (equivalently variance) levels update faster than factor model estimates, so changes in this relationship should give us an improved estimate of future risk. For each asset ℓ we have

$$V^*_{\ell t} = \sum \beta^2_{\ell it}(\sigma^*_{it})^2 + \sigma^2_{s(\ell)t}, \tag{13.4}$$

where $(\sigma_{it}^*)^2$ are the new factor variances implied by the updated asset variances. We solve this set of simultaneous equations to derive the updated factor variances $(\hat{\sigma_{it}}^*)^2$ that minimize mean squared error, subject to the condition these values are non-negative. We also introduce the further constraint

$$(\sigma_{it}^*)^2 \geq (\sigma_{i-1t}^*)^2 \tag{13.5}$$

to allow for the structure that is expected of the principal component factors. Though factor volatility may rise suddenly as market conditions change, there are few economic circumstances where it would be expected to decline dramatically from one time period to the next. It is also prudent to assume that it would not decline substantially, hence we introduce the constraint

$$(\sigma_{it}^*)^2 \geq p_1(\sigma_{it-1}^*)^2. \tag{13.6}$$

In equation (13.4), the asset-specific variances are taken as previous-period known values. Once updated factor variances are derived, the asset-specific variances can be re-calculated as

$$\hat{\sigma}_{s(\ell)t}^2 = V_{\ell t}^* - \sum \beta_{\ell it}^2(\hat{\sigma_{it}}^*)^2. \tag{13.7}$$

As with factor variances, we do not expect asset-specific variances to decline substantially from one period to the next and we set

$$\sigma_{s(\ell)t}^2 := \max[\hat{\sigma}_{s(\ell)t}^2, \sigma_{s(\ell)(t-1)}^2 \times p_2]. \tag{13.8}$$

The updated factor variance estimates are used to re-estimate all asset variances and covariances. We do not need the relationship (13.4) to be given for all assets in the asset universe. As a result we need not directly identify which changes in option-implied volatility impact which factors and to what extent. These changes are derived *implicitly*, by considering the relationship of changes between factor model variance estimates and option-implied variance estimates.

13.3 UPDATING MODEL VOLATILITY USING QUANTIFIED NEWS

There is a strong, yet complex relationship between market sentiment and news. Traders and other market participants digest news rapidly and update their asset positions accordingly. Most traders have access to newswires at their desks. However, whereas raw news is qualitative data, for models to incorporate news directly and automatically we require quantitative inputs.

RavenPack has developed linguistic analytics that process the textual input of news stories to determine quantitative sentiment scores. In particular, they classify individual stories by the market aspects to which they relate; they also assign sentiment indicators that define a story as positive, negative, or neutral. These methods are then applied to derive specific scores about different market entities such as a company or an industry sector. Scores that indicate the relative sentiment for a stock over time have been produced; for further details of how these scores are calculated and more specific details of their methodology, see Section 13.A (appendix on p. 301).

The score for an individual company varies over time, but this time-series is defined over time points with uneven intervals as news stories arrive unexpectedly. We wish to use the information about changing market sentiment to update our beliefs about factor volatility. The score a_{nt} measures market sentiment about company n at time t ($n \in \{1, \ldots, N_2\}$ denotes the assets for which option-implied volatility and market sentiment data are available). If this score varies significantly over time, market beliefs about the company are changing quickly, which indicates rising volatility of the stock.

We calculate the average value of the score over 15-minute intervals and then calculate the variance of these values over one day b_{nt}. It is assumed that the working day starts at 16:00 the previous day and finishes at 15:59 on the current day. Unlike market data that are only available for the hours that the markets are open, news data are published outside market hours. Finally, we calculate S_{nt} as the cumulative sum of variances of scores over the past seven days

$$S_{nt} = \sum_{r=0}^{6} b_{n\,t-r} \tag{13.9}$$

If a particular company is in the news and its sentiment is changing significantly over time this could indicate its volatility has risen. The following day this company could become "old" news and its score may not vary much. However, there is no reason to believe its volatility has suddenly dropped. Cumulating over seven days allows us to account for this. We use seven days so that weekend news is always included. Excluding the weekend entirely seems inappropriate as markets will account for news published then. However, weekend news may not be processed in the same way as weekday news, so it seems to be inappropriate to include it for some days but not others. S_{nt} is defined so that it incorporates a directional change (up or down) in asset volatility and also size of the change.

Consider the adjustment using the implied volatility described in equation (13.3); in a comparable way we define a second adjustment based on news sentiment information

$$M_{nt}^{S} = \left[\prod_{r=0}^{w-1} \frac{S_{n\,t-r}}{S_{n\,t-r-1}}\right] \div \left[\prod_{r=0}^{w-1} \frac{V_{n\,t-r}}{V_{n\,t-r-1}}\right] \tag{13.10}$$

We derive updated factor and asset-specific variances using, first, option-implied data and then news sentiment data. We denote the updated factor and asset-specific variances, which are determined using option-implied data as $({}^{O}\sigma_i^*)^2$ and $({}^{O}\sigma_{s(l)}^*)^2$, respectively. Likewise, $({}^{N}\sigma_i^*)^2$ and $({}^{N}\sigma_{s(l)}^*)^2$ are given from news sentiment data. Time subscripts have been dropped to aid readability.

We combine these variances to give risk estimates based on both sources of information. The combined factor variances are defined as

$$({}^{C}\sigma_i^*)^2 = q({}^{O}\sigma_i^*)^2 + (1-q)({}^{N}\sigma_i^*)^2 \tag{13.11}$$

where $0 \leq q \leq 1$.

The asset-specific variances are updated as

$$({}^{C}\sigma_{s(l)}^*)^2 = q({}^{O}\sigma_{s(l)}^*)^2 + (1-q)({}^{N}\sigma_{s(l)}^*)^2. \tag{13.12}$$

In case $({}^{O}\sigma_{s(l)}^*)^2$ is defined but $({}^{N}\sigma_{s(l)}^*)^2$ is not (this is the case when option-implied data are available for a stock but news sentiment data are not), we use $({}^{O}\sigma_{s(l)}^*)^2$ and vice versa.

13.4 COMPUTATIONAL EXPERIMENTS

Two separate computational studies were undertaken. The first covers the period in January 2008 when equity markets were starting to decline (component stocks of the EURO STOXX 50 index are considered). The second study covers a period in September 2008 when the global economy was beginning to move into recession (component stocks of the Dow Jones 30 are considered).

13.4.1 Study I

The first study covers the period January 17, 2008 to January 23, 2008 when sentiment worsened and option-implied volatility measures surged. Over this period worldwide stock markets fell significantly. Since 2003 equity markets had been growing steadily, but at the end of 2007 they started to decline and sentiment started to fall. Over January 2008 market sentiment worsened further. This was driven by a few key events. In the US, George Bush announced a stimulus plan for the economy and the Fed cut interest rates by 75 basis points, the largest cut since October 1984. In Europe, Société Générale was hit by the fraud scandal of alleged rogue trader Jerome Kerviel. In Asia, stock markets also fell in this period.

We consider a portfolio of financial stocks weighted by their market capitalizations. The portfolio constituents and weights are shown in Table 13.1. Table 13.2 shows the volatility values for this portfolio. The second column shows the values predicted by the "basic" factor model, the third the values from the model updated using only option-implied volatility data ($q = 1$), the fourth the values from the model updated using a

Table 13.1. Constituents and weighting factors for the portfolio of financial stocks (out of the EURO STOXX 50)

Company name	Weighting factor (%)
ALLIANZ	8.30
GENERALI	5.60
AXA	6.80
BBVA	7.10
BANCO SANTANDER	10.40
BNP PARIBAS	8.50
CREDIT AGRICOLE	4.60
DEUTSCHE BANK	5.50
DEUTSCHE BOERSE	3.00
SOCIETE GENERALE	5.60
IBERDROLA	6.50
ING GROEP	7.20
INTESA SANPAOLO	7.70
MUENCHENER RUCK	3.60
UNICREDIT	9.60

Table 13.2. Volatility for the portfolio of financial stocks (out of the EURO STOXX 50)

Dates	Volatility under "basic" statistical model	Volatility under model updated by option-implied volatility ($q = 1$)	Volatility under model updated by option-implied volatility and market sentiment ($q = 0.5$)	Volatility under model updated by market sentiment ($q = 0$)
1 17 2008	19.065	19.130	20.853	22.430
1 18 2008	19.032	21.564	21.619	21.625
1 21 2008	19.319	26.575	28.845	30.845
1 22 2008	21.187	26.759	28.911	30.829
1 23 2008	21.453	26.212	27.869	29.370

combination of option-implied volatility data and sentiment data ($q = 0.5$) and the final column the values for the model updated using only sentiment data ($q = 0$).

In this study 25 factors were used as this explained 90% of historic volatility ($p_1 = 90\%$ and $p_2 = 75\%$).

On January 21, 2008 there was a sharp decline in non-US stock markets (the US market was closed). It is reasonable to assume that stock volatility rose on this date. The portfolio volatility estimate from the model updated using option-implied data is higher than that from the "basic" model and it rises significantly on January 21. The estimate from the market sentiment (news) model is higher and this value rises earlier than the option-implied model, though there is still a significant increase on January 21. This could indicate that the model is picking up increased volatility at an earlier date than option-implied volatility. This seems sensible as news and market sentiment changes precede changes in actual price volatility (traders first process news and then trade on their knowledge and beliefs). Hence, this type of model can provide us with an "early" indication or warning that volatility is rising. The improved volatility model accounts for rapid changes in market sentiment which results in relatively large movements in equity portfolio risk.

It should be noted that sentiment indicators have the potential to be used not only to adjust the expected return variance of an investment, but also return higher moments such as skew and kurtosis. To the extent that such higher moment expectations arise from this process, their influence on the variance forecast can be incorporated by standard mathematical means such as the Cornish–Fisher expansion.

13.4.2 Study II

Over 2008 global equity markets continued to fall. This was heavily influenced by the severe loss of liquidity in credit markets and the banking system. Many large and well-established investment and commercial banks suffered bankruptcy or were propped up by governments. Volatility for financial stocks over September and October 2008 was particularly high. Specific events that contributed to the volatility of the financial sector include Lehman's filing for bankruptcy, Bank of America's announcement of its intention to purchase Merrill Lynch, the Fed's announcement of AIG rescue, Lloyds

Table 13.3. Volatility for the portfolio of financial stocks (out of the Dow Jones 30)

Dates	Volatility under "basic" statistical model	Volatility under model updated by option-implied volatility ($q = 1$)	Volatility under model updated by option-implied volatility and market sentiment ($q = 0.5$)	Volatility under model updated by market sentiment ($q = 0$)
9 18 2008	56.031	71.023	70.326	69.622
9 19 2008	57.949	67.770	72.765	77.439
9 22 2008	61.719	66.302	71.014	75.433
9 23 2008	62.270	62.766	67.557	72.030
9 24 2008	62.279	59.531	63.968	68.118

takeover of HBOS, and on September 19 restrictions imposed on short-selling of financial stocks. This second study covers the period September 18, 2008 to September 24, 2008.

Table 13.3 shows volatility for a portfolio of three financial stocks with equal weights on each stock: Bank of America, CitiGroup, and J.P. Morgan Chase. Similiarly Table 13.4 shows the figures for a portfolio of three non-financial stocks: Johnson & Johnson, Kraft Foods, and Coca Cola. The second column in both tables shows the values predicted by the "basic" factor model, the third the values from the model updated using only option-implied volatility data ($q = 1$), the fourth the values from the model updated using a combination of option-mplied volatility data and sentiment data ($q = 0.5$), and the final column the values for the model updated using only sentiment data ($q = 0$).

In this study 14 factors were used as this explained 90% of historic volatility ($p_1 = 90\%$ and $p_2 = 75\%$).

In most cases there is higher volatility for the finance portfolio when the volatility estimate is updated using option-implied data and likewise are found to increase when news sentiment data are processed. On comparing the estimates for the financial and

Table 13.4. Volatility for the portfolio of non-financial stocks (out of the Dow Jones 30)

Dates	Volatility under "basic" statistical model	Volatility under model updated by option-implied volatility ($q = 1$)	Volatility under model updated by option-implied volatility and market sentiment ($q = 0.5$)	Volatility under model updated by market sentiment ($q = 0$)
9 18 2008	13.751	15.474	15.274	15.196
9 19 2008	13.912	14.907	15.392	16.214
9 22 2008	13.935	15.109	15.819	15.933
9 23 2008	14.316	15.159	16.593	16.709
9 24 2008	14.360	14.169	16.021	16.443

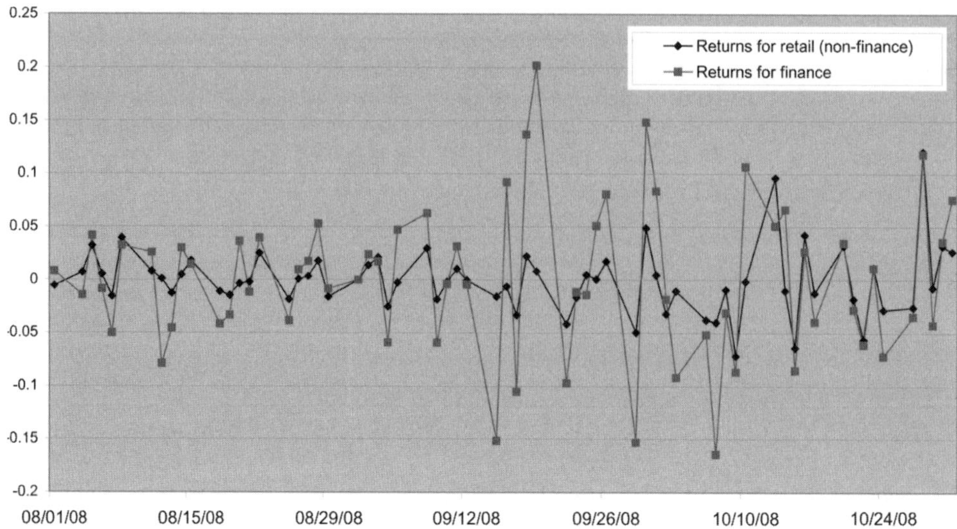

Figure 13.1. Returns for financial and non-financial portfolios over August to October 2008.

non-financial companies we see that financial stocks volatility has risen significantly more than non-financial stocks. This seems a sensible result for this period, given the market conditions and the news. Figure 13.1 shows the changes in prices from August to the end of October. It can be seen that prices for the financial stocks show higher variation and this increases during September.

The differences between the volatility estimates using news sentiment and option-implied volatility serve to highlight the complex nature of news and the way it impacts markets. This study and the scores used are based on the relative volume of negative and positive news items over a period of time. However, they do not account for how different news items may impact market prices and volatility differently. We note the importance of using a variety of sources of information when updating risk estimates.

These computational experiments are illustrative; in order to further exploit the value of quantified news, substantial additional work is needed to refine the process by which news indicators are used to form conditional volatility forecasts and to tune adjustments to subsequent realizations. A formal Bayesian framework for such inclusion is described in Shah (2008).

13.5 DISCUSSION AND CONCLUSIONS

In this chapter we address the problem of making equity portfolio risk estimates sensitive to changes in the market environment and investor sentiment. Traditional multifactor risk models fail to update quickly as new information becomes available. diBartolomeo and Warrick (2005) use option-implied volatility to determine improved estimates of the future covariance matrix. There is a strong, yet complex relationship between market sentiment and news. Traders and other market participants digest news rapidly and update their asset positions accordingly. However, for models to incorporate news directly and automatically, we require quantitative inputs, whereas raw news is qualitative data. RavenPack has developed linguistic analytics that process the textual input of news stories to determine quantitative sentiment scores.

To the extent that we are interested in risk estimation over a relatively short future horizon, conventional factor model methods of estimating security and portfolio risk can be made more responsive to changing conditions by conditioning the forecasts on changes in implied volatility and quantified news. We have presented a tractable method of including both option-implied volatility and quantified news into portfolio risk estimation.

While much research remains to be done to refine our methods, frequent crises in financial markets remind us of the urgency with which all investors, even those with a long-term orientation, should be attentive to short-term fluctuations in financial market risk. Implicit in the wealth accumulation goals of every investor is the assumption of survival: "To finish first, you first must finish."

13.6 ACKNOWLEDGEMENTS

CARISMA and Leela Mitra gratefully acknowledge the financial sponsorship provided by RavenPack International S.L. RavenPack also supplied the news sentiment data used in this study (see Section 13.A for further details—see also Section 1.A, p. 25).

13.A SENTIMENT ANALYTICS OVERVIEW

RavenPack has developed linguistic analytics that process the textual input of news stories to determine quantitative sentiment scores. These scores allow us to incorporate information about the volume and nature of news into quantitative models. We give a brief description of how these have been created.

13.A.1 Tagging process

As a news story is received from a newswire it is tagged to record various linguistic aspects. One particular aspect is a story's "aboutness". This incorporates the entities to which the story applies, the subjects it covers, and the market to which it is relevant.

This analysis is applied to tens of thousands of stories per day aggregated from RavenPack's compilation of diverse and respected sources of news.

13.A.2 Sentiment classifiers

RavenPack's sentiment classifiers detect story type as a preliminary step to distinguishing the story as being "positive" (POS), "negative" (NEG), or "neutral" (NEU) relative to a specific market or asset class. There are two main methods for detecting sentiment. The Expert Consensus Method uses financial experts' tagging of several thousand stories as POS, NEG, or NEU to train a Bayes Classifier which discerns rules from the training set to imitate the experts' tagging. The Traditional Method maps specific words or phrases to pre-defined sentiment values.

13.A.3 Score calculation

The tagging of individual stories can be used to aggregate sentiment scores of specific companies, such as the components of the EURO STOXX 50. Such scores indicate the relative news sentiment about each stock over time. The scores account for stories about the company and the sector in which it operates, thus creating continuous counts of the relative volume of positive and negative stories. For each company six time-series of scores are derived, one based on each of five sentiment classifiers (WLE_SCORE, PCM_SCORE, ECM_SCORE, RCM_SCORE, VCM_SCORE) and one aggregate score (AGG_SCORE). Further descriptions of these classifiers are given below.

As a news item (story) s_t is received on the newswire at time t, it is classified by the WLE classifier as "positive" (POS), "negative" (NEG), or "neutral" (NEU). We define $I_{Pos\ s_t}$ to be an indicator function which takes value 1 when s_t is POS and 0 otherwise. We define a similar function for NEG. Further, the story s_t has a relevance r_{s_t} attached to it. The unscaled score for the company under this classifier is defined as

$$R = \frac{\sum_{q=t-1}^{t-Q} I_{Pos\ s_q} r_{s_q} - \sum_{q=t-1}^{t-Q} I_{Neg\ s_q} r_{s_q}}{\sum_{q=t-1}^{t-Q} r_{s_q}}. \tag{13.13}$$

The times considered are $t-Q, \ldots, t-1$ which are the time points in the 24 hours prior to t when news stories relevant to the company were received. By equation (13.13) R is a signed fraction. This is scaled to give the score

$$T = \mathbf{sign}(R)\sqrt{|\,R\,|} \tag{13.14}$$

which gives values over the range $[-1, 1]$. By applying the relation WLE_SCORE $=$ $(T+1) \times 50$ the values are shifted and scaled to lie in the range $[0, 100]$. This computational process is repeated for each classifier to produce four further time-series of scores (PCM_SCORE, ECM_SCORE, RCM_SCORE, and VCM_SCORE). A weighted average of these scores is finally used to give AGG_SCORE, which is score a in our computation.

13.A.4 Summary of classifiers and scores

WLE_SCORE A raw score that represents the aggregate news sentiment for the given company over the given time period according to the WLE classifier, which specializes in identifying positive and negative words and phrases in articles about global equities. This sentiment score is based on RavenPack's Traditional Methodology.

PCM_SCORE A raw score that represents the aggregate news sentiment for the given company over the given time period according to the PCM classifier, which specializes in identifying the sentiment of stories that are about global equity future earnings developments and projections. This sentiment score is based on RavenPack's Expert Consensus Methodology.

ECM_SCORE A raw score that represents the aggregate news sentiment for the given company over the given time period according to the ECM classifier, which specializes in short commentary and editorials on global equity markets. This sentiment score is based on RavenPack's Expert Consensus Methodology.

RCM_SCORE A raw score that represents the aggregate news sentiment for the given company over the given time period according to the RCM classifier, which specializes in corporate action announcements. This sentiment score is based on RavenPack's Expert Consensus Methodology.

VCM_SCORE A raw score that represents the aggregate news sentiment for the given company over the given time period according to the VCM classifier, which specializes in news stories about mergers, acquisitions, and takeovers. This sentiment score is based on RavenPack's Expert Consensus Methodology.

AGG_SCORE An overall interpreted sentiment score based on weightings of WLE_SCORE, PCM_SCORE, ECM_SCORE, RCM_SCORE, and VCM_SCORE. This identifies the overall news sentiment for the given company over the given time period.

13.B REFERENCES

Black F.; Scholes M. (1973) "The pricing of options and corporate liabilities," *Journal of Political Economy*, **81**(3), 637–659.

Chen N.F.; Roll R.; Ross S.A. (1986) "Economic forces and the stock market," *Journal of Business*, **59**(3), 383–404.

Connor G. (1995) "The three types of factor models: A comparison of their explanatory power," *Financial Analysts Journal*, **51**, 42–46.

diBartolomeo D.; Warrick S. (2005) "Making covariance based portfolio risk models sensitive to the rate at which markets reflect new information," in J. Knight and S. Satchell (Eds.), *Linear Factor Models*, Elsevier Finance.

Ederington L.H.; Lee J.H. (1993) "How markets process information: News releases and volatility," *Journal of Finance*, **48**, 1161–1191.

Fama E.F.; French K.R. (1992) "The cross-section of expected stock returns," *Journal of Finance*, **47**(2), 427–466.

Fama E.F.; French K.R. (1993) "Common risk factors in the returns on stocks and bonds," *Journal of Financial Economics*, **33**, 3–56.

Jalen L. (2008) *News Scores for EURO STOXX 50*, RavenPack International.

Goldman Sachs (2008) *Headline Numbers: The Effects of News on Market Microstructures*, Internal Report, Goldman Sachs.

RavenPack (2008) *RavenPack's Analytics Knowledge Base*, RavenPack International.

Rosenberg. B. (1974) "Extra-market components of covariance in security returns," *Journal of Financial and Quantitative Analysis*, **9**(2), 263–273.

Scowcroft A.; Sefton J. (2006) *Understanding Factor Models*, UBS Investment Research.

Shah A. (2008) "Short term risk from long term models." Available at `http://www.northinfo.com/documents/286.pdf`

Sharpe W.F. (1970) *Portfolio Theory and Capital Markets*, McGraw-Hill.

Sheikh A. (1995) *BARRA's Risk Models*, BARRA Research Insights.

Tetlock P.C.; Saar-Tsechansky M.; Macskassy S. (2008) "More than words: Quantifying language to measure firms' fundamentals," *Journal of Finance*, **63**(3), 1437–1467.

Wilding. T. (2005) "Attributing investment risk with a factor analytic model," in J.L. Knight and S. Satchell (Eds.), *Linear Factor Models in Finance*, Butterworth-Heinemann.

Part IV

Industry insights, technology, products, and service providers

14

Incorporating news into algorithmic trading strategies: Increasing the signal-to-noise ratio

Richard Brown

While the mass adoption of machine-readable news in trading environments is still in its early stages, there are a number of techniques that can be used to significantly improve trading performance, both in offensive as well as in defensive strategies. These techniques range from simple circuit breakers or wolf detection systems (defensive) to systems that will exploit the volatility surrounding significant news items, or those that will predict the direction and magnitude of a price movement (offensive).

Over the last few years, there has been a substantially larger amount of research on the use of news for trading and investment strategies. The research has been less conclusive on signals for returns, however. This has in large part been due to two factors. First, there has traditionally been a lack of comprehensive metrics and metadata, which can be used to determine the direction, magnitude, and duration of such movements. Second, logic suggests that if there is a killer strategy for doing this, one is more likely to trade on it than to tell the whole world about it.

So, how can one incorporate news into algorithmic strategies to improve trading performance?

One of the more common and easily implemented uses of machine-readable news in a trading environment is to use the news feed as a circuit breaker for algorithms. This approach would stop your algorithm from its current course of action when news is published on a particular company. For example, if you are buying 100,000 shares of IBM using a certain algorithm and news comes out on IBM, a news-tripped circuit breaker would stop your continued purchase until you determine (or your machine determines in more advanced approaches) whether or not the information in the news affects your decision. Some also refer to this approach as "wolf detection"—someone has better information than you do and can exploit the market's, or your, ignorance.

In the above example where further automated trades on IBM are stopped when news is published, one can imagine a situation whereby the circuit breaker is tripped too often. This may happen for a stock that is frequently in the news or with others that are often

The Handbook of News Analytics in Finance Edited by L. Mitra and G. Mitra

mentioned in market commentary (i.e., "Microsoft Down in Late Day Trading"). This can become a source of frustration and trading inefficiency when certain stocks' circuit breakers are tripped too often and/or for the wrong reasons. The problem is exacerbated further when one's algo rules state that news on Intel, Dell, and Microsoft (those stocks that may be highly correlated with IBM's) should also stop the algorithm executing orders for IBM, or that news on IBM's customers or suppliers should stop the algorithm as well. And the problem gets exponentially worse as you add more and more sources of information to this logic. A market-maker using this approach to widen its bid–ask spreads when news is published relating to one of its companies would find a very low signal-to-noise ratio and might find itself perpetually out of the market. Unable to keep pace with reviewing news-tripped exceptions, one may eventually turn off the news logic and again be exposed to unforeseen risk.

So, how does one increase the signal-to-noise ratio, ensuring protection from unforeseen exposures without an excessive number of halts or items to review?

There are two defensive approaches to this problem: (1) trip the circuit breaker only when substantive, important, "new", credible, or highly emotive news is published on a company, or (2) trip the circuit breaker on any news about a company and turn the algorithm back on after programmatically determining that the news is duplicative, non-substantive, less emotive, or unimportant. Either approach can be substantially better than many of the processes firms use today, but the second option is ideal for traders who are making markets or are very sensitive to order fulfillment at the millisecond level. This offers the best protection by tripping algorithms immediately, but allows for a much quicker re-entry to market-making or order execution (measured in milliseconds). It can also significantly reduce the number of items that require a more thorough review by human algorithmic trading supervisors.

Sounds logical, right? So how exactly can this be done?

By using the metadata offered in a machine-readable newsfeed, one can quite easily implement the above strategies. In the example outlined, the circuit breaker would initially be triggered by the presence of a news story on IBM, widening the bid–ask spread or stopping the algorithm altogether. Based on a set of rules, the algorithm would then be reversed, resumed, or perhaps accelerated in the presence of certain news types.

Thomson Reuters News Analytics offer a robust set of metadata, which can be used to help address this situation. For example, the "relevance" indicator is used to determine the extent of an article's focus on a particular company. Feature articles on IBM would have a high relevance score while articles in which IBM is one of many companies included would typically have a lower relevance score. If the circuit breaker is tripped automatically, the algo rule might suggest that one turns it back on when the news item has a relevance score below a specified level.

The sentiment, or tone, of the article can also be a powerful signal. A very positively or very negatively-toned article might push the item to the top of a review list so that a trader can more quickly take advantage of a likely price movement. Stopping an aggressive purchase in the face of a very negatively toned item may give you significant protection from being blindsided by an event, while accelerating your purchase in the presence of a highly positive event can help reduce slippage and lower your transaction costs.

Measuring the item's novelty, or uniqueness, can be an important addition to increasing one's responsiveness to news items. An algorithm may resume automatically if the news appears repetitious or await a human response if it appears to have new information. This is especially important as more and more sources are included in the system. One would not necessarily want to react on the 50th repetition of the item.

You can also determine the importance of the article by examining some of the other metadata for clues. Stories about mergers and acquisitions or earnings guidance might mandate review, while the third update to a story might be something to filter out and ignore. Similarly, market commentary might be discounted altogether and broker recommendations by Morgan Stanley's analysts should be ignored when analyzing Morgan Stanley, the company.

Combining the above factors along with a host of other metadata can help significantly enhance the defensive use cases for machine-readable news.

So what about offensive strategies? How can one generate alpha using news?

For more offensive strategies, the same metadata can be used for more aggressive positioning. The main conclusions from published research can each be refined when incorporating some of the intelligence garnered from newly available metadata such as that from Thomson Reuters News Analytics. Academic and other research on the impact of news center around three main ideas

1. News flow, or the rate at which news is published, can predict volume and volatility. Greater news rates would be followed by higher trading volume and increased price volatility.
2. Pricing movements accompanied by news tend to gain momentum in nature while those with a lack of news tend to revert to their previous trends/ranges.
3. The market tends to overreact on high news volumes and underreact on low news volumes.

Increasing the signal strength in these strategies can be accomplished through a number of techniques. First, on news flow being able to predict increases in trading volume and volatility: Studies have shown that more relevant news and more emotive news (highly positive and highly negative in tone) can better predict volume and volatility increases. In addition, negatively toned news has greater impact than does positively toned news. Also, the type of item such as an alert vs. an update to a story can significantly increase the ability to accurately predict volume and volatility spikes. When filtering out market commentary and broker recommendations (as outlined above) and less important, less influential, and biased sources, as well as highly repetitious items, one can further refine the predictive signals in news flow.

Second, on pricing movements with accompanying news flow suggesting momentum: Upward pricing movements with positive news (or downward movements with negative news) from credible sources with the appropriate filters to exclude "irrelevant" news could increase confidence in pricing momentum and reversal strategies.

Third, with the market likely overreacting when lots of news is published on a company and underreacting on small amounts of news: One wouldn't suggest shorting all "bubbles" and going long on all stealth companies, but there are a number of near-term reversals (hours to days) that can be seen with certain types of news. A downward correction after a positive news-induced run-up or an upward bounce after negative news are two observations. Whether these signals induce a programmatic hedge or simply provide a confidence indicator for humans overseeing trading activity, one can implement these types of strategies with relative ease.

In addition to refining some of the more widely published signals on volatility, trading volume, momentum, and reversals that may be present in news, some of the more interesting capabilities lie in the ability to predict the direction, magnitude, and duration of pricing movements. Analyzing sentiment and other text characteristics is growing in popularity, but simple "buy on the good news" and "sell on the bad news" strategies won't likely generate significant alpha as news analytics become more widely adopted. Studies such as those written by Nitish Sinha who looks at the ability to use news volume and sentiment to predict medium-term alpha (one to five months out) or those by David Leinweber who looks at portfolio strategies indicate some of the promise from emerging datasets like news analytics. These techniques can be further refined with more comprehensive selection criteria, including weighting various types of news differently and applying certain filters to the news. These techniques may involve underweighting market commentary, repetitive news items, less important sources, and alerts vs. articles depending on the signal timeframe. One might also overweight other types of news such as exclusives, interviews, strategic news, broker research, and more intense news days. Additionally, adjustments for market and sector sentiment can highlight relative sentiment performance and enhance the signal, particularly during market regime shifts as seen during the downturn in 2008 and upturn in 2009.

While we are in the early stages of the market's adoption of news-based signals for trading and investing, one can clearly see how some simple strategies for enhancing algorithmic trading with news signals may offer a great deal of promise. For those thought leaders already implementing such strategies, it's only a matter of time before these techniques become mainstream and the "easy" alpha will disappear. For those who have yet to explore the power of unstructured text, there is a new frontier for alpha-bearing content.

15
Are you still trading without news?

Armando Gonzalez

To make business decisions, people have been manually extracting patterns from news for centuries, but the increasing volume of news in modern times has called for more automated approaches. News analysis can now be done by collecting and processing information using computer systems equipped to handle the intricacies of the human language.

A vast amount of textual information is available in real time through newswire services and even more is updated on a regular basis on the web. Newswires are delivered by news agencies that provide information from around the world, covering breaking events in business, finance, politics, entertainment, and more. Professional newswire services are organizations of journalists established to supply news reports to other organizations in the news trade: newspapers, magazines, and radio and television broadcasters. The major news agencies generally prepare hard-news stories and feature articles that can be used by other organizations with little or no modification, and then sell them to other news providers.

Today, computers can quantify many aspects of textual content including positive and negative perceptions on facts and opinions reported in the news. They can continuously analyze relevant information from all major news and internet sources like financial sites, blogs, and local and regional newspapers to produce real-time news sentiment scores. These scores not only allow market participants to capture market opportunities, they also help to improve risk management and provide for better trading execution. Financial firms use these data to lead portfolio allocations, which help improve the average life and profit of existing trading models. They can enhance risk metrics such as Value at Risk calculations and control ramp-up or ramp-down times in algorithmic trading engines.

Many high-frequency traders currently boost their gains using news-based algorithms to speed their response time to breaking events. They build defensive applications to ensure that key news events are factored in, and use automated news analysis as a more effective form of low-latency decision support. Firms also reduce the time required for low-frequency fundamental traders to assess their options manually and execute their responses more effectively. Structured news can also help in post-trade analysis to explain why a traditional algorithm or strategy did not work.

Another benefit from automated trading on news is that it can protect portfolio managers or traders from the consequences of missing important news that has an

The Handbook of News Analytics in Finance Edited by L. Mitra and G. Mitra

impact on their position or portfolio. Also, news events on earnings, product recalls, layoffs, stock or credit ratings, and many other categories can be precursors to changes in volatility of securities. Structured news or "news analytics" enable traders to get a head start by acting in advance of these changes.

The underpinnings of news analytics

Being able to express news stories as numbers permits the manipulation of everyday information in a mathematical and statistical way that allows computers not only to make decisions once made only by humans, but to do so both faster and more efficiently. Since market participants are always looking for an edge, the speed of computer connections and the delivery of news analytics, measured in milliseconds, have become an essential part of investment decision making.

News analytics are used in financial modeling, particularly in quantitative and algorithmic trading. They are usually derived through automated text analysis and applied to digital texts using techniques from natural language processing and machine learning such as latent semantic analysis, support vector machines, and Bayesian sorting, among other techniques.

News data are delivered in a variety of formats, often as machine-readable XML documents or delimited files. Analytic data include numerical values, tags, and other properties that represent certain aspects of the underlying news stories. For backtesting purposes, having historical news analytics data is key. Usually, historical data are delivered via flat files, while live data for production purposes are processed and delivered in milliseconds through direct data feeds or APIs.

News analytics work well with most investment strategies and can even help to improve investment and trading performance. To many financial participants, news analytics are considered a relevant, novel, and even critical input to their decision-making process. From a risk management perspective, firms can look for measures to start trading, halt trading, widen spreads, or hedge with other instruments based on how they anticipate the market will react to news. Generally, the value add of automated news analysis has caught the interest of professionals and researchers, who have shown promising results focusing on predicting stock price direction, volatility, and trading volume.

Quantcentration and news

Trading model inputs are traditionally derived from company fundamentals and market data. Traditional quantitative factors are crowded and performance has been degraded due to "quantcentration"—whereby most firms use the same type of data in their models. This is one of the reasons investment models have performed poorly in recent years.

Independent of traditional factors, news analytics are a unique source of explanatory and predictive input. They include structured information and signals that create new trading opportunities on both scheduled and unscheduled news events. Today, these data are used to power a number of applications ranging from high-frequency trading systems requiring low-latency inputs, to risk and asset management applications requiring factors whose time resolution may be daily, weekly, and monthly.

To address quantcentration, RavenPack, a pioneer in the field of news analytics, extracts relevant, actionable content from high-volume, real-time newsfeeds and comprehensive news archives. News analytics are made possible by the practical application of leading edge technologies in the field of computational linguistics. In several cases, RavenPack has pushed the boundaries of this field to help meet the demanding requirements of its primary market, the financial industry.

To recognize when any of over 27,000 global companies are mentioned in the news, RavenPack employs a technology known as named entity recognition. There are many applications of named entity recognition, but the financial industry imposes a requirement that most do not: the names of the entities can change over time, and the same name might refer to different entities at different times. RavenPack has addressed this by building a point-in-time-aware named entity recognition system. Practical, leading solutions like this allow users to address problems like survivorship bias when using RavenPack News Analytics data.

Identifying entities, such as companies, is just the first step. But knowing what role each entity plays in a story is when the real value starts to appear. RavenPack has built a system that looks at financial news stories related to companies and can classify the story into any of hundreds of categories. For each of these, the company roles are extracted. So RavenPack News Analytics can tell you who is the analyst firm and which company is being upgraded, for example. If you are trading on news, knowing this just might come in handy.

Detecting news events automatically

When dealing with the tens of thousands of stories published about companies every day, it makes sense to try to classify them into a set of pre-defined categories. RavenPack has approached this problem by applying technological advancements acquired through many years of experience and has come up with a solution to categorize stories into a simple set of themes which are fundamental to today's investment environment.

The technique of producing this kind of analysis came about by performing a careful study of the types of stories available on companies and by extracting the primary categories that would allow meaningful interpretation of a story. Once the categories had been determined, the goal was to implement technology that could perform the classification automatically. Some categories are more straightforward than others, so different techniques are applied.

Events are defined using thousands of proprietary templates and part-of-speech tagging. These specialized templates are compositions of language tokens or values taken in specific context. Tokens may be a type of language marker, such as a number or date. They may be words or phrases, perhaps broken down to their root form or taken only for a given tense.

Part-of-speech tagging involves marking up the words in a text as corresponding to a particular part of speech, based on both its definition and its context (i.e., relationship with adjacent and related words in a phrase, sentence, or paragraph). This makes templates more scalable, modular, and effective.

As anyone who follows the news knows, stories are often repeated. The impact of a breaking news event is likely to be more valuable than re-hashes of the same story in the following hours. So RavenPack News Analytics take event detection another step beyond and provide, with each event, a novelty score based on the event category and participants within the past 24 hours. Further, all stories which are identified as being in the same chain of events are tagged with a unique key that ties them back to the first notice of the event.

Finding "liquidity" in the news

When constructing trading or investment strategies, distinguishing between companies that can be considered "liquid" or "illiquid" in the news can be important. Not surprisingly, studies have shown that a high correlation exists between market capitalization and news flow, which may be explained by the increased attention given to large-cap companies from research analysts and financial journalists. For this reason, the characteristics of news flow for liquid and illiquid companies may be very different. For example, most publicly traded companies are covered to some degree during the earnings reporting season. However, throughout the year small and mid-caps will have relatively low news volume while large caps will be better covered.

News liquidity can be an important factor when modeling investor decisions about a stock. News liquidity is about relevant news volume and the roles companies play in stories—not mere counts of mentions or keywords. Both scheduled and unscheduled company-related events generate higher news volumes and make stocks more susceptible to price movement. Thus, news liquidity can provide insights not only on directional price changes, but also on stock volatility, trading volume, or liquidity.

16

News analytics in a risk management framework for asset managers

Dan diBartolomeo

Analysis of quantified news holds great promise for the purpose of managing risks within financial institutions, and broadly across the financial system. By facilitating rapid responses to flows of information that reveal risky circumstances, such systems will meaningfully contribute to a lessening of the potential for financial crises. Monitoring flows of information on markets and securities and the sentiment of their content is an excellent indicator for potential dispersion of beliefs among investors, and hence the potential for changes in the prices of assets.

However, the ability to respond quickly to information also increases the requirement that the response be the right one. Responding instantly, but in the wrong fashion, can foster disaster, just as driving a racing car requires greater precision than driving a golf cart. As such, we must frame the general principles of our risk management effort in a thoughtful and thorough fashion.

The first thing to focus on is the difference between risk management in a commercial or investment banking setting, and risk management in an asset management setting. Hedge funds are often in the middle on this spectrum, but we should at least understand the issues.This is the biggest mistake people make. Banks are investing firm capital and are highly leveraged with liabilities at call (a run on the bank). They are worried about bankruptcy and regulatory problems. *It is an issue of firm survival if a firm's capital should be sufficiently impaired.* Quite differently, asset managers are investing other people's money. Those other people are typically long-term investors such as pension funds whose liabilities are not at immediate call. Their liabilities are commitments for future payments, not immediate ones. Even in a life insurer, people aren't going to try to kill themselves to collect early if the insurer is in financial trouble.

In setting up a risk management system, we need to make an explicit choice about what risk we care about. For a bank we care about the bank's risk. However, for agent asset managers, do we really care about the risks for our investors, or do we really care about how risky our revenue stream in business enterprise is? Do we really care about helping investors meet their financial goals, or are we more worried about being fired as a manager by a client because we have a period of poor performance?

Obviously, there is an ethical issue here, but in many asset management firms the revenue aspect takes precedence. Our suggestion is to focus on the client's portfolio risk

The Handbook of News Analytics in Finance Edited by L. Mitra and G. Mitra

needs, but asset managers should consider hedging some of the risk to their revenues from broad market declines. Hedging client active risk is a clear ethical problem since you would be hedging the risk of failure in the very services for which your clients are paying.

Assuming we're paying attention to our investor's risks, we have to figure out what those risks are. The predominant risk for long-term investors is that the more volatile a portfolio's return is, the degree of wealth that is created through the compounding of returns is reduced. *In the long run, it is the compounding that makes investors most of their money.* This is the risk that the Markowitz Mean Variance Optimization is all about.

The second risk investors may run is that they have to spend some of their wealth from time to time to fund consumption. To the extent that we have to liquidate investments at times when their value is down, we have less wealth available for future investment than if we were liquidating at a time when the portfolio value was high. *This is the risk that most investors mistakenly focus on even when they are investing for the long term.* Unfortunately, this sort of short-term thinking fits in better with the Value-at-Risk kind of risk systems that banks are used to having.

The critical problem is that the first kind of risk is a linear function of the variance of portfolio returns, while "drawdown" risk is a function of standard deviation and higher moments. Long-term investors should be paying more attention to variance, while investors with potential consumption needs should be focusing on drawdown risks. The issue of "fat tails" is part of this same discussion. Big down events are much more frequent in financial markets that would be predicted by a normal distribution assumption. This means a lot to investors with drawdown concerns, but less to long-term investors. When you start thinking about decomposing portfolio risk by asset class, sector, or individual position, you need to understand what kind of algebra makes sense and what doesn't.

Asset managers are typically evaluated on "benchmark-relative" (or peer group) returns, but actual investors can't pay their bills with *benchmark-relative money*. For very, very long-term investors the issue of inflation-adjusted returns is also important. Once you know what the investor's objectives around risk really are, you can mix cash or inflation-linked bonds into the benchmark index to proportionately represent concerns for benchmark-relative, absolute, or real returns.

As we have seen in the mortgage securities crisis, liquidity is a crucial issue. Simplistic risk systems that just look at historic price movements just won't work at all for illiquid instruments. The price movements that are observable are just too muted by illiquidity to represent the true risk. Consider how much you would have to discount if you want to sell your house in a couple of days, rather than the typical period of months? Most experts say around 40%. At a minimum, the risk system should be able to answer questions like "What would it cost to liquidate one-third of this portfolio in five trading days, while keeping the same investment allocation?"

For a risk system to correctly manage risk, we should be able to evaluate the risk of an investor's entire portfolio including real estate. We should even be able to consider special risks to human capital or institutional cash flows. For example, if you are the sovereign wealth fund of an oil-rich Middle Eastern government, you probably don't want to ever overweight oil stocks. If you are the endowment of a university that depends a lot on alumni donations from Wall Street executives (e.g., Harvard or Princeton), you know that donation inflows are going to dry up if the market crashes.

The risk systems should be able to create synthetic securities to represent these special exogenous risks.

The ability of a risk system to correctly handle exotic securities has been crucial ever since the advent of derivatives and complex mortgage securities in mainstream investor portfolios. This is often an issue with securities subject to credit risk. Consider the US college-saving plans that were invested in *fixed income mutual funds that lost over 90% of their value in the recent Credit Crisis*. This is often a big failing with risk systems. Frequently, these more exotic securities just get skipped over and remain a ticking time bomb. At worst, procedures should be in place such that if a security cannot be explicitly modeled with reasonable effort, we proxy that security with something simple but reasonable. *We can no longer afford to leave government bonds, money market funds, or other investments perceived as safe out of the process.*

The quality of portfolio risk assessments is sensitive to the extent to which the risk system natively recognizes the full nature of each particular security. If the system does not recognize a security and, therefore, must evaluate risk based on the risks of recognized proxies (or other forms of approximation) the risk assessment will be less robust, even if completeness in security coverage was achieved. As such, all risk reports should be footnoted with information as to what fraction of a portfolio was fully recognized and on what portion of the portfolio it was necessary to resort to cruder assessments.

The risk management system has to have good aggregation capabilities. Not only should we be looking at individual portfolios, but aggregation at the product level, or by regional office, or investment officer. Adherence to benchmarks and compliance constraints should be able to be checked regularly on an almost fully automated basis, with exceptions brought to the attention of appropriate staff on a daily basis.

The reader has probably noticed by now that the subject of news analytics has not been mentioned since the opening paragraphs. This intentional omission is meant to convey that, while news analytics can be important building blocks, they cannot contribute positively to an overall risk management process that is poorly conceived. Prompt response to information flows is a necessary, but not sufficient condition for success.

Managing firm-wide risk is all about deciding what you are trying to accomplish. We need to consider three dimensions of risk for asset managers. The first aspect is the distinction between client portfolio risk and asset manager business risk. The second issue is the balance between long-term risks and short-term risks. Finally, we must consider whether investment risks are perceived in absolute wealth terms, relative to inflation or relative to market benchmarks. We also have to have a process that accurately assesses the risks of all types of investment assets, related liabilities, and potential exogenous economic influences on the investor.

17

NORM—towards a new financial paradigm: Behavioural finance with news-optimized risk management

Mark Vreijling and Thomas Dohmen

NORM is a financial service industry initiative supported by the European Union. NORM aims to enhance market risk assessment metrics by using semantically analysed news-based information. This will compensate for the inflexibility of existing models with regard to strong market fluctuations or market instability and give more dynamic, more reliable market risk estimation.

17.1 INTRODUCTION

In today's chaotic financial climate, systems for predicting market behaviour and the attitudes of financial professionals are under scrutiny. Current market risk assessment characteristics disregard market information that is available from additional sources like, for example, financial news. There are whole new possibilities for producing meaningful market behaviour models by incorporating behavioural and quantitative finance, using the latest techniques and powerful modelling tools. The prevailing market environment can (to some extent) be captured by key innovative techniques of news analytics that quantify news sentiments. The emergence and impact of such behavioural finance is illustrated by the five Nobel Prizes for Economics awarded in this field in recent years.

NORM sets out to improve current risk assessment practices by accurately identifying significant changes in market conditions by using automatic semantic analysis of current financial news streams. The targeted end result is a proof-of-concept application that uses real-time financial news to calculate a more relevant and more reliable risk metric.

17.2 THE PROBLEM OF INCOMPLETE INFORMATION IN MARKET RISK ASSESSMENT

The sole purpose of financial risk management is to identify or anticipate potential risks before they occur, thereby possibly preventing companies from potential disasters or minimizing their effects.

The Handbook of News Analytics in Finance Edited by L. Mitra and G. Mitra

Market risk assessment constitutes a significant part of the estimation of financial risk. It is calculated using risk measures, expressed in risk metrics, and has traditionally been estimated using historical data. This has the disadvantage that it provides a retrospective indication of risk that may not be a proper indication of current and future risk under unstable market conditions. Currently, the popular measures used for estimating market risk are Value at Risk (VaR) and Expected Shortfall (ES) metrics. It is vital for companies to know about risks at the moment that decisions are made, and VaR or ES enable this by incorporating future prospects into their risk calculation by using probability distributions. However, classical VaR calculation assumes that only the risk of single assets and their correlation (or dependence) matters. It does not take sudden market changes into account. As a consequence, this makes VaR inflexible and unresponsive with regard to abnormal market conditions, such as with the instability caused by high-impact news events or an economic crisis.

17.3 REFINING VaR AND ES CALCULATION USING SEMANTIC NEWS ANALYSIS

Abnormal market conditions exert a much higher risk than normal market conditions and it is therefore vital to include them in risk management strategies. The inflexibility of market risk measures with regard to such abnormal conditions can be countered by developing a system that takes financial news messages into account. Financial news reports all events that are relevant for the value of an equity. Such events, or chains of such events, might cause unstable market conditions. Detection of these events can be used to estimate the probability of emerging abnormal market conditions. By incorporating news into the risk calculation, sudden impactful events can help to determine the kind of distribution that should be attributed to individual parameters of the calculation. In order to do so, news messages need to be given an impact value.

17.4 THE IMPLEMENTATION OF SEMANTIC NEWS ANALYSIS

In order to use news as a source for certain market risk evaluation, it needs to be determined what the impact of a news item is on the equities of portfolios in that specific market. Recent technological developments, like SemLab's ViewerPro semantic analysis platform, have enabled the creation of data-mining tools that can interpret live newsfeeds. Combining such technologies with risk metrics, such as VaR, could lead to quicker, more flexible, and more accurate risk assessment calculation.

Historical data can be analysed to determine the magnitude of specific events or event combinations. This would yield an estimate of the probability that abnormal market conditions occur. It would also result in an estimate of the effect of unstable market behaviour on a certain equity. As such, news event analysis could be used as input for risk measures to calculate risk metrics during abnormal market conditions and answer two important questions: "Will there be abnormal market conditions?" and "What will be the effect on a certain portfolio?"

The efficient market hypothesis states that prices of traded assets (stocks, bonds, etc.) reflect all known information. Typically, risk measure calculations only take into account risks that are based on the recent historical data of single assets or portfolios. This works relatively well under stable market conditions in which recent historical behaviour is an acceptable predictor of the expected market behaviour in the near future. However, it is also recognized that under abnormal market conditions historical data cannot be adequately used as an indication for expected market behaviour. Consequently, during such unstable periods, traditionally calculated risk values cannot be trusted. This deceptively suggests that market risk measures are reliable unless there is an abnormal market. In practice, such risk measures have a very limited applicability under unstable market conditions and wrongly suggest approximate risk indication. In essence, the effect of a sudden change in market conditions on future risk predictions is neglected.

17.5 NORM GOALS

NORM aims to improve the reliability of risk metrics by incorporating the impact of sudden market changes. The final goal is threefold

1. To determine the likelihood that a market will suddenly change. This result can be used to adjust the confidence level of traditionally calculated risk metrics.
2. To provide qualitative impact factors to adjust risk metrics. This result can be used to adjust the actual value of the risk metric in combination with an adjusted confidence level.
3. To provide quantitative impact factors to adjust risk metrics. Quantitative impact factors would enable more accurate risk metric calculation while maintaining original confidence levels.

17.6 NORM USES SEMANTIC NEWS ANALYSIS TECHNOLOGY

The technology that NORM uses to achieve these goals is semantic analysis of financial news messages. We define "sudden market changes" as being preceded by significant events that appear in financial news and affect one or more companies. NORM focuses on the equity market, which enables it to restrict the definition of "events" to things that affect the value of one or more equities. These events are, for example, not only company takeovers, mergers, changes in C-level management, etc., but also market-dynamic changes such as oil price changes and regional instability around production facilities.

A state-of-the-art semantic analysis technology is used to automatically detect events in the news and correlate them with the occurrence of sudden market changes. In order to distinguish between relevant and irrelevant events, a dataset of 20 years of financial news history will be analysed and compared with the intraday market values of a set of selected equities. This can be used to test the three goals described above. Subsequently, a proof-of-concept application will be constructed that implements the results, can run on current news and market data, and will be tested by selected early adopters.

17.7 CONCLUSION: NORM CONTRIBUTION TO RISK ASSESSMENT

It is clear that the successful incorporation of financial news will provide risk assessment measures with an appropriate tool to more closely estimate actual risks. Since the technology is available to semantically analyse news so that qualitative information can be extracted, the most interesting development will be to incorporate this qualitative information into risk assessment measures.

The main concrete result of NORM—as a news-based analysis solution—is that it is able to adapt market risk assessment metrics. This solution consist of risk management software and financial services, creating a financially stable model that ensures transparent asset liquidity management. The results will improve the risk management of assets under management and provide an early warning system for the risks involved, based on real-time market developments before they become apparent in quantitative market signals. Apart from early warnings on regulatory issues and fraud detection, it also provides a unique opportunity for traders to limit risk and improve their alpha.

18

Question and answers with Lexalytics

As posed by the editors and answered by Jeff Catlin

This brief chapter poses practical questions on text analysis to Jeff Catlin, CEO of Lexalytics, Inc., a text analytics and sentiment software company based in Boston, MA, providing solutions primarily to the finance, enterprise search, and reputation management industries. Among its many capabilities, Lexalytics technology powers the Thomson Reuters News Analytics system. For more information on Lexalytics' capabilities, please look up "Directory of new analytics service providers" under Thomson Reuters (see p. 344).

So, Jeff, for those looking to analyze text, what are the biggest challenges that they will face when analyzing this largely unstructured content?

To be honest, people that work on text processing and search understand that getting control of the content is often a much bigger hurdle than building out an application. Not all content is created equal. If you consider content sources like Twitter and a Reuters newsfeed, it's pretty hard to imagine that those will ever be handled with identical approaches. Twitter is badly formed, with little if any capitalization, punctuation, or grammar, while something like a Reuters feed is well formed, but more verbose; so, very different approaches must be used to process these two distinctly different types of content. As you focus down on content that is specific to financial services, the problems change slightly.

There are some good and bad points when processing financially oriented news content. First, financial news content tends to be well written with solid grammar and punctuation, which helps significantly in the processing of the text to measure sentiment. Compared with content streams like Twitter, which seldom have punctuation and often some creative grammar, financial news content is clean and easy to work with. The downside of processing this text is that financial news reporters try very hard to be as impartial or muted in their writings as possible so they don't cause undue exuberance or panic as a result of their reporting. This can make it a bit harder to measure the sentiment of the news. Essentially you have to turn up the gain on the engine to be as sensitive to emotion as possible, so that muted signals are detected. We've done this in our build of the Thomson Reuters News Analytics (TRNA) system, and the results in measuring sentiment have been exceptional.

The Handbook of News Analytics in Finance Edited by L. Mitra and G. Mitra

Another important consideration especially in a financial services environment is to have a fit-for-purpose system. In the financial sector, you don't have the luxury of simply re-booting a server or a process if it falls over in the middle of a critical news or trading day. The systems have to stay up all the time and deliver their results consistently and in a timely manner. Lexalytics worked closely with Thomson Reuters in the design and development of TRNA to ensure that the system architecture was fault-tolerant and fully resilient in order to measure sentiment and other valuable text characteristics to produce signals in a matter of milliseconds with no downtime.

What is company-aliasing and why should I care?

Aliasing, which some people call the "Also Known As" problem, is simply the task of making sure that all of the different names for a company are recognized as references to that company. For example, everyone knows that IBM is also known as Big Blue, so it shouldn't be that difficult to build an alias file that we can use to roll up all the references of IBM to a common name. Unfortunately, there are tens of thousands of entities that need to be aliased, with frequent name changes due to mergers, delistings, etc. Working with Thomson Reuters on the development of TRNA meant that we didn't have to solve the company-aliasing problem. It maintains one of the best alias lists in the world, and it's tightly integrated with their real-time newsfeed. Named entity detection, therefore, was a non-issue in the build-out of TRNA. This created a huge advantage to us in the build-out of TRNA because we were able to sidestep a very difficult issue and focus our energy on the problem of finding a sentiment signal in the news content.

There are a few competitors who claim to have sophisticated sentiment technologies that assign sentiment to the article. You've chosen to measure and attribute sentiment to individual entities within the article. Does it really matter? Why is this such an important distinction?

Sentiment can be misleading if only scored at an article level. Many stories are reporting on two or more companies, so measurement of the sentiment for the story isn't particularly useful unless all the companies are in the same industry and are being reported on with the same opinion. It's not hard to imagine that many stories don't fit this definition; most will compare and contrast companies within a sector, so article level sentiment is at best uninteresting, and at worst, misleading. The key to finding and reporting a useful signal is entity level sentiment.

There are several keys to doing entity sentiment well, but the first step is to understand why entity level sentiment vs. document sentiment is so important. If you consider a financial news story reporting quarterly results for Apple, and the story notes that the iPhone is continuing to gain market share vs. competitors like HTC who are clearly struggling, then it's easy to see that sentiment depends entirely on who you are in that document. If you're HTC, things aren't so good, but if you're Apple, the world's a happy place. Applying sentiment to just the overall document would have little, or no value. It is the entities contained within the reports that are important and entity level sentiment becomes critical in analyzing that data.

There are a number of important technical issues to solve when measuring entity level sentiment. Among them are the disambiguation of words and the assignment of sentiment-bearing terms to the correct entity. For disambiguation, consider the word "fine". It can be used in a variety of ways: "things are fine"; "I just paid a fine"; "fine grains of sand". Clearly understanding the context of the word in a particular piece of text is vital to measurement of the term's effect in a given sentence. Additionally, it's important to correctly parse the grammar of a sentence so sentiment phrases are attached to the appropriate entity. Beyond identifying nouns, pronouns, adjectives, and verbs, analysis must also be done on the relationship between entities. For example, to understand in a report that "John Smith, CEO" refers to the same person when written "He announced his resignation" helps significantly when assigning entity level sentiment.

How do you deal with the quantity vs. quality of sources?

The volume of information available today is larger than it's ever been, but most of the content is of unknown quality. Not only is professionally produced news content of better technical quality (good punctuation and grammar) than most other content, it is also more trustworthy. It's far less likely that professional news content will "have an axe to grind", so the sentiment measures we derive from the content are more accurate and honest than those we'd obtain if we added social media sources to the mix. For other sources that are "professional" but likely consistently biased, like company press releases, there are a number of post-processing analysis techniques that you can perform to remove the biases. One can look at the deviation from average sentiment on releases from IBM rather than comparing IBM's release against that from Dell. In addition, an end-user might weight the signal from different sources according to their circulation, page views, or number of households reached. With an unparalleled host of metadata we produce on over 60 fields, we enable clients to slice and dice the data as they see fit for the signal and intelligence that matters most to them.

What advice would you have for someone who wants to develop this capability themselves?

Anyone wishing to build these sorts of capabilities on their own should not underestimate the amount of time and resources required to develop a fit-for-purpose system—one that is scalable to handle the large amounts of content that may need to be processed; one that is fast enough to handle content at the speed required for algorithmic trading; one that is fault-tolerant and fully resilient for 100% uptime; one that incorporates comprehensive aliasing capabilities across tens of thousands of companies; and one that can be managed without a huge staff to maintain it. A development team should be prepared to set aside at least five years to build a system capable of matching the sentiment signal we've achieved on financial content. Alternatively, we'd recommend using a system like ours and focus your skills and expertise on better interpreting the robust output to fit your trading and investment needs.

Directory of news analytics service providers

Company name

Event Zero

Head Office:	Brisbane, Australia
Other sites:	Sydney and Melbourne, Australia; with global coverage provided through a partner network
Managing Director:	David Tucker (CEO)
Marketing Director:	Ramin Marzbani (VP Marketing and Sales)
Chief Technology Officer/Director:	Matthew Cooper (VP Engineering)
Tools/Services:	Event Center

Tool/Services description

- Event Zero's Event Center® is an industry-leading, enterprise-class, event-processing platform delivering broad capability in support of real-time-distributed data aggregation and analysis.
- Event Center has over 70 industry standard data adapters for sources ranging from ICT infrastructure, business applications, sensors, web/market data feeds, and support for a number of proprietary messaging protocols. Data can be captured in real time from massively distributed sources, locally analysed and summarized, and globally aggregated, with native awareness of quality-of-service issues which pervade distributed and heterogeneous data management.
- Event Center supports stream and state-based event-processing paradigms, and a hybrid stream state approach which allows for advanced analytics applications to be written rapidly (typically in days) in response to emergent business needs and ensuring return on investment. The state paradigm allows for long run times for analytics, detecting conditions of interest, and identifying trends over extended periods (months to years). Third-party analytics services (e.g., semantics/reasoning/ontologies) can be connected to Event Center to bring additional power to complex data analysis.
- Event Center also delivers advanced integration technologies which allow for real-time data publishing, either as consumable data, or through response management infrastructure such as real-time alerts, SMS, IVR, tickerboards, web feeds, etc.
- Specific news analytics applications of Event Center include sentiment analysis of public relations and analyst materials, to understanding climate event and climate trend indicators in geographic areas across the globe, to reputation and brand monitoring in social media environments, to regulatory framework changes.

- Event Zero's domestic and international customers deploy solutions in a range of areas including real-time asset-condition-monitoring, customer experience management, data centre monitoring, enterprise process monitoring, environmental monitoring, ICT infrastructure monitoring, intelligent traffic management security and surveillance, sustainability, and utility network management and monitoring.

Contact: `information@eventzero.com` / `http://go.eventzero.com/NewsAnalytics`

Price: From US$25K

Company name

InfoNgen

Head Office:	40 Fulton Street, 24th Floor, New York, NY 10038
Managing Director:	Isaak Karaev (co-founder, Chairman and CEO)
Marketing Director:	Jason Garverich (Head of Sales and Business Development)
Chief Technology Officer/Director:	John Mahoney (co-founder, CTO)
Tools/Services:	Real Time Discovery Engine Discovery Appliance for the Buyside News Trend Analysis Tools Sentiment Analysis

Tool/Services description

- InfoNgen was founded in 2004 by the co-founders of Multex.com, whose highly regarded offerings helped to re-define the financial information and research marketplace.
- InfoNgen's core offering is its Real Time Discovery Engine that constantly monitors over 35,000 online sources and extracts valuable information that's often hidden in secondary and tertiary sources like local papers, foreign language media, blogs, and legal and regulatory sites. InfoNgen's proprietary classification system automatically adds financial-specific tags and topics to all inbound content. By customizing the filters, users receive real-time alerts with finely focused information that's relevant just to them.
- InfoNgen's Discovery Appliance for the Buyside is an "out of the box" solution that provides a highly efficient and cost-effective way to deploy an enterprise-class discovery solution. It includes all of the functionality of InfoNgen's core platform, including automated semantic tagging, industry-specific taxonomies, clustering, and faceting. The bundled solution enables clients to instantly crawl, index, and search across content in the company's network drives as well as email and attachments in Microsoft Exchange Server. The Discovery Appliance for the Buyside is completely secure because it's installed behind a company's firewall.
- InfoNgen News Trend Analysis Tools apply text analytics to all content being processed by InfoNgen and provides advanced statistical comparisons in real time. Our sophisticated trends analysis dashboard provides a visualization tool to help identify patterns in the occurrence of specified tags, enabling users to discover connections between companies and topics that might not otherwise be apparent.

- InfoNgen Sentiment Analysis takes a unique approach, using custom sentiment taxonomies that are relevant to individual industries or document types. For financial research documents, the sentiment engine performs linguistic textual analysis on an analyst's opinion about any company covered in the research report. A sentiment score is calculated for individual data items (e.g., EPS, revenue, operational matrix, business outlook, etc.) as well as for the entire document. For news, rather than applying sentiment at the story level, InfoNgen calculates sentiment at the entity level (e.g., company, product, brand).

Contact: Jason Garverich (+1 212 328 7204)

Price: InfoNgen is a subscription-based service that charges for its core service based on the number of users at an organization. Advanced services—such as custom topics or analytical tools—may incur additional fees depending on company usage. Please contact InfoNgen for further details.

Company name

Kapow Technologies

Head Office: 260 Sheridan Ave., Suite 420, Palo Alto, CA 94306 www.kapowtech.com

Other sites: Denmark: Dr. Neergaards Vej 5A, DK-2970 HÃ, Hørsholm
United Kingdom: 107–11 Fleet Street, London, EC4A 2AB
Germany: Westhafen Tower, Westhafenplatz 1, DE-60327, Frankfurt-am-Main

Managing Director: John Yapaola (CEO)

Marketing Director: Ron Yu (VP, Marketing)

Chief Technology Officer/Director: Stefan Andreasen (Founder and CTO)

Tools/Services: Kapow Web Data Server

Tool/Services description

Kapow Technologies' powerful data-mining technology quickly converts disparate streams of web data into strategic business assets. The result—precision data that drives enhanced business efficiency, intelligence, and performance.

Kapow "robots" use standard web technology to automate navigation and interaction with any website or web application to provide access to its underlying data. Any browsable content can be accessed including

- *Enterprise/SaaS applications* Oracle, SAP, Salesforce.com, any legacy web application, etc.
- *Subscription feeds* Hoovers, BBC, etc.
- *Consumer websites* Amazon, eBay, CNN.com, WSJ.com, etc.
- *Blogs* WordPress, CNN, Flickr, etc.
- *Social networks* Facebook, Twitter, LinkedIn, etc.

Kapow Technologies transforms this web data into a new source of value and intelligence, directly improving business performance by allowing users to

- eliminate time-consuming coding, scripting, or fragile screen-scraping efforts;
- quickly and accurately extract any enterprise or public web data;
- complete data integration projects in hours and days vs. weeks and months.

The Kapow Advantage—Right Data. Right Now. Right Business Decisions.

- *Timeliness* Kapow allows you to extract up-to-the-minute data giving users access to the freshest feeds and a significant competitive advantage.
- *Relevance and accuracy* Kapow Technologies makes it easy to aggregate web data with a new level of precision and feeds it into any data structure, application, business process, or analytic tool including Business Objects, Siebel Analytics, Oracle BI, and others.
- *Flexibility* By selectively combining data from multiple sources (e.g., public web data and internal legacy applications), Kapow Technologies gives organizations access to a new universe of actionable insight.
- *Scalability* Kapow Web Data Server is an immensely scalable, enterprise-grade data integration and transformation platform that can be universally applied to multiple, concurrent web and business intelligence projects without concern for scalability, resource availability, or management.

Contact: sales@kapowtech.com

Price: Dependent upon requirements; please contact Kapow Technologies for more information.

Company name

Northfield Information Services, Inc.

Founded in 1985, Northfield has developed open, analytical models to identify, measure, and control risk. These risk models cover most marketable securities traded worldwide. Based upon sound investment theory, Northfield's products and services have stood the test of time from users within the global institutional investment community.

With over 250 clients worldwide and offices in Boston, London, and Tokyo, Northfield strives to be a preferred partner for institutional investors and asset managers.

Head Office:	Boston, MA
Other sites:	London and Tokyo
Managing Director:	Dan diBartolomeo, President
Marketing and Sales Director:	Nick Cutler
Chief Technology Officer/Director:	Anrei Bunin
Tools/Services:	Risk models Everything Everywhere US Fundamental Equity US Macroeconomic Equity US Short Term Equity Global Equity Risk US REIT Single Country and Regional Equity Global FTSE EPRA/NAREIT REIT Adaptive Near Horizon Transaction Costs Analytical tools Optimizer Service Performance Attribution Service Allocation Research Toolkit Service (ART) Managed Account Rebalancing Service (MARS)

Tool/Services description

- Our risk models and analytical tools are used by investment professionals globally to better forecast portfolio risk vs. a given market benchmark (relative risk) or in the case of (absolute risk) cash. Our models cover all the major global asset classes: equities, sovereign debt, corporates, convertibles, fx, basic commodities, structured fixed income, US mortgage-backed, and US munis. In addition, we provide the user the ability to model illiquids such as real estate, private equity, and hedge funds along with private placement securities and derivatives.

- Our client type ranges from the largest buy-side asset managers and plan sponsors who use our analytical services to assess risk across the entire enterprise to individual portfolio managers and analysts who employ our analytics one portfolio at a time, to finally the large end retail institutions who private-label Northfield analytics into their various high-net-worth platforms.

Contact: `cutler@northinfo.com`; sales: +1-617-208-2050

Price: Please ring or email your requirement and request a price quotation.

Company name

OptiRisk Systems

Founded in 2001, OptiRisk Systems has developed products and provides services for computational problem solving (optimisation) and risk management. OptiRisk works across business sectors including finance, defence and energy, and has customers around the world. It specialises in the areas of portfolio construction, asset and liability management, news analytics and market risk modelling.

Head Office:	London, UK
Other sites:	Bangalore, Chennai, India
Managing Director:	Professor Gautam Mitra
Commercial Director:	Jamie Ridyard
Marketing and Sales Director:	Bala Padmakumar Pillai (India)
Tools/Services:	Optimisation Modelling AMPL Studio SPInE/SAMPL Studio Solvers FortMP FortSP

Tool/Services description

- *Products* OptiRisk offers a range of software products including tools, components and integrated systems which are used for (i) computational problem solving including scheduling, resource planning and other optimisation applications, (ii) financial analytics, (iii) risk control. Products include AMPL Studio and SPInE/SAMPL for optimisation and stochastic optimisation modelling, and fully featured solver and stochastic solver FortMP and FortSP, respectively. The optimisation features include linear, integer, quadratic, second-order cone and full stochastic programming.

  The products can use OptiRisk components, but also allow for third-party components to be plugged in. Complete solutions including third-party library licenses (e.g., CPLEX, MOSEK, etc.) are available, or clients can use their existing licenses.
- *Services* As sponsor of research at CARISMA, Brunel University and other research centres, OptiRisk has developed valuable IP which can be deployed for the benefit of clients.

  News analytics services: Enhanced news analytics modelling service and software implementation service which use news sentiment data and market data. Customisation of models for asset pricing, volatility, trading strategies (high or low frequency) and risk control . Classical models enhanced by news sentiment data.

R&D service: Focused on the client requirement whereby we construct an empirical investigation to study strategies for a given choice of securities comprising market data and news data. We develop the model and provide results of extensive back-testing and stress-testing using archival data and then hand over the working system.

OptiRisk runs specialist workshops in optimisation and news analytics; these are customised training packages; many of these are approved by the CFA for PDU credits.

Contact: Tel: +44 1895 819483; +91 9094532918
Fax: +44 1895 813095
Email: gautam.mitra@optirisk-systems.com
jamie.ridyard@optirisk-systems.com
bpadmakumar@optiriskindia.com
Website: www.optirisk-systems.com

Price: Products and services prices are available on request.

Company name

RavenPack

RavenPack is a leading provider of real-time news analysis services. Financial professionals rely on RavenPack for its speed and accuracy in analyzing news content on more than 27,000 publicly traded companies across 80 countries.

Financial institutions use RavenPack News Analytics to generate better returns by systematically incorporating the effects of news in their investment process. The company's clients include some of the best performing quantitative and algorithmic trading firms in the world.

Diverse types of organizations are incorporating automated news analysis into their decision-making process, from financial trading to risk management firms. Knowing that the vast majority of content is trapped within unstructured text, RavenPack unlocks actionable content from news for instantaneous delivery, whether to a group of analysts at a top global bank or directly into algorithmic trading systems.

Head Office: New York

Other sites: (R&D) Marbella, Spain
(Data Center) Munich, Germany

President and Chief Executive Officer: Armando Gonzalez

Managing Director, Sales and Marketing: Don Williams

Chief Technology Officer: Jason Cornez

Director of Administration and Operations: Tania Calvo Macias

Key services

- *RavenPack News Analytics* Powered by a proprietary text analysis platform, RavenPack analyzes novel and relevant stories published in all major news sources to look for key events, announcements, and opinions that indicate changes in sentiment on more than 27,000 publicly traded companies. Sampled news sources represent the most reliable and authoritative publishers of business and financial news. Published as "computer-readable" data elements on a real-time feed, RavenPack News Analytics are the timeliest company sentiment indicators in the marketplace.
- *Tool/Services description* Trading is increasingly automated, the financial industry is more competitive than ever, and timing is everything. Firms are overloaded with information and have turned to computers to read news and internet information. With RavenPack News Analytics, what would take days for a trader to read and interpret takes RavenPack computers only a few milliseconds. Now, the financial professional can react much faster to the ever-increasing amounts of news and

information available for making trading decisions. RavenPack news analysis services are designed to enhance trading strategies and help financial professionals spot trading opportunities, better manage risk, and generate alpha.

- *News analytics services* RavenPack News Scores—a real-time news sentiment analysis service that improves risk management and trading. The service provides a unique look into the sentiment of more than 27,000 publicly traded companies worldwide. Each score gauges the health of companies by weighing the balance of sentiment in articles published by professional newswires and hundreds of financial sites, online newspapers, and blogs. Dow Jones News Analytics—algorithmic traders and quantitative analysts can now discover new ways to create profitable market opportunities with Dow Jones News Analytics, a flexible solution powered by RavenPack that combines a unique content set of news and sentiment with a powerful real-time API.

Highlights

- *Speed* Low-latency text and sentiment analysis delivered as a real-time data feed.
- *Superior analysis* Multiple sentiment detection techniques provide more accuracy and flexibility.
- *Market-moving events* Over 160 event categories automatically detected by algorithms.
- *Extensive coverage* News analytics available on more than 27,000 publicly traded companies.
- *Elementized format* RavenPack places discrete tagged pieces of news making every record 100% computer-readable.
- *Backtesting data* Over 10 years of millisecond time-stamped data for testing.

Contact: North America
Phone: +1 (646) 216-2140
Email: info@ravenpack.com

EMEA
Phone: +34 952 90 73 90
Email: info@ravenpack.com

Price: Please write to us with your requirements.

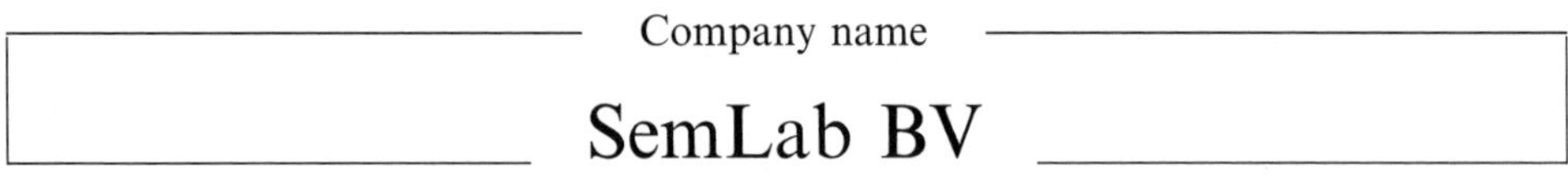

Company name

SemLab BV

Head Office: Alphen aan den Rijn, The Netherlands

Managing Director: Bram Stalknecht, MSc

Marketing Director: Thomas Dohmen, MSc

Chief Technology Officer/Director: Mark Vreijling, PhD

Tools/Services: ViewerPro: semantic news flow algorithm solution
Software consultancy: semantic web, artificial intelligence, computational linguistics

Tool/Services description

- Automated semantic analyses of news
- Transparent, no black box, building your own rules
- Highly flexible and proven
- Connectable to risk-modelling systems

ViewerPro: Semantic processing of news

- ViewerPro is a software platform that automatically analyses news that is relevant for your portfolio to determine the expected impacts of the information in the news on multi-asset classes. ViewerPro automates the effective evaluation of textual news. ViewerPro supports risk managers/(algo)traders' services to assess whether emerging news messages affect the value of a specific equity, bond, or other asset class, and it provides an estimate of the magnitude and direction in which the value of a security may be affected.
- ViewerPro gives traders a powerful tool to capture and edit news-based financial information. Risk managers can express their business rules according to their own market insights in an intuitive way, without interference from an external knowledge engineer. This way, organizations are secure to express their own proprietary knowledge and to create their own trading knowledge base.
- ViewerPro processes text by using leading edge semantic technologies. It was awarded innovation funds from the European Commission. These technologies include metadata filtering, parsing, gazetteering, stemming, natural language processing, automatic pattern matching, etc. This means that ViewerPro can provide the highest possible recall and the highest possible precision in analysing relevant news for trading portfolios, and is scalable to process huge amounts of data instantly.

- ViewerPro can receive (financial) newsfeeds from disparate sources, such as Dow Jones, Reuters, RSS feeds, etc. These streams are processed by using computational linguistics, formal logic, and semantic analysis. This way, ViewerPro determines the positive or negative impacts of the information described in the news on the portfolios that are relevant to the user.
- ViewerPro architecture is service-oriented to enable easy integration and communication with both news providers and your trading systems. ViewerPro can be configured to provide machine-readable information in all desired formats.

Contact: Semlab, Zuidpoolsingel 14a, 2408ZE Alphen a/d Rijn, The Netherlands
T: +31 172 494 777
F: +31 172 497 780
E: `contact@semlab.nl`
W: `http://www.semlab.nl`

Price: Please write to us for a quotation.

Company name

The Chartered Institute for Securities & Investment

To set standards of professional excellence and integrity for the securities and investment industry, providing qualifications and promoting the highest level of competence to our members, other individuals and firms.

Formerly the Securities & Investment Institute (SII) and originally founded by members of the London Stock Exchange in 1992, the Institute is the leading examining, membership and awarding body for the securities and investment industry. It was awarded a royal charter in October 2009, becoming the Chartered Institute for Securities & Investment (CISI).

The CISI currently has around 40,000 members, who benefit from a programme of professional and social events, with continuing professional development (CPD) and the promotion of integrity very much at the heart of everything the organization does.

With ever-increasing regulatory focus on both individuals' and firms' commitment to competence and compliance, the Institute assists companies as well as practitioners to demonstrate their commitment to CPD and professionalism.

The core values of the Institute are to

- set standards of integrity and competence for those working in the financial services industry—ultimately, these standards are for the benefit of investors;
- be the centre of excellence for the design, maintenance and delivery of qualifications, both in the UK and abroad;
- provide members' forums to highlight, share and influence changes in the financial services industry;
- recognize and promote actively the importance of continuing professional development;
- offer appropriate qualifications of the highest calibre, relevance and quality.

The Institute is approved as an awarding body by Ofqual, the UK regulator in education. Its qualifications feature prominently on the Financial Services Skills Council (FSSC) lists of appropriate and recommended exams.

It provides a range of relevant qualifications which attract over 42,000 exam entries each year, delivered in more than 50 countries. The Institute continues to develop its qualifications to meet the demands of the changing financial services industry.

The CISI is committed to assisting individuals to attain and maintain competence and to promoting trust and integrity.

Membership

- CISI membership brings together thousands of practitioners from all parts of a diverse and complex industry into a single effective network.
- Membership of the CISI is the hallmark of professional recognition and signifies that individuals have attained a high standard in their chosen field. This visibly demonstrates an individual's competence and professionalism to employers, colleagues and clients.
- All new exam candidates automatically become student members of the CISI, at no extra cost, to assist them from the outset of their studies. Once candidates pass a benchmark qualification (e.g., the Investment Administration Qualification) they are eligible to progress to Associate (ACSI) membership. Full membership (MCSI) is achieved by attaining a higher level CISI or other relevant professional qualification. It can also be achieved by having very substantial expertise and seniority in the industry.
- Members also have the opportunity to become personally chartered. To achieve this they have to meet a number of criteria, including a number of years successfully logged CPD through the CISI scheme (which requires 35 hours of CPD logged across four learning types on an annual basis) and an A/B pass in IntegrityMatters.
- For those members achieving the full CISI Diploma or the CISI Masters Programme (Wealth Management) it ultimately leads to Chartered Fellowship (FCSI) of the Institute.
- Members are experienced and qualified practitioners in securities, derivatives, corporate finance, investment management, private wealth management and other related areas. All categories of membership must adhere to both the letter and the spirit of the Institute's Code of Conduct and its Principles.

To learn more about the CISI or any aspect of the organization's work or to contact us, please visit `cisi.org/contactus<http://cisi.org/contactus>` or call +44 (0)20 7645 0600.

Company name

Thomson Reuters

Head Office: 3 Times Square, New York, NY 10036
Tel: +1 646 223 4000

Other sites: Over 50,000 employees in more than 100 countries

Chief Executive Officer: Thomas H. Glocer

Executive Vice President and Chief Marketing Officer: Gustav Carlson

Executive Vice President and Chief Technology Officer: James Powell

Relevant tools/services: Thomson Reuters Machine Readable News
Thomson Reuters News Analytics

Tool/Services description

Thomson Reuters Machine Readable News is the industry's most advanced machine-readable news platform. It delivers deep historical news archives, ultra-low-latency structured news, and leading edge news analytics directly to applications. This enables algorithms and humans to exploit the power of news to seize opportunities, exploit market inefficiencies, and manage event risk.

Thomson Reuters Machine Readable News is powered by Reuters News—the world's largest international news agency, with over 2,800 journalists in almost 200 bureaux around the world. We gather and edit news in 21 languages, 24 hours a day, 365 days a year, applying our principles of independence, integrity, and freedom from bias every step of the way. For more than 150 years, Reuters has been associated with breaking the world's top news.

Thomson Reuters News Analytics convert qualitative information into quantitative scores so users—both machines and humans—can quickly analyze thousands of news stories in less time than it takes to read a single headline. By working with key partners (Lexalytics and AlphaSimplex), Thomson Reuters delivers a unique set of real-time news analytics that can be incorporated into trading and investment models to exploit market opportunities and manage event risk.

Thomson Reuters News Analytics use sophisticated natural language processing (NLP) techniques to score news items on over 30,000 companies and nearly 40 commodities and energy topics. Items are scored at an entity level across a number of key dimensions which provides a robust set of metadata in more than 80 fields including

- author sentiment—how positive, negative, or neutral the item is for a given company/commodity;
- relevance—how relevant the story is for a particular company/commodity;
- uniqueness—how new or repetitive the item is;
- item length—how long the text in the item is;
- intensity—how many news items are about the company/commodity;
- topic—what the article is about;
- location of the first mention of the item in the text;
- headline text;
- item genre—interviews, exclusives, wrap-ups, etc.;
- item type—alerts, articles, updates, and corrections;
- index information for cross-linking stories.

The system's output can be used to power quantitative trading across markets, asset classes, and all trading frequencies, support human decision making, and assist with risk management and asset allocation decisions.

The system is available in both hosted and deployed environments with monthly, daily, or real-time updates.

Event Indices

Developed with Andrew Lo and his team at AlphaSimplex, Event Indices measure the frequency of news across various categories such as macroeconomic, natural disaster, violence, and bullish or bearish topics. When the level of news in a given category reaches a certain threshold, signals are sent to a user's trading and risk management system, highlighting potential market movements. Event Indices can predict volatility in key asset classes, such as foreign exchange and equities.

Backed by extensive research and sample data, Event Indices can be tested in users' environments. Delivery is via a data feed for access by trading and risk management systems.

News Archive

With Reuters news content dating back to 1987, and comprehensive news from over 40 third parties dating back to 2003, the News Archive is designed for building and back-testing algorithms and researching how news has moved markets. The archive includes every alert, story, update, correction, and deletion from 2003—each with a rich array of metadata noting the stage of the story, company identifiers, topic codes, headline tags, and other valuable information. Sources include Reuters News as well as select third-party sources such as PR Newswire, Business Wire, and the Regulatory News Service (LSE).

When used alongside Thomson Reuters Tick History, the News Archive enables users to search for hidden correlations between reported events and past trading behavior. With a common symbology and synchronized timestamp, it can be seamlessly integrated into a client's databases so users can track how a story evolved and understand the impact of each piece of the story on the market.

News Feed Direct

Using cutting edge technology, News Feed Direct delivers an ultra-low-latency direct feed of machine-readable news designed solely for application consumption. The feed offers full text and comprehensive metadata via streaming XML broadcast and assured delivery to ensure you never miss an important event. Co-location, dedicated communication lines, and internet connections are among the connectivity options offered at our sites in the New York metro area, London, Chicago, and Washington, D.C.

News Feed Direct content includes

- proprietary, machine-readable, market-moving news from Reuters and select third parties;
- ultra-low-latency machine-readable economics;
- advance feed of results from the Thomson Reuters/University of Michigan surveys of consumers;
- structured company events for data such as earnings and revenue extracted automatically from company press releases;
- credit ratings.

Contact: `MRN@thomsonreuters.com`

Price: Available upon request.

Index

THOMSON REUTERS™
KNOWLEDGE TO ACT